The Sarum Missal, in English [By A.H. Pearson]. Done Into Engl. by A.H. Pearson

Anonymous

THE

Sarum Missal

DONE INTO ENGLISH

BY

A. HARFORD PEARSON M.A. B.C.L.

SECOND EDITION REVISED AND ENLARGED

Presbyter, in Christi mensa quid agis, bene pensa.
Aut tibi vita datur, aut mors æterna paratur.
Dum candela ruit se destruit officiando;
Presbyter ita ruit, si sit reus, celebrando.
Mors tua, mors Christi, fraus mundi, gloria cœli,
Et dolor inferni, sunt memoranda tibi.
E Missali Sarisbariensi, 1526.

LONDON
THE CHURCH PRINTING COMPANY
11 BURLEIGH STREET STRAND.
MDCCCLXXXIV.

LONDON:
PRINTED BY THE CHURCH PRINTING COMPANY,
11, BURLEIGH STREET, STRAND, W.C.

TO

The Dean and Chapter

OF

Salisbury

THIS TRANSLATION OF THE MISSAL

ACCORDING TO THE USE

OF THEIR ILLUSTRIOUS CATHEDRAL CHURCH

IS

Respectfully Dedicated.

CONTENTS.

PREFACE

TO THE SECOND EDITION.

THE demand for a Second Edition of the Sarum Missal is in itself a sufficient witness to the increasing interest in Liturgiology. During the lapse of sixteeen years the York and Hereford Missals, Manuals, and Processionals have been reprinted, also the York Breviary, whilst those of Sarum and Hereford are in progress. With these works may be mentioned two reprints of the Early English Text Society—"The Lay Folkes' Mass Book," and the "Myroure of Oure Ladye." Last, but not least, after the labours of twenty-two years, the reprint of the Sarum Missal from the Burntisland Press is just completed. This claims to be the *Textus receptus*, being a collation of the fifty or more MS. and printed editions of the Sarum Missal.

It had been my intention to have left the Introduction to the First Edition exactly as it stood; but, on consideration, I have thought it advisable to re-cast it partially: the two Introductions can, however, still be compared together, which was my main object.

I had hoped to have found in some copy of the Missals a better representation of the Crucifixion than that from which the woodcut given in the First Edition was engraved. Having, however, examined several, I found that there were only two types—the one given in the New Edition, and one more elaborate, which has the figure of S. Mary Magdalene in the foreground. Their origin I cannot discover, probably they are by some Flemish artist, though the background seems Italian; they are not confined to the English, but appear also in the French, German, and Roman Missals of the period.

The Sequences were translated by my father, the late Rev. C. B. Pearson, Rector of Knebworth and Prebendary of Sarum.

In conclusion, I must offer sincere thanks to Mr. H. Bradshaw, Librarian to the University of Cambridge, for much valuable information and friendly criticism.

LONDON, *Feast of SS. Peter and Paul*, 1884.

PREFACE

TO THE FIRST EDITION.

THE translation of the SARUM MISSAL may interest two classes of readers: that which desires to see the exact formularies from which the English Prayer Book was compiled, and that which is interested in the ancient Ceremonial. In the Missal itself these two subjects are confused together. The Rubrics are sometimes very prolix; sometimes very brief; sometimes contradictory; reference to the *Gradual*, *Processional*, and other books, is often necessary to their right understanding: the directions of the *Registrum S. Osmundi*,* which is perhaps of greater authority than the Rubrics, must be borne in mind; Provincial and Diocesan Constitutions often made their own alterations and additions; and the other printed Uses also occasionally supplement deficiencies in that of Sarum—for which reason a slight notice of those of York and Hereford is necessary.

It has been thought better, therefore, not to confine the work to a translation of the Missal as it stands, but

* Hereafter called *Tractatus de Officiis Ecclesiasticis.*

to endeavour to put it into a more systematic and intelligible form. To this end the Text has been separated from the Rubrics, except in the Ordinary and Canon, and in Holy Week; and the Rubrics have been codified, so as to present a connected view of the Ceremonial— which is of course the object of Rubrics.

This task the translator feels has been inadequately fulfilled, but he trusts he has at all events furnished materials for a more perfect description of the Ceremonial which prevailed in England, at the epoch of the Reformation, than has hitherto been accessible in the vulgar tongue.

The Prayer-Book version of the Psalms, and the Authorised Text of the Bible, have always been followed in translating, as being household words to most English readers, to whom a literal translation of the Vulgate would seem another Bible which is not the Bible: where, however, the Latin of the Missal varies from the Vulgate, it has been literally rendered, and the difference noted by Italics.

On the same principle, so much of the Prayer Book Collects and Prayers as is evidently derived from the Missal has been preserved, even where other words would more closely give the meaning of the text, to the letter of which the Compilers of the Prayer Book by no means habitually confined themselves; and although the precedent they furnish has occasionally been followed, when exact adherence to the Latin would offend the ear of an English reader, the translator has not felt at liberty to omit or add words or phrases merely for the sake of rounding a sentence.

In conclusion, the translator desires to return his sincere thanks to the Dean and Chapter of Salisbury for the loan of their valuable Missals; to the Very Rev. Daniel Rock, D.D., for important elucidations of Ritual which he has kindly communicated, in addition to much assistance derived from his learned work, *The Church of our Fathers;* to the Rev. H. A. Walker, for obligingly correcting the music; to J. D. Chambers, Esq., the Rev. E. Caswall, the Rev. J. Hewett, and the Rev. J. W. Irons, D.D., for permission to use their translations of hymns, and to the Proprietors of *Hymns Ancient and Modern*, and the *Hymnal Noted*, for a similar permission; last, not least, to two friends, who kindly undertook the revision of the sheets as they passed through the press; the able criticisms and friendly suggestions of one, the author of the *Portuary Kalendar*, have been of the greatest value; while to the other, the Public is indebted for the translation of the Sequences, the omission of which would have deprived the book of one of its most marked characteristics.

The translator, if he may refer for a moment to

himself, begs to add that he has not consciously omitted softened, or accommodated a single expression, in accordance with any private opinions, his aim being faithfully and without comment to give an English version of the original in its integrity.

LONDON, *The Epiphany*, 1868.

INTRODUCTION

TO THE SECOND EDITION.

It is obvious, alike from the legend regarding S. Gregory's first acquaintance with the Saxon slaves, as well as from his mandate to S. Augustine to Christianise Britain, that he esteemed it a heathen country; nor in one way was he perhaps far wrong. There is evidence that Pagan rites were mixed up with the Christianity existing in the country, and that the Bishops felt themselves very powerless to check the increase of Paganism. S. Augustine's questions to S. Gregory clearly demonstrate, however, that there was a Liturgy existing to supplant which S. Augustine entirely failed. It is also apparent that S. Augustine knew nothing of any ritual except that of his own Church. His astonishment at finding in Gaul anything except the Office books to which he had been accustomed was very great. No doubt as to S. Gregory's policy remains when we read his answers to St. Augustine's questions. So far as Gaul is concerned it is to be left entirely to its own Bishops. He may suggest changes, but further than this it is no part of his duty to interfere. "Thou shalt not put a sickle into thy neighbour's corn." In Britain the Bishops are "unlearned and weak," so he places them under S. Augustine's charge; but even here it is quite evident that he is to blend the Roman and national uses, not to substitute one for the other. The question at once arises, what was the Roman use? The fact is that this term is a case of what is known in logic as an undistributed middle. The word has different meanings, according to the time and place in which it is used.

597 A.D. Nothing is known of a Roman Liturgy before the fourth or fifth centuries. I am not careful to enquire too closely into the so-called Leonine and Gelasian Sacramentaries under these names; nevertheless, there is something to be gathered from them and their traditions. If we look through the lists of Popes during the second, third, and fourth centuries, we shall find that the names are almost all Greek. There is no doubt that the Liturgy of Rome was also Greek, remains of which are still traceable in the Missal in the Κύριε and Ἅγιος ὁ Θεός. After this Latin became the popular language; but it is curious that the first indication of this change should coincide with the commencement of the long line of Latin Popes commencing with Leo and Gelasius. How the Canon of the Roman Liturgy was composed, and what truth there is in the traditions concerning it, it is difficult to say. There is, however, no doubt that it was in a state of flux during the fifth and sixth centuries, and there is good reason to suppose that this state of things terminated about the time when S. Gregory added the words "diesque nostras in tua pace disponas" in the Canon. It is evident that S. Gregory intended S. Augustine only to adapt to the existing use in Britain such forms as he thought fit; just as he himself had borrowed from the Church of Constantinople. To assume that the Roman Canon was adopted in Britain in 597 A.D. in lieu of the national rite appears to me flatly to contradict the instructions given to S. Augustine; nor does the fact that the Roman Office books were sent to the new mission at all interfere with this theory. Of course S. Augustine and his coadjutors used their own Office books. He appears, however, to have insisted on the use of Gregorian chants instead of the native music, on which they were a decided improvement. But even this raised a storm of opposi-

tion from the native Bishops. Except as a zealous and devout missionary we know comparatively little of S. Augustine; but his attitude towards the native Church was a great contrast to the conciliatory tone which pervades all S. Gregory's letters on the same subject. On the whole, the mission of S. Augustine was far from a success, and the conversion of England had to be re-done by Theodore, 668–690 A.D.

747 A.D. I have assumed in the First Edition that the Council of Cloveshoe may have introduced the Roman Canon into the national use. If so, it is a very early date for it. The summary substitution of the Roman for the Gallican Canon is perhaps the only instance in which a sudden change occurs in the history of Liturgiology, but the very fact that it was a secular and not an ecclesiastical power which accomplished this shows it to be the exception which proves the rule.

The accession of the Carlovingian Kings, the donation of the territorial estates to the Holy See, and the events which culminated in the coronation of Charlemagne on Christmas Day, 800 A.D., produced the most intimate relations between Gaul and Rome. It is true that Pepin had ordered the Roman Canon of the Mass to be substituted for the Gallican. This change was only partially successful, but the decree was rigidly carried out by his son Charlemagne, and that so effectually, that forty years after (840) Charles the Bald had to send for two priests from Toledo to celebrate before him according to the Gallican Use, in order to know what it was.

Considering the line S. Gregory took with regard to National Liturgies, it may at first seem surprising that so sudden a change should have been sanctioned by the Holy See; but the Roman and Gallican Canon were alike equally valid. There was nothing of vital importance in the alteration, and it was therefore acquiesced in by the Pope. This would coincide with the peculiar views of the time on the subject of Church and State. The Holy See was henceforth the seat of a Priest-King, and I can only describe Charlemagne's position by saying he was regarded as a kind of Emperor-Priest. To adopt the Roman Canon would, under such circumstances, be natural, and add an additional tie between the Emperor and the Holy See.

850–1087 A.D. There is not much to note in the English Missals during these 200 years, further than the invention and multiplication of Sequences, dating from the end of the seventh century and spreading rapidly in the subsequent centuries.

Very close relations were maintained between the English and Gallican Churches during the first half of the eleventh century, and specially during the reign of Edward the Confessor. Gallican Bishops were continually appointed to English sees, and the way was paved long in advance for the events which terminated in the Norman Conquest.

1087–1226 A.D. It is, however, with the period between S. Osmund's Episcopate and that of Richard Poore with which we have particularly to deal, and in which the "Sarum Missal" and its use assumed its permanent form. I have in the first Introduction hinted that probably S. Osmund did not take upon himself the prominent part usually assigned to him as the sole compiler of the "Missal." A closer examination of the original charter of the Cathedral, dated 1091, seems to decide the question: "Ego Osmundus . . institui simul et concessi personis et canonicis ejusdem ecclesiæ participato dominorum archiepiscopi et aliorum co-episcoporum nostrorum concilio quorum nomina subscripta sunt." This plainly indicates that the authority under which S. Osmund acted was that of the Archbishop of Canterbury and the comprovincial Bishops. The Charter alludes to a "parvum liber vetus," which doubtless contained the original draft of the Consuetudinary. We have only the *Tractatus* in the form adapted for the new Cathedral at Salisbury. The adoption of this by other Cathedrals and Churches is a testimony to the administrative power of Richard Poore. As an organiser there is no doubt that he was a much abler man than S. Osmund.

It is a matter of great regret that we cannot at present throw more light on the transition state of things between 1092 and 1226. I have no doubt that documents will be found to fill up this gap in the shape of statutes of Cathedrals. The absence of MSS. of the twelfth century is mainly due to its being a time of transition from the use of Greek and Latin to the vernacular. The Lay Folks

VERNACULAR PRIMERS.

Mass Book is a work precisely illustrating this period. The original was in French and was translated into North Country English about the beginning of the thirteenth century. It was probably used in the Province of York, the author being supposed to be Dan Jeremy, who was Canon of Rouen and Archdeacon of Cleveland. The book therefore forms the missing link between the Church of the eleventh and thirteenth centuries. It follows the use and quotes the rubrics of one of the earliest Rouen Missals; the author in his own capacities was at once French and English. When it was first published the present constitution of Cathedral Chapters was in its infancy. The date of its translation would make it a little older than the *Tractatus* of 1226, when these bodies finally developed into their present form. This considerably strengthens the theory I set forth in the first Edition, *i.e.*, that the Rouen use is the parent of the Sarum. This important document has been most ably and dispassionately criticised by Canon Simmons. Nevertheless, I do not agree with his conclusions: if the Greek and Latin languages had not been maintained in their integrity, no Liturgies would probably have come down to us owing to the confusion which arose from the change of tongues; on the other hand vernacular translations began as soon as it was possible, and were succeeded by English Primers, of which new Editions were continually being issued down to the eighteenth century. Notable amongst these works is the "Myroure of Oure Ladye," translated for the nuns of Sion House.

An impression prevails that the English alone translated the Holy Scriptures and Offices into the vernacular. This is, however, a mistake. There are many translations of the Scriptures before the eleventh century; and from the thirteenth to the sixteenth centuries a continuous series exists of what are known as Primers in French, German, and Italian. Until printing was invented, the increase of copies would necessarily be limited. France, in her later days, is conspicuous as being far ahead of other nations in her voluminous translations. In the seventeenth and eighteenth centuries translations and elaborations both in Latin and French, and in French *only*, were made alike of Missals and Breviaries. Even now they may be picked up at the price of waste paper on the Quai Voltaire at Paris.

RITUAL OF XIII., XIV., XV. CENTURIES.

It has been said, and very truly, that elaborate Ritual began with the thirteenth century. I think it may be equally said that it commenced to decline with the sixteenth. Until comparatively late years little or nothing was known of mediæval offices, except as they were supposed to be represented by such services as the Papal Mass at Christmas and Easter. Excepting, however, the absence of a great concourse of Bishops, and the surroundings of a Court, the ordinary ceremonials on week days in mediæval times were throughout the year in France, Germany, and England, not far other than those to be seen on certain days at Rome previously to 1870, not taking into consideration the time taken up by farced Kyries, Processions, and Sequences. In the Sarum Missal there are upwards of one hundred Sequences—some of inordinate length. The Church of Rome seems never to have adopted more than the four which she now has, nor does the ceremonial of the Church of Rome ever appear to have attained the splendour of Teutonic Christianity, although in many ways she borrowed much from it. I have so fully described the structure of the Cathedral at Salisbury and its ceremonial in my first Introduction, that not much need here be added; nevertheless, a few difficulties require clearing up.

First, as to the structure of the Cathedral. There can be no doubt that the Altar at Salisbury stood not where it does, but in the place so plainly pointed out by the frescoe on the roof of our Lord in glory: that is to say it was nearer to the Nave. Whatever the Cathedral of old Sarum may have been, in the new Cathedral of Salisbury a large space was left around the Altar, called Presbyterium, bounded towards the Nave by a step, "gradus Presbyterii." From here to the rood-screen was the Quire. The general appearance of the building would be that of a Basilica, except that there was no throne for the Bishop, nor seats for the clergy around the Apse.

CHAPTER MASS.

Some difficulty arises about these Masses; they were an institution peculiar to Salisbury, as we learn from the *Defensorium Directorii*, which is not very complimentary on the subject. At first sight, one would naturally suppose that they were Masses said under certain circumstances in the Chapter House, but there is no apparent place for an Altar, the centre part of the building being taken up by a pillar, and the walls being surrounded with stone seats.

In the Preface to the Sarum Missal printed at Burnt Island, this is pointed out, and it is argued that probably the Mass was said on these occasions somewhere behind the High Altar. In this, to a certain extent, I coincide; but suggest, as a possibility, that the High Altar at Salisbury may have been so constructed (as at Venice and elsewhere), that the Priest celebrated sometimes facing East, sometimes facing West, in which case the Chapter Mass would have been said behind facing the people.

COLOURS. A great deal of attention has of late years been expended on the colours of Vestments used at Salisbury and elsewhere, *De minimis non curat lex.* I believe that, with the exception of red being used for all Sundays, Martyrs, Ash Wednesday, and the three last days of Holy Week, and white for Christmas and Easter, no particular rule was followed. We find the words *blodius*, *cæruleus*, *purpureus*, *murrein*, *tawny*, *ash-coloured.* The Church at Wells indulged in indigo and saffron, green and saffron, red and white. The Church of Exeter preferred to follow the use of the Roman Curia; this was however quite different from the present Roman Sequence of colour, and included several of the above strange combinations.

Blodius, or blue, ranges, from *cæruleus*, sky blue, to *purpureus*, violet, recalling to mind the similar difficulties as to colour that we find in deciding what is the meaning of the word in Homer, hyacinthine, as applied to hair.

ORIGIN OF NATIONAL USE. I have said as little as possible as to the Liturgy used in this country previous to the eleventh century. The norm of the Liturgy is Gallican. The prayers before the Communion of the Priest, almost identical with those in the Mozarabique Missal, and the Benediction after the *Pax*, are leading features of the Gallican and Mozarabique Uses, and point to an Eastern origin. Nevertheless I much prefer the term National Use—the *communis usus* as it is called in S. Osmund's Charter—to classifications such as British, Celtic, or Anglo-Saxon Use, all misleading, as being connected with theories either incapable of proof or exploded.

INTRODUCTION

TO THE FIRST EDITION.

The Sarum, in common with all Missals, was not the creation of any one particular epoch, but the development of many previous centuries, bearing the impress of divers influences; the translator thinks therefore that a few remarks upon the historical circumstances by which the English missals were influenced, and ultimately moulded into their final shape, may not be unacceptable.

The earliest notice of the existence of a Liturgy in England is involved in the enquiry addressed by S. Augustine to Pope Gregory, 601 A.D.; what should be done when the Roman and the national missal disagreed? The answer of S. Gregory is best conveyed in his own words: "Non pro locis res, sed pro bonis rebus local amanda sunt. Ex singulis ergo quibusque ecclesiis, quæ pia, quæ religiosa, quæ recta sunt, elige: et hæc quasi in fasciculum collecta, apud Anglorum mentes in consuetudinem depone." (Wilk. *Conc.*, vol. I., p. 19.) How S. Augustine carried out these directions does not appear; it is however not improbable that the religious orders would advocate the Gregorian Sacramentary, which may have led the way to the 13th degree of the second Council of Cloveshoe, 747 A.D. "Ut festivitates, in omnibus ad eas rite competentibus rebus, sc. in baptismi officio, in missarum celebratione, in cantilenæ modo, celebrentur juxta exemplar, videlicet quod scriptum de Romanâ ecclesiâ habemus." (Wilk. *Conc.*, p. 97.) It also enjoins the Roman martyrology. These words, however, must have been considered susceptible of some latitude of interpretation, as, in point of fact, the Anglo-Saxon and Roman Use were not identical, though thenceforth the Roman Canon of the Mass, Chants, and methodical arrangement of the Sacramentary, were probably adopted.*

The description given by Amalarius (*de Eccles. Off.*, lib. III.) a pupil of Alcuin, of the ceremonial at Rome in the eighth century, which is nearly the same as that now used by the Pope on great occasions, taken in connection with what may be gleaned from the Troper,† in the Bodleian, furnishes some notion of the interpolations introduced into the Anglo-Saxon Service at that time, particularly the Proses,‡ some of which, *e.g.* that for Ascension Day, were retained in the Sarum rite.

1078-99 A.D. It was after the Norman Conquest, however, that the national missals acquired their celebrity, and assumed their final shape. The effect of the Conquest for the time was the Gallicanizing of England; not that the Anglo-Saxon element was crushed, but the Norman overlaid it, just as the Anglo-Saxon had overlaid the British.

It is hardly correct to represent S. Osmund as having created a new liturgy. The facts are simply these: the Anglo-Saxon hierarchy was deposed in favour of Normans; S. Osmund (originally more distinguished as a statesman, being a Norman count, Earl of Dorset, and Chancellor of England), was made Bishop of Sarum in 1078 A.D. on the death of Herman. During the twenty-two years of his episcopate he built the cathedral, and devoted himself to the care of his diocese, and no doubt especially to the reconciling of his clergy, consisting of two rival races, by rites which should be acceptable to both; § and naturally he would not go farther in quest

* Cf. xv. Decr., "Nihilque quod *communis* usus...... *et* quod Romanæ Ecclesiæ consuetudo permittit, cantent."

† The date of this manuscript is probably about 1000 A.D.

‡ This definition was in later days confined to the sequences; but it was then given to the versicles attached to the Alleluia.

§ In compiling this Use, it is more than probable that he may have been assisted by Lanfranc, who had drawn up something of the same kind for the Benedictines. *Conf.* Wilk. *Conc.*, vol. I. p. 328.

of the former than Rouen, the primatial see of Normandy.* This conjecture approaches certainty when it is found that the Use of Rouen and that of Sarum were almost identical in the eleventh century. A curious and interesting illustration of this will be found in an extract from a Rouen manuscript missal assumed to be 650 years old; which, as the work in which it is quoted, De Moleon,† *Voyages Liturgiques*, was written in 1717, would bring it to about 1067 A.D. The passage is too long for introduction here, and is given in the Appendix.‡

The Rouen Pontifical, of about 1007 A.D., quoted in the same work, shews a like affinity of that of Sarum and of Exeter in later days. The Epistles and Gospels, the custom of Rulers of the choir, the procession from the sacristy with the elements, and that of the Gospel, were the same as in the Sarum rite; and as the description of the latter ceremony illustrates the *Tractatus* it is subjoined—"Puis étant précedé du Thuriferaire, des deux Portechaudeliers, du Soûdiacre, le Diacre va au Jubé, portant le livre des Evangiles, appuyé sur son épaule gauche .... Le Diacre étant monté au Jubé, après avoir encensé le livre, chante l'Evangile, étant tourné vers le Septentrion entre les deux chandeliers .... après l'Evangile ils reviennent tous au même ordre .... sinon que c'est le Soûdiacre qui porte le livre des Evangiles, qu'il présente ouvert à baiser au Prêtre, et ensuite fermé, aux Chappiers du côté droit et dans les hautes chaises du même côté toutes les fois qu'il y a *Credo* à la Messe, puis aux Chappiers du côté gauche et dans les hautes chaises du côté gauche."—*Voyages Liturgiques*, Paris 1717, p. 365.

These facts are to a certain extent strengthened when we discover that in later missals alterations had been made in the Rouen rite which preclude the likelihood of

* John de Bayeux, Archbp. of Rouen (1069-79 A.D.) wrote a book *De rebus Ecclesiasticis*.

† His real name was Le Brun. ‡ See Appendix F.

their having been copied into the English books at a much later date.

Nevertheless, it must not be supposed that French and English Uses were at variance in any essential points with those of Western Christendom; as may be better understood by a slight reference to the architectural and ritual arrangements of churches previously to the eleventh century.

IV.-VIII. CENT. The form generally adopted after the peace of the Church was that known as Basilican, with its one Altar, situated in the chord of an apse, against the wall of which sat the priests on a raised dais, facing the Altar, the Bishop's throne occupying the central place. Over the Altar rose a canopy, on four columns, now known in Italy as the *Baldacchino* (but which was then called the *Ciborium*), usually surmounted by a Cross; and from this canopy hung a dove or pyx, containing the Blessed Sacrament; the Altar, which in primitive times was as often of wood as of stone, and hollow, had nothing on it at Mass except a large cloth, at first of silk—but after a decree of S. Sylvester in 324 A.D., ordered to be of linen material, in proportion approaching to the linen cloth placed on modern Altars. The corporals, being originally used to cover the oblations of the faithful, were also large. Lights, though always used at Mass, were placed about the Altar, or on the ciborium, (D'Achéry, tom. IV., p. 467), never *upon* the Altar; which was accessible on all sides. Between the columns of the ciborium were curtains,* which were drawn aside at certain times.† Such a ciborium seems to have existed at S. Alban's Abbey. *Conf.* Ducange, *sub voce* Superaltare.

The Quire was separated from the nave only by a low wall, and was divided into two parts; that nearer

* It may be doubted, however, whether these ever existed in England, at least in this particular form.

† Bocquillot, *Trait. Hist. de la Liturg. Sacr.*, p. 61.

the altar for the clergy; the other, *schola cantorum*, for the choir. At each side of the Quire was an ambo, or pulpit, whence were read the Lessons, Epistles, and Gospels; some churches, however, were only provided with one pulpit, which was placed in the midst. The Service of Mass, which was always *High*, was not at this period said everywhere daily, but often not more than once or thrice a week, by the Bishop of the diocese, attended by his priests, who joined with him in saying the Canon and words of Consecration;* the musical portions being chanted by the choir. The offering of bread and wine by the people, and Communion in both kinds, were the practice; the hours at which Mass was said varied from 3 to 9 A.M.; and on fasts it was often deferred till after None, Vespers, or even Compline.

Such was, briefly, the Mass of the first eight centuries. The wording of the Canon, previously to the eighth century, differed in France, Italy, and Spain, as to the Saints who were commemorated; and in the Ordinary, in the prayers of oblation, and the communion of the Priest.

It will be seen, then, at once in what points Amalarius' description of the first Roman Ordo may serve to elucidate the Anglo-Saxon ceremonial. To return, now, to the days of S. Osmund: the aspect of things in the eleventh century was very much altered. In the seventh century arose low Masses; in the eighth they increased rapidly; in the ninth they were the rule. This Service, consisting simply of a Mass said by one priest with a server, was without music; and from its first appearance has never ceased to be the popular Service of Christendom. The eighth century witnessed the adoption of the Roman Liturgy† in Gaul, which had been accepted in England at the Council of Cloveshoe; also the practice of daily Mass

* Conf. Amal., lib. I. cap. 12 "simul cum pontifice verbis et manibus conficiunt."

† Practically this means little more than the Roman Chants, and perhaps Canon; see above.

which after Apostolic times had been confined to Spain, Antioch, Africa, and perhaps Gaul. This soon led to the erection of side Altars, which increased to such a degree that they were restrained by a capitulary of Charlemagne, 805 A.D. Portable Altars, also, *super-altaria*, came in at this time, to enable priests to say Mass elsewhere than in church.*

Two other changes may be discerned about the time S. Osmund became Bishop—viz., in Mass, Communion in one kind; and in the arrangement of churches, the closing in of the Quire by stone walls or woodwork, a system which involved more than at first appears.

The Norman reforms, as we find them working in the early part of the thirteenth century, and described in the *Registrum* or *Tractatus de ecclesiasticis officiis*, were of three kinds. First, the classification of the existing ceremonial; under which fall the prayers of oblation, prayers of communion of the priest, and the music. Secondly, the introduction of certain things derived from Rouen, such as the Kalendar,† some sequences, Rulers of the choir, and various minor details which must be passed over for want of space. Thirdly, the arrangement of the Altar differed, over which there was no longer a ciborium;‡ nor was it, as in later times, attached to a wall, but two columns of the ciborium were left, on which was a beam, which

* The Constitutions of English Bishops of later days are full of injunctions respecting them. After the prohibition of wooden Altars, the law of the Church was substantially complied with by letting these super-altars into the wooden altar boards. *Conf.* Stat. Simon, Bp. of Norwich, A.D. 1258; also Regulations for Lincoln Archdeacons, A.D. 1231. "*Ne molentur super ea colores*" is a singular prohibition, which often occurs, indicating a common, and not particularly reverential use, to which they seem to have been sometimes applied. *Conf. supra*; and Constit. Winton., A.D. 1308; Constit. Oxon., A.D., 1322; Synod of Ely, A.D. 1364.

† This reform was somewhat arbitrary; it has been asserted the Anglo-Saxon saints were omitted for no better reason than that their names were unpronounceable to Normans.

‡ Although as has been said we have no trace of curtains, the arrangements with respect to the Lenten Veil (See Rubrics, Sect. xxv.) certainly point to something of this sort.

supported the candlesticks, and sometimes the Cross; the Blessed Sacrament was kept as before, either in a dove or pyx, which hung from the roof, and over which was sometimes spread a covering of silk. (*Conf. Monast. Anglic.*, vol. VIII., 1365.) The Altar was now covered with three linen cloths (this may have been an invention of the twelfth or thirteenth century). The Quire was also slightly altered; the low wall which separated it from the nave was heightened, as were also the pulpits, which had been removed from their former position and placed at the entrance of the Quire; these ultimately were joined, forming the roodloft of the fourteenth and later centuries, which thus developed the screen between the Quire and nave, in which was a door leading to the Quire; over all was a hanging beam, supporting the rood and candlesticks, which in later times became a fixture. This latter change involved the creation of eagles and lecterns; which on ordinary occasions served instead of the pulpits. Behind the pulpits thus heightened, was placed, as at Salisbury, a candelabrum; and on the floor in the Quire a large standard of lights,* like those used in France till a later period.

Such were the main features of the Norman reforms; it remains now to consider their adaptation to other dioceses in England and Scotland, and their subsequent history down to the sixteenth century.

Whoever takes up a Sarum Missal, without a slight acquaintance with the liturgical history of the rest of Western Christendom, might not unnaturally conclude that such features as paucity of Rubrics, the Service being apparently always High Mass, the very elaborate ceremonial, and the posture of the celebrant and ministers—who incline and never kneel or genuflect—were peculiar to Sarum; but in none of those points was there much divergence from the Continental Uses. These were simply

* Pharus or rastrum; Fr. *ratelier.*

characteristics of the age. The individual peculiarities lie in the prayers of oblation, and the communion of the priest, and the beginning and the end of Mass; and it is because these particulars, besides others above noted, are found to be identical with Rouen, that the Use of that Church has been assumed to be the basis on which S. Osmund founded his own. This being so, it is not difficult to understand, first, how various Uses arose; and secondly, how they were subsequently restricted to three.

The reform of the English Use, after the model of Rouen, initiated at Salisbury, was soon adopted in its main features, not only throughout the other dioceses of England, but also of Scotland, and probably in the English pale in Ireland, although in minor points these adaptations of it differed considerably.

Until a careful collation of the various MSS. Missals scattered throughout this country shall have been made, it is impossible to say with certainty how many Uses prevailed; so far as the translator's own limited knowledge of them extends, he does not think more can be found, in the strict sense to which the word should in his opinion be limited, than the three printed Missals—Sarum, York, and Hereford—insomuch as the invention of printing at once gathered together the various local ceremonials into three great groups; and as no fourth printed Missal is known to exist, it may be fairly concluded that there was none strong enough or diverse enough to maintain its ground. The differences between these three are amply shown in the Rubrics and Appendix; there remains, therefore, for consideration, the mode in which they were adapted to collegiate secular bodies, and parish churches.*

It is doubtless true, in a certain sense, as the Preface

* With the regulars this work has no concern; but it is generally found that these *to a certain* extent adapted their Services to the prevalent use of the country.

to the Prayer Book says, that there was a Use of Bangor* and Lincoln; but it might as correctly have predicted the same of S. Paul's, London, Durham; Lichfield, and Worcester. The Prayer Book, however, is here speaking only of "diversity of saying and singing;" words which, taken even in their widest interpretation, very inadequately represent the differences between the Uses of Sarum, York, and Hereford.

Two small tracts, *Defensorium Directorii*,† and *Credo Michi*, appended to some editions of the Sarum Ordinal, show what the diversity of saying and singing was; and at the same time point to other minor diversities, without touching in any way the differences between the three Uses above named.

The former at once proceeds to divide the Sarum Rubrics into two classes, general and ceremonial: of which the latter only applied to the diocese of Salisbury; and it states that the clergy of Winchester and Oxford, though professing to observe the Sarum Use,‡ were yet exempt from the well-known rule in that cathedral, according to which, when two Masses occurred, one of them was said in the Chapter-house. So also the clergy of S. Stephen's, Westminster, and of S. Catherine's, near the Tower, had certain rules of their own about the Collects to be said in Masses for the Dead; those of Wells omitted a Psalm of Prime; and, to sum up, the author says, "I assert most positively, that the sections in the Consuetudinary of Sarum which treat of division of Feasts, Benedictions, Ember Days, the Lenten Veil, Paschal Candle, and Easter Sepulchre, are generally to be observed by all churches

* The Missal given by Maskell as Bangor, in his *Ancient Liturgies of the Church of England*, is merely a Sarum Missal, with variations, such as are customary in all MSS., and, in fact, not so great as are often found between different printed Sarum Missals.

† This was probably written by a priest named Clement Maydestone, who edited the Ordinal. *Conf.*, Wharton's *Angl. Sax.* vol. ii. p. 369

‡ For the meaning in MS. Missals, etc., of this word *ad usum Sarum*, see Page 598.

which can; but those of Vestments, of Four Rulers, of singing Responses by three or four, are only binding on the Sarum clergy; that this assertion of mine is true, the clergy of S. Paul's, London, will bear witness, who observe the Sarum Rite in singing and saying *in cantando et legendo* (*Conf.* Preface to the Prayer Book); but in none of these ceremonies; in respect of which they follow the ancient customs of their Church as instituted in the beginning." He then corrects several typographical and rubrical errors in the Sarum books in anything but deferential language: "Mirabile est valde quomodo tanta cæcitas contigit in ecclesiâ Sarum, quæ *solebat* totius Angliæ esse vera lucerna." The *Crede Michi* is less censorious, and is chiefly occupied with rules about occurrence of holy days.

The earliest existing Register in which the title deeds and other documents of the Dean and Chapter of Salisbury were collected, belongs to the time of the transference of the see to new Sarum, and the building of the new cathedral by Richard Poore about 1225.

This volume is commonly known either as the *Vetus Registrum Sarisburiense*, or the *Registrum Sancti Osmundi*, a name which it has obtained partly from being the oldest Register existing; and partly from its containing copies of the early documents including the two foundation Charters of S. Osmund in 1090.

The volume commences with the famous *Tractatus de ecclesiasticis officiis*, which gives a statement of the privileges and *consuetudines* of the chapter as existing at the time, which is evidently that of Richard Poore. Unfortunately, from being preserved in the *Registrum S. Osmundi* it has been presumed to be the compilation of S. Osmund himself; whereas the very title of it shows that it was a compilation of later date, explaining the state of things as existing in the writer's time (*presens tractatus explanat*). The original deed of S. Osmund exists, and contains not a word respecting ritual. The *Tractatus* on the other hand displays the ritual used at Salisbury about 1225, and we must judge of it accordingly.

The constitutions which are worked into the Rubric prefixed to this Missal show that the Sarum *Consuetudinarium* was almost immediately borrowed and adapted to its own use by most of the secular Churches throughout the country. We trace it at Lincoln, at Lichfield, at Wells, at Exeter, at Chichester, at York, in England: at Dublin and other places in Ireland; and at Glasgow, Moray, Ross, and Aberdeen in Scotland.

In the Council of Durham (*c.* 1237 A.D.) it is noticeable that the laity are ordered to kneel at the Consecration; about this time the elevation of the Host became general, and alterations were made in the mode of reserving the Eucharist; the Council of Oxford (1222 A.D.) enjoining a silver, or at least an ivory pyx, and two candles, *cum lampade*, at Mass.*

Of the Constitutions of Bishops, which are worked into the Rubrics prefixed to this Missal, those of Lichfield are the most interesting, as being only a century later than S. Osmund (*c.* 1250 A.D.), and apparently the first adaptation by another diocese of his reforms. The next of which the translator has found any record are those of Lincoln (1212 A.D.).

It is usually said (and this is true if by them is meant those which stand upon the Altar) that there were no tabernacles till Queen Mary's reign; but the Statutes of Peckham, Archbishop of Canterbury (1281 A.D.) complaining of "great injuries done to the Sacrament," and ordering that "in every parish shall be a tabernacle with a door to shut, in which It is to be placed in a pyx lined with linen" (not, as had been the custom hitherto, in a burse) seem to point, in the abandonment of the doves, in

* This lamp was apparently intended to burn before the Reserved Sacrament. Particular injunctions regarding it are found in the constitutions of Cantilupe, Bishop of Worcester (1240 A.D.), who prescribes "a lamp to burn before the Sacrament night and day," in all churches "quarum amplæ sunt facultates."

favour of a hanging shrine, or perhaps an aumbry in the wall to what eventually paved the way for these later inventions.

These Statutes show that *in cathedrals* the clergy still communicated in both kinds, "solis enim celebrantibus sanguinem sub specie vini consecrati sumere, *in hujusmodi minoribus ecclesiis* est concessum."

It was probably towards the end of the thirteenth, or beginning of the fourteenth century, that the two candles so often pourtrayed in the printed Missals, were first placed on the Altar. (*Conf. Constit.* Wint. and Oxon., 1286, and 1322 A.D.)

The first appearance of the Sarum constitution of Chapter in Scotland seems to have been in the Episcopate of Herbert, Bishop of Glasgow (1147-64 A.D.). This was confirmed 1258 A.D., and again by a Bull of Gregory X. 1274 A.D. In 1258 the Dean and Chapter of Salisbury send under seal a statement of their *consuetudines* to Glasgow; but even this is only the first part of the Sarum *Tractatus* on the constitution and privileges of the Chapter, and the part relating to the *Ordinatio Chori* and the Choir, Procession, and Altar Ritual is wholly omitted. The dioceses of Murray and Dunkeld adopted the Sarum Use properly so called (*in cantando et legendo*) in 1242 and 1249 A.D. respectively.* It need not be repeated that when adopted it was also *adapted* to the requirements of the country.†

* Innes, on "Sarum Liturg. in Scotland," p. 364, quoted in the reprint of Arbuthnot Missal.

† It would have seemed almost superfluous to remark that English Uses were confined to these islands, had not the contrary been sometimes stated, grounded on the fact that English Missals were printed at Rouen, Paris, Antwerp, and Venice. Whatever value may be attached to those printed in France (and, as has been shewn above, there are necessarily great affinities between the French and English Uses), the supposition that an English Use ever prevailed at Venice must at once overthrow this theory. The solution of the difficulty lies, of course, partly in the fact that there were numerous English merchants resident in these places, at whose expense the said Missals were published, and still more in the fact that the printing of these books was a very troublesome matter, and it was a saving of expense to go to those printers who made a speciality of printing them, the vast majority of whom lived at Venice.

Of the printed editions of Missals, those of York and of Hereford may be at once dismissed from consideration. Of the former there are only three, 1516, folio, 1517 and 1532, quarto, which do not much differ; of the latter there is only one, 1502, folio. Of the Sarum there are upwards of fifty; ranging from 1487 to 1557, with a break of twenty years, from 1534 to 1554, during which none were printed.

The translator has not hesitated to make use of the classification adopted in the Burntisland reprint of the Sarum Missal; of which (as the editor of that work will give his own explanation on its completion) no more need be said than is required to explain the abbreviations used. Missals of 1492 (printed for brevity '92, as are all the rest), '94, one in British Museum catalogued 1500. Basel (which two agree) '98, and '2, are not classed. Those of '97, the two editions of Verard, '4 and '8, also '10, form the first class. The four Pynson editions '0, '4, '12, '20, which differ considerably from another edition of '0, and '57, form the second class. Ten others, represented in this Missal by '15, viz., '3, '6, '8 R.M.,* '8 Huvin, '9, '14R., '15, '16R, '19P.C., '21 R., form a third. All the rest, speaking roughly, one *per annum* from 1510 to 1555, form a fourth class. Of these, '13 represents '10, '11, '13, '14 P., 16 P., 19 P.H., '19 P.R., '27 P.P., '27 P.B., '29, '33; and '26 represents '26, '27, '21, '31, '32, '34, '55P. This classification depends chiefly on the general arrangements and endings of the Missals, which vary in having more or less Votive Masses after the "Gospel of Pope John XXII." with which this translation ends.

The text followed almost exclusively is the edition 1519, Rouen, Olivier, and 1527, Paris, Prévost, compared with 1504, Verard,† which latter seems the best of the three; the *Manual*‡ referred to is the edition of 1537, Paris,

* Where there are two editions in one year the initial letter of the place and publisher is added, *e.g.*, '8 R.M., means '8 Rouen, Morin.

† A fragment in the translator's possession.

‡ Also in his possession.

compared with earlier ones; the *Processional*, 1525, Kaetz. It should be added, that though the object of this translation is to present the whole contents of the various editions, two circumstances seemed to favour the omission of the Supplemental Masses.* First, they are not in the earlier editions, except in that of '98; the rest have but a few; and the last (that of '57, a very carefully revised one), omits them wholly; thus reverting after an interval of more than fifty years to the original order. Secondly, their value would hardly have compensated for the additional bulk created by their insertion. They are fifteen in number; Masses of SS. Sebastian, Roch, Erasmus, Christopher, Anthony, Raphael, Gabriel, Barbara, and Compassion of B.V.M., appear in '97, '98, and in most Missals from '10 to '54. '98 adds Masses for Three Kings of Cologne (possibly for the benefit of the Cologne merchants in whose vicinity it was printed), S. Armagil, and the Presentation of the B.V.M.; '97, '1, '4 P. V., '8 V. and '10, omit S. Raphael; '0 P., '3, '4 L., '8 R. M., '8 R. H., '12, '20, give a different Mass for S. Roch; all except the Pynson editions add S. Geneviéve, and have only this and S. Roch. '4 L. has a different one for S. Gabriel; '4 L., 12, and '20 have fewer than the rest. The rubrics in these various editions greatly vary, but a thoughtful student of Missals will know that nothing is proved by their absence, as until some time after the invention of printing, space was, as heretofore, an object, and traditional knowledge was considered sufficient for these puposes. An impression not perhaps unnaturally prevails in some quarters that the edition of 1557, and the other Marian Missals, 1554 and 1555, are less trustworthy than those of earlier date. But the text of the Canon and Ordinary in the Manual is surely preferable to that of the Missal, as it was intended

* The cautels are also omitted to save space, insomuch as they have been already translated; and a Mass for a Woman with Child, which although placed ofter the Marriage Service in the Missal falls under the same category as the Supplemental Masses, and is not in '92, '94, '97, '98, '4 L, '15 or '57

specially for the use of parish priests; and for the same reason the rubrics are there given more at length. As, then, it is found that the additions in the text of '57 are all taken from the Manual, the earliest editions of which contain them, the translator could not but regard them as indications of a desire simply to produce the best text, and has therefore not scrupled to accept them, although they may not appear in earlier Missals.

A few words must be added about the Sequences; which form too prominent a part of the Sarum Missal to be omitted from the present work. Their translator, however, desires to bespeak for their rendering the special indulgence of the reader. There is an abrupt and fanciful wildness in these compositions which may not unfitly be likened to the style of choral odes in Greek plays; their language and grammatical construction is extremely anomalous, abounding in Greek words Latinized, and others of Mediæval coinage; their meaning is often very obscure, and the symbolic allusions are exaggerated, and difficult to discern. If, as Dr. Neale and others maintain, some kind of rhythm was intended, its rules appear so uncertain, that in many the translator felt his only resource was blank verse. Where the metre was discernible it has been reproduced in English as closely as possible. The authors of not more than about twenty sequences appear to be known with any certainty; amongst them are S. Bernard, Notker, who is generally called their inventor (though Dr. Rock would claim Alcuin as their author, a century earlier), Peter Abelard, and Adam de S. Victor, who brought the Sequence into its most perfect shape, and was its most successful composer. Several of them, *e.g.* those in Advent, existed in Saxon times; but in this the utmost latitude was given, as may be gathered from the fact that the Sequence for S. Thomas of Canterbury was different in Sarum, York, Hereford, and Rouen, whilst the MS. Sequentialia abound with Sequences for local saints.

c 2

The Sarum Missal, now for the first time translated in its integrity, presents a picture of the elaborate religious ceremonial which suited the devotional feelings of our countrymen in an earlier and less busy age: as such the translator hopes it may not be uninteresting to the English public; to whose candid judgment he now commends it.

General Rubrics.

Masses are either Festival (*i.e.*, of a Feast), or Ferial (*i.e.*, of a week day). Feasts are divided into Doubles,† Simples, and Sundays.

I.—OF DOUBLES.‡

1. These are of four kinds.

Principal Doubles.—Christmas Day, the Epiphany, Easter Day, Ascension Day, Whitsun Day, the Assumption, the Anniversary of the Patron Saint, and the Dedication of a Church. If either of these last two occur on any of the above six days, they are transferred.

Greater Doubles.—Trinity Sunday, Corpus Christi, the Purification, the Visitation of the B. V. M., the Feast of Relics, the Name of JESUS, the Nativity of our Lady, and All Saints' Day.

Lesser Doubles.—The three days after Christmas, the Circumcision, the three days after Easter and Whitsun Day, Low Sunday, Lady Day, the Invention of the Holy Cross, the Nativity of S. John Baptist, SS. Peter and Paul, the Transfiguration, Holy Cross Day, and the Conception of our Lady.

Inferior Doubles.—The Feast of SS. Andrew, Thomas, Thomas of Canterbury, Matthias, Mark, Philip and James, James the Great, Bartholomew, Matthew, Luke, Simon and Jude, Gregory, Ambrose, George; Augustine, Apostle of England; Augustine, Bp. of Hippo; Michaelmas Day; S. Jerome; the Translation of S. Edward, King Conf.; the Chair of S. Peter at Antioch, and All Souls' Day.

2. According to HEREFORD Use, the first two classes of Sarum were thrown into one, with certain additions, and feasts were divided as follows:—

Principal Doubles.—Christmas Day, Epiphany, Candlemas, *Easter, Ascension Day, S. Ethelbert (being the patron saint of the diocese), *Whitsun Day, *Trinity Sunday, Corpus Christi, the *Feast of Relics, the Assumption and the Nativity of Our Lady, S. Thomas of Hereford and his Translation, All

† So called from the Anthems being doubled, *i.e.*, said throughout at the beginning as well as at the end of the Psalms in the Breviary Office, instead of as on other days, the first words only being said at the beginning. For the Kalendars of York and Hereford, see Appendix C.

‡ The authority for Secs. 1, 2, 3, 4, 6, is the Sarum Brev., *Tractatus*, Heref. Brev, and Miss.

Saints' Day, the Dedication Day, and the Anniversary of the Patron Saint.

Lesser Doubles.†—All the Lesser Doubles of Sarum (except the three days after Easter and Whitsun Day, Low Sunday, Lady Day, and Transfiguration), with the addition of SS. Thomas, Katherine, George, Michael, Denys.

Semi-Doubles were the Inferior Doubles of Sarum (except SS. Thomas Cant. and George), with the addition of SS. Nicholas and Barnabas, Commem. S. Paul, Trans. of S. Thomas, SS. Mary Magd., Anne, Lawrence, Deposition of S. Thomas of Hereford (in Cath. Church), SS. Martin and Katherine. (These last two, together with SS. Jerome, Luke, Simon, and Jude, it was not obligatory to keep as Semi-Doubles.)

Simples were all other feasts, including Sundays, excepting those above marked * (but ? Advent, Passion, Palm S.)

3. What the York Use was with regard to feasts is not very clear; it was probably not very unlike Sarum. The Concept. of B. V. M. was a Principal Greater Double; the Trans. of S. William and his Deposition, and the Feast of S. Peter's Chains, were Doubles. The Trans. of S. Wilfred, S. John de Beverley, Deposition of S. Wilfred, and Feast of Relics, were Lesser Doubles. SS. John ant. Port., Everilda, Germanus, Raphael, and Paulinus were Feasts of Nine Lessons.

II.—OF SIMPLES.‡

These are either movable or immovable. The former are all Feasts of Nine Lessons, and certain ones of Three which occur in Eastertide (called Three with Rulers, see sect. v.) Under this head fall Octave Days and days in an Octave with Rulers. All other feasts are immovable. Amongst movable feasts are some called Triple Invitatories; immovables are divided into Double and Simple Invitatories, distinctions arising from the mode in which the Invitatory or Anthem to the *Venite* at Matins was sung by two or three persons. Under this latter class will fall Octave Days and Days in Octaves without Rulers.

III.—OF SUNDAYS.

1. There are four kinds of Sundays—*Principal Sundays, i.e.*, Advent Sunday, Passion Sunday, and Palm Sunday.

Greater Sundays, i.e., The Second, Third, and Fourth Sunday in Advent, and all Sundays in LXX. and Lent, till Passion Sunday.

† Heref. Miss., Rubric on Processions.

‡ For an enumeration of these, see Kalendar.

Lesser Sundays, *i.e.*, Those when Histories begin, and the Fifth Sunday after Easter.

Inferior Sundays. *i.e.*, The Sundays after the Octave of the Epiphany until LXX., those from the Octave of Low Sunday to the fifth Sunday after Easter, and all the Sundays after Trinity Sunday until Advent.

2. All feasts are translated if they occur on *Principal Sundays*; and all feasts, except Principal and Greater Doubles, if they occur on *Greater Sundays*.

Lesser Sundays are commemorated if they occur on Doubles; on Simples, however, these latter are translated, unless there are many Sundays after Trinity.

Inferior Sundays generally give way before all feasts, or else, where not omitted, the Mass is said in the Chapter-house.

IV.—OF THE TRANSLATION OF FEASTS.

1. If any Double, or Feast of Nine Lessons, or Three with Rulers, occur on Advent Sunday, on the Vigil of Christmas, the Circumcision, the Epiphany on and in its Octave, LXX., or any Sunday in Lent, Ash-Wednesday, the three days before Easter till Low Sunday inclusive, Ascension Day, the Vigil of Whitsun Day and till Trinity Sunday inclusive, Corpus Christi, or the Assumption, it is transferred to the first vacant day.

2. The Dedication of a Church and the Feast of the Patron Saint may, however, be kept on LXX. and till Passion Sunday, also in the Octave of the Epiphany.

3. Doubles are translated according to their rank—*i.e.*, if two occur, the lesser; and if two of the same rank, the least worthy is transferred. Feasts of Nine and Three Lessons are translated under certain circumstances if they occur on Octave Days. See sect. vii.

V.—OF RULING THE CHOIR.*

It is customary for the Choir to have Rulers—*i.e.*, persons whose duty it is at Mass to chant the Office, *Kyrie*, etc.; and in the Breviary Offices the anthems, etc.; also to superintend the choristers. These in cathedrals are appointed by the Precentor, whose duty it is to arrange the table of the singers and ministers of the Altar. This table is generally made out for the week; but at Christmas, Easter, and Whitsuntide, it is made out for each day. There are three forms or grades of stalls at Salisbury Cathedral—the Canons sit in the upper, the minor Canons in the

* Sarum *Tractatus*, secs. xx. xxi.

next, and the boys below. On all Double Feasts the Choir is ruled by four, who, in Principal Doubles, may be any persons the Precentor chooses to name, provided that they be at least Canons. In other Doubles, the first two, called Principals, are the Canons appointed for the week; the other two, called Secondaries, may, at the discretion of the Precentor, be persons holding stalls in the second bench.* In Simple Feasts there are two Rulers only: their office lasts fifteen days, when the table runs by the week (except at Christmas, Easter, and Whitsuntide), the principal of the first week becoming the second in the next. On certain of these days, however, a third Ruler is added, of the superior grade, and these are marked in the Kalendar as Triple Invitatories. Rulers wear silk copes of the colour of the season over a surplice, and have silver staves allotted to them as emblems of office; the following are the days they must all be of the highest rank:—Christmas Day and the two next days, the Epiphany, Easter Day, Easter Monday, Ascension Day, Whitsun Day and the following Monday, the Assumption, the Dedication Day of a Church, and Feast of the Patron Saint.† On the remaining Doubles, two will be of the highest grade, and two of the second.‡ The Choir has Rulers also in and on certain Octaves. See Sect. vii.

VI.—OF FERIAS.

1. Ferias are of four kinds—*Principal Ferias, i.e.*, Maundy Thursday, Good Friday, Holy Saturday, the Vigil of Whitsun Day, and Ash-Wednesday.

Greater Ferias, i.e., all days from Passion Sunday to Maundy Thursday.

Lesser Ferias, i.e., all days from Ash-Wednesday to Passion Sunday, the first and third Rogation Days, and the third week in Advent.

Inferior Ferias, i.e., All days in Advent, except the third week.

2. If Doubles or Simples occur on the first of these four classes, they are transferred, or in the case of untransferables passed over.

If they occur on the second class they are passed over, if

* *Bench, grade, form,* are used indifferently throughout this translation for the same thing.

† These two latter are not in the Sarum *Tractatus*, but, clearly, should be added to the other Principal Doubles.

‡ A list is given in the *Tractatus*, but it is so imperfect a one that no doubt remains in the translator's mind that in enumerating *some* Doubles it meant to include *all* the remainder.

Simples; if Doubles, the Service is of the Feast, with a Memorial of the Week Day.

If they occur on the third class, the Mass of the Feast is said after *Terce*, and the Mass of the Fast after *None*, both at the High Altar, except in places where there is only one Mass; then the Feast is commemorated at the Mass of the Feast.

If they occur on the fourth class, there is always a Memorial of the Week Day.

3. Besides the above four classes there are Vigils. The Vigils falling under the following rule are those of the Epiphany, Ascension Day; SS. Andrew, Thomas, John the Baptist, Peter and Paul, James, Lawrence; the Assumption, S. Bartholomew, the Nativity of Our Lady, S. Matthew, SS. Simon and Jude, All Saints, and the Ember Days. If a Vigil (other than the Vigils of Christmas, Easter, and Whitsun Day) occur on a Feast of Nine Lessons, or Three with Rulers, then the Mass of the Feast is said after *Sext* in the Chapter-house,† and the Mass of the Feast after *Terce*. In small places, however, the Service was of the Feast, with a Memorial of the Fast,‡ as was always the case with Feasts of Three Lessons. The Fast of a Vigil is kept on the Saturday if the Feast fall on the Monday.

4. If an Ember Day and a Vigil occur, the latter has a Memorial. If an Ember Day and a Feast occur, the same rule applies as in the case of Vigils.

VII.—OF OCTAVES AND OCTAVE DAYS.§

1. Of the Octave there is a Service or a Memorial every day for eight days, at Christmas and the four following Feasts,‖ the Epiphany, * Easter, Ascension Day, * Whitsun Day, Corpus Christi; the Dedication Day of a Church (out of LXX. to Easter††), the Feast of the Patron Saint, the Feast of Relics; and the Feasts of the Visitation, Assumption, Nativity of Our Lady, and the Feast of the Name JESUS. On all the above the Octave and Octave Day are celebrated with Rulers of Choir, as also S. Andrew's Day if not in Advent.

2. If any Feast occur in the Octaves of any of the above,

† On certain Vigils the rule of Lent, "both Masses at High Altar," seems to have prevailed, *conf.* Vigils of S. Lawrence and the Assumption.

‡ See Defensorium Directorii, 1488, Bodleian Lib.

§ The authority for this section is a comparison of the scattered rubrics in the Missal, illustrated by the Breviary, Sarum *Tractatus*, etc.

‖ These four Feasts may be regarded either as having Days in the Octave with Rulers or not.

†† *Query.* If the Dedication had anything but a Memorial during Advent, except Octave Day with Rulers? *Conf.* Sarum Breviary.

there is a Memorial of the Octave, and the Service is of the Feast, except in the case of those marked with an asterisk, in the Octaves of which no Feasts can be celebrated.*

No Feast can be translated into the Octaves of Christmas, Epiphany, or Ascension Day.

3. If a Feast with Rulers and an Octave Day occur, the Mass of the Octave Day is said in the Chapter-house, and the Mass of the Feast at the High Altar. If the Feast be a Sunday, however, it is sometimes translated, according as there are few or many Sundays after Trinity.† It appears, however, that on the Octave Day of the Ascension, Simples were translated.

4. If an Octave Day and a Vigil occurred, the rule of Feasts and Vigils is applicable. (See above.)

5. The Feasts of SS. Peter and Paul, and S. Andrew (in Advent), and the Dedication in LXX. to XL., have an Octave Day‡ with Rulers of Choir, though they have none in the Octave.

6. The Feast of S. John Baptist, Relics, S. Lawrence, S. Martin, and the Dedication, in Lent, have Octaves and Octave Days without Rulers of Choir; on the last there is only a Memorial at Mass, and no second Mass in the Chapter-house. In the case of the former, a Day in an Octave and an Octave Day with Rulers was superior to the Octave Day, and the Mass of the Octave was either said in the Chapter-house, or else a Memorial of it was made at the other Mass.

7 According to York Use, S. William and the Feast of the Chains of S. Peter had Octaves with Rulers, while it agreed with Hereford in including S. Agnes amongst those which had Octaves without Rulers.

8. According to Hereford Use, the Feasts with solemn Octaves and Octave Days (*i.e.*, with Rulers) were Christmas and four following days, Epiphany, Easter, Ascension, S. Ethelbert, Whitsun Day, Trinity, Corpus Christi, Peter and Paul, the Assumption, and Nativity of B.V.M., S. Thomas of Hereford and his Translation, also the Feast of the Patron Saint.§

Those with simple Octaves (*i.e.*, without Rulers) were S. Agnes, Nativity S. John Baptist, S. Lawrence, S. Martin, S. Andrew.

* With regard to this statement there is some difficulty: thus Feasts of Three Lessons are allowed to be celebrated in the Octave of the Name of Jesus; whereas in the Octaves of the Epiphany, Ascension Day, Assumption, and Nativity, there was clearly only a Memorial of them, but this may have been due to the fact that it seemed optional to celebrate that Feast either with or without Rulers.

† See Gradual and Missals '97, '2, '13, '26.

‡ See Sarum Breviary.

§ To these the Hereford Breviary adds the Name of Jesus.

VIII.—OF VOTIVE MASSES AND COMMEMORATIONS.

1. On Saturdays when there is no Double Feast, or one with Rulers, Octave, or Octave Day with Rulers, Vigil or Ember Day, and provided it to be out of Lent, there is a Commemoration of the B.V.M., according to the season, as is set forth in the Missal. This Commemoration will not supersede any Sunday Mass unsaid, owing to its having fallen within some Octave with Rulers.

Hereford Use forbade the Commemoration of Our Lady in Advent or LXX., as well as in Lent; and such was also the original rule both in Sarum and in York, until the days of Cardinal Kempe, though in the printed Missals the latter adopted the new custom.*

2. The first vacant ferial day in every week, but preferably on Monday, the Commemoration of the Saint of the place is said. Next after this, the Mass commonly called *Salus Populi* (for the welfare of all our brethren and sisters living) is said. If Tuesday is not vacant, then some other day is taken. After this, in cathedrals, the Saint of the diocese had a Commemoration. The other Votive Masses are said *ad libitum* in the following order: —Sunday, of the Trinity; Monday, of Angels; Tuesday, *Salus Populi*; Wednesday, of the Holy Ghost; Thursday, of the Blessed Sacrament; Friday, of the Holy Cross, of the Five Wounds, or of the Crown of our Lord; Saturday, of Our Lady.

3. According to York Use there was a Commemoration of S. William on Tuesday; there was also a Commemoration of SS. Peter and Paul, and of all Saints. The Commemorations were probably said in the same order as Sarum.

4. According to Hereford Use, these Commemorations were said—on Sunday, of the Trinity; on Monday, of Angels; Tuesday, of S. Ethelbert; Wednesday, of *Salus Populi*; Thursday, of S. Thomas of Hereford, or of the Holy Ghost; Friday, of the Holy Cross; Saturday, of the B.V.M.; there was also a Commemoration of Apostles.

IX.—OF MASSES FOR THE DEAD.

1. In the Cathedral Church of Salisbury there is a daily Mass for the faithful departed (they may have two, the other being for Bishops in the Chapter-house). That this could not be carried on in the country parishes is manifest; hence, it is probable that a Mass was said for them on the first vacant day in every month.

2. On All Souls' Day only one Collect is said.

* See Defensorium Directorii.

X.—OF MEMORIALS.

1. If an ordinary Sunday fall on a Double, there is no Memorial of it at *Mass;* but on Feast of Nine Lessons, not Doubles, there is.

2. There is a Memorial of Ferias in Advent, Lent, Ember Days, Rogations, and Vigils; but in Cathedrals, and where there are many clergy, if a Feast fall on these, there is generally first a Mass of the Feast.

3. There is no Memorial of a Votive Mass.

4. The order of the Breviary is generally kept in regard to Memorials.

5. When there are many Collects, the first and the last only are chanted aloud. Before the first is said, *The Lord be with you,* and *Let us pray;* and *Let us pray* before the second, and so before the P. Comm.; but not again. (For the number of Collects, see sect. xiv.)

XI.—OF THE OFFICE OR INTROIT.

1. The Office is repeated three times on Sundays, Feasts, and Octaves with Rulers, in all Commemorations of Our Lady, and in the Feast of the Place. First the Office, then the Psalm, then the Office again, then the *Glory,* then the Office again.

2. When there are no Rulers, first the Office, then the Psalm and *Glory,* and then the Office is said again.

3. On Passion Sunday and till Easter Day, with the exception of Maundy Thursday (if the Bishop celebrates), and Easter Eve, there is no *Glory,* etc., to the Office, and the latter is only repeated once.

4. In Eastertide, *Alleluia* is added at the end of the Office.

XII.—OF THE *KYRIES.*

1. Three Kyries, three *Christe Eleisons,* and again three *Kyries* are always said before all Masses, except on Good Friday.

2. In some of these are interpolated versicles or farces,* but the form is retained as above (except in one instance where there are ten instead of nine petitions). These are said in the following order:—On Principle Doubles, *O Divine Creator;* on Doubles, any of the succeeding eight appointed; on the Epiphany, Whitsun Day, and Corpus Christi, *O Lord, Fountain;* on Michaelmas Day, *O Lord, King;* on Holy Cross Day and the Invention, *O Light.*

3. At the daily Mass of Our Lady in her Chapel, if a Feast

* See pages 279-83.

(except on the two days before Easter), one of these *Kyries* is chanted without its verses, *i.e.*, *O Lord, Fountain*, or *O Lord, King Resplendent*; and in the same way on Sundays is said, *O Lord, King, Father*; on Mondays, *O King Beneficent*;* on Tuesdays, *O Lord, Maker*; on Wednesdays, *O Lord God Almighty*; on Thursdays, *Maker of the World*; on Fridays, *O Light and Source of Light*; on Saturday, *O Lord Almighty*.†

4. What the YORK Use was does not appear, since no *Kyries* are to be found in its Missal.

5. In the HEREFORD Missal there were 16 *Kyries*, the ones in addition to the Sarum being *Pater Cuncta*, *O Rex clemens*, *Summe Deus*, *Kyrie Genitor*, *Kyrie Rex immense*, and *Puerorum caterva* (this last being appropriated to Innocents' Day).

XIII.—OF THE *GLORIA IN EXCELSIS*.‡

1. This is said out of Advent, from LXX. to Easter Eve exclusive (excepting Maundy Thursday, when the Bishop celebrates), and on Feast of Nine or Three Lessons, with or without Rulers (except the four Feasts of SS. Petronilla, Bertinus, Thecla, and Romanus). Hence it is said, when the *Te Deum* is said, at Matins.

2. In Votive Masses it is not said as a rule. It is, however, said on Our Lady's Commemoration on Saturdays, on Votive Masses of Angels, and apparently on those allotted to the days in the week (with the exception of *Salus Populi*, and the Mass of the Cross, provided this latter be not of LXX. to Easter and Advent). It is not said in Masses for the Dead, or when the Sunday Mass is transferred to the week day.

XIV.—OF COLLECTS.§

2. More than seven Collects are never to be said, for Christ in the Lord's Prayer did not exceed seven petitions. An uneven number of Collects is always to be preserved, except in Christmas week, both at Mass and at Matins. If the number of Collects is naturally even, it is made uneven by adding the Memorial of All Saints, *Grant, O Lord*. When the Mass of any Saint is said in the Chapter-house, Memorials may be said also of others.

* *Rex clemens*. This is found in the later Hereford Missal, but not in the present Sarum books, except as being referred to in this Rubric, which occurs after the Office on p. 521.

† This "saying without verses" means that the chant of the interpolated *Kyrie* was sung without the farces themselves.

‡ The authority for this section is the Rubric in the first Mass on Christmas Day.

§ This section is the substance of a long Rubric in the Mass for Advent Sunday.

2. On all Sundays, and Feasts with Rulers, which fall on Sundays from Easter to Ascension Day inclusive, there are no Memorials at the Mass of the Resurrection which is then said; nor of the Sunday at the Mass of the Saints, if there is one. At the Sunday Mass, or that of the Saints, there is always a Memorial of the Resurrection.

3. In Feasts of Nine Lessons in Lent, or Ember Days, or Advent, there ought to be two Masses—first of the Feast, then of the Fast; but where there are not clergy enough, a Memorial of the Fast may be made at the Mass of the Feast.

4. In Advent Collects are said in the first week thus—1, Advent; 2, Our Lady; 3, All Saints; in the following weeks—1, Collect of the Day; 2, of Advent; 3, of S. Mary.

5. On week-days, and Feasts without Rulers from the First Sunday after the Octave of the Epiphany to XL., are said five Collects—1, of the Day; 2, of Our Lady; 3, of All Saints; 4, of the whole Church; 5, of Peace (this latter is omitted if two Saints are commemorated on the same day). But on Ash-Wednesday and till XL. they are—1, of Day; 2, of Penitents; 3, Our Lady; 4, All Saints; 5, the whole Church.

6. On Sundays in Lent, one Collect only is said.

7. On week-days in Lent, till Maundy Thursday, there are added to the five Collects used on Ash-Wednesday—6, of Peace; 7, for All sorts and conditions of Men.

8. On week-days, and Feasts without Rulers from Low Sunday to Ascension Day, three Collects only are said—1, of the Day; 2, of the Resurrection; 3, of All Saints.

9. On week-days, and Feasts with Rulers from First Sunday after Trinity to Advent, five Collects, as in paragraph 5.

10. On Sundays, and Feasts with Rulers through the year, the same number of Collects is generally said as at Matins. Sometimes there are several Memorials; as on S. Processus' Day at his Mass, there is a Mem. of S. Swithin, Apostles, Our Lady, and All Saints—this latter to make up the number.

There is a Memorial of the Blessed Trinity (whenever the Mass is of the Sunday) from Trinity Sunday till Advent.

11. In the Mass of Our Lady in her Chapel—1, of Our Lady; 2, of the Trinity: 3, For the Bishop and those under him; 4, Deceased benefactors; 5, For all, living and dead.

In the Votive Mass of *Salus Populi* the Collects follow the season.

12. The Secrets and Post Communions are always the same in number as the Collects. If the Collect is addressed to the

Father, it is ended *Through Our Lord;* if to the Son, *Who livest and reignest with God the Father.* If, in the beginning, mention is made of the Son, *Through the same our Lord;* if at the end, *Who liveth with Thee.* If mention is made of the Holy Ghost, at the end is said, *In the unity of the same Holy Ghost.* In saying Collects the rules of section x. are to be kept.

13. According to HEREFORD, one Collect only was said in Trinitytide and Epiphany, on Sundays and Feasts of Nine Lessons, unless a Feast of Three occurred. The Feast of S. Ethelbert was observed in Whitsuntide, and a Memorial made even on Whitsun Day.

XV.—OF THE EPISTLE, GRADUAL, *ALLELUIA*, TRACT, SEQUENCE, AND GOSPEL.

1. After the last Collect is said the EPISTLE, or, at certain seasons, a Lesson or Lessons.* These Epistles and Gospels varied in the different Uses, but, with very few exceptions, only in respect of those on Wednesdays and Fridays. (For which see Appendix B.)

2. The GRADUAL follows, and is always said, except from Friday in Easter Week (exclusive) to Trinity Sunday, after which is a verse, and then (in the Mass of the Day) the Gradual is always repeated, except on Doubles, Thursday and Friday in Easter Week, Wednesday in *Lætare* † Week, the Ember Days (except after the last Lesson), and when there is a Tract. In Votive Masses, if High, it is repeated, except from LXX. to Maundy Thursday and in Our Lady's Mass, when there is no Sequence or Chant, but it is not repeated in the daily Low Mass in her Chapel. The Gradual is said in Masses for the Dead.

3. After the Gradual, the ALLELUIA and ℣. follow. Then the *Alleluia* is repeated with a cadence if there is no Sequence. It is never said when there is a Tract (except on Easter and Whitsun Eves), nor between LXX. and Easter Eve.

In Eastertide, *i.e.*, from Saturday in Easter Week to Trinity Sunday, two *Alleluias* and ℣s. are said, except in the Rogation Days and on Whitsun Eve, on the former of which only one *Alleluia* and ℣. is sung, and on the latter none.

4. The TRACT is said instead of the *Alleluia* on the Sundays between LXX. inclusive and Easter, and on Sundays, Mondays,

* Such was its name if it came out of any part of Scripture other than the Epistles.

† *i.e.*, Mid-Lent week. There was a Lesson on this day, it having in the beginning been the day for the public Scrutiny of those who were to be baptized at Easter.

Wednesdays, and Fridays, between Ash-Wednesday (inclusive) and Easter; also on Ember Saturdays (excepting in Whitsuntide), and in Masses for the Dead.

5. SEQUENCES are said on the Sundays of Advent, on Christmas Day, the Sunday in the Octave, the Circumcision, the Epiphany, Easter Day and in the Octave, Low Sunday; at the Mass of the Resurrection in Eastertide, Ascension Day, Whitsun Day and in the Octave, Trinity Sunday, and Corpus Christi; also in all Feasts with Rulers out of LXX. to Easter but there is no Sequence on the Feast of S. Michael in the Mountain Tomb nor on Feasts of Many Confessors.

The Saints' Days which have proper Sequences, according to Sarum, are SS. Andrew, Nicholas, Concep. B. V. M., the four days after Christmas, S. Vincent, Conv. S. Paul, Candlemas, Lady Day, Invent. Holy Cross, S. Alban, Nativ. S. John Baptist, SS. Peter and Paul, the Visitation of our Lady, through and on Octave Day, Trans. S. Martin, Trans. of S. Osmund, S. Anne, Chains of S. Peter, Transfiguration, Name of JESUS, the Assumption and Octave Day, Nativ. B. V. M., Holy Cross Day, Michaelmas, All Saints' Day, S. Katherine.

According to YORK, Sequences were said, in addition to the above times, in Epiphany and Trinitytide; and on the Eleventh Sunday after Trinity (the Sunday of the Publican), there was a special Sequence.*

The Days with proper Sequences were as above, except that those for Christmas, Circumcision, S. Thomas Cant., Conv. S. Paul, S. Vincent, Candlemas, Lady Day, and S. Mary Magd. were different, and that there were Sequences for the following days—Trans. S. William, S. George, Trans, S. Wilfred, S. John ant. Port, S. William and five days in Octave, S. Bartholomew, Decoll. S. John Baptist, Trans. S. Cuthbert, the Eleven Thousand Virgins, and three Sequences in Octave of S. Martin. The Visit. B. V. M., Transfiguration, and Name of JESUS have none (though the service is supplied at the end of the York Missal).

According to HEREFORD, Sequences were said as at Sarum (except that the Sequence for S. Thomas Cant. differed), and with the addition of Sequences for S. Ethelbert and Day in Octave, S. Thomas Hereford (October 2), and Octave Day, S. Raphael, S. Denys, Trans. S. Thomas Hereford, and S. Edmund.

6. After the Gradual, Tract, Alleluia, or Sequence, follows the GOSPEL and Creed (if it is to be said).

* See Appendix B.

7. The proper Epistles and Gospels for Wednesday may be transferred to Thursday if a Feast occur on that day, but where there are proper ones on Friday they must be said or omitted. Where there are none (as according to Sarum) in Trinitytide, the Epistle and Gospel for Wednesday may be used on Friday, but not on Saturday, on account of Our Lady's Commemoration. The Epistles and Gospels are never anticipated.

8. In the York and Hereford Missals, there are Epistles and Gospels on Fridays as well as on Wednesdays in Trinitytide.

XVI.—OF THE CREED.

1. The Creed is said on all Sundays at High Mass (whether the Mass be of the Sunday or not), through and on the Octave of Christmas, on Maundy Thursday (if the Bishop celebrates), on Easter, Whitsun Day, Ascension Day, Corpus Christi (the Gradual seems to allow it to be said in and on the Octave of this Feast if celebrated with Rulers of Choir), on all Doubles and Feasts of Apostles and Evangelists, on both Feasts of the Holy Cross, on both Feasts of S. Michael, on Nativ. S. John Baptist,* S. Gabriel, and S. Mary Magd., on the Feast of the Crown of our Lord, at Our Lady's Mass when said at the High Altar, at Weddings, at the Consecration of a Church, and on all Saints' Days to whom the Church or an Altar is dedicated.

2. According to York, the Creed was said on all Sundays (whatever the Mass), on Christmas Day and through the Octave, the Epiphany and Octave Day, Easter Day through and on the Octave, Ascension and Octave Day, Whitsun Day through and on the Octave, Corpus Christi and on the Octave Day, on both Feasts of the Holy Cross,† on all Feasts of Apostles and Evangelists, on the Chair of S. Peter, the Chains of S. Peter, on the Octave Day of SS. Peter and Paul, on all Feasts of Our Lady and on the Octave Day of her Assumption and Nativity, on both Feasts of S. John Baptist, S. Mary Magd., S. Michael, All Saints' Day, the Feast of Relics, S. William's Day (in the Mother Church), the Feast of the Four Doctors, S. Ambrose, the two Augustines and S. Jerome, the Dedication (in Cathedral Church), and on the Day of the Absolution of a Corpse.

3. According to Hereford, the Creed was said on all Sundays at High Mass (whatever it was), Christmas Day and eight following days, and so also at Easter and Whitsuntide, on the Epiphany, Ascension Day and Octave Day, Corpus Christi and Octave Day,

* See Proper of Saints. † See York Proper of Saints.

Let us kneel and *Rise* (whenever used), the *Collects, Lessons, Epistle, Gradual, and* ℣., Alleluia and ℣., *Tract, Sequence, Gospel, Creed*, the *Preface*, Our Father, *World without end, The Peace of the Lord*, Agnus Dei, *Comm., P. Comm.*, Ite, Missa est, *Let us give thanks, or May they rest.*

2. In High Mass, the *Gloria in Excelsis* and *Creed* are begun by the Priest, the tone being given him on certain days by the Rulers or Precentor, and then sung by the Choir; *The Lord be with you* and *Let us pray* (whenever used), the *Collects*, the *Preface, World without end, Our Father, The Peace of the Lord, P. Comm., Bow down yourselves* (if Bishop celebrates), are intoned. All the rest is said secretly.

XXII.—OF GENUFLECTING, CROSSING, SITTING, AND STANDING.

A. 1. The Priest genuflects in Mass at *Let us kneel*, on Ash-Wednesday and through Lent; at 1st and 4th stations in Procession on Palm Sunday. The Bishop genuflects at *Come, Holy Ghost*, in the Consecration of Holy Oils on Maundy Thursday.

The word *genuflects* occurs also before the *Gloria in Excelsis*, on Easter and Whitsun Eves, and nowhere else in the Missal. The Deacon genuflects when the Priest turns to the people. This is confirmed by *Tractatus*, secs. xix., lxx., civ.

2. A profound inclination, *corpore inclinato*, is made—1. Before *Take away from us*. 2. From *Thee, therefore*, to *and entreat*, in the Canon. 3. From *We humbly* to *that as many as*. 4. At *Let the obedient performance*.

The word *humilians* (which, though it might mean genuflexion,* is included under this section) is used—1. At High Mass, of the position of the Deacon when the blessing is given at the Gospel. 2. Before receiving the Body. 3. On approaching the Altar for High Mass. (*Tractatus*, sec. xciii.)

3. An inclination of head and body, *capite et corpore*, is made before *In the spirit of humility*.

4. The word *inclinatus* is used—1. Of the Choir at the Altar as it turns to the Gospeller. 2. At the beginning and end of the *Gradual, Alleluia, Sequence*, etc. 3. At the beginning of the *Creed*, till the Choir takes it up. 4. At *Was Incarnate, was made Man, was crucified*, and *Life everlasting* till the *Offertory*.† 5. From the *Offertory* to the end of Mass.

* See pictures in English Missals.

† By Constit. of Lincoln, based upon the Sarum *Tractatus*, and dating from 1236, the Choir of that Cathedral are to bow at *Glory be to God on high, We praise Thee, Receive our prayer*. (Wilk. Conc., vol. i., p. 534.)

B. The Priest *inclines* with the Choir at 1, 2, and 4 of the above; also at offering the Chalice and Bread; before and after the Consecration of the Host; before Consecration of Chalice; at uncovering Chalice before fraction; at *I worship Thee*, in the first prayer of Communion; after Reception of the Blood, and at the end of Mass.

The *Tractatus*, sec. xiii., adds—1, All clergy are to bow to the Altar, and then to the Dean, if entering the Quire at the East; to the Bishop, if entering at the West; the same on going out. 2. In passing and repassing the Altar; and the same on going out.

D. The Priest *makes the sign of the Cross* at —1, The Absolution; 2, *In the Name of*; 3, *The Lord be with you*, throughout Mass;* 4, *Glory be to Thee*; 5, *Blessed is He that cometh*; 6, *Heavenly benediction*, in Canon; 7, *In the Name of*, at end of Mass.

E. The Choir sign themselves at the *Glory of the Father*, and at 3 and 4 above.

F. In Quire, all Clergy *stand*, except at the Epistle, Gradual, *Alleluia*, Tract, and Sequence, when they may *sit*; but on Doubles they must also do so at the *Alleluia*. The boys stand when singing: at the Canon they go into the area and stand inclined to Altar, from *Thee, therefore*, till after the Consecration of the Chalice.

G. The Choir *face the Altar* at the beginning of Mass, the *Kyrie*, and the *Gloria in Excelsis*, at *We praise thee*, *Receive our prayer*, *In the glory of the Father*; at the end of the Gradual, Tract, *Alleluia*, and Sequence; and before turning to the Gospeller (at the Gospel the Choir *faces* the Gospeller). In the Creed, at *I believe in one God*, *Was incarnate ...... Pilate*, and *Life everlasting*, till the Offertory, and from it to the end of Mass.

H. Rulers, when two only, do as the Clergy do; except on Doubles, when they follow the rule of the Choir.

K. The Choir *kneels* from the *Sanctus* to *The peace of God*; and on all week days and feasts without rulers, whilst saying the prayers and psalms appointed, except from Easter Day to second Sunday after Trinity.

L. The Choir changes its side alternate weeks—*i.e.*, it is one week on the *Decani*, the next on the *Cantoris* side. On all

* It may be doubted, as this Verse and Respond follow the *Gloria in Excelsis* and Creed, whether the signing does not properly belong to the conclusion of them. Its being, however, enjoined before turning for the Verse and Respond, after the P. Comm., has induced the other belief.

Double Feasts, however, it is on the *Decani* side, except where there are many Doubles together, *e.g.*, from Christmas to Octave of Epiphany, Maundy Thursday to Low Sunday, Ascension Day and Octave, Whitsun Day to Trinity Sunday, at which times the Choir changes sides every day.

XXIII.—OF THE COLOURS OF VESTMENTS.*

WHITE is used on Easter Day, and till the Octave of Ascension Day† (except Invent. Cross); Feasts and Octaves of Our Lady; both Feasts of S. Michael, S. John in Christmastide;‡ Virgins' Days;§ the Dedication of Church, and Commemorations of our Lady. It will be observed that no colour is given for Christmas. Though the reading adverted to in the foot-note has been abandoned, the Translator thinks that the prescription of *White* instead of *Red* Vestments, for S. John in Christmastide tends to show that the former was the colour of the season, red being considered inappropriate to that Saint, since he was not a Martyr.

According to YORK, the Priest wore a White Cope on Easter Eve, for the blessing of fire, etc.

RED—All Sundays (not in Easter-tide); all Martyrs, Apostles, and Evangelists (out of Easter-tide), Ash-Wednesday, Maundy Thursday, Good Friday, Easter Eve, Simple Feasts of Nine Lessons in Lent,‖ and both Feasts of S. John Baptist and the Holy Cross. *Red* is also assigned to Rulers of Choir, when singing Tracts. This was probably given to Apostles and Evangelists, because most of them were Martyrs, a reason which receives confirmation from the fact that *White* is given to S. John Evangelist.

YELLOW for Feasts of one or many Confessors.

No colour is assigned to the Epiphany, Corpus Christi, the Transfiguration, or Name of JESUS; nor is any ferial colour given. It is known, however, from inventories of Church goods, etc., that Vestments of Blue, Brown, Green, and other colours as well as of Black, were in use.

* The authority for this section is the Rubric in the Ordinary of the Sarum Mass and in the *Tractatus*.

† *Tempore Paschali*, but this ended when the Paschal Candle was taken away on the Friday before Whitsun Day.

‡ *S. Joannis, Apostoli in ebdomada Nativitatis Domini.* This may be read, *S. Joann. Apostoli—in ebd. Nativ. Dni.*—thus giving White as the colour for Christmas; but after originating this reading it has been abandoned, as it was certainly suggested by the desire to find the the colour for Christmas.

§ See *Tractatus*, sec. xix., an inference from the colours of the Rulers' Copes.

‖ *Tractatus* sec. xix.

In endeavouring to fill up the blank days, Trinity Sunday and All Saints' Day have not been included, as the former falls under the general rule of Sundays, and an additional authority for Red rather than White, the modern Roman colour, is afforded by the fact that Red was used in several French dioceses to a late period (De Moleon, *Voyages Liturgiques*, p. 247)—a sufficient argument of itself for not departing from the general rule laid down in the Rubric, as has been shown in the Introduction, where the connection between the English and Gallican Churches is pointed out.

For a like reason, though its grounds are not so strong, All Saints' Day has been placed in the same category. For many centuries that day was equivalent to All Martyrs, and may fairly be supposed to have retained their colour, although embracing Virgins and Confessors.

With respect to the Epiphany, Corpus Christi, Transfiguration, the Name of JESUS, and the ferial colours, a conjecture (though *only* a conjecture) might be based on a careful examination of French Missals, particularly that of Rouen; at all events, the French, rather than the Roman Liturgies, will of course throw most light on the truth.

XXIV.—OF THE VESTMENTS.

1. The Vestments of a Priest for Mass are the Amice, Alb, the Girdle, Stole, Maniple, and Chasuble (this latter is called generally, *the Vestment*, and in inventories and constitutions of Bishops, a pair or two pair of Vestments mean two sets of Chasubles, Amices, Albs, &c.—*i.e.*, all the articles mentioned above);* also occasionally it included the Vestments for Deacon and Sub-Deacon at High Mass.

2. The Vestments of a Bishop are the Sandals and Stockings, the Amice, Alb, Stole, Reliquary pendant from the neck, Tunicle, Dalmatic, Maniple, Chasuble when celebrating, and Cope at other times, Gloves, Episcopal Ring (kept in its place by another smaller one), and Mitre.

3. The Cope is used in Processions, Benedictions, Solemn Matins, and Vespers; also in the Mass of the Pre-sanctified on Good Friday. It is not strictly a sacerdotal Vestment, and is worn by the Rulers of the Choir and others. See sec. v.

4. The Ministers wear Albs and Amices, Girdle, Stole, *Maniple*; the Deacon, a Dalmatic; and Sub-Deacon, a Tunicle.

* Constit. Walter Gray, Archbp. York, A.D. 1250. Wilk. Concil. i., 698.

In Advent and from LXX. to Maundy Thursday they wear folded Chasubles; at the Epistle the Sub-Deacon takes his off: at the Gospel the Deacon crosses his over the left arm, and so keeps it till after the Post-Communion, when he places it as before. Even at these seasons, however, the Dalmatic and Tunicle are worn at the Mass of a Feast.

5. On Ember Days (except in Whitsuntide), Rogations (at the Mass of the Fast), in Processions, and when the Sunday or Saint's Day Mass is said in the Chapter-house; on Ash-Wednesday, Good Friday, and Palm Sunday, only Albs and Amices are worn by the ministers.

6. The Clergy are always in Black Copes,* except on Principal Doubles, and on Doubles occurring on Sunday, when they wear silk Copes of the colour of the day. On the Vigil of Easter, and through and on the Octave, they wear Surplices only, as also on Doubles occurring from Easter to Michaelmas.

7. The Thurifer, Acolytes, and Candle-bearers are always in Albs and Amices, as also the Choir; the Acolyte wears a silk Mantle in addition; † the boys who read the lessons, or chant the Gradual or *Alleluia*, wear Surplices. At Low Mass the Server is in Surplice.‡

8. If a Bishop celebrate, and it be Maundy Thursday or Whitsun Day, he has seven Deacons, seven Sub-Deacons, and three Acolytes; on other Double Feasts only five. On Feasts with Rulers, two at the least; but on Good Friday only one.

XXV.—OF THE ORNAMENTS OF THE ALTAR.

The ALTAR is to be covered with three Linen Cloths,§ of which one at least is blessed; a Cross is always placed before the celebrant ‖—this, with a pair of candlesticks, stands on a beam *over* the Altar, though, in latter times, probably, *on* it. The *Tractatus* prescribes on every Sunday in Advent, and on all other Sundays, four Candles at Mass—two at the steps of the Altar, and two on the Super-Altar.¶

* *i.e.*, the close-fitting black stuff Choral Cope with arm-holes.

† *Mantellum* (? Tunic).

‡ Concil. Oxford A.D. 1222.

§ Conf. Constit. of Westminster, A.D. 1229. Wilk. Conc., p. 622., and Constit. Walter Cantilupe, A.D. 1240, p. 665.

‖ Stat. Richard Bp. Chichester, A.D. 1246, p. 688.

¶ The *Tractatus* reads *in superaltari*; so does the Dublin MS., now at Cambridge. Du Cange gives two meanings to this word—1. *Ciborium*, which it means equivalent to the "Beam" which took its place in Sarum Cathedral; 2. A portable Altar, which it cannot mean here. Of course the word must not be here confounded with the word Super-Altar in the modern sense of Retro-Altar or Re-table.

On Christmas Day, Easter and Whitsun Eves, and on Principal and Greater Doubles,* eight Candles *about* the Altar, of a pound weight each—six on the ledge with the Crucifix and Relics, *i.e.*, on the Beam above (note ¶ p. lvi.); two before Our Lady's image; and five of half-pound weight in the corona before the step of the Altar; also five on the wall over the pulpits where the Lessons are read. From Whitsun Day to and on Our Lady's Nativity, seven Candles are placed in the bronze corona; on all other Lesser and Inferior Doubles there are four Candles *about* the Altar, ten before Our Lady's image, three in the corona, and three in the pulpit.

On days which have a Triple Invitatory, and on the Thursday, Friday, and Saturday in Easter and Whitsuntide, the rule of Sundays in Advent obtains, also on Maundy Thursday.

On all Feasts, on Good Friday, and on week-days, two candles only are used, as also at the Sepulchre on Maundy Thursday; on the next night, and till Easter Day, one only is lit.

The Constitutions of Lichfield, A.D. 1195, in some sort agree with the *Tractatus*—thus the Thesaurarius must provide ten Candles beyond (*ultra*) the Great Altar on Double Feasts, two over (*insuper*) S. Chad's, and one over the others; and four beyond (*ultra*) the High Altar on Feasts with Rulers.

The Council of Oxford, 1222, orders "tempore quo missarum solemnia peraguntur accendantur duo candelæ, una, cum lampade ad minus."

Besides the above there were other ornaments of the Altar which are best enumerated by giving a list of the minimum required in each church by the Constitutions of Westminster, 1229:—2 pair of Vestments,† 2 pair of Corporals of a fit size; 1 Rochet;‡ 2 Altar-frontals—1 Festal, 1 Ferial; 3 Linen Cloths, one at least blessed;§ 2 Chalices; 2 Pyxes—one for the Host, one for the Oblations; 2 Cruets—one for wine, one for water; a pair of Candlesticks, a Censer, a Chrismatory; 2 Crosses—one for Processions, the other for Funerals. In the Quire—2 Surplices, a Banner, Lenten Veil, movable Sacrarium, Lantern, Hand-bell,‖ glass Windows, and decently-dressed Choir.

A dispute arising as to who was to provide the Ornaments of the Church, it was decided by Gray, Archbishop of York, 1253

* Feasts which have a Procession—*i.e.*, even if they fall on a week-day; hence these are equivalent to Principal and Greater Doubles.

† *i.e.*, Albs, Amices, &c. Conf. Cantilupe's Constit., 1240 A.D., which provides 3 sets.

‡ Two; Const. Cantilupe. § Four. *Ibid.* ‖ Two, and also a Bier. *Ibid.*

A.D., that the parishioners were bound to supply 1 Chalice, a Missal, and principal Vestment (*i.e.*, Chasuble, Alb, Amice, etc.), 3 Towels, Corporas; and Vestments for the Deacon and Sub-Deacon, according to their ability, together with a silk Cope for principal feasts, and two others for the Rulers of Choir; 2 Crosses, Bier, Holy-Water Vat, Pax, Paschal Candle-stand, Censer, Lantern, Hand-bell, Lenten Veil, 2 Acolytes' Candlesticks; Books—*i.e.*, Legendary, Antiphoner, Grail, Psalter, Troper, Ordinal, Missal, Manual; Frontal for High Altar; 3 Surplices, Pyx, Lights, etc. The Rector was bound to keep the chancel in repair, roof, walls, windows, and benches. (Conf. Statutes, Walter Peckham, 1279. Synod Exon, 1281.)*

XXVI.—WHEN THE IMAGES ARE COVERED UP.

On the Monday after XL., all Crosses, Images, and Relics, also the Pyx with the Blessed Sacrament, are to be covered up till Matins on Easter Day, except at Mass and till Vespers on Palm Sunday. Also from the preceding Saturday let a veil be hung between the Quire and the Altar, there to remain till the Gospel on Wednesday in Holy Week, when it falls at the words, "*The veil of the Temple was rent in twain.*" It is, however, raised at the Gospel at Mass till "*Brethren and sisters, pray for me;*" and if the next day be a Feast of Nine Lessons, it is kept up till the following Matins. If the Mass of the Feast has to be said after that for the day, it is left down till the Gospel.

According to HEREFORD Use, the veil was raised also at the Elevation and Procession, and (if a Bishop celebrated) after the Confession; on Ember Saturday, in Lent, however, it is not raised till the Tract.

LOW MASS IN ELEVENTH TO SIXTEENTH CENTURIES.†

I.—ON THE PREPARATION OF THE CELEBRANT.

The Priest having confessed and said *Matins*, *Prime*, and *Terce*, (Council Oxon, 1222), enters the Sacristy, says the Prayers of

* In Cathedrals, many other ornaments, of course, appear, *e.g.*, Fans, Pomes (balls of silver filled with charcoal to warm the hands), Crowns (to hang before Altars), Combs, etc. (See Invent. Ornament. in Eccles. Sarum, 1222 A.D.)

† Throughout this chapter, and the next, as well as in the Rubrics, the present tense denotes the SARUM, the past YORK and HEREFORD Uses.

Preparation; washes his hands, saying a prayer (according to YORK Use); prepares the Chalice,* placing on it a clean purificator † *(pannus)*; and on that the Paten with the Bread, and the Burse with two Corporas.

He then vests himself, saying, *Come, Holy Ghost*, and the Psalm *Judge me* (see Ordinary).

According to HEREFORD Use, he said this Psalm before the Altar; in the YORK and HEREFORD Uses, with some Versicles; and in the former two, in the latter one Collect was said in addition.

If a Bishop he vests as above. See Rubrics, sec. xxiii.

The Server must be in a Surplice without colour (*non miniatus*).‡

II.—ENTRANCE OF THE PRIEST, OFFICE, *KYRIE*.

He now approaches the Altar, places the Chalice upon it, first spreading the Corporas; then descending, says the last two ℣℣.§ of the Lord's Prayer; or, according to YORK, a ℣. and ℟. Then the Confession, the Server saying the Absolution, and *vice versa*; then raising and signing himself, he says, *God Almighty*, two ℣℣. and ℟℟., *Let us pray*, and the private prayers, after which he goes up to the Altar.

In YORK and HEREFORD Uses, the verses were different (the HEREFORD had two which the YORK had not), and the Priest went up at once to the Altar.

He then proceeds as in the Ordinary, saying the Office with the Server.

According to HEREFORD Use, the ℟. *Our help* with its ℣. (said according to SARUM, just before going up to the Altar), were said here before the Office.

Then follow the *Kyries*, the Server saying them with the Priest.

III.—THE *GLORIA IN EXCELSIS*, COLLECTS, EPISTLES, GRADUAL, *ALLELUIA*, TRACT OR SEQUENCE, AND CREED.

The Priest goes to the midst of the Altar, and says the *Gloria in Excelsis* with raised hand,‖ inclining his head; which latter he

* When Low Masses first began, the Priest was in the habit of putting in the Wine and Water here before Mass.

† Constit. of Durham, 1221. The Priest must have near the Altar a clean cloth enclosed in another, and covered at the sides on which to wipe their lips and fingers after communicating.

‡ Counc. of Durham and Oxford, 1221 A.D.

§ This Versicle and Respond are not said, according YORK and HEREFORD.

‖ Constit. Lincoln, Wilk. Conc., p. 535.

also does at *We worship Thee; receive our prayer, Jesu*; and at the end, when he signs himself. Then turning, raising his arms, joining (and then disjoining, HEREFORD) his hands, he says, *The Lord be with you*; then returning the same way (with joined hands; he disjoins them at *Let us pray*, closing them at the end of the last HEREFORD), he says the Collects with the Epistle, etc., where he remains, at the Epistle side, till the Gospel.

IV.—THE GOSPEL.

The Server takes the book, inclines, places it on the Gospel side.* The Priest then goes to that side, and says the Gospel (see Ordinary).

According to YORK, before this he said, *Blessed is He that cometh in the Name of the Lord.*

V.—FROM THE CREED TO THE CANON.

The Priest going to the centre of the Altar, says the Creed (with hands for an instant joined, which he disjoins as he proceeds, HEREFORD).

YORK agrees with Sarum about the inclinations in the Creed, but according to the HEREFORD Missal the Priest genuflects from *And was Incarnate* to *for us.*

The Priest uncovers the Chalice (at the end of the Creed), places the Paten before him,† and then uplifting the Chalice‡ with both hands, says, *Receive, O Holy Trinity.*

According to YORK, the Bread was arranged on the Corporas, and the Priest said the same prayer, having first washed his hands; after which he offered the Chalice with the Wine, saying, *Let this Sacrifice be acceptable to Almighty God, In the Name of*, etc.

According to HEREFORD, the Bread and Paten were placed on the top of the Chalice, then kissing it he offered them, saying, *Receive, O Holy Trinity, this oblation which I offer Thee in memory of the Passion of our Lord Jesus Christ; and grant that it may be acceptable in Thy sight on high, and work the salvation of myself and all the faithful. Through.*

After this he replaces the Chalice, covering it; and, taking the Paten, places the Bread on the Corporas before the Chalice, and,

* Conf. MS. Bibl. Reg. 17, B, xvii. Brit. Mus.

† Following Dr. Rock's interpretation of this Rubric. It is quite possible, however, that the SARUM mode of oblating may have been as at HEREFORD; there is at least nothing against it.

‡ Into which wine is poured, either now by the Server, or this had been done before by the Priest in the Sacristy (this is the earlier practice). Conf. Bocquillot, Traité. Histor., pp. 406-7.

blessing the Paten, puts it on the right of the Chalice, under the cloths.

Then he goes to the Epistle side, and says as he washes his hands, the Server ministering to him, *Cleanse me*, etc.

According to York he did the same, saying, *I will wash my hands in innocency, and so will I go to Thine Altar, O Lord,* and the Hymn, *Come, Holy Ghost.*

According to Hereford he said the same Hymn;* adding the ℣. and ℟. *Send forth Thy Spirit*, etc., with the prayer, *Kindle in our hearts* (see p. 393).

Then returning, he says with joined hands, *In the Spirit*, etc.; and then raising himself and censing the Altar on the right, he says, *In the Name of etc.* (see Ordinary).

According to York he did the same, but in blessing the Sacrifice he said, *Let this sacrifice be bles + sed, order + ed, and sancti + fied.*

According to Hereford he did the same, and then held his hands over the Chalice and said, *Come, O Almighty and eternal God, the Sanctifier*, and signed it, saying, *Bless + and sanctify this Sacrifice which is prepared for Thee;* and then himself, saying, *In the Name of*, etc.

He then proceeds as in the Ordinary.

In York and Hereford the ℣. and ℟. to *Brethren and sisters, pray*, were slightly different.

At the *Sanctus* he raises arms and joins his hands till *In the Name*, when he signs himself. Here a bell rings thrice.

According to Hereford, before the Canon he said, adoring the Crucifix, *We adore Thee, O Christ, and bless Thee, for by Thy Holy Cross Thou hast redeemed the world. Have mercy upon us, O Thou Who hast suffered for us.*†

VI.—FROM THE CANON TO THE *PAX*.

The Canon in the three Missals is the same, except that the York orders the Chalice to be uncovered at *By Whom* instead of *By Him;* and the Hereford inserts the rubric, *Here let him incline to the Host*, instead of the Sarum one before *this oblation*, as also before *THIS IS MY BODY*. At the consecration of the Chalice after *Holy and venerable hands*, it adds, *Let him raise his eyes;* and before *Upon which*, and *Remember also*, it has *Let him raise his arms and say.*

* Omitting the verse *dudum sacrata*. What was this verse? It is not in the Sarum or Roman version of this Hymn.

† A Sarum MS. Manual, quoted by Dr. Rock, prescribes the same, and orders the kissing of the feet of the Crucifix or Majesty therein painted.

By the Constit. Stavely, Bp. Coventry, 1237 A.D., and Peckham, Archbp. Cantuar., 1281 A.D., a bell is ordered to be rung thrice at the Elevation.* Conf. Synod Exon. 1287 A.D., which orders Priests to make two standard wax-lights out of the oblations of the faithful, to be lit at this period; and the Constits. Woodlake, 1308, grant an indulgence to all who hold lights at the Consecration. At the Lord's Prayer, according to HEREFORD, the Priest lifts his *arms*, not his *hands*.

VII.—FROM THE *PAX TO THE END OF MASS.*

Before the *Pax* is given, he says the prayer, *O Lord, Holy Father*. This is omitted in the YORK *Use*. In the HEREFORD is said, *O Lord, Who saidst unto Thine Apostles* (see the modern Roman Use).

Then he gives and sends the *Pax*, kissing the Corporas on the right, and the Chalice.†

In the HEREFORD Use he kissed the Chalice before the Altar. The YORK and HEREFORD *Pax* was, *Receive the bond of peace and charity, that ye may be fit for the Holy Mysteries of God.*

Then holding the Body in both hands, he says the prayers of Communion (see Ordinary).

According to YORK, after the *Pax*, he said, *Let us pray;* and holding the Body in both hands, *O Lord, Holy Father* (as in the Ordinary, changing the *I* and *me* to *we and* us, throughout it); then, *Let us pray* and *Let not the reception of Thy Body* (nearly the same as the third Sarum Prayer of Communion); *Let us pray;* and the second Sarum Prayer, *O Lord Jesus Christ.* Here he received the Body, first making the sign of the Cross over his mouth; then the Blood, saying, *The Body of our Lord Jesus Christ be my everlasting healing unto life eternal. Amen. The Blood of our Lord Jesus Christ preserve me unto life eternal. Amen. The Body and Blood of our Lord Jesus Christ preserve my body and soul unto everlasting life. Amen.*

According to HEREFORD, after the *Pax*, he kissed the minister, saying, *The peace of Christ and the Holy Church be with thee and the sons of the Church.* Then followed *O Lord, Holy Father* (in the plural as YORK); then *O Lord Jesu Christ; O God the Father;* and this, *We return thanks to Thee, O God the Father, for those who are already in bliss, and we ask for help by their intercession with Thee;*

* See Wilk. Conc., vol. i., p. 640; and ii., p. 48.

† By the Council of Durham, 1221 A.D., it seems to have been the custom also to kiss the Paten. Priests are forbidden by this Council to kiss the Eucharist. In the case of either Chalice or Paten being used for this purpose, it orders both to be purified with water after Mass. Conf. Constit. of Edmund, Archbp. Cant., 1237 A.D.

for those also who are yet in a place of purification, entreating Thee that by this most Holy Sacrifice their pain may be lighter and shorter; for us also who are weighed down by our sins we offer to Thee, the Father, Thy Son, beseeching Thee that we may be cleansed from the sins committed in the flesh by the Body and Blood of Thy Only-Begotten Son, our Lord Jesus Christ. Who. Then inclining over the Chalice he received the Body, saying, *The Body;* and the Blood, saying, *The Blood* (as YORK, omitting the last prayer).

All follows as in the Ordinary, except that the Server ministers the ablutions.

According to YORK, after one ablution and prayers as Sarum, the Priest placed the Chalice on the Altar, and said, *Let this Communion.*

According to HEREFORD, the Priest went to the Epistle side and washed the Chalice with wine, saying the prayer as in Sarum: then his fingers with wine and water, saying, *Let this Communion.* Then taking water again, and returning to the centre of the Altar, he received it, saying, *Let the Body,* as in the Roman Missal; then he placed the Chalice on the Paten, and went to the *Sacrarium* and washed his hands, saying (Ps. xxv.), *I will wash .... Altar.*

The rest as in the Ordinary, except that in HEREFORD the Priest said, *Ite Missa est;* and he kissed the Altar after *Let the obedient performance.*

In YORK, the Blessing was given on Double Feasts after a ℣. and ℟., with the folded corporals and empty vessels, thus, *The Divine Majesty and the One Deity, the Father +, the Son +, and the Holy Ghost +, bless you. Amen.*

HIGH MASS IN THE ELEVENTH TO SIXTEENTH CENTURIES.

I. ON SIMPLE FEASTS WITH RULERS.

1. THE PROCESSION *

On all Sundays after *Prime* and Chapter (except on Doubles and Palm Sunday), salt and water is blessed † before the Altar in the midst of the Quire by the Priest, vested in alb and cope, with Deacon and Sub-Deacon carrying the Text; Thurifer, Acolytes, and Cross-bearer, all in albs and amices, except the boys with salt and water and the Book, who are in

* From the Processional.

† For the Service, see p. 591; and for that at Easter, p. 174.

surplices. Then the Priest approaches and sprinkles the High Altar, and, as he returns, the clergy as they come up in order; he then goes to the steps of the Quire and says a ℣., ℟., and Collect. Then they go forth in this order—Vergers with rods, Cross-bearer, Acolytes, Thurifer, Sub-Deacon and Deacon, the Priest (the Bishop, if present). As they go, a ℣. and ℟. are sung,* and the Priest sprinkles the Altar, first those on the north side of the Quire round the Presbytery, then those on the south side past the Font, till they come to the Cross,† where they make a station.‡ The Priest turns to the people, saying in the mother tongue, *Let us pray for the Roman Church, the Pope, Archbishops, Bishops, and herein particularly for ours, and for the Dean* (or, in parishes, *the Rector*) *of this Church, for the Holy Land, the peace of the Church, the King, his children, etc.* Then is said Ps. lxvii., ℣.℣., and ℟℟., and a Collect; after which, turning to the people, the Priest says, *Let us pray for the souls of* N. *and* N.; with Ps. cxxx., ℣℣. and ℟℟., and a Collect.§

In Parish Churches the above prayers for the living are said after the Gospel and Offertory, either before the Cross or in the pulpit; those for the dead are always said before the Cross.

Prayers ended, they enter the Quire singing a ℟. and ℣.; ‖ then follows a ℣. and ℟., and the Collect for the day, said at the step of the Quire. In LXX. to XL. this ℣. and ℟., etc., is said by two clergy of the second form, turning to the people. From the Octave of Easter to the fifth Sunday after Easter it is said by two Clerks in surplices. On Christmas Day and Easter Day, three Clerks in copes sing it; on Easter Monday, two Clerks of the lower bench in surplices; on Easter Tuesday and Wednesday, two of the second bench. Then all go to the cemetery and say Ps. lxvii. and a Collect for the departed. It is to be observed that on all Doubles six boys, in silk copes, minister to the Clergy and vest them (but not the Priest or Ministers).

On Christmas Day the order is—first, the Vergers, then Holy Water; three Acolytes with Crosses, in albs and tunics; three

* This varied with the season at Advent, Christmas, LXX., XL., Third Sunday in Lent, Passion Sunday, Easter, Low Sunday, Rogations, Ascension Day, Whitsun Day, Trinity, Corpus Christi.

† *i.e.*, the Rood.

‡ In Trinitytide an Anthem of the Holy Cross, Versicle, Respond, and Collect are said here.

§ These prayers are not said on Doubles, the Sixth Day in the Octave of Christmas, S. Sylvester's Day, or on Palm Sunday.

‖ This varied every Sunday.

Clergy, singing the Prose; Candle-bearers, two Thurifers; Sub-Deacon and Deacon in dalmatic and tunic, with the Text; Priests and Choir in copes—first the boys, then the Clergy of the second and upper grade. The Procession moves down the middle of the Quire, out at west door, and round the Cloister.

On S. Stephen's Day three Deacons, on S. John's three Priests, on Holy Innocents' and S. Thomas Cant. days three boys, sing a prose in procession.

Proses are also said in procession on the Circumcision, *Easter Day, *Ascension Day, *Whitsun Day, *Corpus Christi, *Dedication of the Church, *Visitation B. V. M., Name of JESUS.

On all Minor Doubles there are only two Crosses. On Ascension Day and Corpus Christi, a Shrine with Relics is carried by two Clerks of the second form, in copes, between the Thurifer and Sub-Deacon.

For the Procession on Ash-Wednesday, Palm Sunday, Maundy Thursday, Easter Eve, and Candlemas, see Missal.

On Wednesdays and Fridays in Lent till Maundy Thursday, there is always a Procession after *None* before Mass (except it be a Feast of Nine Lessons) to one of the side Altars, beginning with S. Martin's, without a Cross: at the Altar are said Collects and Litanies. It then goes round, and enters by the west door of the Quire.

There is a Procession on all Principal and Greater Doubles, *on whatever day* they occur.

If a Feast of Nine Lessons occur on the Sunday, the Procession is of the Feast, with an Anthem of Our Lady. If the Feast has no Anthem, it is taken from the Common. The days having proper Anthems are the Feasts of SS. Andrew, Nicholas, Conception B. V. M., SS. Fabian and Sebastian, Agnes, Vincent, Conversion of S. Paul, Lady Day, the Invention of the Cross, S. John Baptist, SS. Peter and Paul; Commemoration of S. Paul; SS. Margaret, Mary Magdalene, Anne; SS. Peter *ad vincula*, S. Laurence, Nativity B. V. M., Holy Cross Day; SS. Matthew, Michael, Denys; Translation S. Edward, All Saints'; SS. Martin, Cecilia, Clement, Katherine.

Apparently Feasts of Three Lessons were not noticed. As exceptions, SS. John and Paul Hippolytus and S. Britius have Anthems from the Common.

According to YORK, the Procession was much the same, Anthems, etc., slightly differing.

* On these days it was said instead of the Verse and Respond in going.

According to HEREFORD, there was a Procession on Principal Doubles, on whatever day they fell; on Semi-Doubles, only on Sundays; on Minor Doubles, the Procession was of the Sunday.

2. FROM THE PROCESSION TO THE EPISTLE.*

After the Procession, whilst the Choir is saying *Terce*, the Priest and Ministers go to the Sacristy to vest. The Rulers put on their copes, and, taking their staves in their hands, go to the Altar, and stand in front below the third step. Here receiving the Office from the Precentor (who in Principal Feasts is bound himself to be present, and enjoin it to the Rulers; and if the Bishop be present, he has to enjoin to him the beginning of the *Gloria in Excelsis*); the Ruler enjoins it to his companion, then both commence it together. After the *Glory be*, when the Office is repeated, the Priest and Ministers approach the Altar. Then the Procession goes in order, as in Missal; on arriving at the Altar the Confession is said, after which the Acolytes put down their candles at the Altar-step. The Priest and Ministers ascend to the Altar, and all follows as in Missal.

According to YORK and HEREFORD Use, there is no mention of Censing here, or of the Kiss of Peace.

The Ministers follow in the *Gloria in Excelsis* the actions of the Priest. After the Collect, having read the Epistle, Gradual, Tract, or Sequence over with his Ministers, the Priest goes with the Deacon to the Sedilia and sits down. After the Office the Candle-bearers leave the Quire, and, going to the Sacristy, one brings the cruets and the silver box with the breads; the other, the ewer and towels, placing them on the shelf over the Piscina; then taking up their candles they go to meet an Acolyte,† who carries the Chalice and Paten in a veil, together with the Burse and Offertory-veil; and, preceding him, they go to the Credence; where the Acolyte leaves the Chalice, and taking the Corporals, places them on the Altar, which he kisses, and returns to the Credence; the Candle-bearers leaving their candles by the side of the Altar.

3. FROM THE EPISTLE TO THE GOSPEL.

The Sub-Deacon, after the last Collect (taking off his chasuble, if he wears one), goes with the Book of the Epistles down to the pulpit and reads it; after which he returns to the Piscina, where

* For Secs. 2-6. Conf. the *Tractatus Sec.* xciii.

† *In mantello serico.* This is the Offertory-veil in which he carried the Chalice.

the Torch-bearers minister to him the towel and water, and the Acolyte gives him the bread and cruets to prepare the oblations; after which he takes the water to the Priest to bless, as he sits in the Sedilia.

According to HEREFORD, the Epistle was read at the lectern, at the step of the Quire.

The Epistle ended, one of the Candle-bearers and another boy go to prepare the lectern in the pulpit.

Two boys in surplices sing the Gradual and Verse there, and return to their places.

After this, two Canons in silk copes chant the *Alleluia*, in the same place.

The Deacon goes to the Piscina, where the Acolyte and the other Candle-bearer minister the ewer and towel to him; after which he goes to the Altar, and censes it and the Relics; or if there is a Sequence, he waits till that is begun, first, however, spreading the Corporals on the Altar. The Sequence is enjoined by the Rulers, as the Office and *Kyrie* were, after which the Choir take it up.

4. FROM THE GOSPEL TO THE CANON.

For the Procession, see the Ordinary. On reaching the pulpit the Sub-Deacon puts the Book of the Gospels on the stand, and takes the Text. The Gospel is then read as in the Ordinary, and all return in procession to the Altar. Here was preached the sermon.

Then follows the Creed, the Sub-Deacon offering the Book of the Gospels to the Priest on the right hand to kiss, the Deacon censing him. There is much confusion here between the *Tractatus* and the Rubrics of the Missals—1st, as to whether it is the Deacon or Sub-Deacon who brings back the Text; 2nd, as to who delivers it to the Priest. It is believed that the right version is as it has been given in the Ordinary of the Mass, but that if the Priest kisses the Text it is given him *on the left by the Sub-Deacon*; if the Book of the Gospels, it is given him *on the right by the Deacon*.

After this the Thurifer censes the Sub-Deacon and the Choir. There is another difficulty here also; as the Rubrics and Missal read, a second censing seems enjoined, at least when the passage is taken into connection with the *Tractatus*. The elucidation may perhaps be this: the Priest, Deacon, and Sub-Deacon are alone censed at the Creed. They remain in their places till the Choir has finished it, and then the Choir is censed. All follows as in the Ordinary.

At the *Sanctus*, which the Rulers chant and lead, a bell rings. The Candle-bearers and Choir go and stand outside the first stalls in the centre of the Quire, with their hands crossed on their chests.

According to HEREFORD Use, the Deacon gave the Paten to the Sub-Deacon, who held it covered with the veil, and did *not* give it to the Acolyte, as at Sarum.

5. FROM THE CANON TO THE *PAX*.

The Ministers remain on their steps, inclining with the Priest at the Consecration, at which a bell rings.

When the Priest crosses his hands, the Candle-bearers minister to the Deacon and Sub-Deacon in washing their hands. The latter goes to the right of the Priest, and raises the Corporals at the signing with the Host. All follows as in the Missal, the Rulers of the Choir leading the *Agnus Dei*.

6. FROM THE *PAX* TO THE END OF THE MASS.

After the Communion of the Priest, all follows as in the Ordinary.

II.—ON DOUBLES, AND IN OCTAVES WITH RULERS.*

The Rulers are four on Doubles, and the Precentor himself stands with them in the centre of the Quire, and enjoins the beginning of the *Kyrie*, etc.

The Gradual is said by three Clerks of the second grade in the pulpit, in copes; and the *Alleluia* by three of the upper grade in the same dress; so also on All Souls' Day. All the rest is as above.

In Octaves, and on Octave Days with Rulers, the *Alleluia* is sung not as above, but by the Rulers in the pulpit.

III.—ON CHRISTMAS DAY AND IN LENT.†

On Christmas Day all as above, but the Lesson before the Epistle is read in the pulpit by any two persons in silk copes. If the Bishop celebrates, the Deacons and Sub-Deaçons (except the Principal) all come into the Quire at the singing of the Office and of the Sequence; and at the Gospel, go in procession by twos behind the Principal Deacon and Sub-Deacon. The Acolyte wears a dalmatic.

At the Second Mass on that Day, the Lesson is read in the pulpit by an Acolyte. The Deacon receives the Blessing from the Bishop before reading the Gospel.

* *Tractatus*, sec. c. † *Tractatus*, sec. xcvi.-xcix.

In Lent, the Tract is sung by four of the upper grade, in silk copes,* at the step of the Altar, all beginning and ending together; but after the first verse the rest are taken up, first by two on the one side, and then by two on the other, the Choir sitting.

On Ash-Wednesday, the First Sunday in Lent, Palm Sunday, Wednesday in Holy Week, and Good Friday, the Tract is sung throughout on both sides, and not as above.

IV.—ON FEASTS WITHOUT RULERS AND WEEK-DAYS.†

The Priest and Ministers enter at the beginning of the Office instead of at the third repetition of the same. The Epistle is read at the step of the Quire, and not at the pulpit.

On Feasts with a Double Invitatory, and in Octave, and on Octave Days without Rulers, the Gradual is sung by two boys in surplices at the step of the Altar, and the *Alleluia* by two Clerks of the second grade in the same place.

On the Saturday in Easter Week, and on Feasts when the *Alleluia* is *Praise the Lord, ye servants*, it is sung by two boys in surplices at the step of the Quire.

On Saturday in Easter Week, on Commemorations of the B. V. M., on Feasts of Three Lessons without Rulers, and week-days, the Gradual and *Alleluia* are sung by one boy at the step of the Quire, but a different boy is required for each.

The Gospel is read on a lectern in the Presbytery, which is prepared by one of the Candle-bearers during the Epistle; and the Sub-Deacon holds the Text opposite the Deacon whilst he reads from the Book of the Gospel which is on the stand. The Deacon then kisses the Text, which is given him by the Sub-Deacon; but he is not censed, neither is the Choir, unless the Creed is said.

* These are red if on a Sunday or Feast of Nine Lessons; black choir copes at other times.

† Conf. *Tractatus* secs. xcv., xcvi., ci.

	Inferior Feria	Lesser Feria[b]	Greater Feria	Principal Feria	Vigil	Commemoration	Feast of iii Lessons	Octave Day without ditto	Octave Day with Rulers	Day in an Octave	Feast of iii Lessons with Rulers	SIMPLES. Feast of ix Lessons	Inferior Double	Lesser Double	Greater Double
Inferior Feria.	0	0	0	0	3	3	3	0	3	4	0	3	3	3	3
Lesser Feria.[b]	0	0	0	0	0	7	7[f]	4	0	4	0	5 or 3	5 or 3	5 or 3	5 or 3
Greater Feria.	0	0	0	0	0	0	7	7	7	7	0	1	5 or 3	5 or 3	5 or 3
Principal Feria.	0	0	0	0	0	0	7	7	7	7	0	1	1	1	1
Vigil.	4	0	0	0	0	0	4	0	5 or 3	5 or 3	0	5 or 3	0	0	0
Commemoration.	4	8	0	0	0	0	4	4	0	0 or 4[d]	0	0	0	0	0
Feast of iii Lessons.	4	8[f]	8	8	3	3	0	3	3	3[e]	3	3	3	3[h]	8
Octave Day without.	0	3	8	8	0	3	4	0	0	6[e] or 3[e]	0	6 or 3	3	3	8
Octave Day with Rulers.	4	0	8	8	5 or 4	0	4	0	0	6[e] or 4[e]	6 or 3	6 or 3	6 or 3	6 or 3	6 or 3
Day in an Octave.	3	3	8	8	5 or 4	0 or 3[d]	4[g]	6a[g] or 4	6a[g] or 3	10	3	3	3 or 8[d]	3 or 8[d]	3 or 8[d]
Feast of iii Lessons with Rulers.	0	0	0	0	0	0	4	0	6a or 4	4	0	2	2	2	2
Feast of ix Lessons	4	5 or 4	2	2	5 or 4	0	4	6a or 4	6a or 4	4	1	9	2	2	2
Inferior Double.	4	5 or 4	5 or 4	2	0	0	4	4	6a or 4	4 or 7[d]	1	1	0	2	2
Lesser Double.	4	5 or 4	5 or 4	2	0	0	4[h]	4	6a or 4	4 or 7[d]	1	1	1	9	2
Greater Double.	4	5 or 4	5 or 4	2	0	0	7	7	6a or 4	4 or 7[d]	1	1	1	1	0
Principal Double.	4	5 or 4	5 or 4	2	5 or 4	0	7	7	6a or 4	4 or 7[d]	1	1	1	1	1
Sunday through the year.	0	0	0	0	6 or 3	0	2 or 6[a]	2 or 6[a]	2 or 6[a]	2 or 6[a]	2 or 3[a]	2 or 3[a]	2 or 8[a]	2 or 8[a]	2 or 8[a]
Lesser Sunday.	0	0	0	0	6a or 3	0	4	4	3[a]	4	1[a]	1[a]	3 or 6[a]	3 or 6[a]	2
Greater Sunday.	0	0	0	0	7	0	7	7	7	7	1	1	1	1	2
…al Sunday.	0	0	0	0	7	0	7	7	7	7	0	1	1	1	0

EXPLANATION OF THE TABLE OPPOSITE.

1. Translation of the First.
2. Translation of the Second.
3. All of the First, Memorial of the Second.
4. All of the Second, Memorial of the First.
5. Mass of the Feast after *Terce*, Mass of the Feast after *Sext* or *None*, both at the High Altar. Where the clergy were not sufficient for this, Mass of the Feast and Memorial of the Fast.
6. Mass of the Second in the Chapter-house. This only applies to the Cathedral Church of Sarum; elsewhere Mass of the Feast and Memorial of the Fast. Cf., *Defens. Direct.*

6A. Mass of the First in the Chapter-house. Elsewhere as above.

7. Nothing of the First.
8. Nothing of the Second.
9. Service of the higher, Transference of the other.
10. Service of the higher, Memorial of the other.

N.B.—When two numbers ("6A[f] or 3," etc.) are given, the first refers to the rule of the Cathedral of Sarum, the second to other Churches, unless the reference indicates the contrary, as O or 4[d].

---

[a] This latter when there were few Sundays after Trinity.

[b] This does not apply to Rogation Days, regarding which see Rubrics on pp. 198-9.

[c] Unless there were many Sundays after Trinity, in which case Rule 2 applies.

[d] If the Octave be without Rulers.

[e] If the Octave be without Rulers, however, Rule 4 applies.

[f] Unless it be in Advent, when Rule 3 applies; or Rogations, when see pp. 198-9.

[g] If the Octave be without Rulers then Rule 3 applies.

[h] In Cathedrals, however, and where there were many Priests, doubtless the Mass of iii Lessons was said by itself, and the High Mass was of the Double—*cf.*, Transfiguration and S. Sixtus. In this case there is no Mem. of iii Lessons at Mass of the Double; and, probably, in the case of the Feast just named, where there could be no second Mass, Rule 8 applied.

January.

THE NIGHT IS XVI THE DAY VIII HOURS LONG.

Golden Number	Sunday Letter	Roman Style	Day of the Month	
iij	A	Kal.	1	**The Circumcision of our Lord.** Lesser Double.
	b	iiij	2	The Octave of S. Stephen, Protomartyr.
xj	c	iij	3	The Octave of S. John, Ap.
	d	Prid.	4	The Octave of the Holy Innocents, MM.
xix	e	Non.	5	The Octave of S. Thomas of Canterbury, Mart.
				[S. Edward, Conf. Vigil.
viij	f	viij	6	**The Epiphany of our Lord.** Principal Double.
	g	vij	7	*Keys of LXX.*
xvj	A	vj	8	Lucian Priest and Companions. *Memorial only.*
v	b	v	9	
	c	iv	10	
xiij	d	iij	11	*Sun in Aquarius.*
ij	e	Prid.	12	
	f	Id.	13	The Octave of the Epiphany. Trip. Invit. *Memorial*
x	g	xix	14	Felix, *Mart. Priest.* [*of S. Hilary.*
	A	xviij	15	Maurus, *Abbat.*
xviij	b	xvij	16	Marcellus, *Mart. Pope.*
vij	c	xvj	17	Sulpicius, *Conf. Bp.* S. Anthony, *Conf.*
	d	xv	18	Prisca, *Virg. Mart.* *First day LXX. can fall.*
xv	e	xiv	19	Wulstan, Conf. Bp. ix Lessons.
iiij	f	xiij	20	Fabian and Sebastian, MM. ix Lessons.
	g	xij	21	Agnes, Virg. Mart. ix Lessons.
xij	A	xj	22	Vincent, Mart. ix Lessons
j	b	x	23	
	c	ix	24	
ix	d	viij	25	The Conversion of S. Paul. Trip. Invit. ix Lessons.
	e	vij	26	[*Mem. of S. Projectus.*
xvij	f	vj	27	Julian, *Conf. Bp.* Double Invit.
vj	g	v	28	The Second Feast of S. Agnes. Double Invit. *Keys*
	A	iv	29	[*of XL.*
xiiij	b	iij	30	Batildis, *Virg. Queen, not Mart.*
iij	c	Prid.	31	

February.

THE NIGHT IS XIV THE DAY X HOURS.

GOLDEN NUMBER	SUNDAY LETTER	ROMAN STYLE	DAY OF THE MONTH*	
	d	Kal.	1	Bridget, *Virg. Mart.*
xj	e	iiij	2	**The Purification of B. V. M.** Greater Double.
xix	f	iij	3	Blase, *Mart. Bp.* Double Invit.
viij	g	Prid.	4	
	A	Non.	5	AGATHA, Virg. Mart. ix. Lessons.
xvj	b	viij	6	Vedastus and Amandus, *Conff. Bps.*
v	c	vij	7	*The Sunday next to the first moon after S. Agatha's Day*
	d	vj	8	[*is XL.*
viij	e	v	9	*Sun in Pisces.*
ij	f	iiij	10	Scholastica, *Virg.*
	g	iij	11	TRANSLATION OF S. FRIDESWIDE, Virg. ix Lessons.
x	A	Prid.	12	
	b	Id.	13	
xviij	c	xvj	14	Valentine, *Mart. Bp.*†
vij	d	xv	15	
	e	xiiij	16	Juliana, *Virg. Mart.*
xv	f	xiij	17	
iiij	g	xij	18	
	A	xj	19	
xij	b	x	20	
j	c	ix	21	*Last day on which LXX. can fall.*
	d	viij	22	THE CHAIR OF S. PETER. Trip. Invit. ix Lessons.‡
ix	e	vij	23	
	f	vj	24	**Matthias**, Ap. Inferior Double.
xvij	g	v	25	
vj	A	iiij	26	*If Leap Year, the fourth day after the Chair of S. Peter will*
	b	iij	27	*be the Feast of S. Matthias, and the letter* f *will be repeated.*
xiv	c	Prid.	28	

* These are put for convenience: they never appear in old Kalendars.
† (*Sic*) He was, as a fact, only a Priest. ‡ ? Inferior Double.

March.

THE NIGHT AND DAY IS XII HOURS.

Golden Number	Sunday Letter	Roman Style	Day of the Month	
iij	d	Kal.	1	David, Conf. Bp. ix Lessons.
	e	vj	2	Chad, Conf. Bp. ix Lessons.
xj	f	v	3	
	g	iiij	4	
xix	A	iij	5	
viij	b	Prid.	6	
	c	Non.	7	Perpetua and Felicitas, *Virg. MM*
xvj	d	viij	8	
v	e	vij	9	
	f	vj	10	
xiij	g	v	11	*Keys of Easter. Sun in Aries. Vernal Equinox.*
ij	A	iiij	12	**Gregory**, Conf. Pope. Inferior Double.
	b	iij	13	*The last day on which XL. can fall.*
x	c	Prid.	14	
	d	Id.	15	
xviij	e	xvij	16	*Entrance of Noah into the Ark.*
vij	f	xvj	17	Patrick, Conf. Bp. ix Lessons.
	g	xv	18	Edward, Mart. King. ix Lessons.
xv	A	xiiij	19	
iiij	b	xiij	20	Cuthbert, Conf. Bp. ix Lessons.
	c	xij	21	Benedict, Abbat. ix Lessons.
xij	d	xj	22	*The first day Easter can fall.*
j	e	x	23	*On this day Adam was created.*
	f	ix	24	
ix	g	viij	25	**The Annunciation of the Lord.** Lesser Double.
	A	vij	26	
xvij	b	vj	27	**The Resurrection of our Lord.** Principal Double
vj	c	v	28	
	d	iiij	29	
xiiij	e	iij	30	
iij	f	Prid.	31	

April.

THE NIGHT IS X THE DAY XIV HOURS.

GOLDEN NUMBER	SUNDAY LETTER	ROMAN STYLE	DAY OF THE MONTH	
	g	Kal.	1	
xj	A	iiij	2	
	b	iij	3	RICHARD, Conf. Bp. ix Lessons.
xix	c	Prid.	4	**Ambrose**, *Bp. and Doctor.* Inferior Double.
viij	d	Non.	5	
xvj	e	viij	6	
v	f	vij	7	
	g	vj	8	
xiij	A	v	9	
ij	b	iiij	10	*Sun in Taurus.*
	c	iij	11	
x	d	Prid.	12	
	e	Id.	13	
xviij	f	xviij	14	Tyburtius, Valerian, and Maximus, *MM.*
vij	g	xvij	15	*The Keys of Rogation Days.*
	A	xvj	16	
xv	b	xv	17	
iv	c	xiiij	18	
	d	xiij	19	Alphege, *Mart. Bp.*
xij	e	xij	20	
j	f	xj	21	
	g	x	22	
ix	A	ix	23	**George**, *Mart.* Inferior Double.
	b	viij	24	
xvj	c	vij	25	**Mark**, *Evang.* Inferior Double. *Greater Litanies. The*
vj	d	vj	26	[*last of Easter.*
	e	v	27	
xiv	f	iiij	28	VITALIS, Mart. iii. Lessons, with Rulers.
iij	g	iij	29	*Departure of Noah from the Ark.*
	A	Prid.	30	DEPOSITION OF S. ERKENWALD, Conf. Bp. ix Lessons.

May.

THE NIGHT IS VIII THE DAY XVI HOURS.

GOLDEN NUMBER	SUNDAY LETTER	ROMAN STYLE	DAY OF THE MONTH	
xj	b	Kal.	1	**Philip and James**, *App.* Inferior Double.
	c	vj	2	
xix	d	v	3	**The Invention of the Holy Cross.** Lesser Double.
viij	e	iiij	4	[*Mem. of SS. Alexander and Eventius.*
	f	iij	5	[sons, with Rulers.
xvj	g	Prid.	6	JOHN ANTE PORTAM LATINAM. Trip. Invit. iii Les-
v	A	Non.	7	JOHN OF BEVERLEY, Conf. Bp. iii Lessons, with Rulers.
	b	viij	8	[with Rulers.
xiij	c	vij	9	TRANSLATION OF S. NICHOLAS, Conf. Bp. iii Lessons,
ij	d	vj	10	GORDIAN AND EPIMACHUS, MM. iii Lessons, with Rulers.
	e	v	11	
x	f	iiij	12	NEREUS, ACHILLES, AND PANCRATIUS, MM. iii Les-
	g	iij	13	*Sun in Gemini.* [sons, with Rulers.
xviij	A	Prid.	14	*It is to be noted that the Translation of S. Chad, Bp., ought*
vij	b	Id.	15	*always to be celebrated with Rulers the Sunday next before*
	c	xvij	16	*Ascension Day.*
xv	d	xvj	17	
iv	e	xv	18	
	f	xiiij	19	DUNSTAN, Conf. Bp. ix Lessons. *Mem. of S. Pudenziana.*
xij	g	xiij	20	
j	A	xij	21	
	b	xj	22	
ix	c	x	23	
	d	ix	24	FEAST OF S. SAVIOUR.
viij	e	viij	25	ALDHELM, Conf. Bp. ix Lessons. *Mem. of S. Urban.*
vj	f	vij	26	**Augustine**, *Apostle of the English.* Inferior Double.
	g	vj	27	
xiv	A	v	28	Germanus, *Conf. Bp.*
iij	b	iiij	29	
	c	iij	30	
xj	d	Prid.	31	Petronilla, *Virg. not Mart.* iii Lessons, with Nocturns [when without the Octave of the Holy Trinity.

June.

THE NIGHT IS VI THE DAY XVIII HOURS.

GOLDEN NUMBER	SUNDAY LETTER	ROMAN STYLE	DAY OF THE MONTH	
	e	Kal.	1	Nichomede, *Mart.*
xix	f	iiij	2	Marcellinus and Peter, *MM.*
viij	g	iij	3	
xvj	A	Prid.	4	
v	b	Non.	5	Boniface and his Companions, *MM.* Double Invit.
	c	viij	6	
xiij	d	vij	7	
ij	e	vj	8	Medardus and Gildardus, *Conff. Bps.*
	f	v	9	TRANSLATION OF S. EDMUND, M. Trip. Invit. ix Less.
x	g	iiij	10	[*Mem. of SS. Primus and Felician.*
	A	iij	11	BARNABAS, Ap. Trip. Invit. ix Lessons.
xviij	b	Prid.	12	Basilides, Cyrinus, and Nabor, *MM.*
vij	c	Id.	13	*Sun in Cancer. Summer Solstice.*
	d	xviij	14	Basil, *Conf. Bp.*
xv	e	xvij	15	Vitus, Modestus, and Crescentia, *MM.*
iv	f	xvj	16	TRANSLATION OF S. RICHARD, Conf. Bp. ix Lessons.
	g	xv	17	[*Mem. of SS. Cyricus and Julita.*
xij	A	xiiij	18	Mark and Marcellian, *MM.* Double Invit.
j	b	xiij	19	Gervasius and Prothasius, *MM.* Double Invit.
	c	xij	20	TRANSLATION OF S. EDWARD, Mart. King. ix Lessons,
ix	d	xj	21	[unless it has been kept in Lent, then iii.
	e	x	22	ALBAN, Proto-Martyr of England. ix Lessons.
xvij	f	ix	23	Etheldreda, *Virg.* With Nocturns. Vigil.
vj	g	viij	24	**Nativity of S. John Baptist.** Lesser Double.
	A	vij	25	
xiv	b	vj	26	John and Paul, *MM.* Double Invit.
iij	c	v	27	
	d	iiij	28	Leo, *Conf. Pope.* With Nocturns. Vigil.
xj	e	iij	29	**Peter and Paul**, *App.* Lesser Double.
	f	Prid.	30	COMMEMORATION OF S. PAUL. Trip. Invit. ix Lessons.

Julp.

THE NIGHT IS VIII THE DAY XVI HOURS.

Golden Number	Sunday Letter	Roman Style	Day of the Month	
xix	g	Kal.	1	The Octave of S. John Baptist. *Mem. of SS. Processus,* [*Martinian, and Swithin.*
viij	A	vj	2	**The Visitation of Blessed Mary.** Greater Double.
	b	v	3	
xvj	c	iiij	4	TRANSLATION AND ORDERING OF S. MARTIN. ix Lessons.
v	d	iij	5	
	e	Prid.	6	THE OCTAVE OF SS. PETER AND PAUL.
xiij	f	Non.	7	TRANSLATION OF S. THOMAS, Mart. ix Lessons.
ij	g	viij	8	*The first Sunday after this Feast is kept as the Feast of Relics,* [*a Principal Double.*
	A	vij	9	THE OCTAVE OF THE VISITATION OF BLESSED MARY.
x	b	vj	10	Seven Brethren. Double Invit.
	c	v	11	TRANSLATION OF S. BENEDICT, Abb. ix Lessons, unless [it has been kept in Lent, then iii.
xviij	d	iiij	12	
vij	e	iij	13	
	f	Prid.	14	*Sun in Leo. Dog-days.* [ix Lessons.
xv	g	Id.	15	TRANSLATION OF S. SWITHIN AND HIS COMPANIONS, Conff.
iiij	A	xvij	16	TRANSLATION OF S. OSMUND, Conf. Bp. ix Lessons.
	b	xvj	17	Kenelm, *Mart. King.* Double Invit.
xij	c	xv	18	Arnulph, *Mart. Bp.*
j	d	xiiij	19	
	e	xiij	20	MARGARET, Virg. Mart. ix Lessons.
xj	f	xij	21	Praxedes, *Virg. not Mart.*
	g	xj	22	MARY MAGDALENE. Trip. Invit. ix Lessons. *Mem.* [*of S. Wandregesilus.*
xvij	A	x	23	Apollinaris, *Mart. Bp.*
vj	b	ix	24	Christina, *Virg. Mart.* With Nocturns. Vigil.
	c	viij	25	**James,** *Ap.* Inferior Double. *Mem. of SS. Chris-* [*topher and Cucufatus.*
xiv	d	vij	26	ANNE, Mother of Mary. Trip. Invit. ix Lessons.
iij	e	vj	27	Seven Sleepers, *MM.* Double Invit.
	f	v	28	Sampson, *Bp.* Double Invit. *Mem. of S. Panthaleon.*
xj	g	iiij	29	Felix and Faustinus, *MM.* Double Invit.
xix	A	iij	30	Abdon and Sennes, *MM.* Double Invit.
	b	Prid.	31	Germanus, *Conf. Bp.*

August.

THE NIGHT IS X THE DAY XIV HOURS.

GOLDEN NUMBER	SUNDAY LETTER	ROMAN STYLE	DAY OF THE MONTH	
				[*of SS. Maccabees.*
viij	c	Kal.	1	THE CHAINS OF S. PETER. Trip. Invit. ix Lessons. *Mem.*
xvj	d	iiij	2	Stephen, *Mart. Pope.* Double Invit
v	e	iij	3	THE FINDING OF S. STEPHEN, Protomartyr. ix Lessons.
	f	Prid.	4	
xiij	g	Non.	5	S. Mary *ad Nives.* Oswald, *Mart. King.* Double Invit.
ij	A	viij	6	**The Transfiguration of our Lord.** Lesser Double.
				[*Mem. of SS. Felicissimus and Agapitus.*
	b	vij	7	**The Name of Jesus.** Greater Double. *Mem. of S.*
x	c	vj	8	Cyriacus and his Companions. *Mem. only.* [*Donatus.*
	d	v	9	Romanus, *Mart.* *Mem. only.* Vigil.
xviij	e	iiij	10	LAURENCE, Mart. Trip. Invit. ix Lessons.
vij	f	iij	11	Tiburtius, *Mart.* *Mem. only.*
	g	Prid.	12	
xv	A	Id.	13	HIPPOLYTUS AND HIS COMPANIONS, *MM.* ix Lessons.
iv	b	xix	14	OCTAVE OF THE NAME OF JESUS. *Mem. S. Eusebius.* Vigil.
	c	xviij	15	**The Assumption of the Blessed Virgin Mary.**
xij	d	xvij	16	*Sun in Virgo.* [Principal Double.
j	e	xvj	17	The Octave of S. Laurence. *Mem. only.*
	f	xv	18	Agapitus, *Mart.* *Mem. only.*
ix	g	xiiij	19	Magnus, *Mart.* *Mem. only.*
	A	xiij	20	
xvij	b	xij	21	[*Mem. of SS. Timothy and Simphorianus.*
vj	c	xj	22	THE OCTAVE OF THE ASSUMPTION OF BLESSED MARY.
	d	x	23	Timothy and Appollinaris, *MM.* With Nocts. Vigil.
xiv	e	ix	24	**Bartholomew,** *Ap.* Inferior Double. *Mem. of S.*
iij	f	viij	25	[*Audoenus.*
	g	vij	26	
xj	A	vj	27	Rufus, *Mart.* Double Invit.
xix	b	v	28	**Augustine,** *Bp. Doct.* Inferior Double. *Mem. S. Hermes.*
	c	iiij	29	THE DECOLLATION OF S. JOHN BAPTIST. Trip. Invit.
				[ix Lessons. *Mem. of S. Sabina.*
viij	d	iij	30	Felix and Adauctus, *MM.* Double Invit.
	e	Prid.	31	Cuthburga, *Virg. not Mart.* Double Invit.

September.

THE NIGHT AND DAY ARE XII HOURS.

GOLDEN NUMBER	SUNDAY LETTER	ROMAN STYLE	DAY OF THE MONTH	
xvj	f	Kal.	1	GILES, Abbat. ix Lessons. *Mem. of S. Priscus.*
v	g	iiij	2	
	A	iij	3	[been kept in Lent.
xiij	b	Prid.	4	TRANSLATION OF S. CUTHBERT. ix Lessons, unless it has
ij	c	Non.	5	Bertinus, *Conf. Abb.* With Nocturns.
	d	viij	6	
x	e	vij	7	
	f	vj	8	**The Nativity of Blessed Mary.** Greater Double.
xviij	g	v	9	Gorgonius, *Mart. Mem. only.*
vij	A	iiij	10	
	b	iij	11	Prothus and Hyacinth, *MM. Mem. only.*
xv	c	Prid.	12	
iv	d	Id.	13	
	e	xviij	14	**The Exaltation of the Holy Cross.** Lesser Double.
				[*Mem of SS Cornelius and Cyprian. Sun in Libra.*
				Autumnal equinox. End of Dog-days.
xij	f	xvij	15	OCTAVE OF THE NATIVITY OF BLESSED MARY. Trip. Invit.
j	g	xvj	16	EDITH, Virg. not Mart. ix Lessons. *Mem. of SS. Euphe-*
	A	xv	17	Lambert, *Mart. Bp.* [*mia, Lucina, and Geminianus.*
ix	b	xiiij	18	*The first Wednesday after the Exaltation is always Ember-*
	c	xiij	19	[*day.*
xvij	d	xij	20	Vigil.
vj	e	xj	21	**Matthew,** *Ap. Ev.* Inferior Double. *Mem. of S. Laudus.*
	f	x	22	MAURICE AND HIS COMPANIONS, MM. ix Lessons.
xiv	g	ix	23	Thecla, *Virg. not Mart.* With Nocturns.
iij	A	viij	24	
	b	vij	25	Ferminus, *Mart. Bp.*
xj	c	vj	26	Cyprian *Bp.* and Justina, *Virg. MM.* Double Invit.
xix	d	v	27	Cosmas and Damian, *MM.* Double Invit.
	e	iiij	28	
viij	f	iij	29	**Michaelmas Day.** Inferior Double.
	g	Prid.	30	**Jerome,** *Priest and Doct.* Inferior Double.

October.

THE NIGHT IS XIV THE DAY X HOURS.

GOLDEN NUMBER	SUNDAY LETTER	ROMAN STYLE	DAY OF THE MONTH	
				[ix Lessons. *Mem. of S. Melorus*
xvj	A	Kal.	1	Remigius, Germanus, Vedastus, & Bavo, Conff. Bps.
v	b	vj	2	Thomas of Hereford, Conf. Bp. ix Lessons. *Mem. of*
xiij	c	v	3	[*S. Ledger*
ij	d	iiij	4	
	e	iij	5	
x	f	Prid.	6	Faith, *Virg. Mart.*
	g	Non.	7	Mark and Marcellus, *MM.* Double Invit.
xviij	A	viij	8	
vij	b	vij	9	Denys and his Companions, MM. ix Lessons.
	c	vj	10	Gereon and his Companions, MM.
xv	d	v	11	Nicasius and his Companions, MM. Double Invit.
iv	e	iiij	12	[Double.
	f	iij	13	**Translation of S. Edward**, *Conf. King.* Inferior
xij	g	Prid.	14	Calixtus, *Mart. Pope.* *Sun in Scorpio.*
j	A	Id.	15	Wulfran, Conf. Bp. ix Lessons. [Lessons
	b	xvij	16	Michael in the Mountain Tomb. Trip. Invit. ix
ix	c	xvj	17	Translation of S. Etheldreda, Virg. not Mart. ix
				[Lessons.
	d	xv	18	**Luke**, *Evang.* Inferior Double. *Mem. of S. Justus.*
xvij	e	xiiij	19	Frideswide, Virg. not Mart. ix Lessons.
vj	f	xiij	20	
	g	xij	21	The Eleven Thousand Virgins, *MM.* Double Invit.
xiv	A	xj	22	
iij	b	x	23	Romanus, *Conf. Bp.* With Nocturns.
	c	ix	24	
xj	d	viij	25	Crispin and Crispinian, MM. ix Lessons. *Mem. of*
xix	e	vij	26	[*S. John of Beverley.*
	f	vj	27	Vigil.
viij	g	v	28	**Simon and Jude**, *App.* Inferior Double.
	A	iiij	29	
xvj	b	iij	30	
v	c	Prid.	31	Quintinus, *Mart.* With Nocturns. Vigil.

November.

THE NIGHT IS XVI THE DAY VIII HOURS.

GOLDEN NUMBER	SUNDAY LETTER	ROMAN STYLE	DAY OF THE MONTH	
	d	Kal.	1	**The Feast of All Saints.** Greater Double.
xiij	e	iiij	2	**Commemoration of All Souls.** Inferior Double. ix Lessons. *Mem. of S. Eustachius and Companions; at Vespers, of S. Mary.*
ij	f	iij	3	WENEFRID, Virg. Mart. ix Lessons.
	g	Prid.	4	
x	A	Non.	5	
	b	viij	6	LEONARD, Abbat. ix Lessons.
xviij	c	vij	7	
vij	d	vj	8	The Four Crowned Martyrs. Double Invit.
	e	v	9	Theodore, *Mart.*
xv	f	iiij	10	
iiij	g	iij	11	MARTIN, Conf. Bp. Trip. Invit. ix Lessons. *Mem.*
	A	Prid.	12	*Sun in Sagittarius.* [*of S. Menna.*
xij	b	Id.	13	Britius, *Conf. Bp.* Double Invit.
j	c	xviij	14	TRANSLATION OF S. ERKENWALD, Conf. Bp.
	d	xvij	15	MACHUTUS, Conf. Bp. ix Lessons. [Invit. ix Lessons.
ix	e	xvj	16	THE DEPOSITION OF S. EDMUND, Conf. Archbp. Trip.
	f	xv	17	HUGH, Conf Bp. ix Lessons. *Mem. of S. Anianus.*
xvij	g	xiiij	18	The Octave of S. Martin. Double Invit.
vj	A	xiij	19	
	b	xij	20	EDMUND, Mart. King. ix Lessons.
xiv	c	xj	21	
iij	d	x	22	CECILIA, Virg. Mart. ix. Lessons.
	e	ix	23	CLEMENT, Mart. Pope. ix Lessons. *Mem. of S. Felicitas.*
	f	viij	24	Chrysogonus, *Mart.*
xix	g	vij	25	KATHERINE, Virg. Mart. ix. Lessons.
	A	vj	26	Linus, *Mart. Pope.*
viij	b	v	27	
	c	iiij	28	
xvj	d	iij	29	Saturninus and Sisinnius, *MM.* With Nocturns. Vigil.
v	e	Prid.	30	**Andrew**, *Ap.* Inferior Double.

December.

THE NIGHT IS XVIII THE DAY VI HOURS.

GOLDEN NUMBER	SUNDAY LETTER	ROMAN STYLE	DAY OF THE MONTH	
	f	Kal.	1	
xiij	g	iiij	2	
ij	A	iij	3	
x	b	Prid.	4	OSMUND, Conf. Bp. ix Lessons.
	c	Non.	5	
xviij	d	viij	6	NICHOLAS, Conf. Bp. Trip. Invit. ix Lessons.
vij	e	vij	7	THE OCTAVE OF S. ANDREW. Trip. Invit.
	f	vj	8	**The Conception of Blessed Mary.** Lesser Double.
xv	g	v	9	
iv	A	iiij	10	
	b	iij	11	
xij	c	Prid.	12	
j	d	Id.	13	LUCY, Virg. Mart. ix Lessons.
	e	xix	14	*Sun in Capricorn. Winter Solstice.*
ix	f	xviij	15	
	g	xvij	16	
xvij	A	xvj	17	*O Sapientia.*
vj	b	xv	18	*After this let there be no Preces at Vespers.*
	c	xiiij	19	
xiv	d	xiij	20	Vigil.
iij	e	xij	21	**Thomas**, *Ap.* Inferior Double.
	f	xj	22	
xj	g	x	23	
xix	A	ix	24	Vigil.
	b	viij	25	**Christmas Day.** Principle Double.
viij	c	vij	26	**Stephen**, *Proto-Martyr.* Lesser Double.
	d	vj	27	**John**, *Ap. and Evang.* Lesser Double.
xvj	e	v	28	**Holy Innocents**, *MM.* Lesser Double.
v	f	iiij	29	**Thomas of Canterbury**, *Mart. Archbp.* Inferior
	g	iij	30	[Double.
xiij	A	Prid.	31	SYLVESTER, Conf. Pope. ix Lessons.

The Proper of Seasons.

First Sunday in Advent.

The Office or Introit. Ps. xxv.

Unto Thee, O Lord, will I lift up my soul; my God, I have put my trust in Thee: O let me not be confounded, neither let mine enemies triumph over me. For all they that hope in Thee shall not be ashamed.

Ps. Shew me Thy ways, O Lord, and teach me Thy paths.

Unto Thee, O Lord, etc.

℣. Glory be to the Father, and to the Son, and to the Holy Ghost: As it was in the beginning, is now, and ever shall be; world without end. Amen.

Unto Thee, O Lord, etc.

¶ *The* Gloria in Excelsis *is not said in Advent at any Mass.*

The Collect.

Stir up, we beseech Thee, O Lord, Thy power, and come, that we may be accounted worthy to be rescued, by Thy protection, from the threatening dangers of our sins; and to be set free by Thy deliverance. Through.

Memorial of S. Mary.

O God, Who at the message of an Angel, etc. (*See Collects before the Ordinary of the Mass.*

¶ *For the number of Collects to be said see General Rubrics.*

The Epistle. Rom. xiii. 11-14.

Brethren, knowing the time .... But put ye on the Lord Jesus Christ.

Gradual. Ps. xxv. For all they that hope in Thee shall not be ashamed, *O Lord.*

℣. Shew me Thy ways, O Lord, and teach me Thy paths.

For all they, etc.

Alleluia! ℣. Ps. lxxxv. Shew us Thy mercy, O Lord, and grant us Thy salvation.

The Sequence.

Eternal Health of man,
Life of the world, which faileth never,
Light everlasting,
Verily our sure Redemption,
Thou, grieving that this world should perish
By the tempter's power,
Though still in Heaven, in lowliest guise cam'st down,
Of thine own clemency.
Then taking on Thee flesh
Of Thine own grace and will,
Thou savedst all on earth
Which else had been undone,
Joy bringing to the world.
Our souls and bodies, Christ,
Deign Thou to purify,
And take us for Thine own,
Thy undefiled abode.
By Thy first coming deign to justify,
And by Thy second deign to set us free;
So when in brightness terrible
Thou shalt judge all the world,
May we in garments incorruptible,
Where'er we trace the prints of Thy blest Feet,
Then follow in Thy train.

The Gospel. Matt. xxi. 1-9.

When they drew nigh unto Jerusalem ...... Blessed is He that cometh in the Name of the Lord.

Offertory. Ps. xxv. Unto Thee will I lift up my soul: my God, I have put my trust in Thee: O let me not be confounded, neither let my enemies triumph over me. For all they that hope in Thee shall not be ashamed.

℣. Lead me forth in Thy truth and learn me: for Thou art the God of my salvation: in Thee hath been my hope all the day long.

℣. Turn Thee unto me and have mercy upon me, *O Lord;* O keep my soul and deliver me: let me not be confounded, for I have put my trust in Thee.

¶ *These two last verses are said alternately with the Offertory on week-days, not on Sunday. This is to be observed whenever they occur throughout the year.*

Secret. May these sacred mysteries, O Lord, cleanse us by their powerful virtue, and bring us with greater purity to Him Who is their Author. Through.

Secret of S. Mary. Strengthen, we beseech Thee, etc. (*See above.*)

Communion. Ps lxxxv. The Lord shall shew loving kindness, and our land shall give her increase.

Post-Communion. May we receive, O Lord, Thy mercy in the midst of Thy temple, and with due honour anticipate the approaching solemnity of our restoration. Through.

Post-Communion of S. Mary. Pour forth, etc.

The Mass ends with, Let us bless the Lord.

WEDNESDAY.

¶ *On week-days the Office is only repeated after the* Glory be.

The Epistle. James v. 7-10.

Be patient therefore, brethren .... the name of *our* Lord *Jesus Christ.*

The Gospel. Mark i. 1-8.

The beginning of the Gospel ...... with the Holy Ghost.

¶ *If any Feast which must be kept fall on this day, the above Epistle and Gospel are said on Thursday: if that is occupied they are omitted altogether that year.*

FRIDAY.

The Lesson. Isaiah li. 1-8.

Thus saith the Lord God, Hearken to Me ...... from generation to generation.

The Gospel. Matt. iii. 1-6.

In those days ...... confessing their sins.

¶ *If Friday is occupied the above Epistle and Gospel are omitted. This applies to all Advent; from* Domine ne in Ira* *to Quinquagesima; and from the Octave of Easter to the Sunday before Ascension. From* Deus omnium† *to Advent, if Wednesday or Thursday are full, the Wednesday Epistle and Gospel may be read on Friday. But the custom of Sarum never anticipates*—e.g., *Wednesday's Epistle and Gospel are never read on Tuesday, nor Friday's on Thursday.*

Second Sunday in Advent.

The Office. Is. xxx. 27, 30.

People of Sion! Behold *the Lord shall come to save the nations,* and the Lord shall cause His glorious voice to be heard *in the gladness of your heart.*

* 1st Sunday after the Octave of the Epiphany.

† 1st Sunday after Trinity.

Ps. lxxx. Hear, O Shepherd of Israel, Thou that leadest Joseph like a sheep.

The Collect.

Stir up, O Lord, our hearts to prepare the way of Thy Only Begotten: that by His coming we may be counted worthy to serve Thee with purified hearts: Who livest.

The Epistle. Rom. xv. 4-13.

Brethren, whatsoever things .... power of the Holy Ghost.

Gradual. Ps. l. Out of Sion hath God appeared in perfect Beauty.

℣. Gather My saints together unto Me; those that have made a covenant with Me with sacrifice

Alleluia! ℣. Luke xxi. 26. For the powers of Heaven shall be shaken; and then shall they see the Son of Man coming in the clouds of heaven with power and great glory.

The Sequence.

Reception giving to the King eternal,
Devout assembly, shout aloud;
To the Creator give His honour due,
To Whom the heavenly hosts sing praise:
Enlightened as they look upon His Face,
For Whom all living souls do wait
Till they at His command shall stand for trial.
In all His judgments strict and terrible,
Yet in His mightiness remembering mercy,
Save us, O Christ, of Thy vast clemency,
Who for our sake didst suffer agony.
Raise to the stars that brightly gleam above us
The world which Thou dost cleanse from its pollution.
  Let Thy saving health appear
  Scattering perils far and near,
  Give purity to all,
  Give peace, we pray.
So we that here are saved by Thy pity,
May reach with joy Thy realm above hereafter,
Where Thou in Majesty dost reign for ever!

The Gospel. Luke xxi. 25-33.

At that time Jesus said to His Disciples, There shall be signs in the sun .... My words shall not pass away.

Offert. Ps. lxxxv. Wilt Thou not turn again, and quicken us: that Thy people may rejoice in Thee? Shew us Thy mercy, O Lord: and grant us Thy salvation.

℣. Lord, Thou art become gracious unto Thy land: Thou hast turned away the captivity of Jacob. Thou hast forgiven the offence of Thy people.

℣. Mercy and truth are met together: truth shall flourish out of the earth, and righteousness hath looked down from Heaven.

Secret. Graciously accept, O Lord, we beseech Thee, our humble prayers and oblations: and forasmuch as our merits avail nothing, succour us with Thy protection. Through.

Comm. Bar. v. 5. Arise, O Jerusalem, and stand on high, and behold the joy that cometh to thee from thy God.

P. Comm. Refreshed with the meat and drink of spiritual nourishment, we humbly beseech Thee, O Lord, that by the participation of this mystery Thou wilt teach us to despise earthly things, and to love heavenly things. Through.

WEDNESDAY.

The Lesson. Zech. viii. 3-8.

Thus saith the Lord .... in truth and in righteousness, *saith the Lord Almighty.*

The Gospel. Matt. xi. 11-15.

At that time Jesus said unto the multitude of the Jews, and to His Disciples, Verily, I say .... let him hear.

FRIDAY.

The Lesson. Isaiah lxii. 6-12.

Thus saith the Lord God, I have set watchmen .... not forsaken.

The Gospel. John i. 15-18.

At that time, John bare witness .... hath declared Him.

Third Sunday in Advent.

The Office. Phil. iv. 4-7.

Rejoice in the Lord alway, and again, I say, rejoice. Let your moderation be known unto all men. The Lord is at hand. Be careful for nothing; but in every thing by prayer let your requests be made known unto God.

Ps. And the peace of God which passeth all understanding shall keep your hearts and minds.

The Collect.

Lord, we beseech Thee, give ear to our prayers, and by Thy gracious visitation lighten the darkness of our hearts. Who livest.

The Epistle. I Cor. iv. 1-5.

Brethren, let a man .... have praise of God.

Gradual. Ps. lxxix. *O Lord,* Thou that sittest upon the cherubim, stir up Thy strength, and come.

℣. Hear, O Thou Shepherd of Israel, Thou that leadest Joseph like a sheep.

Alleluia! ℣. *O Lord,* Stir up Thy strength, and come and help us.

The Sequence.

Thou Who rulest earthly sceptres
With Thy mighty hand alone,
Raise up Thy great power, and come,
To Thy people show Thyself;
Bestow the gifts which bring salvation
On Him Whom all the prophets did foretell,
From the bright palace of the sky,
Lord Jesus to our land draw nigh!

The Gospel. Matt. xi. 2-10.

At that time, when John .... thy way before thee.

Offert. Ps. lxxxv. Lord, Thou art become gracious unto Thy land: Thou has turned away the captivity of Jacob. Thou hast forgiven the offence of Thy people.

℣. *Thou hast* covered all their sins. Thou hast taken away all Thy displeasure.

℣. Shew us Thy mercy, O Lord: and grant us Thy salvation.

Secret. We beseech Thee, O Lord, that we may offer continually to Thee the sacrifice of our devotion, whereby the institution of Thy sacred Mystery may be set forth, and Thy salvation marvellously worked out for us. Through.

Comm. Is. xxxv. 4. Say to them that are of a fearful heart, Be strong, fear not: behold, our God will come and save us.

P. Comm. We implore, O Lord, Thy mercy, that, being cleansed from sin by this Divine assistance, we may be prepared for the approaching feast.

WEDNESDAY IN EMBER WEEK.

The Office. Is. xlv. 8.

Drop down, ye heavens, from above, and let the skies pour down righteousness : let the earth open, and let them bring forth salvation.

Ps. And let righteousness spring up together : I the Lord have created it.

Let us pray.

The Collect.

Grant, we beseech Thee, Almighty God, that the approaching solemnity of our redemption may both afford us succour in this present life, and abundantly bestow on us the rewards of eternal happiness. Through the same.

The Lesson. Is. ii. 2-5.

In those days the Prophet Isaias said, In the last days .... in the light of the Lord *our God.*

Gradual. Ps. xxiv. Lift up your heads, O ye gates, and be ye lift up, ye everalsting doors : and the King of Glory shall come in.

℣. Who shall ascend into the hill of the Lord : or who shall rise up in His holy place? Even he that hath clean hands, and a pure heart.

¶ *The Gradual is not repeated here.*

℣. The Lord be with you.
℟. And with thy spirit.

Let us pray.

The Collect.

Make haste, we beseech Thee, O Lord, and tarry not; and grant us the assistance of thy strength from above, that they who trust in Thy goodness may be sustained by the consolations of Thy coming. Who livest.

¶ *Here follow the usual Memorials.*

The Lesson. Is. vii. 10-15.

In those days the Lord spake .... choose the good.

Gradual. Ps. cxlv. The Lord is nigh unto all them that call upon Him : yea, all such as call upon Him faithfully.

℣. My mouth shall speak the praise of the Lord : and let all flesh give thanks unto His Holy Name.

¶ *The Gradual is repeated.*

The Gospel. Luke i. 26-38.

At that Time, the angel Gabriel .... according to Thy Word.

Offert. Luke i. 28 and 42. Hail *Mary,* highly favoured, the Lord is with thee: blessed art thou among women, and blessed is the fruit of thy womb.

℣. Therefore, that Holy Thing that shall be born of Thee shall be called the Son of God.

Secret. We present, O Lord, offerings befitting this wholesome fast: grant that by these offices we may be prepared for the Nativity of the Eternal Bread. Through.

Comm. Is. vii. 14. Behold, a virgin shall conceive and bear a Son: and shall call His name Emmanuel.

P. Comm. Being filled, O Lord, by the gift of Thy salvation, we humbly beseech Thee, that rejoicing in the taste thereof we may by it be effectually renewed. Through.

FRIDAY IN EMBER WEEK.

The Office. Ps. cxix. 151.

Be Thou nigh at hand, O Lord: for all Thy commandments are true. As concerning Thy testimonies, I have known long since: that Thou *art* for ever.

Ps. Blessed are those that are undefiled in the way: and walk in the law of the Lord.

The Collect.

Stir up, O Lord, we beseech Thee, Thy power, and come; that they who trust in Thy lovingkindness may speedily be delivered from all adversity. Who livest.

The Lesson. Is. xi. 1-5.

Thus saith the Lord God, There shall come forth a rod .... the girdle of His reins.

Gradual. Ps. lxxxv. Shew us Thy mercy, O Lord; and grant us Thy salvation.

℣. Lord, Thou art become gracious unto Thy land: Thou hast turned away the captivity of Jacob.

The Gospel Luke i. 39-47.

Mary arose in those days, and went .... God my Saviour.

Offert. Ps. lxxxv. Wilt Thou not turn again and quicken us, O God, that Thy people may rejoice in Thee: shew us Thy mercy, O Lord, and grant us Thy salvation.

℣. Lord, Thou art become gracious unto Thy land: Thou hast turned away the captivity of Jacob: Thou hast forgiven the iniquity of Thy people.

℣. Mercy and truth are met together: truth shall flourish out of the earth: and righteousness hath looked down from Heaven.

Secret. By the saving Sacrifice, we beseech Thee, O Lord, may we be more heartily prepared for these days, in which that Mystery is to be celebrated on which all fulfilment of commands doth wait. Through.

Comm. Zech. xiv. 5-7 (?) *Behold,* the Lord shall come and all His saints with *Him, and* in that day *there* shall be *a great* light.

P. Comm. Fulfil, O Lord, Thy mercy to Thy people that prayeth: and grant that they being refreshed by the abundance of Thy gifts, may both more instantly ask for a greater measure of grace, and more confidently hope for the same. Through.

SATURDAY IN EMBER WEEK.

The Office. Ps. lxxx.

Come, O Lord, Thou that sitteth on the cherubims: shew the light of Thy countenance, and we shall be whole.

Ps. Hear, O Thou Shepherd of Israel, Thou that leadest Joseph like a sheep.

Let us pray

The Collect.

O God, Who seest that we are afflicted by our own wickedness, mercifully grant that by Thy visitation we may be comforted. Who livest.

The Lesson. Is. xix. 20-22.

In that day they shall cry .... and He shall be intreated of them, and *the Lord our God* shall heal them.

Gradual. Ps. xiv. It goeth forth from the uttermost part of the heaven, and runneth about unto the end of it again.

℣. The heavens declare the glory of God: and the firmament sheweth His handy-work.

Let us pray.

The Collect.

Grant, we beseech Thee, Almighty God, that we who are bowed down under the yoke of the ancient bondage of sin, may by the expected new Birth of Thy only-begotten Son be set free. Who livest.

The Lesson. Is. xxxv. 1-7.

Thus saith the Lord, The wilderness .... and the thirsty land springs of water, *saith the Lord Almighty.*

Gradual. Ps. xix. In them hath He set a tabernacle for the sun : which cometh forth as a bridegroom out of his chamber.

℣. It goeth forth from the uttermost part of the heaven, and runneth about unto the end of it again.

Let us pray.

The Collect.

Grant to us, O Lord, Thy unworthy servants, that we who are cast down by the guilt of our own deeds, may be gladdened by the coming of Thy only-begottten Son. Who livest.

The Lesson. Is. xl. 9-11.

Thus saith the Lord, O Zion ...... and *the Lord our God shall* carry them in His bosom

Gradual. Ps. lxxx. Turn us again, O Lord God of hosts : shew the light of Thy countenance, and we shall be whole.

℣. Stir up Thy strength and come and help us, *O Lord.*

Let us pray.

The Collect.

Grant, we beseech Thee, Almighty God, that the approaching solemnity of Thy Son may both heal us in this present life and reward us eternally. Through the same.

The Lesson. Is. xlv. 1-8.

Thus saith the Lord ...... I the Lord have created it.

Gradual. Ps. lxxx. Stir up Thy strength and come and help us, *O Lord.*

℣. O Thou Shepherd of Israel, Thou that leadest Joseph like a sheep : shew Thyself, Thou that sittest upon the cherubims, before Ephraim, Benjamin, and Manasseh.

Let us pray.

The Collect.

O Lord, we beseech Thee favourably to hear the prayers of Thy people: that we who are justly punished for our offences, by the visitation of Thy goodness may be comforted. Who livest.

The Lesson. Dan. iii. 49 (*i.e.*, Song of the Three Holy Children, v. 26).

But the angel of the Lord came down into the oven together with Azarias and his fellows, and smote the flame of the fire out of the oven, and made the midst of the furnace as it had been a moist whistling wind, so that the flame streamed forth above the furnace forty and nine cubits, and it passed through and burned those Chaldeans it found about the furnace. *But* the fire touched them not at all, neither hurt nor troubled them. Then the three, as out of one mouth, praised, glorified, and blessed God in the furnace. saying—

*Tract.** ℣. Blessed art Thou, O Lord God of our fathers.

℣. And to be praised and exalted above all for ever.

℣. And blessed is Thy glorious and holy Name.

℣. And to be praised and exalted above all for ever.

℣. Blessed art Thou in the temple of Thy holy glory.

℣. And to be praised.........

℣. Blessed art Thou on the glorious throne of Thy kingdom.

℣. And to be praised.........

℣. *Blessed art Thou in the sceptre of the kingdom of Thy Divinity.*

℣. And to be praised.........

℣. Blessed art Thou that beholdest the depths and sittest upon the cherubims.

℣. And to be praised..........

℣. *Blessed art Thou Who walkest upon the wings of the winds.*

℣. And to be praised.........

℣. Let all Thy Angels *and Saints* bless Thee.

℣. And praise and glorify Thee for ever.

℣. *Let the heavens, earth, sea, and all things therein bless Thee.*

℣. And praise.........

* To be sung by two Clerks of the second form in surplices at the step of the choir, alternately with the Choir, the first and last ℣℣. being repeated both by Clerks and Choir.

℣. Glory be to the Father, and to the Son, and to the Holy Ghost.

℣. And praise and honour, power and dominion.

℣. As it was in the beginning, is now, and ever shall be, world without end. Amen.

℣. And praise and honour, power and dominion.

℣. Blessed art Thou, Lord God of our fathers.

℣. And to be praised and exalted above all for ever.

℟. The Lord be with you.

℣. And with thy spirit.

Let us pray.

The Collect.

O God, Who for the three children didst quench the flames of fire: mercifully grant that we Thy servants may not be consumed by the flames of our sins. Through.

¶ *Here follow the customary Memorials.*

The Epistle. 2 Thess. ii. 1-8.

Now we beseech you .... brightness of His coming.

¶ *Then follows this Tract, to be sung by two Clerks of the second bench, in black copes, at the step of the choir.*

Tract. Ps. lxxx. Hear, O Thou Shepherd of Israel, Thou that leadest Joseph like a sheep.

℣. Thou that sittest on the cherubims, show Thyself before Ephraim, Benjamin, and Manasseh.

℣. Stir up Thy strength and come and help us, *O Lord.*

The Gospel. Luke iii. 1-6.

Now in the fifteenth year .... salvation of God.

Offert. Zech. ix. 9. Rejoice greatly, O daughter of Zion; shout, O daughter of Jerusalem: behold, thy King cometh unto thee: He is *holy*, and having salvation; He shall speak peace unto the heathen, and His dominion shall be from sea even to sea, and from the river even to the ends of the earth.

Secret. Look down, O Lord, we beseech Thee, with an eye of favour upon this sacrifice of the faithful, and because we have no strength of our own merits, may we the rather by these gifts be made acceptable to Thee, when Thou meetest us. Who livest.

Comm Ps. xix. He rejoiceth as a giant to run his course. It goeth forth from the uttermost part of the heaven, and runneth about unto the end of it again.

P. Comm. O Lord our God, who hast vouchsafed holy mysteries for our restoration and defence: we beseech Thee make them to us a healing, both now and evermore. Through.

Fourth Sunday in Advent.

The Office. Ps. cvi.

Remember me, O Lord, according to the favour that Thou bearest unto Thy people: O visit me with Thy salvation; that I may see the felicity of Thy chosen: and rejoice in the gladness of Thy people, and give thanks with Thine inheritance.

Ps. We have sinned with our fathers: we have done amiss, and dealt wickedly.

The Collect.

O Lord, raise up, we pray Thee, Thy power, and come, and with great might succour us; that whereas, through our sins we are sore let and hindered, Thy bountiful grace and mercy may speedily help and deliver us. Who livest.

The Epistle. Phil. iv. 4-7.

Brethren, Rejoice in the Lord ... through Christ Jesus *our Lord.*

Gradual. Ps. cxlv. The Lord is nigh unto all them that call upon Him; yea, all such as call upon Him faithfully.

℣. My mouth shall speak the praise of the Lord: and let all flesh give thanks unto His holy Name.

Alleluia! ℣. Come, O Lord, and tarry not: forgive the misdeeds of Thy people.

The Sequence.

Let us all rejoice together
To our God Who all created,
Who hath founded all the worlds,
Made the heavens to shine in brightness,
Divers stars to gleam around;
Sun, the centre of the system;
Moon, the glory of the night:
And the other lesser splendors;
Sea, and earth, and hills, and plains,
Deeps and rivers infinite;
All the ample space of ether,
Where fly the birds; the winds, the rain,
All go forth to do Thy bidding,
Only Father, God alone;
Now, and unto endless ages,
Thee their praise doth glorify,
Who for us and our salvation
Didst Thine only Son send down,

Without spot, for our transgressions
Upon earth to suffer death.
Blessed Trinity, we pray Thee,
Rule our bodies and our souls,
Help us by Thy strong protection,
Grant us pardon for our sins.

The Gospel. John i. 19-28.

At that time, the Jews sent .... where John was baptizing

Offert. Is. xxxv. 4. Be strong, fear not: behold, our God will come with vengeance, even God with a recompence; He will come and save *us*.

℣. Then the eyes of the blind shall be opened, and the ears of the deaf shall be unstopped. Then shall the lame man leap as an hart, and the tongue of the dumb sing.

Secret. We beseech Thee, O Lord, look graciously upon this present sacrifice, whereby being purified we may take part in Thy Son's Nativity. Through.

Comm. Is. vii. 14. Behold a Virgin shall conceive and bear a Son, and shall call His Name Emmanuel.

P. Comm. We beseech Thee, O Lord, accompany Thy people with the plenteousness of Thy gifts, that they being defended from all evil by the virtue of Thy Sacraments, may be prepared both in mind and body for the celebration of the unspeakable Mystery. Through.

WEDNESDAY.

The Lesson. Joel ii. 23-27, and iii. 17-21.

Thus saith the Lord God, Be glad .... dwelleth in Zion *for ever and ever.*

The Gospel. Luke vii. 17-28.

In that time rumour *of Jesus* went forth throughout Judea, and throughout all the region round about, and the disciples of John .... is greater than he.

FRIDAY.

The Lesson. Zech. ii. 10-13.

Thus saith the Lord, Sing and rejoice .... holy habitation, *saith the Lord Almighty.*

The Gospel. Mark viii. 15-26.

At that time Jesus said unto His Disciples, Take heed .... any in the town.

Christmas Eve.

The Office. Ex. xvi. 6.

To-day ye shall know that the Lord *will come and will save you;* and in the morning, then ye shall see *His* glory.

Ps. The earth is the Lord's, and all that therein is: the compass of the world, and they that dwell therein.

The Collect.

God, Who makest us glad with the yearly expectation of our Redemption, grant that as we joyfully receive Thy only-begotten Son for our Redeemer, so we may with sure confidence behold the same Lord Jesus Christ Thy Son when He shall come to be Judge. Who livest.

¶ *This Lesson is read by an Acolyte in alb at the step of the choir; but if the Vigil come on a Sunday, it is read in the pulpit.*

The Lesson. Is. lxii. 1-4.

Thus saith the Lord God, For Zion's sake .... thy land shall be married.

The Epistle. Rom. i. 1-6.

Brethren, Paul, a servant .... the called of Jesus Christ our Lord.

Gradual. Ex. xvi. *To-day* ye shall know that the Lord *will come and will save you;* and in the morning ye shall see *His* glory.

℣. *Ps.* lxxx. Hear, O Thou Shepherd of Israel, Thou that leadest Joseph like a sheep. Thou that sittest on the cherubims, show Thyself before Ephraim, Benjamin, and Manasseh.

Alleluia! ℣. *On the morrow the iniquity of the earth shall be blotted out, and the Saviour of the world shall reign over us.*

The Sequence.

Let us all rejoice. *See p.* 13.

¶ *But neither Alleluia is said, nor Sequence, except on Sunday.*

The Gospel. Matt. i. 18-21.

At that time, when as His Mother Mary .... for He shall save His people from their sins.

Offert. Ps. xxiv. Lift up your heads, O ye gates; and be ye lift up, ye everlasting doors: and the King of Glory shall come in.

℣. The earth is the Lord's, and all that therein is: the compass of the world, and they that dwell therein.

¶ *This verse is not to be said except the Vigil fall on Sunday.*

Secret. Grant, we beseech Thee, Almighty God, that like as we anticipate the adorable Birth of Thy Son, so we may receive with joy His everlasting gifts. Who livest.

Comm. Is. xl. 5. The glory of the Lord shall be revealed, and all flesh shall see *the salvation of our God.*

P. Comm. Grant, we beseech Thee, O Lord, that we may be refreshed by the rehearsal of the Birth of Thy only-begotten Son, Whose heavenly Mysteries are our meat and drink. Through.

IN THE NIGHT OF CHRISTMAS.

¶ *After the ninth ℟. at Matins let the Deacon proceed with the Sub-Deacon, Thurifer, Candle-bearers, Cross-bearer, all in solemn apparel, to cense the Altar; which done, and having received the Blessing from the Priest, let him go to the pulpit to read the Gospel.*

℣. The Lord be with you.

℟. And with Thy spirit.

The beginning of the Gospel according to Matthew (i. 1-16).

Glory be to Thee, O Lord.

The Book of the Generation of Jesus Christ .... Jesus, Who is called Christ.

¶ *The Gospel ended, let the Priest begin the* Te Deum *in a silk cope, after which let the Rulers of the Choir begin Mass.*

Christmas Day.

AT MIDNIGHT.

The Office. Ps. ii.

The Lord hath said unto Me: Thou art My Son, this day have I begotten Thee.

Ps. Why do the heathen so furiously rage together: why do the people imagine a vain thing?

The Collect.

O God, Who hast caused this most holy night to shine with the illumination of the True Light: grant, we beseech Thee, that we who have known the mysteries of this Light on earth, may likewise obtain the full enjoyment of it in Heaven. Who livest.

¶ *Let two Clerks of the second bench, in silk copes, chant this Lesson together in the pulpit.*

I will sing praises to God for ever, Who formed me in His Right Hand, and redeemed me on the Cross with the purple Blood of His Son.

Then alternately.

The Lesson of Esaias the Prophet.

In which is foretold the glorious birth of Christ.

Thus saith the Lord,

Father, Son, and Holy Ghost, by Whom are created all things in Heaven and earth.

The people that walked in darkness

Whom Thou createdest: whom the enemy expelled from Paradise by a subtle fraud: and led captive with him to hell.

Have seen a great light.

And at midnight strange brightness hath shone on the Shepherds,

They that dwell in the shadow of death, the light

Everlasting, and our True Redemption

Upon them hath shined.

O Stupendous Birth,

For unto us a Child is born,

Jesus the Son of God, He shall be great,

A Son

Of the highest Father

Unto us is given.

So had it been foretold from the Throne on high.

And the government shall be upon His shoulder,

That He may rule Heaven and earth.

And His Name shall be called

Messiah, Soter, Emmanuel, Sabaoth, Adonai,

Wonderful,
The Root of David,
Counsellor,
Of God the Father,
God
Who created all things,
Mighty,
Overthrowing the hideous gates of hell
The Everlasting Father,
King Almighty, and governing all,
The Prince of Peace
Here and for ever.
Of the increase of His government
In Jerusalem, Judea, and Samaria,
And peace there shall be no end,
For ever and ever,
Upon the Throne of David, and upon His kingdom,
And there shall be no bounds to His reign
To order it,
In the bonds of the faith,
And to establish it with judgment and with justice,
When He shall come as Judge to judge the world.
From henceforth
To Him be due glory, praise, and rejoicing,
Even for ever.

¶ *Here let them sing together to the end.*

From the rising of the Sun to the going down of the same, let meet praise resound to the Creator throughout all climes to the ends of the whole world. Let everything say, Amen.

¶ *Where there is no chanting let this Lesson be read.*

The Lesson. Is. ix. 2, 6, 7.

Thus saith the Lord God, the people that walked .... from henceforth even for ever.

The Epistle. Tit. ii. 11-15.

Dearly beloved, the grace of God ...... these things speak and exhort, *in Christ Jesus our Lord.*

Gradual Ps. cx. In the day of Thy power shall the people offer Thee free-will offerings with an holy worship: the dew of Thy birth is of the womb of the morning.

℣. The Lord said unto My Lord: Sit Thou on My right hand, until I make Thine enemies Thy footstool.

Alleluia! ℣. Ps. ii. The Lord hath said unto Me: Thou art My Son, this day have I begotten Thee.

The Sequence.

All hosts with one accord
Sing the Incarnate Lord,
With instrument and breath,
Discoursing tidings glad.
This is the hallowed day
On which new happiness
Rose full upon the world;
On this renowned night
Glory was thundered forth,
By angel voices sung;
Wondrous unwonted lights,
At midnight hour,
Around the Shepherd's shone,
Keeping their quiet flocks.
All unexpectedly
God's message they receive.
Who was before the world
Is of a Virgin born;
Glory to God on high
In heaven, and peace on earth.
So doth the heavenly host
Sing praises in the highest,
Let heaven at either pole
Shake with their ringing chant.
On this most holy day
Let glory loudly sung
Through all the earth resound;
Let all mankind proclaim
That God is born on earth.
The foe shall vex mankind
With cruel rule no more;
Peace is restored to earth.
Let all creation joy
In Him Who now is born.
He all upholds alone,
He all did form alone:
May He of His own grace
Loose us from all our sins.

The Gospel. Luke ii. 1.14.

And it came to pass .... good-will towards men.

The Creed.

Offert. Ps. xcvi. Let the heavens rejoice and let the earth be glad before the Lord, for He cometh.

Secret. We beseech Thee, O Lord, that the oblation of this day's festival may be acceptable to Thee, that through the plenitude of Thy Grace, by this sacred communion, we may be found in the likeness of Him in Whom we are united with Thee, Jesus Christ our Lord. Who liveth.

Preface. Because by the mystery.

Within the Canon. In communion with.

Comm., Ps. cix. The dew of Thy birth is of the womb of the morning.

P. Comm. Grant, we beseech Thee, O Lord our God, that we who celebrate with joy the Birth of our Lord Jesus Christ, may by worthy conversation be made meet to attain unto fellowship with Him. Who liveth.

CHRISTMAS DAY.

AT DAY-BREAK.

The Office, Is. ix. 6, 7.

Light shall shine upon us to-day, because unto us the Lord is born, and His Name shall be called Wonderful, the Mighty God, the Everlasting Father, the Prince of Peace. Of *Whose kingdom* there shall be no end.

Ps. xcviii. The Lord is King, and hath put on glorious apparel; the Lord hath put on His apparel, and girded Himself with strength.

The Collect.

Grant, we beseech Thee, Almighty God, unto us on whom is largely shed the light of Thy Incarnate Word, that as by faith It enlightened our minds, so It may shine forth in our deeds. Through.

Memorial of S. Anastasia.

Grant, we beseech Thee, O Almighty God, that we who celebrate the feast of blessed Anastatia Thy Martyr, may be assured of her advocacy with Thee. Through.

¶ *Neither more or fewer Collects are to be said here.*

¶ *Let the following Lesson be read in the pulpit by a Clerk of the second bench.*

The Lesson. Is. lxi. 1-3, and lxii. 11, 12.

Thus saith the Lord, The Spirit ...... redeemed of the Lord.

The Epistle. Titus iii. 4-7.

Beloved, the kindness ...... eternal life *in Christ Jesus our Lord.*

Gradual. Ps. cxviii. Blessed be He that cometh in the Name of the Lord. God is the Lord, Who hath showed us light.

℣. This is the Lord's doing, and it is marvellous in our eyes.

Alleluia! ℣. Ps. xciii. The Lord is King, and hath put on glorious apparel: the Lord hath put on His apparel, and girded Himself with strength.

The Sequence.

Unto the King new born new praises sing,
Whose Father by His Word did frame the worlds,
Whose Mother is a Virgin undefiled;
Begotten of the Father, God of God,
Born of His Mother without carnal stain:
Before all worlds begotten of the Father;
When the full time was come His Mother bare Him.
O wonderful, mysterious generation!
O most astonishing Nativity!
O glorious Child! Divinity incarnate!
So Prophets, moved by Thy Holy Spirit,
Spake of Thy coming Birth, Thou Son of God!
So at Thy dawning Angels sing Thee praises,
And to the earth glad tidings bring of peace.
The very elements themselves are glad.
And all the Saints exultingly rejoice,
Crying, All hail! Save us, we pray, O God,
In Persons Trine, one undivided Substance.

The Gospel. Luke ii. 15-20.

At that time the shepherds said .... told unto them.

Offert. Ps. xciii. *God* hath made the round world so sure: that it cannot be moved. Ever since the world began hath Thy seat been prepared: Thou art from everlasting.

Secret. Grant, O Lord, that we may bring offerings agreeable to the mystery of this day's Nativity, that as He Who was born Man shone forth as God, so this earthly substance may impart to us that which is Divine. Through.

Secret of S. Anastasia. Accept, O Lord, we beseech Thee, gifts worthily offered, and grant that the merits of blessed Anastasia, pleading in our behalf, may avail to the furtherance of our salvation. Through.

Preface and *Within the Canon*, as in first Mass.

Comm. Zech. ix. Rejoice, O daughter of Sion; *praise*, O daughter of Jerusalem: behold, thy King cometh unto thee; He is holy, and having the salvation *of the world*.

P. Comm. O Lord, Whose marvellous Birth cast out the old man, grant, we beseech Thee, that the commemorative renewal of this mystery may evermore renew us. Through.

P. Comm. of S. Anastatia. Thou hast fed, O Lord, Thy family with sacred gifts: ever therefore, we beseech Thee, comfort us by her intercession whose feast we celebrate. Through.

CHRISTMAS DAY.

AT THE THIRD MASS.

The Office. Is. ix.

For unto us a Child is born, unto us a Son is given: and the government shall be upon His shoulder; and His name shall be called *The Angel of Great Counsel.**

Ps. xcviii. O sing unto the Lord a new song: for He hath done marvellous things.

The Collect.

Grant, we beseech Thee, Almighty God, that we who are held in bondage by the old yoke of sin, by the new Birth in the flesh of Thy Only-begotten may be set free. Through.

¶ *Let the following Lesson be read in the pulpit by one of the superior grade in a surplice.*

The Lesson. Is. lii. 6-10.

Thus saith the Lord, Therefore, my people ...... the salvation of our God.

The Epistle. Heb. i. 1-12.

Brethren, God, Who at sundry times .... thy years shall not fail.

Gradual. Ps. xcviii. All the ends of the world have seen the salvation of our God. Shew yourselves joyful unto the Lord, all ye lands.

* *μεγάλης βουλῆς ἄγγελος.—LXX.*

℣. The Lord declared His salvation : His righteousness hath He openly shewed in the sight of the heathen.

Alleluia! ℣. The hallowed day hath shined upon us. Come, ye nations, and adore the Lord, for to-day a great light hath descended on the earth.

The Sequence.

This day celestial melody
Was heard by men on earth,
When the Virgin bare a Son
The hosts above sang praise.
What aileth thee, thou world below
Why joy'st thou not with these?
In pastoral charge the shepherds watch;
Hark! angels' voices clear
Chant forth their strains of holy joy,
Of peace and glory full;
To Christ they render homage due,
To us of grace they sing:
Not unto all such gifts are given,
But to men of good will;
Not irrespectively bestowed,
But measured by desert;
Affections must be weaned from sin,
So shall that peace on us be shed
Which to the good is promised.
Earthly to heavenly things are joined,
In this respect their praises join,
But by desert they are dissever'd.
Rejoice, O man, when thou dost ponder this;
*Rejoice, O flesh, associate with the Word.

His rising by the stars is told
  With indicating light;
Lo! star-lit chiefs to Bethlehem
  Follow that planet bright.
The King of Heaven is cradled found
  Amid the beasts He made,
In a rude manger's narrow bed
  The Lord of all is laid.
Star of the Sea! Thy Blessed Son
  The holy Church adores;
That Thou our service wilt accept
  Devoutly she implores.
Let each redeemed thing the Redeemer's praises sing.

The Gospel. S. John i. 1-14,

In the beginning was the Word ....., full of grace and truth.

* Let this ℣. be said thrice.

Offert. Ps. lxxxix. The heavens are Thine, the earth also is Thine: Thou hast laid the foundation of the round world, and all that therein is. Righteousness and equity are the habitation of Thy seat.

Secret. Sanctify, O Lord, our offerings by the new Birth of Thy only-begotten Son, and mercifully cleanse us from the stains of our sins. Through the same.

Preface and *Within the Canon,* as in first Mass.

Comm. Ps. xcviii. All the ends of the world have seen the salvation of our God.

P. Comm. Grant, we beseech Thee, Almighty God, that as the Saviour of the world Who was born this day, procured for us a heavenly birth, He may also bestow on us immortality. Who liveth.

S. Stephen, Proto-Martyr.

The Office. Ps. cxix.

Princes also did sit and speak against me, *wicked men* have persecuted me: *Help me, O Lord my God, because* Thy servant is occupied in Thy statutes.

Ps. Blessed are those that are undefiled in the way, and walk in the law of the Lord.

The Collect.

Grant to us, Lord, to imitate that which we commemorate, that we may learn to love even our enemies: forasmuch as we celebrate his natal day who knew how to pray even for his murderers to our Lord Jesus Christ Thy Son. Who liveth.

¶ *Then shall follow the Memorial of the Nativity only.*

The Lesson. Acts vi. 8-10, vii. 54-60.

In those days, Stephen, being full of the Holy Ghost .... he fell asleep.

Gradual. Ps. cxix. Princes also did sit, and speak against Me: wicked men have persecuted Me.

℣. Ps. cix. Help me, O Lord, my God: save me for Thy mercies' sake.

℣. *Alleluia!* Acts vii. I see the heavens opened, and Jesus standing on the right hand of *the power of* God.

The Sequence.

Great is the Lord in all the earth,
Great are His works in Heaven above,
And in the earth below.
He is the King of Kings and Lord of all,
Before all worlds begotten of the Father.
He of His love and truth doth Stephen now
Exalt from earth to Heaven,
And in eternal life adorn His brow
With glittering martyr crown.
For Stephen, full of grace and power Divine,
Did wonders great, and spake with faith and wisdom;
But whilst he preached the new and joyful tidings
That our redemption doth no longer tarry,
Looking up steadfastly he saw Heaven opened,
And cried aloud, full of the Holy Ghost,
Unto the multitude which stood around him,
Behold, I see God's glory wonderful
In bright effulgence, and the Son of Man
Stand at the right hand of the power of God.
Which when the impious Jewish people heard
With furious cries they violently ran
And stoned Stephen, crushing all his limbs;
Yet boldly, patiently, the Martyr stands,
And prays, Lay not this sin unto their charge,
But now, Lord Jesus Christ, receive my spirit.
And when he had said this, he fell asleep
In peace eternal, resting in the Lord.
Pray for us too, O Stephen, holy Martyr,
That we may have a part in joys eternal.

The Gospel. Matt. xxiii. 34-39.

At that time Jesus said unto the multitude of the Jews, and to the chief priests, Behold, I send unto you prophets .... the Name of the Lord.

Offert. Acts vi. *The Apostles* chose Stephen, *a Levite,* full of faith and of the Holy Ghost, *whom the Jews* stoned, *praying and* saying, Lord Jesus, receive my spirit. *Alleluia.*

Secret. Receive, O Lord, we beseech Thee, these offerings in memory of Thy holy Martyr Stephen; and as his sufferings have made him glorious, so may our devotion make us blameless. Through.

Comm. Acts vii. I see the heavens opened, and Jesus standing on the right hand of *the power of* God. Lord Jesus receive my spirit, and lay not this sin to their charge, *for they know not what they do.*

P. Comm. May the mysteries we have received, O Lord, be a help to us; and by the intercession of Thy blessed Proto-Martyr Stephen, evermore strengthen and protect us. Through.

S. John the Evangelist.

The Office. Ecclus. xv.

In the midst of the congregation shall *he* open his mouth, and the Lord *filled him with the spirit of wisdom and understanding, and clothed him with the robe of glory.*

Ps. He shall find joy and a crown of gladness.

¶ *In Easter-tide* is added,* Alleluia! Alleluia!

The Collect.

Merciful Lord, we beseech Thee to cast Thy bright beams of light upon Thy Church, that it, being enlightened by the doctrine of Thy blessed Apostle and Evangelist Saint John, may attain to the gift of everlasting life. Through.

¶ *Memorial of Christmas Day and S. Stephen only.*

The Lesson. Ecclus. xv. 1-6.

He that feareth the Lord .... and *the Lord our God* shall cause him to inherit an everlasting name.

Gradual. John xxi. Then went this saying abroad among the brethren, that that disciple should not die.

℣. But, if I will that He tarry till I come, follow thou Me.

Alleluia! ℣. This is the disciple which testifieth of these things: and we know that his testimony is true.

The Sequence.

O John! Disciple chaste, whom Jesus lov'd,
Thou for the love which thou didst bear to Him
Didst leave thy earthly parent in the ship;
Unwedded didst Messiah follow, drinking
Pure streams of wisdom from His holy breast.
Thou saw'st the glory of the Son of God
Whilst yet alive on earth, Whom to behold
The saints do look only in life eternal.
To Thee, Christ, triumphing upon the Cross,

* *i.e.*, S. John ant. Port. Lat. (May 6).

In charge His Holy Mother did commit,
That to the Virgin thou, thyself a virgin,
With filial care should'st minister protection.
In prison cast, and torn with cruel scourges,
Thou didst rejoice to bear Christ's testimony.
Thou, too, didst raise the dead, and deadly poison
Didst drink and take no harm, in Jesus' Name.
To thee the Most High Father doth reveal
His word of prophecy, denied to others.
Do thou, O John, belov'd of Jesus Christ,
Commend us all to God, in never-ceasing prayers!

The Gospel. John xxi. 19-24.

At that time Jesus said unto Peter, Follow Me .... his testimony is true.

Offert. Ps. xcii. The righteous shall flourish like a palm-tree: and shall spread abroad like a cedar in Libanus.

¶ *At the Feast in Easter-tide,* Alleluia!

Secret. Receive, O Lord, we beseech Thee, the offerings we make to Thee on his feast by whose espousal of our cause we trust to be delivered. Through.

Comm. John xxi. Then went this saying abroad among the brethren, that that disciple should not die. Yet Jesus said not, He shall not die; but, If I will that he tarry till I come?

¶ *In Easter-tide,* Alleluia!

P. Comm. Being refreshed, O Lord, with heavenly meat and drink, we humbly beseech Thee, that we may be fortified by his prayers on whose commemoration we have received them. Through.

The Holy Innocents.

The Office. Ps. viii.

O God, out of the mouths of very babes and sucklings hast Thou ordained strength, because of Thine enemies.

Ps. O Lord our Governor: how excellent is Thy Name in all the world!

The Collect.

O God, Whose martyred Innocents on this day showed forth, not by praise, but by death; mortify all evil vices in us, that Thy faith which our tongue uttereth, our lives may in deed confess. Who livest.

¶ *Memorial of Christmas, S. Stephen, and S. John only.*

The Lesson. Rev. xiv. 1-5.

In those days I looked, and lo, ... without their fault before the Throne of God.

Gradual. Ps. cxxiv. Our soul is escaped even as a bird out of the snare of the fowler.

℣. The snare is broken, and we are delivered: our help standeth in the Name of the Lord, Who made Heaven and earth.

Alleluia! ℣. The noble army of Martyrs: Praise Thee, *O Lord.*

The Sequence.

Let children sing high melodies,
The Innocents' triumphant lay,
Whom Christ, the Holy Child, did bear to Heaven to-day.
These for no crime, in cruel fraud,
Herod in madness and in rage,
In Bethlehem and all its coasts,
From two years old and under slew.
Herod, unhappy King, alarm'd
Lest Christ the new-born King should reign,
Is filled with wrath, and seizes arms
With haughty hand and troubled mind,
And seeks the King of Light and Heaven,
Bent to destroy with murderous dart
The life of Him Who giveth life.
Unable with his clouded mind
To look on that bright light he seeks,
Fierce Herod weaves his dark designs
To slay the band of infant saints.
The wicked King his troops prepares,
Pierces with sword the tender limbs;
Babes at the breast he slays, ere yet
The milk can curdle into blood.
The murderous unnatural foe
Infants new-born in pieces tears;
Ere their frail limbs have gathered strength
Under his feet he tramples them.
O blessed Innocents! O blest
The little ones that Herod slew!
O blessed mothers! ye who there
Such pledges of your love did bear.
O sweet array of childen dear!
O holy fight of babes for Christ!
Thousands of tender age lie slain around;
Their mothers' milk flows from them in their throes.

Angelic hosts to welcome stand
The little white-robed martyr band.
A marvellous victory they win,
Gaining the prize of life, ere yet the strife begin.
O Christ! Thee we devoutly pray,
Thou Who didst come the world to mend,
Grant us, with those blest Innocents,
The glories which shall never end!

The Gospel. Matt. ii. 13-18.

At that time the Angel of the Lord .... because they are not.

Offert. Ps. cxxiv. Our soul is escaped even as a bird out of the snare of the fowler. The snare is broken, and we are delivered.

Secret. Be present, O Lord, at the consecration of these gifts, on the festival of the Innocents; and grant that as we venerate their infancy dedicated to Thee, we may be able to imitate their guilelessness. Through.

Comm. Matt. ii. A voice was heard in Rama, lamentation and bitter weeping: Rachel weeping for her children, and refusing to be comforted because they are not.

P. Comm. Grant, O Lord, that, by the prayers of the Holy Innocents, the devout offerings of which we have partaken may alike support our life present, and impart to us that which is to come. Through.

S. Thomas of Canterbury.

The Office.

Let us all rejoice in the Lord, and celebrate this feast in honour of the Martyr Thomas for whose suffering angels rejoice and praise the Son of God.

Ps. lxiv. Hear my voice, O God, in my prayer: preserve my life from fear of the enemy.

The Collect.

O God, in defence of Whose Church the renowned Bishop, Thomas, fell by the swords of wicked men: grant, we beseech Thee, that all who implore his assistance may obtain their petition. Through.

¶ *Memorial of Christmas, S. Stephen, S. John, and the Innocents only.*

The Epistle. Hebrews v. 1-10.

(See *Ep.* i. in Comm. of one Martyr and Bishop.)

Gradual. (See *Grad.* i., in Comm. of one Mart.)

Alleluia! (See *Alleluia* vii., in Comm. of one Mart.)

The Sequence.

This day let solemn strains
Resound on earth below,
And o'er the Martyr's palm
Triumph the heavenly host.
What do ye, joyous folk?
Give thanks with them above.
Let every living soul rejoice,
And with free voice to Christ sing praise.
Let Canterbury at this feast
Devoutly homage pay.
The furious soldier band
Shouts forth the tyrant King's command,
Lawless will and fierce decree
Forced their way full haughtily.
Armed men with passion wild
Places dear to Christ defiled;
But Christ's footsteps following,
Thomas with unswerving tread
Stood unshaken, undismayed,
In obedience to His King
Meets the sword with steady eye,
Counting it all gain to die.
*Thomas, rejoice, thy victory adds a lay
To swell the praise of Christ's own Natal Day!
The Martyr's glory is proclaimed,
By divers signs assured,
Within the fane the Pastor Chief
A cruel death endured;
Nor day nor place from murderous hand
Awe or respect procured.
Star of the Sea! who didst rejoice to feed
Christ at thy holy breast,
Him do we humbly pray, that in the end we may
With Thomas surely rest,
And through his prayer be blest.

The Gospel.

(See *Gosp.* ii., in Comm. of one Mart. and Bp.)

Offert. (See *Offert.* ii., in Comm. of one Mart.)

Secret. Grant, O Lord, we beseech Thee, that blessed Thomas, Bishop and Martyr, may obtain for us that the gift of the saving

* This ℣. is to be said thrice.

offering now to be consecrated may conduce to our salvation; that so we may both know the excellency of his conversation, and partake of the benefit of his intercession. Through.

Comm. (See *Comm.* vi. of Comm. of one Mart.)

P. Comm. O Almighty and most merciful God, grant us that by these holy things which we have received, the revered intercession of Thy Martyr and Bishop, Thomas, may help us, who for the honour of Thy Name was deemed worthy to be crowned by glorious martyrdom. Through.

Sixth Day from Christmas.

WHETHER SUNDAY OR NOT.

The Office. Wisd. xviii.

For while all things were in quiet silence, and that night was in the midst of her swift course, Thine Almighty Word, *O Lord*, leaped down from Heaven out of Thy Royal Throne.

Ps. xciii. The Lord is King, and hath put on glorious apparel: the Lord hath put on His apparel, and girded Himself with strength.

The Collect.

O Almighty and everlasting Lord, direct our actions according to Thy good pleasure, that in the Name of Thy beloved Son we may be deemed worthy to abound in good works. Who.

¶ *Memorials of Christmas, S. Stephen, S. John, The Innocents, and S. Thomas only.*

The Epistle. Gal. iv. 1-7.

Brethren, the heir .... an heir of God through Christ.

Gradual. Ps. xlv. Thou art fairer than the children of men: full of grace are Thy lips.

℣. My heart is inditing of a good matter: I speak of the things which I have made unto the King. My tongue is the pen of a ready writer.

Alleluia! ℣. Ps. xciii. The Lord is King, and hath put on glorious apparel: the Lord hath put on His apparel, and girded Himself with strength.

The Sequence.

Let us celebrate this day, Christ the Lord's Nativity;
Let the heavenly army's cry ring in praise incessantly,
Giving thanks, and honouring the wedding banquet of their King
Now new light illumes the land, darkness flees at its command,
Grace descending opens wide the courts long shut on every side:
O happy Mother, undefiled Virgin, who hast borne a Child!
Great with thy Holy Burden, lo! yet a man thou did'st not know.
Lady, of thee a suppliant crowd doth crave,
Procure from us escape from bands of sin,
O Virgin, blessed of all generations!
For thou alone wast worthy found to bear
Within thy womb Him Who bare all our sins,
Who ruleth things above and things beneath.
Him they above do magnify, rejoicing
In that good state of being which He gave them;
We, lowly multitude, give Him due reverence,
Beseeching favour of His clemency,
That, granting quiet times and present peace,
He will be pleased to give us holy lives,
Bestowing on His servants meet endowments;
Heal our divisions left behind at death,
And lead us where no sin or death is known,
Where at the Father's own right hand He sitteth
And reigneth co-eternal over all,
The world disposing by His power, with Him
In concert, present things and things to come;
On all the just conferring blest rewards
Which shine in brightness, where the true light shineth,
Which is our health eternal and our glory.

The Gospel. Luke ii. 33-40.

At that time Joseph and his mother .... and the grace of God was upon him.

Offert. Ps. xciii. He hath made the round world so sure: that it cannot be moved. Ever since the world began hath Thy seat been prepared, *O God:* Thou art from everlasting.

Secret. Accept, O Lord, we beseech Thee, the sacrifice of Thy people, and vouchsafe them the fellowship of Jesus Christ Thy Son our Lord, Who deigned to be made partaker of our nature. Who.

Comm. Matt. ii. Take the young Child and His Mother, and go into the land of *Judah:* for they are dead who sought the young Child's life.

P. Comm. Now that the Sacrifice hath been received, we beseech Thee, O Lord, let Thy Church everywhere rejoice in Him Who hath taken upon Himself her infirmities, that she might be made partaker of the Divine Nature. Through.

S. Sylvester.

The Office.
(See *Off.* ii., in Comm. Conf. and Bp.)
The Collect.
(See *Coll.* ii., in Comm. Conf. and Bp.)

¶ *Memorials of Christmas, SS. Stephen, John, Innocents, and Thomas.*

The Lesson.
(See *Less.* ii., in Comm. Conf. and Bp.)

Gradual. (See *Grad.* i., in Comm Conf. and Bp.)

Alleluia. (See *All.* v., in Comm. Conf. and Bp.)

The Sequence.
(See *Seq.* in Comm. Conf. and Bp.)
The Gospel.
(See *Gosp.* i., in Comm. Conf. and Bp.)

Offert. (See *Off.* ii., in Comm. Conf. and Bp.)

Secret. Be present, O Lord, we beseech Thee, at our oblations, and suffer not those who are fortified by the glorious confession of blessed Sylvester, Thy Confessor and Bishop, to be exposed to any perils of mind or body. Through.

Comm. See *Comm.* ii., in Comm. Conf. and Bp.

P. Comm. We beseech Thee, Almighty God, that at the intercession of the blessed Sylvester, Thy Confessor and Bishop, the gift which we have received of this day's feast may impart salvation both to our bodies and souls. Through.

The Circumcision of Christ.

The Office.
(See 3rd Mass on Christmas Day.)
The Collect.

O God, Who permittest us to celebrate the Octave of our Saviour's Birth: vouchsafe, we beseech Thee, that as we are renewed by the communion of His Flesh, so we may be defended by His everlasting Divinity. Who.

¶ *There is no Memorial at this Mass.*

The Epistle.

(See 1st Mass on Christmas Day.)

Gradual. (See 3rd Mass on Christmas Day.)

Alleluia! ℣. Heb. i. God, Who at sundry times and in divers manners spake in time past unto the Fathers by the Prophets, hath in these last days spoken unto us by His Son.

The Sequence.

Sing we the joyful day,
Right worthy to be praised,
On which the light arose
Most grateful to our eyes;
The clouds of night retire,
The darkness of our sin
Is past and wholly gone.
This day unto the world
The Day Star of the Sea
The Saviour did bring forth,
New joy to all the earth,
Before Whom hell doth quake,
Dread Death himself doth fear,
For his destruction comes:
The envious serpent groans,
The ancient pest of man,
Spoiled and captive led;
Fall'n man, the erring sheep,
Is to heaven's joys restored.
God's host, the angels bright,
In heaven rejoice to-day,
That the lost piece is found.
O offspring highly blest,
Sent to redeem mankind!
God Who created all
Is of a woman born.
O Nature wonderful,
Most wondrously put on!
To Itself taking that which It was not,
Remaining still that which It was before.
The very Godhead is
With human nature clad.
Whoe'er hath heard the like?
The Shepherd good had come
To seek that which was lost;
His helmet He put on
Like warrior arm'd for fight:
On his own darts the foe,
O'erthrown, did headlong rush,
Taken his armour is
In which he put his trust;

His spoils divided are,
His prey is wrested from him.
Our sure salvation rests
On Christ's most valiant fight,
Who led us to our country, fixed on high,
Triumphing in His glorious victory,
Where thanks and praise we sing to Thee eternally!

The Gospel. Luke ii. 21.

At that time, when eight days were accomplished ...... conceived in the womb.

Offert. (See 3rd Mass on Christmas Day.)

Secret. Grant, we beseech Thee, Almighty God, that by these gifts which we bring in honour of the mystery of the hidden Birth of our Lord Jesus Christ, we may attain to the understanding which is the inheritance of a cleansed soul. Through.

Comm. (See 3rd Mass on Christmas Day.)

P. Comm. Grant, we beseech Thee, O Lord, that that which we have received in the repeated commemoration of our Saviour's Birth may heal, and bestow on us eternal salvation. Through.

¶ *On the Octaves of SS. Stephen, John, Innocents, all as on the day, except the* Sequence, Creed, *and* Preface, *which is the daily one (on the Octave of S. John, however, it is as on Apostles' days). But on a Sunday the* Creed *is said. The* Memorial of S. Mary *is said on week-days, Feasts, and Sundays till the Purification, the Vigil and Feast of Epiphany excepted.*

The Vigil of the Epiphany.

The Office.

(See 2nd Mass on Christmas Day.)

The Collect.

We beseech Thee, O Lord, that the brightness of the approaching Festival may enlighten our hearts, that so we may escape from this world, and may come to the land of eternal light. Through.

Memorial of S. Thomas.

(See p. 29.)

Memorial of S. Edward, King and Confessor.

O God, Who didst manifest Thy only-begotten Son our Lord Jesus Christ in a visible form to the glorious King Edward, grant, we beseech Thee, that for his sake and prayers we may be thought worthy to attain to the eternal vision of our Lord Jesus Christ Himself. Who.

¶ *No further Memorials.*

The Epistle, Gradual and Alleluia.

(See 2nd Mass on Christmas Day.)

The Gospel. Matt. ii. 19–23.

At that time, when Herod was dead .... shall be called a Nazarene.

Offert. (See 2nd Mass on Christmas Day.)

Secret. Grant, we beseech Thee, O Lord, that in this Sacrifice we may both offer and receive Him Whom the devout gifts of the coming Festival proclaim beforehand, our Lord Jesus Christ, Thy Son. Who.

Secret of S. Thomas. (See p. 30.)

Secret of S. Edward. O Lord, we beseech Thee, shed on us, now assisting at the sacred Altar, the light of the Holy Spirit, that what we devoutly offer to Thee in commemoration of the blessed King Edward may, by his intercession, turn to our health and salvation. Through.

Comm. (See 6th day after Christmas.)

P. Comm. Grant us, O Lord, we beseech Thee, worthily to celebrate the mystery which in the infancy of our Saviour is declared by signal miracles, and the manifestation of His humanity, which is shown forth in His bodily growth. Through.

P. Comm. of S. Thomas. (See p. 30.)

P. Comm. of S. Edward. Replenished with the feast of living food, we beseech Thee, O Lord our God, that, for the pleading sake of King Edward Thy Confessor, we may be esteemed worthy to be partakers of the heavenly banquet. Through.

IN THE NIGHT OF THE EPIPHANY.

¶ *Whilst the ninth ℟. is being sung with the Glory and ℣., let the Deacon, having censed the Altar and received the Blessing, proceed with the Sub-Deacon, Thurifer, Candle-bearers, and Acolyte with the Cross, through the midst of the choir to the pulpit to chant the Gospel.*

℣. The Lord be with you.
℟. And with thy spirit.

The Sequence of the Holy Gospel according to Luke (iii. 21-38, iv. 1).

Glory be to Thee, O Lord.

Now when all the people were baptized ...... returned from Jordan.

¶ *The Gospel ended, let the Priest begin the* Te Deum, *vested in a silk cope.*

The Epiphany.

The Office. Mal. iii. (?)

Behold the Lord shall come; *and kingdom, power, and dominion are in His hand.*

Ps. lxxii. Give the King Thy judgments, O God; and Thy righteousness unto the King's son.

The Collect.

O God, Who by the leading of a star didst manifest Thy only-begotten Son to the Gentiles, mercifully grant that we, which know Thee now by faith, may after this life have the fruition of Thy glorious Godhead. Through.

The Lesson. Is. lx. 1-6.

Arise, shine, *Jerusalem* .... praises of the Lord.

Gradual. Is. lx. All they from Sheba shall come: they shall bring gold and incense; and they shall shew forth the praises of the Lord,

℣. Arise, shine, *Jerusalem;* for thy light is come, and the glory of the Lord is risen upon thee.

Alleluia! Matt. ii. We have seen His star in the East, and are come to worship Him.

The Sequence.

All glory to the Lord's Epiphany!
When the wise men adore the Child of God,
Whose majesty and power infinite
For ages the Chaldeans venerate;
Whom all the holy prophets have foretold
Should come to give salvation to the Gentiles:
Who deigned so His majesty to humble,
That on Him He did take the form of servant:
He Who before the world, before all time,
Was God, of blessed Mary was made man.

(The next verse to be said thrice.)

Whom predicting Balaam said:
  Out of Jacob, seen from far,
  There shall come a flaming star
  With mighty power to smite the host
  Of Moab to his utmost coast.
To Him their costly offering,
Gold, incense, myrrh, the Magi bring.
By incense God they Him proclaim,
By gold a King of mighty name,
By myrrh a man of mortal frame.
These in a dream an Angel warns,
To Herod's ear no word to bring,
Troubled about the new-born King,
For much he feared in rage and hate
Lest he should lose his royal state.
Again the star before them went,
And led them on their journey bent,
Rejoicing to their native land,
Unheeding of the King's command.
Transported with exceeding ire
He issues forth his mandate dire,
Throughout all Bethlehem's coasts to seek
And put to death the infants meek.
Let all the choir their voice unite
With organ's swell, in mystic rite,
Bringing to Christ, the King of Kings,
Praises and costly offerings;
Beseeching that He will defend
All kingdoms of the earth, world without end.

The Gospel. Matt. ii. 1-12.

When Jesus was born ...... their own country another way.

Offert. Ps. lxxii. The kings of Tharsis and the isles shall give presents, the kings of Arabia and Saba shall bring gifts. All kings shall fall down before Him: all nations shall do Him service.

Secret. O Lord, we beseech Thee, graciously regard the gifts of Thy Church; whereby are no longer offered gold, frankincense, and myrrh, but what is signified by those offerings is sacrificed and received, Jesus Christ, Thy Son our Lord. Who liveth.

Preface. Because when Thy only-begotten Son.

Within the Canon. In communion with.

Comm. Matt. ii. We have seen His star in the East, and are come *with offerings* to worship *the Lord.*

P. Comm. Grant, we beseech Thee, Almighty God, that what we celebrate in the solemn office, we may apprehend with the full intelligence of a cleansed mind. Through.

¶ *The same Mass is said daily through the Octave without* Creed *or* Sequence.

SUNDAY WITHIN THE OCTAVE.

¶ *The Service for Sunday in Octave all as on the day, except* Sequence *and* Gospel, *which, if the Sunday come not within Octave, is to be read on Wednesday.*

The Gospel. John i. 29-34.

At that time, John saw ...... this is the Son of God.

THIRD DAY WITHIN THE OCTAVE.

¶ *Let the Memorial of Lucian and his companion martyrs be made. See Comm. of many Martyrs.*

The Octave of the Epiphany.

The Office.

As on Epiphany.

The Collect.

O God, Whose only-begotten Son appeared in the substance of our flesh, grant, we beseech Thee, that we may be accounted worthy to be inwardly renewed by Him Whom we acknowledge to have been like to ourselves in outward appearance. Who.

Memorial of S. Hilary.

Be present, O Lord, at our prayers, and by the intercession of blessed Hilary, Thy Confessor and Bishop, whose burial we commemorate, graciously bestow upon us Thy perpetual mercy. Through.

The Lesson. Is. xxv. 1.

O Lord, Thou art my God; I will exalt Thee, I will praise Thy Name; for Thou hast done wonderful things; Thy counsels of old are faithfulness and truth. *O Lord God of Sabaoth, Thy arm is high. Thou art a Crown of Hope with beautified glory.* (Is. xxxv. 1, 2, 10): The wilderness and the solitary place *of Jordan* shall be glad for them; and the desert shall rejoice; *and my people* shall see the glory of the Lord, and the excellency of our God; *and shall be gathered together and redeemed by God;* and come to Zion with songs and everlasting joy upon their heads; they shall obtain joy and gladness. (Is. xli. 18): I will open rivers in high places, and fountains in the midst of the valleys: I will make the dry land springs of water. (Is. lii. 13): Behold, My servant shall be exalted and extolled, and be very high. (Is. xii. 3-5): With joy shall ye draw water out of the wells of salvation. And in that day shall ye say, Praise the Lord, call upon His Name, declare His doings among the people. Sing unto the Lord; for He hath done excellent things; this is known in all the earth, *saith the Lord Almighty.*

Gradual and *Alleluia.* As on Epiphany.

The Gospel. Matt. iii. 13-17.

At that time cometh Jesus ...... in Whom I am well pleased.

Offert. As on Epiphany.

Secret. We bring offerings to Thee, O Lord, in honour of the manifestation of Thy Son; humbly beseeching Thee, that as the same our Lord Jesus Christ is the Author of our gifts, so He may also Himself in mercy graciously accept the same. Who liveth.

Secret of S. Hilary. We pray Thee, O Lord, that the Host offered in remembrance of the burial of S. Hilary, may by his prayers be presented acceptably in Thy sight. Through.

Comm. As on Epiphany.

P. Comm. May Thy heavenly light, we beseech Thee, O Lord, prevent us at all times, and in all places: that we may contemplate with a clear vision, and receive with due effect, the Mystery whereof Thou hast been pleased we should partake. Through.

P. Comm. of S. Hilary. We beseech Thee, O Lord, that at the intercession of blessed Hilary, Thy Confessor and Bishop, the pledge of eternal redemption which we have just received may be our aid both in this life and in the life to come. Through.

First Sunday after Epiphany.*

The Office. Is. vi.

I saw sitting on a Throne, high and lifted up, *a Man whom a multitude of angels worshipped, singing together; behold Him, the Name of Whose kingdom is for everlasting.*

Ps. c. O be joyful in the Lord, all ye lands; serve the Lord with gladness.

The Collect.

O Lord, we beseech Thee mercifully to receive the prayers of Thy people which call upon Thee; that they may both perceive what things they ought to do, and also may have power to fulfil the same. Through.

The Epistle. Rom. xii. 1-5.

I beseech you, therefore .... members one of another in *Jesus Christ our Lord.*

Gradual. Ps. lxxii. Blessed be the Lord God, even the God of Israel: which only doeth wondrous things.

℣. The mountains also shall bring peace: and the little hills righteousness unto the people.

Alleluia! ℣. Ps. c. O be joyful in the Lord, all ye lands: serve the Lord with gladness.

The Gospel. Luke ii. 42-52.

It came to pass, when *Jesus* was twelve .... with God and man.

Offert. Ps. c. O be joyful in the Lord, all ye lands: serve the Lord with gladness, and come before His presence with a song. Be ye sure that the Lord He is God.

Secret. We beseech Thee, O Lord, that the Sacrifice offered to Thee may always quicken and defend us. Through.

Preface. The daily one.

Comm. Luke ii. Son, why hast Thou thus dealt with us? Behold, Thy father and I have sought Thee sorrowing. And He said unto them, How is it that ye sought Me? wist ye not that I must be about My Father's business?

P. Comm. May we, O Lord, partaking of Thy holy things, both receive the effectual working of perfect purification, and the continual aid of Divine protection. Through.

* *i.e.*, First Sunday after the Octave of the Epiphany.

¶ *If the time is so short between the Octave of the Epiphany and LXX.,* that the three Masses* "I saw sitting," "For all the world," "Worship Him," *cannot be sung in each week, then let them be sung in one and the same week. And if a Feast of three lessons occur, then let the Service be of the Feast until Mass, and then at the Mass which shall be of the Sunday let the second Collect be of the Feast, the third of S. Mary, the fourth of All Saints, and the fifth of All the Church. But let the other Masses which follow in that year be omitted, and observe that the Mass* "I saw sitting" *is never said before the first Sunday after Epiphany unless there be no Sunday between the Octave of Epiphany and LXX., in which case, on the week-day after the Octave, let* "I saw sitting" *and the two other Masses as above be said on the two following days, and nothing be done of any Feasts of three Lessons which may occur then.*

If the time be long, however, between the Octave of Epiphany and LXX., then let the Office "Worship" *be sung for three Sundays consecutively.*

If the time be three Sundays exactly, then after the third Sunday let the Epistles of the fourth and fifth Sundays be read on the Wednesday and Friday of that week.

WEDNESDAY.

The Epistle. Romans x. 1-4.

Brethren, my heart's desire and prayer to God for *them* is .... that believeth.

The Gospel. Matt. iv. 12-17.

At that time, when Jesus .... Heaven is at hand.

FRIDAY.

The Epistle. Romans xiii. 1-6.

Brethren, let every soul .... upon this very thing.

The Gospel. Luke iv. 14-22.

At that time, Jesus returned .... out of His mouth.

Second Sunday after Epiphany.

The Office. Ps. lxvi.

For all the world shall worship Thee, *O God;* sing of Thee, and praise Thy Name, *O Most High.*

Ps. lxvi. 1. O be joyful in God, all ye lands: sing praises unto the honour of His Name, make His praise to be glorious.

* *i.e.,* Septuagesima; and so LX., L., XL. signify Sexagesima, Quinquagesima, and Lent.

The Collect.

Almighty and everlasting God, Who dost govern all things in Heaven and earth: mercifully hear the supplications of Thy people, and grant us Thy peace all the days of our life. Through.

The Epistle. Rom. xii. 6-16.

Brethren, having gifts .... men of low estate.

Gradual. Ps. cvii. *The Lord* sent His word, and healed them: and they were saved from their destruction.

℣. O that men would therefore praise the Lord for His goodness: and declare the wonders that He doeth for the children of men!

Alleluia! ℣. Ps. cxlviii. Praise *God*, all ye angels of His: praise Him, all His host.

The Gospel. John ii. 1-11.

At that time, there was a marriage .... believed on Him.

Offertory. Ps. lxvi. O be joyful in God, all ye lands; *be joyful in God, all ye lands*; sing praises unto the honour of His Name. O come hither, and hearken, all ye that fear God: and I will tell you what *the Lord* hath done for my soul. *Alleluia!*

Secret. That the offerings of Thy people may be acceptable to Thee, cleanse them, we beseech Thee, O Lord, from all contamination of frowardness. Through.

Comm. John ii. *The Lord saith*, Fill the water-pots with water, and bear unto the governor of the feast. When the ruler of the feast had tasted the water that was made wine, *he saith unto the bridegroom*, Thou hast kept the good wine until now. *This miracle did Jesus first before His Disciples.*

P. Comm. May the efficacy of Thy power, O Lord, we beseech Thee, be increased in us, that being quickened by the Divine Sacraments, we may, through Thy bounty, alway be made ready to receive that which they promise. Through.

WEDNESDAY.

The Epistle. 1 Tim. i. 15-17.

Dearly beloved, this is a faithful saying .... for ever and ever. Amen.

The Gospel. Mark vi. 1-6.

At that time Jesus went out .... because of their unbelief.

FRIDAY.

The Epistle. Romans xiv. 14-26.

Brethren, I know .... not of faith is sin.

The Gospel. Luke iv. 31-37.

At that time Jesus came down to Capernaum.........country round about.

Third Sunday after Epiphany.

The Office. Ps. xcvii.

Worship Him, all ye gods. Sion heard of it, and rejoiced: and the daughters of Judah were glad.

Ps. The Lord is King, the earth may be glad thereof: yea, the multitude of the isles may be glad thereof.

The Collect.

Almighty and everlasting God, mercifully look upon our infirmities, and stretch forth the right hand of Thy majesty to defend us. Through.

The Epistle. Rom. xii. 16-21.

Brethren, be not wise .... overcome evil with good.

Gradual. Ps. cii. The heathen shall fear Thy Name, O Lord: and all the kings of the earth Thy majesty.

℣. When the Lord shall build up Sion: and when His glory shall appear.

Alleluia! ℣. Ps. xcvii. The Lord is King, the earth may be glad thereof: yea, the multitude of the isles may be glad thereof.

The Gospel. Matt. viii. 1-13.

At that time, when He was come down .... was healed in the self-same hour.

Offert. Ps. cxviii. The right hand of the Lord hath the pre-eminence: the right hand of the Lord bringeth mighty things to pass. I shall not die, but live: and declare the works of the Lord.

Secret. We celebrate again the adorable mysteries of eternal life, beseeching Thee, O Lord, that by devout sacrifice and good works we may attain unto the same. Through.

Comm. Luke iv. *They all* wondered at the words which proceeded out of *the* mouth *of God.*

P. Comm. Grant, we beseech Thee, O Lord, that we, to whom Thou vouchsafest the use of so great mysteries, may be fashioned in truth by their effectual working. Through.

WEDNESDAY.

The Epistle. Romans xv. 30-33.

I beseech you, brethren .... peace be with you all. Amen.

The Gospel. Mark iii. 1-5.

At that time Jesus entered again .... whole as the other.

FRIDAY.

The Epistle. 1 Cor. iii. 16-23.

Brethren, know ye not that .... and Christ is God's.

The Gospel. Matt. iv. 23-25.

At that time Jesus went about .... great multitudes of people.

Fourth Sunday after Epiphany.

The Office.

As on third Sunday.

The Collect.

O God, Who knowest us to be set in the midst of so many and great dangers, that by reason of the frailty of our nature we cannot stand upright; grant to us health of mind and body, that those things which for our sins we suffer, by Thy aid we may overcome. Through.

The Epistle. Rom. xiii. 8-10.

Brethren, owe no man .... love is the fulfilling of the law.

Gradual and *Alleluia.* As on third Sunday.

The Gospel. Matt. viii. 23-27.

At that time, when *Jesus* was entered .... sea obey Him!

Offert. As on third Sunday.

Secret. Grant, we beseech Thee, O Almighty God, that the offering of this Sacrifice may cleanse and defend our frailty from all evil. Through.

Comm. As on third Sunday.

P. Comm. May Thy gifts, O God, detach us from all earthly pleasures, and ever refresh and strengthen us with heavenly food, Through.

WEDNESDAY.

The Epistle. 1 Cor. vii. 1-5.

Brethren, it is good for a man .... tempt you not for your incontinency.

The Gospel. Luke ix. 57-62.

At that time it came to pass .... is fit for the kingdom of God.

FRIDAY.

The Epistle. 1 Cor. vii. 20-24.

Brethren, let every man abide .... abide with God.

The Gospel. Mark x. 12-16.

At that time they brought young children to Jesus .... and blessed them.

Fifth Sunday after Epiphany.

¶ *The* Office, Gradual, Alleluia! Offertory, *and* Communion, *as on the fourth Sunday.*

The Collect.

O Lord, we beseech Thee to keep Thy household in continual godliness; that they who do lean only upon the hope of Thy heavenly grace may evermore be defended by Thy power Through.

The Epistle. Col. iii. 12-17.

Brethren, put on, as the elect of God .... and the Father by *Jesus Christ our Lord.*

The Gospel. Matt xiii. 24-30.

At that time Jesus spake to His Disciples this parable: The kingdom of Heaven .... wheat into my barn.

Secret. Receive, we beseech Thee, O Lord, the oblations and prayers of Thy servants; that by the aid of Thy protection they may not lose what hath been bestowed, and may lay hold on that which they desire. Through.

P. Comm. O God, Who approachest us in the participation of Thy Sacrament, work in our hearts its effectual power; that by the Divine gift which we have received, we may be made meet for the same. Through.

WEDNESDAY.

The Epistle. 1 Tim. ii. 1-7.

Dearly beloved, I exhort .... in faith and verity.

The Gospel. Matt. xxi. 28-32.

At that time Jesus said to the multitude of the Jews, A certain man .... believe him. *He that hath ears to hear, let him hear*

Septuagesima Sunday.

The Office. Ps. xviii.

The sorrows of death encompassed me; the pains of hell came about me: In my trouble I will call upon the Lord: so shall He hear my voice out of His holy temple.

Ps. I will love Thee, O Lord, my strength; the Lord is my stony rock, and my defence: my Saviour.

¶ *From now till Easter Eve no* Gloria in Excelsis *is said, except on Maundy Thursday if the Bishop celebrate.*

The Collect.

O Lord, we beseech Thee favourably to hear the prayers of Thy people; that we, who are justly punished for our offences, may be mercifully delivered for the glory of Thy Name. Through.

The Epistle. 1 Cor. ix. 24-27, x. 1-4.

Brethren, know ye not .... and that Rock was Christ.

Gradual. Ps. ix. A refuge in due time of trouble. And they that know Thy Name will put their trust in Thee: for Thou, Lord, hast never failed them that seek Thee.

℣. For the poor shall not alway be forgotten: the patient abiding of the meek shall not perish for ever. Up, Lord, and let not man have the upper hand.

Tract. Ps. cxxx. Out of the deep have I called unto Thee, O Lord: Lord, hear my voice.

℣. O let Thine ears consider well: the voice of my complaint.

℣. If Thou, Lord, wilt be extreme to mark what is done amiss: O Lord, who may abide it?

℣. For there is mercy with Thee: therefore shalt Thou be feared. I looked for the Lord.

The Gospel. Matt. xx. 1-16.

At that time Jesus spake to His Disciples this parable; The kingdom of Heaven .... but few chosen.

Offert. Ps. xcii. It is a good thing to give thanks unto the Lord: and to sing praises unto Thy Name, O most Highest.

℣. O Lord, how glorious are Thy works: Thy thoughts are very deep.

℣. For lo, Thine enemies, O Lord, lo, Thine enemies shall perish: and all the workers of wickedness shall be destroyed.

Secret. O Lord, Who hast received our offerings and prayers, cleanse us, we beseech Thee, by these heavenly mysteries, and mercifully hear us. Through.

Comm. Ps. xxxi. Shew Thy servant the light of Thy countenance: and save me for Thy mercy's sake. Let me not be confounded, O Lord, for I have called upon Thee.

P. Comm. May Thy faithful people, O God, be strengthened by Thy gifts; that they by receiving may seek them anew, and by seeking may evermore receive them. Through.

¶ *The Service for this day and the following Sundays is not transferred for any double Feast except the Purification or Dedication of a Church, in which case it is transferred to Tuesday, and is said without its Tract. But if a feast of three lessons come on this or the next two Sundays, let there be a memorial of it. Should it come after Ash-Wednesday, no notice is taken of it till the morrow after the Octave of Easter*

WEDNESDAY.

The Epistle. 2 Cor. iv. 3-12.

Brethren, if our Gospel be hid .... but life in you.

The Gospel. Mark ix. 30-37.

At that time Jesus departed thence .... but Him that sent Me. *He that hath ears to hear, let him hear.*

FRIDAY.

The Epistle. 2 Cor. iv 13-18.

Brethren, we having the same spirit .... things which are not seen are eternal.

The Gospel. Matt. xii. 30-37.

At that time Jesus said unto the Pharisees, He that is not with Me .... by thy words thou shalt be condemned.

Sexagesima Sunday.

The Office. Ps. xliv.

Up, Lord, why sleepest Thou? awake, and be not absent from us for ever. Wherefore hidest Thou Thy face: and forgettest our misery and trouble? Our belly cleaveth unto the ground. Arise, O Lord, and help us: and deliver us.

Ps. We have heard with our ears, O God, our fathers have told us,

The Collect.

O God, Who seest that we put not our trust in anything that we do, mercifully grant that by the protection of the Teacher of the Gentiles we may be defended against all adversity. Through.

¶ *On week-days only the last part of the Epistle is to be read, beginning* "At Damascus, *v.* 32.

The Epistle, 2 Cor. xi. 19-33, xii. 1-9.

Brethren, ye suffer fools .... may rest upon me.

Gradual. Ps. lxxxiii. And they shall know that Thou, Whose Name is Jehovah: art only the most Highest over all the earth.

℣. O my God, make them like unto a wheel: and as the stubble before the wind.

Tract. Ps lx. Thou hast moved the land, *O Lord,* and divided it: heal the sores thereof, for it shaketh *that they may flee from the face of Thy bow.*

℣. That they may triumph because of the truth.

℣. Therefore were Thy beloved delivered.

The Gospel. Luke viii. 4-15.

At that time, when much people .... fruit with patience.

Offert. Ps. xvii. O hold Thou up my goings in Thy paths: that my footsteps slip not. Incline Thine ear to me, and hearken unto my words. Shew Thy marvellous loving-kindness, Thou that art the Saviour of them which put their trust in Thee.

℣. Hear the right, O Lord, consider my complaint: and hearken unto my prayer.

℣. Keep me, *O Lord,* as the apple of an eye: hide me under the shadow of Thy wings, deliver my soul from the ungodly.

Secret. Look, O Lord, we beseech Thee, on the offering of this Thy family; and grant that they whom Thou makest partakers of Thy holy gifts may attain unto the fulness of the same. Through.

Comm. Ps. xliii. I will go unto the Altar of God: even unto the God of my joy and gladness.

P. Comm. Grant, we humbly beseech Thee, O Almighty God, that those whom Thou refreshest with Thy Sacrament, may, by a life well pleasing to Thee, worthily serve Thee. Through.

WEDNESDAY.

The Epistle. 2 Cor. i. 23, 24—ii. 1-11.

Brethren, I call God .... not ignorant of his devices.

The Gospel. Mark iv. 1-9.

At that time Jesus began to teach by the sea-side. .... He that hath ears to hear, let him hear.

FRIDAY.

The Epistle. 2 Cor. v. 11-15.

Brethren, knowing the terror .... and rose again.

The Gospel. Luke xvii. 20-37.

At that time when Jesus was demanded of the Pharisees ...... will the eagles be gathered together.

Quinquagesima Sunday.

The Office. Ps. xxxi.

Be Thou my strong rock, and house of defence : that Thou mayest save me. For Thou art my strong rock, and my castle : be Thou also my guide, and lead me for Thy Name's sake.

Ps. In Thee, O Lord, have I put my trust : let me never be put to confusion, deliver me in Thy righteousness, and draw me out of the net.

The Collect.

O Lord, we beseech Thee, mercifully hear our prayers ; loose us from the chains of our sins; and keep us from all adversity. Through.

The Epistle. 1 Cor. xiii.

Brethren, though I speak .... but the greatest of these is charity.

Gradual. Ps. lxxvii. Thou art the God that doeth wonders : and hast declared Thy power among the people.

℣. Thou hast mightily delivered Thy people : even the sons of Jacob and Joseph.

Tract. Ps. c. O be joyful in the Lord, all ye lands : serve the Lord with gladness ;

℣. And come before His presence with a song.

℣. Be ye sure that the Lord He is God.

℣. It is He that hath made us, and not we ourselves: we are His people, and the sheep of His pasture.

The Gospel. Luke xviii. 31-43.

At that time Jesus took .... gave praise unto God.

Offert. Ps. cxix. 12. Blessed art Thou, O Lord: O teach me Thy statutes. *Blessed art Thou, O Lord: O teach me Thy statutes.* With my lips have I been telling: of all the judgments of Thy mouth.

℣. Blessed are those that are undefiled in the way: and walk in the law of the Lord. Blessed are they that keep His testimonies: and seek Him with their whole heart.

℣. Ps. cxix. 22. O turn from *Thy people* shame and rebuke: for *we have not forgotten Thy commandments, O Lord.*

Secret. May this offering, we beseech Thee, O Lord, cleanse away our sins, and sanctify the bodies and souls of Thy servants, for the celebration of this Sacrifice. Through.

Comm. Ps. lxxviii. They did eat, and were well filled; for *the Lord* gave them their own desire: they were not disappointed of their lust.

P. Comm. We beseech Thee, O Almighty God, that we who have received heavenly food, may be thereby defended from all adversity. Through.

Ash-Wednesday.

¶ *After Sexts there may be a sermon to the people. After which let the Clergy prostrate themselves in the choir and say the seven Penitential Psalms, with the anthem,* Remember not, Lord, our offences, nor the offences of our forefathers, neither take Thou vengeance of our sins; *and* Glory be. As it was. *But let the Bishop or superior Priest, clad in his vestments and in a red silk cope, with the Deacon on his right and the Sub-Deacon on his left, and the other ministers of the Altar in albs and amices, say the same apart in prostration before the Altar. The anthem having been repeated,*

Lord, have mercy.
Christ, have mercy.
Lord, have mercy.

Our Father.

¶ *Which having been said by all without chanting, a boy the meantime holding the sackcloth banner near the left corner of the Altar, let the Priest and Ministers rise, and let him alone say, turning to the East on the Gospel side—*

And lead us not into temptation.
Ch. But deliver us from evil.

℟. O Lord, save Thy servants and handmaids.
℣. That put their trust in Thee.
℣. Send unto them help, O Lord, from above,
℟. And out of Zion defend them.
℣. Turn Thee again, O Lord, at the last;
℟. And be gracious unto Thy servants.
℣. Help us, O God, our Saviour;
℟. And for the glory of Thy Name, O Lord, deliver us, and be merciful unto our sins for Thy Name's sake.
℣. O Lord, hear my prayer,
℟. And let my crying come unto Thee.
℣. The Lord be with you.
℟. And with Thy spirit.

Let us pray.

O Lord, we beseech Thee, hear our prayers, and spare all those who confess their sins to Thee, that they whose consciences by sin are accused, by Thy merciful pardon may be absolved. Through.

Let us pray.

We beseech Thee, O Lord, inspire Thy servants with saving grace, that their hearts being melted by plenteousness of tears, may be so softened and subdued that the working of Thy anger may be turned away by a fitting satisfaction. Through.

Let us pray.

Grant, we beseech Thee, O Lord our God, to these Thy servants that by repentance they may be continually mindful of their purification; and that to enable them more effectually to fulfil the same, the grace of Thy presence may prevent and follow them. Through.

Let us pray.

Let Thy compassion, O Lord, we beseech Thee, prevent these Thy servants, that all their iniquities may be blotted out by Thy speedy forgiveness. Through.

Let us pray.

Be present, O Lord, at our supplications, and let not the pitifulness of Thy mercy be far from Thy servants; heal their wounds, and forgive their sins, that they, being separated from Thee by no iniquities, may ever hold fast unto Thee their Lord. Through.

Let us pray,

O Lord, Who art not overcome of our transgressions, but graciously acceptest satisfaction, look we beseech Thee, upon Thy servants who confess that they have grievously sinned against Thee; for to Thee it appertaineth to absolve offences, and to give pardon to sinners: Thou has said Thou wouldest rather the repentance than the death of sinners; grant therefore, O Lord, to these Thy servants, that they may keep unto Thee the vigil of penitence, and, amending their ways, may give thanks for eternal joys bestowed on them by Thee. Through.

Let us pray.

O God, of Whose pardon all men stand in need, remember Thy servants and Thy handmaidens; and because through the deceitfulness and frailty of their mortal bodies they are despoiled of virtue and have done amiss in many things, we beseech Thee give pardon to them who confess, spare them who entreat; that they who by their own deserts are accused, by Thy mercy may be saved. Through.

¶ *Here let the Priest turn to the people and stretch out his hand, and say over them without tone, but in audible voice, thus—*

We absolve you in the place of Blessed Peter, Prince of the Apostles, to whom hath been given by the Lord the power of binding and loosing; and so far as self-accusation pertaineth to you and remission to us, may Almighty God be unto you life and health, and the gracious pardoner of all your sins. Who.

¶ *Here let all rise from prostration, and kiss the earth or the stalls, while the Priest says,* "Who liveth," &c.; *then let the Priest go to the Altar with his ministers, and there, turning to the East on the right side, let him bless the ashes previously placed in silver vessels, saying—*

Almighty and everlasting God, Who hast compassion upon all men, and hatest nothing which Thou hast made, passing over the sins of men for their penitence; Who also succourest them that are in necessity; vouchsafe to bless + and sanctify + these ashes, which for humility and holy religion's sake Thou hast appointed us, after the manner of the Ninevites, to bear on our heads, for the doing away of our offences; and grant that by the invocation of Thy holy Name, all those who have so borne them for the entreating of Thy mercy may be thought worthy to receive from Thee pardon of all their sins, and this day so to begin their holy fast, that on the day of the Resurrection they may be admitted to the holy Paschal Feast with purified minds, and at length receive eternal glory. Through.

¶ *Here let holy water be sprinkled on the ashes.*

The Lord be with you.

Let us pray.

O God, Who desirest not the death but penitence of sinners, graciously look upon the frailty of our condition, and vouchsafe of Thy loving-kindness to bless + and sanctify + these ashes which in token of humility and for the obtaining of pardon, we have placed on our heads; that we whom Thou hast advertised that we are ashes, and who know that we shall return to dust by reason of our depravity, may mercifully be accounted worthy to obtain the pardon of all our sins, and the rewards promised anew on our repentance. Through.

¶ *Then let the ashes be distributed on the heads of the clergy and laity by those of higher dignity, signing the sign of the Cross with ashes, saying thus—*

Remember, O man, that thou art ashes, and unto ashes shalt thou return. In the Name.

¶ *Meanwhile let the following anthem be sung:*

Ps. lxix. 17. Hear me, O Lord, for Thy loving-kindness is comfortable: turn Thee unto me, according to the multitude of Thy mercies.

Ps. Save me, O God; for the waters have come in, even unto my soul.

Glory be. Hear me.

Another Ant. Joel ii. 17. Let the Priests *and Levites* and ministers of the Lord weep between the porch and the altar, and let them say, Spare Thy people, O Lord; *spare them, and turn not away the faces of them that call upon Thee, O Lord.*

Another Ant. Let us change our garments for sackcloth and ashes; let us fast and weep before the Lord, for our God is very merciful to put away our sins.

¶ *The Office ended, let the Priest say at the choir-step—*

The Lord be with you.
And with thy spirit.

Let us pray.

O God, Who art justly angry, and dost mercifully forgive, consider the tears of Thy afflicted people, and graciously turn away Thy wrathful indignation which they have righteously deserved. Through.

Let us pray.

Grant to us, Lord, we beseech Thee, so to enter upon Christian warfare with holy fast, that we who are about to fight against spiritual wickedness may be fortified by the aid of continence. Through.

* ¶ *This being done, let the procession go without Cross through the midst of the Choir, with Torch-bearers and Thurifers, to the West door, the Clergy going according to rank, preceded by the sackcloth banner; then let the Officiant eject the Penitents one by one, handing them out of the Choir by the ministration of some Priest, delivering them to the same by the right hand, but let the Penitents themselves kiss the hand of the Officiant and go out; then if a Bishop be present, let the Archdeacon minister to him as aforesaid, and meantime let these two* ℟. *be said with their* ℣., *without* Glory be.

℟. Behold the man is become as one of us, to know good and evil; *see lest peradventure* he take of the tree of life, and eat and live for ever.

℣. Cherubims and a flaming sword, which turned every way to keep the way of the tree of life. *See, see.*

℟. In the sweat of thy brow shalt thou eat bread, *said the Lord to Adam; when thou shalt till the ground it shall not give its fruit;* thorns also and thistles shall it bring forth to thee.

℣. Because thou hast hearkened unto the voice of thy wife *more than unto Me,* cursed is the ground *in thy work. It shall not.*

¶ *When the Penitents are ejected, the door of the church is shut; and the procession returning as usual, let the Cantor begin—*

℟. Let us who have sinned in ignorance amend our lives, lest we be suddenly overtaken by the day of Death, and seek space of repentance and find it not. Hear us, O Lord, and have mercy upon us, for we have sinned against Thee.

* From the Processional.

℣. We have sinned with our fathers, and done wickedly; we have wrought iniquity. Hear us.

¶ *Immediately let Mass begin.*

The Office. Wisd. xi.

Thou hast mercy upon all, *O Lord, and hatest nothing which Thou hast made,* and winkest at the sins of men, because they should amend. But Thou sparest all, *because Thou art the Lord our God.*

Ps. lvii. Be merciful unto me, O God, be merciful unto me, for my soul trusteth in Thee.

¶ *After* Let us pray, *before the Collect, let the Deacon say,* Let us kneel, *and let all kneel; let him then say,* Arise, *and all rise and kiss the stalls. Let this be observed till Easter every day but Sunday.*

The Collect.

Grant, we beseech Thee, O Lord, unto Thy faithful people, that they may both enter upon the holy solemnities of the fast with befitting reverence, and pass through them with peaceful devotion. Through.

¶ *Five Collects only are said.*

The Lesson. Joel ii. 12-19.

Thus saith the Lord, Turn ye even to Me .... a reproach among the heathen, *saith the Lord Almighty.*

Gradual. Ps. lvii. Be merciful unto me, O God, be merciful unto me, for my soul trusteth in Thee.

℣. He shall send from Heaven; and save me from the reproof of him that would eat me up.

¶ *Choir says by turns:*

Tract. Ps. ciii. *Lord, Thou hast* not dealt with us after our sins: nor rewarded us according to our wickednesses.

℣. Ps. lxxxix. *Lord,* remember not our old sins, but have mercy upon us, and that soon: for we are come to great misery.

¶ *Here no genuflection is made.*

℣. Help us, O God of our salvation, for the glory of Thy Name: O deliver us, and be merciful unto our sins, for Thy Name's sake.

¶ *This Tract to be said every Monday and Friday till Maundy Thursday.*

The Gospel. Matt. vi. 16-21.

At that time Jesus said to His Disciples, When ye fast .... there will your heart be also.

Offert. Ps. xxx. I will magnify Thee, O Lord, for Thou has set me up: and not made my foes to triumph over me. O Lord my God, I cried unto Thee: and Thou hast healed me.

℣. Thou, Lord, hast brought my soul out of hell: Thou hast kept my life from them that go down to the pit.

Secret. Grant, O Lord, we beseech Thee, that we may be duly prepared to present these our offerings, by which we celebrate the beginning of this holy fast. Through.

Preface. Who by this bodily fast.

¶ *This is to be said every week-day in Lent, till Maundy Thursday.*

Comm. Ps. i. In the law of the Lord will he exercise himself day and night: he will bring forth his fruit in due season.

P. Comm. May the mysteries we have received, O Lord, afford us help, that our fast may both be acceptable to Thee, and also avail to our healing. Through.

¶ *After* P. Comm. *let the Priest say*—

Let us pray.

¶ *Then let the Deacon say*—

Bow down your heads to God.

¶ *This is to be said till Maundy Thursday, except on Sundays.*

The Prayer over the People.

Lord, mercifully look upon them who bow down before Thy Majesty, that they who have been refreshed with the Divine gift, may always be sustained by heavenly nourishment. Through.

THURSDAY AFTER ASH-WEDNESDAY.

The Office. Ps. lviii.

When I cried unto the Lord, He heard my voice from the battle that was against me; and *God* that endureth for ever shall bring them down: O cast thy burden upon the Lord, and He shall nourish thee.

Ps. Hear my prayer, O God: and hide not Thyself from my petition. Take heed unto me, and hear me.

The Collect.

O God, Who by sin art offended, and art pacified by repentance, mercifully regard the prayers of Thy people, who make supplication to Thee; and graciously turn away the scourge of Thine anger, which we deserve for our sins. Through.

The Lesson. Isa. xxxviii. 1-6.

In those days was Hezekiah sick .... I will defend *it, saith the Lord Almighty.*

Gradual. Ps. lv. O cast thy burden upon the Lord, and He shall nourish thee.

℣. When I cried unto the Lord, He heard my voice from the battle that was against me.

The Gospel. Matt. viii. 5-13.

At that time when Jesus .... in the self-same hour.

Offert. Ps. xxv. Unto Thee, O Lord, will I lift up my soul; my God, I have put my trust in Thee: O let me not be confounded, neither let mine enemies triumph over me. For all they that hope in Thee shall not be ashamed.

℣. Lead me forth in Thy truth, and learn me: for Thou art the God of my salvation; in Thee hath been my hope all the day.

*℣. Turn Thee unto me, and have mercy upon me. O keep my soul and deliver me: let me not be confounded, for I have put my trust in Thee.

Secret. We offer to Thee, O Lord, the gifts which Thou hast given, that they may both show forth Thy creature for the benefit of our mortal nature, and work in us an immortal cure. Through.

Comm. Ps. li. Then shalt Thou be pleased with the sacrifice of righteousness, with the burnt-offerings and oblations, *O Lord,* upon Thine Altar.

P. Comm. Grant to Thy faithful people, O Lord, we beseech Thee, that they may both continually receive the Paschal Sacraments, and earnestly look forward to that which is approaching, that they, steadfastly abiding in the mysteries by which they have been renewed, may by these means be brought unto newness of life. Through.

The Prayer over the People.

Spare, O Lord, spare Thy people: that having been justly chastised, they may find comfort in Thy mercy. Through.

* Gradual.

FRIDAY AFTER ASH-WEDNESDAY.

The Office. Ps. xxx.

Hear, O Lord, and have mercy upon me: Lord, be Thou my helper.

Ps. I will magnify Thee, O Lord, for Thou has set me up: and not made my foes to triumph over me.

The Collect.

Graciously favour us, O Lord, we beseech Thee, in the fast on which we have entered; that the duties which we observe outwardly, we may also be enabled to fulfil with pure minds. Through.

The Lesson. Is. lviii. 1-9

Thus saith the Lord God, Cry aloud .... and He shall say, Here I am; *for I am merciful, the Lord thy God.*

Gradual. Ps. xxvii. One thing have I desired of the Lord, which I will require: even that I may dwell in the house of the Lord.

℣. To behold the will of the Lord, and *be protected by His holy temple.*

Tract. As on Ash-Wednesday.

The Gospel. Matt. v. 43-48—vi. 1-6.

At that time Jesus said to His disciples, Ye have heard .... shall reward thee openly.

Offert. Ps. cxix. Quicken me, O Lord, according to Thy Word, that I may know Thy testimonies.

℣. O deal with Thy servant according unto Thy loving mercy: and take not the word of Thy truth utterly out of my mouth.

Secret. We offer, O Lord, the Sacrifice of the observance of Lent: grant, we beseech Thee, that it may both make our minds acceptable unto Thee, and dispose us more readily to continence. Through.

Comm. Ps. ii. Serve the Lord in fear: and rejoice unto Him with reverence. Kiss the Son, lest ye perish from the right way.

P. Comm. Grant to us, Lord, we beseech Thee, that the heavenly gifts which we ofttimes approach with due devotion, may prove continually profitable to our salvation. Through.

The Prayer over the People.

Guard Thy people, O Lord, and graciously cleanse them from all sin, inasmuch as no adversity will harm them if no wickedness get the dominion over them. Through.

SATURDAY AFTER ASH-WEDNESDAY.

The Office. Ps. xxx.

Hear, O Lord, and have mercy upon me : Lord, be Thou my helper.

Ps. I will magnify Thee, O Lord, for Thou hast set me up : and not made my foes to triumph over me.

The Collect.

Give ear, O Lord, to our supplications, and grant that we may with true devotion observe this solemn fast, which was instituted to give health and salvation both to our souls and bodies. Through.

The Lesson. Is. lviii. 9-14.

Thus saith the Lord, If thou take away .... hath spoken it, *saith the Lord Almighty.*

Gradual. Ps. xxvii. One thing have I desired of the Lord, which I will require : even that I may dwell in the house of the Lord.

℣. To behold the *will* of the Lord, and to *be protected by His* temple.

The Gospel. Matt. vi. 47-56.

At that time, when even was come ...... was made whole.

Offert. Ps. cxix. 25. Quicken me, O Lord, according to Thy Word, that I may know Thy testimonies.

℣. Give me understanding, and I shall keep Thy law. Let the free-will offerings of my mouth please Thee, O Lord.

Secret. Prepare us, O Lord, we beseech Thee, by the bounden offering of this fast, that we may always celebrate this adorable Sacrifice with sober minds. Through.

Comm. Ps. ii. Serve the Lord in fear: and rejoice unto Him with reverence. Kiss the Son, lest ye perish from the right way.

P. Comm. Being satisfied with the gift of celestial life, we beseech Thee, O Lord our God, that that which is a mystery to us in this present life, may be made our help in eternity. Through.

The Prayer over the People.

Make us, we beseech Thee, O Lord, both at all times to frequent the means of our salvation with due observance, and also more devoutly to attend them after their special commencement. Through.*

First Sunday in Lent, or Invocavit.

The Office. Ps. xci.

He shall call upon Me, and I will hear him: I will deliver him, and bring him to honour. With long life will I satisfy him.

Ps. Whoso dwelleth under the defence of the Most High: shall abide under the shadow of the Almighty.

The Collect.

O God, Who purifiest Thy Church by yearly observance of Lent, grant unto Thy family that what they endeavour to obtain of Thee by fasting, they may follow up by good works. Through.

The Epistle. 2 Cor. vi. 1-10.

Brethren, we beseech you .... possessing all things.

Gradual. Ps. xci. For He shall give His Angels charge over thee: to keep thee in all thy ways.

℣. They shall bear thee in their hands: that thou hurt not thy foot against a stone.

Tract. Ps. xci. Whoso dwelleth under the defence of the Most High: shall abide under the shadow of the Almighty.

℣. I will say unto the Lord, Thou art my hope, and my stronghold: my God, in Him will I trust.

* *Miss.* 1494, 1497 *have the Roman collect,* Fideles tui.

℣. For He shall deliver thee from the snare of the hunter; and from the noisome pestilence.

℣. He shall defend thee under His wings, and thou shalt be safe under His feathers.

℣. His faithfulness and truth shall be thy shield and buckler. Thou shalt not be afraid for any terror by night:

℣. Nor for the arrow that flieth by day; for the pestilence that walketh in darkness: nor for the sickness that destroyeth in the noon-day.

℣. A thousand shall fall beside thee, and ten thousand at thy right hand: but it shall not come nigh thee.

℣. For He shall give His angels charge over thee: to keep thee in all thy ways.

℣. They shall bear thee in their hands: that thou hurt not thy foot against a stone.

℣. Thou shalt go upon the lion and adder: the young lion and the dragon shalt thou tread under thy feet.

℣. Because he hath set his love upon Me, therefore will I deliver him: I will set him up, because he hath known My Name.

℣. He shall call upon Me, and I will hear him: yea, I am with him in trouble.

℣. I will deliver him and bring him to honour, With long life will I satisfy him: and shew him My salvation.

The Gospel. Matt. iv. 1-11.

At that time was Jesus .... and ministered unto Him.

Offert. Ps. xci. He shall defend thee under His wings, and thou shalt be safe under His feathers: His faithfulness and truth shall be thy shield and buckler.

Secret. We offer, O Lord, in the most solemn manner, this Sacrifice at the beginning of Lent, humbly beseeching Thee, that as we abstain from carnal feastings, we may also renounce all hurtful pleasures. Through.

Preface. The daily one.

Comm. Ps. xci. He shall defend thee under His wings, and they shalt be safe under His feathers: His faithfulness and truth shall be thy shield and buckler.

P. Comm. May the holy oblation, O Lord, of Thy Sacrament, give us a new life, that laying aside the old man we may pass to the fellowship of the saving mystery. Through.

MONDAY AFTER INVOCAVIT.

The Office. Ps. cxxiii.

Behold, even as the eyes of servants look unto the hand of their masters: even so our eyes wait upon the Lord our God, until He have mercy upon us. Have mercy upon us, O Lord, have mercy upon us.

Ps. Unto Thee lift I up mine eyes: O Thou that dwellest in the heavens.

The Collect.

Convert us, O God, our Saviour, that this fast of Lent may be beneficial to us, and instruct our minds with thy heavenly doctrine. Through.

The Lesson. Ezek. xxxiv. 11-16.

For thus saith the Lord God ...... with judgment *and justice, saith the Lord Almighty.*

Gradual. Ps. lxxxiv. Behold, O God, our defender: and look upon Thy servants.

℣. O Lord God of Hosts, hear *the prayers of Thy servants.*

Tract. As on Ash-Wednesday.

The Gospel. Matt. xxv. 31-46.

At that time Jesus said to his disciples, When the Son of Man .... into life eternal.

Offert. Ps. cxix. 18, 125. *I will lift up* mine eyes, that I may see the wondrous things of Thy law, *O Lord; that Thou mayest teach me Thy righteousness.* O grant me understanding, that I may know Thy testimonies.

℣. Teach me, O Lord, the way of Thy statutes: and *I will be exercised in Thy precepts.*

Secret. Accept, O Lord, we beseech Thee, the oblations we devoutly offer, that, through Thy operation, they may both sanctify our fast, and obtain for us the favour of Thy comfort. Through.

Comm. Ps. iii. I did call upon the Lord with my voice: and He heard me out of His holy hill. I will not be afraid for ten thousands of the people: that have set themselves against me round about.

P. Comm. May the frequent repetition of Thy mysteries aid us, O Lord, both to wean us from earthly desires, and to implant in us a love of heavenly things. Through.

The Prayer over the People.

Loose, O Lord, we beseech Thee, the chains of our sins, and mercifully turn away from us the punishment we deserve for them. Through.

TUESDAY AFTER INVOCAVIT.

The Office. Ps. xc.

Lord, Thou hast been our refuge: from one generation to another. Thou art God from everlasting, and the world without end.

Ps. Before the mountains were brought forth, or ever the earth and the world were made.

The Collect.

Look down, O Lord, on this Thy family, and grant that, while we chastise ourselves by the mortification of the flesh, our minds may have light in Thy light, by reason of their longing for Thee. Through.

The Lesson. Isa. lv. 6-11.

In those days, Isaiah the Prophet spake, saying, Seek ye the Lord .... whereto I sent it, *saith the Lord Almighty.*

Gradual. Ps. cxli. Let my prayers be set forth in Thy sight as the incense.

℣. Let the lifting up of my hands be an evening sacrifice.

The Gospel. Matt. xxi. 10-17.

At that time, when Jesus was come .... and He lodged there, *and taught them concerning the Kingdom of God.*

Offert. Ps. xxxi. My hope hath been in Thee, O Lord: I have said, Thou art my God. My time is in Thy hand.

℣. Shew Thy servant the light of Thy countenance: and save me for Thy mercy's sake. Let me not be confounded, O Lord, for I have called upon Thee.

Secret. Grant, O Lord, we beseech Thee, that the devotion we offer unto Thee may be in accordance with the gift we have dedicated. Through.

Comm. Ps. iv. Hear me when I call, O God of my righteousness: Thou hast set me at liberty when I was in trouble; have mercy upon me, *O Lord*, and hearken unto my prayer.

P. Comm. We beseech Thee, O Almighty God, that we may effectually obtain that salvation, of which we have received the pledge in these mysteries. Through.

The Prayer over the People.

May our prayers, O Lord, ascend to Thee; and deliver Thou Thy Church from all wickedness. Through.

EMBER WEDNESDAY.

The Office. Ps. xxv.

Call to remembrance, O Lord, Thy tender mercies: and Thy loving-kindnesses, which have been ever of old. Neither let *our* enemies triumph over *us*. Deliver *us*, O God *of Israel*, out of all *our* troubles.

Ps. Unto Thee, O Lord, will I lift up my soul; my God, I have put my trust in Thee: O let me not be confounded.

The Collect.

Mercifully hear our prayers, O Lord, we beseech Thee, and stretch forth the right hand of Thy majesty against all our enemies. Through.

The Lesson. Exod. xxiv. 12-18.

In those days the Lord said unto Moses, ... days and forty nights.

Gradual. Ps. xxv. The sorrows of my heart are enlarged: O bring Thou me out of my troubles, *O Lord.*

℣. Look upon my adversity and misery: and forgive me all my sins.

The Lord be with you.

Let us pray.

We beseech Thee, O Lord, graciously regard the devotion of Thy people: that they who are mortified in body by abstinence, by the fruit of that good work may be renewed in mind. Through.

The Lesson. 1 Kings xix. 3-8.

In those days Elias came to Beersheba .... the mount of God.

Tract. Ps. xxv. O bring Thou me out of my troubles. *O Lord,* look upon my adversity and misery: and forgive me all my sin.

℣. Unto Thee, O Lord, will I lift up my soul; my God, I have put my trust in Thee: O let me not be confounded, neither let mine enemies triumph over me.

℣. For all they that hope in Thee shall not be ashamed: but such as transgress without a cause shall be put to confusion.

¶ *Let this Tract be said on all Wednesdays till Palm Sunday.*

The Gospel. Matt xii. 38-50.

At that time came to Jesus certain of the scribes .... and mother.

Offert. Ps. cxix. 47. And my delight shall be in Thy commandments; which I have loved. My hands also will I lift up unto Thy commandments, which I have loved.

℣. 57. Thou art my portion, O Lord: I have promised to keep Thy law. I made my humble petition in Thy presence with my whole heart.

Secret. We beseech Thee, O Lord, look upon this our only Sacrifice, that we who have waited for those things which we believe may be hoped for in the partaking of these mysteries, may receive the same. Through.

Comm. Ps. v. Consider my meditation. O hearken Thou unto the voice of my calling, my King and my God: for unto Thee will I make my prayer, *O Lord.*

P. Comm. Grant, we beseech Thee, Almighty God, that these holy gifts may cleanse away our guilt, and work in us the fruits of a good life. Through.

The Prayer over the People.

We beseech Thee, O Lord, cast the bright beams of Thy light upon our minds, that we may both perceive the things we ought to do, and also may have power rightly to fulfil the same. Through.

THURSDAY AFTER INVOCAVIT.

The Office. Ps. xcvi.

Glory and worship are before Him : power and honour are in His sanctuary.

Ps. O sing unto the Lord a new song : sing unto the Lord, all the whole earth.

The Collect.

Almighty everlasting God, Who hast appointed the observance of fasting and almsgiving for the remedy of our sins, mercifully grant us ever to be devoted to Thee in mind and body. Through.

The Lesson. Ezek. xviii. 1-19.

In those days, the Word of the Lord .... he shall surely live, *saith the Lord Almighty.*

Gradual. Ps. xvii. Keep me as the apple of an eye : hide me under the shadow of Thy wings.

℣. Let my sentence come from Thy presence : and let Thine eyes look upon the thing that is equal.

The Gospel. John. viii. 31-47.

At that time, said Jesus to those Jews .... heareth God's words.

Offert. Ps. xxxiv. The angel of the Lord tarrieth round about them that fear Him : and delivereth them. O taste, and see how gracious the Lord is.

℣. I will alway give thanks unto the Lord : His praise shall ever be in my mouth.

Secret. We beseech Thee, O Lord, that those offerings which are appointed in this wholesome fast may be favourable to our salvation. Through.

Comm. John vi. The bread that I will give is My Flesh, which I will give for the life of the world.

P. Comm. By the free grant of these Thy gifts, O Lord, lift us up by Thy protection in this world, and renew us everlastingly. Through.

The Prayer over the People.

Grant, O Lord, we beseech Thee, that all Christian people may acknowledge what they profess, and love the heavenly gift they often approach. Through.

EMBER FRIDAY.

The Office. Ps. xxv.

Bring Thou me out of my troubles, *O Lord.* Look upon my adversity and misery: and forgive me all my sin.

Ps. Unto Thee, O Lord, will I lift up my soul; my God, I have put my trust in Thee: O let me not be confounded.

The Collect.

Be favourable, O Lord, to Thy people, and pitifully comfort again with Thy gracious help those whom Thou fillest with devotion to Thee. Through.

The Lesson. Ezek. xviii. 20-28.

Thus saith the Lord God, The soul that sinneth .... he shall not die, *saith the Lord Almighty.*

Gradual. Ps. lxxxvi. My God, save Thy servant that putteth his trust in Thee.

℣. Give ear, Lord, unto my prayer.

Tract. As on Ash-Wednesday.

The Gospel. John v. 1-15.

At that time, there was a feast of the Jews .... which had made him whole.

Offert. Ps. ciii. Praise the Lord, O my soul: and forgot not all His benefits; making thee young and lusty as an eagle.

℣. Who forgiveth all thy sin: Who saveth thy life from destruction: Who crowneth thee with mercy and loving-kindness.

Secret. Receive, O Lord, we beseech Thee, the offerings of our services, and graciously sanctify Thy own gifts. Through.

Comm. Ps. vi. All mine enemies shall be confounded, and sore vexed: they shall be turned back and put to shame suddenly.

P. Comm. May the efficacy of this Sacrament, O Lord, cleanse us from our sins, and obtain for us the accomplishment of our right desires. Through.

The Prayer over the People.

Hear us, O merciful God, and manifest the light of Thy grace to our minds. Through.

EMBER SATURDAY.

The Office. Ps. lxxxviii.

Let my prayer enter into Thy presence, incline Thine ear unto my calling.

Ps. O Lord God of my salvation, I have cried day and night before Thee.

Let us pray.
D. Let us kneel.
D. Rise.

The Collect.

We beseech Thee, O Lord, look graciously on Thy people, and in Thy clemency turn away from them the scourge of Thy wrath. Through.

The Lesson. Dieut. xxvi. 15-19.

In those days Moses spake unto the Lord, saying, Look down from Thy holy habitation .... as He hath spoken *to thee.*

Gradual. Ps. lxxix. Be merciful unto our sins. Wherefore do the heathen say, Where is now their God?

℣. Help us, O God of our salvation, for the glory of Thy Name: O deliver us.

¶ *No repetition of Gradual.*

Let us pray.
D. Let us kneel.
D. Rise.

The Collect.

O God, Who leadest us through things temporal to things eternal, extend Thy mercy to us who are striving after heavenly promises; and because all our faith is of Thee, may all our life be in Thee. Through.

The Lesson. Deut. xi. 22-25.

In those days Moses said to the children of Israel, If ye shall diligently .... *the Lord your God* hath said unto you.

Gradual. Ps. lxxxiv. Behold, O God our Defender: and look upon the face of *Thy servants.*

℣. O Lord God of Hosts, hear *the* prayer *of Thy servants.*

Let us pray.
D. Let us kneel.
D. Rise.

The Collect.

Look on us, O God, our Protector, that we, who labour under the weight of our own evils, may be rescued by Thy mercy, and serve Thee with a free mind. Through.

The Lesson. 2 Mac. i. 23-25.

In those days the priests made a prayer .... *the Lord* open your hearts in His law and commandments, and send you peace. *The Lord* hear your prayers, and be at one with you; and *the Lord our God* never forsake you in time of trouble.

Gradual. Ps. xc. Turn Thee again, O Lord, at the last; and be gracious unto Thy servants.

℣. Lord, Thou hast been our refuge: from one generation to another.

Let us pray.
D. Let us kneel.
D. Rise.

The Collect.

Give ear, O Lord, we beseech Thee, to our prayers; that, through Thy bountiful grace, we may be humble in prosperity, and without fear in adversity. Through.

The Lesson. Ecclus. xxxvi. 1-8.

Have mercy upon us .... Thy wonderful works, *O Lord our God.*

Gradual. O Lord, save Thy people: and bless Thine heritage

℣. Ps. xxviii. Unto Thee will I cry, O Lord my strength: think no scorn of me, lest I become like them that go down into the pit.

Let us pray.
D. Let us kneel.
D. Rise.

The Collect.

Prevent us, O Lord, we beseech Thee, in all our doings, with Thy most gracious power, and further us with Thy continual help; that all our works may be begun, continued, and ended in Thee. Through.

The Lesson.

(See *Less.* v. Emb. Sat. in Advent to v. 34 inclusive.)

Tract. Blessed art Thou in the firmament of heaven, and above all to be praised and glorified for ever.

Choir (*Repeats*).

Clergy. O all ye works of the Lord, bless ye the Lord: O ye heavens, bless ye the Lord: O ye angels of the Lord, bless ye the Lord:

Ch. Praise and exalt Him above all for ever.

Cl. O all ye waters that be above the heaven, bless ye the Lord: O all ye powers of the Lord, bless ye the Lord: O ye sun and moon, bless ye the Lord:

Ch. Praise and exalt Him above all for ever.

Cl. O ye stars of heaven, bless ye the Lord: O every shower and dew, bless ye the Lord; O all ye winds, bless ye the Lord:

Ch. Praise and exalt Him above all for ever.

Cl. O ye fire and heat, bless ye the Lord: O ye nights and days, bless ye the Lord: O ye light and darkness, bless ye the Lord:

Ch. Praise and exalt Him above all for ever.

Cl. O ye ice and cold, bless ye the Lord: O ye frost and snow, bless ye the Lord: O ye lightnings and clouds, bless ye the Lord.

Ch. Praise and exalt Him above all for ever.

Cl. O let the earth bless the Lord: O ye mountains and little hills, bless ye the Lord: O all ye things that grow on the earth, bless ye the Lord:

Ch. Praise and exalt Him above all for ever.

Cl. O all ye fowls of the air, bless ye the Lord: O all ye beasts and cattle, bless ye the Lord: O ye children of men, bless ye the Lord:

Ch. Praise and exalt Him above all for ever.

Cl. O Israel, bless ye the Lord: O ye priests of the Lord, bless ye the Lord: O ye servants of the Lord, bless ye the Lord:

Ch. Praise and exalt Him above all for ever.

Cl. O ye spirits and souls of the righteous, bless ye the Lord; O ye holy and humble men of heart, bless ye the Lord:

Ch. Praise and exalt Him above all for ever.

Cl. O Ananias, Azarias, and Misael, bless ye the Lord:
Ch. Praise and exalt Him above all for ever
Cl. Blessed art Thou in the firmament.
Ch. (*Repeats.*)

The Lord be with you.
And with thy spirit.

Let us pray.

(*Coll.* as Emb. Sat. in Advent.)

The Epistle. I Thess. v. 14-23.

Now we exhort you .... our Lord Jesus Christ.

Tract. Ps. cxvii. O praise the Lord, all ye heathen; praise Him all ye nations.

℣. For His merciful kindness is more and more towards us, and the truth of the Lord endureth for ever.

The Gospel. Matt. xvii. 1-9.

At that time Jesus taketh Peter .... from the dead.

Offert. Ps. lxxxviii. O Lord God of my salvation, I have cried day and night before Thee: O let my prayer enter into Thy presence.

℣. Incline Thine ear unto my calling, O Lord. Thou hast put away mine acquaintance far from me: Lord, I have called daily upon Thee, I have stretched forth my hands unto Thee.

Secret. Sanctify, O Lord, we beseech Thee, our fast by this present Sacrifice, that what we outwardly profess by its observance may be inwardly wrought in us. Through.

Comm. Ps. vii. O Lord my God, In Thee have I put my trust; save me from all them that persecute me, and deliver me.

P. Comm. Defend, O Lord, with Thy perpetual protection those whom Thou feedest with the divine mysteries; and as Thou hast instructed us by heavenly ordinances, guide us by Thy saving consolation. Through.

The Prayer over the People.

May Thy much-desired blessing, O God, give strength to Thy faithful people; both causing them never to swerve from Thy will, and bestowing on them the continual joy of Thy favour. Through.

¶ *If the Bishop is ordaining, the* Prayer over the People *shall not be said*

Second Sunday in Lent, or Reminiscere.

The Office. Ps. xxv.

Call to remembrance, O Lord, Thy tender mercies : and Thy loving-kindnesses, which have been ever of old. Let not our enemies triumph over us. Deliver us, O God *of Israel*, out of all our trouble.

Ps. Unto Thee, O Lord, do I lift up my soul. My God, I have put my trust in Thee, let me not be confounded.

The Collect.

Almighty God, Who seest that we have no power of ourselves, keep us both outwardly and inwardly, that we may be defended from all adversities which may happen to the body, and may be cleansed from all evil thoughts in the soul. Through.

The Epistle. I Thess. iv. 1-7.

We beseech you .... but unto holiness *in Christ Jesus our Lord.*

Gradual. Ps. xxv. The sorrows of my heart are enlarged; O bring Thou me out of my troubles, *O Lord.* Look upon my adversity and misery: and forgive me all my sin.

Tract. Matt. xv. *The Lord* said *to the woman of Canaan,* It is not meet to take the children's bread, and to cast it to dogs.

℣. And she said, Truth, Lord: yet the dogs eat of the crumbs which fall from their masters' table.

℣. Then Jesus answered and said unto her, O woman, great is thy faith; be it unto thee even as thou wilt.

The Gospel. Matt. xv. 21-28.

At that time Jesus went thence .... that very hour.

Offert. Ps. cxix. 47. And my delight shall be in Thy commandments, which I have loved: my hands also will I lift up unto Thy commandments, which I have loved.

Secret. Graciously receive, O Lord, the gifts of Thy Church, which Thou in Thy mercy hast ordained to be offered, and causest by Thy power to pass into the mystery of our salvation. Through.

Preface. The daily one.

Comm Ps. v. Consider my meditation: hearken Thou unto the voice of my calling, my King, and my God: for unto Thee will I make my prayer, *O Lord.*

P. Comm. We beseech Thee, O Lord, let the grace of Thy most sacred Body and Blood which we have received quicken us; and that which it doth promise in this mystic act, may it freely bestow in everlasting effects. Through.

MONDAY AFTER REMINISCERE.

The Office. Ps. xxvi.

Deliver me, *O Lord,* and be merciful unto me. My foot standeth right: I will praise the Lord in the congregations.

Ps. Be Thou my Judge, O Lord, for I have walked innocently: my trust hath been also in the Lord, therefore shall I not fall.

The Collect.

Grant, we beseech Thee, Almighty God, that this Thy family, who mortify the flesh by abstinence from meat, may likewise fast from sin, and follow righteousness. Through.

The Lesson. Dan. ix. 15-19.

At that time Daniel prayed unto the Lord, saying, O Lord our God ...... are called by Thy Name, *O Lord our God.*

Gradual. Ps. lxx. Thou art my helper and my redeemer, O Lord, make no long tarrying. Let them be ashamed and confounded that seek after my soul.

Tract. As on Ash-Wednesday.

The Gospel. John viii. 21-29.

At that time Jesus said to the multitude of Jews, I go My way .... those things that please Him.

Offert. Ps. xvi. I will thank the Lord for giving me warning: I have set God always before me: for He is on my right hand, therefore I shall not fall.

℣. Preserve me, O God: for in Thee have I put my trust. O my soul, thou hast said unto the Lord, Thou art my God. The Lord Himself is the portion of mine inheritance.

Secret. May this sacrifice of propitiation and praise make us, O Lord, worthy of Thy reconciled favour. Through.

Comm. Ps. viii. O Lord our Governor, how excellent is Thy Name in all the world!

P. Comm. May this Communion, O Lord, cleanse us from sin; and make us partakers of the heavenly remedy. Through.

The Prayer over the People.

Hear our supplications, O Almighty God, and mercifully grant that they on whom Thou bestowest boldness to hope for Thy loving-kindness, may experience the effects of Thy wonted compassion. Through.

TUESDAY AFTER REMINISCERE.

The Office. Ps. xxvii.

My heart hath talked of Thee, Seek ye my face: Thy face Lord, will I seek. O hide not Thou Thy face from me.

Ps. The Lord is my light, and my salvation: Whom then shall I fear?

The Collect.

Graciously perfect in us, O Lord, we beseech Thee, the assistance of this holy observance, that what we have perceived to be our duty, by Thy guidance, through Thy working, we may indeed fulfil. Through.

The Lesson. 1 King xvii. 8-16.

In those days, the Word of the Lord came unto Elijah the Tishbite, saying .... which he spake by Elijah.

Gradual. Ps. lv. O cast Thy burden upon the Lord, and He shall nourish Thee.

℣. As for me, I will call upon God, and He shall hear my voice from the battle that was against me.

The Gospel. Matt. xxiii. 1-12.

At that time, spake Jesus to the multitude .... shall be exalted.

Offert. Ps. li. Have mercy upon me, O God, after Thy great goodness: do away mine offences.

℣. For I acknowledge my faults: and my sin is ever before me.

Secret. O Lord, be pleased to work in us Thy sanctifying grace by these mysteries; that it may both cleanse us from all earthly vices, and bring us to the enjoyment of Thy heavenly gifts. Through.

Comm. Ps. ix. I will speak of all Thy marvellous works. I will be glad and rejoice in Thee: yea, my songs will I make of Thy Name, O Thou most Highest.

P. Comm. O Lord, we beseech Thee, may what we have received at Thy Holy Altar be the medicine of mind and body: that we who are fortified by participation of so mighty a restorative, may not be overcome by any adversities. Through.

The Prayer over the People.

O Lord, graciously accept our prayers, and heal the infirmities of our souls; that we, receiving remission, may evermore rejoice in Thy blessing. Through.

WEDNESDAY AFTER REMINISCERE.

The Office. Ps. xxxviii.

Forsake me not, O Lord my God: be not Thou far from me. Haste Thee to help me: O Lord God of my salvation.

Ps. Put me not to rebuke, O Lord, in Thine anger: neither chasten me in Thy displeasure.

The Collect.

Mercifully regard Thy people, O Lord, we beseech Thee; and grant that those whom Thou commandest to abstain from fleshly food, may likewise cease from hurtful vices. Through.

The Lesson. Esther xiii. 8-17.

In those days Esther made her prayer *unto the Lord*, saying, O Lord *God*, the King Almighty: for the whole world is in Thy power, and if Thou hast appointed to save *us*, *we shall forthwith be set free;* for Thou, *Lord*, hast made heaven and earth ...... that praise Thee, O Lord *our God.*

Gradual. Ps. xxviii. O save Thy people, and give Thy blessing unto Thine inheritance.

℣. Unto Thee will I cry, O Lord my strength: think no scorn of me, lest I become like them that go down into the pit.

Tract. As on Ember Wednesday.

The Gospel. Matt xx. 17-28.

At that time, Jesus going up to Jerusalem .... a ransom for many.

Offert. Ps. xxv. Unto Thee, O Lord, will I lift up my soul: O my God, I have put my trust in Thee; O let me not be confounded, neither let my enemies triumph over me; for all they that hope in Thee shall not be confounded.

℣. Lead me forth in Thy truth, and learn me: for Thou art the God of my salvation; in Thee hath been my hope all the day long.

* ℣. Turn Thee unto me, and have mercy upon me: O keep my soul, and deliver me: let me not be confounded, for I have put my trust in Thee.

Secret. Graciously look down, O Lord, on the offerings we make Thee, and by this most Holy Communion absolve us from the chains of our sins. Through.

Comm. Ps. xi. The righteous Lord loveth righteousness: His countenance will behold the thing that is just.

P. Comm. We beseech Thee, O Lord, let our frequent receiving of the mysteries be profitable to us; that we, being cleansed from the evil condition of the old man, may make progress, and increase in newness of life. Through.

The Prayer over the People.

O God, the restorer and lover of innocence, draw to Thyself the hearts of Thy servants, that being inflamed by the fervour of Thy Spirit, they may be found steadfast in faith, and zealous in good works. Through.

THURSDAY AFTER REMINISCERE.

The Office. Ps. lxx.

Haste Thee, O God, to deliver me: make haste to help me, O Lord. Let *my enemies* be ashamed and confounded that seek after my soul.

Ps. Let them be turned backward and put to confusion that wish me evil.

* *Miss.* 94 and *Grad.*

The Collect.

Grant us, we beseech Thee, O Lord, the assistance of Thy grace; that we duly giving ourselves to fasting and prayer, may be delivered from all enemies both of soul and body. Through.

The Lesson. Jeremiah xvii. 5-10.

In those days spake Jeremiah the Prophet, saying, Cursed *be* the man .... to the fruit of his doings, *saith the Lord Almighty.*

Gradual. Ps. lxxix. *O Lord,* be merciful unto our sins. Wherefore do the heathen say: Where is now their God?

℣. Help us, O God of our salvation; for the glory of Thy Name, deliver us, *O Lord.*

The Gospel. John v. 30-47.

At that time Jesus said to the multitude of Jews, I can of Mine own self .... shall ye believe My words?

Offert. Exod. xxxii. *Moses prayed before the Lord his God, and said,* Lord, why doth Thy wrath wax hot against Thy people? Turn from Thy fierce wrath. Remember Abraham, Isaac, and Israel, to whom Thou swarest *to give a land flowing with milk and honey.* And the Lord repented of the evil which He thought to do unto His people.

℣. Exod. xxxiii. 17; xxxiv. The Lord said unto Moses, Thou hast found grace in My sight, and I know thee by name. And Moses made haste, and bowed his head towards the earth, and worshipped, *saying, I know that Thou* keepest mercy for thousands, forgiving iniquity and sin.

Secret. O God, to Whom, seeing divers sacrifices have ceased, we now offer this one only Victim; be present with us who have made our petitions by Thy inspiration, and bid the earnest desires of them who hope in Thee to be fulfilled, and their sins to be blotted out. Through.

Comm. John vi. He that eateth My Flesh and drinketh My Blood, abideth in Me, and I in him, *saith the Lord.*

P. Comm. May Thy grace, O Lord, we beseech Thee, never forsake us, but ever make us intent on Thy holy service; and always procure us Thy abundant help, and defend us from all adversity. Through.

The Prayer over the People.

Be favourable, O Lord, unto Thy servants, and hear their prayers, and grant them everlasting mercy; that they glorying in Thee, their Creator and Guide, may have all blessings restored and perpetuated to them. Through.

FRIDAY AFTER REMINISCERE.

The Office. Ps. xvii.

But as for me, I will behold Thy presence in righteousness; and when I awake up after Thy likeness, I shall be satisfied with it.

Ps. Hear the right, O Lord, consider my complaint.

The Collect.

Grant, we beseech Thee, Almighty God, that we, being cleansed by this holy fast, may come to the approaching feast with pure minds. Through.

The Lesson. Gen. xxxvii. 6-22.

In those days Joseph said unto his brethren, Hear, I pray you .... to his father again.

Gradual. Ps. cxx. When I was in trouble I called upon the Lord: and He heard me.

℣. Deliver my soul, O Lord, from lying lips: and from a deceitful tongue.

Tract. As on Ash-Wednesday.

The Gospel. Matt. xxi. 33-46.

At that time Jesus said unto His disciples and the multitude of Jews, There was a certain householder .... for a prophet.

Offert. Ps. xl. Make haste, O Lord, to help me. Let them be ashamed, and confounded together, that seek after my soul to destroy it.

℣. Let them be driven backward, and put to rebuke, that wish me evil.

Secret. May this Sacrifice, O Lord God, both abide in us indeed, and by its effectual working be confirmed. Through.

Comm. Ps. xii. Thou shalt keep them, O Lord: Thou shalt preserve him from this generation for ever.

P. Comm. Grant, we beseech Thee, O Lord, that we who have received this pledge of eternal salvation may so direct our course agreeably thereto, that we may attain the same. Through.

The Prayer over the People.

Grant, we beseech Thee, O Lord, to Thy people health of mind and body, that they, cleaving to good works, may be ever worthy to be defended by Thy mighty protection. Through.

SATURDAY AFTER REMINISCERE.

The Office. Ps. xix.

The law of the Lord is an undefiled law, converting the soul: the testimony of the Lord is sure, and giveth wisdom unto the simple.

Ps. The heavens declare the glory of God: and the firmament sheweth his handy work.

The Collect.

Grant, O Lord, we beseech Thee, a saving effect to our fast, that the chastisement of the flesh, which we have undertaken, may prevail to the quickening of our souls. Through.

The Lesson. Gen. xxvii. 6-39.

In those days Rebecca spake unto Jacob .... of heaven from above.

Gradual. Ps. xcii. It is a good thing to give thanks unto the Lord: and to sing praises unto Thy Name, O most Highest.

℣. To tell of Thy loving kindness early in the morning: and of Thy truth in the night season.

The Gospel. Luke xv. 11-32.

At that time Jesus spake unto His disciples this parable: A certain man had two sons .... and was lost, and is found.

Offert. Ps. xiii. Lighten mine eyes, that I sleep not in death. Lest mine enemy say, I have prevailed against him.

℣. How long wilt thou forget me, O Lord, for ever: how long shall I seek counsel in my soul?

Secret. Mercifully grant us, O Lord, in answer to this holy Sacrifice, that we, who pray to be absolved from our own may not have the sins of others visited upon us. Through.

Comm. Luke xv. Son, *it was meet that thou shouldst be glad:* for this thy brother was dead, and is alive again; and was lost, and is found.

P. Comm. May the taste of Thy Divine Sacrament, O Lord, penetrate the innermost recesses of our hearts, and make us partakers of its strength. Through.

The Prayer over the People.

Protect, O Lord, we beseech Thee, this Thy family, by Thy continual goodness, that they who do lean only on the hope of Thy heavenly grace, may also be defended by Thy heavenly power. Through.

Third Sunday in Lent, or Oculi.

The Office. Ps. xxv.

Mine eyes are ever looking unto the Lord; for He shall pluck my feet out of the net. Turn Thee unto me, and have mercy upon me: for I am desolate, and in misery.

Ps. Unto Thee, O Lord, will I lift up my soul. My God, I have put my trust in Thee: let me not be confounded.

The Collect.

We beseech Thee, Almighty God, look upon the hearty desires of Thy humble servants, and stretch forth the right hand of Thy Majesty, to be our defence. Through.

The Epistle. Ephes. v. 1-9.

Brethren, be ye followers .... and righteousness and truth.

Gradual. Ps. ix. Up, Lord, and let not man have the upper hand: let the heathen be judged in Thy sight.

℣. While mine enemies are driven back: they shall fall and perish at Thy presence.

Tract. Ps. cxxiii. Unto Thee lift I up mine eyes: O Thou that dwellest in the heavens.

℣. Behold, even as the eyes of servants look unto the hand of their masters,

℣. And as the eyes of a maiden unto the hand of her mistress.

℣. Even so our eyes wait upon the Lord our God, until He have mercy upon us.

℣. Have mercy upon us, O Lord, have mercy upon us.

The Gospel. Luke. xi. 14-28.

At that time Jesus was casting out a devil .... the Word of God, and keep it.

Offert. Ps, xix. The statutes of the Lord are right, and rejoice the heart: sweeter also than honey, and the honey-comb. Moreover, by them is Thy servant taught.

Secret. Receive, O Lord, we beseech Thee, the gifts of Thy devout servants, and of Thy goodness cleanse them who serve the Divine mysteries, by which Thou dost justify even them that are in ignorance. Through.

Preface. The daily one.

Comm. Ps. lxxxiv. Yea, the sparrow hath found her an house, and the swallow a nest where she may lay her young: even Thy Altar, O Lord of Hosts, my King and my God. Blessed are they that dwell in Thy house: they will be always praising Thee.

P. Comm. Mercifully deliver us, O Lord, from all guilt and danger, whom Thou admittest to be partakers of this so great mystery. Through.

MONDAY AFTER OCULI.

The Office. Ps. lvi.

In God's Word will I rejoice: In the Lord's Word will I comfort me. Yea, in God have I put my trust: I will not fear what man can do unto me.

Ps. Be merciful unto me, O God, for man goeth about to devour me: he is daily fighting, and troubling me.

The Collect.

We beseech Thee, O Lord, mercifully to pour forth Thy grace into our hearts; that, as we abstain from fleshly food, so we may withdraw our senses from all hurtful excesses. Through.

The Lesson. 2 Kings v. 1-15.

In those days, Naaman, captain of the host .... now know I that there is no God in all the earth, but *the Lord God of* Israel.

Gradual. Ps. lvi. Thou tellest my flittings, *O God:* put my tears into Thy bottle.

℣. Be merciful unto me, O Lord, for man goeth about to devour me: he is daily fighting, and troubling me.

Tract. As on Ash-Wednesday.

The Gospel. Luke iv. 23-30.

At that time the Pharisees said unto Jesus, Whatsoever we have heard .... went his way.

Offert. Ps. lv. Hear my prayer, O God: and hide not Thyself from my petition. Take heed unto me, and hear me:

℣. How I am vexed. The enemy crieth so, and the ungodly cometh on so fast: I would make haste to escape.

Secret. Grant, O Lord, that the offering we make to Thee of our service, may become to us a sacrament profitable to our salvation. Through.

Comm. Ps. xiv. Who shall give salvation unto Israel out of Sion? When the Lord turneth the captivity of His people: then shall Jacob rejoice, and Israel shall be glad.

P. Comm. Grant, we beseech Thee, O almighty and merciful God, that what we touch with our lips, we may receive with pure minds. Through.

The Prayer over the People.

May Thy mercy, O Lord, we beseech Thee, assist us; that we may be accounted worthy to be rescued from the threatening dangers of our sins by Thy protection, and be set free by Thy deliverance. Through.

TUESDAY AFTER OCULI.

The Office. Ps. xvii.

I have called upon Thee, O God, for Thou shalt hear me; incline Thine ear to me, and hearken unto my words. Keep me as the apple of an eye: hide me under the shadow of Thy wings.

Ps. Hear the right, O Lord, consider my complaint.

The Collect.

Hear us, O almighty and merciful God, and graciously bestow upon us the gift of saving continence. Through.

The Lesson. 2 Kings iv. 1-7.

In those days there cried a certain woman unto Elisha *the Prophet*, saying .... and thy children of the rest.

Gradual. Ps. xix. O cleanse Thou me from my secret faults, O *Lord*. Keep Thy servant also from presumptuous sins.

℣. Lest they get the dominion over me: so shall I be undefiled, and innocent from the great offence.

The Gospel. Matt. xviii. 15-22.

At that time Jesus, looking on His disciples, said to Simon Peter, If Thy brother shall trespass ...... Until seventy times seven.

Offert. Ps. cxviii. The right hand of the Lord hath the pre-eminence: the right hand of the Lord bringeth mighty things to pass. I shall not die, but live: and declare the works of the Lord.

℣. I called upon the Lord in trouble: and *He* heard me at large. The Lord is on my side.

Secret. Lord, we beseech Thee, may the saving effect of our redemption come unto us through this Sacrament; to withdraw us from this world's intemperance, and lead us to all things profitable to our salvation. Through.

Comm. Ps. xv. Lord, who shall dwell in Thy tabernacle? Or who shall rest upon Thy holy hill? Even he that leadeth an incorrupt life, and doeth the thing which is right.

P. Comm. Being cleansed by these holy mysteries, grant us, O Lord we beseech Thee, both pardon and grace. Through.

The Prayer over the People.

Defend us, Lord, by Thy protection, and keep us ever from all iniquity. Through.

WEDNESDAY AFTER OCULI.

The Office. Ps. xxxi.

My trust hath been in the Lord. I will be glad, and rejoice in Thy mercy: for Thou hast considered my trouble.

Ps. In Thee, O Lord, have I put my trust: let me never be put to confusion, deliver me in Thy righteousness.

The Collect.

Grant, O Lord, we beseech Thee, that being disciplined by this wholesome fast, and abstaining from all hurtful vices, we may the more readily obtain Thy favour. Through.

The Lesson. Exod. xx. 12-24.

Thus saith the Lord God, Honour thy father .... I record My Name.

Gradual. Ps. vi. Have mercy upon me, O Lord, for I am weak: O Lord, heal me:

℣. For my bones are vexed. My soul also is sore troubled.

Tract. As on Ember Wednesday.

The Gospel. Matt xv. 1-20.

At that time came to Jesus .... defileth not a man.

Offert. Ps. cix. But deal Thou with me, O Lord, according unto Thy Name: for sweet is Thy mercy.

℣. Hold not Thy tongue, O God of my praise: for the mouth of the ungodly, yea, the mouth of the deceitful is opened upon me.

Secret. Receive, O Lord, we beseech Thee, the prayers of Thy people, together with their oblations; and, while we celebrate these Thy mysteries, defend us from all dangers. Through.

Comm. Ps. xvi. Thou shalt shew me the path of life; in Thy presence is the fulness of joy, *O Lord.*

P. Comm. We beseech Thee, O Lord, may the celestial banquet at which we have fed sanctify us; that we, being cleansed from all errors, may be accounted worthy to attain Thy heavenly promises. Through.

The Prayer over the People.

Grant, we beseech Thee, Almighty God, that we who beg the favour of Thy protection, being delivered from all evils, may serve Thee with a quiet mind. Through.

THURSDAY AFTER OCULI.

The Office.

I am the Saviour of My people, saith the Lord: in whatever distress they shall call upon Me, I will hear them, and I will be their Lord for ever..

Ps. lxxviii. Hear my law, O my people: incline your ears unto the words of my mouth.

The Collect.

Grant, we beseech Thee, Almighty God, that the holy devotion of this fast may both increase our purity and render us acceptable to Thy Majesty. Through.

The Lesson. Jer. vii. 1-7.

In those days the Word of the Lord came unto me, saying, Stand in the gate .... for ever and ever, *saith the Lord Almighty.*

Gradual. Ps. cxlv. The eyes of all wait upon Thee, O Lord: and Thou givest them their meat in due season.

℣. Thou openest Thine hand: and fillest all things living with plenteousness.

The Gospel. John vi. 27-35.

At that time Jesus saith unto the multitude of Jews, Labour not .... shall never thirst.

Offert. Ps. cxxxviii. Though I walk in the midst of trouble, yet shalt Thou refresh me, *O Lord:* Thou shalt stretch forth Thy hand upon the furiousness of mine enemies, and Thy right hand shall save me.

℣. When I called upon Thee, Thou heardest me: and enduedst my soul with much strength.

Secret. Cause us, O Lord, we pray Thee, to approach Thy holy mysteries with pure minds, that we may ever offer Thee a reasonable service. Through.

Comm. Ps. cxix. Thou hast charged: that we shall diligently keep Thy commandments. O that my ways were made so direct: that I might keep Thy statutes!

P. Comm. May the reverent receiving of Thy Sacrament, O Lord, both cleanse us by its mystic working, and defend us by its abiding virtue. Through.

The Prayer over the People.

May Thy heavenly favour, O Lord, we beseech Thee, magnify Thy people that is under Thee, and make them ever to keep Thy commandments. Through.

FRIDAY AFTER OCULI.

The Office. Ps. lxxxvi.

Shew some token upon me for good, that they who hate me may see it, and be ashamed: because Thou, Lord, hast holpen me, and comforted me.

Ps. Bow down Thine ear, O Lord, and hear me: for I am poor, and in misery.

The Collect.

Let Thy gracious favour, O Lord, accompany our fast, that as we abstain from food in body, so we may likewise fast from sin in mind. Through.

The Lesson. Numb. xx. 5-13.

In those days the children of Israel gathered themselves together against Moses and against Aaron, *and said, Give us water that we may drink.* And Moses and Aaron went from the presence of the assembly unto the door of the tabernacle of the congregation, and they fell upon their faces *and cried unto the Lord, and said, O Lord God, hear the cry of this people, and open to them Thy treasury, the fountain of living water, that they may be satisfied, and their murmuring may cease:** and the glory of the Lord .... sanctified in them.

Gradual. Ps. xxviii. My heart hath trusted in *God*, and I am helped : therefore my heart danceth for joy, and in my song will I praise Him.

℣. Unto Thee will I cry, O Lord my strength : think no scorn of me, *depart not from me.*

Tract. As on Ash-Wednesday.

The Gospel. John iv. 5-42.

In those days Jesus cometh to a city of Samaria .... the Saviour of the world.

Offert. Ps. v. O hearken Thou unto the voice of my calling, my King, and my God : for unto Thee will I make my prayer, *O Lord.*

℣. Ponder my words, O Lord : consider my meditation, *and hear me.*

Secret. We beseech Thee, O Lord, mercifully regard the offerings we consecrate to Thee, that they may be acceptable to Thee, and always further our salvation. Through.

Comm. John v. Whosoever drinketh of this water, *saith the Lord to the woman of Samaria,* it shall be in him a well of water springing up into everlasting life.

P. Comm. May the receiving of this Sacrament, O Lord, cleanse us from sin, and bring us to the kingdom of heaven. Through.

The Prayer over the People.

Grant, we beseech Thee, Almighty God, that we who trust in Thy protection, may by Thy aid overcome all things that oppose us. Through.

* *Vide* Vulg.

SATURDAY AFTER OCULI.

The Office. Ps. v.

Ponder my words, O Lord: consider my meditation. O hearken Thou unto the voice of my calling.

Ps. My King and my God.

The Collect.

Grant, we beseech Thee, Almighty God, that they who for the mortification of the flesh abstain from food, may, by following after righteousness, also fast from sin. Through.

The Lesson. Dan. xiii. (*i.e.*, History of Susanna.)

In those days there dwelt a man .... was saved the same day.

Gradual. Ps. xxiii. Yea, though I walk through the valley of the shadow of death, I will fear no evil: for Thou art with me, *O Lord.*

℣. Thy rod and Thy staff comfort me.

The Gospel. John viii. 1-11.

At that time Jesus went unto the Mount of Olives .... go, and sin no more.

Offert. Ps. cxix. 133. Order my steps, *O Lord,* in Thy Word: and so shall no wickedness have dominion over me.

℣. When Thy Word goeth forth: it giveth light and understanding unto the simple.

Secret. May this offering be pleasing unto Thee, O Lord, through our solemn fast; and that it may be the more acceptable, may it be presented to Thee with pure hearts. Through.

Comm. John viii. Woman, hath no man condemned thee? No man, Lord. Neither do I condemn thee: sin no more.

P. Comm. We beseech Thee, Almighty God, that we may be reckoned among His members of Whose Body and Blood we have received communion, Thy Son Jesus Christ our Lord. Who liveth.

The Prayer over the People.

Stretch forth, O Lord, over Thy faithful people, the right hand of Thy heavenly aid, that they may seek Thee with their whole heart, and obtain effectually those things which they ask worthily. Through.

Midlent Sunday, or Lætare.

The Office. Is. lxvi.

Rejoice ye with Jerusalem, and *gather together*, all ye that love *the Lord:* rejoice for joy with her, all ye that mourn for her: that ye may suck, and be satisfied with the breasts of her consolations.

Ps. cxxii. I was glad when they said unto me: We will go into the house of the Lord.

The Collect.

Grant, we beseech Thee, Almighty God, that we, who for our evil deeds do worthily deserve to be punished, by the comfort of Thy grace may be relieved. Through.

The Epistle. Gal. iv. 22-31.

Brethren, it is written .... but of the free; *with which liberty Christ hath made us free.*

Gradual. Ps. cxxii. I was glad when they said unto me: We will go into the house of the Lord.

℣. Peace be within thy walls: and plenteousness within thy palaces.

Tract. Ps. cxxv. They that put their trust in the Lord shall be even as the Mount Sion: which may not be removed, but standeth fast for ever.

℣. The hills stand about Jerusalem: even so standeth the Lord round about His people, from this time forth for evermore.

The Gospel. John. vi. 1-14.

At that time Jesus went over the sea of Galilee .... that should come into the world.

Offert. Ps. cxxxv. O praise the Lord, for the Lord is gracious: O sing praises unto His Name, for it is lovely.

℣. Whatsoever the Lord pleased, that did He in heaven, and in earth.

Secret. Grant, us, be beseech Thee, O Lord, ever to be occupied in the Divine service, and be made meet alike in mind and body for the sacred mysteries. Through.

Preface. The daily one.

Comm. Ps. cxxii. Jerusalem is built as a city: that is at unity in itself. For thither the tribes go up, even the tribes of the Lord: to give thanks unto the Name of the Lord.

P. Comm. Grant, we beseech Thee, merciful God, that we may both handle with true reverence, and ever receive with faithful mind, these Thy holy things with which we are fed unceasingly. Through.

MONDAY AFTER LÆTARE.

The Office. Ps. liv.

Save me, O God, for Thy Name's sake: and avenge me in Thy strength.

Ps. Hear my prayer, O God: for strangers are risen up against me, and tyrants seek after my soul.

The Collect.

Grant, we beseech Thee, Almighty God, that we, who annually celebrate these holy observances, may be well pleasing to Thee, both in body and mind. Through.

The Lesson. I Kings iii. 16-28

In those days came there two women ......, to do judgment.

Gradual. Ps. xxxi. And be Thou my strong rock, and house of defence: that Thou mayest save me.

℣. In Thee, O Lord, have I put my trust: let me never be put to confusion.

Tract. As on Ash-Wednesday.

The Gospel. John ii. 13-25.

At that time the Jews' passover .... for He knew what was in man.

Offert. Ps. c. O be joyful in the Lord, all ye lands: serve the Lord with gladness, and come before His presence with a song. Be ye sure that the Lord He is God.

℣. It is He that hath made us, and not we ourselves; we are His people, and the sheep of His pasture.

Secret. We beseech Thee, O Lord, to work in us by Thy mysteries, that we may offer these gifts to Thee with ready minds. Through.

Comm. Ps. xix. O cleanse Thou me from my secret faults. Keep Thy servant also from presumptuous sins.

P. Comm. We beseech Thee, O Lord, sustain by Thy aid those whom Thou refreshest by the Divine Sacrament, that we who are cherished by temporal may be fed by eternal blessings. Through.

The Prayer over the People.

We beseech Thee, O Lord, graciously hear our prayer, and grant that we, to whom Thou givest an hearty desire to pray, may obtain the help of Thy defence. Through.

TUESDAY AFTER LÆTARE.

The Office. Ps. lv.

Hear my prayer, O God: and hide not Thyself from my petition. Take heed unto me, and hear me:

Ps. How I mourn in my prayer, and am vexed: the enemy crieth so.

The Collect.

We beseech Thee, O Lord, that the sacred fast we observe may be for our improvement in holy conversation, and draw down upon us the constant succours of Thy mercy. Through.

The Lesson. Exod. xxxii. 7-14.

In those days the Lord said unto Moses .... And the Lord *our God* repented of the evil which He thought to do unto His people.

Gradual. Ps. xliv. Arise, and help us, *O Lord:* and deliver us for Thy mercy's sake.

℣. We have heard with our ears, O God, our fathers have told us: what Thou hast done in their time of old.

The Gospel. John vii. 14-31.

At that time, now about the midst of the feast .... And many of the people believed on Him.

Offert. Ps. xl. I waited patiently for the Lord: and He inclined unto me, and heard my calling. And He hath put a new song in my mouth: even a thanksgiving unto our God.

℣. And set my feet upon the rock, and ordered my goings.

Secret. We beseech Thee, O Lord, favourably to look upon the offerings of Thy faithful people, that the oblation made by the reverent service of Thy devout servants may be ratified by Thy favour. Through.

Comm. Ps. xx. We will rejoice in Thy salvation, and triumph in the Name of the Lord our God.

P. Comm. We beseech Thee, O Lord, that the holy food and saving cup may be profitable to us, both to protect us in this life, and to bestow upon us life eternal. Through.

The Prayer over the People.

Have compassion, O Lord, we beseech Thee, on Thy people, and mercifully refresh them who are laden with continual tribulations. Through.

WEDNESDAY AFTER LÆTARE.

The Office. Ezek. xxxvi.

I will be sanctified in you, and gather you out of all countries. Then will I sprinkle clean water upon you, and ye shall be clean: from all your filthiness, and a new spirit will I put within you.

Ps. xxxiv. I will alway give thanks unto the Lord: His praise shall ever be in my mouth.

Let us pray.
D. Let us kneel.
D. Rise.

The Collect.

O God, Who givest to the righteous the reward of their good works, and, through fasting, pardon to sinners; have mercy on Thy suppliants, that the confession of our guilt may obtain remission of sins. Through.

The Lesson. Ezek. xxxvi. 23-28.

Thus saith the Lord God, I will sanctify My great Name ...... and I will be your God, *saith the Lord Almighty.*

Gradual. Ps. xxxiv. Come, ye children, and hearken unto me: I will teach you the fear of the Lord.

℣. They had an eye unto Him, and were lightened: and their faces were not ashamed.

¶ *Here followeth,* The Lord be with you, etc.

FRIDAY AFTER LÆTARE.

The Office. Ps. xix.

Let the meditation of my heart : be alway acceptable in Thy sight, O Lord, my strength, and my Redeemer.

Ps. The heavens declare the glory of God : and the firmament showeth His handy-work.

The Collect.

O God, Who by Thy unspeakable mysteries givest new life to the world; grant, we beseech Thee, that Thy Church may advance in the ordinances which last for ever, and never be left destitute of temporal aid. Through.

The Lesson. I Kings xvii. 17-24.

In those days the son of the woman .... in thy mouth is truth.

Gradual. Ps. cxviii. It is better to trust in the Lord : than to put any confidence in man.

℣. It is better to trust in the Lord : than to put any confidence in princes.

Tract. As on Ash-Wednesday.

The Gospel. John xi. 1-45.

At that time a certain man was sick .... believed on Him.

Offert. Ps. xviii. For Thou shalt save the people that are in adversity, *O Lord*; and shall bring down the high looks of the proud : for who is God, but *Thou, O Lord.*

℣. My complaint shall come before Him, it shall enter even into His ears.

Secret. May the gifts which we have offered, O Lord, we beseech Thee, purify us, and make Thee ever favourable to us. Through.

Comm. John xi. *The Lord, seeing the sisters of Lazarus weeping at the grave, wept in the presence of the Jews,* and cried, "Lazarus, come forth." And he came forth bound hand and foot with grave-clothes, who had been dead four days.

P. Comm. May the receiving of this Sacrament, we beseech Thee, O Lord, continually free us from our own guilt, and protect us from all adversity. Through.

The Prayer over the People.

Grant us, we beseech Thee, Almighty God, that we who are conscious of our infirmity, and trust in Thy loving kindness, may ever rejoice in Thy protection. Through.

SATURDAY AFTER LÆTARE.

The Office. Isa. lv.

Ho, every one that thirsteth, come ye to the waters, *saith the Lord*, and he that hath no money; come ye, *drink with joyfulness.*

Ps. lxxviii. Hear my law, O my people incline: your ears unto the words of my mouth.

The Collect.

O Lord, we beseech Thee, let our devotion bring forth fruit by Thy grace; for then only will our fast profit us, when it is well-pleasing to Thy goodness. Through.

The Lesson. Isa. xlix. 8-15.

Thus saith the Lord God, ... yet will I not forget Thee, *saith the Lord Almighty.*

Gradual. Ps. x. The poor committeth himself unto Thee, O *Lord*; for Thou art the helper of the friendless.

℣. Why standest Thou so far off, O Lord; and hidest Thy face in the needful time of trouble? The ungodly for his own lust doth persecute the poor.

The Gospel. John viii. 12-20.

At that time said Jesus to the multitude of Jews, I am the light of the world: .... for His hour was not yet come.

Offert. Ps. xviii. The Lord is my stony rock, and my defence: my Saviour, in whom I will trust.

℣. I will follow upon mine enemies, and overtake them: neither will I turn again till I have destroyed them.

Secret. O Lord, we beseech Thee, favourably receive these our offerings; and, in Thy mercy, subdue unto Thyself even our rebellious will. Through.

Comm. Ps. xxiii. The Lord is my shepherd: therefore can I lack nothing. He shall feed me in a green pasture: and lead me forth beside the waters of comfort.

P. Comm. O Lord, we beseech Thee, may Thy sacred mysteries which we have received purify us: and by their healing operation cause Thee to look upon us with favour. Through.

The Prayer over the People.

O God, Who choosest rather to show mercy, than to be angry with those that hope in Thee; grant us worthily to lament the evils we have committed, that so we may find the favour of Thy comfort. Through.

Passion Sunday.

The Office Ps. xliii.

Give sentence with me, O God, and defend my cause against the ungodly people: O deliver me from the deceitful and wicked man, for Thou art the God of my strength.

Ps. O send out Thy light and Thy truth, that they may lead me: and bring me unto Thy holy hill, and to Thy dwelling.

¶ *From this day till* Easter *no* Glory *is said at the week-day Mass; except on* Maundy Thursday, *if a Bishop celebrates.*

The Collect.

We beseech Thee, Almighty God, mercifully to look upon this Thy family: that by Thy great goodness they may be governed and preserved evermore, both in body and soul. Through.

The Epistle. Heb. ix. 11-15.

Brethren, Christ being come .... of eternal inheritance, *in Jesus Christ our Lord.*

Gradual. Ps. cxliii. Deliver me, O Lord, from mine enemies. Teach me to do the thing that pleaseth Thee.

℣. Ps. cxviii. It is He that delivereth me from my cruel enemies, and setteth me up above mine adversaries: Thou shalt rid me from the wicked man.

Tract. Ps. cxxix. Many a time have they fought against me from my youth up,

℣. May Israel now say: yea, many a time have they vexed me from my youth up.

℣. But they have not prevailed against me. The plowers plowed upon my back:

℣. And made long furrows. But the righteous Lord: hath hewn the snares of the ungodly in pieces.

The Gospel. John viii. 46-59.

At that time Jesus said unto the multitude of the Jews and the chief priests, Which of you convinceth Me .... and went out of the temple.

Offert. Ps. cxix. I will thank Thee, *O Lord,* with an unfeigned heart. O do well unto Thy servant: that I may live and keep Thy Word. O quicken Thou me, according to Thy Word, *O Lord.*

Secret. Almighty God, graciously behold the offerings of Thy faithful people; and grant that the chains of the world may not hold them captive whom by the Passion of Thy Son Thou didst will to be set free. Who.

Comm. Luke xxii. This is My Body, which is given for you; this cup is the New Testament in My Blood, *saith the Lord;* do this, as oft as ye shall drink it, in remembrance of Me.

P. Comm. Be present with us, O Lord our God, we beseech Thee, and defend by Thy continual aid those whom Thou hast refreshed by Thy mysteries. Through.

MONDAY IN PASSION WEEK.

The Office. Ps. lvi.

Be merciful unto me, O Lord, for man goeth about to devour me; he is daily fighting, and troubling me.

Ps. Mine enemies are daily in hand to swallow me up, *O Lord:* for they be many that fight against me.

The Collect.

Sanctify, O Lord, we beseech Thee, our fasts, and mercifully bestow upon us the pardon of all our sins. Through.

The Lesson. Jonah iii. 1-10.

In those days, the Word of the Lord .... and God repented *concerning His people, ever the Lord our God.*

Gradual. Ps. liv. Hear my prayer, O God: and hearken unto the words of my mouth.

℣. Save me, O God, for Thy Name's sake: and avenge me in Thy strength.

Tract. As on Ash-Wednesday.

The Gospel. John vii. 32-39.

At that time the Pharisees and the chief priests sent officers to take *Jesus* .... which they that believe on Him should receive.

Offert. Ps. vi. Turn Thee, O Lord, and deliver my soul: O save me for Thy mercy's sake.

℣. O Lord, rebuke me not in Thine indignation; neither chasten me in Thy displeasure.

Secret. We present unto Thee, O Lord, this sacrifice of praise on the receiving of the safeguard Thou hast ordained: grant, we beseech Thee, that we may more sincerely and truly receive the same. Through.

Comm. Ps. xxiv. The Lord of Hosts, He is the King of Glory.

P. Comm. May the participation, O Lord, we beseech Thee, of Thy saving Sacrifice both cleanse and heal us. Through.

The Prayer over the People.

Grant, O Lord, we beseech Thee, to Thy people the spirit of truth and peace; that they may know Thee with their whole heart, and fulfil with pious devotion the things which are pleasing unto Thee. Through. In the unity.

TUESDAY IN PASSION WEEK.

The Office. Ps. xxvii.

O tarry Thou the Lord's leisure: be strong, and He shall comfort thine heart; and put thou thy trust in the Lord.

Ps. The Lord is my light, and my salvation; whom then shall I fear?

The Collect.

May our fast, O Lord, we beseech Thee, be acceptable to Thee; that purifying us from sin it may make us worthy of Thy grace, and procure us everlasting recovery. Through.

The Lesson. Dan. xiv. 29-42 (*i.e.*, Hist. of Bel and the Dragon), Dan. vii. 26, 27.

In those days, they of Babylon came to the King .... in a moment before his face. *Then the King said, Let all that dwell in the whole earth* tremble before the God of Daniel; for He delivereth and rescueth, and He worketh signs and wonders in heaven and in earth, Who hath delivered Daniel from the power of the lions.

Gradual. Ps. xliii. O *Lord*, defend my cause: O deliver me from the deceitful and wicked man.

℣. O send out Thy light and Thy truth, that they may lead me: and bring me unto Thy holy hill.

The Gospel. John vii. 1-13.

At that time Jesus walked in Galilee .... for fear of the Jews.

Offert. Ps. ix. And they that know Thy Name will put their trust in Thee: for Thou, Lord, hast never failed them that seek Thee. O praise the Lord which dwelleth in Sion: for He forgetteth not the complaint of the poor.

℣. Thou art set in the throne that judgest right. Thou hast rebuked the heathen, and destroyed the ungodly. Minister true judgment unto Thy people, and be a defence for the oppressed.

Secret. We present this Sacrifice to be offered to Thee, O Lord, to gladden us with temporal consolation, to the end we may more certainly hope for Thy eternal promises. Through.

Comm. Ps. xxv. Deliver *me*, O God *of Israel*, out of all *my* troubles.

P. Comm. Grant, we beseech Thee, Almighty God, that we being continually occupied in divine things, may be made worthy to draw nigh to Thy heavenly gifts. Through.

The Prayer over the People.

Grant, O Lord, we beseech Thee, that the company of Thy servants may persevere in doing Thy will; that in our days Thy faithful people may increase both in worthiness and in number. Through.

WEDNESDAY IN PASSION WEEK.

The Office. Ps. xviii.

It is He that delivereth me from my cruel enemies, and setteth me up above mine adversaries: Thou shalt rid me from the wicked man, *O Lord*.

Ps. I will love Thee, O Lord, my strength: the Lord is my stony rock, and my defence.

The Collect.

Enlighten, O God of mercy, the hearts of Thy faithful people by this holy fast; and, seeing Thou hast given them an hearty desire to pray, graciously give ear unto their supplications. Through.

The Lesson. Lev. xix. 11-19.

In those days the Lord spake unto Moses, saying, Speak unto all the congregation of the children of Israel, and say unto them, ... Ye shall keep My statutes. *For I am the Lord thy God.*

Gradual. Ps. xxx. I will magnify Thee, O Lord, for Thou hast set me up: and not made my foes to triumph over me.

℣. O Lord my God, I cried unto Thee: and Thou hast healed me. Thou, Lord, hast brought my soul out of hell: Thou hast kept my life from them that go down into the pit.

Tract. As on Ember Wednesday.

The Gospel. John x. 22-38.

At that time it was at Jerusalem .... and I in Him.

Offert. Ps. lix. Deliver me from mine enemies, O God: defend me from them that rise up against me.

℣. For, lo, they lie waiting for my soul: the mighty men are gathered against me.

Secret. Grant, we beseech Thee, merciful God, that we may offer Thee, with unfeigned obedience, this Sacrifice of propitiation and praise. Through.

Comm. Ps. xxvi. I will wash my hands in innocency, and so will I go to Thine Altar; that I may shew the voice of thanksgiving, and tell of all Thy wondrous works.

P. Comm. Having received the benediction of the heavenly gift, we humbly offer our supplication unto Thee, Almighty God, that the same may be unto us the means of sacramental grace and salvation. Through.

The Prayer over the People.

O Lord, we beseech Thee, let Thy hoped-for mercy come to Thy people which prayeth; and of Thy heavenly bounty grant unto them both to ask such things as are rightful, and also to obtain their petitions. Through.

THURSDAY IN PASSION WEEK.

The Office. Dan. iii. 28 (*i.e.*, Song of the Three Children, v. 5).

According to judgment didst Thou bring all these things upon us; for we have sinned, and not obeyed Thy commandments: but give glory to Thy Name, and deal with us according to the multitude of Thy mercies.

Ps. xlviii. Great is the Lord, and highly to be praised: in the city of our God, even upon His holy hill.

The Collect.

Grant, we beseech Thee, Almighty God, that the dignity of human nature, which hath been wounded by excess, may be restored by the healing practice of moderation. Through.

The Lesson. Dan. iii. 36-46 (*i.e.*, Song of the Three Children, 12-22).

In those days, Daniel prayed, saying, O Lord God of Israel, despise not Thy people, and cause not Thy mercy .... and glorious over the whole world, *O Lord our God.*

Gradual. Ps. xcvi. Bring presents, and come into His courts. O worship the Lord in the beauty of holiness.

℣. The Lord discovereth the thick bushes: in His temple doth every man speak of His honour.

The Gospel. John vii. 40-53.

In those days, when certain of the people had heard the sayings of Jesus, they said, Of a truth .... went unto his own house.

Offert. Ps. cxxxvii. By the waters of Babylon we sat down and wept: when we remembered thee, O Sion.

℣. Remember the children of Edom, O Lord, in the day of Jerusalem.

Secret. O Lord our God, Who of these creatures which Thou hast formed for the support of our weakness hast been pleased to command gifts to be dedicated to Thy Name; grant, we beseech Thee, that they may be unto us a help in this present life and a sacrament unto life eternal. Through.

Comm. Ps. cxix. 40, 50. O think upon Thy servant, as concerning Thy Word: wherein Thou hast caused me to put my trust. The same is my comfort in my trouble.

P. Comm. Grant, O Lord, that what we have touched with our lips we may also receive with a pure mind; and may the gift bestowed in this world heal us eternally. Through.

The Prayer over the People.

Be favourable, O Lord, we beseech Thee, to Thy people; that, forsaking what displeaseth Thee, they may the rather be filled with delight in Thy commandments. Through.

FRIDAY IN PASSION WEEK.

The Office. Ps. xxxi.

Have mercy upon me, O Lord, for I am in trouble: deliver me from the hand of mine enemies: and from them that persecute me. Let me not be confounded, O Lord, for I have called upon Thee.

Ps. In Thee, O Lord, have I put my trust: let me never be put to confusion, deliver me in Thy righeousness.

The Collect.

O Lord, we beseech Thee, graciously pour into our hearts the help of Thy grace; that we, subduing our sins by voluntary discipline, may rather mortify ourselves in this life than be consigned to eternal punishment. Through.

The Lesson. Jer. xvii. 13-18.

In these days said Jeremiah, O Lord, all that forsake Thee ...... with double destruction, *O Lord our God.*

Gradual. Ps. xxxv. The communing *of mine enemies is not* for peace, *and in wrath they were grievous to me.*

℣. This Thou hast seen, O Lord: hold not Thy tongue then; go not far from me, O Lord.

Tract. As on Ash-Wednesday.

The Gospel. John xi. 47-54.

Then gathered the chief priests .... and there continued with His disciples.

Offert. Ps. cxix. 12, 121, 42. Blessed art Thou, O Lord: O teach me Thy statutes: and give me not over to my *proud* oppressors. So shall I make answer unto my blasphemers.

℣. 158, 84. It grieveth me when I see the transgressors: *O Lord,* when wilt Thou be avenged of them that persecute me?

Secret. Grant, O merciful God, that we may always worthily serve at Thy Altar, and by continual communion thereat may be saved. Through.

Comm. Ps. xxvii. Deliver me not over into the will of mine adversaries: for there are false witnesses risen up against me, and such as speak wrong.

P. Comm. May the continual defence of the Sacrifice we have received never forsake us, O Lord, and ward off from us all things which are hurtful. Through.

The Prayer over the People.

Grant us, we pray Thee, O Lord, pardon of our sins and increase of faith; and that Thou mayest multiply Thy gifts in us, make us more readily to obey Thy commandments. Through.

SATURDAY AFTER PASSION SUNDAY.

The Office. Ps. xxxi.

Have mercy upon me, O Lord, for I am in trouble: deliver me from the hand of mine enemies: and from them that persecute me. Let me not be confounded, O Lord, for I have called upon Thee.

Ps. In Thee, O Lord, have I put my trust: let me never be put to confusion, deliver me in Thy righteousness.

The Collect.

O Lord, we beseech Thee, may the people consecrated to Thy service increase in the spirit of earnest devotion; that they, being exercised in holy actions, may be the more plenteously fulfilled with Thy gifts as they become more acceptable unto Thy Majesty. Through.

The Lesson. Jer. xviii. 18-23.

In those days the impious Jews said one to another, Come, and let us devise devices against *the just one* .... in the time of Thine anger, *O Lord my God.*

Gradual. Ps. xxxv. *The* communing *of mine enemies* is not for peace, *and in wrath they were grievous to me.*

℣. This Thou hast seen, O Lord: hold not Thy tongue then; go not far from me, O Lord.

The Gospel. John vi. 53-71.

At that time Jesus said *to His disciples and to the multitude of Jews*, Verily, verily, I say unto you .... being one of the twelve.

Offert. Remember that I stand before Thee to speak in their favour, and turn Thine indignation from them.

℣. Ps. lxxx. Hear, O Thou Shepherd of Israel, Thou that leadest Joseph like a sheep.

Secret. Receive, O Almighty Creator, the offering which we with fasting present unto Thee out of the largeness of Thine own bounty to us; and that which Thou hast provided for our temporal support, be pleased to turn to our eternal welfare. Through.

Comm. Ps. xxvii. Deliver me not over into the will of mine adversaries: for there are false witnesses risen up against me, and such as speak wrong.

P. Comm. Being filled with the abundance of the Divine gift, we beseech Thee, O Lord our God, that we may ever live by the participation thereof. Through.

The Prayer over the People.

May Thy right hand, O Lord, we beseech Thee, protect Thy people that prayeth; and purify and make them truly wise, that they may both find present comfort, and advance to the good things to come. Through.

Palm Sunday.

¶ *After sprinkling of holy water, let this Lesson be read with its title at the Altar-step, on the south side, over the flowers and leaves, by an Acolyte in alb.*

The Lesson. Exod. xv. 27—xvi. 1-10.

In those days the children of Israel came to Elim ...... appeared in the cloud.

¶ *After the Benediction, let the Gospel follow immediately: read where Gospels are read on week-days; by a Deacon, turning to the East, after the manner of a simple festival, with* The Lord be with you *and* Glory *as usual.*

The Gospel. John xii. 12-19.

At that time much people that were come .... behold, the world is gone after Him.

¶ *The Gospel ended, let the blessing of flowers and leaves follow by the Priest in a red silk cope, on the third step of the Altar, turning to the south; palms and flowers having been previously laid on the Altar for the Clergy, and for others on the step of the Altar at the south side.*

I exorcise Thee, O creature of flowers and leaves, in the Name of God the Father Almighty, and in the Name of Jesus Christ His Son our Lord, and in the power of the Holy Ghost: Henceforth all power of the adversary, all the host of the Devil, and all strength of the enemy, all assaults of demons, be uprooted and expelled from this creature of flowers and leaves; that thou pursue not by subtlety the steps of those who hasten to the grace of God. Through Him who shall come to judge the quick and the dead, and the world by fire. ℟. Amen.

Let us pray.

Almighty, everlasting God, Who in the deluge didst announce to Noe Thy servant the restoration of peace to the earth by the mouth of a dove bearing an olive branch, we humbly entreat Thee that Thy truth may sanct+ify this creature of flowers and leaves, and branches of palms, or leaves of trees, which we offer in the presence of Thy glory, that so Thy devout people may take them in their hands and obtain the grace of Thy benediction. Through.

Let us pray.

O God, Whose Son descended from heaven to earth for the salvation of mankind, and when the hour of His passion was approaching willed to come to Jerusalem sitting on an ass, and to be called King, and to be praised by the people; increase the faith of those that hope in Thee, and mercifully hear the prayers of Thy suppliants. We beseech Thee, O Lord, let Thy blessing come upon us; and vouchsafe to bl+ess these branches of palms and other trees, that all who carry them may be fulfilled with the gift of Thy blessing. Grant therefore, O Lord, that as the Hebrew children met the same Thy Son our Lord Jesus Christ crying, Hosanna in the highest, so we also bearing the boughs of trees in our hands may with good works go to meet Christ, and attain to everlasting joy. Through the same.

Let us pray.

O God, Who gatherest together the scattered and preservest the gathered, Who didst bless the people who carried branches of palm to meet Jesus Christ: Bl+ess also these branches of palm and other trees which Thy servants faithfully bear for the blessing of Thy Name, that into whatsoever place they may be brought, all that dwell there may obtain Thy blessing; that so all ills being put to flight, Thy right hand may protect those whom it hath redeemed. Through.

¶ *Here let the flowers and leaves be sprinkled with holy water and censed.*

℣. The Lord be with you.

℟. And with thy spirit.

Let us pray.

O Lord Jesu Christ, Son of the Living God, Maker and Redeemer of the world, Who for our deliverance and salvation didst deign to come down from the highest Heaven to take flesh and to suffer for us, and Who of Thy own will when approaching the place of that same Passion wast pleased to be blessed, praised, and by the people, who met Thee with palms, proclaimed aloud a King Blessed, coming in the Name of the Lord; do Thou now accept our confession and praise; deign to bl + ess and sancti + fy these branches of palm and other trees and flowers, that whoever shall carry anything hence in reverence of Thy power, being sanctified by heavenly benediction, may be accounted worthy to obtain remission of sins and the reward of everlasting life; through Thee, O Jesu Christ, Saviour of the world. Who.

¶ *This done, let the palms forthwith be distributed; and meantime let the following Anthem be sung, the Precentor beginning—*

I. *Ant.* The Hebrew children carrying olive branches met the Lord, crying out and saying, Hosanna in the highest.

II. *Ant.* The Hebrew children spread their garments in the way and cried, saying Hosanna to the Son of David, Blessed is He that cometh in the Name of the Lord.

THE PROCESSION

¶ *Whilst the palms are being distributed, let a shrine with relics be prepared, in which shall hang in a pyx the Blessed Sacrament; and the distribution ended, let it be borne, preceded by an unveiled Cross, a lantern, and two banners, and followed by the Ministers in albs and amices only, and the Priest in a red silk cope; the Choir following, and as they go let these two Anthems be sung.* Let the Procession go through the west door, round the cloister, through the Canon's gate, to the first station.*

Antiphon. Now the first day of the feast of unleavened bread the disciples came to Jesus, saying unto Him, Where wilt Thou that we prepare for Thee to eat the passover? *But Jesus* said, Go into the city to such a man, and say unto him, The Master saith, My time is at hand: I will keep the passover at thy house with My disciples. And the disciples did as *the Lord* had appointed them; and they made ready the passover.

* These Anthems are supplied in full from the Gradual and Processional.

Antiphon. And when *the Lord* came nigh to Jerusalem, He sendeth forth two of His disciples, and saith unto them, Go your way into the village over against you, and ye shall find a colt tied whereon never man sat; loose him, and bring him *to Me.* If any man *question you,* say ye, That the Lord hath need of him. *Loosing him* they brought the colt to Jesus, and cast their garments on him; and He sat upon Him. And *some* spread their garments in the way: and others strewed branches in the way. And they that followed cried, Hosanna; Blessed is He that cometh in the Name of the Lord. Blessed be the kingdom of our father David; Hosanna in the highest. *Have mercy upon us, O Son of David,*

¶ *If these be not enough till the place of the first station, then let these follow—*

Antiphon. When the people heard that Jesus had come to Jerusalem, they took branches of palm and went to meet Him, and the children cried, saying, This is He Who shall be for the salvation of the world: This is our Salvation, the redemption of Israel. How great is He Whom Thrones and Dominions go forth to meet! Fear not, daughter of Sion, behold thy King cometh unto thee riding upon a colt, the foal of an ass, *as it is written.* Hail, King, Maker of the world, Who hast come to redeem us.

Antiphon. Six days before the feast of the Passover, when the Lord came to the city of Jerusalem, boys met Him, both bearing in their hands branches of palm and crying with a loud voice, saying, Glory to God in the highest.

Antiphon. The sixth day before the Passion came the Lord to the city of Jerusalem, and boys met Him both carrying in their hands branches of palm, and crying with a loud voice, Hosanna in the highest. Blessed *art Thou Who hast* come in the *multitude of Thy mercy:* Hosanna in the highest.

¶ *Then let the Gospel be read (that for the First Sunday in Advent) by the Deacon, in the vestments he has on at the Procession—not close to the Cross, however, but a little apart from his place next the Priest; the Deacon turning to the North and chanting it as on a simple feast of nine lessons, having first received the Benediction as usual.*

¶ *The Gospel ended, let three Clerks of the second grade meet the shrine and carry it, and three Clergy of the same grade go out of the Procession to the west side of the great Cross, and, turning to the people, stand and sing together as follows—*

Anthem. Behold thy King cometh unto thee, O Sion, *mystic daughter,* meek, riding on *beasts,** *of Whose advent the prophetic lesson has foretold.*

* Animalia, cf. Matt. xxi.

¶ *The Officiant, genuflecting, turning to the Relics, says—*

Hail, Jesus, Whom.

¶ *The Choir, genuflecting and kissing the earth, take it up as they rise, saying—*

The people of the Hebrews witness to,
Coming to meet with palms crying salvation.

¶ *The Clergy before the Relics—*

This is He that cometh from Edom, with dyed garments from Bozrah! This that is glorious in His apparel, travelling in the greatness of His strength! *Not on war horses, nor in lofty turrets.**

¶ *The Officiant as before genuflecting says—*

Hail, Light of the world.

¶ *The Choir as before genuflecting say—*

King of Kings, Glory of Heaven,
For whom abideth dominion, praise, and honour, now and for ever.

¶ *The Clergy before the Relics—*

This is He who was delivered as a guiltless lamb to death;
The death of Death, the bane of hell, by death bestowing life.
As of old the blessed seers in their prophecies set forth.

The Officiant. Hail! our Salvation.

The Choir. Peace, Redemption, Strength.
Who didst of Thy own will submit for us to death.

¶ *Then let the Procession proceed to the second station; the shrine with the relics borne, with the lantern and banners on either side, between the Sub-Deacon and the Thurifer, the Precentor beginning—*

Anthem. Thou art worthy, O Lord our God, to receive glory and honour.

Anthem. The multitude come to meet the Redeemer with flowers and palms, and the Gentiles give meet reverence to the triumphal Conqueror, the Son of God, and voices chant Hosanna through the heavens in honour of Christ.

¶ *If these two Anthems are not sufficient, then let one or both of these be chanted—*

℟. *Our Lord* Jesus six days before the Passover came to Bethany, where Lazarus was which had been dead, whom He raised from the dead.

℣. *But there assembled there many of the Jews* that they might see Lazarus. Whom.

* *i.e.*, such as are carried on the backs of elephants.

℟. The chief priests consulted that they might put Lazarus to death; because that by reason of him many *came* and believed on Jesus.

℣. Therefore the people which was with Him when he called Lazarus out of the grave and raised him from the dead, bare record. Because that.

¶ *Here let the second station be made on the south of the Church, where let seven Choristers sing in a conspicuous place—*

Glory, laud, and honour
To Thee, Redeemer King!
To Whom the lips of children
Made sweet Hosannas ring.

¶ *The Choir repeats the same.*

Choristers. Thou art the King of Israel,
Thou David's Royal Son,
Who in the Lord's Name camest,
The King and blessed one.

The Choir. Glory, etc.

Choristers. The company of Angels
Are praising Thee on high,
And mortal men, and all things
Created, make reply.

The Choir. Glory, etc.

Choristers. The people of the Hebrews
With Palms before Thee went;
Our praise, and prayer, and anthem
Before Thee we present.

The Choir. Glory, etc.

¶ *After this let the Procession go through the cloister on the right hand round to the west door, chanting—*

℟. Then gathered the chief priests and the Pharisees a council, and said, What do we? for this Man doeth many miracles. If we let Him thus alone, all men will believe on Him: and the Romans shall come and take away both our place and nation.

¶ *Here let there be the third station before the aforesaid door, and let three Clergy of the superior grade, turning to the people, chant standing in the doorway—*

℣. And one of them *named* Caiaphas, being the high priest that same year, *prophesied, saying*, It is expedient for *you* that one man should die for the people, and that the whole nation perish not. Then from that day forth they took counsel together for to put Him to death. And the Romans.

¶ *This done let them enter the Church by the same door under the shrine with the relics, which is held up on either side for them to pass under, singing,*

℟. * The Lord entering into the holy city, the Hebrew boys chanted the Resurrection of Life; with branches of palm they cried, Hosanna in the highest.

℣. And when they heard that Jesus had come to Jerusalem, they went forth to meet Him. With branches.

¶ *Here let there be the fourth station before the rood in the Church, and let the Officiant begin the Anthem,* Hail! *repeating it thrice each time a tone higher, genuflecting with the Choir; and after the third time let the Choir proceed with the same—*

Anthem. Hail, our King! Son of David, Redeemer of the world, Whom the Prophets proclaim the Saviour of the house of Israel that is to come. For Thee the Father sent into the world to be the saving vcitim, Whom all saints from the beginning of the world and now expect. Hosanna to the Son of David. Blessed is He that cometh in the Name of the Lord. Hosanna in the highest.

¶ *Which done, let them enter the quire. Let all the crosses be uncovered till after Vespers. As they enter they sing—*

℟. Lying men compassed me about: they scourged me without a cause. But Thou, O Lord, my defence, avenge me.

℣. Deliver me from my enemies, O God, defend me from them that rise up against me.

Collect. O Almighty. (See p. 113.)

¶ *Here the Mass begins.*

The Office. Ps. xxii.

But be not Thou far from me, O Lord: Thou art my succour, haste Thee to help me. Save me from the lion's mouth: Thou hast heard me also from among the horns of the unicorns.

Ps. My God, my God, look upon me: why hast Thou forsaken me?

* This and some similar Anthems are not italicized though not in the Bible.

The Collect.

Almighty and everlasting God, Who hast sent our Saviour to take upon Him our flesh, and to suffer death upon the Cross, that mankind should follow the example of His humility, mercifully grant that we may both follow the example of His patience, and also be made partakers of His resurrection, Through.

The Epistle. Phil. ii. 5-11.

Brethren, let this mind .... the glory of God the Father.

Gradual. Ps. lxxiii. For Thou hast holden me by my right hand. Thou shalt guide me with Thy counsel: and after that receive me with glory.

℣. Truly God is loving unto Israel: even unto such as are of a clean heart. Nevertheless, my feet were almost gone: my treadings had well nigh slipt. And why? I was grieved at the wicked: I do also see the ungodly in such prosperity.

Tract. Ps. xxii. My God, my God, look upon me: why hast Thou forsaken me,

℣. And art so far from my health, and from the words of my complaint?

℣. O my God, I cry in the day-time, but Thou hearest not: and in the night season also I take no rest.

℣. And Thou continuest holy: O Thou worship of Israel. Our fathers hoped in Thee: they trusted in Thee, and Thou didst deliver them.

℣. They called upon Thee, and were holpen: they put their trust in Thee, and were not confounded.

℣. But as for me, I am a worm, and no man: a very scorn of men, and the outcast of the people.

℣. All they that see me laugh me to scorn: they shoot out their lips, and shake their heads, saying,

℣. He trusted in God that He would deliver him: let Him deliver him, if He will have him.

℣. They stand staring and looking upon me. They part my garments among them: and cast lots upon my vesture.

℣. Save me from the lion's mouth: Thou hast heard me also from among the horns of the unicorns.

℣. O praise the Lord, ye that fear Him: magnify Him, all ye of the seed of Jacob.

℣. They shall be counted unto the Lord for a generation. They shall come, and the heavens shall declare his righteousness: unto a people that shall be born, whom the Lord hath made.

℣. The Lord be with you
℟. And with thy spirit.

The Passion of our Lord Jesus Christ according to Matthew.

¶ Glory *is not said.*

¶ *The Passion is sung or said in three tones—alto, bass, and tenor—for all are words either of the Jews, or of the Disciples, or of Christ, or of the Evangelist. Therefore, letter* a *signifies Jews and Disciples; letter* b *Christ; letter* t *the Evangelist. The same is observed in the other Passions.*

* *At that time* [t] Jesus said unto His disciples, [b] Ye know that after two days is *the feast of* the passover, and the Son of Man is betrayed to be crucified. [t] Then assembled together the chief priests, and the scribes, and the elders of the people, unto the palace of the High Priest, who was called Caiaphas, and consulted that they might take Jesus by subtilty and kill *Him.* But they said, [a] Not on the feast *day*, lest there be an uproar among the people. [t] Now when Jesus was in Bethany, in the house of Simon the leper, there came unto Him a woman having an alabaster box of very precious ointment, and poured it on His head, as He sat *at meat.* But when His disciples saw *it*, they had indignation, saying, [a] To what purpose is this waste? For this ointment might have been sold for much, and given to the poor. [t] When Jesus understood it, He said unto them, [b] Why trouble ye the woman? for she hath wrought a good work upon Me. For ye have the poor always with you; but Me ye have not always. For in that she hath poured this ointment on My Body, she did it for My burial. Verily, I say unto you, Wheresoever this gospel shall be preached in the whole world, there shall also this that this woman hath done be told for a memorial of her. [t] Then one of the twelve, called Judas Iscariot, went unto the chief priests, and said unto them, [a] What will ye give me, and I will deliver Him unto you? [t] And they covenanted with him for thirty pieces of silver. And from that time he sought opportunity to betray Him. Now the first day of the feast of unleavened bread the disciples came to Jesus, saying unto Him, [a] Where wilt Thou that we prepare for Thee to eat the passover? [t] And He said, [b] "Go into the city to such a man, and say unto him, The Master saith, My time is at hand; I will keep the passover at thy house with My disciples. [t] And the disciples did as Jesus appointed them; and they made ready the passover. Now when the even was come, He sat down with the twelve. And as thy did eat, He said, [b] Verily I say unto you, That one of you shall betray Me.

* Chap. xxvi

[t] And they were exceeding sorrowful, and began every one of them to say unto Him, [a] Lord, is it I? [t] And He answered and said, [b] He that dippeth his hand with Me in the dish, the same shall betray Me. The Son of Man goeth as it is written of Him: but woe unto that man by whom the Son of Man is betrayed! It had been good for that Man if he had not been born. [t] Then Judas, which betrayed Him, answered and said, [a] Master, is it I? [t] He said unto Him, [b] Thou hast said. [t] And as they were eating, Jesus took the bread, and blessed it, and brake it, and gave it to the disciples, and said, [b] Take, eat; this is My Body. [t] And He took the cup, and gave thanks, and gave it to them, saying, [b] Drink ye all of it; for this is My Blood of the New Testament, which is shed for many for the remission of sins. But I say unto you, I will not drink henceforth of this fruit of the vine, until that day when I drink it new with you in My Father's kingdom. [t] And when they had sung an hymn, they went out unto the Mount of Olives. Then saith the Lord unto them [b] All ye shall be offended because of Me this night: for it is written, I will smite the shepherd, and the sheep of the flock shall be scattered abroad. But after I am risen again, I will go before you into Galilee. [t] Peter said unto Him, [a] Though all men shall be offended because of Thee, yet will I never be offended. [t] Jesus said unto him, [b] Verily I say unto Thee, That this night, before the cock crow, thou shalt deny Me thrice. [t] Peter saith unto Him, [a] Though I should die with Thee, yet will I not deny Thee. [t] Likewise said all the disciples. Then cometh Jesus with them unto a place called Gethsemane, and saith unto the disciples, [b] Sit ye here while I go and pray yonder. [t] And He took with Him Peter and the two sons of Zebedee, and began to be sorrowful and very heavy. Then saith He unto them, [b] My soul is exceeding sorrowful, even unto death: tarry ye here, and watch with Me. [t] And He went a little further, and fell on His face, and prayed, saying, [b] O My Father, if it be possible, let this cup pass from Me: nevertheless, not as I will, but as Thou wilt. [t] And He cometh unto the disciples, and findeth them asleep, and saith unto Peter, [b] What, could ye not watch with Me one hour? Watch and pray, that ye enter not into temptation: the spirit indeed is willing, but the flesh is weak. [t] He went away again the second time, and prayed, saying, [b] O My Father, if this cup may not pass away from Me except I drink it, Thy will be done. [t] And He came and found them asleep again: for their eyes were heavy. And He left them, and went away again, and prayed the third time, saying the same words.

Then cometh He to His disciples, and said unto them, [b] Sleep on now, and take your rest; behold, the hour is at hand, and the Son of Man is betrayed into the hands of sinners. Rise, let us be going: behold, he is at hand that doth betray Me. [t] And while He yet spake, lo, Judas, one of the twelve, came, and with him a great multitude with swords and staves, from the chief priests and elders of the people. Now he that betrayed Him gave them a sign, saying, [a] Whomsoever I shall kiss, that same is He: hold Him fast. [t] And forthwith he came to Jesus, and said, [a] Hail, Master, [t] and kissed Him. And Jesus said unto him, [b] Friend, wherefore art thou come? [t] Then came they, and laid hands on Jesus and took Him. And, behold, one of them which were with Jesus stretched out his hand, and drew his sword, and struck a servant of the high priest's, and smote off his ear. Then said Jesus unto him, [b] Put up again thy sword into his place: for all they that take the sword shall perish with the sword. Thinkest thou that I cannot now pray to My Father, and He shall presently give Me more than twelve legions of angels? But how then shall the Scriptures be fulfilled, that thus it must be? [t] In that same hour said Jesus to the multitudes, [b] Are ye come out as against a thief with swords and staves for to take Me? I sat daily with you teaching in the temple, and ye laid no hold on Me. [t] But all this was done, that the scriptures of the prophets might be fulfilled. Then all the disciples forsook Him and fled. And they that had hold on Jesus led Him away to Caiaphas the high priest, where the scribes and the elders were assembled. But Peter followed him afar off unto the high priest's palace, and went in, and sat with the servants, to see the end. Now the chief priests, and elders, and all the council, sought false witness against Jesus to put Him to death, but found none: yea, though many false witnesses came, yet found they none. At the last came two false witnesses, and said, [a] This fellow said, I am able to destroy the temple of God, and to build it in three days. [t] And the high priest arose, and said unto Him, [a] Answerest Thou nothing? what is it which these witness against Thee? [t] But Jesus held His peace. And the high priest answered and said unto Him, [a] I adjure Thee by the living God, that Thou tell us whether Thou be the Christ, the Son of God. [t] Jesus said unto him, [b] Thou hast said: nevertheless I say unto you, Hereafter shall ye see the Son of Man sitting on the right hand of power, and coming in the clouds of heaven. [t] Then the high priest rent his clothes, saying, [a] He hath spoken blasphemy; what further need have we of witnesses? Behold, now we have heard of His blasphemy. What think ye? [t] They answered and said, [a] He is guilty of death. [t] Then did they spit in His face, and buffetted Him; and others smote Him with the palms of their hands saying, [a] Prophesy unto us, Thou Christ, Who is he that smote Thee? [t] Now Peter sat without in the palace: and a damsel came unto him, saying, [a] Thou also wast with Jesus of Galilee. [t] But he denied before them all, saying, [a] I know not what thou sayest. [t] And when he was gone out, into the porch, and another maid saw him, and said unto them that were there, [a] This fellow was also with Jesus of Nazareth. [t] And again he denied with an oath, I do not know the Man. And after a while came unto him they that stood by, and said to Peter, [a] Surely thou also art one of them; for thy speech bewrayeth thee. [t] Then began he to curse and to swear, saying, [a] I know not the Man. [t] And immediately the cock crew. And Peter remembered the word of Jesus, which said unto him, [b] Before the cock crow, thou shalt deny Me thrice. [t] And he went out, and wept bitterly. [*] When the morning was come, all the chief priests and elders of the people took counsel against Jesus to put Him to death. And when they had bound Him, they led Him away, and delivered Him to Pontius Pilate the governor. Then Judas who had betrayed Him, when he saw that He was condemned, repented himself, and brought again the thirty pieces of silver to the chief priests and elders, saying, [a] I have sinned, in that I betrayed the innocent blood. [t] And they said, [a] What is that to us? see thou to that. [t] And he cast down the pieces of silver in the temple, and departed, and went and hanged himself. And the chief priests took the pieces of silver, and said, [a] It is not lawful for to put them into the treasury, because it is the price of blood. [t] And they took counsel, and bought with them the potter's field, to bury strangers in. Wherefore that field was called, The field of blood, unto this day. (Then was fulfilled that which was spoken by Jeremy the prophet, saying, And they took the thirty pieces of silver, the price of Him that was valued whom they of the children of Israel did value, and gave them for the potter's field, as the Lord appointed me.) And Jesus stood before the governor; and the governor asked Him, saying, [b] Art Thou the King of the Jews? [t] And Jesus said unto him, [b] Thou sayest. [t] And when He was accused of the chief priests and elders, He answered nothing. Then said Pilate unto Him, [a] Hearest Thou not how many things they witness against Thee? [t] And He answered him to never a word, insomuch that the

[*] Chap. xxvii.

governor marvelled greatly. Now at that feast the governor was wont to release unto the people a prisoner, whom they would. And they had then a notable prisoner, called Barabbas. Therefore when they were gathered together, Pilate said unto them, [a] Whom will ye that I release unto you? Barabbas, or Jesus which is called Christ? [t] For he knew that for envy they had delivered Him. When he was set down on the judgment seat, his wife sent unto him, saying, [a] Have thou nothing to do with that just Man, for I have suffered many things this day in a dream because of Him. [t] But the chief priests and elders persuaded the multitude that they should ask Barabbas, and destroy Jesus. The governor answered and said unto them, [a] Whether of the twain will ye that I release unto you? [t] They said, [a] Barabbas. [t] Pilate saith unto them, [a] What shall I do then with Jesus, which is called Christ? [t] They all say unto him, [a] Let him be crucified. [t] And the governor said, [a] Why, what evil hath He done? [t] But they cried out the more, [a] Let him be crucified. [t] When Pilate saw that he could prevail nothing, but that rather a tumult was made, he took water and washed his hands before the multitude, saying, [a] I am innocent of the blood of this just person: see ye to it. [t] Then answered all the people, and said, [a] His blood be on us, and on our children. [t] Then released he Barabbas unto them: and when he had scourged Jesus he delivered Him to be crucified. Then the soldiers of the governor took Jesus into the common hall, and gathered unto Him the whole band of soldiers. And they stripped Him, and put on Him a scarlet robe. And when they had platted a crown of thorns they put it upon His head, and a reed in His right hand: and they bowed the knee before Him, and mocked Him, saying [a] Hail, King of the Jews. [t] And they spit upon Him, and took the reed and smote Him on the head. And after that they had mocked Him they took the robe from Him, and put His own raiment on Him, and led Him away to crucify Him. And as they came out they found a man of Cyrene, Simon by name; him they compelled to bear his cross. And when they were come unto a place called Golgotha, that is to say, a place of a skull, they gave Him vinegar to drink mingled with gall: and when He had tasted thereof, He would not drink. And they crucified Him, and parted His garments, casting lots: that it might be fulfilled, which was spoken by the prophet, They parted My garments among them, and upon My vesture did they cast lots. And sitting down they watched Him there; and set up over His head His accusation written, THIS IS JESUS THE KING OF THE JEWS. Then were there two thieves crucified with Him; one on the right hand, and another on the left. And they that passed by reviled Him, wagging their heads, and saying, [a] Thou that destroyest the temple, and buildest it in three days, save Thyself: if Thou be the Son of God, come down from the cross. [t] Likewise also the chief priests mocking Him, with the scribes and elders, said, [a] He saved others, Himself He cannot save: if He be the King of Israel, let Him now come down from the cross, and we will believe Him. He trusted in God; let Him deliver Him now, if He will have Him: for He said, I am the Son of God. [t] The thieves also, which were crucified with Him, cast the same in His teeth. Now from the sixth hour there was darkness over all the land unto the ninth hour. And about the ninth hour Jesus cried with a loud voice, saying, [t] Eli, Eli, lama sabachthani? [t] that is to say, My God, My God, why hast Thou forsaken Me? [t] Some of them that stood there, when they heard that, said, [a] This Man calleth for Elias. [t] And straightway one of them ran, and took a sponge, and filled it with vinegar, and put it on a reed, and gave Him to drink. The others said, [a] Let be, let us see whether Elias will come to save Him. [t] Jesus, when He had cried again with a loud voice, yielded up the ghost.

¶ *Here let the Deacon incline or prostrate himself towards the East, saying privately,* Our Father, Hail Mary, *and* Into Thy hands I commend my spirit: Thou hast redeemed me, O Lord God of truth. *Then let him rise and say the rest of the Passion.*

[t] And behold, the veil of the temple was rent in twain from the top to the bottom, and the earth did quake, and the rocks rent, and the graves were opened, and many bodies of saints which slept arose, and came out of the graves after His resurrection, and went into the holy city, and appeared unto many. Now when the centurion, and they that were with him, watching Jesus, saw the earthquake and those things that were done, they feared greatly, saying, [a] Truly this was the Son of God. [t] And many women were there beholding afar off, which followed Jesus from Galilee, ministering unto Him; among which was Mary Magdalene, and Mary the mother of James and Joses, and the mother of Zebedee's children. When the even was come, there came a rich man of Arimathæa, named Joseph, who also himself was Jesus' disciple: he went to Pilate, and begged the body of Jesus. Then Pilate commanded the body to be delivered. And when Joseph had taken the body, he wrapped it in a clean linen cloth, and laid it in his own new tomb which he had hewn

out in the rock: and he rolled a great stone to the door of the sepulchre, and departed. And there was Mary Magdalene, and the other Mary, sitting over against the sepulchre.

¶ *The Gospels at the end of all the Passions are to be said in alto tone, after the manner of a double Feast, even on Good Friday; but all the Passions are to be said in the manner aforesaid after Sarum Use.*

The Gospel.

Now the next day, that followed the day of the preparation, the chief priests and Pharisees came together unto Pilate, saying, Sir, we remember that that deceiver said, while He was yet alive, After three days I will rise again. Command therefore that the sepulchre be made sure until the third day, lest His disciples come by night, and steal Him away, and say unto the people, He is risen from the dead; so the last error shall be worse than the first. Pilate said unto them, Ye have a watch: go your way, make it as sure as ye can. So they went, and made the sepulchre sure sealing the stone, and setting a watch.

Offert. Ps. lxix. Thy rebuke hath broken My heart; I am full of heaviness: I looked for some to have pity on Me, but there was no man, neither found I any to comfort Me. They gave Me gall to eat; and when I was thirsty they gave Me vinegar to drink.

Secret. We offer unto Thee, O God, Father Almighty, the Paschal Sacrifice of the Immaculate Lamb, by Whose Blood we beseech Thee to deliver us from the ravages of the destroyer, and to lead us into the land of Thy new promise. Through.

Preface. The daily one.

Comm. Matt. xxvi. Father, if this cup may not pass away from Me except I drink it, Thy will be done.

P. Comm. We beseech Thee, O Lord, graciously look upon Thy faithful people, that they calling again to mind the beginning of their redemption, may profit more and more by those things the gift of which hath refreshed them. Through.

MONDAY IN HOLY WEEK.

The Office. Ps. xxxv.

Plead Thou my cause, O Lord, with them that strive with me: and fight Thou against them that fight against me. Lay hand upon the shield and buckler: and stand up to help me, *O Lord, the strength of my salvation.*

Ps. Bring forth the spear, and stop the way against them that persecute me.

The Collect.

Grant, we beseech Thee, O Almighty God, that we who, by reason of our weakness, faint under so many adversities, may recover by the pleading Passion of Thy only-begotten Son. Who.

The Lesson. Is. l. 5-10.

In those days said Isaiah, The Lord God hath opened mine ear .... and stay upon *the Lord* his God.

Gradual. Ps. xxxv. Awake, *O Lord,* and stand up to judge my quarrel : avenge Thou my cause, my God, and my Lord.

℣. Bring forth the spear, and stop the way against them that persecute me.

Tract. As on Ash-Wednesday.

The Gospel. John xii. 1-36.

Then Jesus, six days before the passover .... and did hide Himself from them.

Offert. Ps. cxliii. Deliver me, O Lord, from mine enemies : for I flee unto Thee to hide me. Teach me to do the thing that pleaseth Thee, for Thou art my God.

℣. Hearken unto me for Thy truth and righteousness' sake. And enter not into judgment with Thy servant, *O Lord.*

Secret. May this very oblation commend Thy faithful people unto Thy majesty, O Lord ; which, through Thy Son our Saviour Jesus Christ, hath reconciled them that were at enmity. Who.

Comm. Ps. xxxv. Let them be put to confusion and shame together, that rejoice at my trouble : let them be clothed with rebuke and dishonour, that boast themselves against me.

P. Comm. We, being filled with Thy saving gift, entreat Thy mercy, O Lord ; that by this same Sacrament, which is to us the means of growth in this life, Thou wilt make us partakers of life eternal. Through.

The Prayer over the People.

Help us, O God, our salvation ; and grant that we may come with joy to the commemoration of these benefits, by which Thou hast been pleased to redeem us. Through.

TUESDAY IN HOLY WEEK.

The Office. Gal. vi.

But we ought to glory in the Cross of our Lord Jesus Christ, *in Whom is our salvation, life, and resurrection; through Whom we are saved and set free.*

Ps. lxvii. God be merciful unto us, and bless us: and shew us the light of His countenance, and be merciful unto us.

The Collect.

O almighty and everlasting God, grant that we may so celebrate the mysteries of our Lord's Passion, that we may be found worthy to obtain pardon. Through.

The Lesson. Jer. xi. 18-20.

In those days said Jeremiah, O Lord, Thou hast given me knowledge .... for unto Thee have I revealed my cause, *O Lord my God.*

Gradual. Ps. xxxv. Nevertheless, when they were sick, I put on sackcloth, and humbled my soul with fasting: and my prayer shall turn into mine own bosom.

℣. Plead Thou my cause, O Lord, with them that strive with me: and fight Thou against them that fight against me. Lay hand upon the shield and buckler: and stand up to help me.

℣. The Lord be with you.

℟. And with thy spirit.

The Passion of our Lord Jesus Christ according to Mark.

[*] At that time [t] after two days was the feast of the passover, and of unleavened bread: and the chief priests and the scribes sought how they might take Him by craft, and put Him to death. But they said, [s] Not on the feast day, lest there be an uproar of the people. [t] And being in Bethany in the house of Simon the leper, as He sat at meat, there came a woman having an alabaster box of ointment of spikenard very precious; and she brake the box, and poured it on His head. And there were some that had indignation within themselves, and said, [s] Why was this waste of the ointment made? For it might have been sold for more than three hundred pence, and have been given to the poor. [t] And they murmured against her. And Jesus said, [b] Let her alone; why trouble ye her? she hath wrought a good work on Me. For ye have the poor with you always, and whensoever ye will ye may do them good; but Me ye have not always.

[*] Chap. xiv.

She hath done what she could: she is come aforehand to anoint My body to the burying. Verily, I say unto you, Wheresoever this gospel shall be preached throughout the whole world, this also that she hath done shall be spoken of for a memorial of her. [t]And Judas Iscariot, one of the twelve, went unto the chief priests, to betray Him unto them. And when they heard it, they were glad, and promised to give him money. And he sought how he might conveniently betray Him. And the first day of unleavened bread, when they killed the passover, His disciples said unto Him, [a]Where wilt Thou that we go and prepare that Thou mayest eat the passover? [t]And He sendeth forth two of His disciples, and saith unto them, [b]Go ye into the City, and there shall meet you a man bearing a pitcher of water: follow him. And wheresoever he shall go in, say ye to the goodman of the house, The Master saith, Where is the guestchamber, where I shall eat the passover with My disciples? And he will shew you a large upper room furnished and prepared; there make ready for us. [t]And His disciples went forth, and came into the city, and found as He had said unto them: and they made ready the passover. And in the evening He cometh with the twelve. And as they sat and did eat, Jesus said, [b]Verily I say unto you, one of you which eateth with Me shall betray Me. [t]And they began to be sorrowful, and to say unto Him one by one, [a]Is it I? [t]and another said, [a]Is it I? [t]And He answered and said unto them, [b]It is one of the twelve that dippeth with Me in the dish. The Son of Man indeed goeth, as it is written of Him: but woe to that man by whom the Son of Man is betrayed! Good were it for that man if he had never been born. [t]And as they did eat, Jesus took bread, and blessed, and brake it, and gave to them, and said, [b]Take, eat: this is My body. [t]And He took the cup, and when He had given thanks, He gave it to them; and they all drank of it. And he said unto them, [b]This is My blood of the New Testament, which is shed for many. Verily I say unto you, I will drink no more of the fruit of the vine, until that day that I drink it new in the kingdom of God. [t]And when they had sung an hymn, they went out into the Mount of Olives. And Jesus saith unto them, [b]All ye shall be offended because of Me this night: for it is written, I will smite the shepherd, and the sheep shall be scattered. But after that I am risen, I will go before you into Galilee. [t]But Peter said unto Him, [a]Although all shall be offended, yet will not I. [t]And Jesus saith unto him, [b]Verily, I say unto thee, That this day, even in this night, before the cock crow twice, thou shalt deny Me thrice. [t] But he spake the more vehemently, [a] If I should die with Thee, I will not deny Thee in any wise. [t] Likewise also said they all. And they came to a place which was named Gethsemane: and He said to His disciples, [b] Sit ye here, while I shall pray. [t] And He taketh with Him Peter and James and John, and began to be sore amazed, and to be very heavy; and saith unto them, [b] My soul is exceeding sorrowful unto death: tarry ye here and watch. [t] And He went forward a little, and fell on the ground, and prayed that, if it were possible, the hour might pass from Him. And He said, [b] Abba, Father, all things are possible unto Thee; take away this cup from Me: nevertheless not what I will, but what Thou wilt. [t] And He cometh, and findeth them sleeping, and saith unto Peter, [b] Simon, sleepest thou? couldest not thou watch one hour? Watch ye and pray, lest ye enter into temptation. The spirit truly is ready, but the flesh is weak. [t] And again He went away, and prayed, and spake the same words. And when He returned He found them asleep again (for their eyes were heavy), neither wist they what to answer Him. And He cometh the third time, and saith unto them, [b] Sleep on now, and take your rest: it is enough, the hour is come; behold, the Son of Man is betrayed into the hands of sinners. Rise up, let us go; lo, he that betrayed Me is at hand. [t] And immediately, while He yet spake, cometh Judas, one of the twelve, and with him a great multitude with swords and staves, from the chief priests and the scribes and the elders. And he that betrayed Him had given them a token, saying, [a] Whomsoever I shall kiss, that same is He; take Him, and lead Him away safely. [t] And as soon as he was come, he goeth straightway to Him, and saith, [a] Master, Master, [t] and kissed Him. And they laid their hands on Him, and took Him. And one of them that stood by drew a sword, and smote a servant of the high priest, and cut off his ear. And Jesus answered and said unto them, [b] Are ye come out, as against a thief, with swords and with staves to take Me? I was daily with you in the temple teaching, and ye took Me not: but the Scriptures must be fulfilled. [t] And they all forsook Him, and fled. And there followed Him a certain young man, having a linen cloth cast about his naked body; and the young man laid hold on him: and he left the linen cloth, and fled from them naked. And they led Jesus away to the high priest: and with him were assembled all the chief priests and the elders and the scribes. And Peter followed Him afar off, even into the palace of the high priest; and he sat with the servants, and warmed himself at the fire. And the chief priests and all the council sought for witnesses against Jesus to put Him to death; but found none. For many bare false witness against Him, but their witness agreed not together. And there arose certain, and bare false witness against Him, saying, [a]We heard Him say, I will destroy this temple that is made with hands, and within three days I will build another made without hands. [t]But neither so did their witness agree together. And the high priest stood up in the midst, and asked Jesus, saying, [a]Answerest Thou nothing? What is it which these witness against Thee? [t]But He held His peace, and answered nothing. Again the high priest asked Him, and said unto Him, [a]Art Thou the Christ, the Son of the Blessed? [t]And Jesus said, [b]I am: and ye shall see the Son of Man sitting on the right hand of power, and coming in the clouds of heaven. [t]Then the high priest rent his clothes, and saith [a]What need we any further witnesses? Ye have heard the blasphemy: what think ye? [t]And they all condemned Him to be guilty of death. And some began to spit on Him, and to cover His face, and to buffet Him, and to say unto Him, [a]Prophesy: [t]and the servants did strike Him with the palms of their hands. And as Peter was beneath in the palace, there cometh one of the maids of the high priest: and when she saw Peter warming himself, she looked upon him, and said, [a]And thou also wast with Jesus of Nazareth. [t]But he denied, saying, [a]I know not, neither understand I what thou sayest. [t]And he went out into the porch; and the cock crew. And a maid saw him again, and began to say to them that stood by, [a]This is one of them. [t]And he denied it again. And a little after, they that stood by said again to Peter, [a]Surely thou art one of them: for thou art a Galilæan, and thy speech agreeth thereto. [t]But he began to curse and to swear, saying, [a]I know not this man of whom ye speak. [t]And the second time the cock crew. And Peter called to mind the word that Jesus said unto him, Before the cock crow twice, thou shalt deny Me thrice. And when he thought thereon, he wept. *And straightway in the morning the chief priests held a consultation with the elders, and scribes, and the whole council, and bound Jesus, and carried Him away, and delivered Him to Pilate. And Pilate asked Him, [a]Art Thou the King of the Jews? [t]And He answering said unto him, [a]Thou sayest it. [t]And the chief priests accused Him of many things: but He answered nothing. And Pilate asked Him again, saying, [a]Answerest Thou nothing? behold how many things they witness against Thee. [t]But Jesus yet answered

* Chap. xv.

nothing: so that Pilate marvelled. Now at the feast he released unto them one prisoner, whomsoever they desired. And there was one named Barabbas, which lay bound with them that had made insurrection with him, who had committed murder in the insurrection. And the multitude, crying aloud, began to desire him to do as he had ever done unto them. But Pilate answered them, saying, [a] Will ye that I release unto you the King of the Jews? [t] For he knew that the chief priests had delivered Him for envy. But the chief priests moved the people, that he should rather release Barabbas unto them. And Pilate answered, and said again unto them, [a] What will ye then that I shall do unto Him Whom ye call the King of the Jews? [t] And they cried out again, [a] Crucify Him. [t] Then Pilate said unto them, [a] Why, what evil hath He done? [t] And they cried out the more exceedingly, [a] Crucify Him. [t] And so Pilate, willing to content the people, released Barabbas unto them, and delivered Jesus, when he had scourged Him, to be crucified. And the soldiers led Him away into the hall, called Prætorium; and they call together the whole band. And they clothed Him with purple, and platted a crown of thorns, and put it about His head; and began to salute Him, [a] Hail, King of the Jews. [t] And they smote Him on the head with a reed, and did spit upon Him, and bowing their knees worshipped Him. And when they had mocked Him, they took off the purple from Him, and put His own clothes on Him, and led Him out to crucify Him. And they compel one Simon a Cyrenian, who passed by, coming out of the country, the father of Alexander and Rufus, to bear His Cross. And they bring Him unto the place Golgotha, which is, being interpreted, The place of a skull. And they gave Him to drink wine mingled with myrrh; but He received it not. And when they had crucified Him, they parted His garments, casting lots upon them, what every man should take. And it was the third hour, and they crucified Him. And the superscription of His accusation was written over, THE KING OF THE JEWS. And with Him they crucify two thieves, the one on His right hand, and the other on His left. And the Scripture was fulfilled, which saith, And He was numbered with the transgressors. And they that passed by railed on Him, wagging their heads, and saying, [a] Ah, Thou that destroyest the temple, and buildest it in three days, save Thyself, and come down from the Cross. [t] Likewise also the chief priests mocking said among themselves with the scribes, [a] He saved others; Himself He cannot save. Let Christ the King of Israel descend now from the Cross, that we may see and believe. [t] And they that were crucified with Him reviled Him. And when the sixth hour was come, there was darkness over the whole land until the ninth hour. And at the ninth hour Jesus cried with a loud voice, saying, [b] Eloi, Eloi, lama sabachthani? [t] which is, being interpreted, My God, My God, why hast Thou forsaken Me? [t] And some of them that stood by, when they heard it, said, [s] Behold, He calleth Elias. [t] And one ran and filled a sponge full of vinegar, and put it on a reed, and gave Him to drink, saying, [s] Let alone; let us see whether Elias will come to take Him down. [t] And Jesus cried with a loud voice, and gave up the ghost.

¶ *Here let them kneel, saying*, Our Father, Hail Mary, Into Thy hands.

[t] And the veil of the temple was rent in twain from the top to the bottom. And when the centurion, which stood over against Him, saw that He so cried out, and gave up the ghost, he said, [s] Truly this Man was the Son of God. [t] There were also women looking on afar off; among whom was Mary Magdalene, and Mary the mother of James the less and of Joses, and Salome (who also, when He was in Galilee, followed Him, and ministered unto Him); and many other women which came up with Him unto Jerusalem.

The Gospel.

And now when the even was come, because it was the preparation, that is, the day before the Sabbath, Joseph of Arimathæa, an honourable counsellor, which also waited for the kingdom of God, came, and went in boldly unto Pilate, and craved the body of Jesus. And Pilate marvelled if he were already dead: and calling unto him the centurion, he asked him whether he had been any while dead. And when he knew it of the centurion, he gave the body to Joseph. And he bought fine linen, and took Him down, and wrapped Him in the linen, and laid him in a sepulchre which was hewn out of a rock, and rolled a stone unto the door of the sepulchre.

Offert. Ps. cxl. Keep me, O Lord, from the hands of the ungodly: preserve me from the wicked men:

℣. Who are purposed to overthrow my goings. The proud have laid a snare for me.

Secret. Sanctify, O Lord, we beseech Thee, the oblations of Thy people; that, cleansed from the conversation of the old man, we may be renewed by progress in divine life. Through.

Comm. Ps. lxix. They that sit in the gate speak against me: and the drunkards make songs upon me. But, Lord, I make my prayer unto Thee: in an acceptable time. Hear me, O God, in the multitude of Thy mercy.

P. Comm. We, being filled with the grace of Thy holy gifts, humbly beseech Thee that what in adoration we have thought sweet to our bodily taste, we may perceive to be more exceeding sweet to our souls. Through.

The Prayer over the People.

May Thy mercy, O God, purify us from the corruption of the old man, and enable us to put on the new. Through.

WEDNESDAY IN HOLY WEEK.

The Office. Phil. ii.

At the Name of *the Lord* every knee should bow, of things in heaven, and things in earth, and things under the earth; *because the Lord* became obedient unto death, even the death of the Cross. Therefore Jesus Christ is Lord, to the glory of God the Father.

Ps. cii. Hear my prayer, O Lord: and let my crying come unto Thee.

Let us pray.
D. Let us kneel.
D. Rise.

The Collect.

Grant, we beseech Thee, Almighty God, that we who continually are punished for our evil deeds, may be delivered by the Passion of Thy only-begotten Son. Who.

The Lesson. Is. lxii. 11—lxiii. 1-7.

Thus saith the Lord God, say ye to the daughter of Sion ...... according to all that the Lord *our God* hath bestowed on us.

Gradual. Ps. lxix. Hide not Thy face from Thy servant, for I am in trouble: O haste Thee, and hear me.

℣. Save me, O God: for the waters are come in even unto my soul. I stick fast in the deep mire, where no ground is.

¶ *Here followeth* The Lord be with you, *etc.*

The Collect.

O God, Who didst will Thy Son to suffer on the Cross, that Thou mightest drive away the power of the enemy, grant that we Thy servants may obtain the grace of His resurrection. Through.

¶ *Here follow the usual Memorials.*

The Lesson. Is. lii. 1-10, 12.

In those days said Isaiah, Who hath believed our report? ...... intercession with the transgressors, *that they should not perish, saith the Lord God Almighty.*

Tract. Ps. cii. Hear my prayer, O Lord: and let my crying come unto Thee.

℣. Hide not Thy face from me in the time of my trouble: incline Thine ear unto me.

℣. When I call: O hear me, and that right soon.

℣. For my days are consumed away like smoke: and my bones are burnt up as it were a fire-brand.

℣. My heart is smitten down, and withered like grass: so that I forget to eat my bread.

℣. Thou, *O Lord,* shalt arise, and have mercy upon Sion; for it is time that Thou have mercy upon her.

The Lord be with you.

The Passion of our Lord Jesus Christ according to Luke.

[a] *At that time* [t] the feast of unleavened bread drew nigh, which is called the Passover. And the chief priests and scribes sought how they might kill Him; for they feared the people. Then entered Satan into Judas, surnamed Iscariot, being of the number of the twelve. And he went his way, and communed with the chief priests and captains, how he might betray Him unto them. And they were glad, and covenanted to give Him money. And he promised, and sought opportunity to betray Him unto them in the absence of the multitude. Then came the day of unleavened bread, when the passover must be killed. And He sent Peter and John, saying, [b] go and prepare us the passover, that we may eat. [t] And they said unto Him, [s] Where wilt Thou that we prepare? [t] And He said unto them, [b] Behold, when ye are entered into the city, there shall be a man meet you, bearing a pitcher of water; follow him into the house where he entereth in. And ye shall say unto the goodman of the house, The Master saith unto thee, Where is the guestchamber, where I shall eat the passover with My disciples? And he shall shew you a large upper room furnished: there make ready. [t] And they went, and found as He had said unto them: and they made

[a] Chap. xxii.

ready the passover. And when the hour was come He sat down, and the twelve Apostles with Him. And He said unto them, [b] With desire I have desired to eat this passover with you before I suffer: for I say unto you, I will not any more eat thereof, until it be fulfilled in the Kingdom of God. [t] And He took the cup, and gave thanks, and said, [b] Take this, and divide it among yourselves. For I say unto you, I will not drink of the fruit of the vine, until the Kingdom of God shall come. [t] And He took bread, and gave thanks, and brake it, and gave unto them, saying, [b] This is My body, which is given for you: this do in remembrance of Me. [t] Likewise also the cup after supper, saying, [b] This cup is the New Testament in My blood, which is shed for you. But behold, the hand of him that betrayeth Me is with Me on the table. And truly the Son of Man goeth as it was determined; but woe unto that man by whom He is betrayed. [t] And they began to inquire among themselves, which of them it was that should do this thing. And there was also a strife among them, which of them should be accounted the greatest. And He said unto them, [b] The kings of the Gentiles exercise lordship over them, and they that exercise authority upon them are called benefactors. But ye shall not be so: but he that is greatest among you, let him be as the younger; and he that is chief, as he that doth serve. For whether is greater, he that sitteth at meat, or he that serveth? is not he that sitteth at meat? but I am among you, as He that serveth. Ye are they which have continued with Me in My temptations. And I appoint unto you a kingdom, as My Father hath appointed unto Me; that ye may eat and drink at My table in My kingdom, and sit on the thrones, judging the twelve tribes of Israel. [t] And the Lord said, [b] Simon, Simon, behold, Satan hath desired to have you, that he may sift you as wheat; but I have prayed for thee, that thy faith fail not; and when thou art converted, strengthen thy brethren. [t] And he said unto Him, [a] Lord, I am ready to go with Thee both into prison and to death. [t] And He said, [b] I tell thee, Peter, the cock shall not crow this day, before that thou shalt thrice deny that thou knowest Me. [t] And He said unto them, [b] When I sent you without purse, and scrip, and shoes, lacked ye any thing? [t] And they said, [a] Nothing. [t] Then said He unto them, [b] But now, he that hath a purse, let him take it, and likewise his scrip: and he that hath no sword, let him sell his garment, and buy one. For I say unto you, That this that is written must yet be accomplished in Me, And He was reckoned among the transgressors: for the things concerning Me have an end. [t] And they said, [a] Lord, behold, here are two swords. [t] And He said unto them, [b] It is enough. [t] And He came out, and went, as He was wont, to the Mount of Olives, and His disciples also followed Him. And when He was at the place, He said unto them, [b] Pray, that ye enter not into temptation. [t] And He was withdrawn from them about a stone's cast, and kneeled down and prayed, saying, [b] Father, if Thou be willing, remove this cup from Me: nevertheless, not My will, but Thine be done. [t] And there appeared an angel unto Him from Heaven strengthening Him. And being in an agony, He prayed more earnestly; and His sweat was as it were great drops of blood falling down to the ground. And when He rose up from prayer, and was come to His disciples, He found them sleeping for sorrow, and said unto them, [b] Why sleep ye? rise and pray, lest ye enter into temptation. [t] And while He yet spake, behold, a multitude, and he that was called Judas, one of the twelve, went before them, and drew near unto Jesus to kiss Him. And Jesus said unto him, [b] Judas, betrayest thou the Son of Man with a kiss? [t] When they who were about Him saw what would follow, they said unto Him, [a] Lord, shall we smite with the sword? [t] And one of them smote the servant of the high priest, and cut off his right ear. And Jesus answered and said, [b] Suffer ye thus far. [t] And He touched his ear, and healed him. Then Jesus said unto the chief priests, and captains of the temple, and the elders who were come to Him, [b] Be ye come out as against a thief, with swords and staves? When I was daily with you in the temple, ye stretched forth no hands against Me: but this is your hour, and the power of darkness. [t] Then took they Him, and led Him, and brought Him into the high priest's house: and Peter followed afar off. And when they had kindled a fire in the midst of the hall, and were set down together, Peter sat down among them. But a certain maid beheld him, as he sat by the fire, and earnestly looked upon him, and said, [a] This man was also with Him. [t] And he denied Him, saying, [a] Woman, I know Him not. [t] And after a little while another saw him, and said, [a] Thou art also of them. [t] And Peter said, [a] Man, I am not. [t] And about the space of one hour after, another confidently affirmed, saying, [a] Of a truth this fellow was also with Him; for he is a Galilæan. [t] And Peter said, [a] Man, I know not what thou sayest. [t] And immediately, while he yet spake, the cock crew. And the Lord turned, and looked upon Peter; and Peter remembered the word of the Lord, how He had said unto him, Before the cock crow, thou shalt deny Me thrice.

And Peter went out, and wept bitterly. And the men that hel
Jesus mocked Him, and smote Him. And when they had blind
folded Him, they struck Him on the face, and asked Him, say-
ing, [a] Prophesy, who is it that smote Thee? [t] And many othe
things blasphemously spake they against Him. And as soon a
it was day, the elders of the people, and the chief priests, an
the scribes, came together, and led Him into their council, say-
ing, [a] Art thou the Christ? tell us. [t] And He said unto them
[b] If I tell you, ye will not believe: and if I also ask you, ye wil
not answer Me, nor let Me go. Hereafter shall the Son of Ma
sit on the right hand of the power of God. [t] Then said they all
[a] Art Thou the Son of God? [t] And He said unto them, [b] Y
say that I am. [t] And they said, [a] What need we any further wit-
ness? for we ourselves have heard of His own mouth. *[t] An
the whole multitude of them arose, and led Him unto Pilate
And they began to accuse Him, saying, [a] We found this fellow
perverting the nation, and forbidding to give tribute to Cæsar,
saying that He Himself is Christ a King. [t] And Pilate aske
Him saying, [a] Art Thou the King of the Jews? [t] And H
answered him and said, [b] Thou sayest it. [t] Then said Pilate to
the chief priests and to the people, [a] I find no fault in this Man.
[t] And they were the more fierce, saying, [a] He stirreth up the
people, teaching throughout all Jewry, beginning from Galilee
to this place. [t] When Pilate heard of Galilee, he asked whether
the Man were a Galilæan. And as soon as he knew that He
belonged unto Herod's jurisdiction, he sent Him to Herod, who
himself also was at Jerusalem at that time. And when Herod
saw Jesus, he was exceeding glad: for he was desirous to see
Him of a long season, because he had heard many things of
Him; and he hoped to have seen some miracle done by Him.
Then he questioned with him in many words; but He answered
him nothing. And the chief priests and scribes stood and vehe-
mently accused Him. And Herod with his men of war set Him
at nought, and mocked Him, and arrayed Him in a gorgeous
robe, and sent Him again to Pilate. And the same day Pilate
and Herod made friends together: for before they were at
enmity between themselves. And Pilate, when he had called
together the chief priests and the rulers and the people, said unto
them, [a] Ye have brought this Man unto me, as one that perverteth
the people: and, behold, I, having examined Him before you,
have found no fault in this Man touching those things whereof
ye accuse Him. No, nor yet Herod: for I sent you to him; and,
lo, nothing worthy of death is done unto Him. I will therefore

* Chap. xxiii.

chastise Him, and release Him. [a](For of necessity he must release one of them at the feast.) And they cried out all at once, saying, [a]Away with this Man, and release unto us Barabbas. [a](Who for a certain sedition made in the city, and for murder, was cast into prison.) Pilate therefore, willing to release Jesus, spake again to them. But they cried, saying, [a]Crucify Him, crucify Him. [a]And he said unto them the third time, [a]Why, what evil hath He done? I have found no cause of death in Him: I will therefore chastise Him, and let Him go. [a]And they were instant with loud voices requiring that He might be crucified. And the voices of them and of the chief priests prevailed. And Pilate gave sentence that it should be as they required. And he released unto them him that for sedition and murder was cast into prison, whom they had desired; but he delivered Jesus to their will. And as they led Him away, they laid hold upon one Simon, a Cyrenian, coming out of the country, and on him they laid the cross, that he might bear it after Jesus. And there followed Him a great company of people, and of women, which also bewailed and lamented Him. But Jesus turning unto them said, [b]Daughters of Jerusalem, weep not for Me, but weep for yourselves, and for your children. For, behold, the days are coming, in which they shall say, Blessed are the barren, and the wombs that never bare, and the paps that never gave suck. Then shall they begin to say to the mountains, Fall on us; and to the hills, Cover us. For if they do these things in a green tree, what shall be done in the dry? [a]And there were also two other, malefactors, led with Him to be put to death. And when they were come to the place which is called Calvary, there they crucified Him, and the malefactors one on the right hand, and the other on left. Then said Jesus, [b]Father, forgive them: for they know not what they do. [a]And they parted His raiment, and cast lots. And the people stood beholding. And the rulers also with them derided Him, saying, [a]He saved others; let Him save Himself, if He be Christ, the chosen of God. [a]And the soldiers also mocked Him, coming to Him, and offering Him vinegar, and saying, [a]If Thou be the King of the Jews, save Thyself. [a]And a superscription also was written over Him in letters of Greek, and Latin, and Hebrew, THIS IS THE KING OF THE JEWS. And one of the malefactors which were hanged railed on Him, saying, [a]If Thou be Christ, save Thyself and us. [a]But the other answering rebuked him, saying, [a]Dost not thou fear God, seeing thou art in the same condemnation? And we indeed justly;

for we receive the due reward of our deeds: but this Man hath done nothing amiss. [t]And he said unto Jesus, [b]Lord, remember me when Thou comest into Thy kingdom. [t]And Jesus said unto him, [b]Verily I say unto thee, To-day shalt thou be with Me in Paradise. [t]And it was about the sixth hour, and there was a darkness over all the earth until the ninth hour. And the sun was darkened, and the veil of the temple was rent in the midst.

¶ *Here let the veil before the Altar fall.*

[t]And when Jesus had cried with a loud voice, He said, [b]Father, into Thy hands I commend My spirit. [t]And having said thus, He gave up the ghost.

¶ *Here let them kneel, saying,* Our Father; Hail, Mary; Into Thy hands.

[t]Now when the centurion saw what was done, he glorified God, saying, [a]Certainly this was a righteous man. [t]And all the people that came together to that sight, beholding the things which were done, smote their breasts and returned. And all His acquaintance, and the women that followed Him from Galilee, stood afar off, beholding these things.

The Gospel.

And, behold, there was a man named Joseph, a counsellor; and he was a good man and a just (the same had not consented to the counsel and deed of them): he was of Arimathæa, a city of the Jews; who also himself waited for the kingdom of God. This man went unto Pilate, and begged the body of Jesus. And he took it down, and wrapped it in linen, and laid it in a sepulchre that was hewn in stone, wherein never man before was laid.

Offert. Ps. cii. Hear my prayer, O Lord: and let my crying come unto Thee.

℣. Hide not Thy face from me: *hide not Thy face from me.*

Secret. Accept, O Lord, we beseech Thee, the gift now offered; and mercifully grant that we may apprehend with pious affections that which by the mystery of the Passion of Thy Son our Lord we do set forth. Through.

Comm. Ps. cii. I mingled my drink with weeping; for Thou hast taken me up, and cast me down: and I am withered like grass. But Thou, O Lord, shalt endure for ever. Thou shalt arise, and have mercy upon Sion: for it is time that Thou have mercy upon her.

P. Comm. Quicken our understandings, Almighty God, that by the death in this world of Thy Son, which the adorable mysteries do testify, we may surely trust Thou hast given us eternal life. Through.

The Prayer over the People.

O Lord, we beseech Thee, behold this Thy family, for which our Lord Jesus Christ was contented to be betrayed into the hands of wicked men, and to suffer death upon the Cross. Who.

Maundy Thursday.

RECONCILIATION OF PENITENTS.

¶ *After Nones let the Priest of highest rank, in red silk cope, with two Deacons in amice, without Sub-Deacon or Cross, go to the west door through the quire, preceded by the sackcloth banner; let the Penitents be in the vestibule. If the Bishop is present, let the senior Archdeacon, in silk cope, without the door, read as follows in behalf of the Penitents:—*

The accepted time is come, O reverend Prelate, the day of Divine propitiation and salvation of men: when death was abolished and eternal life began; when a planting of new vines is so to be made in the vineyard of the Lord of Hosts, that the blindness of the old man may be purged away. For albeit no time is devoid of the riches of the Lord's goodness, yet now forgiveness of sins is more ample by reason of His indulgence, and the admission of those that are beginning a new life is more free by reason of His grace. By those to be regenerated we gain numbers, by those who return we gain strength. Water washeth, tears wash; hence there is joy over the receiving of the called, and joy at the absolution of penitents. Hence it is that thy suppliants, after that by neglect of the Divine Commandments and transgression of approved ordinances they have fallen into divers sins, in lowly prostration cry unto God in the words of the Prophet, saying, We have sinned with our fathers, we have dealt wickedly, we have committed iniquity; have mercy upon us, O Lord, who turn not a deaf ear to the saying of the Gospel, Blessed are they that mourn, for they shall be comforted. As it is written, They have eaten the bread of affliction, they have watered their couch with tears: they have afflicted their soul by grief and their body by fasting, that they may recover the health of their souls which they had lost. Therefore it is the singular privilege of penitence, that it is both profitable to individuals, and conduceth to the common welfare of all. Renew, therefore, in them, O Apostolic Prelate, whatsoever hath been decayed by the suggestion, rage, and malice of the devil; by the merit of thy prayers on their behalf make these men near to God through the grace of Divine reconciliation: that they who were before displeasing in their perverse ways may now get the victory over the author of their death, and rejoice to please the Lord in the land of the living.

¶ *Then let the Bishop or Officiant begin the Ant.,* Come ye, *below the said door, turning to the North, making sign of the Cross as it were beckoning. Then let the Deacon, for the Penitents, outside the door, say,* Let us kneel. *Let another Deacon, for the Bishop, say,* Rise, *and this thrice; but after the third* Come ye, *let the Choir proceed with the whole Ant., the Precentor beginning,* Children hearken unto me, I will teach you the fear of the Lord; *Ps.,* I will bless; *with* Glory, *the Ant. repeated after each verse. While Ps. is chanted with Ant. by Choir, let the Penitents be handed one by one to the Officiating Priest by some Priest of the Choir, without change of habit; and by him be restored to the bosom of the Church. If the Bishop be present, let the Penitents be handed by the Priest to the Archdeacon, and by him to the Bishop, and by Him be restored to the bosom of the Church; then let the procession return as usual to the quire. Then let all kneel, and the Clergy in the quire say the seven Pentitential Psalms, with* Glory; *the officiating Priest and his ministrants saying them by themselves, with Ant.,* Remember not, *as on Ash-Wednesday, down to*

Let us pray.

Be present, O Lord, at our supplications, and graciously listen unto me, who specially stand in need of Thy pity; and grant unto me, whom not by election of merit, but by the gift of Thy grace Thou hast appointed unto this ministry, confidence in fulfilling the duty Thou hast laid upon me, and do Thou of Thy loving kindness work in our administration. Through.

Let us pray.

O God, most gracious Creator and most compassionate Restorer of mankind, Who by the Blood of Thine only Son hast redeemed man, by the envy of the devil cast down from immortality, quicken these Thy servants whom Thou desirest in no wise to die to Thee; and as Thou dost not leave them to stray, receive them when chastised. Let the sorrowful sighings of these Thy servants, O Lord, we beseech Thee, move Thy loving kindness. Heal Thou their wounds, stretch out Thy saving hand to them as they lie before Thee. Let not Thy Church be robbed of any part of her body; let not Thy flock suffer loss; let not the enemy rejoice over the losses of Thy family; let not a second death have possession of those that were regenerated by the saving laver.

Unto Thee, therefore, O Lord, we humbly offer our prayers; before Thee we pour forth the sorrows of our heart. Spare Thou them that confess; by Thy aid let them so weep over their sins in this mortal life, that in the day of terrible judgment they may escape the sentence of eternal damnation. Most holy Father, spare them the knowledge of the terrors of darkness, of wailing in flames; let them returning from the error of their ways unto the path of righteousness suffer no more mortal wounds, but let that which Thy grace hath bestowed on them, and the reformation which Thy pity hath worked in them, be made whole and entire, and abide in them for ever. Through.

Let us pray.

O Lord, Holy Father, Almighty, everlasting God, Who hast deigned to heal our wounds; we Thy humble priests entirely desire Thee of Thy goodness to incline Thine ears unto our prayers, and by our confession be Thou moved to repent Thee. Forgive all our offences, have mercy on the sins of the whole world; grant to these Thy servants, O Lord, pardon for punishment, joy for mourning, life for death, that they who at the mighty prospect of the heights of Heaven have sunk down from their confidence in Thy compassion, may be accounted worthy to attain unto the blessings of the reward of Thy peace, and unto the gifts of Heaven. Through.

¶ *Here let the priest turn to the people, and stretch out his hand, and say the Absolution without tone—*

We absolve you in place of blessed Peter, Prince of Apostles, to whom hath been given by the Lord the power of binding and loosing; and so far as self-accusation pertaineth to you and remission to us, may Almighty God be unto you life and health, and the gracious pardoner of all your sins. Who.

¶ *Then let all rise and kiss the benches or earth. If the Bishop be present, let him give the Blessing whilst they kneel.*

¶ *Here let the Mass begin.*

The Office. Gal. vi.

But we ought to glory in the Cross of Jesus Christ our Lord, *in Whom is our salvation, life, and resurrection, through Whom we are saved and set free.*

Ps. lxvii. God be merciful unto us, and bless us: and shew us the light of His countenance, and be merciful unto us.

¶ Glory be *if Bishop celebrates. Chant of* Conditor Kyrie *is used without the verses whether Bishop celebrates or not.* Gloria in Excelsis *is said if Bishop celebrates.* Let us pray *is said without* Kneel, etc.

The Collect.

O God, from Whom both the traitor Judas received the punishment of his crime, and the thief the reward of his confession, grant us the full effect of Thy propitiation, that as our Lord Jesus Christ at the time of His Passion rendered unto each according to their deservings, so having destroyed the old man in us, He may bestow upon us the grace of His resurrection. Who

The Epistle. 1 Cor. xi 20-32.

Brethren, when ye come together .... that we should not be condemned with the world.

¶ *Let this Epistle be read in the pulpit, and then this* Gradual *be said by two boys in surplices—*

Gradual. Phil. ii. *Christ* became obedient *for us* unto death, even the death of the Cross.

℣. Wherefore God also hath highly exalted Him, and given Him a name which is above every name.

¶ *If the Bishop celebrates, let the* Gradual *not be repeated. Let the Gospel be said in the pulpit as on Sundays unless the Bishop celebrate, when it must be sung after the manner of a double feast.*

The Gospel. John xiii. 1-15.

Now before the feast of the Passover .... that ye should do as I have done to you.

¶ Creed *if the Bishop celebrates.*

Offert. Ps. cxviii. The right hand of the Lord hath the pre-eminence: the right hand of the Lord bringeth mighty things to pass. I shall not die, but live; and declare the works of the Lord.

¶ *Three Hosts are to be consecrated this day; one to be received by the Priest, two to be reserved with the Cross in the sepulchre.*

Secret. We beseech Thee, O Lord, Holy Father, Almighty, eternal God, that He Himself may make our Sacrifice acceptable unto Thee, Who, according to this day's tradition, set forth this to be done by His disciples in remembrance of Him, even Jesus Christ our Lord. Who.

Preface. The daily one; *and the* Sanctus *is to be solemnly sung.*

In the Canon, Communicating with; *and* This therefore; *and* Who the day before.

¶ *For the Service of Consecration of Holy Oils which comes here, see Appendix*

¶ *No* Agnus Dei *or* Peace *is given unless the Bishop celebrate, in which case see Appendix with Service of Holy Oils.*

Comm. John xiii. *The Lord Jesus, after He had supped with His disciples, washed their feet, and* said unto them, Know ye what I have done unto you? I, *your Lord and Master,* have given you an example, that ye should do as I have done.

¶ *After* Comm. *let Vespers begin as for a feast, without rulers of the Choir, and without* O God, make speed. *Let the Ant.,* I will take the cup of salvation and call upon the Name of the Lord, *be begun by one of the superior form.*

Ps. cxvi. I believed (*without* Glory, *and so all the rest*).

Ant. With them that are enemies unto peace, I labour for peace; but when I speak unto them thereof, they make them ready for battle.

Ps. cxx. When I was in trouble.

Ant. Keep me, O Lord, from the hands of the ungodly.

Ps. cxl. Deliver me, O Lord, from the evil man.

Ant. Keep me from the snare that they have laid for me, and from the traps of the wicked doers.

Ps. cxli. Lord, I call upon Thee.

Ant. I looked also upon my right hand, and saw there was no man that would know me.

Ps. cxlii. I cried unto the Lord.

Ant. As they did eat, Jesus took bread, and blessed it, and brake it, and gave to His disciples.

Magnificat.

¶ *Ant. being repeated, let the Priest say—*

The Lord be with you.

Let us pray.

P. Comm. We, being refreshed by life-giving sustenance, beseech Thee, O Lord our God, that we may, in Thy gift of immortality, attain that which in the time of our mortal life we follow after. Through.

¶ *If a Bishop celebrates, let Mass and Vespers finish together with* Ite Missa est: *if not, with* Let us give thanks unto the Lord.

ABLUTION OF THE ALTARS.

¶ *After refection, let the Clergy assemble at church to wash the Altars, and perform the Maundy, and say Compline. First, let the water be blessed in the usual way, privately, outside the choir. Then let two Priests of higher rank be ready with Deacon and Sub-Deacon of second form, and Candle bearer of first form, all in albs and amices, and two Clergy bearing wine and water; and begin at the High Altar and wash it, pouring on it wine and water, whilst the* ℟., On the Mount of Olives, *is sung by the whole Choir before the Altar, with its* ℣., *and without* Glory.

1. ℟. *On the Mount of Olives I prayed to the Father:* Father, if it be possible, let this cup pass from Me: the spirit indeed is willing, but the flesh is weak. Thy will be done.

℣. Nevertheless, not as I will, but as Thou wilt. Thy will.

¶ *Which ended, the* ℣. *and Collect of the Saint in whose honour the Altar is consecrated is said in low voice, without tone or* The Lord be. *So let all the Altars in the church be washed, with* ℟. *and* ℣. *and prayers as aforesaid; provided no* ℟. *begin except before the Altar, and be there chanted entire. At the end of each ablution, let the* ℟., Lying men, *be sung with its* ℣.

2. ℟. Lying men compassed Me about; they scourged Me without a cause: but Thou, O Lord, My defence, avenge Me.

℣. For trouble is hard at hand, and there is none to help. But Thou.

3. ℟. My soul is exceeding sorrowful, even unto death, tarry ye here and watch with Me: *now shall ye see the multitude which will compass Me about. Ye will flee, and I will go and be sacrificed for you.*

℣. Behold, the hour is at hand, and the Son of Man shall be delivered into the hands of sinners. Ye will.

4. ℟. Lo! we have seen He hath no form nor comeliness, there is no beauty in Him. He hath borne our sins, and *sorroweth for us;* but He was wounded for our offences; by His stripes we are healed.

℣. Surely He hath borne our griefs and carried our sorrows. By His.

5. ℟. One of My disciples shall betray Me *to-day:* woe to that man by whom I am betrayed. Good were it for that man if He had never been born.

℣. He that dippeth his hand with Me in the dish, the same shall betray Me *into the hands of sinners.* Good.

6. ℟. Judas the wicked trafficker kissed the Lord: He as an innocent lamb refused not the kiss of Judas: for a sum of money He betrayed Christ to the Jews.

℣. Drunken with the poison of covetousness, whilst he thirsts after gain, he comes to hanging. For a sum.

7. ℟. Could not ye, *who declared ye would die for Me,* watch with Me one hour? *And see ye not Judas, how he sleepeth not, but hasteneth to betray Me to the Jews?*

℣. Sleep on now and take your rest; behold, he that betrayeth Me is at hand. And see ye.

8. ℟. The elders of the people took counsel, that they might take Jesus by subtilty and kill Him. *They came* out as against a thief with swords and staves.

℣. They imagined wickedness with themselves, and went out. They came out.

9. ℟. O Judas, who hast cast away the counsels of peace, and hast covenanted with the Jews for thirty pieces of silver, thou hast sold the just blood: and thou gavest the kiss of peace, which thou hadst not in thy breast.

℣. Thy mouth was full of malice, and thy tongue did set forth deceit. And thou gavest.

10. ℟. The heavens will uncover the iniquity of Judas, and the earth will rise up against him, and his sin shall be manifest, in the day of the Lord's anger; with them who said to the Lord God, Depart from us, for we desire not the knowledge of Thy ways.

℣. He shall be reserved for the day of destruction, and at the day of vengence he shall be led out. With.

¶ *If these Responses are not sufficient, let them begin again; always ending with* Lying men compassed. *After the ablution of Altars, let them go into the chapter-house; and let the Deacon read the Gospel for the day. Then follows the sermon.*

THE MAUNDY, OR WASHING OF THE FEET.

¶ *At the end of which let the two Priests aforesaid rise up, and, beginning from those of the highest rank, wash the feet of all, one on one side of the choir, the other on the other; and, lastly, each other's feet. In the meantime, let the following Anthems, with their respective Psalms, be sung by the Choir sitting.*

Ant. A new commandment I give unto you, that ye love one another; as I have loved, that ye also love one another, *saith the Lord.*

Ps. lxvii. God be merciful.

¶ *The whole Psalms are said, and the Ant. repeated after each verse, without* Glory.

Ant. Let us love one another, for love is of God; and he that loveth his brother is born of God, and *seeth* God.

Ps. cxxxiii. Behold how good.

Ant. In those days a woman in the city, which was a sinner, when she knew that Jesus sat at meat in the house *of Simon the leper*, brought an alabaster box of ointment, and stood behind *at the feet of the Lord Jesus* weeping, and began to wash His feet with tears, and did wipe them with the hairs of her head, and kissed His feet and anointed them with ointment.

Ps. li. Have mercy upon me.

Ant. Then *Mary anointed the feet of Jesus, and wiped them with her hair*; and the house was filled with the odour of the ointment.

Ps. cxix. Blessed are those.

Ant. After the Lord rose from supper, He poured water into a basin and began to wash His disciples' feet: *this example He left them.*

Ps. xlix. O hear ye this.

¶ *Let the following Anthems be chanted, if necessary; if not, let them be altogether left out.*

Ant. Ye call Me Master and Lord, and ye say well, for so I am. If, then, your Lord and Master, have washed your feet, ye ought also to wash one another's feet.

Ant. If I, your Lord and Master, have washed your feet *for you, how much more* ought ye to wash one another's feet.

Ant. Now before the feast of the Passover, when Jesus knew that His hour was come that He should depart out of this world unto the Father, and supper being ended, He riseth *and girdeth Himself with* a towel, poureth water into a bason, began to wash the disciples' feet.

Ant. He cometh to Peter. Peter saith unto Him, Thou shalt never wash my feet. Jesus answered him, If I wash Thee not, thou hast no part with Me. Lord, not my feet only, but also my hands and my head.

¶ *After the washing of the feet a sermon is preached (if thought fit); after which, let a Priest say prayers, thus—*

℟. We wait for Thy loving kindness, O God.

℣. In the midst of Thy temple.

℟. Thou hast charged,
℣. That we should diligently keep Thy commandments.

℟. Behold, how good and joyful a thing it is.
℣. Brethren, to dwell together in unity.

℟. O Lord, hear my prayer;
℣. And let my crying come unto Thee.

℟. The Lord be with you.
℣. And with thy spirit.

Let us pray.

Be present, O Lord, we beseech Thee, at the performance of our bounden duty; and because Thou didst deign to wash Thy disciples' feet, despise not Thou the work of Thy hands which Thou hast committed unto us to be retained; but as the outward impurities of our bodies are here washed away, so may the inward sins of us all be cleansed by Thee, which do Thou Thyself deign to grant. Who.

¶ *Then let the following Gospel be read, without title, by some Deacon of the second grade, in a surplice, the Blessing being first asked of the Officiant: let it be read after the manner of a lesson, whilst the brethren take the love-cup.*

The Gospel. John xiii. 16-38—xiv. 1-31.

At that time Jesus said to His disciples, Verily, verily, I say unto you .... Arise, let us go hence.

¶ *And so let them rise, and go into the church and say Compline privately.*

Good Friday.

¶ *After Nones, let the Priest go to the Altar, in priestly robes, in red chasuble, with Deacon, Sub-Deacon, and other Ministers of the Altar, all in albs and amices. Let the Acolyte, in alb, proceed to read this lesson without title at the step of the choir, thus—*

* In their affliction they will seek Me early. Come, and let us return .... and the knowledge of God more than burnt offerings.

* Hosea v. 15, vi. 1-6.

¶ *Let the Choir say the Tracts alternately.*

Tract. * Hab. iii. O Lord, I have heard Thy speech, and was afraid : *I considered Thy works and was astonished.*

℣. In the midst *of two living creatures shalt Thou appear : when the years approach, Thou shalt be known : when the time shall come, Thou shalt show Thyself.*

℣. *Whilst my mind was troubled at it :* in wrath *Thou wilt* remember mercy.

℣. God came from *Lebanon*, and the Holy One from *the shady and dark mountain.*

℣. His glory covered the heavens, and the earth was full of His praise.

Let us pray.

D. Let us kneel.

D. Rise.

O God, from Whom (*as on Maundy Thursday*).

¶ *Let the Sub-Deacon read this lesson at the step of the choir, without* title, thus—

† The Lord spake unto Moses and Aaron .... it is the Lord's Passover.

Tract. Ps. cxl. Deliver me, O Lord, from the evil man : and preserve me from the wicked man.

℣. Who imagine mischief in their hearts : and stir up strife all the day long.

℣. They have sharpened their tongues like a serpent : adder's poison is under their lips.

℣. Keep me, O Lord, from the hands of the ungodly : preserve me from the wicked men.

℣. Who are purposed to overthrow my goings. The proud have laid a snare for me.

℣. And spread a net abroad with cords : yea, and set traps in my way.

℣. I said unto the Lord, Thou art my God : hear the voice of my prayers, O Lord.

℣. O Lord God, Thou strength of my health : Thou hast covered my head in the day of battle.

℣. Let not the ungodly have his desire, O Lord : let not his mischievous imagination prosper, lest they be too proud.

* Chiefly follows the LXX. version. † Exod. xii. 1-11

℣. Let the mischief of their own lips fall upon the head of them: that compass me about.

℣. The righteous also shall give thanks unto Thy Name: and the just shall continue in Thy sight.

¶ *Let the Passion follow, without* The Lord be with you, *and without title, thus**—

[t] Jesus went forth with His disciples over the brook Cedron, where was a garden, into the which He entered with His disciples. And Judas also, which betrayed Him, knew the place: for Jesus ofttimes resorted thither with His disciples. Judas then, having received a band of men and officers from the chief priests and Pharisees, cometh thither with lanterns and torches and weapons. Jesus therefore, knowing all things that should come upon Him, went forth, and said unto them, [b] Whom seek ye? [t] They answered Him, [a] Jesus of Nazareth. [t] Jesus saith unto them, [b] I am He. [t] And Judas also, which betrayeth Him, stood with them. As soon then as He had said unto them, I am He, they went backward, and fell to the ground. Then asked He them again, [b] Whom seek ye? [t] And they said, [a] Jesus of Nazareth. [t] Jesus answered, [b] I have told you that I am He; if therefore ye seek Me, let these go their way: [t] that the saying might be fulfilled, which He spake, Of them which Thou gavest Me have I lost none. Then Simon Peter having a sword drew it, and smote the high priest's servant, and cut off his right ear. The servant's name was Malchus. Then said Jesus unto Peter, [b] Put up thy sword into the sheath: the cup which my Father hath given Me, shall I not drink it? [t] Then the band and the captain and officers of the Jews took Jesus, and bound Him, and led him away to Annas first; for he was father in law to Caiaphas, which was the high priest that same year. Now Caiaphas was he which gave counsel to the Jews, that it was expedient that one man should die for the people. And Simon Peter followed Jesus, and so did another disciple: that disciple was known unto the high priest, and went in with Jesus into the palace of the high priest. But Peter stood at the door without. Then went out that other disciple, which was known unto the high priest, and spake unto her that kept the door, and brought in Peter. Then saith the damsel that kept the door unto Peter, [a] Art not thou also one of this Man's disciples? [t] He saith, [a] I am not. [t] And the servants and officers stood there, who had made a fire of coals: for it was cold: and they warmed themselves: and Peter stood with them, and warmed himself. The

* John xviii.

high priest then asked Jesus of His disciples, and of His doctrine. Jesus answered him, [b] I spake openly to the world; I ever taught in the synagogue, and in the temple, whither the Jews always resort; and in secret have I said nothing. Why askest thou Me? ask them which heard Me, what I said unto them: behold, they know what I said. [t] And when He had thus spoken, one of the officers which stood by struck Jesus with the palm of his hand, saying, [a] Answerest Thou the high priest so? [t] Jesus answered him, [b] If I have spoken evil, bear witness of the evil: but if well, why smitest thou Me? [t] Now Annas had sent Him bound unto Caiaphas the high priest. And Simon Peter stood and warmed himself. They said therefore unto him, [a] Art not thou also one of His disciples? [t] He denied it, and said, [a] I am not. [t] One of the servants of the high priest, being his kinsman whose ear Peter cut off, saith, [a] Did not I see thee in the garden with Him? [t] Peter then denied again: and immediately the cock crew. Then led they Jesus from Caiaphas unto the hall of judgment: and it was early; and they themselves went not into the judgment hall, lest they should be defiled; but that they might eat the passover. Pilate then went out unto them, and said, [a] What accusation bring ye against this Man? [t] They answered and said unto him, [a] If He were not a malefactor, we would not have delivered Him up unto thee. [t] Then said Pilate unto them, [a] Take ye Him, and judge Him according to your law. [t] The Jews therefore said unto him, [a] It is not lawful for us to put any man to death: [t] that the saying of Jesus might be fulfilled, which He spake signifying what death He should die. Then Pilate entered into the judgment hall again, and called Jesus, and said unto Him, [a] Art Thou the King of the Jews? [t] Jesus answered him, [b] Sayest thou this thing of thyself, or did others tell it thee of Me? [t] Pilate answered, [a] Am I a Jew? Thine own nation and the chief priests have delivered Thee unto me: what hast Thou done? [t] Jesus answered, [b] My kingdom is not of this world: if My kingdom were of this world, then would My servants fight, that I should not be delivered to the Jews: but now is My kingdom not from hence. [t] Pilate therefore said unto Him, [a] Art Thou a King then? [t] Jesus answered, [b] Thou sayest that I am a King. To this end was I born, and for this cause came I into the world, that I should bear witness unto the truth. Every one that is of the truth heareth My voice. [t] Pilate saith unto Him, [a] What is truth? [t] And when he had said this, he went out again unto the Jews, and saith unto them, [a] I find in Him no fault at all.

But ye have a custom, that I should release unto you one at the passover; wilt ye therefore that I release unto you the King of the Jews? [t]Then cried they all again, saying, [a]Not this Man, but Barabbas. [t]Now Barabbas was a robber. *Pilate therefore took Jesus, and scourged Him. And the soldiers platted a crown of thorns, and put it on His head, and they put on Him a purple robe, and said, [a]Hail, King of the Jews: [t]and they smote Him with their hands. Pilate therefore went forth again, and saith unto them, [a]Behold, I bring Him forth to you, that ye may know that I find no fault in Him. [t]Then came Jesus forth, wearing the crown of thorns, and the purple robe. And Pilate saith unto them, [a]Behold the Man! [t]When the chief priests therefore and officers saw Him, they cried out, saying, [a]Crucify Him, crucify Him. [t]Pilate saith unto them, [a]Take ye Him, and crucify Him: for I find no fault in Him. [t]The Jews answered him, [a]We have a law, and by our law He ought to die, because He made Himself the Son of God. [t]When Pilate therefore heard that saying, he was the more afraid; and went again into the judgment hall, and said unto Jesus, [a]Whence art Thou? [t]But Jesus gave him no answer. Then saith Pilate unto Him, [a]Speakest Thou not unto me? Knowest Thou not that I have power to crucify Thee, and have power to release Thee? [t]Jesus answered, [b]Thou couldest have no power at all against Me, except it were given Thee from above: therefore he that delivered Me unto thee hath the greater sin. [t]And from thenceforth Pilate sought to release Him: but the Jews cried out, saying, [a]If thou let this Man go, thou art not Cæsar's friend: whosoever maketh himself a king speaketh against Cæsar. [t]When Pilate therefore heard that saying, he brought Jesus forth, and sat down in the judgment seat, in a place that is called the Pavement, but in the Hebrew, Gabbatha. And it was the preparation of the passover, and about the sixth hour: and he saith unto the Jews, [a]Behold your King. [t]But they cried out, [a]Away with Him, away with Him, crucify Him. [t]Pilate said unto them, [a]Shall I crucify your King? [t]The chief priests answered, [a]We have no King but Cæsar. [t]Then delivered he Him therefore unto them to be crucified: and they took Jesus, and led Him away. And He, bearing His Cross, went forth into a place called the place of a scull, which is called in the Hebrew, Golgotha: where they crucified Him, and two other with Him, on either side one, and Jesus in the midst. And Pilate wrote a title, and put it on the Cross; and the writing was, JESUS OF NAZARETH THE KING OF THE

* Chap. xix.

JEWS. This title then read many of the Jews: for the place where Jesus was crucified was nigh to the city: and it was written in Hebrew, and Greek, and Latin. Then said the chief priests of the Jews to Pilate, [a] Write not, The King of the Jews; but that He said, I am the King of the Jews. [t] Pilate answered, [a] What I have written, I have written. [t] Then the soldiers, when they had crucified Jesus, took His garments, and made four parts, to every soldier a part; and also His coat: now the coat was without seam, woven from the top throughout. They said therefore among themselves, [a] Let us not rend it, but cast lots for it, whose it shall be: [t] that the Scripture might be fulfilled, which saith, They parted My raiment among them.

¶ *Here let two Acolytes, in surplices, one at the right, the other at the left side of the Altar, approach, and remove from it two linen cloths which were placed upon the Altar for that purpose.*

And for My vesture they did cast lots. These things therefore the soldiers did. Now there stood by the Cross of Jesus, His mother, and His mother's sister, Mary the wife of Cleophas, and Mary Magdalene. When Jesus therefore saw His mother and the disciple standing by, whom He loved, He saith unto His mother, [b] Woman, behold thy son. [t] Then saith He to the disciple, [b] Behold thy mother. [t] And from that hour that disciple took her unto his own home. After this, Jesus, knowing that all things were now accomplished, that the Scripture might be fulfilled, saith, [b] I thirst. [t] Now there was set a vessel full of vinegar: and they filled a sponge with vinegar, and put it upon hyssop, and put it to His mouth. When Jesus therefore had received the vinegar, He said, [b] It is finished: [t] and He bowed His head, and gave up the ghost.

¶ *Let* Our Father; Hail, Mary; *and* Into Thy hands, *follow.*

[t] The Jews therefore, because it was the preparation, that the bodies should not remain upon the Cross on the Sabbath-day (for that Sabbath-day was an high-day), besought Pilate that their legs might be broken, and that they might be taken away. Then came the soldiers, and brake the legs of the first, and of the other which was crucified with him. But when they came to Jesus, and saw that He was dead already, they brake not His legs. But one of the soldiers with a spear pierced His side, and forthwith came there out blood and water. And he that saw it bare record, and his record is true: and he knoweth that he saith true, that ye might believe. For these things were done

that the Scripture should be fulfilled, A bone of Him shall not be broken. And again, another Scripture saith, They shall look on Him Whom they pierced.

The Gospel.

After this Joseph of Arimathæa, being a disciple of Jesus, but secretly for fear of the Jews, besought Pilate that he might take away the body of Jesus: and Pilate gave him leave. He came therefore, and took the body of Jesus. And there came also Nicodemus, which at the first came to Jesus by night, and brought a mixture of myrrh and aloes, about an hundred pound weight. Then took they the body of Jesus, and wound it in linen clothes with the spices, as the manner of the Jews is to bury. Now in the place where He was crucified there was a garden; and in the garden a new sepulchre, wherein was never man yet laid. There laid they Jesus therefore because of the Jews' preparation day; for the sepulchre was nigh at hand.

¶ *The appointed solemn Collects follow.*

Let us pray, most dearly beloved unto us, first of all, for the Holy Church of God, that our God and Lord will vouchsafe to preserve it in peace throughout the whole world; subjecting to it principalities and powers; and grant to us that we, leading a quiet and peaceable life, may glorify God the Father Almighty

Let us pray.

D. Let us kneel.
D. Rise.

O almighty and eternal God, Who, in Christ, hast revealed Thy glory to all nations; preserve, we beseech Thee, the works of Thine own mercy, that Thy Church, which is spread over the whole world, may persevere by steadfast faith in the confession of Thy Name. Through. ℟. Amen.

Let us pray also for our most blessed Pope N., that our God and Lord Who hath made choice of him in the order of the Episcopate, may preserve him in health and safety for his Holy Church, to rule the holy people of God.

Let us pray.

D. Let us kneel.
D. Rise.

O almighty and eternal God, by Whose counsel are all things established, mercifully regard our prayers, and by Thy goodness preserve the Prelate chosen for us; that the Christian people which is so governed, may increase in the worthy profession of their faith under so great a Pontiff. Through. ℟. Amen.

Let us also pray for all Bishops, Priests, Deacons, Sub-Deacons, Acolytes, Exorcists, Readers, Door-keepers, Confessors, Virgins, Widows, and for all the holy people of God.

Let us pray.
D. Let us kneel.
D. Rise.

O almighty and eternal God, by Whose Spirit the whole body of the Church is governed and sanctified, receive our supplications for all estates of men; that, by the gift of Thy grace, every member of the same may faithfully serve Thee. Through. In the unity. ℟. Amen.

Let us pray.
D. Let us kneel.
D. Rise.

Let us pray, too, for our most Christian King N., that our Lord and God may make subject to him all barbarous nations for our perpetual peace.

Let us pray.
D. Let us kneel.
D. Rise.

Almighty, everlasting God, in Whose hand is the power of all and the rights of all kingdoms, graciously behold the empire of Christendom: that the nations which trust in their own fierceness may be restrained by the right hand of Thy power. Through. ℟. Amen.

Let us pray.
D. Let us kneel.
D. Rise.

Let us pray also for our Catechumens, that our Lord and God may open the ears of their hearts, and the door of His mercy; that having received the remission of all their sins by the laver of regeneration, they may themselves also be found acceptable in Jesus Christ our Lord.

Let us pray.
D. Let us kneel.
D. Rise.

O almighty and eternal God, Who continually enrichest Thy Church with new offspring; increase the faith and understanding of our Catechumens, that, being born again in the font of Baptism, they may be joined to Thy adopted children. Through. ℟. Amen.

Let us pray.

D. Let us kneel.

D. Rise.

Let us pray, most dearly beloved unto us, to God the Father Almighty; that He would purge the world of all errors, remove diseases, drive away famine, open prisons, loose chains, grant a safe return to them that travel, health to the sick, and a haven of safety to such as are at sea.

Let us pray.

D. Let us kneel.

D. Rise.

O almighty and eternal God, the comfort of the sorrowful, the strength of those that travail; let the prayers of such as call upon Thee in any manner of tribulation come to Thee, that all may rejoice that Thy mercy hath been present with them in their necessities. Through. ℟. Amen.

Let us pray.

D. Let us kneel.

D. Rise.

Let us pray also for heretics and schismatics, that our God and Lord Jesus Christ may deliver them from all errors, and be pleased to call them back to the Holy Mother, the Catholic and Apostolic Church.

Let us pray.

D. Let us kneel.

D. Rise.

O almighty and eternal God, Who savest all men, and willest not that any should perish; look on those souls that are deceived by the fraud of the devil; that laying aside all malice and heresy, the hearts of the erring may recover and return to the unity of Thy truth. Through. ℟. Amen.

Let us pray also for the perfidious Jews; that God and our Lord would take away the veil from their hearts, that they also may acknowledge our Lord Jesus Christ.

Let us pray.

¶ Let us kneel, etc., *is here omitted.*

O almighty and eternal God, Who dost not reject from Thy mercy even the perfidious Jews; hear our prayers which we offer unto Thee for the blindness of that people; that they acknowledging the light of Thy truth, which is the Christ, may be brought out of their darkness. Through. ℟. Amen.

Let us pray.

D. Let us kneel.

D. Rise.

Let us pray also for Pagans, that Almighty God would remove iniquity from their hearts: that leaving their idols, they may be converted to the living and true God, and His only Son, Jesus Christ our God and Lord. Who liveth and reigneth with the Holy Ghost, God, world without end.

Let us pray.

D. Let us kneel.

D. Rise.

O almighty and eternal God, who willest not the death of sinners, but always desirest them life; mercifully accept our prayers, and deliver them from the worship of idols; and, to the praise and glory of Thy Name, admit them to the flock of Thy holy Church. Through. ℟. Amen.

¶ *The Collects being ended, let the Priest put off his chasuble and lay it aside, sitting in his seat by the Altar with the Deacon and Sub-Deacon; meantime let two Priests of the upper grade, with bare feet, in albs, without apparel, holding aloft the veiled Cross behind the High Altar, on the right side, solemnly chant between them these verses. Let two Deacons of the second grade, in their black copes, at the quire step, turning to the Altar, say the Greek* Ἅγιος; *let the Choir respond,* Sanctus Deus, *genuflecting, and kissing the benches at each response three times, and rising again, but let the Priests holding the Cross behind the Altar, and the Deacons at the step of the quire, saying,* Ἅγιος, *always remain standing.*

Priests. O My people, what have I done unto thee, and wherein have I wearied thee? testify against Me. *Because* I brought thee up out of the land of Egypt, *thou hast prepared a Cross for thy Saviour.*

Deacons. Ἅγιος ὁ Θεὸς, Ἅγιος Ἰσχυρος Ἅγιος Ἀθάνατος ἐλέησον ἡμᾶς.

Choir. Sanctus Deus, Sanctus Fortis, Sanctus et Immortalis, miserere nobis.

Priests. Because I led thee through the wilderness forty years, and fed thee with manna, and brought thee into a land exceeding good, thou has prepared a Cross for thy Saviour.

Deacons. Ἅγιος.

Choir. Sanctus.

Priests. What could I have done more unto thee that I have not done? I indeed planted thee, O My vineyard, with fair fruit, and thou are become very bitter unto Me; for thou gavest Me to drink in My thirst vinegar mingled with gall, and piercedst thy Saviour's side with a lance.

Deacons. Ἅγιος.

Choir. Sanctus.

¶ *Then let the Priests uncover the Cross by the Altar on the right side, and sing this Anthem—*

Behold the wood of the Cross on which hung the Saviour of the world. O come, let us adore.

¶ *Let the Choir repeat the Anthem following, genuflecting and kissing the benches—*

We adore Thy Cross, O Lord, and we praise and glorify Thy holy Resurrection, for lo! by the Cross joy hath come to the whole world.

Ps. lxvii. God be merciful unto us, and bless us; and show us the light of His countenance, and be merciful unto us.

¶ *Let the whole Ps. be said by the Choir, without* Glory, *and after each v. let the Anth. be similarly repeated with genuflexion. Meantime let the Cross be placed on the third step of the Altar, the Priests sitting on either side of it. Then let the Clergy with bare feet draw near and adore the Cross, beginning with those of highest rank; at end of Ps. and Anth. let the two Priests, still sitting by the Cross, chant this verse, in the manner aforesaid, Choir repeating it sitting, after every succeeding verse of the hymn—*

Priests. Hail, faithful Cross! above them all
One and only noble Tree;
The woods no foliage yield, no fruit
Which can be compared with thee:
O sweet the nails, O sweet the wood,
O sweet the load which here we see!

Choir. Hail, faithful.

Priests. Sing, my tongue, the glorious battle,
With completed victory, rife;
And above the Cross's trophy
Tell the triumph of the strife,
How the world's Redeemer conquered
By surrendering of His life.

Choir. Hail, faithful.

Priests. God His Maker sorely grieving
That the first-made Adam fell,
When he ate the fruit of sorrow,
Whose reward was death and hell,
Noted then this wood, the ruin
Of the ancient wood to quell.

Choir. Hail, faithful.

Priests. For the work of our salvation
Needs would have its order so,
And the multiform deceivers
Art by art would overthrow,
And from thence would bring the medicine,
Whence the insult of the foe.

Choir. Hail, faithful

Priests. Wherefore when the sacred fulness
Of the appointed time was come,
This world's Maker left His Father,
Sent the heavenly mansion from;
And proceeded, God incarnate,
Of the Virgin's holy womb.

Choir. Hail, faithful.

Priests. Thirty years amongst us dwelling,
His appointed time fulfilled;
Born for this, He meets His Passion,
For that this He freely willed:
On the Cross the Lamb is lifted,
Where His life-blood shall be spilled.

Choir. Hail, faithful.

Priests. He endured the nails, the spitting,
Vinegar, and spear, and reed;
From that holy Body, broken,
Blood and water forth proceed;
Earth and stars, and sky and ocean,
By that flood from stain are freed.

Choir. Hail, faithful.

Priests. Bend Thy boughs, O Tree of glory,
Thy relaxing sinews bend;
For awhile the ancient rigour
That Thy birth bestow'd suspend,
And the King of heavenly beauty
On thy bosom gently tend.

Choir. Hail, faithful.

Priests. Thou alone wast counted worthy
This world's ransom to uphold,
For a shipwrecked race preparing
Harbour like the Ark of old,
With the sacred Blood anointed
From the stricken Lamb that roll'ed.

Choir. Hail, faithful.

Priests. To the Trinity be glory
Everlasting, as is meet;
Equal to the Father, equal
To the Son and Paraclete,
Trinal unity, Whose praises
All created things repeat.

Choir. Hail faithful.

¶ *The hymn ended, let the Cross be carried through the Quire by the two aforesaid Priests to some Altar to be adored by the people. And let this be sung during the time in the quire, with its* ℣., *the Precentor beginning the Anthem*—

Anth. Whilst the Maker of the world suffered the punishment of death upon the Cross, and crying with a loud voice gave up the ghost; lo! the veil of the Temple was rent, and the graves were opened, for there was a great earthquake, because the world cried aloud that it could not endure the death of the Son of God.

℣. Therefore the side of the crucified Lord being pierced by the lance of the soldier, there came forth blood and water for our redemption and salvation.

℟. O admirable price! by the weighing of which the captivity of the world is ransomed, the infernal gates of hell are burst, and the door of the Kingdom is opened unto us.

℣ The side of the Crucified.

¶ *As the Cross-bearer returns to the vestibule, let the Priests in surplices, with bare feet, with amices, precede, bearing the Body of Christ in a pyx to the appointed Altar, whilst the aforesaid Anthem is chanted. The Adoration and Anthem ended, let the aforesaid Priests, with the same reverence used in bearing it forth, carry back the Cross through the quire to the High Altar.*

¶ *Then let all the Clergy come together from the quire to the Altar; and let the Priest put on again the Chasuble which he had put off, and approach to the step of the Altar with the Deacon and Sub-Deacon, and say the* Confession *and* Absolution, *with Suffrages and Collect,* Take away from us, O Lord, *as usual; but let the kiss of Peace not be given.*

¶ *Then, the Sacrifice being placed in the usual manner upon the Altar and censed, with mixture of wine and water in the chalice, after washing his hands let him say with a reverence before the Altar,* In the spirit of humility, etc., *kissing the Altar and blessing the Sacrifice; and turn himself, saying,* Brethren, pray, *in the accustomed manner.*

¶ *Then let him say in a low voice without tone,* Let us pray, Instructed by; *with the Lord's Prayer. Let the Choir answer,* But deliver. *Then let him say,* Deliver us, we beseech Thee; *in which prayer whilst he says,* Through the same, *let him make the accustomed Fraction, as on other days. Then let him say in a low voice, without tone,* World without end. *Let the Choir respond,* Amen.

¶ *Then let him place in the chalice, as usual, a particle of the Host.*

¶ The Peace of God *and* Agnus Dei *are not said, nor is the* Peace *given; but let the Priest at once communicate himself, saying,* The Body of the Lord, etc.; *and for reception of the Body and Blood,* The Body and Blood of our Lord Jesus Christ preserve us to everlasting life. Amen. *With no previous prayer.*

¶ *Then after washing of hands, let them say Vespers, not chanting them, but two and two privately before the Altar, thus—Ant.,* I will take; *Ps.,* I believed; *and other Ants. and Pss. as on Maundy Thursday, including* Magnificat *and its Ant. Then let* Our Father *be said, standing, with Ps.* li.; *which ended, let the Priest say audibly, without tone, the Post-Communion, without* The Lord be with you, *and without* Let us pray, *beginning,* We beseech Thee, O Lord, look upon this Thy family, *without* Who with Thee. *And so let Mass and Vespers end together. Nothing more is said.*

¶ *Vespers being ended, let the Priest put off his chasuble; and, taking with him one of the superiors, in surplices, both with bare feet, let him replace the Cross in the sepulchre, together with the Lord's Body in the pyx; himself beginning alone the* ℟., I am counted as one of them that go down into the pit: I have been even as a man that hath no strength, free among the dead. ℣. Thou hast laid Me in the lowest pit, in a place of darkness and in the deep. I have been. *Both genuflecting at the beginning, and then rising. And so with the next* ℟., *let the Choir take it up and go on with its* ℣., *and kneel to the end of the Service.*

¶ *Then the sepulchre having been censed and the door shut, let the Priest begin the* ℟.. The Lord being buried, *and the Choir sing the rest with its* ℣., The sepulchre was sealed: rolling a stone to the door of the sepulchre: setting soldiers to watch it. ℣. Lest peradventure His disciples should come by night and steal Him away, and say unto the people, He is risen from the dead. Setting.

¶ *At each of these three Ant. let the aforesaid Priests kneel continuously. Let the Priest begin the Ant.* In peace; *and the Choir go on,* I will lay me down. *Also the Priest Ant.,* At Salem; *Choir,* Is His tabernacle. *The Priest Ant.,* My flesh; *Choir,* Shall rest in hope.

¶ *This ended, and Prayers being said at pleasure secretly by all with genuflexion, all others going back as they see fit, in no fixed order, let the Priest put his chasuble on again, and in the same order with which he went up at the beginning of the Service, with Deacon and Sub-Deacon and the other Ministers of the Altar, let him depart.*

¶ *From that time one wax candle at the least shall burn continually before the sepulchre until the Procession on Easter Day; howbeit, when the* Benedictus *is sung, and during the other things which follow on the next night, let it be extinguished. Likewise let it be extinguished on the Vigil of Easter while the new fire is blessed, until the Paschal Candle be lighted.*

HOLY SATURDAY.

¶ *The Clergy being assembled in the quire, and None being said, let the Officiant in red silk cope, Deacon in dalmatic, Sub-Deacon in tunic, the rest of the Ministers of the Altar in albs and amices, without light, candles, cross, or fire in the censer. Also a certain one of the first grade in surplice carrying on a wand a branch formed by three extinguished wax tapers, preceding the Procession after the bearer of the holy water, go through the quire in Procession to bless the new fire and font, the Choir following without change of habit, the Superior going first, to the pillar on the south side, next the font, where let the Officiant between the two pillars bless the fire which is there to be kindled. On the way let the Ps.,* The Lord is my light, *be said without tone, and without* Glory. *Standing thus—*

R			Candle-bearer.			
I			Boy with Book.			
O	Sub-Deacon.	Deacon.	Officiant.	Water-bearer.	Thurifer.	Fire.
H			Candle-bearer.			
C	Pillar.		Acolyte with Branch.		Pillar.	

THE BLESSING OF THE FIRE.

Priest. The Lord be with you.

Let us pray.

O Lord our God, Father Almighty, Unfailing Light, Maker of all lights, hear us Thy servants, and bl + ess this fire which is consecrated by Thy sanctifying benediction: do Thou Who lightest every man that cometh into this world, enlighten the conscience of our hearts with the fire of Thy love; that we, being inflamed by Thy fire, and illuminated by Thy light, the darkness of sin being expelled from our hearts, may by Thy guidance be deemed meet to come to life eternal; and as Thou madest fire to shine for Thy servant Moses by the pillar of fire going before him in the Red Sea, so enkindle our light, and let the candle which shall be lit thereat ever remain blessed in honour of Thy majesty; and whosoever shall bear light from it let him be illuminated by the light of spiritual grace. Through.

¶ *Here let holy water be sprinkled on the fire.*

The Lord be with you.

Let us pray.

O Lord, Holy Father, almighty, ever-living God, vouchsafe to bl + ess and sancti + fy this fire; which we, unworthy as we are, through the invocation of Thy only-begotten Son our Lord Jesus Christ, presume to bl + ess: do Thou most merciful Father, sanctify it with Thy bl + essing; and grant that it may prevail for the profit of mankind. Through.

Let us pray.

Prevent us, we beseech Thee, O Lord, alway, here and everywhere, with celestial light: that we may both discern with clear vision and worthily and effectually receive the mystery whereof Thou hast willed us to be partakers. Through. Who.

THE BLESSING OF THE INCENSE.

I exorcise thee, most unclean spirit and every illusion of the enemy, in the Name of God the Father Almighty, and in the Name of Jesus Christ His Son, and in the power of the Holy Ghost; that thou shouldest depart and withdraw from this creature of frankincense or incense, together with all thy fraud and malice: that this creature may be sancti + fied in the Name of our Lord Jesus Christ, that all who taste, touch, or smell it, may receive the virtue and aid of the Holy Ghost: so that wheresoever this incense or frankincense shall be, there thou shalt in no wise dare to draw nigh, nor presume to raise opposition: but, O unclean spirit, whosoe'er thou art, fly far hence and depart with all thy subtilty, being adjured by the Name and power of God the Father Almighty, and His Son our Lord Jesus Christ, Who shall come in the Holy Spirit to judge the quick and the dead, and thee the father of lies, and the world by fire. ℟. Amen.

Let us pray.

We beseech Thy everlasting and most righteous loving kindness, O Lord, Holy Father, almighty, ever-living God, that Thou wouldest be pleased to bl + ess and sancti + fy this species of frankincense or incense; that it may be an incense acceptable to

Thy majesty for a sweet savour: let this species be bl+essed by Thee, sancti+fied by the invocation of Thy Holy Name, that wheresoever the fumes thereof shall reach, every kind of evil spirit may be cast out and put to flight, even as the incense of the fish's liver which Raphael the archangel showed Thy servant Tobias when he went to set Sarai free. Through

Let us pray.

Let Thy benediction, O Lord, descend upon this spirit of incense or frankincense, like unto that of which Thy prophet David sang, saying, Let my prayer be set forth in Thy sight as incense; let it be unto us an odour of comfort, sweetness, and grace; that every illusion of the enemy of mind and body may be put to flight by this smoke; that we may be, as the Apostle Paul saith, a sweet savour unto God. From the face of this incense or frankincense let every assault of the devil flee away, as dust before the wind and smoke before the fire; and bestow this incense of sweet savour, most Holy Father, to abide for ever for the work of Thy Church and the cause of religion, that by mystic significance the fragrant odour may show forth unto us the sweetness of spiritual virtue. Wherefore, Almighty God, we beseech Thee by the powerful right hand of Thy majesty deign to bl+ess this creature compounded of a mixture of divers things; that in virtue of Thy Holy Name, wheresoever the smoke of its sweet scent shall be given forth, it may miraculously prevail to put to flight all vain assaults of unclean spirits, and to drive away all diseases and restore health, and in most fragrant odour to come up into Thy nostrils with perpetual sweetness. Through.

¶ *After the Blessing of Incense, let a censer be filled from the coals with incense, and let the new fire be censed. Then let the taper on the wand alone be lighted from the new fire, the other lights of the church being first put out. Then let the Procession return as usual into the quire. Whilst returning, let two Clergy of the second grade, in surplices, behind the Priest, sing—*

Thou Leader kind, Whose word call'd forth the radiant light,
Who by set bounds dividest night and day,
When the sun set, in gloom rose chaos on our sight:
Give back, O Christ, Thy light, Thy servants pray.

¶ *Let the Choir repeat this, and also after each v. Whilst the Clergy chant, let them stand still, and the Choir move on; and whilst the Choir chant, let them stand, and the Clergy move on.*

Cl. Although with countless stars and with the silv'ry tint
Of lunar lamp Thou dost the heavens dye,
Yet dost Thou teach us how by sudden stroke of flint
The rock-born seed of light to vivify.

Ch. Thou Leader kind, etc.

Cl. Lest man forget the hope for man of heavenly light,
That in Christ's Body lies a hidden thing;
Who willèd to be called the steadfast Rock of might
Whence by our little sparks our race should spring.

Ch. Thou Leader kind, etc.

Cl. So in that room, O Lord, Thou didst Thy gifts display—
To wit, the flickering tongues that flame-like fall;
Till then obscur'd and lost, new light brings back the day,
And vanquish'd night withdraws her riven pall.

Ch. Thou Leader kind, etc.

Cl. Through whom Thy honour, praise, and wisdom all divine,
Majesty, goodness, mercy, shine and blend;
And to maintain Thy realm in threefold might combine,
Knitting time now with time which cannot end.

Ch. Thou Leader kind, etc.

THE BLESSING OF THE PASCHAL CANDLE.

¶ *At the step of the quire, let them stand thus—*

		Candle-bearer.		
Acolyte with Branch.	Sub-Deacon with Book.	Deacon.	Paschal Candle.	Thurifer.
	CHANCEL STEP.		CHANCEL STEP.	
		Candle-bearer.		

Deacon (*chanting*). Now let the angelic host of Heaven rejoice, let the Divine Mysteries be joyfully celebrated, and for the victory of so great a King let the trumpet of salvation be sounded. Let the earth, brightened with such effulgence, delight herself; and being illumined by the splendour of the eternal King, perceive the darkness of the universe to be done away. Let our Mother Church also be joyful, adorned with the radiance of so great light, and let this court resound with the mighty voices of the peoples.

Wherefore as ye stand by, most dearly beloved brethren, at the so marvellous clearness of this holy light, I pray you, together with me, invoke the tender mercy of Almighty God, that he Who hath deigned to enrol me not for my own deserts in the number of Levites, pouring out upon me the grace of His light, may enable me to declare the praise of this taper. Through our Lord Jesus Christ His Son, Who with Him liveth and reigneth in the unity of the Holy Ghost, God.

℟. World without end.

℣. Amen.

℟. The Lord be with you,

℣. And with thy spirit.

℟. Lift up your hearts.

℣. We lift them up unto the Lord.

℟. Let us give thanks unto our Lord God.

℣. It is meet and right so to do.

Because it is very meet and right to proclaim with full desire of heart and mind and voice the invisible God Almighty, the Father, and His only begotten Son, with the Holy Ghost; Who for us paid the debt of Adam to the eternal Father, and blotted out the bond of the old sin in His holy Blood.

For this is the Paschal Feast, in which that true Lamb is slain, and by His Blood the door-posts are hallowed. This is the night on which Thou madest our fathers, the children of Israel, whom Thou broughtest up out of Egypt, to pass through the Red Sea, dry-shod. This, therefore, is the night wherein were cleared away the shades of sin by the illumination of the pillar. This is the night which as at this day restores to grace, unites in sanctity the believers in Christ throughout the universe, set apart from the evil of the world and the darkness of sins. This is the night in which Christ burst the bonds of death, and ascended conquering from the grave. For it had advantaged us nothing to be born, except we had been redeemed.

O marvellous condescension of Thy loving kindness concerning us! O unspeakable tenderness of love! to redeem the servant Thou gavest up the Son! O truly needful sin of Adam and of ourselves, which was blotted out by the Death of Christ! O happy guilt, the desert of which was to gain such and so great a Redeemer! O truly blessed night, which alone was permitted to know the time and the hour on which Christ rose from the grave!

This is the night of which it is written, The night is as clear as the day; and, My night shall be turned to day. Therefore the hallowing of this night puts to flight wickedness, washes away guilt, restores innocency to the fallen, and joy to the sorrowing: banishes hatred, brings about concord, and bows down sovereignties.

Therefore, in favour of this night, receive, Holy Father,

¶ *Here let the Deacon put the grains of incense into the candle in the form of a Cross, and into the branch which the Acolyte carries.*

the evening sacrifice of this incense, which the Holy Church offers to Thee in this solemn oblation of wax, the work of bees, at the hands of the ministers.

But now we have heard the praise of this pillar, which in honour of God the glowing fire kindles.

¶ *Here let the candle be lit from the new fire, and not put out till Compline next day; and let the Candle-bearers light their candles throughout the church.*

Which, albeit it is divided into parts of borrowed light, hath suffered no loss. It is fed by the liquid wax which the Queen Bee produced for the composition of this precious taper.

O blessed night, which spoiled the Egyptians, enriched the Hebrews: night in which heavenly things are united with earthly.

We pray Thee, Lord, that this candle, consecrated to the honour of Thy Name, may last unfailing for the dispelling of the darkness of this night. Being acceptable for its sweet odour, let it be mingled with the lights above. Let the Morning Star find it burning; to wit, that Morning Star Who knows no setting; He Who returned from the grave, and shone serene upon mankind.

We, therefore, pray Thee, O Lord, that Thou wilt grant us quietness of times, and be pleased to preserve in these paschal joys us Thy servants, all the clergy and most devout people, together with our Father Pope N., and our King N., and also our Bishop N.

Who ever livest, reignest, rulest, and are glorified, God alone, alone most high, Jesu Christ, with the Holy Ghost, in the glory of God the Father. Amen.

¶ *The Paschal Candle shall burn continually through Easter week at Matins, Mass, and Vespers; and on the Octave Day of Easter. On all Sundays from the Octave of Easter to the Lord's Ascension let it be lighted only at Mass; also on the Feast of S. Mark the Evangelist and SS. Philip and James at Mass only. But on the Annunc. of B. Mary and Inv. of the Holy Cross as in the Octave of Easter. The stand with the Paschal Candle shall be taken away on the Friday after Ascension Day.*

¶ *The blessing of the Paschal Candle ended, let the Priest who is to finish the Office, putting on his chasuble, go to the Altar with his Ministers, without saying the Confession, but only* Our Father, *and kiss the Altar with his Ministers, and go and sit down. Let the triple candle on the wand depart; but let a Minister bring another candle and stand on the step at the left side of the Altar, turning to the South until the Sevenfold Litany is ended.*

¶ *Then let the Lessons be read, without title, by persons of higher grade at the step of the quire.*

*The Lesson.**

In the beginning .... He had rested from all His work which God created and made.

Let us pray.

O God, Who didst wonderfully create man, and more wonderfully didst redeem him, give unto us, we beseech Thee, strength of mind to stand against the allurements of sin, that we may attain unto joys eternal. Through.

The Lesson.†

And it came to pass, that in the morning watch ...... Then sang Moses and the children of Israel this song unto the Lord, and spake.

¶ *All Tracts are said by Choir alternately, except the last. Let the first begin at the side of the Choir of the Reader of the Lesson.*

Tract. Exod. xv. I will sing unto the Lord, for He hath triumphed gloriously: the horse and his rider hath He thrown into the sea. The Lord is my strength and song, and He is become my salvation.

℣. He is my God, and I will prepare Him an habitation: my father's God, and I will exalt Him.

℣. The Lord is a man of war: The Lord is His Name.

Let us pray.

O God, Whose ancient miracles we perceive to cast their beams even on our age; and while Thou didst stretch out the right hand of Thy power to deliver one people from Egyptian persecution, didst turn it unto the working out of the salvation of the Gentiles through the water of regeneration; grant, we beseech Thee, that the fulness of the whole world may become children of Abraham, and succeed to the honourable estate of Israel. Through.

* Gen. i., ii. 1, 2. † Exod. xiv. 24-31, xv. 1.

*The Lesson.**

And in that day seven women .... from storm and from rain.

Tract. Is. v. My wellbeloved hath a vineyard in a very fruitful hill.

℣. And he fenced it, and gathered out the stones thereof, and planted it with the choicest vine, and built a tower in the midst of it.

℣. And also made a winepress therein : for the vineyard of the Lord of Hosts is the house of Israel.

Let us pray.

O God, who hast indoctrinated us in the pages of both Testaments in the Celebration of the Paschal Sacrament; give unto us such a sense of Thy mercies, that from our experience of gifts present our hope of future blessings may be confirmed. Through.

The Lesson.†

Moses therefore wrote this song ...... until they were ended.

Tract. Deut. xxxii. Give ear, O ye heavens, and I will speak; and hear, O earth, the words of my mouth.

℣. My doctrine shall drop as the rain, my speech shall distil as the dew, as the small rain upon the tender herb.

℣. *And as snow upon the hay:* because I will publish the Name of the Lord.

℣. Ascribe ye greatness unto our God. He is the Rock, His work is perfect: for all His ways are judgment.

℣. A God of truth and without iniquity, just and *holy* is *the Lord.*

Let us pray.

O God, Who dost always multiply Thy Church by the calling of the Gentiles, mercifully be pleased to defend those whom Thou dost wash in the water of Baptism with Thy continual protection. Through.

Tract. Ps. xlii. Like as the hart desireth the water-brooks; so longeth my soul after Thee, O God.

℣. My soul is athirst for God, yea, even for the living God: when shall I come to appear before the presence of God?

* Is. iv. 1-6. † Deut. xxxi. 22-30.

℣. My tears have been my meat day and night : while they daily say unto Me, Where is now thy God?

Let us pray.

Grant, we beseech Thee, Almighty God, that we who keep the Paschal Feast, being inflamed with celestial desires, may thirst after the fountain of life, our Lord Jesus Christ Thy Son. Who.

Almighty, everlasting God, look graciously upon the devotion of Thy people about to be regenerated, who pant as the hart after the waters; and mercifully grant that the thirst of their faith may sanctify their souls and bodies in the mystery of Baptism. Through.

¶ *Then let the Sevenfold Litany follow, chanted in the midst of the quire by seven boys in surplices: meanwhile let the Priest put off his chasuble and lay it on the Altar, and let him put on his red silk cope, standing before the Altar, until the Litany is sung through.*

* Lord, have mercy upon us.
Christ, have mercy upon us.
Christ, hear us.

Holy Mary,
Holy Mother of God,
Holy Virgin of Virgins,
Holy Michael,
Holy Gabriel,
Holy Raphael,
All ye Holy Angels and Archangels,
Holy John the Baptist,
All Holy Patriarchs and Prophets,
Holy Peter,
Holy Andrew,
Holy John,
Holy James,
Holy Philip,
Holy Bartholomew,
Holy Matthew,
All ye Holy Apostles and Evangelists,
Holy Stephen,
Holy Linus,
Holy Cletus,
Holy Laurence,
Holy Vincent.
Holy Sixtus,
} Pray for us.

* This down to page 172 is taken from the Processional.

Holy Denys with his Companions All ye Holy Martyrs, Holy Sylvester, Holy Gregory, Holy Hilary, Holy Martin, Holy Remys, Holy Andoen, Holy Augustine, All ye Holy Confessors, Holy Mary Magdalene, Holy Felicitas, Holy Perpetua, Holy Agatha, Holy Agnes, Holy Cecilia, Holy Scholastica, All ye Holy Virgins, All ye Saints,	Pray for us.

If the Bishop be present, let him stand in his seat whilst the aforesaid Litany is said. This Litany over, immediately let the Five-part Litany begin, chanted as the other only by five Deacons. When they shall come to Holy Mary, *immediately let the Procession go to bless the font in this order: First the Cross-bearer in alb and tunic, then two Candle-bearers in albs and amices, then the Thurifer in the same dress; after him two Boys in surplices walking together, one carrying the book, the other on his right the candle for blessing the font. Then two Deacons of the second grade in albs and amices, one bearing the oil, the other on the right the chrism; then the Sub-Deacon in tunic, the Deacon in dalmatic, the Priest in red cope, the Clergy in order; let them come to the font on the south side of the church, the five Deacons of the second grade singing this Litany, containing five out of each order of Saints, in the midst of the Clergy, walking after the Officiant—*

Lord, have mercy upon us.
Christ, have mercy upon us.
Christ, hear us.
Holy Mary, pray for us.

¶ *Here let the Procession rise and begin to go.*

Holy Mother of God, Holy Virgin of Virgins, Holy Michael, Holy Gabriel, Holy Raphael, All ye Holy Angels and Archangels of God,	Pray for us.

Holy John the Baptist,
All ye Holy Patriarchs and Prophets,
Holy Paul,
Holy James,
Holy Thomas,
Holy Simon,
Holy Thaddeus,
All ye Holy Apostles and Evangelists,
Holy Clement,
Holy Cornelius,
Holy Cyprian,
Holy Sebastian,
Holy Maurice with his Companions,
All ye Holy Martyrs,
Holy Benedict,
Holy Nicholas,
Holy Germanus,
Holy Romanus,
Holy Aldhelm,
Holy Augustine,
All ye Holy Confessors,
Holy Lucy,
Holy Petronilla,
Holy Katherine,
Holy Christina,
Holy Bridget,
All ye Holy Virgins,
All ye Saints,

} Pray for us.

¶ *In these two Litanies,* O God the Father of Heaven, *and the three following clauses are omitted, because Christ laid in the grave until the third day: so says Pope Gelasius.*

¶ *At the font let them keep in the same order till the end of the Litany, when the following change is made—*

	Candle-bearer.		Candle-bearer.	
	Cross-bearer.		Thurifer.	
Holy Oil.				Chrism.
Boy with Book.				Candle for Font.
Sub-Deacon.		Font.		Deacon.
		Officiant.		
		Five Deacons.		
		Bishop (if present).		

¶ *Then let the Officiant begin—*

The Lord be with you.

And with Thy spirit.

Let us pray.

Almighty, everlasting God, be present at the mysteries of Thy exceeding goodness, be present at the sacraments, and for the regenerating of the new people which the font of Baptism bringeth forth for Thee send out the Spirit of Adoption, that whatsoever is here done by our humble ministry may be fulfilled by the effectual working of Thy virtue

¶ *Let him proceed to chant as follows—*

Through our Lord Jesus Christ Thy Son, Who liveth and reigneth with Thee in the unity of the Holy Ghost, God,

℣. World without end.

℟. Amen.

℣. The Lord be with you,

℟. And with thy spirit.

℣. Lift up your hearts.

℟. We lift them up unto the Lord.

℣. Let us give thanks unto our Lord God.

℟. It is meet and right so to do.

It is very meet, right, and our bounden duty that we should at all times and in all places give thanks unto Thee, O Lord, Holy Father, Almighty, everlasting God, Who dost most wonderfully and effectually work in the invisible power of Thy sacraments. And albeit we are unworthy to discharge so great mysteries, yet do Thou not leave us destitute of Thy gifts of grace, and incline Thy merciful ears to our prayers.

O God, Whose Spirit moved upon the face of the waters amidst the very first elements of the world, that even then nature might take into herself the sanctification of the waters; O God, Who by washing away the crimes of the guilty world in water didst shadow forth the figure of regeneration in the very out-pour of the Deluge, that the mystery of one and the same element might be both the end of vice and the source of virtue; look down, we beseech Thee, O Lord, on the face of Thy Church, and increase and multiply in her Thy regenerated people; Thou Who by the mighty power of Thy abundant grace dost gladden Thy city, and openest the font of Baptism for the calling in of the Gentiles throughout the whole world, that at the command of Thy Majesty it may receive the grace of Thy Only-begotten of the Holy Ghost.

¶ *Here let him divide the water with his hand in the form of a Cross, saying,*

May He fertilize this water prepared for the regeneration of man by the hidden intermixture of His light, that by a holy conception a heavenly offspring may rise up out of the spotless womb of the divine font, into a new-born creature. And let all who differ in sex or age be brought forth by parent grace unto the same infancy. Wherefore at Thy command, O Lord, let every unclean spirit depart far hence; let the whole malice and fraud of the devil stand afar off. Let no power of the enemy intrude and find place here, nor haunt or lie in wait around, nor creep in surreptitiously, nor infect with poison.

Let this creature be holy and innocent, free from all assault of the adversary, and purified by the abolishing of all wickedness. Let it be a living + font, a regenerating + water, a purifying + stream; that all those that are to be washed in this laver of salvation, through the operation in them of the Holy Ghost, may obtain the favour of perfect purification.

Wherefore I bless thee, O creature of water, by the living + God, by the true + God, by the holy + God, by + God Who in the beginning did divide thee by His word from the dry land, Whose spirit moved upon thee, Who caused thee to flow out of Paradise, and commanded thee to water the earth in four rivers.

¶ *Here let the Priest throw water out of the font with his hand, in the form of the Cross, into the four quarters.*

Who, when thou wast bitter in the desert, poured sweetness into thee and made thee fit to drink; and brought thee forth out of the rock for the people that were athirst.

I bl+ess thee by Jesus Christ His only Son our Lord, Who in Cana of Galilee did turn thee into wine by His powerful sign and miracle; Who did walk upon thee with His feet, and was by John baptized in thee in Jordan; Who did bring thee forth out of His side together with blood, and commanded His disciples in thee to baptize believers, saying, Go ye teach all nations, baptizing them in the Name of the Father, and of the Son, and of the Holy Ghost.

¶ *Here let him change his voice, and read.*

Do Thou, O God, almighty and merciful, be present with us who keep these commandments; do Thou graciously breathe upon us.

¶ *Here let him breathe three times upon the font in the form of the Cross.*

Do Thou bl+ess these pure waters with Thy mouth; that, over and above the natural cleansing power they may exercise over bodies washed therein, they may be effectual to the purifying of souls.

¶ *Here he shall let fall drops of wax from the candle into the font in the form of a Cross, and then say, chanting again—*

Let the power of the Holy Ghost descend into this font and the fulness thereof, and make the whole body of this water fruitful in regenerating power.

¶ *Here let him dip the candle into the middle of the font, making a Cross, and then go on—*

Here let the stains of all sin be done away: here let nature, formed after Thine image, and reformed for the honour of its Author, be cleansed from all the filthiness of the old man.

¶ *Here let the candle be taken out of the font, with these words—*

That every man that approacheth this sacrament of regeneration may be born again into the new infancy of true innocency. Through

¶ *Here let him read,*

our Lord Jesus Christ Thy Son. Who.

¶ *No oil or chrism is to be poured into the font, unless there be a baptism.*

¶ *The blessing of the font ended, let three Clergy of higher grade in silk copes, chant this Litany as they go in procession, in the same way as* Thou, Leader kind.

Cl. King of all the holy angels,
This whole world in mercy aid.

¶ *Let the Choir repeat; and so after every verse.*

Cl. Do thou first plead for us, Mother
Of the Branch, most holy maid;
And the Father's choir most high,
Bright angelic company.

Ch. King of all.

Cl. Supplicate your Heavenly King,
All ye Apostolic band;
Let the out-pour'd blood of martyrs
Plead for us at Thy Right Hand.

Ch. King of all.

Cl. All ye confessors implore Him;
  Virgins, consonant in grace,
Pray indulgence greater for us,
  For probation longer space.

Ch. King of all.

Cl. All ye saints and perfect spirits,
  We beseech you to entreat
That our sins be purged from us
  Through your prayers before God's feet.

Ch. King of all.

Cl. Hear us, O Christ Jesus, Shepherd
  Of Thy people breathing grace,
Who didst form the clay that made us,
  And the authors of our race.

Ch. King of all.

Cl. Grant us, Holy Spirit, equal
  Of the Father and the Son,
Truly Thee to know, Thee only
  To love till Time's course be run.

Ch. King of all.

¶ *Then let Mass be begun solemnly by the Precentor, without rulers of Choir, with the* Kyrie, *taking the chant from* O Light and Source, *without the* ℣.; *meantime let the Priest in chasuble, at the Altar, say* Confession *and* Absolution, *with suffrages, and the collect,* Take away from us O Lord, *as usual, without the kiss of Peace. Then let him cense the Altar, and begin the* Gloria in Excelsis. *Then let all take off their black copes and genuflect; then let all the bells be rung together as the Choir chant,* And on earth peace.

The Lord be with you.

Let us pray.

O God, Who dost enlighten this most holy night with the glory of the Lord's Resurrection, keep in the children of Thy new family the spirit of adoption which Thou hast given; that they, being renewed in body and mind, may offer unto Thee a pure service. Through.

¶ *Let the Epistle be read in the pulpit.*

The Epistle. Coloss. iii. 1-4.

Brethren, if ye be risen with Christ, seek those things which are above, where Christ sitteth on the Right Hand of God. Set your affections on things above, not on things on the earth: for ye are dead, and your life is hid with Christ in God. When Christ, Who is our life, shall appear, then shall ye also appear with Him in glory.

¶ *Then let two Clergy of second grade, in silk copes, chant in the pulpit—*

Alleluia! ℣. Ps. cxviii. O give thanks unto the Lord for He is gracious, because His mercy endureth for ever.

¶ *Let the Choir end with Cadence. Clergy again begin the* Alleluia, *without Cadence. Then let the Tract follow, chanted, whole and entire, by two Clergy of the second grade, in black copes, at the step of the quire, the Choir sitting.*

Tract. Ps. cxvii. O praise the Lord, all ye heathen; praise Him, all ye nations.

℣. For His merciful kindness is ever more and more towards us, and the truth of the Lord endureth for ever.

¶ *Meanwhile let the Deacon and Sub-Deacon go through the quire without the Cross, as usual, to read the Gospel; let two candle-bearers precede them, with extinguished lights; and let it be read in pulpit as on Sundays.*

The Gospel. Matt. xxviii. 1-7.

In the end of the Sabbath, as it began to dawn toward the first day of the week, came Mary Magdalene and the other Mary to see the sepulchre. And, behold, there was a great earthquake: for the angel of the Lord descended from Heaven, and came and rolled back the stone from the door, and sat upon it. His countenance was like lightning, and his raiment white as snow: and for fear of him the keepers did shake, and became as dead men. And the angel answered and said unto the women, Fear not ye: for I know that ye seek Jesus, which was crucified. He is not here: for He is risen, as He said. Come, see the place where the Lord lay. And go quickly, and tell His disciples that He is risen from the dead; and behold, He goeth before you into Galilee; there shall ye see Him: lo, I have told you.

¶ *No Offertory or Creed is said.*

The Lord be with you.

Let us pray.

Secret. Accept, we beseech Thee, O Lord, the prayers of Thy people, with the oblations of the Sacrifice; that being solemnly adopted into the Paschal mysteries, they may by the working of Thy mighty power be profitable unto us for our health to all eternity. Through.

Preface. And Thee at all times, but chiefly on this night.

Within the Canon, In communion with; *and* This therefore.

¶ *On this day the* Sanctus *is solemnly said. No* Agnus Dei *is said, nor is the* Peace *given; but after a short pause let Vespers as for a feast begin, without rulers of Choir, or ringing of bells, or* O God make speed, *by some one of upper grade, in behalf of the Choir.*

Ant. Alleluia!

Ps. cxvii. O praise the Lord, all ye heathen: praise Him, all ye nations. For His merciful kindness is ever more and more towards us: and the truth of the Lord endureth for ever. Praise the Lord. Glory.

Ant. Alleluia! Alleluia! Alleluia! Alleluia!

¶ *Then let the Anthem before* Magnificat *immediately be begun by the one of upper grade next in rank to the Celebrant, but it is not to be chanted through by the Choir before the Psalm is intoned. Let neither Altar nor Choir be censed.*

Ant. In the end.

Ps. Magnificat.

Ant. In the end of the Sabbath, when it began to dawn towards the first day of the week, came Mary Magdalene and the other Mary to see the sepulchre. Alleluia!

The Lord be with you.

Let us pray.

Pour into us, O Lord, the spirit of Thy love, that they whom Thou hast satisfied with the Paschal Sacrament may by Thy goodness be made of one mind. Through.

¶ *So let Mass and Vespers end together, the Deacon saying,* Ite Missa est, *with the tone of the* Alleluia.

Easter Day.

¶ *On Easter Day, before Mass and ringing of bells, let the Clergy assemble at church, and let all the lights be lit throughout the church. Let two of the upper grade, with Candle-bearers, Thurifer, and Clergy around them, go to the sepulchre, and after censing it with great veneration, i.e., genuflecting, place the Lord's Body on the Altar. Then let them take the Cross again out of the sepulchre, and let the one of highest grade begin,* Christ being raised. *Then let all the bells be rung together, and let the Procession go through the quire by the S of the presbytery, with the Cross borne with veneration on their arms, with Thurifer and Candle-bearers, going out by N. door of presbytery, to a certain Altar, on N. side of the church, i.e., S. Martin's, Choir following. The Lord's Body, which has been placed on the Altar in pyx, is committed to the care of the Sub-Treasurer, who suspends it in the tabernacle.*

Ant. Christ being raised from the dead, dieth no more; death hath no more dominion over Him; for in that He liveth, He liveth unto God. *Alleluia! Alleluia!*

℣. Now let the Jews declare, how the soldiers who kept the sepulchre lost the King when the stone was rolled, wherefore kept they not the rock of righteousness; let them either produce the buried, or adore the risen One, saying with us,

¶ *Let the Choir answer—*

Alleluia! Alleluia!

¶ *Then let the person of highest grade standing, at the station, turning to the Altar, say—*

℣. The Lord hath risen from the grave.

Let us pray.

O God, Who didst will Thy Son to suffer death upon the Cross for us, that Thou mightest cast out of us the power of the enemy, grant to us Thy servants that we may ever live rejoicing in His Resurrection. Through.

¶ *Then let all joyfully genuflect, and adore the Cross in order; let them return without procession quietly into the quire; then let all crosses and images throughout the church be uncovered, and the bells ring as usual for Matins.*

¶ *On Easter Day and all Sundays from now till Feast of Trinity let this Anthem be sung at sprinkling of holy water—*

I saw waters issuing out of the temple on the right hand. Alleluia!

And all those unto whom that water cometh shall live. And they shall say, Alleluia! Alleluia!

Ps. O give thanks unto the Lord for He is gracious, because His mercy endureth for ever.

I saw water. Glory. I saw.

℣. ℟. Coll. *as usual.*

The Office. Ps. cxxxix.

When I wake up, I am present with Thee, *Alleluia!* Thou hast laid Thy hand upon me, *Alleluia!* Such knowledge is too wonderful for me. *Alleluia! Alleluia!*

Ps. O Lord, Thou hast searched me out, and known me: Thou knowest my down-sitting, and mine up-rising.

The Collect.

God, Who on this day through Thine Only-begotten hast overcome death, and opened unto us the gate of everlasting life; as by preventing us Thou dost put into our minds good desires, so by Thy help bring the same to good effect. Who.

The Epistle. 1 Cor. v. 7, 8.

Brethren, Purge out .... sincerity and truth.

Gradual. Ps. cxviii. This is the day which the Lord hath made: we will rejoice and be glad in it.

℣. O give thanks unto the Lord for He is gracious, because His mercy endureth for ever.

Alleluia! ℣. 1 Cor. Christ our Passover is sacrificed.

The Sequence.

This day the dawn glows bright above the sun,
Telling how Christ hath fought and glorious victory won.
Jesus hath triumphed o'er the haughty foe,
And his foul camp majestic hath laid low.
Unhappy sin of Eve,
Of which all death do reap;
O happy Mary's child
With Whom now feast we keep.
Blest be the Queen exalted high,
His Mother, Who triumphantly
Hath spoiled hell and reigneth in the sky.
O King for ever, graciously
Accept the praise we offer Thee,
To Thee at God's Right Hand on high,
Crying aloud incessantly.
Thou, death's power now overthrown,
Triumphing on high art gone,
To joys of Heaven which are Thine own.
O vast, O fair, O high,
Light-giving clemency,
Breathing benignantly!
Honour to Thee and praise
Who didst that load upraise
Which burdened our old days.
Brightly shine the courts of God
Purchased by the crimson flood
Of the Lamb's most precious Blood.

By His mighty virtue He
Cleansed all our misery,
Granting gifts benign and free.
Awestruck within myself I gaze
Upon the wonders of these days,
That before our unworthy eyes
Such mighty sacraments should rise.

From the root of David springing,
Of Judah's tribe the Lion Thou
Hast arisen, glory bringing,
Who didst seem a Lamb but now.
Thou Who laid'st the earth's foundations
Seekest now the realms on high,
To eternal generations
Recompensing righteously.
Prince of evil, wicked fiend,
What avails thy impious lie?
In fiery chains thou art confined
By Christ's glorious victory.
Ye peoples, marvel at the tale!
Whoe'er such miracles hath heard?
That death o'er death should so prevail,
Such grace on sinners be conferred!
Judæa, unbelieving land,
Look forth and on the Christians gaze,
See how in joyous crowds they stand
And chant the blest Redeemer's praise!

Wherefore, O Christ, our holy King,
Loose us from guilt, and pardon bring.
Grant that Thy chosen bands with Thee
May rise in blest felicity,
And of Thy grace rewarded be.
The Holy Paraclete's blest comfort, Lord,
We look for, trusting to Thy gracious Word,
Soon as Ascension's holy day
In solemn joy hath passed away,
When Thou, returning to the skies,
O'ershadowed by a cloud to endless praise didst rise.

The Gospel. Mark xvi. 1-7.

At that time, Mary Magdalene .... as He said unto you.

The Creed.

Offert. Ps. lxxvi. The earth trembled and was still, when God arose to judgment. *Alleluia!*

Secret. Accept, we beseech Thee, O Lord, the prayers of Thy people, with the oblations of the Sacrifice, that being solemnly adopted into the Paschal mysteries, they may, by the working of Thy mighty power, be profitable unto us for our health to all eternity. Through.

The Preface. And Thee indeed.

Within the Canon, Communicating with; *and* This therefore.

Comm. 1 Cor. v. Christ our Passover is sacrificed, *Alleluia!* therefore let us keep the feast with the unleavened bread of sincerity and truth. *Alleluia! Alleluia! Alleluia!*

P. Comm. Pour into us, O Lord, the spirit of Thy love; that those whom Thou hast satisfied with the Paschal Sacrament, may of Thy goodness be made of one mind. Through.

EASTER MONDAY.

The Office. Ex. xiii.

The Lord *hath brought you* into a land flowing with milk and honey. *Alleluia!* And that the Lord's law may *always* be in Thy mouth. *Alleluia! Alleluia!*

Ps. cxviii. O give thanks unto the Lord for He is gracious, because His mercy endureth for ever.

The Collect.

O God, Who in the Paschal Feast hast bestowed restoration upon the world; we beseech Thee, continue unto Thy people Thy heavenly gift, that they may both attain unto perfect freedom and advance unto life eternal. Through.

The Lesson. Acts x. 37-43.

In those days Peter, standing in the midst of the people, said, Men and brethren, that word .... receive remission of sins.

Gradual. Ps. cxviii. This is the day which the Lord hath made: we will rejoice and be glad in it.

℣. Let Israel now confess that He is gracious, and that His mercy endureth for ever.

Alleluia! ℣. Luke xxiv. Did not our hearts burn within us, while He talked with us by the way *concerning Jesus.*

The Sequence.

Let the old leaven be purged out,
With purity to bring about
  A resurrection new:
This is our hopes expected hour,
Behold this Day of mighty power
  By the Law's witness true;
This Day hath spoil'd th' Egyptian foe,
And let the Hebrew captives go
  From iron bondage free,

Who toiling for deliverance, pin'd
Midst clay and bricks and straw, confin'd
  In cruel slavery.
Now let the praise of God most high,
And voices shouting victory,
  Break forth in triumph free:
This is the Day the Lord hath made,
This Day hath all our grief repaid,
  Now we salvation see.
The Law foreshadow'd things to come,
Christ of all promises the sum
  Doth all things consummate;
The precious Blood of Christ out-pour'd
Hath wholly quenched the flaming sword,
  Unguarded is the gate.
Jesus, Who brought us life and joy,
By Isaac is foreshown, the boy
  For whom the ram was slain:
Forth from the pit doth Joseph rise,
So vanquishing Death's penalties
  Jesus comes back again.
Free from the serpent's deadly power
He Pharaoh's serpents doth devour
  Like Moses' rod of yore;
To those by fiery serpents' bite
Wounded, the brazen serpent's sight
  Doth life and health restore.
Piercing his jaw with iron hook,
Christ the great dragon captive took:
  In cockatrice's den
The weaned child puts in his hand,
Forthwith affrighted from the land
  Flees the old foe of men.
When to God's house Elisha went,
The mocking tribe by she-bears rent,
  Soon felt the bald-head's wrath:
David escapes in subtilty,
The scape-goat swiftly flees away;
  The sparrow flieth forth.
With jaw-bone arm'd hath Samson slain
A thousand men, yet doth not deign
  In his own tribe to wed;
From Gaza's gates he burst the bar,
And bearing posts and doors afar,
  To the hill's top he sped;
So from the portals of the grave
The tribe of Judah's Lion brave
  The third day doth arise;
The Father's voice doth roar on high,
He to the Heavenly treasury
  Doth bear the captured prize.
From the Lord's Face a fugitive
The whale doth Jonah forth alive,
Of Jonah true figurative,

Out of his belly cast;
The cluster ripe of Cyprus vine
Doth grow and bring forth noble wine;
The Synagogue's pale blossoms pine,
The Church doth ever last.
Twixt death and life the fight is done,
The Lord is risen—the victory won;
Witnesses with that Holy One
Rise too the saints beneath;
Let the new morn, the new-born Day
Wipe yester-even's tears away,
It is the time of holy day,
For Life hath vanquish'd Death.
O Jesu! Victor, Life, we pray;
Jesu, of life the oft-trod way,
Whose Death hath Death abolished,
Deign us with faith assur'd to lead
Unto the Paschal Board.
O Bread of Life! O Springing Well!
True fruitful Vine, we greet Thee well;
Deign us to feed, to cleanse us deign;
From second death and bitter pain
Deliver us, O Lord!

The Gospel. Luke xxiv. 13-35.

At that time two of *the* disciples *of Jesus* went .... known of them in breaking of bread.

Offert. Matt. xxviii. The angel of the Lord descended from Heaven, and said to the women: *Whom seek ye?* He is risen, as He said. *Alleluia!*

Secret. We who offer this Paschal Sacrifice, beseech Thee, O Lord, that what we frequent in outward act, we may effectually apprehend. Through Him Who rose from the dead, our Lord Jesus Christ, Thy Son. Who.

Comm. Luke xxiv. The Lord is risen, and hath appeared to Peter. *Alleluia!*

P. Comm. We beseech Thee, O Lord, let the devout partaking of the Paschal Sacrament have its perfect work in us, and translate our affections from earthly to heavenly ordinances. Through.

EASTER TUESDAY.

The Office. Ecclus. xv.

She shall give Him the water of wisdom to drink. *Alleluia!* He shall be stayed upon her, and shall not be moved. *Alleluia! Alleluia!* She shall exalt Him for ever. *Alleluia! Alleluia!*

Ps. cxviii. O give thanks unto the Lord for He is gracious, because His mercy endureth for ever.

The Collect.

O God, Who dost continually multiply Thy Church with new offspring; grant unto Thy servants that they may hold fast in their lives the Sacrament which they have received by faith. Through.

The Lesson. Acts xiii. 16, 26-33.

In those days Paul stood up, and beckoning with his hand that they should hold their peace, said, Men and brethren, children of the stock of Abraham .... raised up again Jesus *Christ our Lord.*

Gradual. Ps. cxviii. This is the day which the Lord hath made: we will rejoice and be glad in it.

℣. Let them give thanks whom the Lord hath redeemed: and delivered from the hand of the enemy, and gathered them out of the lands.

Alleluia! ℣. John. xx. Jesus *our Lord rose, and* stood in the midst *of His disciples,* and said, Peace be with you.

The Sequence.

Pour forth, chaste band, your holy canticles,
With deep-toned organ peal accompanied;
Unto the King Who burst the gates of hell,
Our God, repeat your joyful melodies.
When death He had o'ercome, He rose again,
Bearing perpetual joy to all the world.
Lost souls that crowd Cocytus' dismal brink,
Unwonted brightness wondering descry
As He doth enter, blessed Lord of life.
The mighty demon multitude,
Smitten with fear and trembling, quake.
Deeply they sigh and wail aloud;
And much they marvel, Who so bold
To break the iron prison-bars?
Meanwhile into the courts above,
Begirt with glittering bands, He comes,
And comforts the disciples' fainting hearts.
Let us awestruck, His trophies contemplating,
With lowly voice our supplication make
That we amidst the honoured Virgin band
May celebrate our Easter Festival,
And on the hallowed Galilean day*
Gaze on the glorious beams of dawning light.

* This is an ancient name for Easter Tuesday.

The Gospel. Luke xxiv. 33-47.

At that time Jesus Himself stood in the midst .... in His Name among all nations.

Offert. Ps. xviii. The Lord thundered out of Heaven, and the Highest gave His thunder. The springs of water were seen. *Alleluia!*

Secret. Receive, O Lord, the prayers of Thy Church, that rejoiceth in the grace of its redemption, that it may be sustained by confidence in these present gifts, and steadfast faith in Thy resurrection. Through.

Comm. Col. iii. If ye be risen with Christ, seek, those things which are above, *Alleluia!* where Christ sitteth on the Right Hand of God. Set your affections on things above. *Alleluia!*

P. Comm. We pray Thee, O Lord, that the mysteries of which we have partaken may sanctify us, and enable us duly to observe the Paschal Feast. Through.

WEDNESDAY IN EASTER WEEK.

The Office. Matt. xxv.

Come, ye blessed of My Father, inherit the kingdom, *Alleluia!* which is prepared for you from the beginning of the world. *Alleluia! Alleluia! Alleluia!*

Ps. xcviii. O sing unto the Lord a new song: for He hath done marvellous things.

The Collect.

O God, Who by the yearly solemnity of the Resurrection of our Lord fillest us with joy; mercifully grant that, through the feasts which we celebrate in this world, we may come at last to those joys that are eternal. Through.

The Lesson. Acts iii. 13-19.

In those days Peter *opened his mouth and said, Men of Israel, and ye that fear God, give audience,* The God of Abraham, and of Isaac .... Repent, therefore, and be converted, that your sins may be blotted out.

Gradual. Ps. cxviii. This is the day which the Lord hath made: we will rejoice and be glad in it.

℣. The Right Hand of the Lord bringeth mighty things to pass: the Right Hand of the Lord hath the pre-eminence.

Alleluia! ℣. Matt. xxviii. *The Lord arose and met the women,* saying, All hail! And they came and held Him by the feet.

The Sequence.

Let all the world with prayer and praise,
Keeping the Easter Festival,
United Alleluias sing.
Washed and made white in holy font,
Renouncing hell's impurities,
Let the sweet band of innocents rejoice.
Let us too tune our slackened strings,
With music's art and mellowed note,
And to our proses modulate
With ringing voice fit cadences,
For Christ is the meek Victim made,
And for our restoration He
The Cross's infamy hath borne.
He, Life abiding ever,
Did suffer pains of death,
Refusing not to taste
The bitter cup of gall.
Those cruel wounds He bare,
Transfixed with nails and lance;
So suffering, bearing all our sins,
He did to lowest hell descend.
Thence taking from the enemy his arms,
Mighty in triumph beareth back the spoil.
Then death o'ercome, and taking flesh again,
On the third day the Conqueror doth rise,
To Him then let us chant exulting hymns
Through Whom eternal life hath shone on us,
And the bright courts of Heaven open'd wide—
Excellent glory unto Him be given.

The Gospel. John xxi. 1-14.

At that time Jesus showed Himself again .... after that He was risen from the dead.

Offert. Ps. lxxviii. *The Lord* opened the doors of Heaven. He rained down manna also upon them for to eat: and gave them food from Heaven. So man did eat angels' food. *Alleluia!*

Secret. May the Sacrifice, O Lord, offered in the Paschal rejoicings obtain for us the gift of Thy gracious favour, seeing that thereby Thy Church is wonderfully fed and nourished. Through.

Comm. Rom. vi. Christ being raised from the dead, dieth no more, *Alleluia!* Death hath no more dominion over Him. *Alleluia! Alleluia!*

P. Comm. Grant, we beseech Thee, O Lord, that we being cleansed wholly from the old man, may by the receiving of Thy adorable Sacrament be transformed into the new creature. Through.

THURSDAY IN EASTER WEEK.

The Office. Wisd. x.

They magnified with one accord Thine hand, that fought for them. *Alleluia!* For wisdom opened the mouth of the dumb, and made the tongues of them that cannot speak eloquent. *Alleluia! Alleluia!*

Ps. cxviii. O give thanks unto the Lord for He is gracious, because His mercy endureth for ever.

The Collect.

O God, Who hast knit together in one divers nations in the confession of Thy Name, grant that they who have been born again by the water of Baptism, may have one inward faith and one outward devotion. Through.

The Lesson. Acts viii. 26-40.

In those days the Angel of the Lord spake unto Philip .... preached in all the cities, till he came to Cæsarea, *the Name of our Lord Jesus Christ.*

Gradual. Ps. cxviii. This is the day which the Lord hath made: we will rejoice and be glad in it.

℣. The same stone which the builders refused: is become the head-stone in the corner. This is the Lord's doing: and it is marvellous in our eyes.

¶ *The* Gradual *is not to be repeated after its* ℣. *this day or next.*

Alleluia! ℣. Mark xiv. *On the day of My Resurrection, saith the Lord,* I will go before you into Galilee.

The Sequence.

Say, from what regions hastening,
With tidings of new joy to men,
Doth thou revisit our abode?
With look serene and thrilling voice,
She,* "Alleluia!" did reply:
"To me an Angel hath declared
Things marvellous concerning Christ,
And with exulting voice did sing,
The Lord of Heaven is risen indeed!"

* *i.e.*, S. Mary Magdalene.

Forthwith with winged joyousness,
Swift as a bird she sped away,
Rejoined her fellows, and declared
How the old law is now made void,
And the new law of grace doth reign.
Now therefore, fellow-servants, cry aloud.
This day did Christ redeem us all from death.
The Father did deliver up the Son
For us men, to be slain by wicked hands.
The Son did willingly submit to die
So from eternal death to ransom us.
Now may we all in safety take our rest,
And win the joys of never-ending life.
Ye then, my fellow-servants, keep with me
This holy Easter Feast: Christ is our peace.

The Gospel. John xx. 11-18.

At that time Mary stood without .... spoken these things unto her.

Offert. Exod. iii. *On the day of your feast, saith the Lord,* I will bring you into a land flowing with milk and honey. *Alleluia!*

Secret. Graciously accept, we beseech Thee, O Lord, the offering of Thy people; that they being renewed by the confession of Thy Name in Baptism, may obtain everlasting bliss. Through.

Comm. 1 Pet. ii. *O* peculiar people, shew forth the praises of Him. *Alleluia!* Who hath called you out of darkness into His marvellous light. *Alleluia!*

P. Comm. Hear our prayers, O Lord, that, by frequenting these sacred mysteries of our redemption, we may obtain help for this life present, and gain the favour of joys eternal. Through.

FRIDAY IN EASTER WEEK.

The Office. Ps. lxxviii.

The Lord brought them out safely, *Alleluia!* and overwhelmed their enemies with the sea. *Alleluia! Alleluia! Alleluia!*

Ps. Hear my law, O my people: incline your ears unto the words of my mouth.

The Collect.

O almighty and eternal God, Who hast bestowed on us the Paschal Mystery in token of the covenant of man's reconciliation;

give unto us the will to show forth in our lives that which we profess with our lips. Through.

The Epistle. I Pet. iii. 18-22.

Dearly beloved, Christ also hath once suffered for sins .... is on the right hand of God.

Gradual. Ps. cxviii. This is the day which the Lord hath made: we will rejoice and be glad in it.

℣. Blessed be He that cometh in the Name of the Lord. God is the Lord, Who hath shewed us light.

¶ Gradual *not to be repeated.*

Alleluia! ℣. Ps. xcvi. Tell it out among the heathen that the *Lord hath reigned from the tree.*

The Sequence.

Unto the Paschal Victim bring,
Christians, your thankful offering,
The Lamb redeemed the flock,
So Christ the spotless, without guile,
To God did sinners reconcile.
In wondrous deadly shock
Lo! death and life contend and strive;
The Lord of life, Who died, doth reign and live.
Declare unto us, Mary, say,
What thou sawest on the way?
I saw the grave which could not Christ retain,
I saw His glory when He rose again;
I saw th' Angelic witnesses around;
The napkin and the linen clothes I found.
Christ our hope hath risen, and He
Before you goes to Galilee.
Believe we Mary's word alone; refuse
To heed the sayings of the lying Jews.
Christ from the dead we know is risen indeed:
Victorious King, have mercy in our need!

The Gospel. Matt. xxviii. 16-20.

At that time the eleven disciples went away .... unto the end of the world.

Offert. Lev. xxiii. This shall be a day to be remembered by you, *Alleluia!* and ye shall keep it a solemn feast-day for the Lord in your generations: a day for a statute for ever. *Alleluia! Alleluia! Alleluia!*

Secret. We beseech Thee, O Lord, graciously accept the offerings which we present for an atonement for the sins of those that have been regenerated, and for the hastening of heavenly succour. Through.

Comm. Matt. xxviii. All power is given to Me in heaven and in earth, *Alleluia!* Go ye, teach all nations, baptizing them in the Name of the Father, and of the Son, and of the Holy Ghost. *Alleluia! Alleluia!*

P. Comm. O God, Who by the remission of sins hast begotten the children of Thy adoption, grant that all Thy faithful may truly apprehend the blessings they have received in this present sacrament. Through.

SATURDAY IN EASTER WEEK.

The Office. Ps. cv.

He brought forth His people with joy, *Alleluia!* and His chosen with gladness. *Alleluia! Alleluia!*

Ps. O give thanks unto the Lord, and call upon His Name; tell the people what things He hath done.

The Collect.

Grant, we beseech Thee, Almighty God, that we, who with reverence have celebrated this Feast of Easter, may through it arrive at everlasting joys. Through.

The Lesson. I Pet. ii. 1-10.

Dearly beloved, laying aside, *therefore*, all malice .... now have obtained mercy.

¶ *Let this* Alleluia! *be sung by two boys in surplices in the pulpit.*

Alleluia! ℣. Ps. cxviii. This is the day which the Lord hath made: we will rejoice and be glad in it.

¶ *Let this* Alleluia! *be sung by two boys in surplices at the step of the quire*

Alleluia! ℣. Ps. cxiii. Praise the Lord, ye servants: O praise the Name of the Lord.

¶ *Let the Choir finish it.*

℣. Blessed be the Name of the Lord; from this time forth for evermore.

¶ Alleluia! *is repeated here without cadence.*

The Sequence.

Upon the week's first dawning gray
The Son of God that blessed day
  Our hope and glory rose;
The king of evil and his crew
Vanquish'd, hell's portals open threw,
  And triumph'd o'er His foes.
He by His Resurrection blest,
Throughout the world with joy confest,
  Doth consolation shed.
Harbinger of His rising then,
Right quickly Mary Magdalen
  With her glad tidings sped.
She to Christ's brethren, grieving sore,
That their dear Lord should be no more,
  Did joy long look'd for bring;
O blessed eyes! which first did see
Set free from death's captivity
  The world's Almighty King!
This is indeed that woman wailing
At Jesus' feet, Whose grace availing
  Did wash her sins away;
While silent she doth pray and weep
For Christ her Lord, affection deep
  Her actions all display.
Not ignorant Whom she worships there,
Nor yet for what should be her prayer,
  Her guilty soul is heal'd.
O Mary! Mother of devotion!
Star thou art callèd of the ocean
  By merit of thy deed!
Made equal to Christ's Mother when
That name Thou didst receive from men,
  Far lower is Thy meed;
She, the world's Mistress glorified;
The sinner, she, beatified;
The Church doth each one welcome in
Of happiness the origin.
The portal, she, through which the light
Upon our darkness dawnèd bright:
She, herald of her risen Lord,
Made the world glad in full accord.
O Mary Magdalen! we pray
Hear thou our joyful vows to-day;
To merit grace, before Christ's Face,
  This company commend;
That so the Fount of Mercy great!
Which wash'd thee in thy lost estate,
May cleanse us too, His servants true,
  And gracious pardon send.

The Gospel. John xx. 1-9.

At that time, the first day of the week cometh Mary Magdalene .... rise again from the dead

Offert. Ps. cxviii. Blessed be He that cometh in the Name of the Lord: we have wished you good luck, ye that are of the house of the Lord. God is the Lord, Who hath showed us light. *Alleluia! Alleluia!*

Secret. Grant, we beseech Thee, O Lord, that we may always show forth our thankfulness by these Paschal mysteries: that the work of restoration being continually carried on in us, may be unto us an occasion of perpetual gladness. Through.

Comm. Gal. iii. As many of you as have been baptized into Christ, have put on Christ. *Alleluia!*

P. Comm. Being quickened by the gift of our redemption, we beseech Thee, O Lord, to grant that through this help to eternal salvation, a true faith may ever be increased in us. Through.

Sunday in the Octave of Easter.

¶ *All as Easter Day except no* Gradual, *and the* Alleluia! *is*—

Alleluia! ℣. 1 Cor. v. Christ our Passover is sacrificed for us.

Alleluia! ℣. Matt. xxviii. The angel of the Lord descended from Heaven, and came and rolled back the stone from the door and sat upon it.

The Sequence.

Let us with lowly voice
The Saviour's praises sing;
And glorify with melodies devout
Messiah, heavenly Lord,
Who made Himself of no repute
Us lost men to set free:
Shrouding with fleshly veil
His glorious Deity.
In swathing mean disguis'd
He in a manger lies,
For the transgressors' sake;
Naked from Paradise,
Outcast, expatriate,
In Joseph's, Mary's, Simeon's arms,
A helpless babe He lies.
By circumcision's rite,
By legal offering,
As sinner He is cleans'd
Who yet Himself is wont

Our misdeeds to remit,
At John His servant's hands
He deigns to be baptiz'd;
Bears with the tempter's snares,
Flies persecuting stones,
Hunger's sharp pangs endures,
Sleeps weary, sadly weeps;
E'en washes His disciples' feet,
He, the God-Man, the mightiest, the meekest.
Yet midst these lowly acts
Of poor humanity,
His mighty Deity,
In no wise could be hid,
By divers signs display'd,
And teaching marvellous.
At marriage feast He gives
To water taste of wine;
The blinded eyes He rob'd
With vivifying light;
The whitened leprosy
With gentle touch he heal'd;
The dead He from corruption rais'd,
And cured the paralytic limbs;
He staunched the bloody flux,
And with five loaves five thousand satisfied.
Upon the stormy lake He walk'd
As on dry land, and bade the winds be still;
He loos'd the stammering tongue,
The deaf He made to hear,
The fevers He drove out.
These mighty wonders and the like achiev'd,
Of His own will being taken and condemn'd,
He scorn'd not bitter crucifixion's shame;
But on His death the sun refused to look.
The Day hath shone on us,
The Day the Lord hath made.
Putting the foe to flight,
Victorious He appears
Unto His loving brethren alive;
To Mary first, to the Apostles next,
Expounding Scripture, opening their hearts,
That so they might unlock deep truths touching Himself.
Therefore with one consent
All things rejoicingly
Welcome the rising Christ.
The flowers, the fruitful fields
With new-born freshness spring;
Now the keen frost is gone,
The birds sing jubilee;
The sun and moon, o'ercast
With gloom at Jesus' death,
Shine forth more brilliantly;
The verdant earth salutes

With joy the rising Christ,
Which quaking uttered threats
Of ruin at His death.
Exult we on that day
When Jesus rose again,
And opened to our feet the path of life.
Let stars, earth, sky, rejoice,
And all the choirs on high
Upraise their grateful voice
To praise the Trinity.

THE SUNDAY CELEBRATION FOR THE WEEK.

The Office. 1 Peter ii.

As new-born babes, *Alleluia! as reasonable beings* desire the sincere milk of the word. *Alleluia! Alleluia! Alleluia!*

Ps. lxxxi. Sing we merrily unto God our strength: make a cheerful noise unto the God of Jacob.

The Collect.

Grant, we beseech Thee, Almighty God, that we who have fulfilled the Paschal Feast, may by Thy bounty hold it fast in our lives and conversation. Through.

The Epistle. 1 John v. 4-10.

Dearly beloved, whatsoever is born of God .... hath the witness in himself.

Alleluia! ℣. John xx. After eight days Jesus came, the doors being shut, and stood in the midst *of His Disciples*, and said, Peace be unto you.

Alleluia! ℣. Matt. xxviii. The angel of the Lord descended from Heaven, and came and rolled back the stone and sat upon it.

℣. The angel answered and said unto the women, *Whom seek ye? But they said, Jesus of Nazareth.*

¶ *These two verses are said alternately, when the Service is of the week-day; but if there be no week-day vacant, the last verse is wholly omitted.*

The Gospel. John xx. 19-31.

At that time, the same day at evening .... ye might have life through His Name.

Offert. Matt. xxviii. The angel of the Lord descended from Heaven, and said to the women, *Whom seek ye?* He is risen, as He said. *Alleluia!*

Secret. Receive, we beseech Thee, O Lord, the gifts of Thy

Church in her gladness: and as Thou hast given her cause for so great joy, bestow upon her the fruition of eternal happiness. Through.

Preface. The daily one.

Comm. John xx. Reach hither thy finger, and behold *the place of the nails, Alleluia!* and be not faithless, but believing, *Alleluia! Alleluia!*

P. Comm. Grant, we beseech Thee, O Lord our God, that the sacred mysteries Thou hast given us for the defence of our renewed life, may be made by Thee our healing remedy now and evermore. Through.

WEDNESDAY.

The Epistle. I Cor. xv. 12-23.

Brethren, if Christ be preached .... But every man in his own order: *through Jesus Christ our Lord.*

The Gospel. Mark xvi. 9-13.

At that time, when Jesus was risen .... neither believed they them.

FRIDAY.

The Epistle. Hebrews xiii. 17-21.

Brethren, obey them .... for ever and ever. Amen.

The Gospel. Matt. xxviii. 8-15.

At that time the women departed quickly .... until this day.

¶ *On all feasts with rulers of Choir from the Octave of Easter to Ascension Day, the second* Alleluia! *will be one of the following; after which recourse must be had to those for Easter Week,* i.e., *those for Monday, Wednesday, and Thursday in order; and when these are all said, then let the following, nine in number, be begun again.*

Alleluia! ℣. Luke xxiv. Abide with us, O Lord, for it is toward evening, and the day is far spent.

Alleluia! ℣. Luke xxiv. Christ ought to have suffered and to rise from the dead: and to enter into His glory.

Alleluia! ℣. Rom. vi. Christ being raised from the dead, dieth no more: death hath no more dominion over Him.

Alleluia! ℣. *The Most High hath risen from the grave, Who hanged for us on the wood.*

Alleluia! ℣. *Christ hath risen, and hath shined on His people: whom He redeemed with His Blood.*

Alleluia! ℣. Rom. iv. Christ died for our sins, and rose again for our justification.

Alleluia! ℣. Luke xxiv. *Jesus our Lord rose* and stood in the midst of His disciples, and said, Peace be unto you.

Alleluia! ℣. Matt. xxviii. *The Lord arose, and meeting the women, said,* All hail! Then they came and held Him by the feet.

Alleluia! ℣. Matt. xvi. *On the day of My Resurrection, saith the Lord,* I will go before you into Galilee.

¶ *On all Sundays up to Ascension Day let the Mass of the Resurrection be said as on Easter Day, except the* Gradual, Communicating with, *and* This oblation. *The Sequence,* Unto the Paschal Victim, *is said. If a feast with rulers occur, let all be of the Saint's Day and Memorial of Resurrection, but not of Sunday. But let the Sunday Mass be said through the week with the common Preface; and if no such day is vacant, it is said in the Chapter-house on the Sunday.*

Second Sunday after Easter.

The Office. Ps. xxxiii.

The earth is full of the goodness of the Lord. *Alleluia!* By the word of the Lord were the heavens made. *Alleluia! Alleluia!*

Ps. Rejoice in the Lord, O ye righteous: for it becometh well the just to be thankful.

The Collect.

O God, Who in Thy Son's humiliation hast lifted up the world which lay prostrate, grant to Thy faithful people perpetual joyfulness, and cause them whom Thou hast rescued from the calamity of everlasting death to have the fruition of joys eternal. Through.

The Epistle. 1 Pet. ii. 21-25.

Brethren, Christ also suffered for us .... and Bishop of your souls.

Alleluia! ℣. John x. I am the good Shepherd, and know My sheep, and am known of Mine.

Alleluia; ℣. John x. *The good Shepherd hath risen: Who hath given His life for His flock.*

The Gospel. John x. 11-16.

At that time Jesus said, I am the good Shepherd .... and one Shepherd.

Offert. Ps. lxiii. O God, Thou art my God, early will I seek Thee: I will lift up my hands in Thy Name.

Secret. May this holy oblation, O Lord, ever draw down upon us a saving blessing; and effectually work in us that which in mystery it sheweth forth. Through.

Comm. John x. I am the good Shepherd, *Alleluia!* and I know My Sheep, and am known of Mine. *Alleluia! Alleluia!*

P. Comm. Grant, we beseech Thee, Almighty and merciful God, that we who receive Thy quickening grace may ever glory in Thy gift. Through.

WEDNESDAY.

The Epistle. 1 Peter i. 18-25.

Dearly beloved, Forasmuch as ye know .... endureth for ever.

The Gospel. Luke xxiv. 1-12.

At that time, upon the first day of the week .... which was come to pass.

FRIDAY.

The Epistle. Romans v. 18-21.

Brethren, as by the offence .... eternal life by Jesus Christ our Lord.

The Gospel. Matt. ix. 14-17.

At that time came to Him .... and both are preserved.

Third Sunday after Easter.

The Office. Ps. lxvi.

O be joyful in God, all ye lands, *Alleluia!* sing praises unto the honour of His Name, *Alleluia!* make His praise to be glorious. *Alleluia! Alleluia! Alleluia!*

Ps. Say unto God, O how wonderful art Thou in Thy works: through the greatness of Thy power.

The Collect.

God, Who shewest to them that be in error the light of Thy truth, to the intent that they may return into the way of righteousness; grant unto all them that are admitted into the fellowship of Christ's religion, that they may eschew those things that are contrary to their profession, and follow all such things as are agreeable to the same. Through.

The Epistle. 1 Peter ii. 11-19.

Dearly beloved, I beseech you .... Honour the King. Servants, be subject to your masters with all fear; not only to the good and gentle, but also to the froward. For this is thankworthy, *in Jesus Christ our Lord.*

Alleluia! ℣. John xvi. A little while, and ye shall not see Me: and again, a little while and ye shall see Me, because I go to the Father.

Alleluia! ℣. John xvi. But I will see you again, and your heart shall rejoice, and your joy no man taketh from you.

Alleluia! ℣. *Christ is risen, Who created all things, and pitied mankind.*

¶ *In this week and the next these two last verses are said alternately; the first of the three is equivalent to a* Gradual.

The Gospel. John xvi. 16-22.

At that time Jesus said to His disciples .... no man taketh from you.

Offert. Ps. cxlvi. Praise the Lord, O my soul; while I live will I praise the Lord: yea, as long as I have any being, I will sing praises unto my God. *Alleluia!*

Secret, O Lord, we beseech Thee, that it may be vouchsafed unto us by these mysteries to put a bridle on earthly desires, and learn to love things heavenly. Through.

Comm. John xvi. A little while, and ye shall not see Me, *Alleluia!* and again, a little while and ye shall see me, because I go to the Father. *Alleluia! Alleluia!*

P. Comm. Look upon Thy people, we beseech Thee, O Lord, and graciously absolve from the sins of this world those whom Thou hast vouchsafed to renew by eternal mysteries. Through.

WEDNESDAY.

The Epistle. I John i. 1-8.

Dearly beloved, these things write I.........the true light now shineth. *Through Jesus Christ our Lord.*

The Gospel. John iii. 25-36.

At that time there arose a question.........wrath of God abideth on him.

FRIDAY.

The Epistle. I Thess. v. 5-11.

Brethren, ye are all the children of light.........edify one another *in Christ Jesus our Lord.*

The Gospel. John xii. 46-50.

At that time said Jesus unto His disciples, I am come a light...... so I speak.

Fourth Sunday after Easter.

The Office. Ps. xcviii.

O sing unto the Lord a new song, *Alleluia!* for He hath done marvellous things, *Alleluia!* His righteousness hath He openly shewed in the sight of the heathen. *Alleluia! Alleluia!*

Ps. With His own right hand, and with His holy arm: hath He gotten Himself the victory.

The Collect.

O Almighty God, Who makest the faithful to be of one mind; grant unto Thy people, that they may love the thing which Thou commandest, and desire that which Thou dost promise; that so, among the manifold changes of the world, our hearts may there be fixed where true joys are to be found. Through.

The Epistle. James i. 17-21.

Dearly beloved, every good gift..............able to save your souls.

Alleluia! ℣. John xvi. I go to Him that sent Me; but because I have said these things unto you, sorrow hath filled your hearts.

Alleluia! ℣. John xvi. I tell you the truth, it is expedient for you that I go away.

¶ *For the week.*

Alleluia! ℣. Luke xxiv. The Lord hath risen indeed, and hath appeared unto *Peter*.

The Gospel. John xvi. 5-15.

At that time Jesus said unto his disciples, Now I go My way ...... shall shew it unto you.

Offert. Ps. lxvi. O be joyful in God, all ye lands: *O be joyful in God, all ye lands:* sing praises unto the honour of his Name. O come hither, and hearken, all ye that fear God: and I will tell you what *the Lord* hath done for my soul. *Alleluia.*

Secret. O God, Who, when Thou hadst risen from the dead after Thy Passion, didst return again in greater power unto Thy disciples; mercifully grant that this Easter Sacrifice may reconcile us to Thy Majesty, and make us better prepared in good works for the obtaining of Thy grace. Who.

Comm. John xvi. When the Comforter is come, the Spirit of Truth, He shall reprove the world of sin, and of righteousness, and of judgment. *Alleluia! Alleluia!*

P. Comm. Help us, O Lord our God, that, by that which we have received with faith, we may be both cleansed from sin, and delivered from all dangers. Through.

WEDNESDAY.

The Epistle. James ii. 1-13.

Dearly beloved, have not the faith of our Lord Jesus Christ .... mercy rejoiceth against judgment.

The Gospel. John vii. 11-15.

At that time, Jesus looking upon His disciples, said, Holy Father .... keep them from the evil.

FRIDAY.

The Epistle. James ii. 24-26.

Dearly beloved, ye see .... without works is dead also.

The Gospel. John xiii. 33-36.

At that time said Jesus to His disciples, Little children .... follow Me afterwards.

Fifth Sunday after Easter.

The Office. Isa. xlviii.

With a voice of singing declare ye, *and let Alleluia! be heard:* utter it even to the end of the earth! the Lord hath redeemed His *people. Alleluia! Alleluia!*

Ps. lxvi. O be joyful in God, all ye lands: sing praises unto the honour of His Name, make His praise to be glorious.

The Collect.

O Lord, from Whom all good things do come; grant to us Thy humble servants, that by Thy holy inspiration we may think those things that be good, and by Thy guiding may perform the same. Through.

The Epistle. James i. 22-27.

Dearly beloved, be ye doers of the Word .... unspotted from the world.

Alleluia! ℣. John xvi. Hitherto have ye asked nothing in My Name: ask and ye shall receive.

Alleluia! ℣. Rom. vi. Christ being raised from the dead, dieth no more: death hath no more dominion over Him.

The Gospel. John xvi. 23-30.

At that time said Jesus to His disciples, Verily, verily, I say unto you .... Thou camest forth from God.

Offert. Ps. lxvi. O praise our *Lord* God, ye people: and make the voice of His praise to be heard; Who holdeth our soul in life: and suffereth not our feet to slip. Praised be God, Who hath not cast out my prayer: nor turned His mercy from me. *Alleluia!*

Secret. Receive, O Lord, we beseech Thee, the prayers of the faithful, together with these oblations; that by means of this holy office we may attain unto eternal life. Through.

Comm. Ps. xcvi. O sing unto the Lord, *Alleluia!* sing unto the Lord, and praise His Name: be telling of His salvation from day to day. *Alleluia! Alleluia!*

P. Comm. Grant to us, Lord, we beseech Thee, that we being satisfied with the fulness of the heavenly Table, may both desire such things as be rightful, and also may obtain our desire. Through.

ROGATION MONDAY.

¶ *The Sunday Mass is said for High Mass this day, and the following Mass is said in Procession; but if a feast with rulers come upon this day the Sunday Mass is transferred, and used as the Mass in Procession on Rogation Tuesday, or the Vigil of Ascension Day.*

The Office. Ps. xviii.

So shall He hear my voice out of His holy temple, *Alleluia!* and my complaint shall come before Him, it shall enter even into His ears. *Alleluia! Alleluia!*

Ps. I will love Thee, O Lord, my strength: the Lord is my stony rock, and my defence: my Saviour.

The Collect.

Grant, we beseech Thee, Almighty God, that we, who in our afflictions put our trust in Thy goodness, may by Thy protection ever be defended against all adversities. Through.

¶ *Memorial of the Patron Saint of the church and of All Saints.*

The Epistle. James. v. 16-20.

Dearly beloved, confess your faults .... hide a multitude of sins.

Alleluia! ℣. Ps. cxviii. O give thanks unto the Lord for He is gracious, because His mercy endureth for ever.

The Gospel. Luke. xi. 5-13.

At that time Jesus said to His disciples, Which of you shall have a friend ...... give the Holy Spirit to them that ask Him?

Offert. Ps. cix. I will give great thanks unto the Lord with my mouth: and praise Him among the multitude: for He shall stand at the right hand of the poor: to save his soul from unrighteous judges. *Alleluia!*

¶ *Here may be the sermon.*

Secret. May these gifts, O Lord, both loose the bonds of our wickedness, and procure for us the favour of Thy mercy. Through.

Comm. Luke xi. Ask, and ye shall receive: seek, and ye shall find: knock, and it shall be opened to you. For every one that asketh, receiveth: and he that seeketh, findeth: and to him that knocketh, it shall be opened. *Alleluia!*

P. Comm. We beseech Thee, O Lord, further our prayers with Thy gracious favour, that we, receiving Thy gifts in trouble, may by reason of the comfort we find increase in love to Thee. Through.

ROGATION TUESDAY.

¶ *High Mass of Our Lady and Procession-Mass* Salus Populi, *unless the Sunday Mass was transferred, when it takes the place of the Mass* Salus Populi. *If a feast with rulers occur, the Mass of the feast takes the place of Our Lady's Mass. Only one* Alleluia! *is said at the Mass* Salus Populi.

THE VIGIL OF THE ASCENSION.

¶ *If there is no feast with rulers, the following is said for High Mass, and the Mass* Salus Populi *is said in the Procession. If there is a feast with rulers, then that is said for High Mass, and the Mass of the Vigil is said in Procession. If the Sunday Mass is transferred to this day, then that is said in Procession instead of the Mass* Salus Populi.

The Office. Ps. xlvii.

O clap your hands together, all ye people: O sing unto God with the voice of melody. *Alleluia! Alleluia!*

Ps. He shall subdue the people under us: and the nations under our feet.

The Collect.

Grant, we beseech Thee, Almighty Father, that our minds may be ever intent upon that blessed place whither Thine Only-begotten Son our Lord, the glorious Author of the approaching festival, hath gone before; that they may in conversation attain to that towards which by faith they reach forth. Through.

¶ *Memorials of Our Lady and All Saints.*

The Lesson. Acts iv. 32-35.

In those days the multitudes of them that believed .... according as he had need.

Alleluia! ℣. Ps. xlvii. O clap your hands together, all ye people; O sing unto God with the voice of melody.

The Gospel. John xvii. 1-11.

At that time Jesus lifted up His eyes to heaven ...... I come to Thee.

Offert. Acts i. Ye men of Galilee, why stand ye gazing up into heaven? This same Jesus, which is taken up from you into heaven, shall so come in like manner as ye have seen Him go into heaven. *Alleluia!*

Secret. We humbly present, O Lord, the Sacrifice in honour of Thy Son's adorable Ascension, for which we are preparing; grant, we beseech Thee, that by this most Holy Communion we may ascend unto the things of heaven through Him. Who.

Comm. John xvii. Father, while I was with them, I kept those whom Thou gavest Me. *Alleluia!* But now I come to Thee. I pray not that Thou shouldest take them out of the world, but that Thou shouldest keep them from the evil. *Alleluia! Alleluia!*

P. Comm. Grant, we beseech Thee, O Lord, that by this Sacrament which we have received, our devout affections may thither ascend, where Jesus Christ our Lord is with Thee in substance of our nature. Who.

Ascension Day.

The Office. Acts i.

Ye men of Galilee, why stand ye gazing up into heaven? *Alleluia! He* shall so come in like manner as ye have seen Him go into heaven. *Alleluia! Alleluia! Alleluia!*

Ps. And while they looked steadfastly toward heaven as He went up, behold, two men stood by them in white apparel. Which also said.

The Collect.

Grant, we beseech Thee, Almighty God, that like as we do believe Thy Only-begotten Son our Redeemer to have ascended into the heavens, so we may also in mind dwell in heavenly things. Through.

The Lesson. Acts i. 1-11.

The former treatise have I made .... see Him go into heaven.

Alleluia! ℣. Ps. xlvii. God is gone up with a merry noise: and the Lord with the sound of the trump.

Alleluia! ℣. Eph. iv. Christ when He ascended up on high led captivity captive, and gave gifts unto men.

¶ *This is said on this day and on the Octave day, even if it be a double feast.*

Alleluia! ℣. Ps. lxviii. *The Lord in the holy place of Sinai* ascended up on high, and led captivity captive.

¶ *This last is said daily through the Octave, except on the Sunday and Octave day, whatever feast occurs, except SS. Philip and James and the Invention of the Cross.*

The Sequence.

The Almighty King, victorious on this day,
Having redeem'd the world with puissant might,
Ascended to the skies from whence He came.
After His Resurrection He confirm'd
Th' Apostles' hearts for forty holy days,
And gave them power of remitting sins,
And sent them to baptize in all the world,
In grace of Father, Son, and Holy Ghost;
Commanding, as He sat with them at meat,
They should not from Jerusalem depart,
But wait for gifts which had been promised—
"After not many days the Comforter,
The Spirit, I will send to you on earth;
Ye shall bear witness to Me in Judea,
And in Jerusalem, and in Samaria."
And when He had said this, it came to pass
While they beheld, lo! He was taken up,
And a bright cloud out of their sight receiv'd Him,
As towards heaven steadfastly they look'd.
And, lo! to men in white apparel clad
Stood by them, saying, Wherefore gaze ye so
Into the height of heaven? for this Jesus
Who now from you to God's right hand is taken
Shall so come, in like manner as He goeth,
Th' entrusted talent's usury to require.

O God of heaven, of sea, of earth!
Thou dost man, whom Thou createdst—
Whom by fraud and subtilty
The foe drave forth from Paradise,
And, captive with himself,
Dragged down to Tartarus;
Whom by Thine own blood-shedding
Thou didst as God redeem—

To that same state bear back
From whence by sin he fell,
The joys of Paradise.
When Thou as Judge dost come
To doom the universe,
Grant, we beseech Thee, Lord,
Eternal joys to us
In the saints' blessed land,
In which we all to Thee
Shall Alleluias sing.

The Gospel. Mark xvi. 14-20.

At that time Jesus appeared unto the eleven *disciples* .... confirming the Words with signs following.

The Creed.

Offert. Ps. xlvii. God is gone up with a merry noise; and the Lord with the sound of the trump. *Alleluia!*

Secret. Receive, O Lord, the gifts which we offer in memory of the glorious Ascension of Thy Son; and mercifully grant that we may be both delivered from present dangers, and attain unto everlasting life. Through.

Preface. Who after His Resurrection.

Within the canon, In communion with.

Comm. Ps. lxviii. Sing unto the Lord, Who sitteth in the heavens over all from the beginning.

P. Comm. Grant, we beseech Thee, Almighty and most merciful God, that what we perceive to have been received in visible mysteries, we may obtain in their invisible efficacy. Through.

¶ *The same Mass is said throughout the Octave, except a feast with rulers occur, and except on the Sunday in the Octave; but without* Sequence *or* Creed.

Sunday After Ascension Day.

The Office. Ps. xxvii.

Hearken unto my voice, O Lord, when I cry unto Thee. *Alleluia!* My heart hath talked of Thee: *I have sought Thy face.* Thy face, Lord, will I seek: O hide not Thou Thy face from me. *Alleluia! Alleluia!*

Ps. The Lord is my light and my salvation: whom then shall I fear?

The Collect.

Almighty and eternal God, inspire Thy servants with willing devotion to Thee, that we may serve Thy Majesty with sincere hearts. Through.

¶ *Memorial of Ascension Day.*

The Epistle. 1 S. Peter iv. 7-11.

Dearly beloved, be ye sober .... through Jesus Christ *our Lord.*

Alleluia! ℣. Ps. xlvii. God reigneth over the heathen: God sitteth upon His holy seat.

Alleluia! ℣. John xiv. I will not leave you comfortless: I go away and come again unto you, and your heart shall rejoice.

¶ *No* Sequence *is said.*

The Gospel. John xv. 26-27—xvi. 1-4.

At that time said Jesus to His disciples, When the Comforter is come .... remember that I told you of them.

Offert. Ps. cxlvi. Praise the Lord, O my soul: while I live will I praise the Lord: as long as I have any being I will sing praises unto my God.

Secret. Grant, we beseech Thee, Almighty God, that we may offer with acceptance this sacrifice which is consecrated to be the Body and Blood of Him Whom, sitting at the right hand of Thy power, we assuredly believe to intercede for us, Thy Son our Lord Jesus Christ. Who.

Comm. John xvii. Father, when I was with them I kept those that Thou gavest Me. *Alleluia!* But now I come to Thee: I pray not that Thou wouldest take them out of the world, but that Thou wouldest keep them from the evil. *Alleluia! Alleluia!*

P. Comm. Grant, we beseech Thee, Almighty God, that by this most Holy Communion we may confidently believe that will be accomplished in the body of the whole Church which hath already been accomplished in her Head. Through.

¶ *If any feast with rulers occur on this Sunday, let all the Service be of the feast, and let the Sunday Mass be said in the Chapter-house with the chant upon the* Kyrie, etc., *as on a feast of three lessons without rulers; and one* Alleluia! ℣. The Lord reigneth. *Let the second* Alleluia *be used at the Mass of the feast, except it be the Invention of the Cross. On the Octave of Ascension all as on Ascension Day, except the* Sequence *and* Creed.

FRIDAY.

¶ *Service of S. Mary, if there be no feast with rulers. Let the second Alleluia be Alleluia!* ℣. The Lord reigneth.

THE VIGIL OF WHITSUN DAY.

¶ *Let the Priest and Ministers go to the Altar vested as on Easter Eve, without the Confession and only* Our Father. *Let the following Lessons be read by persons of higher grade in surplices, at the step of the quire, without titles.*

*The Lesson.**

God did tempt Abraham .... Beersheba; and Abraham dwelt there.

The Collect.

Let us pray.

O God, Who by the deed of Thy servant Abraham hast given to mankind an example of obedience; grant us both to vanquish our corrupt wills, and to fulfil Thy righteous commands in all things. Through.

¶ *The Lesson,* Moses therefore wrote this song. *Tract,* Give ear, O ye heavens! *as on Easter Eve.*

¶ *All the Tracts are said by the Choir alternately, except the last.*

Let us pray.

O God, the glory of the faithful and the life of the righteous, Who by Thy servant Moses has instructed us also in the measure of holy song: grant Thy mercy to all nations, by giving them happiness and removing terror far from them, that Thy warnings of vengeance may turn to their eternal salvation. Through.

¶ *The Lesson,* In those days seven women. *Tract,* My well-beloved hath, *as on Easter Eve.*

Let us pray.

O God, Who hast indoctrinated us in the pages of both Testaments for the celebration of this present festival, give unto us such a sense of Thy mercies that from our experience of gifts present our hope of future blessings may be confirmed. Through.

The Lesson.†

Hear Israel, the commandments of life .... and conversed with men.

* Gen. xxii. 1-19. † Baruch iii. 9-37.

Let us pray.

O God, Who, by the mouth of Thy prophets, hast commanded us to forsake the things of this world, and to press towards those that are eternal; grant unto Thy servants that what we have surely known to be commanded by Thee, by Thy heavenly inspiration we may be enabled to fulfil. Through.

Tract. Ps. xlii. Like as the hart desireth the water brooks; so longeth my soul after Thee, O God.

℣. My soul is athirst for God, yea, even for the living God: when shall I come to appear before the presence of God?

℣. My tears have been my meat day and night: while they daily say unto me, Where is now thy God?

Let us pray.

Grant, we beseech Thee, Almighty God, that we who celebrate the feast of the gift of the Holy Ghost, being inflamed with celestial desires, may ever thirst for the fountain of Life, Jesus Christ Thy Son.

Almighty and everlasting God, Who hast willed Thy Paschal Sacraments to be comprehended in the mystery of fifty days; grant, we beseech Thee, that the people which were scattered abroad by the confusion of tongues may by Thy heavenly gift be gathered together again into one confession of Thy Name. Through.

¶ *Here let the Litanies and Benediction of the Font all follow, exactly as on Easter Eve. In returning is said* King of all the holy. *Then let Mass begin. The* Kyrie *and* Confession *is said as usual. At the* Gloria in Excelsis, *let all genuflect, and take off their black copes, and let all the bells be rung.*

The Lord be with you.

Let us pray.

The Collect.

Grant, we beseech Thee, Almighty God, that the rays of Thy brightness may shine upon us; and that the light of Thy light may, by the illumination of the Holy Ghost, strengthen the hearts of those who have been born again by Thy grace. Through.

The Lesson. Acts xix. 1-8.

In those days it came to pass that, while Apollos .... things concerning the Kingdom of God.

¶ *Then let two Clergy of the second grade, in silk copes, chant in pulpit this* Alleluia! *Let the Choir take it up.*

Alleluia! ℣. Ps. cxviii. O give thanks unto the Lord for He is gracious, because His mercy endureth for ever.

¶ *Let the Choir end with a Cadence, and Clergy repeat the* Alleluia! *without Cadence. The Tract is sung as on Easter Eve.*

Tract. Ps. cxvii. O praise the Lord, all ye heathen: praise Him, all ye nations. For His merciful kindness is ever more and more toward us: and the truth of the Lord endureth for ever.

¶ *The Gospel read as on Easter Eve.*

The Gospel. John xiv. 15-21.

At that time said Jesus to His disciples, If ye love Me, keep My commandments ...... will manifest Myself to him.

¶ *No Creed.*

Offert. Ps. civ. When Thou lettest Thy breath go forth they shall be made, and Thou shalt renew the face of the earth: the glorious Majesty of the Lord shall endure for ever. *Alleluia!*

Secret. We beseech Thee, O Lord, mercifully to give heed to the offerings of Thy people; and that they may be accepted of Thee, may the saving Advent of the Holy Ghost purge our consciences. Through.

Preface. The daily one.

¶ *On this day the* Sanctus *and* Agnus *are solemnly said.*

Comm. John vii. In the last day of the feast, Jesus stood and cried, saying, He that believeth on Me, as the Scripture hath said, out of his belly shall flow rivers of living water. But this spake He of the Spirit, which they that believe on Him should receive. *Alleluia! Alleluia!*

P. Comm. Grant, we beseech Thee, Almighty God, that the Holy Ghost may come, and by His manifestation declare unto us the Majesty of Thy Son. Through.

Whitsun Day.

The Office. Wisd. ii.

For the Spirit of the Lord filleth the world: *Alleluia!* and that which containeth all things hath knowledge of the voice. *Alleluia! Alleluia! Alleluia!*

Ps. lxviii. Let God arise, and let His enemies be scattered: let them also that hate Him flee before Him.

The Collect.

God, Who as at this time didst teach the hearts of Thy faithful people, by the sending to them the light of Thy Holy Spirit; grant us by the same Spirit to have a right judgment in all things, and evermore to rejoice in His comfort. Through. In the unity.

The Lesson. Acts ii. 1-11.

In those days, when the day of Pentecost ...... the wonderful works of God.

Alleluia! ℣. Ps. civ. When Thou letteth Thy breath go forth they shall be made: and Thou shalt renew the face of the earth.

Alleluia! ℣. *The Holy Ghost proceeding from the Throne illuminated the hearts of the Apostles this day with invisible power.*

The Sequence.

May the Holy Spirit's grace
Be present with us now,
And for Himself our hearts
An habitation make,
And from our inmost souls cast out
All spiritual wickedness.
O gracious Spirit, Thou
Who dost enlighten all,
The darkness chase away
Which fills our minds with gloom.
O Thou Who ever lov'st
Thoughts holily conceiv'd,
Thy unction graciously
Infuse into our hearts.
Spirit of purity,
Who dost all evil cleanse,
Enable Thou the eyes
Which light our inner man
The Father to discern
Who dwelleth in the highest,
Whom they alone can see
Who are the pure in heart.
Thou didst inspire the prophets to make known
Their glorious predictions of the Christ;
Thou the Apostles didst with strength endue
To bear Christ's trophy throughout all the world
When God by His Almighty Word did frame
The fabric of the heaven and earth and seas;
Thou, Spirit, brooding o'er the waters' face,
Didst spread abroad Thy fostering Deity;
Thou, to give life to souls,
Water dost fertilize;

And breathing on them deign'st
To make men spiritual;
Thou the world, rent by variance, by tongues
And rites, O Lord, has set at one again;
Thou, best of masters, dost recall
Idolaters to worship God;
Then, Holy Spirit, graciously
Hear us who lift our prayers to Thee,
Without Whom every prayer is counted vain,
Unworthy by God's ear to be received.
Thou, Spirit, Who the Saints of every age
In Thy embrace enfolding hast instructed
By inspiration of Thy Holy Name,
Thyself a gift unwonted pouring out
Upon the Apostolic band devout,
A gift throughout all ages yet unknown,
Hast made this day a day of high renown.

The Gospel. John xiv. 23-31.

At that time Jesus said unto His disciples, If a man love Me, he will keep My words .... even so I do.

The Creed.

Offert. Ps. lxviii. Stablish the thing, O God, that Thou hast wrought in us, for Thy temple's sake at Jerusalem: so shall kings bring presents unto Thee. *Alleluia!*

Secret. Sanctify, we beseech Thee, O Lord, these oblations, and purify our hearts by the light of the Holy Ghost. Through.

Preface. Who when He ascended.

Within the Canon, In communion with, *and* This oblation.

Comm. Acts ii. Suddenly there came a sound from heaven, as of a rushing mighty wind, where they were sitting, *Alleluia!* and they were all filled with the Holy Ghost, *and published the wonderful works of God. Alleluia!*

P. Comm. May the outpouring of the Holy Ghost cleanse our hearts, O Lord, and render them fruitful by the inward dew of His grace. Through.

WHITSUN MONDAY.

The Office. Ps. lxxxi.

He should have fed them with the finest wheat flour, *Alleluia!* and with honey out of the stony rock should I have satisfied Thee. *Alleluia! Alleluia! Alleluia!*

Ps. Sing we merrily unto God our strength: make a cheerful noise unto the God of Jacob.

The Collect.

O God, Who didst give the Holy Ghost to Thy Apostles, grant unto Thy people an effectual answer to their petition, that they to whom Thou hast vouchsafed faith, may enjoy abundance of peace. Through.

The Lesson. Acts x. 42-48.

In those days Peter opened his mouth and said, Men, brethren, and fathers, the Lord commanded us to preach unto the people ...... baptized in the Name of *our Lord Jesus Christ.*

Alleluia! ℣. Ps. civ. When Thou lettest Thy breath go forth they shall be made: and Thou shalt renew the face of the earth.

Alleluia! ℣. John xiv. The Comforter, which is the Holy Ghost, Whom the Father will send in My Name, He will teach you *all truth.*

The Sequence.

Now let the sacred choir
With holy symphony
The promised joys sound forth
In fulness sent from heaven.
Assembled in one place,
The Apostolic band
Awaits the glorious gifts.
Forthwith a voice divine,
Filling their hearts with power,
Attests the Comforter.
In every tongue they speak
Some mighty mystery
And wondrous works of God.
In canticles divine
His praises to rehearse
The assembly ceases not.
O God of all the earth,
  Thee sun and moon do praise;
  The universal host
  Of heaven in concert join
  Their voice with waters deep.
  Thee sings the genial earth;
  Thee all the glittering stars;
  Thee ransom'd souls adore,
  Rejoicing in Thy love.
The Jews amazed declare, that cursed band
Is of new wines' inebriation full;
Counting those fill'd with grace as full of wine.

These holy mysteries receiving, Peter
Doth conquer and subdue those hardened hearts,
Affirming this to be foretold by Joel.
Now triumphing our soul
Doth utter songs devout,
That for the heavenly visitant
A place she may prepare.
Let every string proclaim
Thy holy praise abroad,
That we may entertain
Those hallow'd gifts of grace.
All this pure offering
Of melody accept,
That so we may attain
Thine heavenly seat on high,
Whence light for ever flows.
Thou Who didst consecrate
Those hallow'd feasts of old,
Fulfil us now with light:
Or in Thy heavenly realms
Grant us perpetual joys.
O Holy Ghost! thanksgiving meet
And Glory in Thy starry seat
Is ever due to Thee.
Deign Thou in stately happiness
Our souls and bodies to possess,
O Christ, eternally!

The Gospel. John iii. 16-21.

At that time Jesus saith to a certain ruler of the Pharisees, God so loved the world ...... wrought in God.

Offert. Ps. xviii. The Lord thundered out of heaven, and the Highest gave His thunder: and the springs of waters were seen.

Secret. O Lord, we beseech Thee, grant, according to the promise of Thy Son Jesus Christ our Lord, that the Holy Ghost may more abundantly reveal to us the hidden mystery of this sacrifice, and may graciously discover to us all truth. Through.

Comm. John xiv. The Holy Ghost will teach you, *Alleluia!* whatsoever I have said unto you. *Alleluia! Alleluia!*

P. Comm. Work in us in its fulness, O Lord, we beseech Thee, the healing virtue of redemption, that we may be made worthy of the indwelling of the Holy Ghost. Through.

WHITSUN TUESDAY.

The Office.

Receive the joy of your glory, *Alleluia!* giving thanks to God, *Alleluia!* Who hath called you to His heavenly Kingdom. *Alleluia! Alleluia! Alleluia!*

Ps. lxxviii. Hear my law, O my people: incline your ears unto the words of my mouth.

The Collect.

We beseech Thee, O Lord, let the power of the Holy Ghost come upon us, that it may both cleanse our hearts, and defend us from all adversity. Through.

The Lesson. Acts viii. 14-17.

In those days, when the Apostles .... they received the Holy Ghost.

Alleluia! ℣. Ps. civ. When Thou lettest Thy breath go forth, they shall be made: and Thou shalt renew the face of the earth.

Alleluia! ℣. *Come, Holy Ghost, fill the hearts of Thy faithful people, and kindle in them the fire of Thy love.*

The Sequence.

Now prompt, O muse, the fitting strain,
And let the organ lend its tempered might;
Swell, pipe and string, the joyous note of praise;
Whilst we, with lifted heart and voice,
Devoutly sing the honour of this day,
For on this day descends the Paraclyte
Upon Christ's faithful ones, filling their souls with grace.
A sudden sound is heard, and tongues of fire are seen,
  And lo! with accents not their own,
Untaught of man, they speak the wondrous works of God.
Yet carnal unbelief cries scornfully,
"Full of new wine are these:" misdeeming them
Whose hearts the Blessed Spirit with love inflames.
    It is the fiftieth day
  From the great Resurrection morn;
Into their heart of hearts down glides the mystic fire;
  While to the city a clear sign is given.
Then forth they go, a light amid the gloom,
Dropping the Word's good seed in every land
    With many a sign of power,
    While the supernal dew
  Blesses the thirsty new-sown field.
And now, O Christ, Thy servants waiting on Thee

Here in Thine House, would fain their voice attune
To that new song which saints in glory sing.
To Him be endless glory, honour, power,
Who to all men that serve Him faithfully
In every clime the Spirit's aid vouchsafes—
Meekly, with one accord, the wondrous gift we seek,
That He, the Holy Ghost, our inmost hearts
First cleansing, with all wisdom may enlighten.
Alleluia !

The Gospel. John x. 1-10.

At that time Jesus said to His disciples, Verily, verily, I say unto you .... have it more abundantly.

Offert. Ps. lxxviii. *The Lord* opened the doors of Heaven. He rained down manna also upon them for to eat: and gave them food from Heaven. So man did eat angels' food. *Alleluia!*

Secret. We beseech Thee, O Lord, that the Holy Ghost may descend upon this Altar; and both sanctify the gifts of Thy people, and mercifully cleanse the hearts of those that receive the same. Through.

Comm. John xv. The Spirit, which proceedeth from the Father, *Alleluia!* He shall glorify me. *Alleluia! Alleluia!*

P. Comm. Grant, we beseech Thee, O Lord, that the Holy Ghost may renew our souls by this Divine Sacrament, since He Himself is the remission of all sin. Through.

EMBER WEDNESDAY.

¶ *This Mass of the Fast is always said for High Mass, according to Sarum Use, on this day and the next two Ember days.*

The Office. Ps. lxviii.

O God, when Thou wentest before *Thy* people, *Alleluia! making a way before them, Alleluia! dwelling among them. Alleluia! Alleluia!*

Ps. Let God arise, and let His enemies be scattered: let them also that hate Him flee before Him.

Let us pray.

The Collect.

Grant, we beseech Thee, Almighty God, that the Holy Ghost may remove from our minds all carnal affections, and mightily pour into us all spiritual gifts. Through.

The Lesson. Wisdom i. 1-7.

Love righteousness .... knowledge of His voice.

¶ *Let the above be read by an Acolyte in a surplice, in the pulpit; then let three Clergy of second grade in silk copes, in the same place, say—*

Alleluia! ℣. Ps. civ. When Thou lettest Thy breath go forth they shall be made; and Thou shalt renew the face of the earth.

¶ Alleluia! *is not to be repeated.*

The Collect.

Let the Holy Ghost, Who proceedeth from Thee, O Lord, we beseech Thee, illumine our minds, and lead us into all truth, as Thy Son hath promised. Who.

The Lesson. Acts ii. 14-21.

In those days, Peter, standing up with the eleven .... that whosoever shall call on the Name of the Lord shall be saved.

Alleluia! ℣. Acts ii. *The Apostles* began to speak with other tongues the wonderful works of God.

The Sequence.

Th' illustrious day, when from the Throne
The fiery tongues came rushing down
  On Christ's assembled band,
To enrich their tongues, their hearts to fill;
To kindred praise invites us still,
  With heart, and tongue, and hand.
Christ on this Pentecostal day,
Revisiting without delay
  The Bride, His promise sent;
After the honey's treasured worth
The Rock a store of oil gave forth,
  The Rock now permanent.
From Sinai's Mount proclaimed the Law
Graven on stone the people saw,
  Not sent in tongues of fire:
Newness of heart and quickened mind,
With unity of tongue combined,
  The chosen few inspire—
O happy, O most festive day!
Whereon the early founders lay
  The Church's basis sure.
The rising Church's first-fruits born
To life anew this holy morn,
  Three thousand souls figure—
The two loaves by the law ordained,
Two peoples represent, retained

By faith's adopting tie.
The Head Stone of the corner, set
Between the two, together met,
Hath wrought out unity.
New bottles, not the worn and old,
New wine are suitable to hold:
With oil Elisha fills
The widow's vessels not a few:
So on fit hearts His holy dew
God graciously distils.
We are not worthy of this wine,
Or oil, or of this dew divine,
If discord reigns within.
His consolation cannot find
A place in a divided mind,
Or heart obscured by sin.
Come, Holy Comforter, benign!
Our tongues control, our hearts incline!
If on us Thy blest Presence shine,
No poison harms, no gall:
There is no joy, no pure content,
No health, no calm stabiliment,
Sweetness hath no constituent,
Except Thy grace do all.
Thou art the light, the oil to cure;
Thou working in the water pure,
Mysterious virtue dost assure
To bless Thy chosen race.
By new creation born again,
To praise Thee now our hearts are fain;
By nature's sons of wrath, we gain
The privilege of grace.
Thou art the gift, and giver too,
All good on earth to Thee is due;
With gratitude our hearts endue,
To praise Thy Name with accents true
Do Thou our lips ordain:
Cleanse us, we pray, from all our sin,
Of purity Thou origin;
Grant we, in Christ renewed, may win
A perfect life, and bring us in
Where joys in fulness reign.

The Gospel. John vi. 44-51.

At that time said Jesus to His disciples and to the multitude of Jews, No man can come to Me .... the life of the world.

Offert. Ps. cxix. My delight shall be in Thy commandments: which I have loved. My hands also will I lift up unto Thy commandments, which I have loved. *Alleluia!*

Secret. We beseech Thee, O Lord, that the Holy Ghost may sanctify these gifts offered to Thee; and may our communicating in them shield us from the deadly poison of all sin. Through.

Comm. John xiv. My peace I give unto you, *Alleluia!* My peace I leave with you. *Alleluia! Alleluia!*

P. Comm. By virtue of this Mystery, O Lord, let the perpetual splendour of Thy brightness shine upon us; and may the Holy Ghost, of one substance with the Son, illuminate us. Through.

WHITSUN THURSDAY.

The Office.

¶ *As on Whitsun Day.*

The Collect.

Grant, we beseech Thee, Almighty and merciful God, that Thy Holy Spirit may come unto us, and dwell in us, and make us to be a worthy Temple of His glory. Through.

The Lesson. Acts viii. 5-8.

In those days, Philip went down .... great joy in that city.

Alleluia! ℣. Ps. civ. When Thou lettest Thy breath go forth they shall be made: and Thou shalt renew the face of the earth.

Alleluia! ℣. Acts ii. Suddenly there came a sound from Heaven as of a rushing mighty wind.

The Sequence.

Now let the holy band the Lord's high names declare:
Messiah, Saviour, Lord of Hosts, Emanuel,
Only-begotten, Way, Life, Hand, ‘Ομοούσιος,
Beginning, the First-born, Wisdom, and Power;
The Head and End, Alpha and Omega,
Fountain of Good, Advocate, Mediator,
Lamb, Sheep, Calf, Serpent, Lion, Ram, and Worm;
Mouth, Word, Sun, Brightness, Glory, Light and Image;
Bread, Branch, Vine, Mount, Door, Rock, and Corner-stone;
Messenger, Bridegroom, Shepherd, Prophet, Priest,
The Lord, Immortal, God, Almighty, Jesus.
May He our Saviour be; to Whom be glory ever.

The Gospel. Luke ix. 1-6.

At that time Jesus called His twelve disciples together .... healing everywhere.

Offert. Ps. lxviii. Stablish the thing, O God, that Thou hast wrought in us, for Thy temple's sake at Jerusalem: so shall kings bring presents unto Thee. *Alleluia!*

Secret. Endue our gifts, O Lord, with the power of the Holy Ghost, that what in this present festival we hallow to Thy Name, He may make discernible to us now and for evermore. Through.

Comm. Acts ii. Suddenly there was a sound from Heaven as of a rushing mighty wind, where they were sitting, *Alleluia!* and they were all filled with the Holy Ghost, and spake the wonderful works of God. *Alleluia! Alleluia!*

P. Comm. We beseech Thee, O Lord, that, through the operation of the Holy Ghost, our vices may be purged away by this heavenly Sacrifice, that we may ever be made meet for Thy gifts. Through.

EMBER FRIDAY.

The Office. Ps. lxxi.

O let my mouth be filled with Thy praise, *Alleluia!* that I may sing, *Alleluia!* My lips will be fain when I sing unto Thee. *Alleluia! Alleluia!*

Ps. In Thee, O Lord, have I put my trust, let me never be put to confusion: but rid me, and deliver me in Thy righteousness.

The Collect.

Grant, we beseech Thee, Merciful God, that when Thy Church is gathered together by Thy Holy Spirit, she may in no manner be hurt by the assaults of her enemies. Through.

The Lesson. Acts ii. 22-28.

In those days Peter opened his mouth and said, Ye men of Israel, hear these words .... full of joy with Thy countenance.

Alleluia! ℣. Ps. civ. When Thou lettest Thy breath go forth, they shall be made: and Thou shalt renew the face of the earth.

Alleluia! ℣. Wisd. i. The Spirit of the Lord hath filled the whole world: and that which containeth all things hath knowledge of His voice.

The Sequence.

Let all the people give
Praises devout to God,
With sweet high-sounding voice.
The Holy Spirit's grace
Was on the Apostles sent
This day in tongues of fire.
May He, the Comforter,
By His blessed Presence cleanse
Our souls from stain of sin,
And fit them for Himself
A habitation pure;
And graciously pour out
His gifts into our breasts,
That so our lives may be
Well-pleasing in His sight.
May we world without end
Our Alleluias sing.
Praise, power, honour, might,
And glory be to God.

The Gospel. Luke v. 17-26.

At that time, it came to pass on a certain day .... we have seen strange things to-day.

Offert. Ps. cxlvi. Praise the Lord, O my soul; while I live will I praise the Lord: yea, as long as I have any being, I will sing praises unto my God. *Alleluia!*

Secret. May the sacrifice offered in Thy presence, O Lord, be consumed by that divine fire by which the Holy Ghost inflamed the hearts of the disciples of Christ Thy Son. Through.

Comm. John iii. The wind bloweth where it listeth, and thou hearest the sound thereof, but canst not tell whence it cometh, and whither it goeth. *Alleluia! Alleluia!*

P. Comm. Grant, we beseech Thee, Almighty God, that by the receiving of this Sacrament the vices of our weak nature may be so purged away, that we may perceive in ourselves the gift of Thy grace promised anew through the Holy Ghost. Through.

EMBER SATURDAY.

The Office. Rom. v.

The love of God is shed abroad in *your* hearts, *Alleluia!* by His Spirit which dwelleth in you. *Alleluia! Alleluia!*

Ps. lxxxviii. O Lord God of my salvation, I have cried day and night before Thee.

¶ *The* Kyrie *is sung without verses. Let the* Gloria in Excelsis *be said as in an Octave with rulers of Choir. Let the first Lesson be read by an Acolyte at the step of the quire, the others by Clerks of the second bench alternately, the fifth by one of the upper grade. The* Alleluia! *is sung by two boys in surplices: it is not repeated.*

Let us pray.

The Collect.

We beseech Thee, O Lord, graciously pour the Holy Spirit, into our hearts by Whose wisdom we were created, and by Whose providence we are governed. Through.

The Lesson. Joel. ii. 28-32.

Thus saith the Lord God, I will pour out My Spirit .... Name of the Lord shall be delivered.

Alleluia! ℣. Ps. civ. When Thou lettest Thy breath go forth they shall be made, and Thou shalt renew the face of the earth.

Let us pray.

The Collect.

Let Thy Holy Spirit, O Lord, we beseech Thee, inflame us with that fire which our Lord Jesus Christ sent on earth, and earnestly desired that it should be kindled. Who.

The Lesson. Lev. xxiii. 9-17, 21.

In those days the Lord spake unto Moses, saying .... throughout your generations, *saith the Lord Almighty.*

Alleluia! Come, Holy Ghost, fill the hearts of Thy faithful people, and kindle in them the fire of Thy love.

Let us pray.

The Collect.

O God, Who for the healing our souls hast commanded us to mortify our bodies by devout fasting, mercifully grant that we may ever faithfully serve Thee, both with body and soul. Through.

The Lesson. Deut. xxvi. 1-11.

In those days said Moses to the children of Israel: Hear, O Israel, that which I command thee this day: when thou art come into the land .... the Lord thy God hath given thee.

Alleluia! ℣. Acts ii. Thine *Apostles* spake with other tongues the wonderful works of God.

Let us pray.

The Collect.

Grant, we beseech Thee, Almighty God, that being instructed by this wholesome fast, we may abstain from all vice, and more readily obtain Thy favour. Through.

The Lesson. Lev. xxvi. 3-12.

In those days the Lord said unto Moses; Speak unto the children of Israel and say unto them, If ye walk in My statutes .... and ye shall be My people, *saith the Lord Almighty.*

Alleluia! ℣. Acts ii. Suddenly there came a sound from Heaven as of a mighty rushing wind.

Let us pray.

The Collect.

Grant, we beseech Thee, O Almighty God, that we may in such wise abstain from carnal feasting, that we may in like manner fast from the assaults of vice. Through.

The Lesson. Dan. iii. 26-66 (*i.e.*, the Song of the Three Children).

The Angel of the Lord came down into the oven .... O Ananias, Azarias, and Misael, bless ye the Lord: praise and exalt Him above all for ever.

¶ *Let two Clergy of the second grade say this at the steps of the quire—*

Alleluia! ℣. Dan. iii. Blessed art Thou, O Lord God of our fathers: Thy Name is worthy to be praised and glorified for evermore.

℣. The Lord be with you.
℟. And with thy spirit.

Let us pray.

The Collect.

O God, Who, in the behalf of the three children, didst assuage the flames of fire; mercifully grant that, by the advent of the Holy Ghost, we Thy servants may not be set on fire by the flames of vice. Through.

The Lesson. Acts xiii. 44-52.

In those days came the whole city together ...... with the Holy Ghost.

¶ *Let two of the upper grade, in silk copes, say—*

Alleluia! ℣. Ps. cxvii. O praise the Lord, all ye heathen: praise Him, all ye nations.

¶ *Let* Alleluia! *be repeated.*

The Sequence. Now let the holy band (*see p.* 215).

The Gospel. Luke iv. 38-43.

In those days Jesus arose out of the synagogue, and entered into Simon's house .... I must preach the Kingdom of God to other cities also.

Offert. Ps. lxxviii. O Lord God of my salvation, I have cried day and night before Thee: O let my prayer enter into Thy presence, *O Lord. Alleluia!*

Secret. We beseech Thee, O Lord, send the Holy Spirit, that He may both make these present gifts Thy Sacraments to us, and purify our hearts for the receiving of the same. Through.

Comm. John xiv. I will not leave you comfortless, I will come to you again: *Alleluia!* and your heart shall rejoice. *Alleluia! Alleluia!*

P. Comm. May Thy sacred mysteries, O Lord, bestow upon us the Divine fervour, that we may delight both in their celebration and in their effect. Through.

Trinity Sunday.

The Office. Tobit xii.

Blessed be *the Holy Trinity, and the Undivided Unity. We will give thanks to Him,* for the mercy He hath done unto *us.*

Ps. Let us bless the Father and the Son, together with the Holy Ghost.

The Collect.

Almighty and everlasting God, Who hast given unto us Thy servants grace, by the confession of a true faith, to acknowledge the glory of the eternal Trinity, and in the power of the Divine Majesty to worship the Unity; we beseech Thee, that Thou wouldest keep us steadfast in this faith, and evermore defend us from all adversities. Who.

The Lesson. Rev. iv. 1-10.

In those days I saw a door opened in Heaven .... worship Him that liveth for ever and ever.

Gradual. Dan. iii. Blessed art Thou, O Lord, Who beholdest the depths, and sittest upon the cherubim.

℣. O ye heavens, bless ye God: for the mercy He hath done unto *us.*

Alleluia! ℣. Tobit viii. Blessed art Thou, O Lord God of our fathers: Thy Name is worthy to be praised and glorified for evermore.

The Sequence.

Adored be the blessed Trinity,
Glory co-equal, Godhead co-eternal—
The Father God, the Son begotten, ever
Above all with the Holy Ghost abiding.
Always one Will have all the Persons Three,
And never with each other are at variance.
For God is one, not into three divided,
So the right faith, which Christ set forth, confesses.
This is the faith which doth abolish sin;
This the unclouded country doth restore
Where heavenly hosts chant their sweet symphony,
Christ's footsteps clad in robes of white they follow;
And, after this world's strife is o'er, put on
The change of raiment after which they yearn.
Let us, too, whom the grace of God enlightens,
Pay, as in duty bound, our debts to heaven,
That so for us may after death abide
Communion with that celestial band;
And when the final sentence is awarded,
We may have entrance to the courts above,
Where light beams forth conspicuous, enkindled
By that undying flame, the Lord our God,
Our everlasting Vision, our Salvation,
Which lighteth up the holy angels' breasts
While upon Christ alone they fix their eyes
Such thirst will saints in soul and body feel,
When for their holy deeds a prize eternal
Shall by the Judge of all have been awarded.

The Gospel. John iii. 1-15.

In those days there was a man of the Pharisees, named Nicodemus .... but have eternal life.

Preface. Who with Thy Only-begotten Son.

Offert. Tobit xii. Blessed be God *the Father, and the Only-begotten Son of God, as likewise the Holy Ghost;* for the mercy He hath done unto *us.*

Secret. Sanctify, we beseech Thee, O Lord God, Holy Trinity, by the invocation of Thy Holy Name, the offering of this oblation; and through it perfect us to be an eternal gift presented unto Thee. Through.

Comm. Tobit xii. Let us bless the God of Heaven; and we will give thanks unto Him in the sight of all that live; for the mercy He hath done unto *us.*

P. Comm. May the receiving of this Sacrament, O Lord our God, and the confession of the everlasting Holy Trinity, and of the undivided Unity of the same, be profitable to us, for the salvation of body and soul. Who.

¶ *Throughout the week till Corpus Christi let this Mass be said, unless* Salus *or the Feast of B. V. M. on Saturday, occur, but without* Sequence *or* Creed; *and for the Epistles* O the depth *and* The grace of our Lord *are said alternately through the week, together with the Gospel* When the Comforter is come. *See Votive Mass of the Trinity.*

Corpus Christi.

The Office Ps. lxxxi.

He should have fed them also with the finest wheat-flour, *Alleluia!* and with honey out of the stony rock should I have satisfied thee. *Alleluia! Alleluia! Alleluia!*

Ps. Sing we merrily unto God our strength: make a cheerful noise unto the God of Jacob.

The Collect.

O God, Who under this wondrous Sacrament hast left us a memorial of Thy Passion, grant us, we beseech Thee, so to reverence the holy mysteries of Thy Body and Blood, that in ourselves we may ever sensibly have fruition of the redemption which Thou hast wrought. Who.

The Epistle. 1 Cor. xi. 23-29.

Brethren, I have received of the Lord .... not discerning the Lord's Body.

Gradual. Ps. cxlv. The eyes of all wait upon Thee, O Lord: and Thou givest them their meat in due season.

℣. Thou openest Thine hand: and fillest all things living with plenteousness.

Alleluia! ℣. John vi. My Flesh is meat indeed, and My Blood is drink indeed: he that eateth My Flesh and drinketh My Blood, dwelleth in Me, and I in him.

The Sequence.

Sion, lift thy voice and sing;
Praise thy Saviour and thy King;
  Praise with hymns thy Shepherd true:
Strive thy best to praise Him well;
Yet doth He all praise excel;
    None can ever reach His due.

See to-day before us laid
The living and life-giving Bread!
  Theme for praise and joy profound!

The same which at the sacred board
Was, by our Incarnate Lord,
  Given to His Apostles round.

Let the praise be loud and high,
Sweet and tranquil be the joy
  Felt to-day in every breast,
On this Festival divine,
Which records the origin
  Of the glorious Eucharist.

On this Table of the King,
Our new Paschal offering
  Brings to end the olden rite:
Here, for empty shadows fled,
Is reality instead;
Here, instead of darkness, Light.

His own act, at Supper seated,
Christ ordained to be repeated,
  In His memory divine;
Wherefore now, with adoration,
We the Host of our Salvation
  Consecrate from bread and wine.

Hear what Holy Church maintaineth,
That the bread its substance changeth
  Into Flesh, the wine to Blood.
Doth it pass thy comprehending?
Faith, the law of sight transcending,
  Leaps to things not understood.

Here beneath these signs are hidden
Priceless things, to sense forbidden—
  Signs, not things, are all we see:
Flesh from bread, and Blood from wine;
Yet is Christ, in either sign,
  All entire, confess'd to be.

They, too, who of Him partake,
Sever not, nor rend, nor break,
  But entire their Lord receive.
Whether one or thousands eat,
All receive the self-same meat,
  Nor the less for others leave.

Both the wicked and the good
Eat of this celestial Food;
  But with ends how opposite!
Here 'tis life, and there 'tis death;
The same, yet issuing to each
  In a difference infinite.
Nor a single doubt retain,

When they break the Host in twain,
But that in each part remain
  What was in the whole before;

Since the simple sign alone
Suffers change in state or form,
The Signified remaining one
 And the same for evermore.

Lo! upon the Altar lies,
Hidden deep from human eyes,
Bread of Angels from the skies,
 Made the food of mortal man:
Children's meat to dogs denied,
In old types foresignified;
In the manna heav'n-supplied,
 Isaac and the Paschal Lamb.

Jesu! Shepherd of the sheep!
Thou Thy flock in safety keep.
Living Bread! Thy life supply;
Strengthen us. or else we die;
 Fill us with celestial grace.
Thou who feedest us below!
Source of all we have or know!
Grant that with Thy Saints above,
Sitting at the Feast of Love,
 We may see Thee face to face.

The Gospel. John vi. 55-58.

At that time said Jesus to His disciples and to the multitude of the Jews, My Flesh is meat indeed .... shall live for ever.

The Creed.

Preface. Because by the mystery.

Offert. Lev. xxi. The priests of the Lord do offer the offerings made by fire and the bread of their God, therefore they shall be holy unto their God, and they shall not profane His Name. *Alleluia!*

Secret. O Lord, we beseech Thee, mercifully grant unto Thy Church the gifts of unity and peace, which are mystically represented in these offerings which we present. Through.

Comm. I Cor. xi. As often as ye eat this Bread, and drink this Cup, ye do shew the Lord's death till He come. Wherefore whosoever shall eat this Bread and drink this Cup of the Lord unworthily, shall be guilty of the Body and Blood of the Lord. *Alleluia!*

P. Comm. Grant, O Lord, we beseech Thee, that we may be fulfilled with the eternal fruition of Thy Godhead, which in this life the partaking of Thy precious Body and Blood doth prefigure. Who.

¶ *This Mass is said throughout the Octave, but without* Sequence *and* Creed, *unless the Octave is kept with rulers of Choir; in which case the Sequence* Sion, lift, *and* Creed *may be used.*

First Sunday after Trinity.

The Office. Ps. xiii.

Lord, my trust is in Thy mercy: and my heart is joyful in Thy salvation. I will sing of the Lord, because He hath dealt so lovingly with me

Ps. How long wilt Thou forget me, O Lord, for ever: how long wilt Thou hide Thy face from me?

The Collect.

O God, the strength of them that put their trust in Thee, mercifully accept our prayers; and because the weakness of our mortal nature can do nothing without Thee, grant us the help of Thy grace, that in keeping of Thy commandments we may please Thee, both in will and deed. Through.

¶ *There is always a Memorial of Trinity Sunday from now till Advent when the Sunday Mass is said.*

The Epistle. I John. iv. 8-21.

Beloved, love is of God .... love his brother also.

Gradual. Ps. xli. I said, Lord, be merciful unto me: heal my soul, for I have sinned against Thee.

℣. Blessed is he that considereth the poor and needy; the Lord shall deliver him in the time of trouble.

Alleluia! ℣. Ps. v. Ponder my words, O Lord: consider my meditation.

The Gospel. Luke xvi. 19-31.

At that time Jesus spake this parable unto His disciples, There was a certain rich man ...... though one rose from the dead.

Offert. Ps. v. O hearken Thou unto the voice of my calling, my King, and my God: for unto Thee will I make my prayer, *O Lord.*

Secret. O God, Who renewest us who are created after Thine image, both by sacraments and precepts, graciously accept the prayers and oblations of Thy suppliants, that the propitiatory sacrifice may obtain for them that which no trust in their own merits can assure to them. Through.

Comm. Ps. ix. I will speak of all Thy marvellous works. I will be glad and rejoice in Thee: yea, my songs will I make of Thy name, *O* Thou most Highest.

P. Comm. Grant, we beseech Thee, O Lord, that we who are fulfilled with such bounties may both receive the gift of salvation, and never cease from praising Thee. Through.

WEDNESDAY.

The Epistle. 2 Peter i. 16-19.

Dearly beloved, we *have* made known unto you the power ...... arise in your hearts.

The Gospel. Matt. v. 17-19.

At that time said Jesus to His disciples, Think not that I am come .... great in the Kingdom of Heaven.

Second Sunday after Trinity.

The Office. Ps. xviii.

The Lord was my upholder. He brought me forth also into a place of liberty: He brought me forth, even because He had a favour unto me.

Ps. I will love Thee, O Lord, my strength; the Lord is my stony rock, and my defence *and* my Saviour.

The Collect.

O Lord, Who never failest to govern them whom Thou dost bring up in Thy steadfast love; make us to have alike a perpetual fear and love of Thy Holy Name. Through.

The Epistle. 1 John iii. 13-18.

Dearly beloved, marvel not if the world hate you .... but in deed and in truth.

Gradual. Ps. cxx. When I was in trouble I called upon the Lord: and He heard me.

℣. Deliver my soul, O Lord, from lying lips: and from a deceitful tongue.

Alleluia! ℣. Ps. vii. God is a righteous Judge, strong, and patient: and God is provoked every day.

The Gospel. Luke xiv. 16-24.

At that time Jesus spake this parable unto His disciples, A certain man made a great supper .... shall taste of my supper.

Offert. Ps. vi. Turn Thee, O Lord, and deliver my soul: O save me for Thy mercy's sake.

Secret. May the oblation to be offered to Thy Name purify us, O Lord: and make us day by day to advance in heavenly life. Through.

Comm. Ps. xiii. I will sing of the Lord, because He hath dealt so lovingly with me: yea, I will praise the Name of the Lord most Highest.

P. Comm. Grant, O Lord, we beseech Thee, that we who have received the holy gift may, whilst we attend the mystery, more effectually work out our salvation. Through.

WEDNESDAY.

The Epistle. Eph. iv. 17-24.

Brethren, this I say and testify in the Lord .... righteousness and true holiness *in Christ Jesus our Lord.*

The Gospel. Matt. xxi. 23-27.

At that time when *Jesus* was come into the Temple .... by what authority I do these things.

Third Sunday after Trinity.

The Office. Ps. xxv

Turn Thee unto me, and have mercy upon me, *O Lord,* for I am desolate, and in misery. Look upon my adversity and misery: and forgive me all my sin, *my God*

Ps. Unto Thee, O Lord, will I lift up my soul; my God, I have put my trust in Thee: O let me not be confounded.

The Collect.

O Lord, we beseech Thee mercifully to hear our supplications; and grant that we, to whom Thou hast given an hearty desire to pray, may by Thy aid be defended. Through.

The Epistle. 1 Peter v. 6-11.

Dearly beloved, humble yourselves .... dominion for ever and ever.

Gradual. Ps. lv. O cast thy burden upon the Lord, and He shall nourish thee.

℣. When I cried unto the Lord, He heard my voice from the battle that was against me.

Alleluia! ℣. Ps. xviii. I will love Thee, O Lord, my strength; the Lord is my stony rock, and my defence, *and* my Saviour.

The Gospel. Luke xv. 1-10.

At that time drew near unto *Jesus* all the publicans .... sinner that repenteth.

Offert. Ps. ix. They that know Thy Name will put their trust in Thee: for Thou, Lord, hast never failed them that seek Thee. O praise the Lord which dwelleth in Sion: for He forgetteth not the complaint of the poor.

Secret. Sanctify, O Lord, we beseech Thee, the gifts offered to Thee: that for our healing they may become the Body and Blood of Thy Only-begotten Son. Who.

Comm. Ps. xvii. I have called upon Thee, O God, for Thou shalt hear me: incline Thine ear to me, and hearken unto my words.

P. Comm. We, having received Thy gifts, beseech Thee, O Lord, that by their virtue Thou wouldest purify us from all vices, and fill us abundantly with the gifts of Thy grace. Through

---

WEDNESDAY.

The Epistle. 2 Tim. iv. 17, 18.

Dearly beloved, the Lord stood with me .... glory for ever and ever. Amen.

The Gospel. Matt. v. 25-30.

At that time said Jesus to His disciples, Agree with thine adversary .... cast into hell.

Fourth Sunday after Trinity.

The Office. Ps. xxvii.

The Lord is my light, and my salvation; whom then shall I fear? the Lord is the strength of my life; of whom then shall I be afraid? When mine enemies and my foes came upon me, they stumbled and fell.

Ps. Though an host of men were laid against me, yet shall not my heart be afraid.

The Collect.

O God, the protector of all that trust in Thee, without Whom nothing is strong, nothing is holy; multiply upon us Thy mercy, that, Thou being our ruler and guide, we may so pass through things temporal, that we lose not the things eternal. Through.

The Epistle. Rom. viii. 18-23.

Brethren, I reckon that the sufferings .... the redemption of our body, *in Christ Jesus our Lord.*

Gradual. Ps. lxxix. Be merciful unto our sins, O Lord. Wherefore do the heathen say: Where is now their God?

℣. Help us, O God of our salvation, for the glory of Thy Name: deliver us, *O Lord.*

Alleluia! ℣. Ps. xxi. The King shall rejoice in Thy strength, O Lord: exceeding glad shall he be of Thy salvation.

The Gospel. Luke vi. 36-42.

At that time Jesus said to His disciples, Be ye therefore merciful .... mote that is in thy brother's eye.

Offert. Ps. xiii. Lighten mine eyes, that I sleep not in death; lest mine enemy say: I have prevailed against him.

Secret. Look down, O Lord, we beseech Thee, on the offerings of Thy suppliant Church; and grant that they may ever be consecrated and received for the salvation of the faithful. Through.

Comm. Ps. xviii. The Lord is my strong rock, and my defence; my Saviour, my God, my might.

P. Comm. May Thy holy things, O Lord, which we have received, give us life: cleansing us from our sins, and making us ready for Thy everlasting mercy. Through.

WEDNESDAY.

The Epistle. 1 John ii. 3-6.

Beloved, hereby we do know that we know Him .... so to walk, even as He walked.

The Gospel. Matt. xvii. 10-18.

At that time His disciples asked *Jesus,* saying .... the child was cured from that very hour.

Fifth Sunday after Trinity.

The Office. Ps. xxvii.

Hearken unto my voice, O Lord, when I cry unto Thee: Thou hast been my succour: leave me not, neither forsake me, O God of my salvation.

Ps. The Lord is my light, and my salvation: whom then shall I fear?

The Collect.

Grant, O Lord, we beseech Thee, that the course of this world may be so peaceably ordered by Thy governance, that Thy Church may joyfully serve Thee in all quietness. Through.

The Epistle 1 Peter iii. 8-15.

Dearly beloved, be ye all of one mind *in prayer,* having compassion .... the Lord God in your hearts.

Gradual. Ps. lxxxiv. Behold, O God, our defender, and look upon *Thy servants.*

℣. O Lord God of hosts, hear *the* prayers *of Thy servants.*

Alleluia! ℣. Ps. lxxi. and xxxi. In Thee, O Lord, have I put my trust: let me never be put to confusion, rid me and deliver me in Thy righteousness. Bow down Thine ear to me: make haste to deliver me.

The Gospel. Luke v. 1-11.

At that time, as the people pressed upon *Jesus* to hear .... forsook all, and followed Him.

Offert. Ps. xvi. I will thank the Lord for giving me warning: I have set God always before me: for He is on my right hand, therefore I shall not fall.

Secret. Let our humble prayers, O Lord, we beseech Thee, ascend up into Thy merciful presence; and let the virtue of Thy Godhead, which Thou dost all-abundantly bestow upon us to the purification of our minds, descend upon these oblations. Through.

Comm. Ps. xxvii. One thing have I desired of the Lord, which I will require: even that I may dwell in the House of the Lord all the days of my life.

P. Comm. We beseech Thee, O Lord, let the holy mysteries cleanse and defend us by their special efficacy. Through.

WEDNESDAY.

The Epistle. 1 Tim. ii. 1-7.

Beloved, I exhort that, first of all .... in faith and verity.

The Gospel. Luke viii. 22-25.

At that time it came to pass on a certain day .... and they obey Him.

Sixth Sunday after Trinity.

The Office. Ps. xxviii.

The Lord is my strength: and He is the wholesome defence of His Anointed. O save Thy people, and give Thy blessing unto Thine inheritance: feed them for ever.

Ps. Unto Thee will I cry, O Lord, my strength: think no scorn of me; lest, if Thou make as though Thou hearest not, I become like them that go down into the pit.

The Collect.

O God, Who hast prepared for them that love Thee good things yet unseen, pour into our hearts such love toward Thee, that we, loving Thee in and above all things, may obtain Thy promises, which exceed all that we can desire. Through.

The Epistle. Rom. vi. 3-11.

Brethren, so many of us as were baptized .... alive unto God through Jesus Christ our Lord.

Gradual. Ps. xc. Turn Thee again, O Lord, at the last: and be gracious unto Thy servants.

℣. Lord, Thou hast been our refuge: from one generation to another.

Alleluia! ℣. Ps. lix. Deliver me from mine enemies, my God: defend me from them that rise up against me.

The Gospel. Matt. v. 20-24.

At that time Jesus said unto His disciples, Except your righteousness .... then come and offer thy gift.

Offert. Ps. xvii. O hold Thou up my goings in Thy paths: that my footsteps slip not. Incline Thine ear to me, and hearken unto my words. Shew Thy marvellous loving-kindness, Thou that art the Saviour of them which put their trust in Thee, *O Lord.*

Secret. Favourably hear our humble prayers, O Lord, and graciously receive these oblations of Thy servants: that what each hath offered to the honour of Thy Name, may be profitable for the salvation of all. Through.

Comm. Ps. xxvii. Therefore will I offer in His dwelling an oblation with great gladness: I will sing, and speak praises unto the Lord.

P. Comm. Grant, O Lord, we beseech Thee, that we, whom Thou hast fed with this heavenly gift, may be cleansed from our secret sins, and delivered from the snares of our enemies. Through.

WEDNESDAY.

The Epistle. 1 John ii. 21-25.

Dearly beloved, I have not written unto you ...... eternal life.

The Gospel. Mark x. 17-21.

At that time, when Jesus was gone forth into the way .... come and follow Me.

Seventh Sunday after Trinity.

The Office. Ps. xlvii.

O clap your hands together, all ye people: O sing unto God with the voice of melody.

Ps. He shall subdue the people under us: and the nations under our feet.

The Collect.

God of all power, Who art the Author of all good things, graft in our hearts the love of Thy Name, increase in us true religion, nourish us with all goodness, and of Thy great mercy keep us in the same. Through.

The Epistle. Rom. vi. 19-23.

Brethren, I speak after the manner of men .... eternal life, through Jesus Christ our Lord.

Gradual. Ps. xxxiv. Come, ye children, and hearken unto me: I will teach you the fear of the Lord.

℣. They had an eye upon Him, and were lightened: and their faces were not ashamed.

Alleluia! ℣. Ps. lxv. Thou, O God, art praised in Sion: and unto Thee shall the vow be performed in Jerusalem.

The Gospel. Mark viii. 1-9.

In those days, the multitude *with Jesus* being very great ...... He sent them away.

Offert. Dan. iii.* Like as in the burnt offerings of rams and bullocks, and like as in ten thousands of fat lambs: so let our sacrifice be in Thy sight this day, and grant that we may wholly go after Thee: for they shall not be confounded that put their trust in Thee, *O Lord.*

Secret. Favourably hear our humble prayers, O Lord, and graciously receive these oblations of Thy people: and that the vow of none may be without effect, the request of none be sent empty away, grant that the things which we ask faithfully, we may obtain effectually. Through.

Comm. Ps. xxxi. Bow down Thine ear to me: make haste to deliver me.

P. Comm. We, being replenished with Thy gifts, beseech Thee, O Lord, to grant that we may both be cleansed by their efficacy, and strengthened by their aid. Through.

WEDNESDAY.

The Epistle. Rom. viii. 1-6.

Brethren, there is now no condemnation .... to be spiritually minded is life and peace *in Christ Jesus our Lord.*

The Gospel. Matt. xii. 1-7.

At that time Jesus went on the Sabbath Day .... would not have condemned the guiltless.

Eighth Sunday after Trinity.

The Office. Ps. xlviii.

We wait for Thy loving-kindness, O God: in the midst of Thy temple. O God, according to Thy Name, so is Thy praise unto the world's end: Thy right hand is full of righteousness.

* *i.e.*, Song of the Three Children (v. 17).

Ps. Great is the Lord, and highly to be praised: in the city of our God, even upon His holy hill.

The Collect.

O God, Whose providence ordereth all things, we humbly beseech Thee to put away from us all hurtful things, and to give us those things which be profitable for us. Through.

The Epistle. Rom. viii. 12-17.

Brethren, we are debtors .... and joint-heirs with Christ.

Gradual. Ps. xxxi. And be Thou my strong rock, and house of defence: that Thou mayest save me.

℣. In Thee, O Lord *God*, have I put my trust: let me never be put to confusion.

Alleluia! ℣. Ps. lxxviii. Hear my law, O my people.

The Gospel. Matt. vii. 15-21.

At that time Jesus said to His disciples, Beware of false prophets .... but he that doeth the will of My Father, Which is in Heaven, *he shall enter into the Kingdom of Heaven.*

Offert. Ps. xviii. For Thou shalt save the people that are in adversity: and shalt bring down the high looks of the proud. For who is God *beside Thee, O Lord?*

Secret. O God, Who by one perfect sacrifice hast confirmed the divers sacrifices of the Law, accept from Thy devout servants the oblation presented unto Thee, and sanctify it by the like blessing which Thou didst give to the offering of righteous Abel: that what each hath offered in honour of Thy Divine Majesty, may be profitable for the salvation of all. Through.

Comm. Ps. xxxiv. O taste, and see, how gracious the Lord is: blessed is the man that trusteth in Him.

P. Comm. Let Thy wholesome working, O Lord, both set us free from our froward ways, and lead us unto those things which be rightful. Through.

WEDNESDAY.

The Epistle. Rom. v. 8-11.

Brethren, God commendeth His love toward us .... through our Lord Jesus Christ.

The Gospel. Mark ix. 38-48.

At that time the disciples said unto Jesus, Master, we saw one casting out devils .... the fire is not quenched.

Ninth Sunday after Trinity.

The Office. Ps. liv.

Behold, God is my helper : the Lord is with them that uphold my soul. He shall reward evil unto mine enemies : destroy Thou them in Thy truth, *O God, my defender.*

Ps. Save me, O God, for Thy Name's sake : and avenge me in Thy strength.

The Collect.

Grant to us, Lord, we beseech Thee, the spirit to think and do always such things as be rightful ; that we, who cannot exist without Thee, may be enabled to live according to Thy will. Through.

The Epistle. 1 Cor. x. 6-13.

Brethren, we should not lust after evil things .... able to bear it.

Gradual. Ps. viii. O Lord our Governour, how excellent is Thy Name in all the world :

℣. Thou that hast set Thy glory above the heavens!

Alleluia! ℣. Ps. lxxxi. Sing we merrily unto God our strength : make a cheerful noise unto the God of Jacob. Take the psalm : the merry harp with the lute.

The Gospel. Luke xvi. 1-9.

At that time Jesus spake this parable unto His disciples, There was a certain rich man which had a steward .... receive you into everlasting habitations.

Offert. Ps. xix. The statutes of the Lord are right, and rejoice the heart : sweeter also than honey, and the honey-comb. Moreover, by them is Thy servant taught.

Secret. Receive, we beseech Thee, O Lord, the offerings which of Thine own bounty we present unto Thee, that these most holy mysteries may, by the power of Thy grace, make us holy in conversation in this life, and bring us to those joys that never end. Through.

Comm. Matt. vi. Seek ye first the Kingdom of God, and all things shall be added unto you, *saith the Lord.*

P. Comm. May the heavenly mystery, O Lord, we beseech Thee, renew us both in soul and body: that we may perceive the effectual virtue of that which we have outwardly performed. Through.

WEDNESDAY.

The Epistle. Rom. vi. 16-18.

Brethren, know ye not, that to whom ye yield yourselves servants to obey .... the servants of righteousness *in Christ Jesus our Lord.*

The Gospel. Luke xvi. 10-15.

At that time said Jesus to His disciples, He that is faithful in that which is least .... abomination in the sight of God.

Tenth Sunday after Trinity.

The Office. Ps. lv.

When I called upon the Lord, He heard my voice from the battle that was against me, and brought them down, even God that endureth for ever: O cast thy burden upon the Lord, and He shall nourish thee.

Ps. Hear my prayer, O God: and hide not Thyself from my petition: take heed unto me, and hear me.

The Collect.

Let Thy merciful ears, O Lord, be open to the prayers of Thy humble servants; and that they may obtain their petitions, make them to ask such things as shall please Thee. Through.

The Epistle. 1 Cor. xii. 2-11.

Brethren, ye know that ye were Gentiles .... every man severally as He will.

Gradual. Ps. xvii. Keep me, *O Lord,* as the apple of an eye: hide me under the shadow of Thy wings.

℣. Let my sentence come forth from Thy presence: and let Thine eyes look upon the thing that is equal.

Alleluia! ℣. Ps. lxxxviii. O Lord God of my salvation, I have cried day and night before Thee.

The Gospel. Luke xix. 41-47.

At that time, when *Jesus* was come near .... and He taught daily in the temple.

Offert. Ps. xxv. Unto Thee, O God, will I lift my soul; my God, I have put my trust in Thee: O let me not be coufounded, neither let mine enemies triumph over me. For all they that hope in Thee shall not be ashamed.

Secret. Grant us, O Lord, we beseech Thee, frequently and worthily to approach these mysteries: seeing that as often as this commemorative sacrifice is celebrated, the work of our redemption is carried on. Through.

Comm. Ps. li. Then shalt Thou be pleased with the sacrifice of righteousness, with the burnt-offerings and oblations upon Thine Altar, *O Lord.*

P. Comm. May the Communion of Thy Sacrament, O Lord, both bestow upon us purity, and contribute to our unity. Through.

WEDNESDAY.

The Epistle. I Cor. xv. 39-46.

Brethren, all flesh is not the same flesh .... afterward that which is spiritual *in Christ Jesus our Lord.*

The Gospel. Luke xxi. 34-36.

At that time said Jesus to His disciples, Take heed to yourselves, lest at any time .... to stand before the Son of Man.

Eleventh Sunday after Trinity.

The Office. Ps. lxviii.

God in His holy habitation, God that maketh men to be of one mind in an house: He will give strength and power unto His people.

Ps. Let God arise, and let His enemies be scattered: let them also that hate Him flee before Him.

The Collect.

O God, Who declarest Thy almighty power most chiefly in shewing mercy and pity; mercifully grant unto us Thy grace, that we, running the way of Thy promises, may be made partakers of Thy heavenly treasure. Through.

The Epistle. 1 Cor. xv. 1-10.

Brethren, I declare unto you the Gospel .... was not in vain.

Gradual. Ps. xxviii. My heart hath trusted in *God*, and I am helped: therefore my heart danceth for joy, and in my song will I praise Him.

℣. Unto Thee will I cry, O Lord, my strength: think no scorn of me.

Alleluia! ℣. Ps. xc. Lord, Thou hast been our refuge: from one generation to another.

The Gospel. Luke xviii. 9-14.

At that time Jesus spake this parable .... he that humbleth himself shall be exalted

Offert. Ps. xxx. I will magnify Thee, O Lord, for Thou hast set me up; and not made my foes to triumph over me. O Lord my God, I cried unto Thee: and Thou hast healed me.

Secret. May the oblation we are about to consecrate, O Lord, be presented before Thee, which Thou hast in such wise appointed to be offered in honour of Thy Name, that the same may be graciously made to work our healing. Through.

Comm. Prov. iii. Honour the Lord with thy substance, and with the first-fruits of all thine increase: so shall thy barns be filled with plenty, and thy presses shall burst out with new wine.

P. Comm. We beseech Thee, O Lord our God, that in Thy mercy Thou wouldest never leave those destitute of Thy aid whom Thou ceasest not to restore by Divine sacraments. Through.

WEDNESDAY.

The Epistle. 1 Cor. vi. 15-20.

Brethren, know ye not that your bodies are the members of Christ .... therefore glorify God in your body.

The Gospel. Luke xviii. 1-8.

At that time Jesus spake a parable unto *His disciples* to this end, that men ought always to pray .... He will avenge them speedily.

Twelfth Sunday after Trinity.

The Office. Ps. lxx.

Haste Thee, O God, to deliver me: make haste to help me, O Lord. Let them be ashamed and confounded that seek after my soul.

Ps. Let them be turned backward and put to confusion that wish me evil.

The Collect.

Almighty and everlasting God, Who in the abundance of Thy mercy art wont to give more than either we desire or deserve; pour down upon us Thy mercy; forgiving us those things whereof our conscience is afraid, and giving us those things which we are not worthy to ask. Through.

The Epistle. 2. Cor. iii. 4-9.

Brethren, such trust have we through Christ .... exceed in glory.

Gradual. Ps. xxxiv. I will alway give thanks unto the Lord: His praise shall ever be in my mouth.

℣. My soul shall make her boast in the Lord: the humble shall hear thereof, and be glad.

Alleluia! ℣. Ps. xcv. O come, let us sing unto the Lord: let us heartily rejoice in the strength of our salvation.

℣. Let us come before His presence with thanksgiving: and shew ourselves glad in Him with psalms.

The Gospel. Mark vii. 31-37.

At that time Jesus, departing from the coasts of Tyre .... the dumb to speak.

Offert. Exod. xxxii. Moses besought the Lord his God, and said. *Moses besought the Lord his God and said:* Lord, why doth Thy wrath wax hot against Thy people? *Spare the wrath of Thy soul:* remember Abraham, Isaac, and Jacob, to whom Thou swarest *to give a land flowing with milk and honey.* And the Lord repented of the evil which He thought to do unto His people.

Secret. Mercifully look down, O Lord, we beseech Thee, on our bounden service: that the gift we offer may be acceptable to Thee, and may succour our frailty. Through.

Comm. Ps. civ. The earth is filled with the fruit of Thy works, *O Lord:* that he may bring food out of the earth, and wine that maketh glad the heart of man, and oil to make him a cheerful countenance, and bread to strengthen man's heart.

P. Comm. Grant, O Lord, we beseech Thee, that in partaking of Thy Sacrament we may have a sense of support both in mind and body; that receiving the salvation of both we may glory in the fulness of the heavenly healing. Through.

WEDNESDAY.

The Epistle. 2 Cor. iv. 5-11.

Brethren, we preach not ourselves, but Christ Jesus the Lord .... made manifest in our mortal flesh.

The Gospel. Matt. xi. 20-24.

At that time Jesus began to upbraid the cities .... in the day of judgment, than for thee.

Thirteenth Sunday after Trinity.

The Office. Ps. lxxiv.

Look upon Thy covenant, *O Lord,* and forget not the congregation of the poor for ever. Arise, O God, maintain Thine own cause: forget not the voice of thine enemies.

Ps. O God, wherefore art Thou absent from us so long: why is Thy wrath so hot against the sheep of Thy pasture?

The Collect.

Almighty and merciful God, of Whose gift it cometh that Thy faithful people do unto Thee true and laudable service; grant, we beseech Thee, that we may without stumbling run the way of Thy promises. Through.

The Epistle. Gal. iii. 16-22.

Brethren, to Abraham and his seed .... might be given to them that believe.

Gradual. Ps. lxxiv. Look upon *Thy* covenant, O Lord: and forget not the congregation of the poor for ever.

℣. Arise, O God, maintain Thine own cause: and forget not the voice of Thine enemies.

Alleluia! ℣. Ps. xcv. For the Lord is a great God: and a great King above all *the earth*.

The Gospel. Luke x. 23-37.

At that time said Jesus to His disciples, Blessed are the eyes that see .... Go, and do Thou likewise.

Offert. Ps. xxxi. My hope hath been in Thee, O Lord: I have said, Thou art my God. My time is in Thy hand.

Secret. Mercifully look down, O Lord, we beseech Thee, on the offerings we lay on Thy holy Altar; that they may be to the honour of Thy Name, by obtaining abundant pardon for us. Through.

Comm. Wisd. xvi. Thou didst send us from Heaven bread, *O Lord,* able to content every man's delight, and agreeing to every taste.

P. Comm. Let the participation of this holy mystery, O Lord, we beseech Thee, give us life, and bestow upon us both pardon and protection. Through.

WEDNESDAY.

The Epistle. 1 Thess. ii. 9-13.

Ye remember, brethren, our labour and travail .... effectually worketh also in you that believe.

The Gospel. Matt. xii. 14-21.

At that time the Pharisees went out .... in His Name shall the Gentiles trust.

Fourteenth Sunday after Trinity.

The Office. Ps. lxxxiv.

Behold, O God our defender: and look upon the face of Thine Anointed. For one day in Thy courts: is better than a thousand.

Ps. O how amiable are Thy dwellings; Thou Lord of hosts! My soul hath a desire and longing to enter into the courts of the Lord.

The Collect.

Almighty and everlasting God, give unto us the increase of faith, hope, and charity; and, that we may obtain that which Thou dost promise, make us to love that which Thou dost command. Through.

The Epistle. Gal. v. 16-24.

Brethren, walk in the Spirit .... the affections and lusts.

Gradual. Ps. xcii. It is a good thing to give thanks unto the Lord: and to sing praises unto Thy Name, O most Highest.

℣. To tell of Thy loving-kindness early in the morning; and of Thy truth in the night-season.

Alleluia! ℣. Ps. cv. O give thanks unto the Lord, and call upon His Name: tell the people what things He hath done.

The Gospel. Luke xvii. 11-19.

At that time, as Jesus went to Jerusalem .... thy faith hath made thee whole.

Offert. Ps. xxxiv. The angel of the Lord tarrieth round about them that fear Him: and delivereth them. O taste, and see how gracious the Lord is.

Secret. Favourably behold, O Lord, Thy people and their offerings: that being reconciled by this oblation, Thou mayest bestow upon us pardon, and grant our petitions. Through.

Comm. John vi. The bread that I will give is My Flesh, which I will give for the life of the world.

P. Comm. Grant, O Lord, we beseech Thee, that we, having received Thy heavenly Sacrament, may advance in our progress towards eternal redemption. Through.

WEDNESDAY.

The Epistle 2 Cor. vi. 14-18: vii. 1.

Brethren, be ye not unequally yoked together .... perfecting holiness in the fear of God.

The Gospel. Luke xii. 13-24.

At that time one of the company said unto *Jesus* .... God feedeth them.

Fifteenth Sunday after Trinity.

The Office. Ps. lxxxvi.

Bow down Thine ear, O Lord, and hear me: my God, save Thy servant that putteth his trust in Thee. Be merciful unto me, O Lord: for I will call daily upon Thee.

Ps. Comfort the soul of Thy servant: for unto Thee, O Lord, do I lift up my soul,

The Collect.

Keep, we beseech Thee, O Lord, Thy Church with Thy perpetual mercy; and, because the fraility of man without Thee cannot but fall, keep us ever by Thy help from all things hurtful, and lead us to all things profitable to our salvation. Through.

The Epistle. Gal. v. 25, 26; vi. 1-10.

Brethren, if we live in the Spirit .... them that are of the household of faith.

Gradual. Ps. cxviii. It is better to trust in the Lord: than to put any confidence in man.

℣. It is better to trust in the Lord: than to put any confidence in princes.

Alleluia! ℣. Ps. cviii. O God, my heart is ready, my heart is ready: I will sing and give praise with the best member that I have.

The Gospel. Matt. vi. 24-37.

At that time said Jesus to His disciples, No man can serve two masters .... these things shall be added unto you.

Offert. Ps. xl. I waited patiently for the Lord: and He inclined unto me, and heard my calling. And he hath put a new song in my mouth: even a thanksgiving unto our God.

Secret. Grant to us, O Lord, we beseech Thee, that this oblation may be profitable to our salvation, both cleansing us from our sins, and reconciling us to Thy loving-kindness. Through.

Comm. John vi. He that eateth My Flesh and drinketh My Blood dwelleth in Me, and I in him, *saith the Lord.*

P. Comm. Let Thy Sacrament, O God, continually purify and strengthen us, and lead us to the attainment of eternal salvation. Through.

WEDNESDAY.

The Epistle. 1 Tim. i. 8-14.

Dearly beloved, we know that the law is good .... which is in Christ Jesus *our Lord.*

The Gospel. Luke xx. 1-8.

At that time it came to pass .... by what authority I do these things.

Sixteenth Sunday after Trinity.

The Office. Ps. lxxxvi.

Be merciful unto me, O Lord: for I will call daily upon Thee. For Thou, Lord, art good and gracious; and of great mercy unto all them that call upon Thee.

Ps. Bow down Thine ear, O Lord, and hear me: for I am poor, and in misery.

The Collect.

O Lord, we beseech Thee, let Thy continual pity cleanse and defend Thy Church; and, because it cannot continue in safety without Thy succour, govern it evermore by Thy favour. Through.

The Lesson. Ephes. iii. 13-21.

Brethren, I desire that ye faint not .... world without end. Amen.

Gradual. Ps. cii. The heathen shall fear Thy Name, O Lord: and all the kings of the earth Thy Majesty.

℣. When the Lord shall build up Sion: and when His glory shall appear.

Alleluia! ℣. Ps. cxv. Ye that fear the Lord put your trust in the Lord: He is their helper and defender.

The Gospel. Luke vii. 11-16.

At that time Jesus went into a city called Nain .... God hath visited His people.

Offert. Ps. xl. Make haste, O Lord, to help me. Let them be ashamed, and confounded together, that seek after my soul to destroy it.

Secret. Let Thy Sacrament, O Lord, keep us in safety, and ever defend us against the assaults of the devil. Through.

Comm. Ps. lxxi. Lord, I will make mention of Thy righteousness only. Thou, O God, hast taught me from my youth up until now: forsake me not, O God, in mine old age, when I am grey-headed.

P. Comm. Let the inward working of the heavenly gift, O Lord, possess both our souls and bodies: that what it alloweth, and not that which our own mind deviseth, may continually prevail in us. Through.

WEDNESDAY.

The Epistle. Col. ii. 8-13.

Brethren, beware lest any man spoil you .... having forgiven you all trespasses, *through Jesus Christ our Lord.*

The Gospel. Mark viii. 22-26.

At that time Jesus cometh to Bethsaida .... nor tell it to any in the town.

Seventeenth Sunday after Trinity.

The Office. Ps. cxix. 137, 124.

Righteous art Thou, O Lord; and true is Thy judgment. O deal with Thy servant according unto Thy loving mercy.

Ps. Blessed are those that are undefiled in the way: and walk in the law of the Lord.

The Collect.

Lord, we pray Thee that Thy grace may always prevent and follow us, and make us continually to be given to good works. Through

The Epistle. Ephes. iv. 1-6.

Brethren, I therefore the prisoner of the Lord .... through all, and in you all. *Who is blessed for ever and ever. Amen.*

Gradual. Ps. xxxiii. Blessed are the people whose God is the Lord Jehovah: and blessed are the folk that *the Lord* hath chosen to Him to be His inheritance.

℣. By the word of the Lord were the heavens made: and all the hosts of them by the breath of His mouth.

Alleluia! ℣. Ps. cxviii. The Right Hand of the Lord bringeth mighty things to pass: the Right Hand of the Lord hath the pre-eminence.

The Gospel. Luke xiv. 1-11.

At that time, as *Jesus* went into the house .... he that humbleth himself shall be exalted.

Offert. Dan. ix. I Daniel prayed unto my God, and said: Hear, O Lord, the prayers of Thy servant: cause Thy face to shine upon Thy sanctuary; and *mercifully look down upon this Thy people*, whereupon Thy name is called, *O God.*

Secret. Cleanse us, O Lord, we beseech Thee, by the effectual working of this present sacrifice; and by Thy mercy make us meet to be partakers thereof. Through.

Comm. Ps. lxxvi. Promise unto the Lord your God, and keep it, all ye that are round about Him: bring presents unto Him that ought to be feared. He shall refrain the spirit of princes: and is wonderful among the kings of the earth.

P. Comm. O Lord, we beseech Thee, of Thy mercy purify our souls, and renew them by this holy Sacrament; that we may receive help thereby, both in this body and hereafter. Through.

WEDNESDAY.

¶ *The Epistle and Gospel as on Wednesday after the Twenty-third Sunday.*

Eighteenth Sunday after Trinity.

The Office. Eccles. xxxvi.

Give peace, O Lord, to them that wait for Thee, and let Thy prophets be found faithful: hear the prayer of Thy servant, *and of Thy people Israel.*

Ps. cxxii. I was glad when they said unto me: We will go into the house of the Lord.

The Collect.

Lord, we beseech Thee, grant Thy people grace to withstand the temptations of the devil, and with pure minds to follow Thee the only God. Through.

The Epistle. I Cor. i. 4-8.

Brethren, I thank my God always .... blameless in the day of our Lord Jesus Christ.

Gradual. Ps. cxxii. I was glad when they said unto me: We will go into the house of the Lord.

℣. Peace be within Thy walls: and plenteousness within Thy palaces.

Alleluia! ℣. Ps. cxxii. I was glad when they said unto me: We will go into the house of the Lord.

Alleluia! ℣. Our feet shall stand in thy gates, O Jerusalem.

¶ *These two verses are said alternately on week-days, but* Our feet *is always said first. If there is no vacant week-day, then let* Our feet *be omitted that year altogether.*

The Gospel. Matt. xxii. 35-46.

At that time the Pharisees came to Jesus; and one of them, who was a lawyer .... ask Him any more questions.

Offert. Exod. xxiv. Moses *consecrated* an Altar to the Lord, offering burnt-offerings thereon, and sacrificing a peace-offering: *he made an evening sacrifice for a sweet odour to the Lord God in the sight of the children of Israel.*

Secret. We humbly beseech Thy Majesty, O Lord, that these holy things which we present may set us free from past and future transgressions. Through.

Comm. Ps. xcvi. Bring presents, and come into His courts. O worship the Lord in the beauty of holiness.

P. Comm. We beseech Thee, Almighty God, that by Thy sanctifying ordinances our vices may be cured, and eternal healing spring up for us. Through.

WEDNESDAY.

The Epistle. Rom. xv. 30-33.

I beseech you, brethren .... the God of peace be with you all. Amen.

The Gospel. Matt. xiii. 31-35.

At that time Jesus spake this parable to His disciples: The Kingdom of Heaven is like to a grain .... kept secret from the foundation of the world.

Nineteenth Sunday after Trinity.

The Office.

I am the Salvation of the people, saith the Lord: in whatsoever distress they call on Me, I will hear them: and will be their Lord for ever.

Ps. lxxviii. Hear my law, O my people: incline your ears to the words of my mouth.

The Collect.

O Lord, forasmuch as without Thee we are not able to please Thee, we beseech Thee let Thy pity direct our hearts. Through.

The Epistle. Ephes. iv. 23-28.

Brethren, be renewed in the spirit of your mind .... have to give to him that needeth.

Gradual. Ps. cxli. Let my prayer be set forth in Thy sight as the incense, *O Lord.*

℣. Let the lifting up of my hands be an evening sacrifice.

Alleluia! ℣. Ps. cxxv. They that put their trust in the Lord shall be even as the Mount Sion: which may not be removed, but standeth fast for ever *in Jerusalem.*

The Gospel. Matt. ix. 1-8.

At that time Jesus entered into a ship .... had given such power unto men.

Offert. Ps. cxxxviii. Though I walk in the midst of trouble, yet shalt Thou refresh me, *O Lord:* Thou shalt stretch forth Thy hand upon the furiousness of mine enemies, and Thy right hand shall save me.

Secret. O God, Who by the communion of this sacred sacrifice, makest us partakers of the one supreme Divine Nature: grant, we beseech Thee, that as we know Thy truth, so we may shew it forth by a right mind and conversation. Through.

Comm. Ps. cxix. 4, 5. Thou hast charged: that we shall diligently keep Thy commandments. O that my ways were made so direct: that I might keep Thy statutes!

P. Comm. We who have been fed with Thy holy gift, give thanks unto Thee, O Lord, humbly beseeching Thy mercy, that Thou wouldest make us worthy of that which we have received. Through.

WEDNESDAY.

The Epistle. 2 Thess. ii. 15-17; iii. 1-5.

Brethren, stand fast .... into the patient waiting for Christ.

The Gospel. Matt. xiii. 37-43.

At that time the disciples of Jesus came unto Him, saying, Declare unto us the parable .... Who hath ears to hear, let him hear.

Twentieth Sunday after Trinity.

The Office. Dan. iii.*

In all the things that Thou hast brought upon us, *O Lord*, Thou hast executed true judgment: we have trespassed, and not obeyed Thy commandments, but give glory to Thy Name, and deal with us according to the multitude of Thy mercy.

Ps. xlviii. Great is the Lord, and highly to be praised: in the city of our God, even upon His holy hill.

The Collect.

O almighty and merciful God, of Thy bountiful goodness keep us, we beseech Thee, from all things that may hurt us; that we, being ready both in body and soul, may cheerfully accomplish those things that Thou wouldest have done. Through.

The Epistle. Ephes. v. 15-21.

Brethren, see then that ye walk circumspectly .... one to another in the fear of *Christ*.

Gradual. Ps. cxlv. The eyes of all wait upon Thee, O Lord: and Thou givest them their meat in due season.

℣. Thou openest Thine hand: and fillest all things living with plenteousness.

Alleluia! ℣. Ps. cxxx. Out of the deep have I called unto Thee, O Lord: Lord, hear my voice.

The Gospel. Matt. xxii. 1-14.

At that time Jesus spake with His disciples in parables, saying, The Kingdom of Heaven is like unto a certain king .... but few are chosen.

* *i.e.*, Song of the Three Children, *v.* 5, 7, 8, 9, 20.

Offert. Ps. cxxxvii. By the waters of Babylon we sat down and wept: when we remembered thee, O Sion.

Secret. Grant, we beseech Thee, O Lord, that these gifts which we offer before Thy Majesty may be profitable for our salvation. Through,

Comm. Ps. cxix. 49, 50. O think upon Thy servant, as concerning Thy Word: wherein Thou hast caused me to put my trust. The same is my comfort in my trouble.

P. Comm. Let Thy merciful healing, O Lord, work in us to set us free from our frowardness, and make us ever hold fast to Thy commandments. Through.

WEDNESDAY.

The Epistle. 2 Tim. ii. 1-7.

Dearly beloved, be strong in the grace .... the Lord give thee understanding in all things.

The Gospel. Luke xiv. 12-15.

At that time Jesus said to a certain ruler of the Pharisees, When thou makest a dinner or a supper .... blessed is he that shall eat bread in the Kingdom of God.

Twenty-first Sunday after Trinity.

The Office. Esther. xiii.*

O Lord, the whole world is in Thy power, and there is no man that can gainsay Thee: for Thou hast made *all things*; Heaven and earth, and all the wondrous things under the heaven. Thou art Lord of all things.

Ps. cxix. Blessed are the undefiled in the way, who walk in the law of the Lord.

The Collect.

Grant, we beseech Thee, merciful Lord, to Thy faithful people pardon and peace, that they may be cleansed from all their sins, and serve Thee with a quiet mind. Through.

The Epistle. Ephes. vi. 10-17.

My brethren, be strong in the Lord .... which is the Word of God.

Gradual. Ps. xc. Lord, Thou hast been our refuge: from one generation to another.

* See Apocrypha, *v.* 9, 10, 11.

℣. Before the mountains were brought forth, or ever the earth and the world were made: Thou art God from everlasting, and world without end.

Alleluia! ℣. Ps. cxlvi. Praise the Lord, O my soul; while I live will I praise the Lord: yea, as long as I have any being, I will sing praises unto my God.

The Gospel. John iv. 46-53.

At that time there was a certain nobleman .... himself believed, and his whole house.

Offert. Job i. There was a man in the land of Uz whose name was Job, perfect and upright, and one that feared God: *and Satan asked that he might tempt him, and power was given him by the Lord over his possessions, and over his flesh;* and he destroyed *all his substance, and his sons: and he* smote *his flesh with a grievous* boil.

Secret. Let these mysteries, O Lord, we beseech Thee, provide for us a heavenly medicine, and cleanse away the vices of our hearts. Through.

Comm. Ps. cxix. 81, 84, 86. My soul hath longed for Thy salvation: and I have a good hope because of Thy Word. When wilt Thou be avenged of them that persecute me? They persecute me falsely: O be Thou my help, *O Lord, my God.*

P. Comm. That we may be worthy of Thy sacred gifts, O Lord: make us, we beseech Thee, continually to obey Thy commandments. Through.

WEDNESDAY.

The Epistle. 1 Thess. i. 4-10.

Knowing, brethren beloved, your election of God .... Whom He raised from the dead, even Jesus *Christ our Lord.*

The Gospel. Luke vi. 6-11.

At that time it came to pass that *Jesus* entered into the synagogue and taught .... what they might do to Jesus.

Twenty-second Sunday after Trinity.

The Office. Ps. cxxx.

If Thou, Lord, wilt be extreme to mark what is done amiss: O Lord, who may abide it? For there is mercy with Thee, *O God of Israel.*

Ps. Out of the deep have I called unto Thee, O Lord : Lord, hear my voice.

The Collect.

Lord, we beseech Thee to keep Thy household the Church in continual godliness ; that through Thy protection it may be free from all adversities, and devoutly given to serve Thee in good works, to the glory of Thy Name. Through.

The Epistle. Phil. i. 6-11.

Brethren, we are confident *in the Lord Jesus,* that He who hath begun a good work .... unto the glory and praise of God.

Gradual. Ps. cxxxiii. Behold, how good and joyful a thing it is : brethren, to dwell together in unity !

℣. It is like the precious ointment upon the head, that ran down unto the beard : even unto Aaron's beard.

Alleluia ! ℣. Ps. cxlvii. He healeth those that are broken in heart : and giveth medicine to heal their sickness.

℣. The Lord promised His blessing : and life for evermore.

¶ As regards this second verse, see page 247.

The Gospel. Matt. xviii. 23-35.

At that time Jesus spake to His disciples this parable : The Kingdom of Heaven is like unto a certain king .... forgive not every one his brother their trespasses.

Offert. Esther xiv.* Remember *me*, O Lord, *Who art above all power ;* and give me proper and eloquent speech in my mouth, *that my words may be pleasing when I come before the princes*

Secret. Mercifully accept, O Lord, the offering which Thou hast willed to be for a propitiation before Thee, that salvation should be restored to us in the might of Thy loving-kindness. Through.

Comm. Luke xv. I say unto you, there is joy in the presence of the angels of God over one sinner that repenteth.

P. Comm. We, being partakers of the food of immortality, beseech Thee, O Lord, that with pure minds we may live according to that which we have received with our lips. Through.

* See Apocrypha.

WEDNESDAY.

The Epistle. Rom. iii. 19-26.

Brethren, we know that what things soever the law saith ...... justifier of him which believeth in Jesus *Christ.*

The Gospel. Matt. xi. 23-26.

At that time said Jesus to His disciples, Verily I say unto you, that whosoever shall say .... which is in Heaven forgive your trespasses.

Twenty-third Sunday after Trinity.

The Office. Jer. xxix.

I know the thoughts that I think toward you, saith the Lord, thoughts of peace, and not of evil. Then shall ye call upon Me, and I will hearken unto you, and I will turn away your captivity, from all places.

Ps. lxxxv. Lord, Thou art become gracious unto Thy land; Thou hast turned away the captivity of Jacob.

The Collect.

O God, our refuge and strength, Who art the author of all godliness, be ready to hear the devout prayers of Thy Church; and grant that those things which we ask faithfully we may obtain effectually. Through.

The Epistle. Phil. iii. 17-21.

Brethren, be followers together with me .... to subdue all things unto Himself, *in Christ Jesus our Lord.*

Gradual. Ps. xliv. It is Thou that savest us from our enemies, *O Lord:* and puttest them to confusion that hate us.

℣. We make our boast of God all day long: and will praise Thy Name for ever.

Alleluia! ℣. Ps. cxlvii. He maketh peace in thy borders: and filleth thee with the flour of wheat.

The Gospel. Matt. xxii. 15-21.

At that time went the Pharisees .... unto God the things that are God's.

Offert. Ps. cxxx. Out of the deep have I called unto Thee, O Lord: Lord, hear my voice.

Secret. We beseech Thee, O Lord, incline us heartily unto Thy service; and that we may wait on Thee without offence, do Thou Thyself make us such as Thou requirest us to be. Through.

Comm. Mark xi. *Verily* I say unto you, what things soever ye desire when ye pray, believe that ye receive them, and ye shall have them.

P. Comm. Having received, O Lord, the gifts of the holy mystery, we humbly beseech Thee, that what Thou hast commanded us to do in remembrance of Thee, may be an effectual aid to our weakness. Through.

WEDNESDAY.

The Epistle. Rom. v. 17-21.

Brethren, if by one man's offence death reigned, by one ...... eternal life by Jesus Christ our Lord.

The Gospel. Matt. xvii. 24-27.

At that time, when Jesus and His disciples were come to Capernaum .... give unto them for Me and Thee.

Twenty-fourth Sunday after Trinity.

The Office. Jer. xxix.

I know the thoughts that I think towards you, saith the Lord, thoughts of peace, and not of evil; then shall ye call upon Me, and I will hear you, and I will turn your captivity from all places.

Ps. lxxxv. Lord, Thou are become gracious unto Thy land: Thou hast turned away the captivity of Jacob.

The Collect.

O Lord, we beseech Thee, absolve Thy people from their offences; that through Thy bountiful goodness we may be delivered from the bands of those sins which by our frailty we have committed. Through.

The Epistle. Col. i. 9-11.

Brethren, we do not cease to pray for you .... long-suffering with joyfulness, *in Christ Jesus our Lord.*

Gradual. Ps. xliv. But it is Thou that savest us from our enemies, *O Lord;* and puttest them to confusion that hate us.

℣. We make our boast of God all day long, and will praise Thy Name for ever.

Alleluia! ℣. Ps. vii. O Lord my God, in Thee have I put my trust: save me from all them that persecute me, and deliver me.

The Gospel. Matt. ix. 18-22.

At that time, while Jesus spake *to the multitudes,* behold, there came a certain ruler .... And the woman was made whole from that hour.

Offert. Ps. cxxx. Out of the deep have I called unto Thee, O Lord: O Lord, hear my voice.

Secret. Let the oblation of this gift cleanse us, O Lord, we beseech Thee, and make us wholly worthy of the sacred things we have received. Through.

Comm. Mark xi. *Verily* I say unto you, what things soever ye desire when ye pray, believe that ye receive them, and ye shall have them.

P. Comm. We receiving the heavenly gift, beseech Thee, O Lord, suffer not that to turn to our condemnation which Thou hast ordained for the healing of Thy faithful people. Through.

WEDNESDAY.

The Epistle 2 Cor. x. 20-31.

Brethren, I would not that ye should have fellowship with devils .... do all to the glory of God.

The Gospel. Matt. xxi. 28-32.

At that time said Jesus to the multitudes of the Jews, A certain man had two sons .... that ye might believe him. *He that hath ears to hear, let him hear.*

Sunday next before Advent.

The Office. Jer. xxix.

I know the thoughts that I think towards you, saith the Lord, thoughts of peace, and not of evil: then shall ye call upon me, and I will hearken unto you, and I will turn away your captivity from all places.

Ps. lxxxv. Lord, Thou art become gracious unto Thy land: Thou hast turned away the captivity of Jacob.

The Collect.

Stir up, we beseech Thee, O Lord, the wills of Thy faithful people; that they, plenteously bringing forth the fruit of good works, may of Thy loving-kindness be more plenteously rewarded. Through.

The Lesson. Jer. xxiii. 5-8.

Behold, the days come .... they shall dwell in their own land, *saith the Lord Almighty.*

Gradual. Ps. xliv. It is Thou that savest us from our enemies: and puttest them to confusion that hate us.

℣. We make our boast of God all day long: and will praise Thy Name for ever.

Alleluia! ℣. Ps. cii. The heathen shall fear Thy Name, O Lord: and all the kings of the earth Thy Majesty.

¶ *Through the week, when the Service is ferial, is said one of the two following Alleluias.*

Alleluia! ℣. Ps. cxiv. When Israel came out of Egypt: and the house of Jacob from among the strange people.

Alleluia! ℣. Ps. cxxxviii. I will give thanks unto Thee, O Lord, with my whole heart: even before the gods will I sing praise unto Thee.

The Gospel. John. vi. 5-14.

At that time, when Jesus lift up His eyes .... Prophet that should come into the world.

Offert. Ps. cxxx. Out of the deep have I called unto Thee, O Lord: Lord, hear my voice.

Secret. Favourably behold, O Lord, the sacrifice we are about to celebrate; that it may both cleanse us from the corruptions of our present state, and make us acceptable unto Thy Name. Through.

Comm. Mark xi. *Verily* I say unto you, What things soever ye desire when ye pray, believe that ye receive them, and ye shall have them.

P. Comm. Grant, we beseech Thee, Almighty God, that our souls, which are satisfied with the Divine gift, may be filled with a longing desire to be kindled by the flame of Thy Spirit, and to shine as bright lights in the presence of Christ Thy Son at His coming. Through.

¶ *If there are more than twenty-five Sundays after Trinity, the Service for the twenty-fourth is to be repeated; and if less, the extra Masses can be said on the week-days, provided that this Service shall always be used on the Sunday next before Advent. If a Saint's Day fall on the Sunday, the Sunday Service is to be said on the first vacant day in the week.*

EMBER WEDNESDAY IN SEPTEMBER.

The Office. Ps. lxxxi.

Sing we merrily unto God our strength: make a cheerful noise unto the God of Jacob. Take the psalm: the merry harp with the lute. Blow up the trumpet in the new-moon: for this was made a statute for Israel: and a law of the God of Jacob.

Ps. This He ordained in Joseph for a testimony: when he came out of the land of Egypt.

Let us pray.

The Collect.

Let the frailty of our nature, O Lord, we beseech Thee, be sustained by the relief of Thy mercy; that as in itself it continually decayeth, by Thy merciful goodness it may be renewed. Through.

The Lesson. Amos ix. 13-15.

Behold the days come, saith the Lord ...... land which I have given them, saith the Lord *Almighty.*

Gradual. Ps. xxxiv. Come, ye children, and hearken unto me: I will teach you the fear of the Lord.

℣. They had an eye unto Him, and were lightened: and their faces were not ashamed.

℣. The Lord be with you.

℟. And with thy spirit.

Let us pray.

Grant, we beseech Thee, O Lord, the humble request of Thy family: that whilst they observe abstinence from bodily food, their souls may also fast from sin. Through.

The Lesson. Nehemiah viii. 1-10.*

In those days all the people gathered themselves together ...... the joy of the Lord is your strength.

Gradual. Ps. cxiii. Who is like unto the Lord our God, that hath His dwelling so high : and yet humbleth Himself to behold the things that are in Heaven and earth ?

℣. He taketh up the simple out of the dust : and lifteth the poor out of the mire.

The Gospel. Mark ix. 17-29.

At that time one of the multitude answered and said *unto Jesus*, Master, I have brought unto Thee my son ...... by nothing, but by prayer and fasting.

Offert. Ps. cxix. 47, 48. And my delight shall be in Thy commandments : which I have loved. My hands also will I lift up unto Thy commandments, which I have loved.

Secret. O God, Who hast been pleased to constitute Thy Sacrament of these fruits of the earth ; vouchsafe, we beseech Thee, through It to bestow upon us aid both in this present life and in life eternal. Through.

Comm. Neh. viii. Eat the fat, and drink the sweet, and send portions unto them for whom nothing is prepared : for this day is holy unto our Lord ; neither be ye sorry, for the joy of the Lord is your strength.

P. Comm. Having received, O Lord, the heavenly gifts, we humbly beseech Thee, that what by Thy special grace we celebrate with due service, we may also by Thy bounty be worthily disposed to receive. Through.

EMBER FRIDAY IN SEPTEMBER.

The Office. Ps. cv.

Let the heart of them rejoice that seek the Lord. Seek the Lord and His strength : seek His face evermore.

Ps. O give thanks unto the Lord, and call upon His Name : tell the people what things He hath done.

The Collect.

Grant, we beseech Thee, Almighty God, that we who observe these holy appointed times with yearly worship, may please Thee both in body and mind. Through.

* *i.e.*, 1-3 ; 4 to "*they* stood beside him ;" 5, 6, 7, "The Levites" to the end ; 8-10.

The Lesson. Hosea xiv. 1-9.*

Thus saith the Lord, O Israel, return unto the Lord ...... and the just shall walk in them.

Gradual. Ps. xc. Turn Thee again, O Lord, at the last: and be gracious unto Thy servants.

℣. Lord, Thou hast been our refuge: from one generation to another.

The Gospel. Luke vii. 36-50.

At that time one of the Pharisees desired *Jesus* that He would eat with him ...... Thy faith hath saved thee; go in peace.

Offert. Ps. ciii. Praise the Lord, O my soul: and forget not all His benefits; making Thee young and lusty as an eagle.

Secret. Let the offering of our fast, O Lord, we beseech Thee, be acceptable unto Thee to atone for sin; make us worthy of Thy grace, and bring us to the eternal things which Thou hast promised. Through.

Comm. Ps. cxix. 22-24. O turn from me shame and rebuke: for I have kept Thy testimonies, *O Lord*; for Thy testimonies are my delight.

P. Comm. We beseech Thee, Almighty God, that we rendering Thee thanks for the bounties we have received, may be made partakers of blessings more to be desired. Through.

EMBER SATURDAY IN SEPTEMBER.

The Office. Ps. xcv.

O come, let us worship *God*, and fall down: and kneel before the Lord our Maker. For He is the Lord our God.

Ps. O come, let us sing unto the Lord: let us heartily rejoice in the strength of our salvation.

Let us pray.

The Collect.

Almighty and everlasting God, Who by a wholesome abstinence healest both body and soul: we humbly beseech Thy Majesty, graciously accept our devout prayers and fasting, and succour us both here and hereafter. Through.

* In verse 8, "Ephraim ...... idols," is omitted.

The Lesson. Levit. xxiii. 27-32.

In those days the Lord spake unto Moses .... shall ye celebrate your Sabbath, *saith the Lord Almighty.*

Gradual. Ps. lxxix. Be merciful, *O Lord,* unto our sins, for Thy Name's sake. Wherefore do the heathen say: Where is now their God?

℣. Help us, O God of our salvation: for the glory of Thy Name, *Lord* deliver us.

Let us pray.

The Collect.

Grant, we beseech Thee, O Almighty God, that in fasting we may be filled with Thy grace; and by abstinence become stronger than all our enemies. Through.

The Lesson. Levit. xxiii. 39-43.

In those days the Lord spake unto Moses, saying, In the fifteenth day of the seventh month ...... I am the Lord your God.

Gradual. Ps. lxxxiv. Behold, O God, our defender; and look upon *Thy servants.*

℣. O Lord God of hosts, hear *the* prayer *of Thy servants.*

Let us pray.

The Collect.

Grant, we beseech Thee, O Lord, that Thy faithful servants may rejoice in the blessings they have humbly implored: that they reverencing Thee by their outward fasting, may be fulfilled with the abundance of Thy good things. Through.

The Lesson. Micah vii. 14-16; 18-20.

O Lord our God, feed Thy people with Thy rod .... hast sworn unto our fathers from the days of old, *O L.rd our God.*

Gradual. Ps. cxli.. Let my prayers be set forth in Thy sight as the incense, *O Lord.*

℣. Let the lifting up of my hands be an evening sacrifice.

Let us pray.

The Collect.

Grant, O Lord, we beseech Thee, that we may so abstain from carnal feastings, as to fast in like manner from all vices that assault us. Through.

The Lesson. Zach. viii. 14-20.

In those days the word of the Lord came unto me, saying, Thus saith the Lord of hosts; as I thought to punish you .... therefore love the truth and peace, *saith the Lord of hosts.*

Gradual. Ps. xxviii. Save Thy people, *O Lord*, and give Thy blessing unto Thine inheritance.

℣. Unto Thee will I cry, *my God:* think no scorn of me, lest I become like them that go down into the pit.

Let us pray.

The Collect.

As it is by Thy grace, O Lord, that we offer Thee the tribute of this solemn fast; so grant us, we beseech Thee, the aid of Thy pardoning mercy. Through.

The Lesson. Dan. iii. 26-66 (*i.e.*, the Song of the Three Children).

¶ *As on Saturday after Whitsun Day*, The Angel of the Lord.

Tract. The Almighty ever adore, and bless for ever and ever.

Choir. The Almighty ever adore.

Clergy. ℣. The stars of Heaven, the whole race of men, both sun and moon, the lights of Heaven,

Choir. The Almighty ever adore.

Clergy. ℣. So, too, the waters all above, the dew and rain, every breeze.

Choir. And bless for ever and ever.

Clergy. ℣. Fire and heat, burning and freezing, cold and warmth, and hoar-frost,

Choir. The Almighty.

Clergy. ℣. Snow and ice, night and day, light and darkness, lightning, clouds.

Choir. And bless.

Clergy. ℣. Deserts, mountains, green herbs, hills, rivers, fountains, the sea and waves.

Choir. The Almighty.

Clergy. ℣. All things living which the sea beareth, the air quickeneth, and the earth nourisheth.

Choir. And bless.

Clergy. ℣. Every race of men, Israel himself, and all servants and worshippers of Christ.

Choir. The Almighty.

Clergy. ℣. Holy and humble men of heart, and the three children that overcame.

Choir. And bless.

Clergy. ℣. The flames of the fiery furnace that was ordered by the tyrant ready duly to despise.

Choir. The Almighty.

Clergy. ℣. Praise be to Father and to Son, and praise to the Blessed Holy Ghost.

Choir. And bless.

¶ *Let the Clergy begin again* The Almighty, *then let the Choir repeat it.*

℣. The Lord be with you.

℟. And with thy spirit.

Let us pray.

The Collect.

O God, Who for the three children didst quench the flames of fire; mercifully grant us that we Thy servants may not be consumed by the flames of our sins. Through.

The Epistle. Heb. ix. 2-12.

Brethren, there was a tabernacle made ....obtained eternal redemption for us.

Tract. Ps. cxvii. O praise the Lord, all ye heathen: praise Him, all ye nations.

℣. For His merciful kindness is ever more and more towards us: and the truth of the Lord endureth for ever.

The Gospel. Luke xiii. 6-17.

At that time Jesus spake also *to the multitude* this parable: A certain man had a fig-tree .... the glorious things that were done by Him.

Offert. Ps. lxxxviii. O Lord God of my salvation, I have cried day and night before Thee: O let my prayer enter into Thy presence, *O Lord.*

Secret. We beseech Thee, O Lord, to look favourably on our gifts and fast, since Thou disposest the same as seemeth good to Thee. Through.

Comm. Lev. xxiii. In the seventh month *ye shall keep a feast,* because I made the children of Israel dwell in booths, when I brought them out of the land of Egypt: I am the Lord your God.

P. Comm. Let Thy Sacrament, O Lord, we beseech Thee, perfect in us that which it containeth: that we may enjoy in truth and reality what we now offer under a figure. Through.

The Dedication of a Church.

The Office. Gen. xxviii.

How dreadful is this place! this is the House of God, and this is the gate of Heaven: *and it shall be called the court of God.*

¶ *In Easter-tide,* Alleluia!

Ps. xciii. The Lord is King, and hath put on glorious apparel: the Lord hath put on His apparel, and girded Himself with strength.

The Collect.

O God, Who restoreth year by year the day of the consecration of this Thy holy temple, and always permittest us to present ourselves again in safety at the holy mysteries: hear the prayers of Thy people, and grant that whosoever entereth into this temple to ask any blessing of Thee, may joyfully obtain all his petitions. Through.

The Lesson. Rev. xxi. 2-5.

In those days, I John saw the holy city .... Behold, I make all things new.

Gradual. This place was made by God, a mystery above all value; it is unreprovable.

℣. *O God, on Whom the choirs of angels attend, hear the prayers of Thy servants.*

Alleluia! ℣. Ps. cxxxviii. I will worship towards Thy holy temple, and praise Thy Name.

¶ *These two following* Alleluias *are said alternately through the Octave, except on the Sunday and the Octave Day.*

Alleluia! Gen. xxviii. ℣. How dreadful *and adorable* is this place! truly this is none other but the House of God, and this is the gate of Heaven.

Alleluia! ℣. Is. ii. The mountain of the Lord's House *hath been* established in the top of the mountains, and exalted above the hills.

¶ *This Sequence is to be said even in Lent.*

The Sequence.

Jerusalem and Sion's daughters fair,
Assembled band, who in the faith have share,
With joyful voice unceasingly declare,
Alleluia!

For on this day Christ for His Spouse doth take
Our Mother, for His faith and justice sake,
Whom He brought out of misery's deep lake,
The Holy Church.

She in the Holy Spirit's clemency,
Bride in the Bridegroom's grace rejoicing high,
In glorious place by queens exultingly
Is called blessed.

Midst plaudits loud forthwith is given her dower,
A dower most wonderful! a threefold power,
Reaching to heaven, to earth, and to the lower
Dungeons of hell.

Doubt not my words, though marvellous they be,
Her from His side, endowed thus wealthily,
As the God-Man, a mighty mystery,
Himself brought forth.

That in such wise should be the Church's birth—
The woman showed in figure upon earth
When she from Adam's side first issued forth,
Ill-omened Eve.

Eve was but step-mother to all her seed;
To the elect this Mother is indeed
The port of life, and unto those in need
A hiding-place.

Fair, wonderful in offspring, great in might,
As moon, as sun, she shines in beauty bright,
More terrible than army for the fight
Set in array.

One and alone she is, yet manifold;
Receiving all, yet one unbroken fold;
To multitudes, herself one, young and old
She doth give birth.

This was by Jordan's parted waters shown;
This she who came from distant lands makes known,
Attracted by the marvellous renown
Of Solomon's lore.

By divers types prefigured this is she
In bridal vesture clad resplendently,
Above the heavenly hosts upraised to be
With Christ conjoined.

O solemn festival of high delight!
Which does with Christ Himself the Church unite!
Wherein our own salvation's marriage rite
We celebrate!

O entertainment sweet, assembly blest!
Which to the fallen gives consoling rest;
To them that have lost hope, the sore distressed,
A breathing time.

There are rewards unto the righteous given,
There joy anew God's angels in the heaven,
There hearts are gladdened by the gracious leaven
Of charity.

The Source of Wisdom from eternity,
By gracious, all-disposing scrutiny,
In the due course of things did this foresee
Should come to pass.

Therefore when Christ His marriage-feast shall make,
May we with joy of true delights partake,
And never the blest company forsake
Of His elect. Amen.

¶ *After Septuagesima till Ash-Wednesday the following Tract is said on the Octave only.*

Tract. Ps. lxxxiv. O how amiable are Thy dwellings: Thou Lord of hosts! My soul hath a desire and longing to enter into the courts of the Lord.

℣. My heart and my flesh rejoice in the living God.

℣. Yea, the sparrow hath found her an house, and the swallow a nest where she may lay her young.

℣. Even Thy altars, O Lord of hosts, my King and my God.

℣. Blessed are they that dwell in Thy house: they will be alway praising Thee.

¶ *In Easter-tide the second* Alleluia *of the Resurrection shall be said daily through the Octave, and on the Octave Day, and also on the first day.*

The Gospel. Luke xix. 1-10.

At that time Jesus entered and passed through Jericho .... to seek and to save that which was lost.

Offert. 1 Chron. xxix. O Lord God, in the uprightness of mine heart I have willingly offered all these things: and now have I seen with joy Thy people, which are present here. O God of Israel, keep the imagination of the heart of Thy people.

¶ *In Easter-tide,* Alleluia!

Secret. Grant, we beseech Thee, O Lord, our petition, that, whosoever we be who are met within the walls of this church whereof we celebrate the dedication Anniversary, we may please

Thee with full and perfect devotion both of body and soul ; that whilst we pay these our present vows, we may, by Thy help, be counted worthy to attain unto the everlasting reward. Through.

Comm. Matt. xxi. My House shall be called the House of Prayer, *saith the Lord: in it* whosoever asketh, receiveth ; and he that seeketh, findeth ; and unto him that knocketh, it shall be opened.

¶ *After* Comm. *in Easter-tide*, Alleluia ! Alleluia !

P. Comm. O God, Who hast deigned to call the Church Thy Spouse, that she who had obtained grace through her steadfast Faith should also gain honour in Name ; grant that all this people, who serve Thy Name, may be found worthy to have a share in that title. Who.

¶ *If this feast fall from the Octave of the Epiphany to LXX., from the Octave of Easter to Ascension Day, or from Trinity Sunday to Advent, the same Mass is said through the Octave (unless a feast of nine lessons occurs) without Sequence or Creed; except that on the Sunday within the Octave is sung:*

The Sequence.

Now let the faithful choir their serenade
To high Heaven sing:
The chamber of the Queen is ready made
For glory's King.
The lowly Burr doth thus with Lily wed,
With sun a Star;
To God the soul, in mystic union led,
A shrine doth rear.
Christ and the Church, in chaste espousal knit,
This day we praise.
Thus man to God his spirit doth unite
In yoke of grace;
Flesh to the Son of God in marriage high
Hath thus attained;
The peerless Son to deep humility
Did condescend.
The Mightiest one of low estate did seek,
And by His Word the Bride, so dark and meek,
Made clean and white.
What He ordained He hath so fulfilled,
Who the impure could make, if so He willed,
All pure as light.
O Handmaid ! haste thy liberty to gain,
That sceptred with thy Husband Thou mayest reign.
Thy Spouse consider ; Him whom types disguise
True faith discerneth with unclouded eyes.

The Gospel. Luke vi. 47, 48.

At that time Jesus said to His disciples, Whosoever cometh .... upon a rock.

The Octave of the Dedication of a Church.

¶ *All as on the Day except—*

The Sequence.

The dwellings of the Lord of hosts how fair!
The Master-builder's courts how sure they are!
Unharmed by wind, or floods, or rain,
For ever settled they remain.
How majestic their foundations,
Shadowy prefigurations
Of the mystic types pourtray.
Formed from sleeping Adam's side,
Eve of the approaching Bride
Doth a sign convey.
Framed of wood, the Ark doth save
Noah, guided o'er the wave,
When the world was drowned.
Sarah, stricken now in years,
Laughs when she an infant bears;
Her joy doth ours expound.
Long widowed, veiled in robes unfitting,
Thamar by the wayside sitting,
To Judah twins doth bear.
The royal maiden doth deliver
The infant Moses from the river,
In bulrush ark laid near;
This is the male lamb sacrificed,
With which all Israel was sufficed,
And by its blood brought near:
Of Sheba's utmost parts the Queen
In quest of wisdom here is seen,
King Solomon to hear:
Black, but yet comely, see we her
Perfumed with frankincense and myrrh,
With balmy odours fraught.
Thus things to come which types concealed
The day of grace hath now revealed,
And illustration brought.
Now let us take our rest and sing,
With the beloved tarrying,
The marriage-hour is come;
The trumpets as the guests go in
With solemn tones the Feast begin,
The psaltery lulls them home.
Ten thousand thousand voices raise
With one consent the Bridegroom's praise,
And Alleluia! Alleluia! cry
In everlasting joy, unceasingly.

The Gospel. John x. 22-30.

At that time it was at Jerusalem .... I and My Father are One.

¶ *From LXX. to Ash-Wednesday the Octave Day is kept (but not the days within the Octave, except by a memorial). From Ash-Wednesday to the Octave of Easter there is only a memorial.*

The Consecration of a Church.

¶ *All as on the Dedication of a Church, except the Sequence, which is,* The dwellings of the Lord.

The Collect.

O God, Who art Thyself the author of the gifts to be hallowed unto Thee, pour forth Thy benediction upon this house of prayer, that the help of Thy defence may be perceived by all who call upon Thy Name. Through.

¶ *In Easter-tide,* Alleluia!

Secret. O God, Who in every place of Thy dominion art wholly present, and workest in all Thy power; graciously accept this sacrifice offered to Thy Name, and be the protector of this house whereof Thou art the founder, that in the power of the Holy Ghost they who worship here may have free access even unto Thyself. Through.

P. Comm. We being refreshed by Thy saving Sacrament, give thanks unto Thee, O Lord: fill, we beseech Thee, this temple with the glory of Thy Majesty; that in honour of Thy Name it may become unto Thy people a house of prayer. Through.

The Reconciliation of a Church.

The Office. Ezek. xxxvi.

When I shall be sanctified in you I will gather you out of all countries. Then will I sprinkle clean water upon you, and ye shall be clean from all your filthiness, and a new spirit will I give you.

¶ *In Easter-tide,* Alleluia!

Ps. xxxiv. I will alway give thanks unto the Lord: His praise shall ever be in my mouth.

The Collect.

O God, Who hast said, My House shall be called a house of prayer, deign to cleanse and sanctify this house, which hath been polluted and defiled by the abomination of the heathen; that Thou mayest mercifully hear the prayers and vows of all them that call upon Thee in this place, and graciously bring the same to good effect. Who.

The Epistle.

(As on the Dedication.)

Gradual. Ps. xcvi. Bring presents, and come into His courts. O worship the Lord in the beauty of holiness.

℣. Ps. xxix. *The Lord* discovereth the thick bushes; in His temple doth every man speak of His honour.

Alleluia! ℣. Ps. cv. O give thanks unto the Lord, and call upon His Name: tell the people what things He hath done.

The Gospel. Luke vi. 43-48.

At that time said Jesus to His disciples, A good tree bringeth not forth corrupt fruit ...... for it was founded upon a rock.

Offert. Dan. ix. I Daniel prayed unto my God, saying, Hear, *Lord,* the prayers of Thy servant: cause Thy face to shine upon Thy sanctuary, and *graciously* behold *this people whereupon Thy Name* is called, *O God.*

Secret. We beseech Thee, O Lord, let this offering cleanse this place from the impurities of the wicked [*or* of the offence which has been committed], and make our supplications here and everywhere acceptable unto Thee. Through.

Comm. Ps. li. Then shalt Thou be pleased with the sacrifice of righteousness, with the burnt-offerings and oblations: then shall they offer young bullocks upon Thine Altar.

P. Comm. O Lord, we that are partakers of the gifts of eternal salvation, humbly implore of Thee that this church [*or* cemetery], being cleansed from the pollutions of the heathen [*or* the wicked], may abide under the sanctification of Thy blessing: and that our hearts, being wholly alienated from all defilements of sin, may ever devoutly serve Thee. Through.

THE END OF THE PROPER OF SEASONS.

Prayers to be said before Mass.

I. BEFORE THE HOURS.*

Seven times this day will I praise Thee, O Lord, being mindful of Thy exceeding great and wonderful works, by which in the beginning Thou didst found the universe in seven days; mindful also of the sevenfold grace of Thy Holy Spirit, at each of the seven Canonical Hours, which I, unworthy, propose, according to the sacred rule and institution of Thy Church, to say in Thy presence this day to the praise of Thy Holy Name. Deign, I entreat Thee, to bestow upon me the singular gifts of grace, that being abundantly filled by that Thy most Blessed Spirit and His sevenfold gifts, and supported as on the seven pillars which Wisdom hath hewed out for the building of her house, throughout the cycle of the seven days of the week, by the succession of which times fulfil their course; and throughout the seven ages by which the frailty of man continually goeth on its way towards death, I may in such wise please Thee, that, through the painful exercise of the mystic septenary in practice of the seven works of the Spirit, I may be enabled to avoid the seven deadly sins, which are the seven devils cast out of that Mary of the Gospel by Christ; and to vanquish those seven more wicked spirits which the strong man armed taketh to himself for the ruin of man, and may at length be brought into the triumph of the eight-ranked Virtues† after the warfare of this present life is ended. But I ask of Thy most merciful loving-kindness, that whilst I fulfil these Canonical Hours to the praise of Thy Majesty, Thou wilt deign ever to assist my heart; guide my tongue, that fitly, entirely, perfectly, intelligibly, and distinctly it may utter words; deliver my soul from wandering and distracted thoughts, and cause her without ceasing to attend upon Thee whilst she speaketh with Thee, lest whilst through worldly imaginations she goeth forth and departeth from Thee, Who delightest in the secret of the conscience, she may have cause to weep bitterly because Thou hast also justly departed from her. Receive, therefore, at my lips the saving sacrifice of praise, to the end it may do honour unto Thee, and present me before Thee a living sacrifice, holy, acceptable, and well-pleasing to Thee; and pour out Thy grace upon my lips, that out of a good heart I may indite a good matter, and by reason of the grace of my

* 19' Missal, P.O. † Or eight Beatitudes?

lips may have Thee, the King, for my friend; and whilst I open my mouth unto Thee in the voice of joy and thanksgiving, do Thou deign to fill it with Thy benediction. Amen.

II. INSTRUCTIONS TO PRIESTS DESIROUS TO CELEBRATE MASS.*

First, *Before Mass three things are to be considered*—

Examination of the Intention.
General Contrition.
A sincere Confession.

1. *Examination of the Intention*—

That he celebrate not for vain glory.
That he celebrate not for outward appearance.
That he celebrate not out of respect to any person.
That he celebrate not for temporal gain.
That he celebrate not out of mere habit.

2. *General Contrition*—

For the good works omitted which he ought to have done.
For sins committed in thought, word, and deed.

3. *Sincere Confession*—

Of all distinct sins, known and unknown.

Secondly, *At Mass he should be*—

Careful respecting place, so that he may be able to receive in both kinds.

Yet more careful touching the chalice, that it be not cracked or mended.

Most careful of all of the matter, that the Host be not foul, the wine sour, or without water

In the Communion there should be care—

Great, touching acts, that he perform them humbly.
Greater, touching words, that he say them correctly.
Greatest, touching intention, that he intend in steadfast faith to consecrate.

In Consecration let him have—

Carefulness in making the Body of Christ.

Reverence in handling the Body of Christ.
Devotion in receiving the Body of Christ.

In handling the Body of Christ let there be reverence—

Great, in respect of Its comprehending Christ's so excellent Body.

Greater, in respect of Its comprehending Christ's so excellent Soul.

Greatest, in respect of Its comprehending Christ's so excellent Godhead.

In consecrating he must intend—

By tears to worship God.
To commemorate the Death of Christ,
To unite in one the whole Church.

In consecrating he must intend to obtain—

Increase of Love.
Inseparability of Union.
Hastening of Fruition.

First, let his prayer be humble; and secondly, let him take heed—

Lest so unworthy a minister should unworthily receive so great a mystery.

Lest so undevout a priest should turn the sentence of so just a Judge to his own condemnation.

Lest so unclean a host should drive away so excellent a guest from himself by his foul transgressions.

And that the Lord most pitiful may make him to have part with His elect priests.

First, let him remember to pray for himself and for the living—

That they may be partakers of so great a mystery.
Hearers capable of receiving the benefit of Masses.
Meek, yet despisers of the vanities of the world.
Steadfast in making satisfaction for their own failings.
Vigilant in following after the Divine benefits.

Secondly, let him remember to pray for the dead.

That through the most comfortable mystery they may enjoy continual succour.

That through the prayers of faithful members of the Church they may obtain sweet relief from their pains.

That through this our Divine Viaticum they may have restoration, and communion with the saints.

After Mass, let thanks be given in the highest—

For that in so great, so sweet Bread of Angels, he hath received the Creator of creatures.

For that in so great perpetual Food of all Saints, he hath received the Creator of creatures.

For that in so great and effectual Viaticum of Christ's elect, he hath received the Creator of creatures.

Saint Bernard saith :—

O Priest, thy body is daily made the sepulchre of Christ.

How doth falsehood proceed out of thy mouth by which the Truth entereth ?

How do thine eyes behold vanity which daily look upon the Truth ?

How should thy hands be stretched out to unlawful things which hold Him that upholdeth all things ?

How art thou filled with excess of wine who oughtest to be filled with God ?

III. A PRAYER OF THE MOST BLESSED AUGUSTINE.*

TO BE SAID BY THE PRIEST BEFORE MASS FOR HIS OWN DEVOTIONS.

O most mighty High Priest and true Bishop, Jesus Christ, Who didst offer Thyself to God the Father a pure and spotless Victim upon the Altar of the Cross for us miserable sinners, and didst give us Thy Flesh to be eaten and Thy Blood to be drunken, and didst appoint this mystery in the power of the Holy Ghost, saying, Do this, as oft as ye shall do it, in remembrance of Me; I, being mindful of this Thy adorable Passion, do flee to draw nigh unto Thy Altar, as an unworthy sinner, to offer unto Thee the Sacrifice which Thou Thyself didst institute and command to be offered in memory of Thee for our salvation, in which indeed Thy Flesh is verily received, and Thy Blood verily drunken; the basest things are united with the highest; divine things with things human. But who can worthily celebrate this unless Thou, O God Almighty, shalt make the offerer worthy? I know of a surety, and confess the same to Thy goodness, that I am not worthy to draw nigh to so great a mystery, by reason of my grievous sins and my negligences, which cannot be numbered; but I know and believe of a truth, and

* '12 Missal.

NOTE.—This prayer is as a fact one of S. Anselm's (see S. Anselm, Opera., p. 274).

confess with my whole heart and lips, that Thou art able to make me worthy, Who alone makest of the unworthy worthy, of the unclean clean, and of sinners just and holy men. Therefore by this Thy almighty power and ineffable love I implore Thy mercy, and beg that Thou wouldest deign to grant to me, a sinner, whom besides other gifts Thou hast deigned to call to the priestly office, not for any merits of mine, but only of the good pleasure of Thy compassion, to celebrate this heavenly sacrifice and handle so great a mystery with that reverence, respect, devotion, fear, and purity of heart which is fitting, and so firmly to believe in the same; to understand, to perceive, steadfastly to retain, to speak, and to think what pleaseth Thee, and is for my soul's good, that Thou mayest with gracious favour receive It at my hands, for the salvation of myself and all others both quick and dead. Who.

IV. THE SONG OF S. AUGUSTINE ON THE CHARGE OF THE PRIESTHOOD.*

O venerable brothers, ye priests of God above,
I pray ye hear the message I speak to you in love;
Ye heralds of the Highest, ye shining lights of day,
Who beam with hope enduring, and charity's pure ray.

Ye do to God your service in His own holy shrine;
And Christ hath called you branches, Who is Himself the Vine;
O see ye be not barren, nor bitter fruit ye give,
If with the Root that bears you ye would for ever live.

The Catholic religion yours is it to uphold,
The world's true light and ransom, the shepherds of the fold;
The walls of Jacob's dwelling. the art of Life who teach;
Who judge the Church in meekness, who to the nations preach.

The Catholic religion is lost if ye betray;
The salt that lacks its savour serves but to cast away;
The path of life is doubtful unless the light shine clear;
Except the Shepherd watcheth, the robber draweth near.

The care of God's own Vineyard is given unto you,
That with the streams of doctrine its soil ye should bedew;
The thorns and choking thistles should root from out the ground,
That so the faith of Jesus may flourish and abound.

* '34 Missal.

Ye are the patient oxen who tread the threshing-floor,
The wheat and chaff with caution to part for evermore:
The laymen frail and simple, and all inconstant still,
Have you for an ensample to shew them good or ill.

Whatever they shall notice is grievous unto you,
That doubtless they will argue they must with care eschew;
Whatever they shall see you by holy deeds proclaim,
That they will reckon lawful, and free from sin or shame.

Since ye have been appointed the shepherds of the sheep,
Oh, see ye be not slothful, nor silent watch ye keep;
Be loud and plain the warnings ye raise when harm is nigh—
The wolf sees folds in safety with jealous rav'ning eye.

A threefold food the faithful have need of day by day—
The Body of the Saviour, to keep their life for aye;
The Word of due instruction, the which discreetly give;
The earthly meats that perish, whereby their bodies live.

The honour of your office unclouded let it be,
And give to those that seek them the gifts of grace all free;
For should you ever venture the rights of faith to sell,
Ye seek Gehazi's sentence, with lepers doom'd to dwell.

Baptize the people freely, and freely them confess;
The Eucharist give freely, to save them and to bless;
As Christ's Apostles taught ye, ye are all things to try,
The good alone that proveth that are ye to hold by.

Be all your conversation in holiness maintained;
Your conscience clear and quiet, your lives in virtue trained;
Your manners framed to order, your hearts devoid of guile,
Let no corrupt indulgence your saintliness defile.

Let no disdainful temper your noble souls depress;
Be dignified in manner, and meetly grave in dress;
No thoughts of filthy lucre permit your hearts to seize,
Ye to whose care are given the heavenly Kingdom's keys

Be brief in speech, lest haply to evil ye be led,
By over-freely talking man's vanity is fed;
The words which ye shall utter must be concise and few,
For ever on much speaking sin waiteth to ensue.

Be patient, full of kindness, and sober, pious, wise;
Be upright, single-minded, let pureness light your eyes;
Be hospitable, humble, see that the simple learn;
Oh, comfort all in sorrow, from sin the sinner turn.

I pray ye so be able the Shepherd's charge to keep,
And living in the Spirit, to feed the Saviour's sheep,
That when your fleshly garment at length ye lay aside,
The Lord a robe eternal of glory may provide.

V. A PRAYER TO BE SAID BEFORE MASS.*

O God, Who makest of the unworthy worthy, and of sinners just men (and holy), and pure of the impure, cleanse my heart and body from all taint and defilement of sin, and make me a worthy (and earnest) minister at Thy holy Altar; and mercifully grant that on this Altar to which I, so unworthy, now draw near, I may offer a sacrifice acceptable (and pleasing) to Thy loving-kindness for my sins and offences, and for my numberless daily transgressions, [for all here present, and for everyone united with me by friendship or kindred, or who persecute or oppose me with any manner of hatred], (and likewise for wiping away of the sins of all Christian people) [and for all faithful Christians quick and dead]; and let my prayer and sacrifice be acceptable unto Thee, through Him Who offered Himself unto Thee, God the Father, a sacrifice for us, Jesus Christ Thy Son our Lord. Who.

VI. Another Prayer.†

[O Lord, I am not worthy that Thou shouldest come under my roof, but trusting in Thy loving-kindness] [(O almighty and merciful God, lo!)], I draw nigh [unto Thy Altar] {(to the Sacrament of the Body and Blood of Thy Only-Begotten Son, our Lord Jesus Christ)}, sick to the Physician of Life, (unclean to the Fountain of Mercy)}, [(blind to the Light of Eternal Brightness)], [(poor to the Lord of Heaven and earth, naked to the King of Glory)], [a sheep to the Shepherd,

* The parts in ( ) are in '26 Missal, and those in [ ] are in '15 Missal. The rest is common to both.

† The parts in [ ] are in '26; in {} in some editions of '26; in ( ) in 4L. The rest is common to both.

a thing formed to Him that formed it, desolate to the kind Comforter, miserable to Him who pitieth, guilty to Him that bestoweth pardon, unholy to Him that justifieth; hard-hearted to the out-pourer of grace], imploring the abundance of Thy boundless mercy, to the intent Thou wouldest vouchsafe to heal my infirmities, [to wash away] (deliver me from) [(defilement, to enlighten my blindness)], to enrich my poverty, [(to clothe my nakedness)], [to bring back the wandering, to comfort the forsaken, to reconcile the guilty, to give pardon to the sinner, forgiveness to the wretched, life to the accused, justification to the dead], that I may [be deemed worthy to] receive [Thee] the Bread of Angels, the King of kings, [(the Lord of lords)], {(with that reverence and fear, that contrition and love)}, (that faith and purity, that purpose and humility) [(which is expedient for my soul)], [with that chastity of body and purity of mind, that contrition of heart and flow of tears, that spiritual joy and heavenly gladness, which is most expedient for my soul, that it may be profitable to me for eternal life, and the remission of all my sins. Amen.] {(Grant unto me, I beseech Thee, that I may receive not only the Sacrament of this the Body and Blood of the Lord, but also the virtue of the Sacrament. O most gracious God, grant me so to receive the Body of Thine Only-begotten Son our Lord Jesus Christ, which He took of the Virgin Mary, that I may be found worthy to be incorporated into His mystical Body, and to be reckoned among His members. O most loving Father, grant unto me that Thy beloved Son Whom now I purpose to receive beneath a veil, I may at length behold with unveiled face. Who.)}

VII. Another Prayer.*

I beseech Thee, O most pitiful Lord Jesu Christ, that for the sake of Thy Mother, the most Blessed Virgin Mary, and all Thy Saints, Thou wouldest teach and permit me to draw nigh to the so marvellous Sacrament of Thy Body and Blood, with that purity of heart, and cleanness of mind, with that devotion and reverence, which becometh and is expedient for my soul. O most gracious Lord Jesu Christ, let my heart discern the sweetness of Thy blessed Presence; let it cleanse away all my slothfulness of spirit, wash out all mine offences, shield me from all the numberless perils of this world. Let my soul taste how sweet Thou art, O Lord, that after the taste of Thee all carnal

* From '13 Missal.

pleasures may give place. O Bread of Delight! O Food of Life! O Meat to be desired! O Banquet of exceeding sweetness, refreshing all things, and never failing! Angels and Spirits of just men partake of Thy plenteousness. Let it please Thee, O Lord, that now my sinful soul in this her pilgrimage may partake of Thee in faith, that so receiving virtue from Thee, she may through Thee finish her course even unto Thee, without hindrance from Satan. Mortify in my members and in my heart all carnal desires and all lustful passions; that Thou, the King of Virgins and lover of chastity, mayest have a peaceful abiding-place in this my tabernacle. O Lord, Thou knowest by how many and how great disquietnesses my soul is vexed. But do Thou, O Lord, Who art the great Physician, come and heal her; Thou to whom is committed all power and dominion through endless ages. Amen.

The Preparation for Mass.

¶ *Let the Priest who desires to confess say—*

Bless, Father.

Priest. The Lord be in thy heart and lips to confess all thy sins, in the Name of the Father, and of the Son, and of the Holy Ghost. Amen.

¶ *Then let him tell his sins, which being ended the Priest shall say—*God Almighty have mercy, *and* The Almighty and merciful Lord, *as in the Ordinary of the Mass.*

The merits of our Lord Jesus Christ's Passion, the prayers of our Holy Mother the Church, the good deeds which Thou hast done and shall do by the grace of God, be to thee for the pardon of thy sins.

¶ *Here let him enjoin the Penance, saying—*

And for a special Penance thou shall say or do this or that.

¶ *Then let him absolve him, and say—*

Our Lord Jesus Christ, Who is the High Priest, absolve thee of His tenderest mercy; and I, by the authority committed unto me, absolve thee first from the sentence of the lesser excommunication if thou art in need of it, then from all thy sins, in the Name of the Father, and of the Son, and of the Holy Ghost. Amen.

The Kyries.

I.

On all principal Feasts.

O Divine Creator of all things, Thou our God, in Thy pity,
Have mercy upon us.

Unto Thee, O Christ, the King of kings, rejoicing in praise together, we pray Thee,
Have mercy upon us.

Thou to Whom ever belongeth praise, virtue, peace, and dominion without end.
Have mercy upon us.

O Christ, King, only Son, co-eternal with Thy gracious Father,
Have mercy upon us.

Thou Who didst save lost man, restoring him from death unto life.
Have mercy upon us.

Jesu, the Good Shepherd, that the sheep of Thy pasture perish not,
Have mercy upon us.

O Spirit, the Comforter, we Thy suppliants most humbly beseech Thee,
Have mercy upon us.

O Lord our strength and our salvation evermore,
Have mercy upon us.

O Supreme and one God, bestow on us the gifts of life in Thy compassion, and deign to
Have mercy upon us.

II.

On all other double Feasts, any of the following.

O Lord, King, Father unbeggotten! very Essence of being,
Have mercy upon us.

O Lord, Fountain of Light, Maker of all things,
Have mercy upon us.

O Lord, Who hast sealed us with the print of Thine image,
Have mercy upon us.

O Christ, upon us, in the form of man partakers of the Divine Nature,
Have mercy.

O Christ, Orient Light, by Whom are all things,
Have mercy upon us.

O Christ, Who art perfect wisdom,
Have mercy upon us.

O Lord, quickening Spirit, Power of Life,
Have mercy upon us.

O Lord, Thou Who proceedeth from Both, in Whom are all things,
Have mercy upon us.

O Lord, Thou cleanser of iniquities, and bestower of grace,
Have mercy upon us.

We beseech Thee forsake us not by reason of our offences; O Comforter of the sorrowing soul,
Have mercy upon us.

III.

On the Epiphany, Whitsun Day, Corpus Christi especially,

O Lord, Fountain of Goodness, Father Unbegotten, from Whom all good things do come,
Have mercy upon us.

O Lord, Who didst send Thy Son Himself to suffer for the guilt of the world, that He might save it,
Have mercy upon us.

O Lord, Who bestoweth sevenfold gifts by the Spirit with which Heaven and earth are fulfilled,
Have mercy upon us.

O Christ, Only-Begotten of God the Father, Whom the Holy Prophets wondrously foretold should be born into the world of a virgin,
Have mercy upon us.

O Holy Christ, Lord of Heaven, Theme of Regal Glory, before Whom the Hierarchy of Angels ever stand praising Thee for Thy Divinity,
Have mercy upon us.

O Christ from Heaven be present with our prayers, Thou before Whom here on earth we humbly worship, devoutly crying unto Thee, Jesu,
Have mercy upon us.

O Lord, gracious Spirit, consisting with the Father and the Son together of one nature, and from Both proceeding,
Have mercy upon us.

O Lord, Who when Christ was baptized in the water of Jordan didst shine forth and appear in the shape of a Dove,
Have mercy upon us.

O Lord, Fire Divine, light up our hearts, that we may ever be worthy equally to proclaim Thee,
Have mercy upon us.

IV.

O Lord Almighty, Father unbegotten, upon us miserable
Have mercy.

O Lord, Who hast redeemed the work of Thy hands by Thine own Son,
Have mercy upon us.

O Lord Adonai, blot out our offences, and upon Thy people
Have mercy.

O Christ, Brightness of the Father's glory, and the express Image of His Person,
Have mercy upon us.

O Christ, Who didst save the world at the command of the Father,
Have mercy upon us.

O Christ, Saviour of men, eternal Life of Angels,
Have mercy upon us.

O Lord, Spirit, the Comforter, Dispenser of pardon,
Have mercy upon us.

O Lord, Fountain of mercy and of sevenfold grace,
Have mercy upon us.

O Lord, most pitiful Forgiver, proceeding from Both, O most bountiful Giver of gifts, Teacher, Quickener, of Thy goodness
Have mercy upon us.

V.

On the Feast of S. Michael and All Angels especially.

O Lord, King resplendent on the Heavenly citadel! Hail! for evermore, and in Thy pity upon Thy people ever
Have mercy.

Thou Whom the hymning hosts of Cherubim with praise everlasting continually proclaim,
Have mercy upon us.

To Whom the companies of Seraphim on high illustriously respond, lauding Thee.
Have mercy upon us.

O Christ, King throned on High, Whom the nine orders of Angels unceasingly and gloriously praise, vouchsafe ever on Thy servants to
Have mercy.

O Christ, Whom the one only Church throughout all the world doth hymn forth, to Whom sun and moon, stars, earth, and sea, evermore do service,
Have mercy upon us.

Thou the same Whom all the Saints, themselves heirs of the glorious eternal country, triumphantly proclaim in worthiest strains,
Have mercy upon us.

O Thou gracious Offspring of the Holy Virgin Mary, King of kings, Blessed Redeemer, on those whom Thou hast ransomed from the power of death with Thine own Blood, for ever
Have mercy.

O most Illustrious Unbegotten, Begotten already without beginning, without effort excelling all things, on this Thy congregation in Thy pity
Have mercy.

Sun of most unclouded glory, Dispenser of justice, when Thou shalt strictly judge all nations, in Thy pity, we earnestly beseech Thee, upon Thy people now standing before Thee
Have mercy.

VI.

On Holy Cross Day, and the Invention of the Cross especially.

O Light and Source of Light, God over all,
Have mercy upon us.

By Whose will all things ever consist,
Have mercy upon us.

Thou Who alone art able to pity,
Have mercy upon us.

Redeemer of mankind and their salvation, in Thy mercy
Have mercy upon us.

We that are redeemed by Thy Cross from everlasting death beseech Thee,
Have mercy upon us.

Thou Who art the Word of the Father, Author of Pity, Light of Truth,
Have mercy upon us.

O God, Holy Ghost, the Comforter,
Have mercy upon us.

Thou our compassionate Physician,
Have mercy upon us.

O Holy Trinity and Unity, ever
Have mercy upon us.

VII.

O God, Almighty Father, Creator of all things,
Have mercy upon us.

Fount and kindly Source of good, Light everlasting,
Have mercy upon us.

O benevolent Ruler, let Thy goodness save us:
Have mercy upon us.

O Christ, the Brightness of God, the Father's Virtue and Wisdom,
Have mercy upon us.

Thou that formest the image of man, and restorest him when fallen,
Have mercy upon us.

That the work of Thy Hands perish not, Jesu, graciously
Have mercy upon us.

O Holy Ghost, proceeding from Both, Thou Bond of Love,
Have mercy upon us.

O kindling Fire and Spring of Life, Thou purifying Energy,
Have mercy upon us.

O Thou Cleanser of guilt, most excellent Bestower of pardon, blot out our offences; with Thy Holy gifts fulfil us, O gracious Spirit:
Have mercy upon us.

VIII.

O Lord, Maker of all creatures,
Have mercy upon us.

O Thou who dost blot out our offences, without ceasing
Have mercy upon us

Suffer not the work of Thy Hands to perish, but in Thy pity
Have mercy upon us.

O Christ, Only Son of the Father, born of a Virgin,
Have mercy upon us.

Thou Who didst save the lost world from death by Thy Blood,
Have mercy upon us.

Pitifully hearken unto the prayers of them that now call upon Thee,
Have mercy upon us.

O gracious Spirit, fulfil us with Thy grace:
Have mercy upon us.

Thou Who from the Father and the Son continually dost proceed,
Have mercy upon us.

Holy Trinity, Trine Unity, together to be adored, loose the bands of our sins and redeem us from death; now let us all cry aloud with well-tuned voice, O God,
Have mercy upon us.

IX.

Maker of the world, Eternal King,
Have mercy upon us.

Fount of boundless goodness,
Have mercy upon us.

All that may harm us do Thou cast out:
Have mercy upon us.

O Christ, Who art the Light of the world and the Giver of life,
Have mercy upon us.

Look upon us who are wounded by the fraud of the devil:
Have mercy upon us.

Thou that dost preserve and strengthen them that believe in Thee,
Have mercy upon us.

Thy Father, and Thee, and the Spirit proceeding from Both,
(Have mercy upon us)

We know to be God, One and Trine,
Have mercy upon us.

O Thou the Comforter, in Thy clemency be present with us, that we may live in Thee:
Have mercy upon us.

Collects

WHICH MAY BE SAID THROUGHOUT THE YEAR

AFTER THE

COLLECT FOR THE DAY.

IN ADVENT.

¶ *See the* Collect, Secret, and Post-Communion *on pp.* 1, 2, 3.

IN LENT.

The Collect.

O Lord, we beseech Thee, hear our prayers, and spare all those who confess their sins to Thee, that they whose consciences by sin are accused, by Thy merciful pardon may be absolved. Through.

Secret. We have offered Thee the oblation of reconciliation, O Lord, and pray that Thou wouldest mercifully pardon our offences, and direct our wavering hearts. Through.

P. Comm. Grant, O eternal Saviour, that we who have received by this gift pardon of our offences, may henceforth flee from sin. Through.

OF THE BLESSED VIRGIN MARY.

FROM ADVENT TO CHRISTMAS, EXCEPT CONCEPTION OF B. V. M.

The Collect.

O God, Who at the message of an Angel was pleased that Thy Word should take flesh in the womb of Blessed Mary, ever-Virgin, grant, we humbly beseech Thee, that we who truly believe her to be the Mother of God may be aided by her intercession with Thee. Through.

Secret. Strengthen, we beseech Thee, O Lord, in our minds the mysteries of the true Faith, that we who steadfastly confess Him Who was conceived of a Virgin to be very God and very Man, may by the power of the same saving Incarnation be accounted meet to attain unto everlasting happiness. Through.

P. Comm. Pour forth, we beseech Thee, O Lord, Thy grace into our hearts, that as we have known the Incarnation of Thy Son Christ by the message of an Angel, so by His Cross and Passion we may be brought unto the glory of His Resurrection. Through.*

FROM CHRISTMAS TO THE PURIFICATION.

The Collect.

O God, Who by the fruitful Virginity of Blessed Mary didst bestow upon mankind the reward of eternal salvation, grant, we beseech Thee, that we may perceive that she intercedes for us, by whom we have been counted worthy to receive the Author of life, Jesus Christ Thy Son. Who.

Secret. We humbly beseech Thee, O Lord, that we who have offered these gifts, and steadfastly believe the very Incarnation of Thy Word, may perceive for our salvation in this mystery the same true substance of Flesh and Blood which the Virgin Mother brought forth by the operation of the Holy Ghost. Through.

P. Comm. Grant, we beseech Thee, Almighty God, that we may be quickened by her intercession through whose Virginity we have received the Author of our salvation, Jesus Christ our Lord. Who.

FROM THE PURIFICATION TO ADVENT.

The Collect.

Grant, O Lord God, we beseech Thee, that we Thy servants may enjoy continual health of mind and body, and by the glorious intercession of Blessed Mary, ever-Virgin, may be delivered from present sorrow, and have the fruition of joy everlasting. Through.

Secret. By Thy mercy, O Lord, and at the intercession of Blessed Mary, ever-Virgin, let this oblation avail to our everlasting happiness and peace. Through.

P. Comm. Grant, we beseech Thee, O Lord, that we who have received this assistance towards our salvation may be preserved everywhere by her intercession in reverence of whom we have presented this oblation to Thy Majesty. Through.

OF ALL SAINTS.

The Collect.

Grant, we beseech Thee, Almighty God, that the intercession of Holy Mary, Mother of God, and of all holy and heavenly

* This Post-Communion is said also in Eastertide and until the Vigil of the Ascension instead of the P. Comm. "Grant, we beseech Thee," above.

powers, the blessed patriarchs, prophets, apostles, evangelists, martyrs, confessors and virgins, and all other Thy saints, may gladden us in every place; and whilst we call to remembrance their good works, let us also have a sense of their protection. Through.

Secret. O Lord, graciously accept the oblations we present, and, at the intercession of the holy, glorious, and ever-Virgin Mary, Mother of God, with all Thy saints, defend us from all dangers. Through.

P. Comm. Grant, we beseech Thee, O Lord, that we who have received the heavenly Sacrament, reverencing the memory of the Blessed ever-Virgin Mary, Mother of God, and all Thy saints, may by the aid of their prayers attain in eternal joy unto that which we have celebrated on earth. Through.

FOR THE WHOLE CHURCH.

The Collect.

O Lord, mercifully hear the prayers of Thy Church; that She being delivered from all manner of adversity and error, may joyfully serve Thee in all godly quietness. Through.

Secret. Protect us, we beseech Thee, O Lord, who serve at Thy mysteries; that cleaving unto the things which are of God, we may wait upon Thee both in body and soul. Through.

P. Comm. O Lord our God, we beseech Thee, suffer not those to fall into the perils of this life whom Thou dost permit to rejoice in the partaking of heavenly food. Through.

FOR PEACE.

The Collect.

O God, from Whom all holy desires, all good counsels, and all just works do proceed; Give unto Thy servants that peace which the world cannot give; that both our hearts may be set to obey Thy commandments, and also that by Thee we being defended from the fear of our enemies may pass our time in rest and quietness. Through the merits of Jesus Christ our Saviour. Amen.

Secret. O God, Who sufferest not them that believe in Thee to be troubled by any terrors; be pleased to accept the prayers and offerings of the people which is dedicated unto Thee, and let peace, vouchsafed to us by Thy pity, keep the borders of Christians safe from all enemies. Through.

P. Comm. O God, Who art the author of peace and lover of concord, in knowledge of Whom standeth our eternal life, Whose service is perfect freedom; Defend us Thy humble servants in all assaults of our enemies; that we, surely trusting in Thy defence, may not fear the power of any adversaries. Through the might of Jesus Christ our Lord. Amen.

FOR ALL SORTS AND CONDITIONS OF MEN.

The Collect.

O Lord, we beseech Thee, of Thy goodness loose the chains of all our sins; and at the intercession of Blessed, glorious, and ever-Virgin Mary, Mother of God, with all Thy saints, keep the Lord Pope, kings and princes, bishops and abbots, and all people committed to their charge, and us Thy servants, and our dwelling-places, in all holiness; do Thou cleanse from all their sin, and enlighten with virtue, all united to us by kindred, friendship, profession, or prayer, and all Catholic people; bestow upon us peace and health; drive away pestilence and famine; to our friends and enemies give true charity; bestow health upon the sick, dispose the way of Thy servants towards the attainment of everlasting salvation; and to all the faithful, quick and dead, grant life and eternal rest in the land of the living. Through.

Secret. O God, Who by the one offering of Thy Body hast loosed the sins of the whole world, graciously accept this oblation, wipe away the stain of our sins, forgive the sins of all faithful Christians, both quick and dead, and at the intercession of the Blessed, glorious, and ever-Virgin Mary Mother of God, with all Thy saints, bestow on us the everlasting reward, O Saviour of the world. Who.

P. Comm. We beseech Thee, O Lord, let the Sacrament which we have received blot out all our offences; and, for the sake of Blessed and ever-Virgin Mary, Mother of God, and at the intercession of all Thy saints, let It drive far from us all iniquity, the assaults of enemies visible and invisible, sickness and sudden death, and let It be profitable for the pardon of all faithful people, quick and dead, in furtherance of whose salvation this oblation hath been offered to Thee. Through.

The Collect.

We beseech Thee, Almighty God, for the sake and prayers of the most holy Mother of God, ever-Virgin Mary, and all the blessed heavenly powers .... and all other Thy saints,* grant us Thy mercy; give unto Thy people constancy of faith which cannot be moved, and peace; remove far from us war, famine, and pestilence; in Thy power give us constancy and fortitude, send fear and weakness upon our enemies, grant to all of us who do rightly the blessing of eternal life, give to those who hate us and persecute us consideration and pardon; and vouchsafe to our departed friends, and to all who sleep in Christ, pardon of all their sins and eternal rest. Through.

Secret. In the presence of Thy Divine Majesty, we beseech Thee, Almighty God, at the intercession of † .... Thy saints, let our oblations and prayers go up acceptably; mercifully grant us pardon and peace; put far from us war, famine, and pestilence; pour forth upon us abundantly faith, hope, and charity; ever protect us with Thy defence, tread under foot the insolence and power of our enemies; grant to all of us who do rightly the abundance of Thy grace; turn the hearts of those that are at variance to the blessings of peace; vouchsafe rest to our departed friends, and on all Thy faithful people bestow life everlasting. Through.

P. Comm. We beseech Thee, O Lord our God Almighty, by the mysterious power of this Sacrament, at the intercession of .... Thy saints, let the saints of our sins be blotted out, and our prayers be found acceptable in the presence of Thy Majesty; let Thy people be set free from sin and enemies, and be strengthened in the right faith; the insolence and might of our enemies be put down; pestilence and famine be driven far away; our benefactors be filled with the abundance of Thy grace; those who are at variance be restored to brotherly unity; our departed friends enjoy rest, and let all Thy faithful people be counted worthy to attain unto eternal life. Through.

The Collect.

We beseech Thee, O Lord, at the intercession of all Thy saints, protect us ever by Thy grace; and bestow Thy mercy upon all Christians in every place, living and dead, that the living may by Thy aid be defended from all that assault them, and the dead may be counted worthy to receive pardon of all their sins. Through.

* As on p. 286. † As above.

Secret. O Lord, we beseech Thee, graciously look upon our offerings, for the honour of all Thy saints grant us pardon of our sins, and for all Christians living or dead let this present oblation obtain help in this life, and an eternal reward in that which is to come. Through.

P. Comm. Let this sacrifice, O Lord, which we have received be profitable to our salvation for the sake and at the intercession of all Thy saints, and in Thy mercy obtain for all Christians, living and dead, a reward here and in the world to come. Through.

The Collect.

Almighty and everlasting God, Who art Lord both of the living and the dead, and pitiest all those whom Thou dost foreknow to be Thine by faith and works; we humbly entreat Thee, that they in whose behalf we have purposed to offer prayers, both those whom this world still holdeth in the flesh, and those already delivered from the body whom the world to come hath received, may by Thy goodness and mercy be counted worthy to obtain pardon of their sins and everlasting happiness. Through.

Secret. O God, to Whom alone is known the number of the elect which shall have a place in happiness above; grant, we beseech Thee, that the book of blessed predestination may have the names of all whom we have undertaken to commend to Thee in our prayers, and of all the faithful, written therein. Through.

P. Comm. O Thou our King and Priest, we give thanks unto Thee for the joy of Thy heavenly banquet, humbly imploring Thy Majesty that this most holy offering of Thy Body and Blood be not accounted unto us for condemnation, but be a saving intercession for our pardon. Let it be the washing away of sins, strength to the weak, a sure support against all perils of the world; and the forgiveness of sins to all the faithful, quick and dead. Through Thee, O Saviour of the world, King of Glory. Who.

The Ordinary of the Mass.

Whilst the Priest is putting on the sacred vestments, let him say the following hymn.

Come, Holy Ghost, our souls inspire,
And lighten with celestial fire.
Thou the anointing Spirit art,
Who dost Thy sevenfold gifts impart.

Thy blessed Unction from above
Is comfort, life, and fire of love.
Enable with perpetual light
The dulness of our blinded sight.

Anoint and cheer our soiled face
With the abundance of Thy grace.
Keep far our foes, give peace at home:
Where Thou art Guide, no ill can come.

Teach us to know the Father, Son,
And Thee, of both, to be but One.
That, through the ages all along,
This may be our endless song:

Praise to Thy eternal merit,
Father, Son, and Holy Spirit.

℣. Send forth Thy Spirit, and they shall be made;
℟. And Thou shalt renew the face of the earth.

The Collect.

O God, unto Whom all hearts be open, all desires known, and from Whom no secrets are hid; cleanse the thoughts of our hearts by the inspiration of Thy Holy Spirit, that we may perfectly love and worthily magnify Thee; through Christ our Lord. *Amen.*

Then shall follow the Anthem.

Ant. I will go unto the Altar of God.

Ps. xliii. Give sentence with me, O God, and defend my cause against the ungodly people: O deliver me from the deceitful and wicked man.

For Thou art the God of my strength, why hast Thou put me from Thee: and why go I so heavily, while the enemy oppresseth me?

O send out Thy light and Thy truth, that they may lead me: and bring me unto Thy holy hill, and to Thy dwelling.

And that I may go unto the Altar of God, even unto the God of my joy and gladness: and upon the harp will I give thanks unto Thee, O God, my God.

Why art thou so heavy, O my soul: and why art thou so disquieted within me?

O put thy trust in God: for I will yet give Him thanks Which is the help of my countenance and my God.

Glory be.

Ant. I will go unto the Altar of God, even unto the God of my joy and gladness.

Lord, have mercy.
Christ, have mercy.
Lord, have mercy.

Our Father .... trespass against us.

Hail, *Mary*, thou that art highly favoured, the Lord is with thee.

Blessed art Thou among women, and blessed is the fruit of thy womb, *Jesus*.

Let the principal Ruler of the Choir ask the **Office** *for the Mass of the Precentor, then enjoin it on his fellow-ruler, and begin it together; and let the* **Kyrie, Sequence, Offertory, Sanctus, Agnus Dei,** *and* **Communion** *be asked, enjoined, and begun in like manner.*

This done, and the **Office** *having been begun, when after the repetition of the* **Office** *the* **Glory** *is said, let the Priest with his ministers approach the step of the Altar in the following order. First the Candle-bearers, two and two; then the Thurifers; after them the Sub-Deacon, Deacon, Priest. Then let the Priest say the* **Confession,** *the Deacon assisting him on the right, and the Sub-Deacon on the left beginning thus.*

℣. And lead us not into temptation.

℟. But deliver us from evil.

℣. Confess unto the Lord, for He is gracious.

℟. For His mercy endureth for ever.

The Confession.

I confess to God, Blessed Mary, all Saints, and to you, that I have sinned exceedingly in thought, word, and deed, of my fault: I pray Holy Mary, all Saints of God, and you, to beseech for me.

Ministers. God Almighty have mercy upon you and forgive you all your sins; deliver you from every evil; confirm and strengthen you in goodness; and bring you to everlasting life.

Priest. Amen.

After which the Ministers say the **Confession,** *and the Priest* **God Almighty.** *Then let the Priest say:*

The Almighty and merciful Lord grant you pardon and forgiveness of all your sins, space for true repentance, amendment of life, and the grace and consolation of the Holy Ghost.

Ministers. Amen.

And whoever the Priest is who celebrates, if the Bishop is present, let him always say the **Confession, God Almighty,** *and the* **Absolution** *at the step of the Altar. Then shall follow:*

℣. Our help is in the Name of the Lord.

℟. Who hath made heaven and earth.

℣. Blessed be the Name of the Lord.

℟. From this time forth, now and for evermore.

Let us pray.

Having finished his prayers, let the Priest kiss the Deacon and then the Sub-Deacon saying thus:

Receive the kiss of peace and love, that ye may be fit to perform the Divine Office at the most holy Altar.

Let this be always done except in Masses for the Dead and the three days before Easter.

After the Office of the Mass, let one of the Candle-bearers bring bread and wine and water for the Eucharist; and the other fetch the basin with water and a towel.

This done, let the Candle-bearers set down their Candles at the Altar-step; then let the Priest go and say in the midst of the Altar, silently and with inclined body and joined hands:

Let us pray.

Take away from us, we beseech Thee, O Lord, all our sins, that we may be deemed worthy to enter into the holy of holies with pure minds. Through.

Then let the Priest rise and kiss the Altar in the midst, and sign himself on the face, saying:

In the Name of the Father, and of the Son, and of the Holy Ghost. Amen.

Then let the Deacon place incense in the censer, and say first to the Priest:

Bid a blessing.

And let the Priest say:

The Lord, in Whose honour this incense shall be burnt, by Him be it blessed. In the Name of the Father, and of the Son, and of the Holy Ghost.

Then let the Deacon, giving him the censer, kiss his hand; and let the Priest cense the Altar, first on the right side, then the midst, then on the left side. Then let the Priest himself be censed by the Deacon; and after this, let the Priest kiss the Text which the sub-Deacon brings him.

This being done by the Priest and Ministers on the right side of the Altar, let the Choir proceed with the third repetition of the Office; after which the **Kyrie.** *On certain days these had verses, for which see pp. 279-83.*

Lord, have mercy upon us *(iij).*
Christ, have mercy upon us *(iij).*
Lord, have mercy upon us *(iij).*

Let the Priest and Ministers, having said the **Office** *and* **Kyrie,** *sit in the sedilia and wait whilst the Choir sings them.*

Then follows the **Gloria in Excelsis** *when it is to be said, the Priest beginning it in the midst of the Altar, and then saying the rest privately with his Ministers on the right side. On Doubles let the principal Ruler of the Choir enjoin it to the Priest.*

On all Sundays through the year one of these Chants is sung.

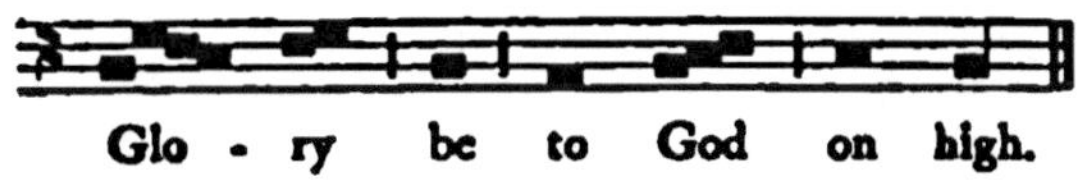

On all greater Doubles one of these.

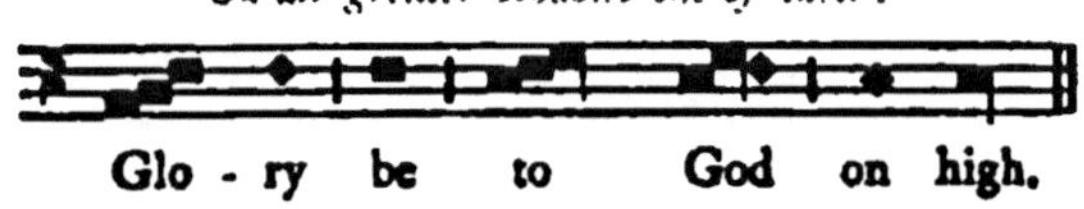

Glo - ry be to God on high.

In all other Doubles, and on all Feasts and on Octaves when there is a triple Invitatory, is sung either the second Chant as above for Sundays or else—

Glo - ry be to God on high.

On both Feasts of S. Michael and on that of S. Dunstan.

(As the last Chant.)

In all simple Feasts when the Choir is ruled is said:

Glo - ry be to God on high.

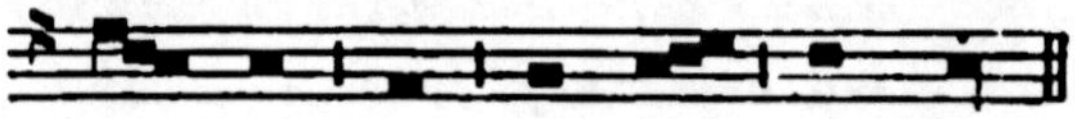

Glo - ry be to God on high.

In all Feasts of three lessons when the Choir is not ruled, and in Octaves is said:

Glo - ry be to God on high.

Glo - ry be to God on high.

In Commemorations of our Lady.

(As first Chant on Sundays through the year.)

*In the quire in the last service of our Lady before Advent and LXX., and and on the Octave of the Assumption and Nativity of our Lady. In the Chapel of our Lady on every Saturday.**

Glo - ry be to God . . on high.

And in earth peace, good will towards men.

* **Literal reading—" And it is said with its prose in the daily Masses in the Chapel of S. Mary every Saturday." Query if it means every Saturday, *or* " in the daily," etc., *and* " every Saturday."**

We praise Thee, we bless Thee, we worship Thee, we glorify Thee, we give thanks to Thee for Thy great glory, O Lord God, heavenly King, God the Father Almighty.

O Lord, the only-begotten Son Jesu Christ; * *O Spirit, and kind Comforter of orphans.* God, Lamb of the Father, *First-born of the Virgin-Mother Mary.* Thou that takest away the sins of the world,

Have mercy upon us.

Thou that takest away the sins of the world,

Receive our prayer, *to the glory of Mary.*

Thou that sittest at the right hand of the Father,

Have mercy upon us.

For Thou only art holy, *sanctifying Mary;* Thou only art the Lord, *ruling Mary;* Thou only *crowning Mary.* O Jesu Christ, with the Holy Ghost, art most high in the glory of God the Father. *Amen.*

All turn to the Altar and incline at Glory be to God on high, We praise Thee, Receive our prayers, *and at the end when they sign themselves.*

They sign themselves also at Glory be to Thee, O Lord, *and after the* Sanctus *at* Blessed is He.

After the Gloria, *signing himself on the face, let the Priest turn to the people, and raising his arms a little, say, with joined hands:*

The Lord be with you.

The Choir answers, And with thy spirit, *in the same tone. And then let the Priest turn again to the Altar and say:*

Let us pray.

The Lord be with you *is always said in the same way, and similarly* Let us pray, *except before the Prefaces and at a Marriage Mass before the* Peace, *when it is thus:*

The Lord be with you. Let us pray.

Then follows the Collect, ending thus

world with-out end. A - men.

* The proses (*i.e.*, verses in italics) are never said except when this last Chant is sung.

If there be any Memorial, then Let us pray *is said as before, only all the remaining Collects are said without it, and* World without end *only to the last. It is allowable to enter the quire up to the end of the first Collect.*

The normal position of the Ministers is each behind the other on their step; when the Priest turns to the people the Deacon does the same, but the Sub-Deacon genuflects and raises the Priest's chasuble: If a Bishop celebrates, all the Deacons and Sub-Deacons observe the same rule, with the principal Deacon or Sub-Deacon standing in the midst; nevertheless, the principal Sub-Deacon alone adjusts the Celebrant's chasuble.

All Clergy are bound to stand at Mass, except whilst the Epistle, Gradual, Alleluia, *or* Tract *is chanted. On Double Feasts all must, however, stand too at the* Alleluia. *And at the end of the* Gradual, Alleluia, *etc., they turn to the Altar before turning to the chanter of the Gospel.*

The Rulers of the Choir when there are only two follow the rule in all things of Clergy of the second grade, for which see General Rubrics, except that they stand when the Choir sings the Alleluia, *and turn to the Altar at the beginning of the Chants.*

Then follows the Epistle, which is read on certain days in the pulpit, on others at the step of the quire, by the Sub-Deacon thus:

The Lesson *or* The Epistle of —— to ——.

After which follows the Gradual *and* Alleluia, *or* Tract. *This ended, the* Sequence *is said. With what ceremonies and when, see General Rubrics.*

The Gradual, Alleluia, Tract, *or* Sequence, *having been said privately by the Priest with his Ministers, let the Sub-Deacon take the bread and wine and water with the chalice, and prepare them for the Service of the Eucharist; the blessing of the water being first asked of the Priest thus, the Priest in the meantime sitting:*

Bid a blessing.

The Priest answers.

The Lord. By Him be it blessed from Whose side came forth blood and water. In the Name of the Father, and of the Son, and of the Holy Ghost.

Then let the Deacon, before he goes to chant the Gospel, cense the midst of the Altar only, for the lectern is never censed either at Mass or Matins before the Gospel. Then let him take the Text—i.e., *the Book of the Gospels—and bending to the Priest standing before the Altar and turning his face south, let him say, not intoning:*

Bid a blessing.

The Priest answers.

The Lord be in thy heart and mouth, that thou mayest preach the Holy Gospel of God. In the Name of the Father, and of the Son, and of the Holy Ghost. Amen.

If the Priest is celebrating without Ministers he says the same, beginning with **Lord, bid a blessing,** *and altering* **Thy** *to* **My heart and mouth.** *Let the Deacon go through the midst of the quire carrying the Text solemnly on his left hand, the Thurifer and Candle-bearers preceding him.* and, if it be a Double Feast, the Cross-bearer. At the pulpit, let the Sub-Deacon take the Text and hold it on the left of the Deacon opposite him, the Cross-bearer standing on the right opposite; the Candle-bearers on either side, and the Thurifer behind the Deacon turned towards him; and let the Gospel be always read turning to the north. Then shall he say, signing the book, his forehead, and chest with his thumb:*

℣. The Lord be with you.

℟. And with thy spirit.

The Sequence of the Gospel according to Matthew, Mark, Luke, or John.

Glory be to Thee, O Lord.

After the Gospel, let him kiss the Text, which the Sub-Deacon offers him, and then carries leaning against his breast.

Then let the Priest, standing in the midst of the Altar, begin the **Creed.** *After its commencement, the Ministers having returned from the pulpit to the Altar, let the Deacon give the Priest the book to kiss, or else taking the Text from the Sub-Deacon give it to the Priest to kiss, standing on his right hand, the Sub-Deacon ministering to the Deacon, and the Acolyte to the Sub-Deacon.*

the Father Almighty, Maker of heaven and earth, And of all things visible and invisible:

And in one Lord Jesus Christ, the only-begotten Son of God, Begotten of His Father before all worlds, God of God, Light of Light, Very God of very God, Begotten, not made, Being of one substance with the Father; by Whom all things were made. Who for us men, and for our salvation came down from heaven, And was incarnate by the Holy Ghost of the Virgin Mary, And was made man, and was crucified for us under Pontius Pilate. He suffered and was buried, And the third day He rose again according to the Scriptures, And ascended into Heaven, And sitteth on the right hand of the Father. And He shall come

* "And the Sub-Deacon with the book out of which he was to read."—(Reg. Osm.; see Introduction and General Rubrics.)

again with glory to judge both the quick and the dead: Whose kingdom shall have no end.

And I believe in the Holy Ghost, The Lord and Giver of Life, Who proceedeth from the Father and the Son, Who with the Father and the Son together is worshipped and glorified, Who spake by the Prophets.

And I believe one Holy Catholick and Apostolick Church. I acknowledge one Baptism for the remission of sins, And I look for the Resurrection of the dead, And the life of the world to come. Amen.

For the days on which the **Creed** *is to be said see the General Rubrics.*

At the beginning of it the Choir sign themselves, and turn to the Altar inclining. They also incline at **And was incarnate, And was made man, And was crucified,** *and at the* **world to come.** *They remain turned to the Altar till the end of the Mass, except at the* **Offertory.**

Then shall the Priest chant:

℣. **The Lord be with you.**
℟. **And with thy spirit.**

Let us pray.

Then is said the **Offertory.**

After the **Offertory,** *let the Deacon give the Priest the chalice and the paten and Sacrifice, kissing his hand each time. Then receiving from the Deacon the chalice, let the Priest place it carefully in its proper place in the midst of the Altar, and, inclining, raise it a little with either hand, and offer the Sacrifice to the Lord, saying this prayer:*

Receive, O Holy Trinity, this oblation which I, an unworthy sinner, offer in Thy honour, Blessed Mary's, and all Thy Saints, for my sins and offences; for the salvation of the living and the repose of all the faithful departed. In the Name of the Father, and of the Son, and of the Holy Ghost, let this new Sacrifice be acceptable to Almighty God.

Having said this prayer, let him replace the chalice and cover it with the corporas, and place the bread upon the corporas decently before the chalice containing wine and water; and let him kiss the paten and place it to the right of the Sacrifice, covering it a little under the corporas. This done, let him take the censer from the Deacon and cense the Sacrifice thrice, making the sign of the Cross over it; then thrice round and on either side: then thrice between himself and the Altar, and whilst he censes let him say this verse:

Let my prayer, *O Lord,* **be set forth in Thy sight as the incense.**

After this let the Priest be censed by the Deacon, and let the Sub-Deacon bring him the Text to kiss. Then let the Acolyte cense the Choir, beginning with the Rulers; after which the upper grade on the Dean's side, beginning with the Dean, or in his absence the person in the nearest stall to him; then the upper grade on the Precentor's side; in like manner the second and first grades, the boy inclining to each of the Clergy as he censes them, the Sub-Deacon following with the text for each to kiss.*

If it is a Principal Double Feast, let the Precentor first be censed who stands in the midst with the Rulers of the Choir.

In Doubles, if a Bishop celebrates, let two boys come with two Censors and two Sub-Deacons with two Texts or Relics. If the Bishop shall not celebrate and it is a Double, let a boy carry the Text on the Cantor side. When there is no **Creed** *said let the Sacrifice only be censed. This done, let the Priest go to the right side of the Altar, and let him wash his hands, saying:*

Cleanse me, O Lord, from all pollution of mind and body, that I may in purity perform the holy work of the Lord.

In the meantime let the Deacon cense the Altar on the left side and the Relics in order.

Then let the Priest return to the Altar, and let the Ministers place themselves on their steps. Then standing before the Altar, inclining his head and body, and with joined hands, let the Priest say this prayer:

In the spirit of humility and with a contrite heart let us be accepted of Thee, O Lord; and let our sacrifice be in such wise in Thy sight that it may be accepted of Thee this day, and please Thee, O Lord, my God.

Raising himself, let him kiss the Altar to the right of the Sacrifice, and let him give the Blessing over it afterwards, signing himself, saying:

In the Name of the Father, and of the Son, and of the Holy Ghost.

Then let the Priest turn to the people and say in a low voice:

Brethren and sisters, pray for me that my and your sacrifice may alike be accepted by the Lord our God.

The Clergy answer privately:

The grace of the Holy Ghost illumine thy heart and lips, and the Lord graciously accept this sacrifice of praise at thy hands for our sins and offences.

In Masses for the Dead, when the body is present, and on all Anniversaries and Trentals, but at no other time, after the washing of the hands let the Priest say:

We of- fer to Thee ob - la - tions and pray-ers, O Lord.

* See General Rubrics.

And let the Choir answer chanting:

Do Thou receive them for those souls whose memory we keep this day; make them, O Lord, to pass from death unto life.

Meanwhile let the Priest say:

In the spirit of humility.

Then let him say in a low voice, turning to the people:

Brethren and sisters, pray for the faithful departed.

The Clergy answer chanting:

Grant them eternal reset, O Lord, and let light perpetual shine upon them, which of old time Thou didst promise to Abraham and to his seed.

Turning to the Altar, let the Priest say the Secrets in number and order according to the Collects that have been said before the Epistle, beginning:

Let us pray.

At the end let him say aloud:

world with - out end.

A - men.

The Lord be with you.

And with thy spi - rit.

And then let the Sub-Deacon take the paten and the offertory-veil from the hands of the Deacon, which let him give, covered with the same, to the Acolyte to hold until **Our Father** *is said, the Acolyte standing the while on the step behind the Deacon (Reg. S. Osmund reads "Sub-Deacon," which seems the best). Let this be done always through the year at every Mass, except in Masses for the dead. It is to be done, however, on All Souls' Day.*

Here let the Priest raise his hands as he says:

Lift up your hearts.

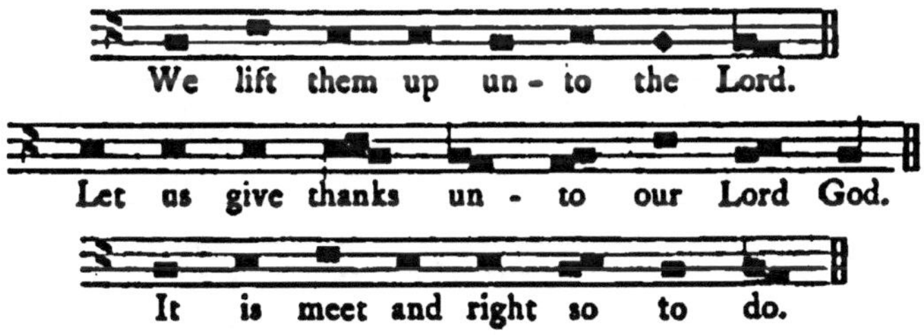

This **Preface** *following is said on Christmas Day at every Mass, and daily through the week, and on the Circumcision; and on all feasts of our Lady from then till and on the Purification; also on Corpus Christi and in and on the Octave (where it is kept with one); also in Votive Masses and Commemorations of the same.* **In communion with** *is said only on Christmas Day and till and on the Circumcision; on Christmas Night at the Midnight Mass* **Most holy night** *is said instead of* **Most holy day.**

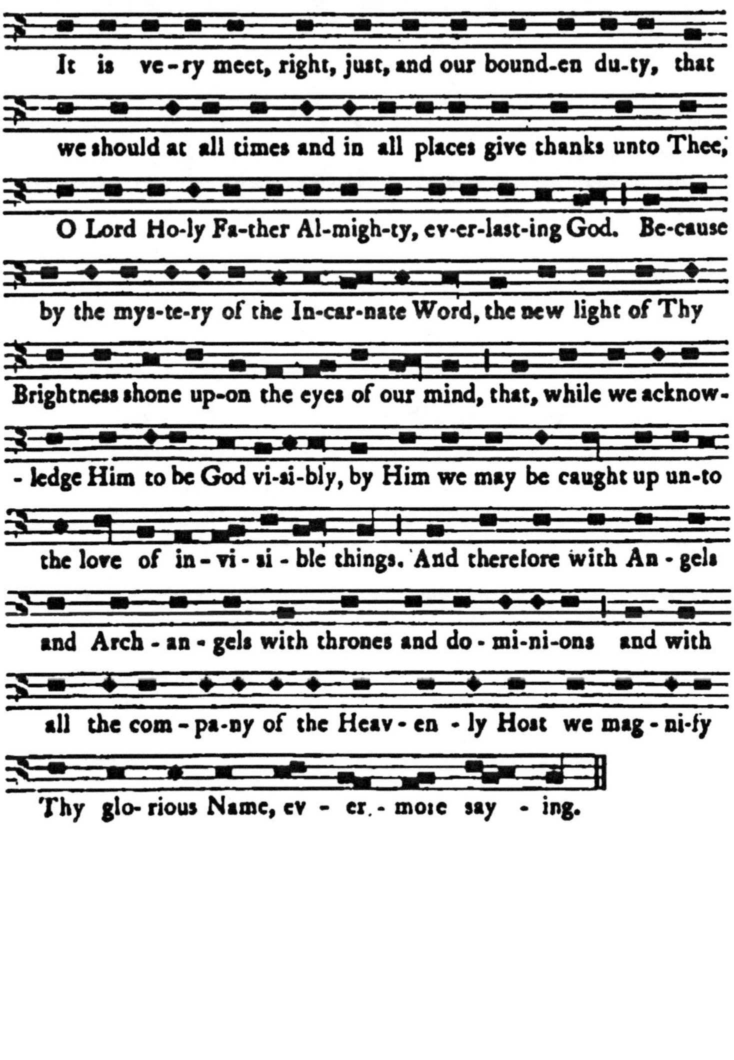

Within the Canon.

In communion with, and celebrating the most holy day [*or* the most holy night] in which the Immaculate Virginity of Blessed Mary brought forth a Saviour for this world, and reverencing, etc., *as in the Canon.*

The following **Preface** *is said on the Day of the Epiphany and through and on the Octave Day.* **In communion with** *is said similarly.*

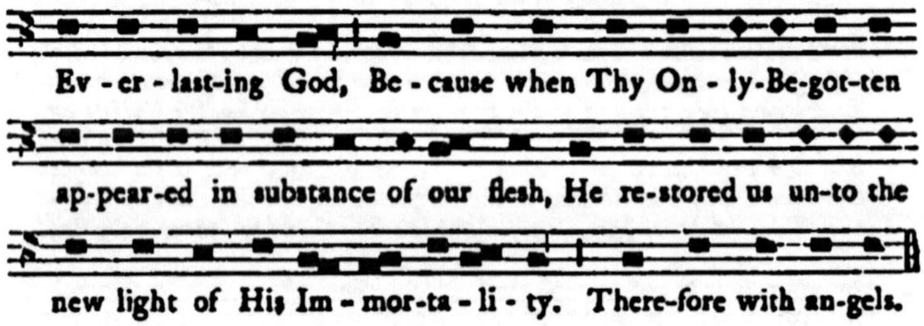

Within the Canon.

In communion with, and celebrating the most holy day in which Thy Only-begotten, co-eternal with Thee in Thy glory, visibly was made manifest in the body in the reality of our flesh, and reverencing, etc.

The following **Preface** *is said on Ash-Wednesday, and on every Mass that is of the fast till Maundy Thursday, except on Sundays :*

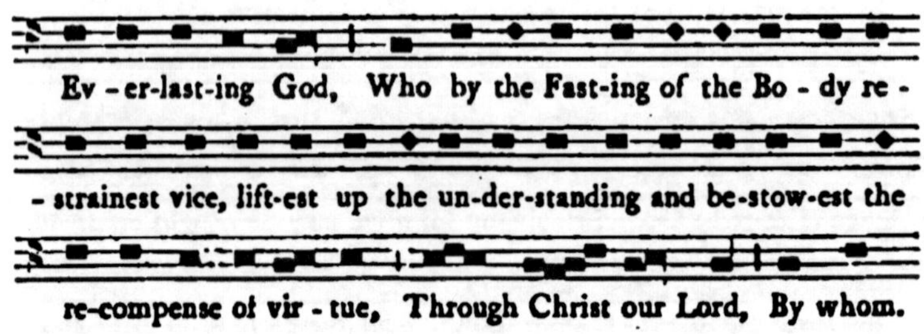

On Sundays in Lent and on Maundy Thursday the daily **Preface** *is said. On which latter day is said—*

Within the Canon.

In communion with, and celebrating the most holy day in which our Lord Jesus Christ was betrayed for us, and reverencing, etc.

Also,

This oblation, therefore, of our service and that of Thy whole

family which we offer to Thee* on the day on which our Lord Jesus Christ delivered unto his disciples the adorable† mystery of His Body and Blood, We beseech Thee, O Lord, etc.

Also,

Who, the day before He suffered for our salvation and that of all men, that is to-day, took bread into His holy and adorable hands.

The following **Preface** *is said on Easter Eve, Easter Day, and daily through the week till and on the Octave Day; also on all Sundays till Ascension Day, when the Service is of the Sunday or of Easter* (i.e., *the Resurrection*). **In communion with** *and* **This Oblation** *is said only through and on the Octave But* **Chiefly on this night** *is said only on Easter Eve; at other times,* **This day.**

Within the Canon.

In communion with, and celebrating the most holy day [*or* the most holy night] of the Resurrection of our Lord Jesus Christ according to the flesh, and reverencing, etc.

* "On behalf also of those whom Thou hast deigned to regenerate by water and the Holy Ghost, granting them remission of all their sins."—97, '55 Missals.

† Most MSS. read "celebration of the."

Also,

This oblation, therefore, of our service and that of Thy whole family which we offer to Thee, on behalf of those also whom Thou hast deigned to regenerate by water and the Holy Ghost, granting them forgiveness of all their sins; We beseech Thee, O Lord, etc.

The following **Preface** *is said on Ascension Day. It is also said through and on the Octave, and on the Sunday within the Octave, unless there come a Feast which has one of its own. Similarly is said* **In communion with.**

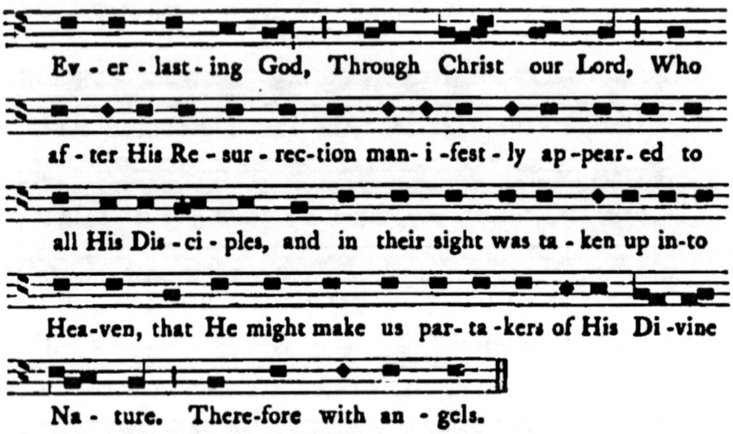

Within the Canon.

In communion with, and celebrating the most holy day whereon our Lord Jesus Christ, Thy Only-begotten Son, set upon the right hand of Thy glory the substance of our frailty, which He had united unto Himself, and reverencing, etc.

The following **Preface** *is said on Whitsun Day and through the week, and in all Masses of the Holy Ghost.* **In communion with** *and* **This oblation, therefore,** *are said only on Whitsun Day, and from now till Trinity Sunday.*

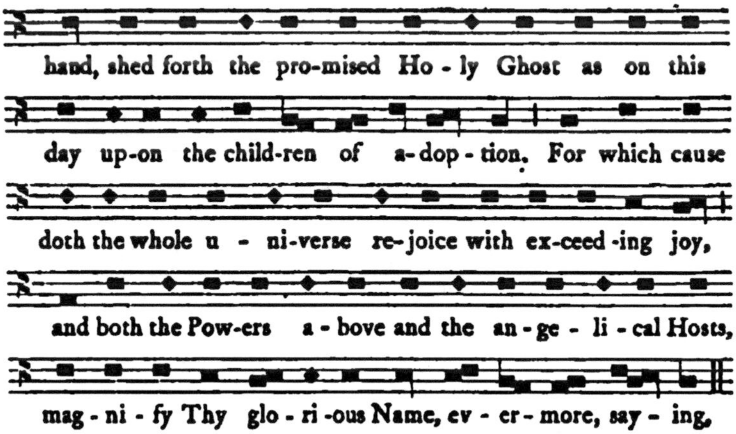

Within the Canon.

In communion with and celebrating the most holy day of Pentecost, whereon the Holy Ghost appeared to the Apostles in the likeness of fiery tongues, and reverencing, etc.

Also

This oblation, therefore of our bounden duty and that of Thy whole family, which we offer unto Thee on behalf of those also whom Thou hast deigned to regenerate by water and the Holy Ghost, granting them forgiveness of all their sins, we beseech Thee, O Lord, etc.

The following Preface *is said on Trinity Sunday and on the Sundays following until Advent, when the Mass is of the Sunday although it be said in the Chapter-house. It is also said on all Commemorations of the Holy Trinity through the year, and in every Marriage Mass.*

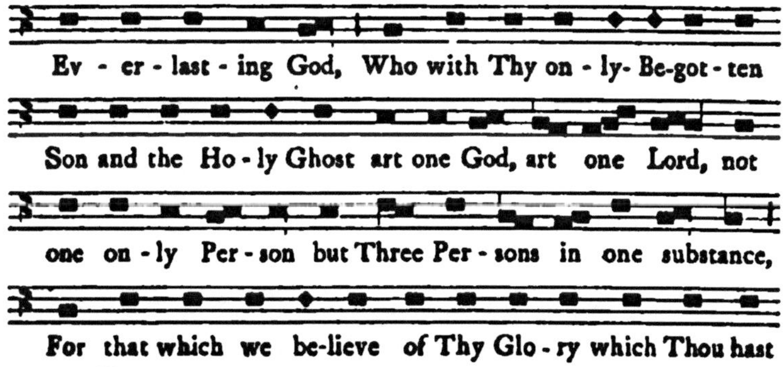

re-veal-ed, the same do we be-lieve of Thy Son, and of

the Ho-ly Ghost, with-out dif-fer-ence or in - e - qual - i - ty:

that in the con - fes - sion of a true and ev - er - last - ing

God-head both Dis-tinc-tion in the Per-sons, and U - ni - ty

in Be-ing, and E-qual-i - ty in Ma - jes - ty, be wor-ship-ped

which An-gels and Arch-an-gels praise, Che-ru- bin al - so and Se -

- ra - phin, Who cease not to cry with one voice, say - ing,

The following **Preface** *is said on all Feasts of the Apostles and Evangelists (except on S. John the Evangelist's Day in Christmas week: it is, however, said on the Octave Day, and on his other Feast in Eastertide), and through and on the Octave Days of SS. Peter and Paul, and S. Andrew.*

Ev - er - last - ing God, and hum- bly be-seech Thee that

Thou wouldest not leave Thy flock des -ti-tute, O Lord, E - ter-nal

Shep-herd, but through Thy Blessed A-pos-tles wouldest keep it

un-der Thy con- tin - u - al Pro - tec-tion: that it may be go -

- vern-ed by the same Ru-lers whom Thou hast made to pre-side

o-ver it as its Vic-ars and Pas-tors. There-fore with an - gels,

The following **Preface** *is said on both Feasts of the Holy Cross, and in Commemorations of the same throughout the year.*

Ev - er-last-ing God, Who hast es - ta-blish-ed the sal - va-tion

of man-kind by the Wood of the Cross, that so whence Death

came, from thence Life might rise a-gain, and he who had

gain-ed the vic - to-ry by a tree, by the Tree might al - so be

o - ver - come : Through Christ our Lord, By Whom.

The following **Preface** *is said on every Feast of the Blessed Virgin Mary (except on her Purification); it is also said through the Octaves of the Assumption and the Nativity, and on the Commemorations through the year (except from Christmas Day to the Purification).*

Ev - er - last- ing God, and Thee on the { Conception. / Annunciation / Assumption / Nativity / Visitation / Veneration }

of the Bless-ed and glo - ri- ous Ev - er - Vir - gin Ma - ry ought

we with ex - ult -ing souls to praise, to bless, and to pro-claim.

Who by the o - ver - sha-dow- ing of the Ho - ly Ghost did

both con - ceive Thy On - ly Be - got - ten and in glo - ry of

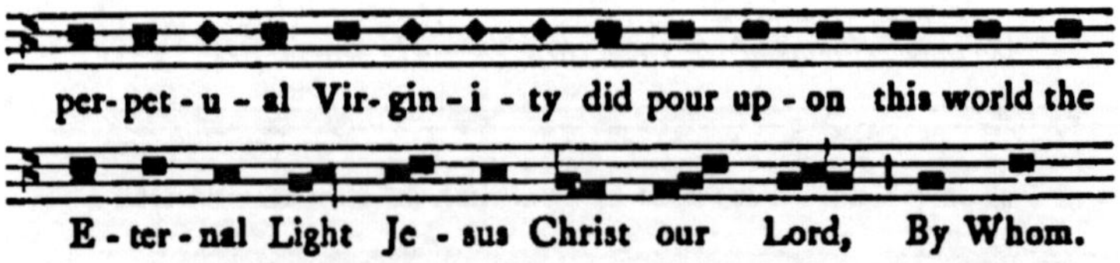

The following **Preface** *is the daily one, and is said on all Feasts and week-days, and through Octaves which have none proper to them.*

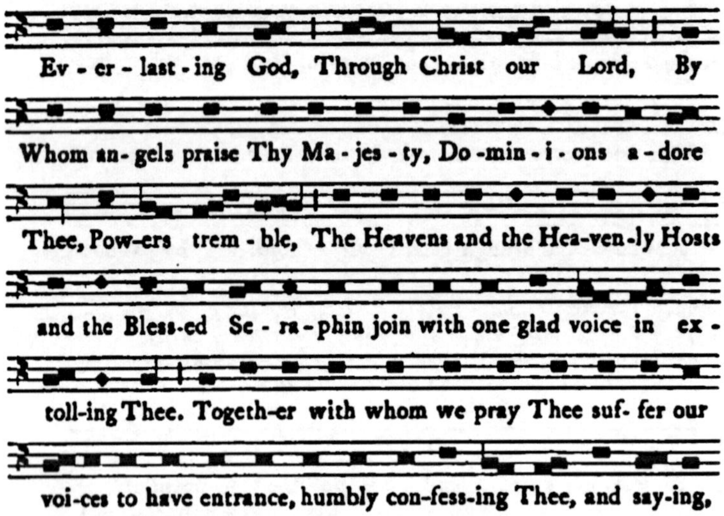

Then follows the **Sanctus.**

Whilst the Priest says **Holy, Holy,** *let him raise his arms a little and join his hands until these words,* **In the Name of the Lord:** *then let him sign himself on the face.*

Holy, Holy, Holy, Lord God of Hosts; heaven and earth are full of Thy glory. Hosanna in the highest.

Blessed is He that cometh in the Name of the Lord. Glory be to Thee, O Lord, in the highest.

When the Service of S. Mary is said for the last time before Advent and Septuagesima, and on the Octaves of the Visitation, Assumption, and Nativity, then is said instead of **Blessed is He:**

Blessed is *the Son of Mary* **that cometh, etc.**

Then immediately, with joined hands and uplifted eyes, let him begin, inclining himself

I·N·R·I

The Canon of the Mass.

Thee therefore, O most Merciful Father, through Jesus Christ Thy Son our Lord, we most humbly pray and entreat, *Here let the Priest rise and kiss the Altar on the right of the Sacrifice, saying,* to accept and bless, *Here let the Priest make three crosses over the chalice and bread, saying,* these gi ✠ fts, these pre ✠ sents, this ho ✠ ly immaculate Sacrifice, *Having made them, let him raise his hands, saying,* which we offer to Thee in the first place in behalf of Thy Holy Catholic Church, to which do Thou deign to give peace, to guard, to unite, and to govern it, throughout the whole world: together with Thy Servant our Pope *N.*, our Bishop *N.*, *Here his own Bishop only is mentioned,* our King *N.*, *naming these persons,* all the Orthodox and maintainers of the Catholic and Apostolic Faith.

Remember, O Lord, Thy servants and handmaidens *N.*, and *N.*, *in praying for whom a due order dictated by charity should be observed. Let the Priest pray five times —first, for himself; secondly, for his father and mother, carnal and spiritual, and other relations; thirdly, for special friends, his parishioners and others; fourthly, for all present; fifthly, for all Christian people; and here the Priest can commend all his friends to God: with the caution, however, that no one should pause there too long, both for fear of distraction of mind, and of suggestions which may be made by evil angels, as well as other dangers,* and all here present, whose faith is approved and whose devotion is known unto Thee; in whose behalf we offer unto Thee, or who are engaged in offering unto Thee, this sacrifice of praise, for themselves and all pertaining to them, for the redemption of their souls, for the hope of their salvation and security; and are paying their vows unto Thee, the eternal, living, and true God.

In communion with and reverencing the memory, in the first place, of the glorious and ever-Virgin Mary, *Inclining a little*, Mother of our God and Lord Jesus Christ; as also of Thy blessed Apostles and Martyrs, Peter and Paul, Andrew, James, John, Thomas, James, Philip, Bartholomew, Matthew, Simon and Thaddæus, Linus, Cletus, Clement, Sixtus, Cornelius, Cyprian, Laurence, Chrysogonus, John and Paul, Cosmas and Damian, and all Thy Saints; for whose sake and prayers grant that in all things we may be strengthened by the aid of Thy protection. Through the same Christ our Lord. Amen.

Here let the Priest regard the Host with great veneration, saying:

This oblation, therefore, of our service and that of Thy whole family, we beseech Thee, O Lord, graciously to accept, and to dispose our days in Thy peace, delivering us from eternal damnation, and causing us to be numbered amongst the flock of Thine elect. Through Christ our Lord. Amen.

Here let him again regard the Host, saying

Which oblation, we beseech Thee, O Almighty God, that thou wouldest vouchsafe, in all respects, *Here let him make three crosses over each oblation.* to bl ✠ ess, ap ✠ prove, rat ✠ ify, and make reasonable and acceptable, that it may become to us the Bo ✠ dy, *Here let him sign over the bread,* and the Blo ✠ od, *Here let him sign over the chalice, and joining his hands, say,* of Thy most dearly Beloved Son our Lord Jesus Christ, *Here let the Priest raise and join his hands, and afterwards wipe his fingers, and elevate the Host, saying,*

Who on the day before He suffered took bread into His holy and adorable hands, and lifting up his eyes to Heaven, *Here let him raise his eyes,* unto Thee, His Father, God Almighty, *Here let him incline, and afterwards raise himself a little,* gave thanks to Thee, bles✠sed, brake, *Here let him touch the Host but not so as to break it, as some do;*

for although the order of the words seems to imply that Christ brake before consecrating, tradition teaches the contrary, **and gave it to His disciples, saying, Take and eat ye all of this,**

FOR THIS IS MY BODY.

These words ought to be said in one and the same breath without pause. After these words, let the Priest incline to the Host, and with bowed head adore It, and afterwards elevate It above his forehead that It may be seen by the people, and reverently replace It before the chalice, making a cross with the same; and then let him uncover the chalice and hold it between both hands, not disjoining the thumb from the forefinger, save only to make the sign of the cross, saying :

Likewise after Supper, taking also this most excellent chalice into His holy and adorable hands, and giving thanks to Thee, *Here let him incline,* **He bles ✠ sed, and gave it to His disciples, saying, Take and drink ye all of it,** *Here let the Priest elevate the chalice a little saying.*

FOR THIS IS THE CUP OF MY BLOOD OF THE NEW AND EVERLASTING TESTAMENT, THE MYSTERY OF FAITH, WHICH SHALL BE SHED FOR YOU AND FOR MANY FOR THE REMISSION OF SINS.

Here let him elevate the chalice to his chest, or above his head, saying :

As oft as ye shall do this, ye shall do it in remembrance of Me.

Here let him replace the chalice, and rub his fingers over it in case of any crumbs, and cover the chalice. Then let him raise his arms in the form of a cross, joining his fingers, until the benedictions.

Wherefore also, O Lord, we Thy servants together with Thy holy people, calling to mind the most blessed Passion of the same Christ Thy Son our Lord God, together with His Resurrection from the dead, and His glorious Ascension into Heaven, offer to Thy excellent Majesty of Thy gifts and bounties, *Here let him make five crosses : three over the Host and chalice, saying.* **a pu ✠ re, a**

ho ✠ ly, a spot ✠ less Sacrifice, *The fourth over the bread, saying*, the holy Br ✠ ead of eternal life, *The fifth over the chalice, saying*, and the Cup ✠ of everlasting salvation.

Upon which do Thou vouchsafe to look with favourable and gracious countenance, and accept them as Thou didst accept the gifts of Thy righteous servant Abel, the sacrifice of our Patriarch Abraham, and the holy sacrifice, the pure oblation, which Thy High Priest Melchisedech offered to Thee,

Here let the Priest, inclining his body and crossing his hands, say:

We humbly entreat Thee, Almighty God, command these things to be carried by the hands of Thy Holy Angel to Thy Altar on High before the sight of Thy Divine Majesty, that as many of us, *Here he shall raise himself and kiss the Altar on the right of the Sacrifice*, as shall by partaking at this Altar receive the most sacred Bo ✠ dy, *Here let him sign over the Host*, and Bl ✠ ood of Thy Son, *Here let him sign over the chalice*, may be fulfilled with all grace and heavenly bene ✠ diction, *Here let him sign himself on his face*, through the same Christ our Lord. Amen.

Here let him pray for the dead:

Remember also, O Lord, the souls of Thy servants and handmaidens, N. and N., who have gone before us with the sign of the faith, and sleep the sleep of peace; to them, O Lord, and to all who rest in Christ, we pray Thee, grant a place of refreshment, of light, and of peace. Through the same Christ our Lord. Amen.

Here let him strike his breast once, saying:

To us, also, Thy sinful servants, who hope in the multitude of Thy mercies, vouchsafe to grant some part and fellowship with Thy holy Apostles and Martyrs, with John, Stephen, Matthias, Barnabas, Ignatius, Alexander, Marcellinus, Peter, Felicitas, Perpetua, Agatha,

Lucy, Agnes, Cecilia, Anastasia, and all Thy Saints, into whose company, not weighing our merits but pardoning our offences, we beseech Thee to admit us. Through Christ our Lord, by Whom, O Lord, Thou ever createst, *Here let the Priest sign the chalice, thrice saying,* sanctifi ✠ est, quick ✠ enest, bles ✠ sest, and bestowest upon us all these good things. *Here let the Priest uncover the chalice, and sign it five times with the Host. First, beyond the chalice on either side; secondly, in a line with it; thirdly, below it; the fourth time as the first, and the fifth before it. Meanwhile, let the Deacon stand at the right of the Priest, having first washed his hands, and assist him in raising the corporals; and as he retires let him kiss the Altar and the right shoulder of the Priest.* By Him ✠ and with Him ✠ and in Him ✠ is unto Thee, God the Father Al ✠ mighty, in the unity of the Holy ✠ Ghost, all honour and glory. *Here let the Priest cover the chalice, and keep his hands on the Altar whilst he says,*

Here let the Deacon receive the Paten from the hands of the Sub-Deacon, and hold it up uncovered with extended arms on the right of the Priest. Then let the Priest raise his hands, and

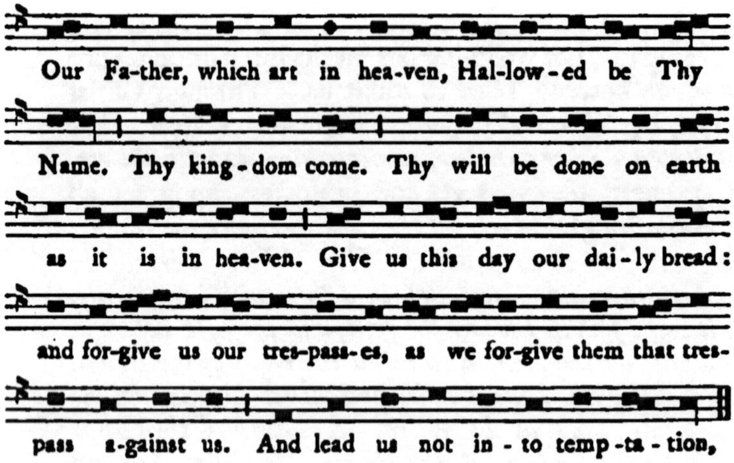

Let the Choir answer:

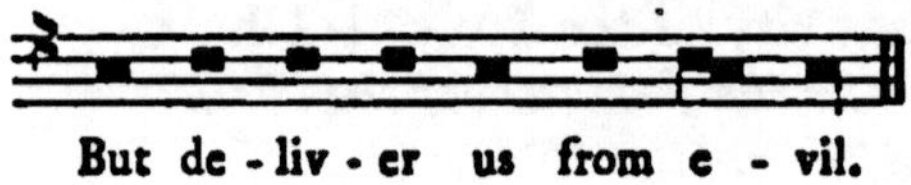

Let the Priest say **Amen** *privately.*

Deliver us, O Lord, we beseech Thee, from all evils past, present, and to come; and at the intercession of the blessed and glorious ever-Virgin Mary, Mother of God, and of Thy blessed Apostles Peter, and Paul, and Andrew, with all Saints, *Here let the Deacon give the paten to the Priest, kissing his hand; and let the Priest kiss the paten: then let him place it first before his left, then his right eye: after which let him make the sign of the cross over his head, and then let him replace it, saying,* **graciously give peace in our time, that, aided by the help of Thy loving-kindness, we may both be ever set free from sin and secure from all disquietude.** *Here let him uncover the chalice and take the Body, with an inclination, placing It over the bowl of the chalice, holding It between the thumbs and fore-fingers, and let him break It into three parts, the first fraction whilst he says,* **Through the same Thy Son Jesus Christ our Lord,** *The second fraction,* **Who with Thee**

liveth and reigneth in the unity of the Holy Ghost, God, *Here let him hold the two broken pieces in his left hand, and the third over the top of the chalice in his right hand, saying aloud,*

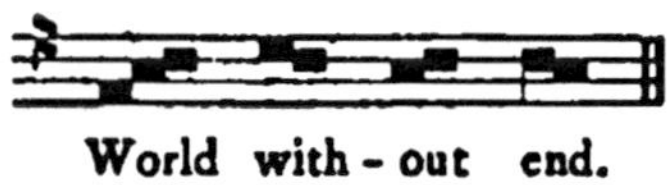

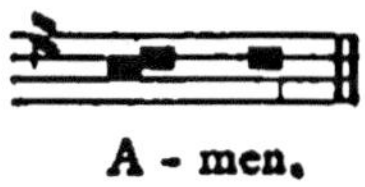

[*It is to be known that in every Ferial Mass the Choir kneel from the* **Sanctus** *to the* **Peace** *through the year (except from Easter to the First Sunday after Trinity). On Feasts of three lessons without rulers, and on and in Octaves when the Choir is not ruled, and on week-days from the First Sunday after Epiphany to Maundy Thursday, and from Trinity Sunday to Christmas Eve, the following prayers are said kneeling :*

Antiphon. **Thine is the power.**

Ps. lxxix. O God, the heathen are come, etc.
Glory.
Ps. lxvii. God be merciful unto us, etc.
Glory.
Ps. xxi. The King shall rejoice, etc.
Glory.

Antiphon. **Thine is the power, and the kingdom, O Lord: Thou art above all nations : Give peace in our time, O Lord.**

Lord, have mercy upon us.
Christ, have mercy upon us.
Lord, have mercy upon us.

Our Father.

And all this is said without tone as well by the Clergy in the quire as by the Priest with his Ministers. Then let the Priest say intoning:

℣. **And lead us not into temptation.**
℟. **But deliver us from evil.**
℣. **Let God arise, and let His enemies be scattered.**
℟. **Let them also that hate Him flee before Him.**
℣. **Not unto us, O Lord, not unto us,**
℟. **But unto Thy Name give the glory.**
℣. **Let us pray for the afflicted and captives.**
℟. **Deliver Israel, O God, out of all his troubles.**

℣. Send them help, O Lord, from Thy Sanctuary.
℟. And strengthen them out of Sion.
℣. Be unto us, O Lord, a strong tower,
℟. From the face of the enemy.
℣. O Lord, save the King,
℟. And mercifully hear us when we call upon Thee.
℣. O Lord, hear our prayer,
℟. And let our cry come unto Thee.
℣. The Lord be with you.
℟. And with thy spirit.

Let us pray.

O God, Who in Thy wondrous Providence orderest all things, we humbly pray Thee that, rescuing the land which Thy Only Begotten Son hath consecrated with His own Blood out of the hands of the enemies of the Cross of Christ, Thou wouldst restore it to the worship of Christ, by mercifully directing the prayers of the faithful who are instant for its deliverance into the way of eternal peace. Through.

Govern, we beseech Thee, O Lord, Thy servant our Bishop, and at the intercession of the Blessed Mary Mother of God, ever-Virgin, and of all Thy Saints, multiply upon him the gifts of Thy grace, that he being delivered from all offences, and not being left destitute of temporal aids, may rejoice in never-failing ordinances. Through.

Grant, we beseech Thee, Almighty God, to Thy servant our King health of mind and body, that he, cleaving to good works, may ever be defended by Thy mighty protection. Through.]

Here let him make three crosses within the chalice with the third particle of the Host, saying:

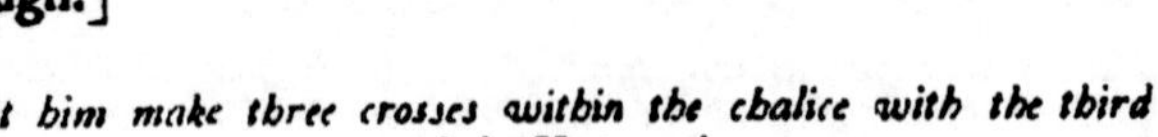

The peace of the Lord be al - way with you.

Let the Choir answer

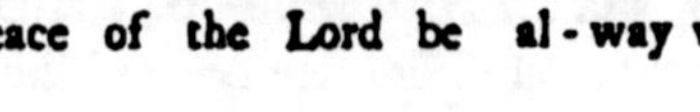

And with thy spi - rit.

Then, if the Bishop shall celebrate, let the Deacon, turning to the people and holding the Bishop's staff in his right hand, with the crook turned towards himself say:

Bow down your-selves for a bless-ing.

Let the Choir answer:

Thanks be to Thee, O God.

Afterwards, the Eucharist being replaced on the paten, let the Bishop give the Blessing to the people.

At the **Agnus Dei,** *let both the Ministers approach the Priest on the right the Deacon nearer, the Sub-Deacon further, and let them say privately.*

O Lamb of God, that takest away the sins of the world,
Have mercy upon us.
O Lamb of God, that takest away the sins of the world,
Have mercy upon us.
O Lamb of God, that takest away the sins of the world,
Grant us Thy peace.

In Masses for the Dead, instead of **Have mercy upon us,** *is said:*

O Lamb of God, that takest away the sins of the world,
Grant them rest.

Adding in the third petition, **Eternal.**

Here, making the sign of the cross, let him place the said third particle of the Host in the Sacrament of the Blood, saying:

Let this most ✠ holy union of the Body and Blood of our Lord Jesus Christ be to me and all who receive It health of mind and body, and a saving preparation for worthily attaining unto eternal life. Through.

Before the **Peace** *is given, let the Priest say:*

O Lord, Holy Father, Almighty, everlasting God, grant me so worthily to receive this most holy Body and Blood of Thy Son our Lord Jesus Christ that I may thereby receive forgiveness of all my sins, and be filled with Thy Holy Spirit and have Thy

peace; for Thou only art God, and there is no other beside Thee, Whose kingdom and glorious dominion abideth ever world without end. Amen.

Here let the Priest kiss the corporals on the right side and the top of the chalice, and afterwards the Deacon, saying:

℣. Peace be unto thee and to the Church of God.

℟. And with thy spirit.

Let the Deacon receive the Peace *from the Priest on his right, and let him give it to the Sub-Deacon. Then let the Deacon carry it to the Rulers at the step of the quire, and let them give it each to his side, beginning with the seniors. On Feasts and week-days when there are no rulers,* ¶ *let the* Peace *be borne to the Choir from the Deacon by the two last of the second grade: the rest as before. If a Bishop celebrate, let the Deacon kiss first the principal Sub-Deacon, from whom let the rest take it; then the two secondary Rulers (if it be a Double Feast), who shall give it to the principal Rulers, they bearing it after to the decani and cantoris side, and the secondaries to the Chancellor's and Treasurer's end. After the giving of the* Peace, *let the Priest say these prayers privately, before communicating, holding the Host in both hands.*

O God the Father, Fount and Source of all goodness, Who moved by Thy loving-kindness didst will Thine Only Begotten to descend for us to this lower world and to take Flesh, Which I unworthy here hold in my hands, *Here let the Priest incline himself to the Host,* I worship Thee, I glorify Thee, I praise Thee with the whole purpose of my mind and heart, and beseech Thee not to forsake us Thy servants, but forgive us our sins, that so we may be enabled to serve Thee, the only Living and True God, with a pure heart and chaste body. Through the same Christ our Lord. Amen.

O Lord Jesu Christ, Son of the Living God, Who by the will of the Father and the co-operation of the Holy Ghost hast by Thy death given life to the world; deliver me, I beseech Thee, by this Thy most holy Body and Blood, from all my iniquities and from every evil; make me ever obedient to Thy commandments, and suffer me not to be for ever separated from Thee, O Saviour of the world. Who with God the Father and the same Holy Ghost livest and reignest God, world without end. Amen.

Let not the Sacrament of Thy Body and Blood, O Lord Jesu Christ, which I albeit unworthy receive, be to me for judgment and condemnation, but by Thy goodness be profitable to the health of my body and soul. Amen.

To the Body let him say, before he receive, bowing down.

Hail for evermore, most holy Flesh of Christ, to me before all and above all the highest source of joy. The Body of our Lord Jesus Christ be unto me a sinner the Way and the Life, in the Name ✠ of the Father, and of the Son, and of the Holy Ghost. Amen.

Here let him receive the Body, making a cross with the same before his mouth. Then to the Blood let him say, with great devotion:

Hail for evermore, Heavenly Drink, to me before all and above all the highest source of joy. The Body and Blood of our Lord Jesus Christ be unto me a perpetual healing unto everlasting life. Amen. In the Name ✠ of the Father, and of the Son, and of the Holy Ghost. Amen.

Here let him receive the Blood; which taken, let the Priest incline, and say with devotion the prayer following—

I give thanks unto Thee, O Lord, Holy Father, Almighty, everlasting God, Who hast refreshed me with the most sacred Body and Blood of Thy Son our Lord Jesu Christ; and I pray that this Sacrament of our salvation of which I, unworthy sinner, have partaken, turn not to judgment nor condemnation according to my deserts, but be profitable to the preservation of my body and soul unto everlasting life. Amen.

Which said, let the Priest go to the right side of the Altar with the chalice between his hands, his fingers joined as before; and let the Sub-Deacon approach and pour into the chalice wine and water, and let the Priest rinse his hands lest any relics of the Body or Blood remain on his fingers or in the chalice. When, however, any Priest, has to celebrate twice in one day, then at the first Mass he ought not to receive any ablution, but place it in the aumbry or in a clean vessel till the end of the next Mass, and then take both ablutions. After the first ablution is said:

What we have partaken of with our mouth, O Lord, may we receive with a pure heart, and by a temporal gift may our everlasting healing be effected.

Here let Him wash his fingers in the chalice with the wine poured in by the Sub-Deacon; after drinking which follows,

Let this communion, O Lord, cleanse us from sin, and make us partakers of a heavenly healing.

* *Here let the Deacon pour water into the chalice,* * *which having drunk, let the Priest place the chalice on the paten, that if ought remain it may drain off. And afterwards, inclining himself, let him say:*

Let us adore the sign of the Cross, whereby we have received the Sacrament of salvation.

Then let him wash his hands, the Sub-Deacon ministering to him; and in the meantime let the Deacon fold up the corporas and put them in the burse, and, while the **Communion** *is being said, let him place them upon the chalice, with the offertory-veil, and give them to the Acolyte to take back with the like ceremony with which he brought the same. After* **World without end. Amen,** *let the Sub-Deacon carry the book to the right side of the Altar, and the Deacon take the chalice and offer it to the Priest to drink if ought remains. Then let the Priest say the* **Communion,** *and, signing himself on the face, turn to the people, and, with arms a little raised and joined hands, say:*

℣. The Lord be with you.

℟. And with thy spirit.

Turning to the Altar, let him say:

Let us pray.

Then let him say the **Post-Communions,** *after the same order and number as the* **Collects,** *ending with,*

℣. World without end,

℟. Amen.

The last **Post-Communion** *ended, having made the sign of the cross on his forehead, let the Priest again turn to the people and say.*

℣. The Lord be with you.

℟. And with Thy spirit.

Then let the Deacon say, turning to the Altar:

℣. Let us give thanks unto the Lord.

℟. Thanks be to God.

* The Manuals of '37 and other earlier dates, and Missal of '54, make the *Deacon* perform the ablutions which follow immediately after the communion of the Blood. After the asterisked rubric is this: "Which having drunk, let the Priest go to the midst of the Altar and place the chalice......... and, after inclining himself before the Altar, say with great devotion, 'I return thanks to Thee......... unto life everlasting.' Then let him go to the right side of the Altar and wash his hands," etc.

Or else, turning to the people

℣. Depart ye, Mass is over.

℟. Thanks be to God.

In Masses for the Dead, turning to the Altar.

℣. May they rest in peace.

℟. Amen.

This having been said, let the Priest, with body inclined and hands joined, say secretly in the midst of the Altar :

Let the obedient performance of my bounden duty be pleasing unto Thee, O Holy Trinity, and grant that this Sacrifice which I, unworthy that I am, have offered in the sight of Thy Majesty, may be acceptable unto Thee; and may, through Thy mercy, obtain Thy favour for myself and all those in whose behalf I have offered it. Who livest and reignest God, world without end. Amen.

Which ended, let the Priest rise, signing himself on his face, saying :

In the Name of the Father, and of the Son, and of the Holy Ghost. Amen.

And so, with an inclination, let them depart, with the Torch-bearers and other Ministers, in the order in which they came in at the beginning of Mass. And immediately after Thanks be to God *let Nones be said when they come after Mass; and in returning let the Priest say the Gospel,* In the beginning, etc.

A Thanksgiving to be said after Mass.

When the Priest shall take off his chasuble and vestments, let him say the following Psalms, with the Antiphon:

Ant. Let us sing the Song of the Three Children.

O ye Priests of the Lord, bless ye the Lord: praise Him, and magnify Him for ever.

O ye Servants of the Lord, bless ye the Lord: praise Him, and magnify Him for ever.

O ye Spirits and Souls of the Righteous, bless ye the Lord: praise Him, and magnify Him for ever.

O ye holy and humble Men of heart, bless ye the Lord: praise Him, and magnify Him for ever.

O Ananias, Azarias, and Misael, bless ye the Lord: praise Him, and magnify Him for ever.

Ps. cl. O praise God in His holiness, etc.

Lord, now lettest Thou Thy servant, etc.

Ant. Let us sing the Song of the Three Children, which they sang in the furnace of fire and gave thanks unto the Lord.

Lord, have mercy,
Christ, have mercy.
Lord, have mercy.

Our Father.

℣. And lead us not into temptation,
℟. But deliver us from evil.

℣. Let us bless the Father, and the Son, and the Holy Ghost.

℟. Let us praise and magnify Him for ever.

℣. Blessed art Thou, O Lord, in the firmament of Heaven, and to be praised and exalted for ever.

℟. The Holy Trinity bless and keep us. Amen.

℣. Enter not into judgment with Thy servant, O Lord.

℟. For in Thy sight shall no man living be justified.

℣. Turn us, O Lord God of hosts.

℟. Shew the light of Thy countenance, and we shall be whole.

℣. Lord, hear my prayer.

℟. And let my cry come unto Thee.

℣. The Lord be with you.

℟. And with thy spirit.

Let us pray.

O God, Who for the Three Children didst quench the flames of fire, mercifully grant that we Thy servants may not be consumed by the flame of our sins. Through.

Kindle in our reins and in our heart, O Lord, the fire of the Holy Ghost, that we may serve Thee with a chaste body and please Thee with a pure heart. Through.

Prevent us, O Lord, we beseech Thee, in all our doings with Thy favour, and further us with Thy help; that all our works may be begun, continued, and ended in Thee. Through.

Prayers to be said after Mass.

I.

Almighty and everlasting God, Saviour of souls and Redeemer of the world, graciously look upon me Thy servant prostrate before Thy Majesty; and of Thy loving-kindness behold this Sacrifice which in honour of Thy Name I have offered for the salvation of the faithful, both quick and dead, and also for our sins and offences. Put away Thine anger from me, grant me Thy grace and mercy; open unto me the door of Paradise, and deliver me in Thy might from all evils; whatever guilt I have in mine own person incurred do Thou forgive; and make me so to persevere in Thy precepts in this world that I may be found worthy to be joined to the flock of the elect. Grant this, O my God, on Whose blessed Name honour and dominion waiteth for ever and ever. Amen.

II.

O Almighty and everlasting Lord God Jesus Christ our Lord, be merciful unto my sins, through the partaking of Thy Body and Blood; for Thou hast spoken, saying, "Whoso eateth My Flesh, and drinketh My Blood, dwelleth in Me and I in him." Wherefore I humbly beseech Thee to create in me a clean heart, and renew a right spirit within me; and deign to stablish me with Thy free Spirit, and to deliver me from all the snares and malice of the Devil; that I may be found worthy to have a share in the joys of heaven. Who.

III.

I give thanks unto Thee, Lord God, Almighty Father, that Thou hast vouchsafed to satisfy me with the Body and Blood of

Thy beloved Son, our Lord Jesus Christ. I beseech Thy boundless goodness, Almighty and merciful God, that this Holy Communion be not unto me for judgment or condemnation; but be an earnest of faith and shield of good will to cast out of my mind all the deceits of the enemy, to root out the plague of pride, the lust of appetite, and perversity of tongue, that I may enter in unto that banquet where are the true Light and the perpetual joys of the just. I pray also, O Lord, that this Holy Communion may be unto me my guide and viaticum to the haven of eternal salvation. Let it be unto me consolation when I am troubled in mind; exceeding delight in every good purpose; patience in tribulation and difficulties; medicine in sickness. By these most sacred Mysteries which I have received, grant unto me right faith, steadfast hope, and perfect charity; renunciation of the world, a pure desire, contentment of mind, and ardent love to Thee. In memory of, and hearty fellowship with, the Passion of Thy beloved Son, fulfil my life with virtue to Thy praise and with faith unfeigned; and in the hour of my departure let me receive the grace of so great a mystery with true faith, firm hope, and sincere charity, that I may behold Thee for ever. Amen.*

Priest, at Christ's Table to thine acts give heed,
To life, or to eternal death, they lead.
While it gives light, the taper wastes away,—
Th' unworthy celebrant himself doth slay.
Thy death, Christ's death, this false world, pains of hell,
And joys of heaven,—these things consider well.

IV.

I render thanks to Thee, O most sweet Lord Jesu Christ, Very Light, Health of believers, Comfort of the sorrowful, Hope of all men, Joy of angels, that Thou hast vouchsafed this day to feed me Thy servant, a miserable and great sinner, with Thy most sacred Body and Blood. Wherefore I most wretched, full of numberless offences, with tears and prayers implore Thy most tender mercy and supreme clemency, that this most sweet refreshment, this most excellent and incomprehensible Communion, turn not to the condemnation of my soul, but aid me in driving out all the fraud and malicious snares of the Devil, so that none of his iniquities ever have dominion in my heart, body, soul, or senses; but let Thy gracious favour bring me to the heavenly banquet of the angels, where Thou dost dwell, Who art True Blessedness, Light unclouded, everlasting Joy. Amen.

* These three prayers are from the Missal of 1526.

V.

I give thanks unto Thee, O Lord Jesu Christ, Who didst advance me, an unclean and unworthy sinner, to the dignity of the priesthood, and Who this day, of the bounty of Thy goodness, and not for any merit of mine, hast vouchsafed unto me the grace of consecrating and receiving Thy most holy Body and Blood; and grant, I beseech Thee, of Thy most tender mercy and unspeakable goodness, and for Thy most holy Cross and Passion, that this ineffable Sacrament of which I, unworthy sinner, have partaken, be not unto me guilt unto punishment, but a saving intercession for my forgiveness and salvation; and whatever I have done amiss this day at Thy holy Altar in depraved, unlawful, and unclean thoughts; in want of reverence, in gesture, act or negligence, in vain repetition of words or distraction of mind, or in any other manner whatsoever, I implore Thy most holy goodness mercifully deign to pardon and grant me entire absolution from these and all my sins. Who.

VI.

Almighty, everlasting, and most merciful God, Who didst come to redeem sinners, I pray Thee by the most sweet Sacrament of Thy Body and Blood, the mystery which I unworthy have received, grant me forgiveness and remission of all my sins, both now and hereafter; that I may be duly penitent, gain perseverance in good works, know Thee with my whole heart, do all such things as are pleasing to Thee with a perfect love, meditate upon Thee with a pure mind, and after this life never be separated from Thee. Through.*

VII.

A Prayer to obtain a good end, and remission of sins, both for himself and for his friends.

O Lord God, Father Almighty, Who hast promised rewards to the just and pardon to the penitent, Who wouldest not the death of sinners, neither hast pleasure in the destruction of any that die, I humbly entreat Thee, for the sake of the most Holy Mary, Mother of God, and of all Thy elect Saints, and of Thy own mercy, grant unto me Thy servant, *N.*, remission of all my sins, and bring me to that penitence by which Thou didst save David, didst look graciously upon Peter when he wept, and didst cleanse Mary Magdalene. O Lord Jesu Christ cast out of my heart all things which offend Thee; and pour into me such love that I may be enabled perfectly to love and fear Thee, and neither to think nor desire anything save that which

* These two last prayers are from the Missal of 1520.

I know to be pleasing unto Thee, O Lord. I entreat thee, Blessed Virgin Mary, Temple of the Lord, Sanctuary of the Holy Ghost; I entreat ye also holy Archangels Michael, Gabriel, and Raphael, and all our appointed guardian Angels, and the nine angelic orders, to intercede for me: as also Peter, Paul, Andrew, John, and all Apostles, Martyrs, Confessors, Virgins, Saints, and Elect of God, to deign to protect me when I shall be set before the Tribunal of the Eternal King to be judged. I commend unto Thee, most loving Jesu Christ, all who love or care for me, all who give me pitying aid, all who are indebted to me, or related to me. And likewise for mine enemies, I beseech Thee that Thou wouldest turn them unto peace, and cause them to attain to true penitence. I entreat Thee, O Lord Jesu Christ, mercifully to remember all who are mindful of me, and who have commended themselves to my unworthy prayers, and who have done me any charity or kindness; as well as all who are connected with me by relationship, friendship, or the bonds of faith, whether they be still in the body or have departed this life, and visit them, that they, faithfully serving Thee, may be defended from all adversities; and grant unto them and me deliverance from all punishment, and bring us to everlasting rest. And this I earnestly implore, that whenever the day of my death shall come, Thou Thyself, Who givest judgment against the accusers, wilt become my defender, Who art blessed for ever and ever. Amen.*

VIII.

O God of Compassion and Truth, I humbly entreat Thee in Thy mercy to grant unto me, most wretched, the pardon of my innumerable sins, whereby I have provoked Thy mighty wrath; that, through Thy pity, I may be cleansed according to Thy will in this life, and attain unto a part and lot in eternal happiness. Unto all the faithful also, whether in the body or out of the body, who are united to me in the bonds of the spirit or the flesh, and who in confession, or by request, have commended themselves to me; to all those also whose money and alms I have received, or who have received hurt through my malice or negligence, stretch forth the hand of Thy compassion, and of Thy unspeakable bounty grant them that pardon of their sins which they desire, and bring them to the repose of the blessed. Amen.†

* This and the following prayer are from the Missal of 1533.

† Here follow the Cautels in some Missals.

The Proper of Saints.

THE VIGIL OF S. ANDREW, Ap.

The Office. Matt. iv.

The Lord, walking by the Sea of Galilee, saw two brethren, Peter and Andrew, and he *called* them. Follow Me, and I will make you fishers of men.

Ps. xix. The heavens declare the glory of God, and the firmament sheweth His handywork.

The Collect.

We beseech Thee, Almighty God, let S. Andrew, Thy Apostle, implore Thy aid in our behalf, that we may be absolved from our sins, and delivered from all evil. Through.

Memorial of SS. Saturninus and Sisinnius.

O God, Who permittest us to celebrate the day of Thy blessed Martyrs Saturninus and Sisinnius, grant us Thy help for their sake. Through.

¶ *This Memorial is not made if the Vigil fall in Advent.*

The Lesson.

(See *Less.* i., as on the Vigil of an Apostle.)

Gradual. (See *Grad.* i., in the Common.)

Alleluia. (If on Sundays, *All.* ii., in the Common.)

The Gospel. John i. 35-51.

At that time John stood .... upon the Son of Man.

Offert. As on Vig. Ap.

Secret. We offer, O Lord, this gift to be consecrated unto Thee; whereby we who celebrate the feast of S. Andrew, Thy Apostle, with fasting and holy services, implore also the purification of our minds. Through.

Secret of SS. Saturninus and Sisinnius. Graciously accept, O Lord, the gifts offered unto Thee on the passion of Thy Martyrs, Saturninus and Sisinnius; and, at their intercession, let them be acceptable to Thy Majesty. Through.

Comm. John i. *Andrew said to* his own brother Simon, We have found the Messias, *Who is called* Christ. And he brought him to Jesus.

P. Comm We, who have received the saving Sacrament, humbly pray Thee, O Lord, that, at the intercession of S. Andrew Thy Apostle, our service on his revered feast may further our salvation. Through.

P. Comm. of SS. Saturninus and Sisinnius. We beseech Thee, O Lord, let the holy intercession of S. Saturninus and his fellows ever plead in our behalf, that this Communion make us meet to be visited by Thee. Through.

S. Andrew, *Ap.*

The Office.

(As in the Common.)

¶ *The* Gloria in Excelsis *is said, if this feast occur before Advent.*

The Collect.

We make our humble supplications unto Thy Majesty, O Lord, that like as the Apostle S. Andrew was set to be both preacher and Bishop of Thy Church, so he may ever be our intercessor with Thee. Through.

The Epistle. Rom. x. 10-18.

Brethren, with the heart .... unto the ends of the world.

Gradual. (See *Grad.* iii. in the Comm.)

Alleluia! The Lord loved Andrew as a sweet savour.

The Sequence.

The sacred honours of this festival
With praises due let the whole Church ordain;
The gentlest of the Saints she celebrates,
Andrew, for wondrous grace conspicuous.
When from John Baptist the Apostle learned
That One had come Who should take sins away,
Entering His house forthwith, he heard His word;
And, having found his brother Barjonah,
Rejoicing saith, "Messiah we have found!"
And led him to the Saviour's gentle presence.
By the sea-side Christ called him, and exchanged
His fisher's craft for Apostolic rank—

His soul, after the glorious Paschal Feast,
The Holy Ghost did hallow by His power,
And sent him forth to call men to repentance,
And through the Son show God the Father's mercy,
In such a Father boast thyself, Achaia!
Illuminated by his saving doctrine,
Honoured by divers signs and miracles.
Lament and groan, fierce murderer Egeas,
Thee plagues of hell and death eternal hold;
Whilst Andrew through the Cross in joy abides.
Now thou dost see thy King; now thou adorest;
Now, Andrew, in His presence Thou dost stand.
Sweet odours now Thou dost inhale
Of love divine the spicy gale.
Be thou to us an excellent perfume;
Health-breathing balsam of the life to come.

The Gospel. Matt. iv. 18-22.

At that time Jesus .... and followed Him.

The Creed.

Offert. (See *Offert.* iii. in the Common.)

Secret. We beseech Thee, O Lord, let the holy prayers of S. Andrew obtain for our sacrifice Thy favour, that it may be made acceptable for his sake, in honour of whom it is solemnly set forth. Through.

Comm. Matt. iv. Follow Me, and I will make you fishers of men; *and* they left their nets *and the ship*, and followed *the Lord.*

P. Comm. We who have received with joy the Divine Mysteries on the feast of S. Andrew, beseech Thee, O Lord, that as Thou causest Thy saints to be thereby glorified, so they may also prevail for our pardon. Through.

¶ *Throughout the Octave the same Mass is said, except the Mass* Salus populi *should be sung, or Our Lady's Mass on Saturday. In Advent, there is only a Memorial of the Octave, except on the Octave Day; but should this be Saturday or Sunday, the Mass of the Octave is said in the Chapter-house, with one Collect only. This is also done, though S. Andrew's Day itself be translated; as well as when S. Nicholas and the Octave Day fall together. Cf.: the Octave of S. Laurence and passim.*

THE DEPOSITION OF S. OSMUND, *Conf. Bp.*

¶ *All as* i. *in the Common, except* Grad. *and* Offert. ii. *in the same.*

S. NICHOLAS, *Conf. Bp.*

¶ *The* Office, Epistle, Alleluia, Gospel, *and* Offert, i., Grad. iv. *and* Comm. ii. *in the Common.*

The Collect.

O God, Who didst distinguish Blessed Nicholas, Thy Bishop, by divers miracles, grant, we beseech Thee, that for his sake and prayers we may be delivered from the flames of hell. Through.

The Sequence.

Now triumphing in concord meet
  Let us our voices raise,
Upon this yearly festival
  S. Nicholas to praise.
Who fasted while an infant yet
  He did in cradle lie;
And at the very breast began
  To merit joys on high.
To learning he rejoiced in youth
  His reason to apply;
Refraining from all vicious stains
  Of sensuality.
A blest Confessor; such his dignity
  A voice from Heaven proclaimed;
By which advancing to the highest grade
  Of Bishop he is named.
Firm in his soul all excellence
  Of piety was found;
And many kindnesses he showed
  To the oppressed around.
By gifts of gold he from disgrace
  The virgins' honour saved,
Relieving too their fathers' need,
  By poverty depraved.

Whilst certain shipmen made voyage,
Contending with the ocean's rage,
  Their vessel lost well nigh;
When now of safety they despair,
In danger's height uplifting prayer
  All with one voice outcry:

O Nicholas, thou blessed saint!
In bitterness of death we faint,
  Us to some harbour lead;
Lead us to some safe sheltering place,
Thou who dost by thy kindly grace
  So many help in need;

While yet, and not in vain, they cried,
"Lo! I am present," one replied,
  "For your protection sent."

Forthwith a gentle breeze arose,
The roaring seas sank to repose,
The tempest's rage was spent.

Out of his tomb of holy oil
Distils a fountain rare;
Diseases at its touch recoil,
By virtue of his prayer:

We who in this sad world abide,
Already shipwrecked in the tide
Of guilt and sin and pain,
Thee, glorious Nicholas, we pray
To that safe harbour shew the way,
Where peace and glory reign.

That unction unto us accord,
By intercession to the Lord,
Whereby the sins He healèd then
Which wounded Mary Magdalen.

Let those who celebrate his feast
Rejoice for evermore;
And Christ reward them with a crown
When this life's race is o'er.

Secret. Sanctify, O Lord, we beseech Thee, these gifts which we offer in reverence of Thy holy Bishop Nicholas, that through them our life may ever be guided both in prosperity and adversity. Through.

P. Comm. We beseech Thee, O Lord, that the sacrifice we have received on the feast of Thy holy Bishop Nicholas may strengthen us with everlasting protection. Through.

THE OCTAVE OF S. ANDREW.

¶ *All as on the Day except—*

The Collect.

We beseech Thee, O Lord, that the repeated feast of Thy Apostle S. Andrew be our protection; that we may have a sense of his perpetual defence, whose succour we call to mind with pious devotion. Through.

The Gospel. Mark i. 14-18.

At that time, after that John was put in prison, came Jesus .... and followed Him.

Secret. We beseech Thee, O Lord, that these gifts which are offered together with the prayers of Thy Apostle S. Andrew, procure for us abundant pardon. Through.

P. Comm. O Lord, we beseech Thee, let Thy Apostle S. Andrew bestow on us the protection which we desire; to which end let the saving Sacrament we have received be profitable to us. Through.

The Conception of Blessed Mary.

The Office.

Let us all rejoice in the Lord, and celebrate this feast in honour of the Virgin Mary, at whose Conception Angels rejoice and praise the Son of God.

Ps. xlv. My heart is inditing of a good matter: I speak of the things which I have made unto the King.

The Collect.

O God, mercifully hear the supplication of Thy servants; that we who are assembled together on the Conception of the Virgin Mother of God, may at her intercession be delivered by Thee from the dangers which beset us. Through.

The Lesson. Eccles. xxiv. 17-21.

As the vine .... they that work by me shall not do amiss.

Gradual. (See *Comm.* iv. Virg. Mart.)

Alleluia! ℣. *The Conception of the glorious Virgin Mary who sprang from the seed of Abraham, of the tribe of Judah, of the root of David.*

The Sequence.

Let us celebrate this day
Whereon piously we say
Mary was conceived.
Begotten is the Mother Maid,
Conceived, created, channel made
Of pardon to the world.
Adam's primeval banishment
And Joseph's childless discontent
There find a remedy.

* This the Prophets have foreshown,
This was to the Patriarchs known:
The Virgin whence a flower should spring,
The Star which forth the Sun should bring,
On this day is conceived;
The flower which from the rod should bloom,
The Sun which of the Star should come,
Is Christ interpreted.

O how happy, O how fair!
Sweet to us, to God how dear,
Hath this Conception been!
Misery now is at an end,
Mercy doth on earth descend,
For sorrow joy is seen.
A Mother new new offspring bears,
From a new Star new Sun appears,
New grace doth all inspire;
The Mother bears the Generator,
The Creature brings forth the Creator,
The Daughter bears the Sire;

O Unexampled novelty!
O new, unheard of dignity!
The Mother's holy chastity
The Son's Conception shows.
Rejoice, O gracious Virgin mild!
Fair rod with blossoms undefiled,
Mother ennobled by her Child,
Such grace no other knows.

That which lay hid, in figure sealed,
By clouds mysterious concealed,
The future Mother hath revealed,
For once a Virgin pure and good
Reversed the laws of Motherhood:
Nature, surprised, beheld a flood
Of Deity outpoured.

. . . .

* It is impossible satisfactorily to translate this stanza, the point of which depends upon a play on the words *Eva* and *Ave*, which often occurs elsewhere, and is necessarily lost in English:—

Triste fuit in Eva ve,
Sed ex Eva formans Ave,
Versa vice, sed non prave
Intus ferens in conclave
Verbum bonum et suave
Nobis, Mater Virgo, fave
Tua frui gratia.

Whoe'r thou art, without delay
Open thy lips, her praises pay;
Offer her homage, to her pray
At every hour, on every day.
With swelling voice, with spirit sage,
By supplicating prayer engage
  A portion in her patronage.

Thou of the sad art comfort sure,
True Mother of the orphans poor,
Of the opprest the help secure,
Thou of the sick the healing cure,
  All things to all thou givest.
With one consent we ask of thee,
Whom praise awaits especially,
Conduct us wanderers o'er this sea
Unto salvation's port, where we
  By grace may be at rest. Amen.

The Gospel. Matt. i. 1-16.

The book of the generation .... Who is called Christ.

The Creed.

Offert. (See *All.* iv. Virg. Mart.)

Secret. O Lord, let the Human Nature of Thine Only-begotten succour us, that He, Who being born of a Virgin diminished not but sanctified the chastity of His Mother, may put away our offences from us on the feast of her Conception, and make our oblations acceptable to Himself, even Jesus Christ our Lord. Who.

Comm. Thy Son's true faith hath cleansed the world of sin. Immaculate thy virginity abideth.

P. Comm. Grant, we beseech Thee, O Lord, that the Sacrament which we have received of our bounden duty on this yearly Celebration, may, at the intercession of Blessed Mary, ever Virgin, afford us relief in this present life and in the world to come. Through.

S. LUCY, *Virg. Mart.*

¶ *All as* i. *in the Common, except* Offert. ii. *in the same.*

Secret. O Lord, we beseech Thee, look upon the gifts to be joyfully dedicated, which we humbly offer unto Thy Name on the feast of S. Lucy, Thy Virgin and Martyr. Through.

P. Comm. O Lord, we beseech Thee, let the prayers of S. Lucy, Virgin and Martyr, be pleasing and reconcile us unto Thee, that we may so perceive the saving efficacy of the holy Sacrament we have received. Through.

THE VIGIL OF S. THOMAS.

¶ *All as on Vig. Ap. If this occur on the Ember Days, let there be only a Memorial at Mass; otherwise let the Mass be of the Vigil.*

S. Thomas, *Ap.*

¶ *All as in the Common, except—*

The Collect.

Grant unto us, we beseech Thee, O Lord, so to rejoice in the feast of S. Thomas Thy Apostle, that we may both be ever aided by his protection, and follow his faith with befitting devotion. Through.

The Gospel. John xx. 24-29.

At that time Thomas .... and yet have believed.

The Creed.

Secret. O Lord, we render unto Thee our bounden duty and service, humbly imploring that Thou wouldest watch over Thy gifts in us, at the prayers of S. Thomas, Thy Apostle, in honour of whose confession we offer unto Thee the sacrifice of praise. Through.

Comm. John xx. Reach hither Thy hand, and *behold the print of the nails. Alleluia!* And be not faithless, but believing. *Alleluia, Alleluia.*

P. Comm. O merciful God, let the receiving of the Divine Sacrament, and the intercession of S. Thomas, Thy Apostle, be profitable to Thy people, that they may unceasingly ask for the salvation of soul and body, and have the same abundantly bestowed upon them. Through.

S. FELIX, Mart. Bp.

¶ *The* Office iii., Grad. *and* Alleluia ii. *in the Comm. Conf. Bp.*, Epistle iv., Gospel ii., Offert. v., *and* Comm. iii. *in Comm. Mart.*

The Collect.

Grant, we beseech Thee, Almighty God, that the example of S. Felix, Thy Martyr and Bishop, may stir us up to a better life, to the intent that we may also imitate the acts of him whose feast we celebrate. Through.

Secret. Graciously receive, O Lord, the sacrifice dedicated to Thee, for the sake of S. Felix, Thy Martyr and Bishop; and grant that it may prevail for our perpetual succour. Through.

P. Comm. We, who receive Thy Holy Sacrament, humbly pray Thee, O Lord, that we may have a sense of the protection of S. Felix, Thy Martyr and Bishop, whose feast we celebrate. Through.

S. MAUR, Conf. Abb.

¶ *All as in the Common, except* Office i. *and* Comm. vi. *in Comm. Mart., and* Alleluia ii. *in Comm. Conf. Bp.*

The Collect.

O God, Who hast granted to S. Maur, Deacon and Abbot, a portion in eternal glory, mercifully grant us an entrance into the heavenly kingdom at his intercession, by whose example we are taught to live aright. Through.

Secret. Graciously sanctify the gifts of Thy Church, O Lord; and grant that by this Holy Communion, at the intercession of S. Maur, Thy Confessor and Abbot, we may be refreshed with the Bread of Heaven. Through.

P. Comm. We humbly beseech Thee, Almighty God, that, at the intercession of S. Maur, Thy Confessor and Abbot, Thou wouldest both multiply Thy gifts in us and direct our days. Through.

S. MARCELLUS, Mart. Pope.

¶ *The* Office, Offert., *and* Comm. i. *Comm. Conf. Bp.*; Grad. iii., Alleluia iv., *and* Gospel iii. *in the same*; Epistle i. *in the Common*.

The Collect.

We beseech Thee, O Lord, mercifully hear the prayers of Thy people; that we may be assisted, for the sake of Thy Martyr and Bishop Marcellus, in whose passion we rejoice. Through.

Secret. We beseech Thee, O Lord, that, by the saving intercession of S. Marcellus, Thy Martyr and Bishop, the gifts we have offered may be profitable to our salvation. Through.

P. Comm. Grant, we beseech Thee, O Lord, that we who have received and are nourished by Thy Sacrament, may be aided by the prayers of S. Marcellus, Thy Martyr and Bishop. Through.

S. SULPICIUS, Conf. Bp.*

¶ *The* Office *and* Comm. iii., Grad. *and* Gospel i., Alleluia vi., *and* Offert. ii. *in the Common*; Epistle i., *in Comm. Conf.*

The Collect.

Grant, we beseech Thee, Almighty God, that we who commemorate the burial of S. Sulpicius, Thy Confessor and Bishop, may be aided by his intercession with Thee. Through.

Secret. O Lord, we beseech Thee, let the oblation which we present on the commemoration of S. Sulpicius, Thy Confessor and Bishop, together with our supplications, appear with acceptance before Thee; and, at his prayers, abundantly bestow upon us Thy favour. Through.

P. Comm. O Lord, we beseech Thee, let Thy holy Sacrament afford us protection; and for the sake, and at the intercession of S. Sulpicius, Thy Confessor and Bishop, absolve us from all our sins. Through.

* In the Calendar, S. Anthony Conf. is mentioned as being kept this day. Presumably, the Service was taken out of the Common of Saints.

S. PRISCA, Virg. Mart.

¶ *The* Office *and* Grad. ii., Epistle, Gospel, *and* Offert. i., Alleluia *and* Comm. iii. *in the Common. If this or any other feast of three lessons fall between LXX and Ash-Wednesday, no* Alleluia *is said, nor* Tract. *The* Grad. *is only doubled.*

The Collect.

Grant, we beseech Thee, Almighty God, that we who keep the day of S. Prisca, Thy Virgin and Martyr, may both rejoice in her annual feast, and profit by the example of so great faith. Through.

Secret. We beseech Thee, O Lord, graciously accept our gifts; and, at the intercession of S. Prisca, Thy Virgin and Martyr, turn the hearts of us all to the observance of true religion. Through.

P. Comm. We beseech Thee, O Lord, let these sacred Mysteries which we have received, and the holy intercession of S. Prisca, Thy Virgin and Martyr, aid us. Through.

S. WULSTAN, *Conf. Bp.*

¶ *All as* i. *in the Common, except* Grad. iv., Alleluia v., *and* Comm. ii. *in the same.*

The Collect.

We beseech Thee, O God, pour out the spirit of Thy love upon us, that, at the intercession of S. Wulstan, Thy Confessor and Bishop, we may be counted worthy to taste of Thy delights in everlasting happiness. Through.

Secret. Receive, O Lord, we beseech Thee, the oblation of Thy family which prayeth; and, at the intercession of S. Wulstan, let Thy loving-kindness bestow on us that which by reason of our guilty consciences we dare not hope for. Through.

P. Comm. We, who have been fed with the Mystery of Thy Salvation, humbly implore Thy mercy, O Lord, that his prayers whose guidance and protection Thou hast given may never fail us. Through.

SS. FABIAN AND SEBASTIAN, MM.

¶ *All as* i. *in the Common, except* Gospel v., Offert. iii., *and* Comm. ii. *in the same. If this or any other feast of nine lessons fall before LXX. or XL., until Palm Sunday, the* Tract *is said as in the Common, and no* Sequence *or* Alleluia; *and if a Double, it is said until Maundy Thursday. On Candlemass, Lady-day, or the Dedication of a Church, a* Sequence *is said, however. If it is a feast of three lessons, no* Tract *is said, but the* Gradual *is doubled.*

The Collect.

O God, Who didst strengthen SS. Fabian and Sebastian, Thy Martyrs, with the virtue of constancy in suffering, grant us, for the love of Thee, in imitation of them to despise the good things of the world, and to fear none of its adversities. Through.

Secret. We beseech Thee, O Lord, let the offering of our service be acceptable in Thy sight, and further our salvation at their prayers on whose martyrdom it is offered. Through.

P. Comm. We humbly beseech Thee, O Lord, that we who are fulfilled with the blessing of Thy Sacrament, and defended by the glorious confession of Thy holy Martyrs Fabian and Sebastian, may thereby be cleansed from all sin. Through.

S. AGNES, *Virg. Mart.*

¶ *The* Office, Gradual, *and* Offert. iii., Epistle *and* Alleluia ii., Gospel i., *and* Comm. v. *in the Common.*

The Collect.

Almighty and everlasting God, Who dost choose the weak things of the world to confound the things which are mighty, mercifully grant that we who keep the feast of S. Agnes, Thy Martyr, may have a sense of her protection with Thee. Through.

Secret. Accept, O Lord, we beseech Thee, the Sacrifice, by the offering of which Thou hast deigned to be pleased; and grant that, at the intercession of S. Agnes, Thy Virgin and Martyr, the service of our souls which we offer may, by the effectual working of this ordinance, be well-pleasing to Thee. Through.

P. Comm. We, being refreshed by the Divine Offering, beseech Thee, O Lord our God, that, at the intercession of S. Agnes, Thy Virgin and Martyr, we may find help in this life and happiness in life eternal. Through.

S. VINCENT, *Mart.*

¶ *The* Office *and* Offert. v., Epistle iii., Grad., Gospel, *and* Comm. i., *and* Alleluia ii. *in the Common.*

The Collect.

Be present, O Lord, at our supplications, that we whose consciences by sin are accused, may, at the intercession of Thy Martyr S. Vincent, be delivered. Through.

The Sequence.

This day the Lord girds with a robe of gladness
His faithful soldier Vincent: Alleluia!
With more than wonted acclamation, now
Let the assembled company rejoice.

This day the Martyr brave to God
Brought pleasing offering;
This day the fiery torment bare
And cruel suffering:

And from the aged Saint's address
Drawing encouragement,
Refused not to submit his limbs
To sharpest punishment.

Before the judge's presence cited,
Touching the Church's faith united
They inquisition make:
He is not caught by guile concealed,
Doth not to bitter torture yield,
Nor Constancy forsake.

Thus Dacianus mocked appears,
While the undaunted Martyr fears
No bitterness of pain;
And to his baffled torturers' crowd
Abundant thanks to give aloud
His love doth not refrain.

The Prefect, fiercely angered,
Bade next prepare the fiery bed:
The bowels of that insolent
Are by the flaming wicker brent.

The Martyr strains in that fell strife
Hoping to win the crown of life,
Which faithful combatants shall gain
Who for Christ's sake the fight maintain.

For his triumphant warfare's sake
The courts of Heaven rejoicings make;
Because this day he gained success
O'er ministers of wickedness.

That we his countenance may gain,
And so the gift of life obtain,
On this his yearly Festival
Let joy throughout our choir prevail:
And in the Church with cheerful sound
Let Alleluias echo round.

Secret. We beseech Thee, O Lord, at the intercession of Thy glorious Martyr Vincent let the Sacrifice of Reconciliation which we have offered be made acceptable unto Thee. Through.

P. Comm. We beseech Thee, O Lord, defend us, by virtue of the Sacrament which we have received, in answer to the prayers of Thy Martyr, S. Vincent. Through.

THE CONVERSION OF S. PAUL.

The Office.

Let us all rejoice in the Lord, and solemnly celebrate this day, in the which S. Paul made this world glorious by his Conversion.

Ps. Concerning the enlightenment of holy preaching, and Conversion of S. Paul.

The Collect.

O God, Who, through the preaching of Thy Apostle S. Paul, hast instructed the whole world; grant, we beseech Thee, that we this day, having his Conversion in remembrance, may by his example attain unto Thee. Through.

Memorial of S. Prejectus.

We beseech Thee, O Lord, that the glorious intercession of S. Prejectus, Thy Martyr, may commend us unto Thee; that we may obtain at his prayers what we deserve not by our own actions. Through.

The Lesson. Acts ix. 1-22.

In those days, Saul .... that this is very Christ.

Gradual. Gal. ii. He that wrought effectually in Peter to the Apostleship, was also mighty in me toward the Gentiles; and *they* perceived the grace that was given unto me.

℣. 1 Cor. xv. *The* grace *of God* which is in me was not in vain, *but His grace ever abideth in me.*

Alleluia! ℣. *Great Saint Paul, the* chosen vessel, *is very worthy to be extolled.*

The Sequence.

The Feast of holy Paul let us devoutly keep,
Whom with such grace the Lord endowed, that he
Is by the Church called Teacher of the Gentiles.
The wolf a lamb, the persecutor preacher
Becomes; with actions changed the name is changed—
Paul he is called who Saul was called before,
By madness urged he poisonous rage breathed forth:
Christ's members with fell cruelty pursuing.
A light from heaven shining round about him
Of sight deprived him, but within enlightened.
Christ buffets him, lest he should be exalted;
He casts him down, but raises him while falling:
Rebukes him prostrate, but rebuking heals him.
To him the teaching of the faith commits,
Ordains him a defender of the Church.
To him, who once had been an enemy,
Believing, the deep mysteries reveals
Which were not lawful for a man to utter.
Him whom at first the Synagogue brought up
Afterwards Mother Church rejoices over.
Those mysteries which he had learned, he went
Through the whole world to publish by his preaching.
He comes to Rome, and there one God proclaims;
Nero resists, who worshipped images.
Forthwith he puts him to a cruel death;
From the world takes him, sends him to the stars.
Whither may God bring us, too, of his mercy
Through aid of holy Paul's prayers. Alleluia!

¶ *If in LXX. or XL. the following* Tract *is said instead of the* Sequence.

Tract. Thou art the chosen vessel, holy Paul, an Apostle very worthy to be extolled.

℣. The preacher of Truth, and Teacher of the Gentiles in faith and verity.

℣. Through thee all nations have known the grace of God.

℣. Intercede for us to God, Who chose thee.

The Gospel. Matt. xix. 27-29.

At that time, Simon Peter said *to Jesus,* Behold .... everlasting life.

The Creed.

Offert. Ps. cxxxix. How dear are Thy counsels unto me, O God; O how great is the sum of them!

Secret. We beseech Thee, O Lord, at the prayers of Thy Apostle S. Paul, sanctify the gifts of Thy people; that those things which are pleasing to Thee by reason of Thine own ordinance, may, by the aid of his prayers, be made yet more acceptable. Through.

Secret of S. Prejectus. O Lord, graciously receive our prayers, together with the oblations laid upon Thine Altar; and, at the prayers of S. Prejectus, Thy Martyr, cause them graciously to be acceptable to Thee. Through.

Comm. Matt. xix. Verily, I say unto you, that ye which have *forsaken all and* followed Me, shall receive an hundredfold, and shall inherit everlasting life.

P. Comm. We, being refreshed by the saving Mystery, beseech Thee, Almighty God, that, as Thou hast willed this day to be had in honour for the Conversion of Thy Apostle S. Paul, so Thou wouldst cause us to turn away from sin, and evermore to rejoice in Thy service. Through.

P. Comm. of S. Prejectus. Grant, we beseech Thee, O Lord our God, that, like as on the feast of S. Prejectus, Thy Martyr, we rejoice in the present Mystery, so we may be gladdened by its perpetual vision. Through.

S. JULIAN, Conf Bp.

¶ *The* Office *and* Gradual i., Alleluia, Offert., *and* Comm. ii., *and* Gospel iii. *in the Common;* Epistle i. *in Comm. Conf. Doct.*

The Collect.

O God, Who didst give S. Julian to be a wondrous teacher of Thy Church; mercifully grant that we may ever have him as our devout intercessor with Thee. Through.

Secret. Look, we beseech Thee, O Lord, upon our offerings; and, for the sake of the holy Bishop Julian, put away all our sins from us. Through.

P. Comm. We, being filled with the Divine Sacrament, humbly beseech Thee, O Lord, for the sake of the holy Bishop Julian, to make us worthy of Thy heavenly ordinances. Through.

THE SECOND FEAST OF S. AGNES, Virg. Mart.

¶ *The* Office, *Comm. Many Virg.;* Epistle i., *Comm. Virg. not Mart.;* Grad. *and* Offert. ii., Gospel *and* Alleluia v., *and* Comm. iv. *in the Common.*

The Collect.

O God, Who dost gladden us with the yearly feast of S. Agnes,

Thy Martyr, grant that we may follow the example of her holy conversation, whom in this Office we honour. Through.

Secret. We beseech Thee, O Lord, let our gifts be acceptable to Thee, whereby the glorious feast of S. Agnes, Thy Virgin Martyr, is again celebrated. Through.

P. Comm. We beseech Thee, O Lord, let the holy Mysteries which we have received preserve us outwardly in our bodies, and inwardly in our souls; and, at the intercession of S. Agnes, Thy Martyr, bestow upon us present and eternal mercy. Through.

S. BATILD, Virg. Queen.

¶ *The* Office, Alleluia i., Epistle *and* Grad. ii. *in the Common*; Gospel, Offert. iii., *and* Comm. iv. *in Comm. Virg. Mart.*

The Collect.

We beseech Thee, O Lord, let Thy Church devoutly celebrate the holy day of S. Batild, both waxing more fervent through love of the great glory bestowed on her, and profiting by the example of so great faith. Through.

Secret. O Lord, let these gifts be acceptable to Thee, for the sake of S. Batild, who presented herself a living, holy, and well-pleasing sacrifice to Thee. Through.

P. Comm. We, being satisfied with heavenly food, beseech Thy loving-kindness, Almighty Father, that, at the intercession of S. Batild, we may obtain the grace of Thy compassion. Through.

S. BRIDGET, Virg.

¶ *The* Office *Comm. Many Virg.*; Alleluia iii. *and* Comm. v., *Comm. Virg. Mart.*; Epistle *and* Grad. i., Gospel *and* Offert, ii. *in the Common.*

The Collect.

We beseech Thee, O Lord, let the prayers of S. Bridget, Thy Virgin, which are pleasing to Thee, aid us, and never cease to entreat Thy loving-kindness towards us. Through.

Secret. We beseech Thee, O Lord, that, being reconciled unto Thee by the Sacrifice we have offered, Thou wouldst, at the intercession of S. Bridget, Thy Virgin, graciously succour us in our time. Through.

P. Comm. Let the gifts we have received, O Lord, commend to Thee Thy faithful, for the sake of blessed Bridget, Thy Virgin, and let her who pleased Thee implore aid for us. Through.

The Purification of the Blessed Virgin Mary.

THE BLESSING OF THE CANDLES.

¶ *Sext being sung, let the Blessing of the Candles, be solemnly begun by the Bishop or Priest, in a silk cope and the other vestments, on the highest step of the Altar, turning to the East, and saying:*

℣. The Lord be with you.

℟. And with thy spirit.

Let us pray.

Bl + ess, O Lord Jesu Christ, this creature of wax for us who pray to Thee; and pour Thy heavenly blessing upon it, by virtue of the Holy Cross, that, as Thou hast permitted it to be used by men to dispel darkness, such may be the measure of power and benediction which it receiveth by the sign of Thy Holy Cross, that whereinsoever it shall be lighted or set up, the Devil may depart in fear and trembling, and flee away, with all his, out of those dwellings, nor presume any more to disquiet [*Here let him chant*] them that serve Thee. Who, with God the Father and the Holy Ghost, livest and reignest God, world without end. Amen

Let us pray.

O Lord, Holy Father, Almighty and everlasting God, Who didst create all things out of nothing, and by the labour of bees at Thy command hast brought this fluid to the perfection of wax; and Who, on this day, didst fulfil the desire of righteous Simeon: we humbly beseech Thee, that by the invocation of Thy Holy Name, and at the intercession of Blessed Mary, ever Virgin, whose festival we this day devoutly celebrate, and at the prayers of all Thy saints, Thou wouldst vouchsafe to bl + ess and sanc + tify these candles, fashioned for the service of men, and for the good of their souls and bodies, whether on land or water; and mercifully hear from Thy holy Heaven, and from the seat of Thy Majesty, the voice of this Thy people, who desire reverently to bear them in their hands, and to praise and exalt Thee; and show mercy to all that cry unto Thee, whom Thou hast redeemed with the precious Blood of Thy beloved Son. Who.

Let us pray.

Almighty and everlasting God, Who on this day wast pleased that Thy Only Begotten should be presented in the Temple, and be taken into the arms of holy Simeon; we humbly beseech Thy mercy to bl + ess, sanc + tify, and give the light of Thy heavenly benediction to these candles, which we Thy servants desire to take up and carry in honour of Thy name: to the end that by offering them to Thee, our Lord God, we being inflamed by the fire of Thy amiable brightness, may be made worthy to be presented in the holy Temple of Thy glory.* [*Here let him begin to chant.*] Through the same, Thy Son, Jesus Christ our Lord, Who liveth and reigneth with Thee in the unity of the Holy Ghost, God.

℣. World without end.

℟. Amen.

℣. The Lord be with you.

℟. And with thy spirit.

℣. Lift up your hearts.

℟. We lift them up unto the Lord.

℣. Let us give thanks unto our Lord God.

℟. It is meet and right so to do.

It is very meet, just, right, and our bounden duty that we should at all times, and in all places, give thanks unto Thee, O Lord, Holy Father, Almighty Everlasting God, Fount and Source of all Light, Who hast enlightened the world with the beams of Thy Brightness, by sending Thy Only Begotten Son to us, in the womb of a pure Virgin. Him Whom long before Thou hast promised by the mouth of the Prophets, Thou hast sent in these last days a Light to the people which sat in darkness. We therefore pray Thee, O Lord, vouchsafe to bl + ess with Thy benediction these candles prepared for Thy Name, Who hast translated us from the power of darkness into the light and Kingdom of Thy dear Son, by Whom light hath sprung up in darkness to the upright in heart, and the joys of eternal salvation; and Who hast fulfilled the desire of just Simeon that he should not see death before he had beheld with his eyes the Incarnation of the same Christ Thy Son, the Light and Salvation of the whole world; so fill us with the brightness of Thy light that all dark clouds of unbelief may be driven away; and as on this day Thou didst let Thy servant depart in peace, even so vouchsafe to guide us in the peace of Thy holy Church, that we may be enabled to enter the haven of eternal rest; that so the true light may pour its beams upon us; and in the last day we, in company with hymning bands of angels, may attain with joy unto the vision of the face of the Sun which never faileth. [*Here let him read.*] Who with Thee, in the unity of the Holy Ghost, liveth and reigneth, God, world without end.

℟. Amen.

¶ *Here let the candles be sprinkled with holy water and censed.*

℣. The Lord be with you.
℟. And with thy spirit.

Let us pray.

O Lord, Holy Father Almighty, unfailing Light, Who art the Maker of all light, bl + ess this light to be borne by Thy faithful in honour of Thy Name, to the intent that we, being sanctified by Thee and blessed by the brightness of Thy light, may be kindled and illuminated: and mercifully grant that, as of old time Thou didst cause the face of Thy servant Moses to shine with the same fire, our hearts and senses may be so illuminated that we may be found meet to attain unto the vision of eternal brightness. Through.

Let us pray.

Almighty and everlasting God, Who didst send into the world Thy Only Begotten Son before the worlds, but in due time incarnate of the Virgin Mary, to be the true and unfailing Light to dispel the darkness of mankind, and to kindle the light of faith and truth; mercifully grant that, like as we are outwardly enlightened by this natural light, so Thy spiritual rays may inwardly shine upon us. Through.

¶ *The benediction of the candles being ended, let them be lighted and distributed, and meanwhile let this Anthem be sung:*

Ant. A light to lighten the Gentiles, and to be the glory of Thy people Israel.

Ps. Lord, now lettest Thou Thy servant depart in peace according to Thy Word.

A light.
For mine eyes have seen Thy salvation.
A light.
Which Thou hast preoared before the face of all people. To be.
A light.
Glory be. A light. As it was. A light.

¶ *Let Mass follow.*

The Office. Ps. xlviii.

We wait for Thy loving-kindness, O God: in the midst of Thy temple; O God, according to Thy Name so is Thy praise unto the world's end: Thy right hand is full of righteousness.

Ps. Great is the Lord, and highly to be praised: in the city of our God, even upon His holy hill.

The Collect.

Almighty and everlasting God, we humbly beseech Thy Majesty that, as Thy Only Begotten Son was this day presented in the Temple in the substance of our flesh, so we may be presented unto Thee with pure heart. Through.

The Lesson. Mal. iii. 1-4.

Thus saith the Lord God, Behold .... as in former years, *said the Lord Almighty.*

Gradual. Ps. xlviii. We wait for Thy loving-kindness, O God: in the midst of Thy temple. O *Lord,* according unto Thy Name so is Thy praise unto the world's end.

℣. Like as we have heard, so have we seen in the city of our God: even upon His holy hill.

Alleluia! ℣. Ps. cxxxviii. I will worship toward Thy holy temple, and praise Thy Name.

The Sequence.

¶ *This is said even in LXX.*

On this bright day the festive band gives praise,
And in sweet concert calls on Mary's name.
  Purest of Virgins, thou alone divine
  Queen of the world; salvation's cause thou art,
  The gate of light and heaven, full of grace.
To her was erst th' angelic message sent,
"Hail, Mary! of God's grace for ever full,

(*The above verse is said thrice on this day only.*)

Thou among women blessed ever, Virgin,
And Mother spotless; glorious in thine offspring."
To which address thus Mary answering said:
"How can these things thou tell'st of be in me,
Seeing I certainly know not a man.
And am myself born undefiled of man?"
To whom the Angel thus gives holy answer:
"The Holy Ghost shall come upon Thee, Mary;
And thou shalt give new cause of joy to heaven
By bringing in thy Son into the world;
Bearing within the cloister of thy womb
Him Who doth govern the expanse of heaven,
Who upon earth in all times giveth peace."

¶ *Then let the Priest and his Ministers, in their seats near the Altar, say privately:*

Tract. Luke ii. Lord, now lettest Thou Thy Servant depart in peace, according to Thy Word.

℣. For mine eyes have seen Thy salvation.

℣. Which Thou hast prepared: before the face of all people.

℣. To be a light to lighten the Gentiles: and to be the glory of Thy people Israel.

The Gospel. Luke ii. 22-32.

At that time, when the days .... Thy people Israel.

The Creed.

Offert. Ps. xlv. Full of grace are Thy lips: because God hath blessed thee for ever.

Secret. Grant, we beseech Thee, Almighty God, that as on this day the gifts are consecrated by the adorable Oblation of Thy Son, so at the prayers of his glorious Mother the brightness of everlasting light may be bestowed upon us. Through.

Comm. Luke ii. It was revealed unto *Simeon* by the Holy Ghost that he should not see death before he had seen the Lord's Christ.

P. Comm. We beseech Thee, O Lord our God, that, at the intercession of the blessed ever-Virgin Mary, Thou wouldest make the sacred Mysteries we have received for our strengthening and amendment of life a restoring aid in this world and in that which is to come. Through.

S. BLASE, Mart. Bp.

¶ *The* Office iii., Grad. iv. *Comm. Conf. Bp.*; Epistle *and* Alleluia i. *in the Common*; Sequence *or* Tract *and* Comm. *as in the same*; Gospel *and* Offert v. *in Comm. Mart.*

The Collect.

Let Thy blessed Martyr Blase, O Lord, implore the aid of Thy loving-kindness for us, that we may be sensible of his protection whose feast we celebrate. Through.

Secret. We offer these oblations unto Thy Majesty, O Lord, and pray that they may be accepted at the intercession of Thy Martyr and Bishop S. Blase, in whom the love of Thy Son our Lord Jesus Christ did burn brightly. Who.

P. Comm. We beseech Thee, O Lord, let the Mysteries which we have received on the commemoration of Thy Martyr and Bishop S. Blase, preserve us who this day commemorate his suffering with devout service. Through.

S. AGATHA, *Virg. Mart.*

The Office.

Let us all rejoice in the Lord and keep this feast day in honour of Agatha the Martyr, on whose passion Angels rejoice and praise the Son of God.

Ps. xlv. My heart is inditing of a good matter : I will speak of the things which I have made unto the King.

The Collect.

O God, Who amidst other miracles of Thy power hast bestowed even on weak woman the victory of martyrdom, mercifully grant that we who keep the day of S. Agatha, Thy Virgin Martyr, may by her example attain unto Thee. Through.

¶ *The* Lesson *and* Offert. ii., Alleluia i, Sequence *or* Tract, *and* Gospel *as in the Common.*

Gradual. Ps. xlvi. God shall help her *with his countenance:* God is in the midst of her, therefore shall she not be removed.

℣. The rivers of the flood thereof shall make glad the city of God : the holy place of the Tabernacle of the Most Highest.

Secret. In commemoration of S. Agatha, Thy Virgin Martyr, O Lord, we lay upon Thy Altar the mystical gifts, humbly beseeching Thy Majesty that for her sake we may be found worthy to be freed from all evil. Through.

Comm. He Who was pleased to heal me of all my sickness, and to restore my breast, upon Him I call, the living God.

P. Comm. We beseech Thee, O Lord, protect Thy family who have received the food of Thy heavenly Mystery, that at the intercession of S. Agatha, Thy Virgin Martyr, we may of Thy bounty attain unto the healing medicine of eternal salvation, which by Thy inspiration we long after. Through.

SS. VEDASTUS AND AMANDUS, Conff. Bps.

¶ *All as in the Common.*

The Collect.

Be present, O Lord, with Thy people that prayeth under the protection of Thy holy Confessors and Bishops Vedastus and Amandus, that what they have no confidence in themselves to ask they may attain for the sake of their intercessors, who are pleasing unto Thee. Through.

Secret. We bring to Thine Altar, O Lord, the sacrifice of praise, humbly praying that it may be commended unto Thee by their aid in whose honour we make this offering by Thy tender mercy. Through.

P. Comm. O Lord, we, receiving the Divine Mystery, humbly beseech Thee that, at the prayers of Thy holy Confessors and Bishops Vedastus and Amandus, it may ever work in us our sanctification. Through.

S. SCHOLASTICA, Virg.

¶ *All as* i. *in the Common, except* Epistle *and* Grad. ii. *in the same.*

The Collect.

O God, Who for the setting forth of the way of innocence didst cause the soul of Thy Virgin S. Scholastica to enter into heaven in the shape of a dove, grant us, we beseech Thee, for her sake, to live innocently, that we may be counted meet to attain to the same joys. Through.

Secret. Receive, O Lord, we beseech Thee, the desires and petitions of the faithful, together with their oblations, that at the intercession of Thy Virgin S. Scholastica, who unfeignedly loved Thee, faith may never grow cold nor chastity become lukewarm in us. Through.

P. Comm. O Lord, we beseech Thee, for the sake of Thy blessed Virgin Scholastica, graciously regard this Thy family which Thou hast satisfied with spiritual food, that like as at her prayers Thou didst cause the rain to come down from heaven and accomplish her desire, so at her supplication Thou wouldst deign to pour out upon our barren hearts the dew of heavenly grace. Through.

THE TRANSLATION OF S. FRIDESWIDE.

¶ *Presumably the Service was the same as on her feast in October.*

S. VALENTINE, Mart.

¶ *The* Office iv., Epistle *and* Offert. i., Grad. ii., Alleluia v., Gospel iii., Comm. vi. *in the Common.*

The Collect.

Grant, we beseech Thee, Almighty God, that we who keep the day of Thy Martyr S. Valentine may at his intercession be delivered from all evils that threaten us. Through.

Secret. We beseech Thee, O Lord, let the prayers of Thy Martyr S. Valentine make the Sacrifice which we offer acceptable unto Thee. Through.

P. Comm. We beseech Thee, O Lord, for the sake of Thy Martyr S. Valentine graciously deliver from all adversities those whom Thou hast refreshed with heavenly sustenance. Through.

S. JULIANA, Virg. Mart.

¶ *The* Office ii., Epistle. Gospel, *and* Offert. i., Grad. iii., Comm. iv., Alleluia v. *in the Common.*

The Collect.

Almighty and everlasting God, Who choosest the weak things of the world to confound the things which are mighty, grant that we may rejoice with meet devotion on the feast of Thy Martyr S. Juliana, both extolling Thy power in her passion and perceiving the aid which Thou hast provided for us. Through.

Secret. O Lord, we extol Thy might and bring Thee gifts and offerings on the precious death of Thy Martyr, S. Juliana; grant, we beseech Thee, that, like as she is well-pleasing unto Thee, so also our bounden duty and service may be made acceptable. Through.

P. Comm. We beseech Thee, O Lord, that for the sake and intercession of S. Juliana, Thy Martyr, Thou wouldst bestow on us who have tasted Thy Divine Mystery mercy both in this world and in that which is to come. Through.

The Chair of S. Peter.

The Office.

¶ *As* i. *in Comm. Conf. Bp.*

The Collect.

O God, Who having given to S. Peter Thy Apostle the keys of the Kingdom of Heaven, and deliver unto him the power of a Bishop to bind and loose souls, mercifully grant that by the aid of his intercession we may be loosed from the bands of our sins. Who.

The Epistle. 1 Peter i. 1-7.

Peter, an Apostle .... Jesus Christ *our Lord.*

Gradual. Ps. cvii. That they would exalt Him in the congregation of the people, and praise Him in the seat of the elders.

℣. O that men would therefore praise the Lord for His goodness: and declare the wonders that He doeth for the children of men!

Tract. Matt. xvi. Thou art Peter, and upon this Rock I will build My Church.

℣. And the gates of hell shall not prevail against it: and I will give unto thee the keys of the Kingdom of Heaven.

℣. Whatsoever thou shall bind on earth, shall be bound in Heaven.

℣. And whatsoever thou shalt loose on earth, shall be loosed in Heaven.

The Gospel. Matt. xvi. 13-19.

At that time Jesus came .... loosed in Heaven.

The Creed.

A A

Offert. Ps. xlv. *Thou shalt* make them princes in all lands: *they shall* remember Thy Name from one generation to another.

Secret. We beseech Thee, O Lord, let the prayers of S. Peter, Thy Apostle, commend unto Thee the petitions and gifts of Thy Church, that the feast which we celebrate in his honour may be profitable unto our pardon. Through.

Comm. Matt. xvi. Thou art Peter, and upon this Rock I will build My Church.

P. Comm. O Lord, we beseech Thee, let the gift we have received cause us to rejoice, that, like as we extol Thy wonderful works in Thy Apostle Peter, so through him we may obtain Thy abundant pardon. Through.

S. Matthias, *Ap.*

¶ *All as in the Common.*

The Collect.

O God, Who didst choose S. Matthias to be of the number of Thy Apostles, grant, we beseech Thee, that at his intercession we may ever perceive about us the yearnings of Thy compassion. Through.

The Lesson. Acts i. 15-26.

In those days Peter stood up .... with the eleven Apostles.

The Gospel. Matt. xi. 25-30.

At that time Jesus answered .... My burden is light.

The Creed.

Secret. O God, who, that the sacred number of Thy Apostles might not lack perfection, didst by the election of S. Matthias supply the loss of the apostate traitor, sanctify these present gifts, and through them strengthen us with the power of Thy grace. Through.

P. Comm. Grant, we beseech Thee, Almighty and merciful God, that by these holy Mysteries which we have received we may, at the intercession of S. Matthias, Thy Apostle, obtain pardon and peace. Through.

S. DAVID, *Conf. Bp.*

¶ *All as* i. *in the Common, except* Coll. *and* Comm. ii., *and* Grad. iv. *in the same.*

S. CHAD, *Conf. Bp.*

¶ *All as* i. *in the Common, except the* Office iii., Epistle iv., Gospel *and* Offert. ii. *in the same*

SS. PERPETUA AND FELICITAS, MM

¶ *All as* i. *in Comm. Many Virg., except* Grad. ii. *in the same.*

The Collect.

Help us, we beseech Thee, O Lord our God, to honour the victory of Thy Martyrs, SS. Perpetua and Felicitas with unceasing devotion, that those whom we are unable worthily to imitate we may at the least commemorate with humble obeisance. Through.

Secret. Look down, we beseech Thee, O Lord, on the gifts presented at Thine Altar on the feast of Thy Martyrs, SS. Perpetua and Felicitas, that as by this holy Mystery Thou didst bestow glory on them, so by the same Thou wouldst also abundantly pour forth upon us pardon and grace. Through.

P. Comm. We, who are sustained by the Divine gift of Thy Sacrament on the feast of Thy Martyrs, SS. Perpetua and Felicitas, beseech Thee, O Lord, that as by Thy grace we are comforted by the good things in this world, so we may also have fruition of those which are eternal. Through.

S. Gregory, *Conf. Pope.*

¶ *All as* Comm. Conf. Doct. *except* Gospel iii. *Common Conf. Bp.*

The Collect.

O God, Who hast given unto the soul of Thy servant Gregory the reward of eternal happiness, mercifully grant that we who are weighed down by the burden of our sins may be aided by his protection. Through.

Secret. We beseech Thee, O Lord, let the intercession of Thy most blessed Confessor and Bishop Gregory commend our gifts to Thy mercy, that what we for our unworthiness cannot obtain, his prayers may procure for us. Through.

P. Comm. We that are filled with the food of Thy sacred Body and precious Blood, beseech Thee, O Lord our God, that, at the intercession of S. Gregory, Thy Confessor and Bishop, we may, in sure and certain redemption, attain unto that which we devoutly celebrate. Through.

S. PATRICK, *Conf. Bp.*

¶ *All as* i. *in the Common, except* Comm. iii. *and* Grad. iv. *in the same.*

The Collect.

O God, Who didst distinguish S. Patrick, the Apostle of Ireland, with divers miracles, and translate him to the glory of heaven, grant, we beseech Thee, that for his sake, and aided by his prayers, we may attain unto the reward of everlasting happiness. Through.

Secret. Almighty God and Father, we beseech Thee, let the prayers of S. Patrick, Thy Confessor and Bishop, make this oblation which we offer this day in his honour profitable unto Thy Majesty. Through.

P. Comm. We, being refreshed with the joys of Thy Divine Sacrament, humbly pray Thee, Almighty God, that the offerings which we have presented to Thy Majesty in honour of S. Patrick, Thy Confessor and Bishop, may be for the increase of our salvation. Through.

S. EDWARD, *Mart. King.*

¶ *All as* iii. *in the Common, except* Grad. i., Offert. v. *and* Comm. vi. *in the same.*

The Collect.

O God, Who rulest over the everlasting kingdom, graciously behold Thy family, who celebrate the martyrdom of King Edward; and grant that, as Thou hast vouchsafed to glorify him with the gift of heaven, so at his intercession Thou wouldst make us meet to partake of everlasting happiness. Through.

Secret. Look down, we beseech Thee, eternal God, on this our humble offering, presented to Thee in honour of Thy King and Martyr Edward, which oblation Thou hast, by a wondrous dispensation, been pleased to sanctify unto Thyself;

and grant us, for his prayers, so innocently to live that we may attain to joys eternal. Through.

P. Comm. O Lord, let Thy holy Sacrament which we have received purify us; and, at the intercession of Thy blessed King and Martyr Edward, bring us to have part in eternal happiness. Through.

S. CUTHBERT, *Conf. Bp.*

¶ *All as* i. *in the Common, except* Offert. *and* Comm. ii. *in the same.*

The Collect.

O God, Who, by the inestimable gift of Thy grace, dost glorify Thy Saints, grant, we beseech Thee, that, at the intercession of S. Cuthbert, Thy Confessor and Bishop, we may attain unto most excellent virtues. Through.

Secret. Receive, O Lord, we beseech Thee, the Sacrifice for man's redemption; and, at the intercession of S. Cuthbert, Thy Confessor and Bishop, mercifully work in us salvation of soul and body. Through.

P. Comm. We beseech Thee, O Lord, let the holy Sacrament which we have received protect us by its virtue; and at the intercession of S. Cuthbert, Thy Confessor and Bishop, whose life hath shone forth gloriously, keep us in peace and holiness. Through.

S. BENEDICT, *Conf. Abb.*

¶ *All as in the Common, except* Comm. ii. *Conf. Bp.*

The Collect.

Almighty and everlasting God, Who on this day didst release Thy most blessed Confessor Benedict from the bondage of the flesh and take him up to heaven, grant, we beseech Thee, to us Thy servants who celebrate this feast pardon of all our sins, that we who with joyful hearts take pleasure in his renown may for his sake, and at his intercession, have fellowship with him. Through.

Secret. O Lord, let the gifts offered in honour of S. Benedict, Thy Confessor and Abbot, be pleasing unto Thee; and, at his intercession, grant us pardon of all our sins. Through.

P. Comm. Let the receiving of Thy Sacrament, O Lord, at the intercession of S. Benedict, Thy Confessor and Abbot, lead us to follow the example of his conversation, and also to attain unto his reward. Through.

¶ *If the last three feasts fall in Passion Week, let no notice be taken of them until the feasts of their Translations.*

The Annunciation of Blessed Mary.

¶ *All as in Comm.* Blessed Virgin Mary *for Advent. If in Eastertide, the second* Alleluia *is of the Resurrection. In her chapel, the second* Alleluia *is* ℣. Hail *Mary*, that art full of grace, the Lord is with thee. Blessed art thou among women. *The* Sequence *is always said, even in Lent.*

The Sequence.

Hail, Mary! hope of all mankind!
Hail, gentle maid of holy mind!
Hail, full of grace divine!
Hail, Virgin such as ne'er was known!
Who by the bush wast erst foreshown,
Which unconsumed did shine.

Hail, thou rose most fair to see!
ail, thou rod of Jesse's une!
Whose fruit innate our sad estate
Didst bring to liberty.

Hail! for whom no peer is found;
Of joy thou hast restored the sound
To the long-sorrowing earth.
Hail! thou who bearedst in Thy womb
A Son Whose might should overcome,
And loose the bands of Death.

Hail! light the virgins to enlighten,
Through whom light from on high did brighten
Those o'er whom darkness spread.
Hail! Virgin, of whom to be born
The King of Heaven did not scorn,
And by Thee to be fed.

Hail! jewel, heaven's luminary!
Hail! Holy Spirit's sanctuary.
O what cause for amaze, how worthy all praise,
Is this virginity!
In which, quickened to light by the Paraclete,
Shone forth fecundity!

O how holy, how serene!
How gentle, how benign of mien,
Needs must that Virgin be,
Who hath bondage cast aside,
The gate of heaven hath opened wide,
And brought back liberty.

O lily pure of chastity!
Entreat thy Holy Son, for He
Delighteth in humility,
That he will not in that sad day
Of judgment cast us all away;
But at thy prayer all graciously
Will cleanse us from iniquity,
That we in light's abode may reign:
Let every creature say, Amen.

Tract. Luke i. Hail, *Mary*, full of grace, the Lord is with thee.

℣. Blessed art thou among women, and blessed is the fruit of thy womb.

℣. The Holy Ghost shall come upon thee and the power of the Highest shall overshadow thee.

℣. Therefore, also, that Holy Thing that shall be born of thee shall be called the Son of God.

¶ *If this feast fall on any Sunday in Lent, let it always be transferred to the next day. If it occur on Maundy Thursday, and from then till the Octave of Easter, let it be transferred to the first vacant day after the same.*

S. RICHARD, *Conf. Bp.*

¶ *All as* i. *in the Common, except* Grad. iv. *and* Comm. ii. *in the same. In Easter-tide, the second* Alleluia *will be one of those at* p. 191, *and so with all feasts in Easter-tide. The* Gospel "I am the true vine."

The Collect.

O God, Who hast made Thy Church illustrious by the deeds and glorious miracles of S. Richard, Thy Confessor and Bishop, grant that we Thy servants, at his intercession, may attain unto the glory of everlasting happiness. Through.

Secret. Grant, we beseech Thee, merciful God, at the intercession of S. Richard, Thy Confessor and Bishop, that the gift offered in the sight of Thy Majesty may both give us grace to live aright, and obtain for us everlasting glory. Through.

P. Comm. O Lord, let this Holy Mystery which we have received, and which Thy Confessor and Bishop, S. Richard, was wont reverently to administer, effectually work out our salvation. Through.

S. Ambrose. *Bp. Doct.*

¶ *All as* i. *in the Common, except* Office *and* Comm. ii. *Conf. and Bp.*, *and* Gospel iii. *in the same. In Easter-tide, the* Alleluia *is* i. *in the Common. The* Gospel, "I am the true vine." *The* Creed *is said.*

The Collect.

O God, Who didst give S. Ambrose unto Thy people to be a minister of eternal salvation, grant, we beseech Thee, that we may be found worthy ever to have him for an intercessor in heaven who hath been to us a teacher of life on earth. Through.

Secret. O God, let this Sacrifice, at the intercession of Thy most blessed Confessor, S. Ambrose, both indeed abide and be established in us by effectual working. Through.

P. Comm. We beseech Thee, Almighty God, let the prayers of S. Ambrose continually follow us; and let that which our petitions cannot obtain, be granted to us at his intercession. Through.

SS. TYBURTIUS AND VALERIAN, MM.

¶ *All as* vi. *in the Common, except the* Office viii., Alleluia ii., *and* Comm. i. *in the same. The* Gospel, "I am the true vine."

The Collect.

Grant, we beseech Thee, Almighty God, that we who keep the feast of Thy holy Martyrs, Tyburtius, Valerian, and Maximus, may likewise follow their excellence. Through.

Secret. O Lord, we beseech Thee, look down upon these gifts; and, by the protection of the holy Martyrs, Tyburtius, Valerian, and Maximus, whose feast we celebrate, let Thy faithful people obtain pardon and salvation, and be found worthy of an everlasting reward. Through.

P. Comm. O Lord, we beseech Thee, let the blessing we have received in Thy Sacrament sanctify our bodies and souls, and at the intercession of Thy holy Martyrs, Tyburtius, Valerian, and Maximus, make us to be numbered in eternal glory. Through.

S. ALPHEGE, Mart. Bp.

¶ *The* Office vi., Offert. iv., *and* Comm. v. *in Comm. Mart.*; Epistle ii. *in the Common*; Alleluia iv. *in Comm. Conf. and Bp.* Gospel, "I am the true vine."

The Collect.

O God, Who didst adorn S. Alphege, Thy Bishop, with the dignity of the Priesthood and the palm of Martyrdom, mercifully grant us so to be assisted by his intercessions with Thee, that we may rejoice with him in everlasting happiness. Through.

Secret. Bless, O Lord, and Thyself accept, we beseech Thee, these gifts which we have laid upon Thine Altar, that, at the intercession of S. Alphege, Thy Martyr and Bishop, they may be profitable to our present enjoyment and everlasting salvation. Through.

P. Comm. We humbly pray Thee, O Lord, of Thy mercy, that we who have received the Sacrament may, at the intercession of Thy Martyr and Bishop, S. Alphege, attain in eternal life unto the service we offer in this world. Through.

S. George, *Mart.*

¶ *All as* vi. *in the Common, except* Grad. iii., Offert. *and* Comm. iv. *in the same.* Gospel, "I am the true vine." *The* Creed *is said.*

The Collect.

O God, Who causest us to rejoice in the good deeds and intercession of S. George, Thy Martyr, mercifully grant that, by the gift of Thy grace, we may obtain the benefits we ask of him. Through.

The Epistle. James i. 2-12.

Beloved, count it all joy .... them that love Him.

Secret. We offer unto Thee, O Lord, the wonted Sacrifice on the death of Thy Martyr, S. George, entreating of Thy mercy, that through these holy Mysteries we may, in Thy victory, overcome the temptations of the old Enemy, and of Thy bounty obtain an everlasting recompense of reward. Through.

P. Comm. We humbly pray Thee, Almighty Father, that we who are satisfied with the sweetness of the heavenly Table, may at the intercession of Thy Martyr, S. George, also be partakers of His resurrection by Whose death we are redeemed. Through.

S. Mark, *Evang.*

¶ *All as in the Common, except the* Office vi. *in Comm. Mart.*, Offert. iv *and* Comm. v. *in the same. The* Gospel, "I am the true vine." *The* Creed *is said.*

The Collect.

O God, Who hast exalted S. Mark, Thy Evangelist, by the grace of preaching the Gospel; grant, we beseech Thee, that we may both profit by his teaching, and ever be defended by his prayers. Through.

The Epistle. Ephes. iv. 7-13.

Brethren, unto every one of us .... the fulness of Christ.

Secret. We, presenting these gifts to Thee, O Lord, on the feast of S. Mark, Thy Evangelist, beseech Thee that, as the preaching of the Gospel hath made him glorious, so his intercession may make us acceptable to Thee both in word and deed. Through.

P. Comm. We, that have been refreshed by the nourishment of spiritual food, beseech Thee, O Lord our God, that we may, at the intercession of S. Mark, Thy Evangelist, attain unto the fulness ot the grace of that which here we approach in a mystery. Through.

¶ *If this feast occur after Easter Week, then let the Procession follow High Mass. If in it, let no notice be taken of it that year, unless it fall on the Octave Day, then let it be translated to the morrow.*

S. VITALIS, Mart.

¶ *The* Office vi., Epistle v., *and* Sequence *in the Common.* Alleluia ii., Offert. vii., *and* Comm. viii. *in Comm. Many Martyrs. The* Gospel, "I am the true vine."

The Collect.

Grant, we beseech Thee, Almighty God, that, at the intercession of S. Vitalis, Thy Martyr, we may be defended from all adversities which may happen to the body, and be cleansed from evil thoughts in the soul. Through.

Secret. We beseech Thee, O Lord, let the gifts with which we commemorate the glorious death of S. Vitalis, Thy Martyr, be pleasing unto Thee. Through.

P. Comm. We beseech Thee, Almighty God, that the divine gift which we have received, at the intercession of S. Vitalis, Thy Martyr, may be profitable to our salvation. Through.

THE BURIAL OF S. ERKENWALD.

¶ *Presumably all as in the Common.*

SS. Philip and James, *App.*

The Office. Nehem. ix.

In the time of their trouble, they cried unto Thee, *O Lord, and* Thou heardest them from heaven. *Alleluia, Alleluia.*

Ps. xxxiii. Rejoice in the Lord, O ye righteous, for it becometh well the just to be thankful.

The Collect.

O God, Who dost make us glad in the annual feast of Thy Apostles Philip and James, grant, we beseech Thee, that we may be instructed by the example of those in whose deeds we rejoice. Through.

The Lesson. Wisdom v. 1-5.

The righteous man .... among the Saints.

Alleluia! ℣. Wisdom v. The righteous man shall stand in great boldness before the face of such as have afflicted him.

Alleluia! ℣. Luke xxiv. Did not our heart burn within us, while He talked with us by the way *concerning Jesus.*

The Sequence.

(*See* i. *in the Common.*)

The Gospel. John xiv. 1-13.

At that time, Jesus said to His disciples, Let not your heart .... whatsoever ye shall ask *the Father* in My Name, that will I do.

The Creed.

Offert. Ps. lxxxix. O Lord, the very heavens shall praise Thy wondrous works, and Thy truth in the congregation of the Saints.

Secret. O God, the Redeemer and Perfecter of Thy Church, grant that we may receive the gifts of the Paschal Sacrament at the prayers of Thy Apostles Philip and James, under whose rule and governance Thou didst will that they should be preached. Through.

Comm. John xiv. Have I been so long with you, and yet hast thou not known Me, Philip? He that hath seen Me, hath seen the Father, *Alleluia.* Believest thou not that I am in the Father, and the Father in Me? *Alleluia, Alleluia.*

P. Comm. We beseech Thee, O Lord, that we who are recalling the mysteries of Easter may be comforted by the prayers of Thy blessed Apostles, Philip and James, under whose rule and governance we have come to the knowledge of this duty. Through.

The Invention of the Holy Cross.

The Office. Gal. vi

But *we ought to* glory in the Cross of our Lord Jesus Christ, by Whom *is our Salvation, Life, and Resurrection; by Whom we have been saved and set free. Alleluia, Alleluia.*

Ps. lxvii. God be merciful unto us and bless us; and shew us the light of His countenance, and be merciful unto us.

The Collect.

O God, Who hast renewed the miracles of Thy Passion in the glorious Invention of the saving Cross, grant that, by the price paid on the life-giving word, we may obtain favour unto life everlasting. Who.

Memorial of SS. Alexander, Eventius, and Theodolus.

Grant, we beseech Thee, Almighty God, that we who observe the day of Thy Saints, Alexander, Eventius, and Theodolus, may, at their intercession, be delivered from all evils that beset us. Through.

The Epistle.

(Epistle vi. *in Comm. Mart.*)

Alleluia! O sweet the wood, O sweet the nails: thou (Cross) that bearest a sweet burden; alone wast worthy to support the King and Lord of Heaven.

Alleluia! Ps. xcvi. Tell it out among the heathen that the Lord *reigneth from the Tree.*

The Sequence.

Hail, Holy Cross, thou Tree of dignity!
Bearing the costly price of all the world;
That so the foe who triumphed by a tree
Should in his turn by a Tree conquered be.
And what in the beginning had been cause
Of death to men banished from Paradise,
Should also be the cause of life to all
Who by Christ's death are truly made alive.
Thou ever art a spectacle of dread,
O Holy Cross! to our fell enemies.
That which death views with awe, and hell doth fear,
Doth sign anew Christ's servants for his own.
To whom be praise and glory evermore.

The Gospel. John iii. 1-15.

At that time there was a man .... everlasting life.

The Creed.

Offert. Protect Thy people, O Lord, by the sign of the Holy Cross, from all their enemies who lie in wait for them; that the service we present may be pleasing unto Thee, and that our Sacrifice may be acceptable unto Thee. Alleluia.

Secret. Graciously look down, O Lord, on the Sacrifice which we offer to Thee; let it preserve us from the wickedness of men, and place us under the safety of Thy protection, that we may scatter the powers of the air and the snares of our adversaries, through the banner of Thy Son's Holy Cross. Through.

Secret of SS. Alexander, Eventius, and Theodolus. We beseech Thee, O Lord, let Thy glorious blessing descend upon this oblation, mercifully to work holiness in us, and to cause us to rejoice on the feast of Thy Martyrs, Alexander, Eventius, and Theodolus. Through.

Comm. By the Tree we are saved, and by the Holy Ghost we are set free; the fruit of a tree beguiled us, the Son of God hath redeemed us. Alleluia.

P. Comm. We whom Thou hast refreshed with heavenly food and spiritual drink, beseech Thee, Almighty God, to defend from all malice of the enemy those whom Thou hast made to triumph in the wood of Thy Son's Cross, which is the armour of righteousness, for the salvation of the world. Through.

P. Comm. of SS. Alexander, Eventius, and Theodolus. Grant, we beseech Thee, O Lord, that we who have received the sacred gifts, may, by the prayers and example of Thy holy Martyrs, Alexander, Eventius, and Theodolus, be stirred up more earnestly to long after the same. Through.

S. JOHN BEFORE THE LATIN GATE.

¶ *All as on the feast at Christmas (see* p. 26*) except the* Sequence, *which is in the Common. The* Creed *is said.*

The Collect.

O God, Who seest that our adversities trouble us on every side, grant, we beseech Thee, that the intercession of S. John, Thy Apostle and Evangelist, may protect us. Through.

Secret. O Lord, make us so to celebrate, by Thy Mysteries, the feast of S. John, Thy Apostle and Evangelist, that we may alike believe and follow the doctrine which he preached. Through.

P. Comm. We beseech Thee, O Lord, that we who have been fed with heavenly food, may, at the intercession of S. John, Thy Apostle and Evangelist, be nourished unto life eternal. Through.

S. JOHN OF BEVERLEY, *Conf. Bp.*

¶ *The* Office, Sequence, *and* Offert. i., Collects, *and* Alleluia ii., Epistle *and* Comm. iii. *in the Common.*

THE TRANSLATION OF S. NICHOLAS

¶ *Presumably all as on his feast in December.*

SS. GORDIAN AND EPIMACHUS, MM.

¶ *The* Office viii., Epistle ii., Alleluia *and* Offert. i.; Gospel, "I am the true vine;" *and* Comm. iv. *in the Common.*

The Collect.

Grant, we beseech Thee, Almighty God, that we who keep the feast of Thy Martyrs, SS. Gordian and Epimachus, may be aided by their intercessions with Thee. Through.

Secret. Grant, we beseech Thee, O Lord our God, that, as the death of Thy Saints is precious in Thy sight, so the oblations of those who reverence their good deeds may be made acceptable to Thee. Through.

P. Comm. Refresh Thy people, O Lord, we beseech Thee, with spiritual means of grace; and make them partakers in the joys of those whose feast Thou permittest them to celebrate. Through.

SS. NEREUS, ACHILLES, AND PANCRATIUS, MM.

The Office: Ps. xxxiii.

Behold, the eye of the Lord is upon them that fear Him, and upon them that put their trust in His mercy. *Alleluia.* To deliver their soul from death, *for He is their helper and defender. Alleluia, Alleluia.*

Ps. Rejoice in the Lord, O ye righteous, for it becometh well the just to be thankful.

The Collect.

We beseech Thee, O Lord, let the holy feast of Thy Martyrs, SS. Nereus, Achilles, and Pancratius, comfort us and make us worthy of Thy service. Through.

¶ *The* Epistle iii., Alleluia iv.; Gospel, "I am the true vine;" Offert. vi. *and* Comm. i. *in the Common.*

Secret. Let the confession of Thy Martyrs, SS. Nereus, Achilles, and Pancratius, be pleasing to Thee, O Lord, both to present our gifts, and ever to implore Thy pardon for us. Through.

P. Comm. We beseech Thee, O Lord our God, that at the prayers of Thy Martyrs, SS. Nereus, Achilles, and Pancratius, the Holy Sacrament which we have received may reconcile us more and more unto Thee. Through.

S. DUNSTAN, *Conf. Bp.*

¶ *All as* ii. *in the Common, except* Epistle, Gospel, *and* Comm. i., *and* Alleluia vi. *in the same.*

The Collect.

O God, Who hast translated S. Dunstan, Thy Bishop, unto the kingdom of heaven; grant us, for his glorious sake, to pass unto everlasting joy. Through.

Memorial of S. Pudenziana, Virg.

Grant us, we beseech The, Almighty God, both that we may rejoice in the good deeds of Thy Virgin, S. Pudenziana, and be sustained by her kindly aid. Through.

Secret. Receive, O Lord, we beseech Thee, the gifts of Thy family that prayeth, which we present on the feast of S. Dunstan, Thy Bishop and Confessor, imploring Thee that we, being aided by his protection, may be defended from all snares of the enemy. Through.

Secret of S. Pudenziana. Sanctify, O Lord, these oblations with Thy blessing, that for the sake of Thy Virgin, S. Pudenziana, in reverence for whom they are offered, the same may be acceptable unto Thee. Through.

P. Comm. Help us, O Lord, we beseech Thee, for the prayers of S. Dunstan, Thy Confessor and Bishop, in whose honour we have partaken of Thy Sacrament. Through.

P. Comm of S Pudenziana. We that have received the Mystery of eternal Salvation beseech Thee, O Lord, to make us so to use Thy Sacrament that, at the intercession of Thy Virgin, S. Pudenziana, we may be found meet to sit down at Thy everlasting Banquet. Through.

S. ALDHELM, *Conf. Bp.*

¶ *All as* i. *in the Common, except* Epistle *and* Gospel iii., Grad. iv., *and* Comm. ii. *in the same. In Easter-tide*, Gospel, "I am the true vine."

The Collect.

O God, Who on this day didst raise S. Aldhelm, Thy Bishop, unto everlasting joys, we beseech Thee for his sake in Thy mercy to lead us thither. Through.

Memorial of S. Urban, Mart.

Grant, we beseech Thee, Almighty God, that we who keep the feast of S. Urban, Thy Martyr and Bishop, may be assisted by his intercessions with Thee. Through

Secret. We beseech Thee, O Lord, let this oblation be acceptable to Thee at his prayers on whose feast it is offered. Through.

Secret of S. Urban. Sanctify, O Lord, we beseech Thee, the gifts dedicated to Thee; and, at the intercession of S. Urban, Thy Martyr and Bishop, look upon us as reconciled unto Thee by the same. Through.

P. Comm. Graciously be present, we beseech Thee, O Lord, with us who celebrate the feast of Thy Bishop, S. Aldhelm; and for his sake grant us the joys of everlasting life. Through.

P. Comm. of S. Urban. We who receive the heavenly Sacrament with humble devotion beseech Thee, O Lord, of Thy loving-kindness graciously to breathe into us that mighty love which burned in S. Urban, Thy Martyr and Bishop. Through.

S. Augustine, *Apostle of the English.*

¶ *All as in Comm. Conf. Doct., except* Grad. i., Sequence, *and Offert.* ii. *in Comm. Conf. Bp., and* Gospel *as in Comm. Evang., except in Easter-tide*, "I am the true vine." *The* Creed *is said.*

The Collect.

O God, Who gavest S. Augustine to be the first Bishop and teacher of the English nation; grant, we beseech Thee, that we may perceive the assistance of his prayers with Thee in heaven whose good deeds we set forth on earth. Through.

Secret. We beseech Thee, O Lord, let the oblations be pleasing unto Thee wherewith we reverence the good deeds of S. Augustine,

Thy Bishop and Confessor, and call to mind the pledges alike of our liberty and life. Through.

P. Comm. We beseech Thee, O Lord, let Thy holy Sacrament which we have tasted this day, on the feast of S. Augustine, Thy Bishop and Confessor, renew us; may we always long to be fulfilled with the same, and continually be satisfied. Through.

S. GERMANUS, Conf. Bp.

¶ *All as* i. *in the Common, except* Grad. *and* Comm. ii. *and* Alleluia iii. *in the same. In Easter-tide,* Gospel, "I am the true vine."

S. PETRONILLA, Virg.

¶ *All as* i. *in the Common, except* Grad. ii. *in the same, and* Alleluia iii. *in Comm. Virg. Mart.*

The Collect.

O God, Who hast given unto the soul of S. Petronilla, Thy Virgin, a place in heaven, loose us, at her intercession, from the chains of our sins, and ever defend us from all adversity. Through.

Secret. Graciously receive, O most merciful God, the Sacrifice which we offer unto Thy Majesty, and, for the sake of S. Petronilla, Thy Virgin, grant us help in this present life, and happiness in that which is to come. Through.

P. Comm. We, who have received heavenly sustenance, beseech Thee, O Lord, that by the same, at the intercession of S. Petronilla, Thy Virgin, we may be found meet to attain unto joy everlasting. Through.

S. NICHOMEDE, Mart.

¶ *The* Office v., Epistle, Alleluia, *and* Offert. i., Grad. ii., Gospel, *and* Comm. iii. *in the Common. In Easter-tide,* Gospel, "I am the true vine."

The Collect.

O God, Who causest us to rejoice in the good deeds and intercession of S. Nichomede, Thy Martyr, mercifully grant that by the gift of Thy grace we may obtain the benefits which we ask of him. Through.

Secret. Sanctify, O Lord, these gifts which have been offered; and at the intercession of S. Nichomede, Thy Martyr, cleanse us thereby from the stains of our sins. Through.

P. Comm. Vouchsafe, we humbly beseech Thee, Almighty God, that those whom Thou refreshest with Thy Sacrament, may also, at the intercession of S. Nichomede, Thy Martyr, by their worthy conversation, serve and please Thee. Through.

SS. MARCELLINUS AND PETER, MM.

¶ *The* Office *and* Offert. iii., Grad. *and* Comm. iv., Alleluia vii., *and* Gospel vi. *in the Common. In Easter-tide,* Gospel, "I am the true vine."'

The Collect.

As on SS. Philip and James' Day.

The Lesson. Rev. vii. 13-17.

In those days, one of the elders answered .... from their eyes.

Secret. We present unto Thee, O Lord, our gifts and prayers on the passion of Thy Martyrs Marcellinus and Peter, and do homage to Thy mighty power, imploring thereby the aid of Thy loving-kindness. Through.

P. Comm. We beseech Thee, O Lord, that the partaking of the heavenly Banquet vouchsafed unto us, together with the prayers of Thy Saints, may protect Thy people. Through.

S. BONIFACE AND HIS COMPANIONS, MM.

¶ *The* Office viii., Epistle v., Grad., *and* Alleluia ii., Gospel iii., Offert. vi., *and* Comm. i. *in the Common. In Easter-tide,* Gospel, "I am the true vine."

The Collect.

Almighty and everlasting God, Who upon S. Boniface and his companions didst bestow the palm of Martyrdom, grant us, we beseech Thee, pardon for their sake on whom Thou hast deigned to bestow a crown. Through.

Secret. Receive, O Almighty God, the oblation of Thy servants which we humbly present unto Thee in honour of S. Boniface, Thy Martyr, and his companions; that at their prayers who offered themselves to Thee a sacrifice of praise for a sweet-smelling savour, we may be found worthy to be united to Thy Only Begotten Son Jesus Christ our Lord. Through.

P. Comm. Let Thy mercy, O God, through this Sacrament which we have received, at the intercession of S. Boniface, Thy Martyr, and his companions, both cleanse us from all lurking remains of the old man, and fit us for holiness and newness of life. Through.

SS. MEDARDUS AND GILDARDUS, Conff. Bpp.

¶ *All as in the Common. In Easter-tide,* Gospel, "I am the true vine."

The Collect.

O God, Who hast set apart this day's holy feast in honour of Thy Bishops and Confessors, SS. Medardus and Gildardus, be present at the prayers of Thy family, and grant that we may be supported for the sake and by the aid of those whose feast we celebrate. Through.

Secret. Regard, we beseech Thee, O Lord, Thy people who hasten to Thy Sacrament, on this present feast of Thy Bishops and Confessors, SS. Medardus and Gildardus, that their offerings in honour of Thy Name may be profitable for the pardon of all. Through.

P. Comm. We render thanks unto Thee, O Lord our God, Who hast deigned to restore us by a heavenly healing; vouchsafe us, we beseech Thee, pardon of our sins, as Thou didst vouchsafe the chair of the Episcopate to Thy Confessors, SS. Medardus and Gildardus. Through.

THE TRANSLATION OF S. EDMUND, *Conf. Abp.*

The Office.

Let us all rejoice in the Lord, and celebrate the feast in honour of S. Edmund, for whose translation angels rejoice and praise the Son of God.

Ps. xxxiii. Rejoice in the Lord, O ye righteous, for it becometh well the just to be thankful.

The Collect.

O God, Who permittest us to celebrate the Translation of S. Edmund, Thy Bishop and Confessor, we humbly beseech Thee, for his sake and prayers, to turn us from wickedness to virtue, and from bondage unto the kingdom. Through.

Memorial of SS. Primus and Felician, MM.

O Lord, we beseech Thee, make us duly to attend the feast of SS. Primus and Felician, Thy Martyrs, and at their prayers perceive the gift of Thy protection. Through.

¶ *All as* ii. *in the Common, except* Grad. iv., Gospel *and* Offert. i. *in the same. In Easter-tide,* Gospel, "I am the true vine."

Alleluia! This Edmund, poor and gentle, entereth heaven rich, and is praised in hymns above.

Secret. O God, Who, by Thy heavenly blessing, dost turn bread and wine into Thy Flesh and Blood, grant, we beseech Thee, that for the sake of S. Edmund, Thy Bishop and Confessor, we, returning unto Thy pity, may be established in Thy favour. Through.

Secret of SS. Primus and Felician. We beseech Thee, O Lord, let the Sacrifice to be consecrated on the feast of Thy precious Martyrs, SS. Primus and Felician, be accepted in Thy sight; and, for their glorious deeds, both cleanse us from our sins and make the prayers of Thy servants pleasing unto Thee. Through.

P. Comm. O God, Who hast translated S. Edmund, Thy Confessor and Bishop, from suffering to joy, grant, we beseech Thee, that we who reverence his Translation on earth may, by his protection, be translated to heaven. Through.

P. Comm. of SS. Primus and Felician. We beseech Thee, Almighty God, let the feast of Thy Martyrs, SS. Primus and Felician, which has been celebrated with the heavenly Mystery, procure for us Thy pardon and favour. Through.

S. BARNABAS, *Ap.*

¶ *All as* i. *in the Common, except* Alleluia *and* Sequence ii., Offert. iii. *in the same.*

The Collect.

We beseech Thee, O Lord, let the prayers of Thy Apostle,

S. Barnabas, commend Thy Church to Thee, and let him continue to intercede for her whom by his doctrine and death he doth glorify. Through.

The Gospel. John xv. 12-16.

At that time, Jesus said to His disciples, This is My commandment .... He may give it unto you.

The Creed.

Secret. O Lord, we offer unto Thee the Sacrifice of Reconciliation on this festival of S. Barnabas, Thy Apostle; grant, we beseech Thee, at his prayers, both to understand and attain unto this help* of our redemption. Through.

P. Comm. We beseech Thee, O Lord, let the heavenly Sacrament which we have offered to Thy Majesty on the passion of Thy Apostle, S. Barnabas, be profitable to our salvation, at his intercession on whose day we have received it. Through.

SS. BASILIDES, CYRINUS, NABOR, AND NAZARIUS, MM.

¶ *The* Office i., Epistle ii., Grad. vi., Alleluia v., Gospel xiii., Offert. iv., *and* Comm. iii. *in the Common*

The Collect.

We beseech Thee, O Lord, let the feast of Thy Martyrs, SS. Basilides, Cyrinus, Nabor, and Nazarius, shine forth in us, in answer to our prayers; that the grace bestowed on them by Thy eternal goodness may also grow in us by the fruits of our devotion. Through.

Secret. Give unto us, we beseech Thee, O Lord, the spirit of true religion; and at the intercession of Thy Martyrs, SS. Basilides, Cyrinus, Nabor, and Nazarius, look favourably upon our gifts. Through.

P. Comm. We, being refreshed by Thy Divine Sacrament, beseech Thee, O Lord our God, that at the intercession of Thy Martyrs, SS. Basilides, Cyrinus, Nabor, and Nazarius, we may be found worthy of a place in the joys of heaven. Through.

* *i.e.*, the Blessed Sacrament.

S. BASIL, Conf. Bp.

¶ *All as* i. *in the Common, except* Grad. iv. *and* Comm. ii. *in the same.*

The Collect.

O God, Who didst see fit to choose S. Basil, Thy Confessor, to be a chief doctor and preacher of the Catholic Faith, grant, we beseech Thee, that at his intercession we may be set free from the evil of our sins, and serve Thee with sincerity of heart. Through.

Secret. We beseech Thee, O Lord, that the gifts offered unto Thee be made profitable, at the prayers of S. Basil, Thy Confessor and Bishop, unto eternal salvation. Through.

P. Comm. O Lord, let the glorious intercessions of S. Basil, Thy Confessor and Bishop, obtain for us that the Sacrament of heavenly healing which we have received, minister grace unto us continually. Through.

SS. VITUS, MODESTUS, AND CRESCENTIA, MM.

¶ *The* Office iv., Epistle iii., Grad. *and* Offert. ii., Alleluia *and* Comm. vii., *and* Gospel ix. *in the Common.*

The Collect.

Grant, we beseech Thee, Almighty God, that we may share the reward of Thy Martyrs, SS. Vitus, Modestus, and Crescentia, whose victory we celebrate. Through.

Secret. O Lord, be favourable unto our supplications, and accept the oblations and prayers of Thy people; and, at the intercession of Thy Martyrs, SS. Vitus, Modestus, and Crescentia, turn our hearts unto Thyself, that we, being delivered from worldly lusts, may pass unto an earnest longing after heavenly things. Through.

P. Comm. We beseech Thee, O Lord, keep us, who are refreshed by partaking of the food of salvation, under the defence of Thy Martyrs, SS. Vitus, Modestus, and Crescentia, in whose earthly festival Thou hast this day permitted us to rejoice. Through.

THE TRANSLATION OF S. RICHARD, *Conf. Bp.*

¶ *All as* i. *in the Common, except* Grad. iv. *and* Comm. ii. *in the same.*

The Collect.

O God, Who permittest us to celebrate with due honour the Translation of Thy Bishop and Confessor, S. Richard, grant us, we beseech Thee, for his sake and prayers, to pass out of this miserable world, and attain unto the joys of heaven. Through.

Memorial of SS. Ciricus and Julita, MM.

Hear us, O Lord our God, who pray to Thee, with the aid of Thy holy Martyrs, S. Ciricus and S. Julita his mother, that we may maintain like constancy with those whose triumphs we celebrate. Through.

Secret. We offer unto Thee, O Lord, our prayers and gifts, humbly beseeching Thee that, at the intercession of S. Richard, Thy Bishop and Confessor, whose translation we keep, we may be turned from wickedness to virtuous living, and from bondage to the kingdom. Through.

Secret of SS. Ciricus and Julita. We present unto Thee, O Lord, the holy gifts of the faithful, trusting in the intercession of Thy Martyrs, SS. Ciricus and Julita, that what with unworthy service we perform may, for their sake, be made more acceptable. Through.

P. Comm. We humbly beseech Thee, O Lord, by this Sacrament which we have received, for the sake and intercession of S. Richard, Thy Bishop, the day of whose translation we reverently keep, to translate us from the darkness of this life unto perpetual light. Through.

P. Comm of SS. Ciricus and Julita. O Lord, let Thy people obtain an increase of holy blessing by this Sacrament which we have received; and, at the intercession of Thy Martyrs, SS. Ciricus and Julita, be ever upholden by the abundant help of Thy benefits. Through.

SS. MARK AND MARCELLIAN, MM.

¶ *The* Office *and* Offert. vii., Epistle *and* Alleluia vi., Grad. iv., Gospel *and* Comm. xi. *in the Common.*

The Collect.

As Memorial of SS. Alexander, etc., p. 365.

Secret. O Lord, we beseech Thee, let Thy grace continually prevent and follow us, and mercifully receive these oblations which we offer to be consecrated to Thy Name for our sins, that at the intercession of Thy Martyrs, SS. Mark and Marcellian, they may be profitable unto the salvation of all. Through.

P. Comm. Let the glorious deeds of Thy Martyrs, SS. Mark and Marcellian, assist us, O Lord, that Thy holy ordinance which we have received may quicken us. Through.

SS. GERVASIUS AND PROTHASIUS, MM.

The Office. Ps. lxxxv.

The Lord shall speak peace unto His people and to His saints, that they turn not again.

Ps. Lord, Thou art become gracious unto Thy land: Thou hast turned away the captivity of Jacob.

The Collect.

As Memorial of MM., p. 365.

The Epistle. Romans viii. 28-32.

Brethren, we know .... delivered Him up for us all.

¶ Grad. i., Alleluia, Offert. *and* Comm. iii. *and* Gospel x. *in the Common.*

Secret. We offer unto Thee, O Lord, the sacrifice of praise for the grace bestowed on Thy Martyrs, SS. Gervasius and Prothasius, to the end they might not fear to die for Thy Name, and after death might shine in glory everlasting. Through.

P. Comm. We beseech Thee, O Lord, let Thy blessing imparted by these holy Mysteries fill the hearts of Thy faithful people, that they may both do honour to the death of Thy Martyrs, SS. Gervasius and Prothasius, and under their guardianship obtain the everlasting salvation which they desire. Through.

THE TRANSLATION OF S. EDWARD, *Mart. King.*

¶ *The* Office *and* Epistle iii., Grad. *and* Comm. i., Alleluia v., Gospel iv., *and* Offert. ii. *in the Common.*

The Collect.

O God, the Ruler of the Eternal Kingdom, mercifully behold Thy family, who keep the Translation of King Edward; and as Thou deignest to glorify him by the gift of heaven, so at his prevailing intercession graciously make us to be numbered with him in everlasting happiness. Through.

Secret. Look down, we beseech Thee, O Lord God, on our humble sacrifice offered unto Thee in honour of Thy King and Martyr, S. Edward, which Thou art pleased to hallow unto Thyself by a marvellous dispensation; and grant us, at his prayers, so innocently to live, that we may be found worthy to attain unto everlasting joy. Through.

P. Comm. O Lord, let the holy Sacrament we have received make us pure; and, at the intercession of S. Edward, Thy King and Martyr, bring us to a portion in everlasting happiness. Through.

S. ALBAN, *Proto-Martyr of England.*

¶ *The* Office iv., Grad. ii., Alleluia *and* Offert i., Gospel iii., *and* Comm. vi. *in the Common.*

The Collect.

O God, Who hast hallowed this day by the martyrdom of S. Alban, grant, we beseech Thee, that we may ever be comforted by his continual help, in whose yearly feast we rejoice. Through.

The Lesson. Wisdom iv. 7-15.

But though the righteous .... respect unto His chosen.

The Sequence.

Come forth, come forth in triumph, joyous band,
Sing to the Lord high-sounding canticles,
And to the world tell out his wondrous works.

With all your heart, and strength, and soul
  The praise of Christ make known,
Who of his saints is life and power,
  Glory, reward, and crown.

Whose plenteous loving-kindness decks
  Alban with golden bay;
Whose all-prevailing gift of grace
  Cleans'd all his guilt away,
And set his horn of glory up
  For ever and for aye.

For when God's gift he had received,
  The mystery of grace,
Idols he spurned, not fearing then
  The heathen monarch's face.

Whilst to the punishment of death
  A prisoner he was led,
He dried the brimming stream, and passed
  In safety o'er its bed;

And by a like effect of grace
  The dry and sandy earth,
Did also to a springing well
  Of water sweet give birth.

O Alban! who these works achieved
  Leaving this earthly plain,
Ascending up, the highest heaven
  With glory erst dost gain,
To thee, as to our patron, now
  We seek with earnest prayer,
That for the pardon of our sins
  Thy favour we may share.
For England's people intercede,
And for her everlasting peace.

*For us Thy suppliants obtain
The life where endless joys remain
And Alleluias never cease.

Secret. We beseech Thy mercy, O Lord, that, like as, in reverencing S. Alban Thy Martyr, we declare Thy marvellous acts, so by this holy office of reconciliation he may ever himself devoutly intercede for us. Through.

P. Comm. We beseech Thee, O Lord, let S. Alban, Thy Martyr, ever intreat Thy Majesty, that Thy Sacrament may cleanse us from sin. Through.

* This verse is said thrice.

THE VIGIL OF S. JOHN THE BAPTIST.

The Office. Luke i.

Fear not, Zacharias, for thy prayer is heard, and thy wife Elizabeth shall bear thee a son, and thou shalt call his name John; and he shall be great in the sight of the Lord, and he shall be filled with the Holy Ghost, even from his mother's womb; and many shall rejoice at his birth.

Ps. xxi. The King shall rejoice in Thy strength, O Lord; exceeding glad shall he be of Thy salvation.

The Collect.

Grant, we beseech Thee, Almighty God, that Thy family may walk in the way of salvation; and, following the exhortations of S. John, the forerunner of Christ, may in all quietness attain unto Him Whom he foretold, our Lord Jesus Christ, Thy Son. Who.

Memorial of S. Etheldreda, Virg.

O God, Who on this day causest us to rejoice in the yearly feast of S. Etheldreda, Thy Virgin, mercifully grant that we may be succoured for her sake, the example of whose chastity doth enlighten us. Through.

The Lesson. Jerem. i. 4-10.

In those days, the word of the Lord .... to plant, *saith the Lord Almighty.*

Gradual. John i. There was a man sent from God, whose name was John. The same came—

℣. To bear witness of the Light, *and** to make ready a people prepared for the Lord.

¶ *If Sunday, is said—*

Alleluia! ℣. Luke i. Thou, child, shalt be called the Prophet of the Highest; for thou shalt go before the face of the Lord to prepare His ways.

The Gospel. Luke i. 1-17.

There was in the days of Herod .... prepared for the Lord.

Offert. Ps. viii. *Thou crownest* him with glory and worship,

* Luke i.

and makest him to have dominion of the works of Thy hands, *O Lord.*

Secret. Grant, we beseech Thee, Almighty God, that according to the witness of S. John the Baptist, Thy Lamb, Who is set forth in these Mysteries, may ever take away our sins. Through.

Secret of S. Etheldreda. We beseech Thee, O Lord, graciously to accept, at the prayers of S. Etheldreda, Thy Virgin, the offering we have presented before the eyes of Thy Majesty. Through.

Comm. Ps. xxi. His honour is great in Thy salvation: glory and great worship shalt Thou lay upon him, *O Lord.*

P. Comm. Let the excellent prayers of S. John the Baptist, O Lord, accompany us, to the end he may reconcile us unto Him Whose coming he foretold, Jesus Christ Thy Son our Lord. Who.

P. Comm. of S. Etheldreda. We beseech Thee, Almighty God, that, at the intercession of S. Etheldredra, Thy Virgin, our partaking of the heavenly Table may ever draw our desires to Thee. Through.

S. John the Baptist.

The Office. Isa. xlix.

The Lord hath called me from the bowels of my mother by my name, and He hath made my mouth like a sharp sword; in the hollow of His hand hath He hid me, and made me as a polished shaft.

Ps. xcii. It is a good thing to give thanks unto the Lord, and to sing praises unto Thy Name, O Thou most Highest.

The Collect.

O God, Who hast made this day honourable to us in the Nativity of S. John, grant unto Thy people the grace of spiritual joy, and dispose the minds of all the faithful unto the way of everlasting salvation. Through.

The Lesson. Isa. xlix. 1-7.

Listen, O isles .... to be His servant. I will also give Thee for a light to the Gentiles, that Thou mayest be My salvation unto the end of the earth .... Kings shall see and arise, princes also shall worship *the Lord Thy God*, and the Holy One of Israel, and He shall choose Thee.

Gradual. Jeremiah i. Before I formed thee in the belly, I knew thee: and before thou camest out of the womb I sanctified thee.

℣. The Lord put forth His hand, and touched my mouth, and said unto me—

Alleluia! ℣. Matt. xi. Among them that are born of women there hath not risen a greater than John the Baptist.

The Sequence.

The Holy Baptist's yearly festival,
Herald of Christ, we celebrate to-day:
Whose life and conversation let us follow,
That to the life he spoke of he may bring us.
Most holy man, thou friend of Jesus Christ,
Devoutly we desire to share the joys
Which, unto Zechariah, Gabriel promised
To those who thy nativity should keep;*
That through this feast we may rejoice for ever,
Where happy saints of God in bliss unite.
Thou who the hearts of faithful men preparest,
Lest God should error find or treachery there,
We ask that thou wouldst intercede for us
That our continual sins may be absolved;
That He may graciously be pleased to visit
His faithful people, and abide in them;
That He Whom thou didst point out with thy finger,
The Lamb that the world's sins doth take away,
With his pure fleece may mercifully clothe us,
That we may follow Him arrayed in white,
Associate with angels, through the gate
Of brightest light, O John, thou friend of Christ!

(*The last line is said three times.*)

The Gospel. Luke i. 57-68.

At that time Elizabeth's full time was come .... redeemed His people.

The Creed.

Offert. Ps. xcii. The righteous shall flourish like a palm-tree, and shall spread abroad like a cedar in Libanus.

* *On the day of the Decollation is said, instead of the above two lines—*
Which may in heaven be given to those of us
Who glory on thy day of martyrdom

Secret. We place our gifts upon Thy Altar, O Lord, in due reverence of his Nativity, and asking his assistance who spake of the coming of the Saviour of the world, and shewed forth His presence, Jesus Christ Thy Son. Who.

Comm. Luke i. Thou, child, shalt be called the Prophet of the Highest, for Thou shalt go before the face of the Lord to prepare His ways.

P. Comm. Let Thy Church, O God, rejoice in the generation of S. John the Baptist, by whom was made known to her as the Author of her own regeneration Thy Son Jesus Christ our Lord. Who.

¶ *The same Mass is said through the Octave, unless the Sunday Mass must be sung, or unless the Masses* Salus, *or of our Lady, or of the Patron Saint occur.*

SS. JOHN AND PAUL, MM.

The Office. Ps. xxxiv.

Great are the troubles of the righteous, but the Lord delivereth him out of all. *The Lord* keepeth all his bones, so that not one of them is broken.

Ps. I will alway give thanks unto the Lord; His praise shall ever be in my mouth.

The Collect.

We beseech Thee, Almighty God, let a twofold joy await us on to-day's feast, proceeding from the glory of SS. John and Paul, whom the same faith and passion in very deed made brethren. Through.

¶ *Memorial of S. John the Baptist.*

¶ *The* Epistle viii., Grad. *and* Gospel vii., *the* Sequence *(if a Sunday)* i., Offert. ii., *and* Comm. vi. *in the Common.*

Alleluia! ℣. Rev. xi. These are the two olive-trees and the two *candles burning* before God; *they* have power to shut heaven *with clouds and to open its gates, for their tongues are made the keys of heaven.*

Secret. We place the offering of reconciliation upon Thy Altar, O Lord, adoring Thy might in the suffering of Thy Saints John and Paul, and by them imploring for ourselves pardon of our sins. Through.

P. Comm. We beseech Thee, O Lord, let the Sacrament which Thy faithful people have received be profitable unto them; and, leaning on the guardianship of those whose day they celebrate, be found meet to attain that everlastingly after which in this world they devoutly follow. Through.

THE VIGIL OF SS. PETER AND PAUL, App.

The Office. John xxi.

The Lord saith unto Peter, When thou wast young, thou girdedst thyself, and walkedst whither thou wouldest; but when thou shalt be old, thou shalt stretch forth thy hands, and another shalt gird thee and carry thee whither thou wouldest not. This spake He, signifying by what death he should glorify God.

Ps. xix. The heavens declare the glory of God, and the firmament sheweth His handiwork.

The Collect.

O God, Who permittest us to keep by anticipation the glorious day of Thine Apostles, SS. Peter and Paul, grant, we beseech Thee, that we may ever be prevented by their favour and aided by their prayers. Through.

Memorial of S. Leo, Conf. Bp.

O God, Who madest S. Léo, Thy Bishop, an equal with Thy Saints in good deeds, mercifully grant that we who keep his commemorative feast may also imitate the example of his life. Through.

¶ *Memorial of S. John the Baptist.*

The Lesson. Acts iii. 1-10.

In those days Peter and John .... which had happened unto him.

Gradual. (See ii. in the Comm.)

Alleluia. (See i. in the Common.)

The Gospel. John xxi. 16-19.

At that time Jesus said to Simon Peter .... should glorify God.

Offert. (See *Grad.* iii. in the Common.)

Secret. We beseech Thee, O Lord, let the prayers of those whose feast we keep make the gifts of reconciliation which we present, acceptable to Thee for our fasting. Through.

Secret of S. Leo. Grant, O Lord, that, at the intercession of S. Leo, Thy Bishop and Confessor, this oblation, by the offering of which Thou didst give remission of sins to the whole world, may be profitable unto us. Through.

Comm. John xxi. Simon, son of Jonas, lovest Thou Me more than these? Lord, Thou knowest all things; Thou knowest that I love Thee.

P. Comm. We have received, O Lord, the Divine Mysteries in anticipation of the feast of Thy Apostles, SS. Peter and Paul, which we desire to keep; grant, we beseech Thee, that we may be defended by their prayers whose rule doth govern us. Through.

P. Comm. of S. Leo. O Lord, we that have received the Divine Mystery, entreat that the pious intercession of S. Leo, Thy Bishop and Confessor, may accompany us, and that we may have a sense of his wished-for protection whose feast we keep. Through.

SS. Peter and Paul, *App.*

The Office. Acts. xii.

Now I know for a surety that the Lord hath sent His angel, and hath delivered me out of the hand of Herod, and from all the expectation of the people of the Jews.

Ps. And when Peter was come to himself, he said—

The Collect.

O God, Who hast hallowed this day by the martyrdom of Thy Apostles Peter and Paul, grant unto Thy Church in all things to follow the precepts of those from whom she received the beginning of her faith. Through.

The Lesson. Acts xii. 1-11.

In those days Herod the King .... the people of the Jews.

Gradual. (See *Grad.* iii. in the Common.)

Alleluia! ℣. Matt. xvi. Thou art *Simon Bar-Jonah, to whom* flesh and blood hath not revealed *the Word of the Father*, but the Father *Himself*, which is in heaven.

The Sequence.

O jocund band, sing forth melodious praise,
With symphonies conjoining rhythmic words!
With special strains chant those true lights of heaven,
Who cast their golden gleams o'er all the world,
Whose trophies flourish in the courts above.
This bright day may their merit sins absolve.
Upon each head a chaplet shines of triumph—
One o'er the cross, the other o'er the sword.
Victorious now, beyond the stars on high
They stand superior in the heavenly realm.
Hence by thy word, O blessed Peter! thou
The mighty door of heaven dost shut and ope:
With favour now receive our faithful vows,
Unloosing all the thraldom of our sin.
O holy Paul! thy sacred teaching bring,
Illuminate the people's hearts with truth,
And in so far as God may grant perfection
Raise thou their thoughts to things above the stars,
Where music of the angels doth resound,
In concert of stringed instruments and voice;
In which concordant symphony combined
That chief quartette doth excellently blend—
Virtue and Justice, Prudence, Temperance—
Wherein the hosts of heaven in ritual due
Harmonious sing canticles to Christ.
That they may with our choir associate be,
May those great luminaries grant, to whom
High-sounding acclamations we upraise.
Let all redeemed creation cry, Amen.

The Gospel.

(See *Gosp.* iv. in the Common.)

The Creed.

Offert. (See *Offert.* ii. in the Common.)

Secret. O Lord, let the prayers of Thy Apostles accompany this Sacrifice, whereby Thou dost permit us to gain purification and protection, which we present to be consecrated to Thy Name. Through.

Comm. Matt. xvi. Thou art Peter, and upon this rock I will build My Church.

P. Comm. We beseech Thee, O Lord, at the intercession of Thy Apostles, to defend us, whom Thou hast filled with the Bread of Heaven, from all adversities. Through.

¶ *Within the Octave (when the Mass is of the same) is said all as* i. *in the Common, except* Grad. iii. *and* Offert. iv., *and the Collects, which are as on the day.*

THE COMMEMORATION OF S. PAUL, *Ap.*

The Office. 2 Tim. i.

I know whom I have believed, and am persuaded that He is able to keep that which I have committed unto Him against that day.

Ps. cxxxix. O Lord, Thou hast searched me out, and known me; Thou knowest my downsitting and mine uprising.

The Collect.

O God, Who through the preaching of Thy Apostle S. Paul didst teach the Gentile multitudes, grant, we beseech Thee, that we may perceive his protection whose feast we keep. Through.

¶ *Memorial of S. Peter (as on the feast of the Chair of S. Peter), and of S. John Baptist (as on the day).*

The Epistle. Gal. i. 11-26.

I certify you, brethren .... and they glorified *our Lord Jesus Christ* in me.

¶ *All as on the Conv. of S. Paul. The* Creed *is said.*

Secret. We present unto Thee, O Lord, our due oblation, and pray that it, being consecrated, may contribute to the praise of Thy Name, the reverence due to the dignity of the Apostles, and unto our own protection. Through.

P. Comm. Grant, we beseech Thee, Almighty God, that Thy Church, being refreshed by Thy saving Sacrament, and supported by the prayers of S. Paul Thy Apostle, may in such wise receive these present gifts that she may be found meet to attain unto those which are eternal. Through.

THE OCTAVE OF S. JOHN BAPTIST.

¶ *All as on the Day, except—*

The Gospel. Luke i. 13-25.

At that time the angel said unto Zacharias, Fear not ...... my reproach among men.

¶ *If this feast fall on Saturday or Sunday the Mass of the Octave is said in the Chapter-house.*

The Visitation of the Blessed Virgin Mary.

The Office.

Let us all rejoice in the Lord, and celebrate the Feast in honour of the Virgin Mary, concerning whose Visitation angels rejoice and praise the Son of God.

Ps. xlv. My heart is inditing of a good matter: I will speak of the things which I have made unto the King.

The Collect.

O God, Who for the consolation of both didst move the most Holy Virgin Mary, Mother of Thy Only Begotten Son, to visit S. Elizabeth, mercifully grant that we Thy servants may ever draw comfort from her Visitation, and be by Thy protection defended from all adversities. Through.

¶ *There is no Memorial.*

The Lesson. The Song of Solomon ii. 1-14.

I am the Rose of Sharon .... thy countenance is comely.

Gradual. Blessed and worthy of reverence art thou, O Virgin Mary, who in chastity wast found the Mother of the Saviour.

℣. *O Virgin Mother of God, He Whom the world cannot contain was hidden in thy womb, and was made Man.*

Alleluia! ℣. *Wondrous Mother, highest in grace, multiply thy gifts, enrich the Church with holy virtues, and take away division; give thy protection to the penitent.*

The Sequence.

Let the glad feast employ our lay
Which Zachariah's house this day
Witnessed with happiness:
Great doings there we contemplate:
Let then a feast new feast create,
The Church's house to bless.

No higher feast our joy can move
Than that whereon abundant love
  Did gracious token show:
Which blest Elizabeth perceived,
When in old age she seed conceived,
  As we from Scripture know.

Let the whole world give welcome meet,
And let the Visitation sweet
  Be heartily adored;
Her pitying heart's benignity,
Her lowly state's humility
  A sacred balm afford.

The spirit of prophetic fire,
Both Babe and Mother did inspire
  When Mary enterèd;
Endued with comfort so, and strength,
The happy Mother saw at length
  Her time accomplishèd.

Then of this feast the author true,
O Sion, praise with honour due,
  The Mother of our Lord;
Extol her loudly as ye may,
Her favour ye can ne'er repay,
  Nor worthy praise accord.

Thou who didst visit on the hill,
Deign in these plains to visit still
  Our Mother Church below;
Of Christian souls thou medicine,
May that be ours by grace divine
  Which man cannot bestow.

Of earthly women, thou most blest
Star of the Sea, Light manifest,
Comfort thy mournful servants' breast,
  On all thy brightness send.
Grant us that blessedness to know
Which from thy Holy Child doth flow,
That so he may on us bestow
  A glory without end.

The Gospel. Luke i. 38-47.

At that time Mary arose and went .... my Saviour.

The Creed.

Offert. Luke i. Hail, *Mary*, that art highly favoured, the Lord is with thee: blessed art thou among women, and blessed is the fruit of thy womb.

Secret. O Lord, we beseech Thee, graciously behold the oblation of Thy Church; and at the intercession of the glorious Virgin Mary, Mother of God, grant her always the gifts of union and peace. Through.

Comm. Blessed is the womb of the Virgin Mary, which bare the Son of the Eternal Father.

P. Comm. O God, who by means of the Blessed Virgin Mary hast succoured a lost world, for her glorious sake and prayers be pleased to grant that all offence and disorder be removed from the Kingdom of Thy Church, and that she may ever duly serve Thee in Thy peace. Who.

¶ *Throughout the Octave let the same Mass be said with the following* Sequences. *All these, except that for the Fifth, Sixth, and Octave Day, stand in the Missals for the same days in the Octave of the Assumption—*

THE SECOND DAY.

The Sequence.

Mary, after travail, Virgin,
Mother who gavest birth to God,
Made by his power full of grace,
Hail, Lady of all earth below!
Hail, gracious Queen of heaven above!
Let Heaven and all the concourse of the saints
To thee pour forth harmonious symphonies;
Let earth, woods, waters, cry aloud to thee.
Illustrious Parent, blessed Mother, hail!
Whence light and truth were to the world made known.
Thou at thy holy paps hast Jesus fed,
Virgin which hast brought forth—a Mother yet a Maid!
Wherefore, O Lady, listen to our vows;
For man's salvation intercede with Christ.
Through thee, O Mother, let, we pray,
Thy children's sins be done away;
And unto us be entrance given
To everlasting joys of heaven;
And glory may be there secure
Where life for ever doth endure.

THE THIRD DAY.

The Sequence.

Hail, Mary, highly favoured!
The Lord is with Thee, gentle Maid!
Thou art above all women blest,
Who peace to all mankind broughtest,
  Joy to the angel's heart.
The fruit of thy womb blessed be,
Who hath ordained us graciously
  With thee to have a part.

By this salutation,
Sweet sign of salvation,
  A thing wondrous to hear,
Thou didst bring forth a child:
A new Star undefiled,
  A new Sun thou didst bear—
Thou the temple wast made,
An immaculate Maid,
Of Christ our salvation,
The Lamb and the Lion.
The Flower and the Dew,
By a miracle new,
Bread and Shepherd, were born
Of thee, rose without thorn,
Of all virgins the Queen.
Of righteousness thou art the city,
Thou art the Mother, too, of pity:
Theophilus thou didst reclaim
Out of the pit of guilt and shame.
Wherefore, Star of the Sea!
Sojourn of Deity,
Of the sun dawning ray,
Portal of Paradise,
From which light did arise,
To Thy Holy Son pray,
That we, from all our sins set free,
May by his grace accepted be,
And gain a habitation bright
Where ever shines unclouded light!

THE FOURTH DAY.

The Sequence.

Now let the faithful choir with joy exulting sing,
  Alleluia!

The Undefiled brings forth of mighty kings the King,
  O wonder rare!

The Heaven-descended Councillor, born of a Virgin, doth appear,
  Sun of a Star:

A Sun that doth no setting know, a Star whose rays do ever glow,
  Gleaming afar.

As a star puts forth its ray, so the Virgin in like way
  Her Son doth bear.

Bright the Star doth still endure, so the Virgin still is pure,
  No stain is there.

Of Lebanon the cedar tall is with the hyssop on the wall
  Made lowly here:

The self-existent Word on high took on Him flesh, and bodily
  His Passion bare.

Esaias this foretold, the Synagogue of old knew this, yet fast did hold
  Its blindness drear.

Though prophets may rehearse, and heathen Sybil's verse confirm, hearts still averse
Will not give ear.

Believe without delay; unhappy nation say, why will ye go away?
Lost people, hear.

No more the Scripture scorn, think on the Child new-born, Whom for this world forlorn
Mary did bear.

THE FIFTH DAY.

¶ *The* Sequence *as on the Purification of Our Lady.*

THE SIXTH DAY.

¶ *The* Sequence *as on the Annunciation.*

THE SEVENTH DAY.

The Sequence.

The light of this auspicious day
Beholds the honours which we pay
To her who God did bear;
On this high festival we raise
To Mary ever-Virgin praise,
And her deserts declare.

Let every man, at every hour,
Before her humble vows outpour,
Seek her protecting face;
Bring their best energies to sing,
With heart and soul, with voice and string,
Hail, Mary, full of grace!

Hail! Lady, Mistress of the skies!
Hail! ever-maiden, chaste and wise!
Thou peerless Mother fair.
Unwedded thou didst seed conceive,
Thou didst the wondrous grace receive,
Daughter the Sire to bear.

Fresh garden which south breezes fan,
Path secret kept, untrod by man,
Gate closed most jealously;
Sweet earth by dews of heaven renewed;
Pure fleece of Gideon, bedewed
By showers of Deity.

Hail! brightness of the firmament!
With thy rays circumambient,
Visit our darkened soul.
Star of the Sea! the storm appease,
Lest tempest-tost the raging seas
Destructive o'er us roll.

THE OCTAVE DAY OF THE VISITATION OF BLESSED MARY.

The Sequence.

Come, thou Mother of all grace!
Succour of our wretched race,
Fount of tenderness!
Light of the Church, come thou, and pour
Upon thy servants grieving sore,
A ray of happiness.

As our Queen we honour thee,
Sing praises to thee joyously
With fervency of heart;
Thou in troubles and distress,
And when doubts our souls depress,
Health and comfort art.

Star brightly gleaming in the sky,
Allay the raging tempest high,
Which stirs this stormy sea;
Look on Symon Peter's boat,
On thy Son's holy seamless coat,
Let them not rended be.

Haven of those who navigate,
Thy children, when they supplicate,
Deign graciously to guide:
Do thou the sorrowing console,
Give succour to the fainting soul,
The erring gently chide.

By that blest Infant born of thee,
With man thou joinest Deity,
With earthly things the sky;
Let heresies and schism cease,
And to the covenant of peace
Give thou security.

SS. PROCESSUS AND MARTINIAN, MM.

¶ *The* Office *and* Alleluia vi., Epistle i., Grad. v., Gospel viii., Offert. ii., *and* Comm. vii. *in the Common.*

The Collect.

(See *Coll.* ii. in Comm. Many Conff.)

Memorial of S. Swithin.

O God, Who permittest us to celebrate the most holy day of the burial of S. Swithin, Thy Confessor and Bishop, graciously be present with the prayers of Thy Church, that she may be protected by the guardianship of him in whose deeds she glories. Through.

¶ *Memorial of SS. Peter and Paul and of Our Lady.*

Secret. Receive, O Lord, our prayers and oblations, and that they may be worthy in Thy sight let us be succoured by the prayers of Thy Martyrs SS. Processus and Martinian. Through.

Secret of S. Swithin. Accept, O most merciful God, the gift which we present to Thy Majesty, and at the intercession of S. Swithin, Thy Bishop and Confessor, grant that it may be profitable to our welfare in this life and in the next. Through.

P. Comm. We who have been refreshed with the Divine Mystery, and who rejoice in the earthly commemoration of Thy Martyrs SS. Processus and Martiniac, beseech Thee, O Lord, that we may at their intercession be numbered in the lot of salvation in which they by Thy grace have glory. Through.

P. Comm. of S. Swithin. O God, Who by the partaking of Thy Sacrament dost cleanse us from the pollution of sin, grant, we beseech Thee, that for the sake of S. Swithin, Thy Bishop and Confessor, we may be delivered from all adversities, and enjoy the delights of heavenly life. Through.

TRANSLATION AND ORDERING OF S. MARTIN, *Conf. Bp.*

¶ *All as* i. *in the Common, except* Grad. *and* Comm. iii., *and* Alleluia iv. *in the same.*

The Collect.

O God, Who gavest S. Martin unto Thy people to be a minister of eternal salvation, grant, we beseech Thee, that he who performed Thy commands on earth may ever deign to be our intercessor in heaven. Through.

¶ *Memorials of the Visitation and of the Apostles.*

The Sequence.

Let the whole Church, in Catholic peace united,
Proclaim the praise of Martin, priest of Christ,
And at his name let heretics fly pale.
In such a son rejoice, Pannonia;
Exult in such a scholar, Italy.

In holy strife each of Gaul's three divisions
Contend of which he should be held the Bishop;
But let all joy alike to call him Father:
His body rests in care of Tours alone.
Let Franks and Germans join in his applause,
Clad in whose cloak the Lord Himself was seen.
He in the parts of Egypt is renowned;
And by wise men of Greece, who count themselves
Inferior in gifts and skill to Martin:
For fevers he allays, and devils casts out,
And paralytic limbs restores to vigour.
By his prevailing prayer three dead are raised.
He impious rites destroys, and images
Unto the flames delivers, for Christ's glory;
With unclad arms the Mysteries celebrating,
He with a light from heaven is endued.
With eyes and hands, and his whole soul uplifted
To heaven, all things earthly he despises.
Of Christ he ever spake and righteousness.
And all which to true life doth appertain:
Therefore we all entreat thee, blessed Martin,
That as thou here hast many wonders shown us,
So by thy supplication thou wouldst ever
Pour out on us the grace of Christ from heaven.

The Gospel. Luke xii. 32-34.

At that time Jesus said to His disciples, Fear not .... there will your heart be also.

Secret. We beseech Thee, O Lord, let the intercession of S. Martin, Thy Bishop and Confessor, commend our gifts, and make us ever acceptable to Thy Majesty. Through.

P. Comm. We beseech Thee, O Lord, let the Sacrament which we received bestow on us a saving defence, and at the intercession and for the sake of Thy Bishop and Confessor, S. Martin, absolve us from all sin. Through

---

THE OCTAVE DAY OF SS. PETER AND PAUL.

¶ *The* Office v., Epistle viii., Grad., Offert., *and* Comm. iv., Sequence i., *and* Alleluia *as on SS. John and Paul.*

The Collect.

O God, Whose right hand raised S. Peter the Apostle as he walked on the waves that he sank not, and delivered His Apostle Paul, who thrice suffered shipwreck, from the deep of the sea, graciously hear us, and grant that for the sake of both we may attain unto everlasting glory. Who.

The Gospel. Matt. xiv. 22-33.

At that time Jesus constrained .... the Son of God.

Secret. We beseech Thee, O Most High God, look upon the vows which we pay unto Thee, and grant that they may be pleasing unto Thee for the prayers of those in whose honour they are presented. Through.

P. Comm. O Lord, let the Sacrament which we have received prepare for us a heavenly healing at the prayers of Thy Apostles Peter and Paul. Through.

THE TRANSLATION OF S. THOMAS OF CANTERBURY, *Mart.*

¶ *All as on his feast in Christmas-week, except the* Collects, *which are the same as on the Translation of S. Edmund, changing* Edmund *into* Thomas.

The Feast of Relics.

¶ *On the first Sunday after the Translation of S. Thomas shall be celebrated the feast of Relics of the Church of Sarum. The* Office *and* Grad. v., Epistle viii., Alleluia iii., Sequence, Offert., and Comm. i., Gospel ii., *in Comm. Many Mart.*

The Collect.

Grant, we beseech Thee, Almighty God, that the good deeds of the Holy Mother of God, and ever-Virgin Mary, and of all Thy Saints whose relics are contained in this church, may protect us, that at their prayers we may continually rejoice in peace and quietness in Thy praise. Through.

Secret. We beseech Thee, merciful God, behold with gracious eye the gifts offered to Thy Majesty, that at the prayers of those whose most precious relics are preserved in this church they may be profitable unto our salvation. Through.

P. Comm. We who have tasted the Divine Mysteries beseech Thee, O Lord, let the intercession of those in whose holy guardianship we delight everywhere protect us. Through.

THE SEVEN BRETHREN, MM.

The Office. Ps. cxiii.

Praise the Lord, ye servants, O praise the Name of the Lord; *Who* maketh the barren woman to keep house, and to be a joyful mother of children.

Ps. Blessed be the Name of the Lord from this time forth for evermore.

The Collect.

Grant, we beseech Thee, Almighty God, that as we have known that Thy glorious Martyrs, Felix, Philip, Vitalis, Marcial, Alexander, Sylvanus, and Januarius, were bold in their confession, so we may have a sense of their holy zeal in interceding with Thee on our behalf. Through.

The Epistle.

(See iv. in the Common.)

Gradual. (See viii. in the Common.)

Alleluia! ℣. Ps. cxiii. Praise the Lord, ye servants: O praise the Name of the Lord.

℣. Blessed be the Name of the Lord from this time forth for evermore.

¶ *Both* ℣℣. *are said as in Easter-week.*

The Gospel. Matt. xii. 46-50.

At that time, while *Jesus* talked to the people .... the same is my brother, and sister, and mother.

Offert. (See v. in the Common.)

Secret. Regard, O Lord, the oblations of the faithful, and let them be acceptable to Thee on the death of Thy saints, who loving Thee with the love of brethren gave their bodies to martyrdom. Through.

Comm. Matt. xii. Whosoever shall do the will of My Father Which is in Heaven, the same is My brother, and sister, and mother, *saith the Lord.*

P. Comm. We that are refreshed, O Lord, by Thy grace with the Food of Life, make our supplications unto Thee that we may have a share in the reward of those whose victory we celebrate. Through.

THE TRANSLATION OF S. BENEDICT, *Abbot.*

¶ *All as in the Common, except* Comm. ii. *in Comm. Conf. Bp.*

The Collect.

We beseech Thee, O Lord, let the intercession of the Abbot S. Benedict commend us in Thy sight, that by his protection we may obtain that which by our own good deeds we cannot. Through.

Secret. We beseech Thee, O Lord, at the prayers of S. Benedict, let the Sacrifice which we have laid upon the holy Altar be made profitable unto our salvation. Through.

P. Comm. O Lord, let the Abbot S. Benedict protect us by his intercession whilst we receive Thy Sacrament, that we may both prove the wonderful excellence of his conversation, and receive the benefit of his intercession. Through.

THE TRANSLATION OF S. SWITHIN AND HIS COMPANIONS, *Conff.*

¶ *All as in the Common, except—*

The Collect.

Almighty and everlasting God, Who hast made this day honourable by the translation of S. Swithin, Thy Bishop and Confessor, and his companions; grant joyfulness unto Thy Church in this celebration, and at their intercession whose feasts we revere on earth let us be exalted unto heaven. Through.

Secret. (As on the feast of SS. Theodolus and Gildardus.)

P. Comm. O Lord, we that have received the pledge of everlasting life, humbly implore Thee that, at the intercession of S. Swithin, Thy Bishop and Confessor, and his companions, we may verily partake of that which we have handled under the form of a sacrament. Through.

THE TRANSLATION OF S. OSMUND, *Conf. Bp.*

¶ *The* Office *as on Visit. B. V. M., changing the word* Visitation *to* Translation. Epistle *and* Comm. ii., Grad. iv., Alleluia, Gospel, *and* Offert. i. *in the Common.*

The Collect.

O God, Whose miracles of old we perceive to shine forth even in our days to the magnifying of Thy Name, and the praise and honour of S. Osmund, Confessor and Bishop, mercifully grant us, at the intercession of him whose Translation we keep, both to glorify Thee in this present world and to enjoy Thy presence in that which is to come. Through.

The Sequence.

Let us Messiah's praise essay,
Who is the Truth, the Life, the Way,
The glory of the blest:
This joyful day let Osmund's name
And memory of illustrious fame
Be by the Church confest.

On this the feast of his Translation
The heavenly host with veneration
Stand up in reverence:
The Son of God they celebrate,
In Whom all hope doth culminate;
Who of his excellence

Made this Confessor brighter shine
Than Osmund's own illustrious line,
In parentage more high.
Above his military shield
The merits of his virtues yield
A nobler dignity.

Prudent, heroic, self-denying,
On faith and hope for strength relying,
In justice eminent;
In charity most excellent,
Such panoply from heaven sent
All wickedness repels.

Envy and quarrels, haughtiness,
Base avarice and unfeelingness,
Jests, vauntings, gluttony,
A soldier without spot or stain,
He doth beat down, give up, refrain,
Cast out, and make to flee.

Jewels, possessions, robes, and gold,
He. storing treasures still untold,
To the Church dedicates:
With these he beautifies the shrine,
But from himself a stream divine
Of wonders emanates.

He makes the lame to walk, the blind
To see, the dumb a tongue to find,
The sad to mourn no more;
Lepers he heals, the dead brings back,
Nor faileth those who his help lack
From sickness to restore.

O saintly Bishop, hear when we
Our suppliant voices lift to thee,
To us thy comfort give:
May we be cleansed from stain of sin,
To heavenly courts admittance win,
And in their brightness live.

Secret. Sanctify our gifts, O Lord, we beseech Thee, for the sake and at the intercesion of Thy bountiful Confessor Osmund, that they may be changed into the Body and Blood of Thy Son Jesus Christ our Lord, and may be profitable to the salvation of our souls. Through.

P. Comm. We that have received the holy gifts humbly beseech Thee, O Lord, that we, being strengthened by their virtue, may both follow the example of Thy Bishop and Confessor S. Osmund, and attain unto joys eternal. Through.

S. KENELM, Mart. King.

¶ *The* Office *and* Epistle iii., Gospel iv., Grad. i., Alleluia *and* Offert. v., *and* Comm. vi. *in the Common.*

The Collect.

Almighty and merciful God, Who hast specially gladdened us this day by the feast of S. Kenelm, Thy King and Martyr, look with serenity on the vows of Thy faithful people, and grant that for his sake and prayers whose feast we keep we may ever be sustained. Through.

Secret. Look down, O Lord God, on These present gifts, and at the intercession of S. Kenelm, Thy Martyr, whose revered feast we observe, let them bestow on the faithful forgiveness unto salvation, and worthily obtain for them the joys of everlasting life. Through.

P. Comm. We beseech Thee, O Lord, let Thy people be glad in keeping the feast of Thy Martyr S. Kenelm, and make them whom Thou hast refreshed with the food of the heavenly Table to have fellowship with Thee in everlasting life. Through.

S. ARNULPH, Mart. and Bp.

¶ *The* Office *and* Alleluia v., *the rest* iii. *except* Offert. i., *in Comm. Mart*

The Collect.

Almighty God, be present at our supplications, and at the intercession of S. Arnulph, Thy Bishop and Martyr, mercifully grant that the effects of Thy accustomed compassion may be seen in them whom Thou dost encourage to hope for Thy pity. Through.

Secret. O Lord, let not the gracious prayers of Thy Bishop and Martyr, S. Arnulph, be wanting to us to reconcile our gifts to Thee, and ever to obtain Thy pardon for us. Through.

P. Comm. We beseech Thee, O Lord, let Thy blessed Bishop and Martyr, Arnulph, draw nigh to pray that Thy Sacrifice might give us salvation, Through.

S. MARGARET, Virg. Mart.

¶ *The* Office, Offert. *and Comm.* iii., Epistle i., Grad. *and* Alleluia ii., *and the rest as in the Common.*

The Collect.

O God, Who on this day didst cause the Virgin S. Margaret to enter into heaven by the palm of martyrdom; grant us, we beseech Thee, to follow her example, and be counted worthy to attain unto Thee. Through.

Secret. We beseech Thee, O Lord, let the Sacrifice offered on the feast of Thy Virgin Martyr, S. Margaret, give us both holiness of mind and continual chastity of body. Through.

P. Comm. As on S. Kenelm's Day.

S. PRAXEDES, Virg.

¶ *The* Office ii. *and* Comm. iv. *in Comm. Virg. Mart.*; Epistle, Grad., *and* Alleluia ii., *and the rest as in the Common.*

The Collect.

Almighty God, let the supplication of Thy Virgin S. Praxedes, be present with Thy people, that whoever rejoices in her honour may be protected by Thy aid. Through.

Secret. Receive, O Lord, we beseech Thee, the gift offered in honour of Thy holy Virgin, Praxedes, and for her sake and prayers abundantly bestow upon us in Thy mercy that which we cannot of ourselves obtain. Through.

P. Comm. We beseech Thee, O Lord, let Thy holy ordinance, for the sake and by the aid of S. Praxedes, Thy Virgin, put away all our sins from us, and bring us to the Kingdom of Heaven. Through.

S. MARY MAGDALENE.

The Office.

As in the Common.

The Collect.

Grant us, most merciful Father, like as S. Mary Magdalene, by loving Thy Only Begotton Son above all things, obtained forgiveness of her sins, so she may procure for us in Thy compassionate presence everlasting blessedness. Through.

Memorial of S. Wandregesilus.

O God, by Whose grace the life of S. Wandregesilus, Thy Abbot and Confessor, hath been highly praised, at his intercession let Thy loving-kindness work in us that which is pleasing in Thy sight. Through.

The Lesson.

As in the Common.

Gradual. As iv. in Comm. Virg. Mart.

Alleluia! ℣. Luke x. Mary hath chosen that good part which shall not be taken away from her.

The Sequence.

As on Saturday in Easter-week.

The Gospel. Luke vii. 36-50.

At that time one of the Pharisees desired *Jesus* that He would eat with Him .... go in peace.

The Creed.

Offert. As ii. in the Common.

Secret. Bless, O Lord, the Sacrifice offered unto Thee; and grant that S. Mary Magdalene may obtain for us of Thee that blessing which she gained from Thy Only Begotten Son, while she offered unto Him a mystical service. Through.

Secret of S. Wandregesilus. We beseech Thee, Almighty God, let the oblation of Thy family, which is adorned by the life and example of S. Wandregesilus, Thy Confessor and Abbot, be commended to Thee by his holy intercession. Through.

Comm. As in Comm. Virg., not Mart.

P. Comm. O Lord, let the following of the example of S. Mary Magdalene afford us wholesome teaching, that we may be found meet to have a share in that good part which shall not be taken away from her. Through.

P. Comm. of S. Wandregesilus. We who have received Thy Sacrament humbly pray Thee, O Lord, that we may perceive the guardianship of S. Wandregesilus, Thy Confessor and Abbot, whose memory we reverence. Through.

S. APOLLINARIS, Mart. Bp.

¶ *The* Office ii., Grad. iii., Alleluia iv., *and* Offert. i. *Comm. Conf. Bp.*; Epistle iv. *Comm. Mart.*; Gospel v. *Comm. Ap.*

The Collect.

Let the appointed day of Thy Martyr and Bishop, S. Apollinaris, O Lord, ever be prolonged to us, and both pour into our hearts the joy of his glory and make us acceptable to Thee. Through.

Secret. We beseech Thee, O Lord, let the reverend confession and prayers of S. Apollinaris, Thy Martyr, ever commend our oblation. Through.

Comm. Ps. lxxxix. I have sworn once by My holiness, his seed shall endure for ever; and his seat is like as the sun before Me; he shall stand fast for evermore as the moon, and as the faithful witness in heaven.

P. Comm. O Lord, we that have received the pledge of eternal redemption beseech Thee that at the intercession of Thy Martyr, S. Apollinaris, it may aid and comfort us in this life and in life eternal. Through.

THE VIGIL OF S. JAMES, Ap.

¶ *All as Vig. Ap., except Memorial of S. Christina.*

The Collect.

O Lord, let Christina, Thy Virgin and Martyr, who hath ever

been pleasing to Thee both for her chastity's sake and for Thy power shown forth in her, implore forgiveness for us. Through.

Secret. We beseech Thee, Almighty God, that we who honour the yearly feast of S. Christina, Thy Virgin and Martyr, by this Sacrifice may be ever confirmed by the integrity of her faith, and aided before Thee by her holy prayers. Through.

P. Comm. We humbly beg of Thee, Almighty God, at the intercession of S. Christina, Thy Virgin and Martyr, to keep under Thy perpetual protection those whom Thou hast satisfied with the heavenly gift. Through.

¶ *If this Vigil fall on a Sunday let nothing be done of the Vigil, except a Memorial only.*

S. James, *Ap.*

¶ *All as* i. *in the Common, except* Grad. *and* Sequence ii., *and* Offert. iii. *in the same.*

The Collect.

Be Thou, O Lord, the sanctifier and guardian of Thy people, that under the protection of Thy Apostle, James, they may please Thee in their conversation, and serve Thee in all quietness. Through.

Memorial of SS. Christopher and Cucufatus, MM.

O God, Creator and Ruler of the world, Who, hast hallowed this day by the passion of Thy Martyrs, SS. Christopher and Cucufatus, grant that all we who reverence them for their martyrdom's sake may at their intercession be delivered from the eternal flames of hell. Through.

The Gospel. Matt. xx. 20-23.

At that time came to *Jesus* the brother .... prepared of My Father.

The Creed.

Secret. We beseech Thee, O Lord, let the death of S. James, Thy Apostle, obtain favour for the oblation of Thy people, that those things which for our sake are unfitting may at his intercession become pleasing unto Thee. Through.

Secret. of SS. Christopher and Cucufatus. O Lord, we beseech Thee, favourably accept the gifts we offer, and for the sake and prayers of Thy Martyrs, SS. Christopher and Cucufatus, grant that they may aid and further our salvation. Through.

P. Comm. We, rejoicing in him on whose feast we have received Thy holy Mysteries, O Saviour of the world, beseech Thee, O Lord, to aid us, at the intercession of S. James, Thy Apostle, on whose day Thou hast refreshed us with Thy Body and Blood. Who.

P. Comm. of SS. Christopher and Cucufatus. O Lord, we that have received the heavenly Sacrament on the feast of Thy Martyrs, SS. Christopher and Cucufatus, beseech Thee, at their prayers, to grant that we may attain in joy everlasting unto that which here on earth we minister. Through.

S. ANNE, MOTHER OF MARY.

The Office.

As in the Common, inserting *Anne, Mother of Mary.*

The Collect.

O God, Who on this day didst exalt the excellent S. Anne, who bare Thy dearly-beloved Mother, to the joys of life in heaven, grant, we beseech Thee, that we may attain to eternal blessedness for her glory's sake of whose saving offspring Thou wast pleased to take unto Thee the nature of man for the salvation of the world. Who.

The Epistle.

As in the Common.

Gradual. As iv. Comm. Virg. Mart.

Alleluia! Hail, holy Mother Anne, of whom was born the Virgin Mary, who conceived seed from heaven, and brought forth the Saviour of the world.

The Sequence.

Under the old law's discipline,
Descended from a royal line,
Anne was born on earth:
Long did this illustrious dame
Bring forth no child to bear her name,
Which to much grief gave birth.

At length the Lord saw fit to give,
Her heart in mercy to revive,
The blessing of a child.
Offspring of patriarchal line,
Anne, who dost in lustre shine,
In glory undefiled,

We unto thee petition make,
That for thy signal merit's sake
Grace may on us descend.
O Anne, Mother, pure for ever!
O rose, right fair, of beauteous air!
With whom the lilies blend,

Thou who didst bear Christ's Mother dear,
When we despair, with gracious prayer
To our protection come.
Lo, here of light the spotless shrine,
Hope for the weak and medicine,
Thy offspring as a Queen doth shine
In the celestial home.

May she who is preferred o'er all
Receive, through thee, our humble call;
And in the courts ethereal
Our advocate become.

The Gospel. Matt. i. 1-16.

The book of the generation .... which is called Christ.

Offert. (See ii. in the Common.)

Secret. Sanctify, O Redeemer of the World, the gifts of this Sacrifice, and make the same profitable to our salvation, at the prayers of S. Anne, from whose womb, as from a palace, Thy Mother, the shrine of Virgin purity, issued forth. Who.

Comm. As Comm. Virg., not Mart.

P. Comm. Protect us, O Lord, who have received the appointed Sacrament of the heavenly Table, at the glorious intercession of S. Anne, Mother of Mary, of whom came forth the Virgin, who bare a Son for the salvation of all that are born of woman; who, without loss of chastity, brought forth for us the Light of Life, our Lord Jesus Christ, Thy Son. Who.

THE SEVEN SLEEPERS.

¶ *The* Office vii., Epistle ii., Grad. *and* Alleluia v., Gospel vi., Offert. i., *and* Comm. iv. *in the Common.*

The Collect.

O God, Who didst richly crown with reward the Seven Sleepers, the glorious heralds* of the everlasting Resurrection, grant, we beseech Thee, that we may attain, at their prayers, unto the holy resurrection which by them was marvellously set forth. Through.

Secret. O God, in Whom all the righteous have rest, and the Saints assured peace, grant us worthily to offer the oblation of reconciliation, that here on earth we may continually meditate upon the perfect peace which Thy Saints always enjoy in heaven. Through.

P. Comm. We, calling to mind the victory of Thy Saints, have received the adorable Sacrament, which we beseech Thee, O Lord, may obtain us pardon of our sins for their sake, concerning whose sleep we praise Thy Majesty. Through.

S. SAMPSON, Conf. Bp.

¶ *All as* i., *in the Common, except* Alleluia *and* Offert. ii., Comm. iii. *in the same.*

The Collect.

Almighty and everlasting God, grant unto us, Thy servants, at the intercession of S. Sampson, Thy Bishop, when we entreat, pardon of our sins; when we seek, the way of salvation; when we knock, the opening of the court of the heavenly kingdom, that by Thy aid we may be found meet to attain unto the eternal abode of Thy Majesty. Through.

Memorial of S. Panthaleon, Mart.

O God, Who hast hallowed this day by the martyrdom of S. Panthaleon, grant, we beseech Thee, at his intercession, that what shall have a recompense of reward in heaven, may here be manifest in our conversation. Through.

Secret. O God of Apostles, God of Martyrs, God of Confessors, God of Virgins, God of all the elect, we humbly entreat Thee, vouchsafe to sanctify and bless this holy Sacrifice in honour of S. Sampson, Bishop, and let it be profitable in the sight of Thy Majesty both for the health of our bodies and the salvation of our souls. Through.

Secret of S. Panthaleon. O Lord, let S. Panthaleon, Thy Martyr, who, being wasted by divers torments, was verily a living victim, by his intercession make the oblations which we present pleasing to Thee. Through.

* *i.e.*, Types.

P. Comm. O Lord, Who hast satisfied us with holy gifts on this feast of S. Sampson, Thy Bishop and Confessor, we beseech Thee be pleased to multiply unto Thy Church peace, faith, hope, and charity, whereby we may be found worthy to please Thee in Thy Church. Through.

P. Comm. of S. Panthaleon. We, that have been filled with the sacred food of our redemption, beseech Thee, O Lord, that at the intercession of S. Panthaleon, Thy Martyr, we may, by the holy Mysteries which we have received, be made meet for joys eternal. Through.

A SECOND MASS OF S. PANTHALEON.

¶ *The* Office ii., Epistle *as on S. Alban's Day*, Grad. *and* Offert. i., Alleluia iii., Gospel iii., *and* Comm. vi. *in the Common. The* Collects *as in the last Mass.*

SS. FELIX, SIMPLICIUS, FAUSTINUS, AND BEATRICE, MM.

¶ *All as in Comm. Many Conf., except* Epistle vi., Alleluia iv., *and* Gospel vii. *in the Common.*

The Collect.

Grant, we beseech Thee, Almighty God, that like as Christians rejoice on earth in the feast of Thy Martyrs, Felix, Simplicius, Faustinus, and Beatrice, so in eternity they may have the fruition thereof, and devoutly apprehend that which they celebrate in deed. Through.

Secret. We humbly beseech Thee, O Lord, let the Sacrifice which we present in honour of Thy Martyrs, SS. Felix, Simplicius, Faustinus, and Beatrice, confer upon us pardon and salvation. Through.

P. Comm. O Lord, let the people set apart for Thy service bear away with them the benefit and joy of Thy blessing, that in the continual protection of Thy holy Martyrs, Felix, Simplicius, Faustinus, and Beatrice, they may reap the fruit of the service they have presented on earth. Through.

SS. ABDON AND SENNES, MM.

¶ *All as* i. *in the Common, except* Alleluia vi., Gospel xi., Comm. iii. *in the same*, Epistle ii. *Comm. Mart.*

The Collect.

O God, Who of Thy grace didst bestow upon Thy Martyrs,

Abdon and Sennes, the great favour of attaining unto this glory, grant unto Thy servants pardon of their sins, that for the sake and intercession of Thy Saints we may be delivered from all adversity. Through.

Secret. O Lord, we touch with devotion of heart these mysteries, which we have attended in reverence for Thy Martyrs, Abdon and Sennes, whereby let protection and joys be multiplied to us. Through.

P. Comm. Let Thy faithful people, O Lord, receive the gift of heavenly healing, whereby they may, at the intercession of Thy Martyrs, SS. Abdon and Sennes, be cleansed from all their sins. Through.

S. GERMANUS, Conf. Bp.

¶ *The* Office, Offert, *and* Comm. i., Epistle *and* Gospel iii., Grad., *and* Alleluia ii. *in the Common.*

The Collect.

Hear us, O God of our salvation, and forasmuch as the voice of our prayers deserveth not to be heard, we beseech Thee, let the intercession of S. Germanus, Thy Bishop and Confessor, be accepted in our behalf. Through.

Secret. O Lord, we that offer unto Thee the Sacrifice in memory of Thy Bishop and Confessor, S. Germanus, beseech Thee that, by his holy support and intercession, we may obtain the reconciliation which of ourselves we deserve not. Through.

P. Comm. We humbly beseech Thee, Almighty God, that we who have received the food of Thy heavenly Table may, at the intercession of Thy Confessor and Bishop, S. Germanus, attain unto life everlasting. Through.

THE CHAINS OF S. PETER, *Ap.*

All as on SS. Peter and Paul, except—

The Collect.

O God, Who didst loose S. Peter the Apostle from his chains, and let him go unhurt, we beseech Thee loose the chains of our sins, and mercifully defend us from all evil. Through.

Memorial of the Maccabees, MM.

Let the crown of the brother Martyrs, O Lord, cause us to rejoice, and increase and strengthen our faith, and comfort us with their manifold protection. Through.

The Lesson. Acts xii. 12-17.

In those days, Peter, when he had gone forth from prison, came to the house of Mary .... had brought him out of prison.

Alleluia! ℣. At the command of God, loose, O Peter, the chains of the world, thou who dost cause the kingdom of heaven to be opened to the blessed.

The Sequence.

Lo! now this glorious day o'er all the world
Pours forth its splendour with soft genial light:
Let us with thankful lays S. Peter honour,
Who, by the love he bare to thing above,
Did win the trophy of the Holy Cross,
And heavenly glory worthily bestowed,
To which, with pious hearts and gladsome voice,
Let all our brotherhood add their acclamations.
May he who from the Lord received the gift
To bind and loose, the bearer of the Keys,
Our fetters burst asunder by the power
Committed to him; raise us up to heaven,
And with the assembly of the just unite us
In the fair realms of highest Paradise,
Where now the angelic host doth Thee adore,
O Christ, with voice harmonious chanting forth
The Saint's new song, mellifluous resounding.
With all humility desiring favour
Of Thy most gracious Majesty on high,
Let us with them in rhythmic strains unite
Such as befit Thy lofty dignity;
And here on earth continually praise
The Three in One in heavenly glory seated.
The angelic powers high in eminence
Praise Thee, in glory triumphing, for ever;
The awful principalities of heaven
Glorify Thee above the starry spheres.
Thou at the right hand of the Father sitting
Vouchsafe to hear Thy servants supplications,
And blend them with the voices of the angels,
And let our choir, with theirs associate,
Ever Thee glorify Who reignest with Thy Saints.

The Creed.

Secret. We offer Thee, O Lord, the gift of reconciliation, and pray that as Thou gavest constancy to S. Peter, Thy Apostle, in bonds, so Thy grace may be effectual for our forgiveness Through.

Secret of the Maccabees. Let the Mystery offered with devotion of heart on the feast of Thy Martyrs both protect and give us joy. Through.

P. Comm. We beseech Thee, O Lord, at the intercession of S. Peter, Thy Apostle, let the receiving of the Divine gift ever loose us from the chains of our sins, and put away all evil from us. Through.

P. Comm. of the Maccabees. Grant, we beseech Thee, Almighty God, that we may both profess and follow the faith of those whose memory we celebrate, by partaking of the Sacrament. Through.

S. STEPHEN, Mart. Pope.

¶ *The* Office *and* Offert. ii., Grad. iii., Alleluia iv., Gospel, *and* Comm. i *in Comm. Bp. and Conf.*; Epistle i. *in the Common.*

The Collect.

O God, Who dost gladden us by the yearly feast of S. Stephen, Thy Bishop and Martyr, mercifully grant that we may rejoice in the protection of him whose day we keep. Through.

Secret. We beseech Thee, O Lord, let the intercession of S. Stephen, Thy Bishop and Martyr, make our oblations acceptable to Thee, who, by worthily offering the same, pleased Thee. Through.

P. Comm. O Lord, we receiving the Divine Mysteries, beseech Thee, that at the intercession of Thy Bishop and Martyr, S. Stephen, they may minister to the increase of our everlasting happiness. Through.

THE INVENTION OF S. STEPHEN, PROTO-MARTYR, AND HIS COMPANIONS, *MM.*

¶ *All as on S. Stephen's Day. No* Creed *is said.*

The Collect.

O God, Who art the marvellous brightness of Thy Saints, and Who didst on this day reveal the place in which the bodies of SS. Stephen, Thy Martyr, Nicodemus, Gamaliel, and Alibon, were found, grant us, we beseech Thee, in their company to rejoice in eternal happiness. Through.

Secret. O Lord, look graciously upon the Sacrifice offered to Thee by the prayers of the faithful, that that which this day brought glory unto Thy beloved Martyrs, Stephen, Nicodemus, Gamaliel, and Alibon, may obtain favour and redemption for us. Through.

P. Comm. We, being nourished and satisfied by Thy Feast, humbly beseech Thee, O Lord our God, ever to help us for the sake of S. Stephen, Thy Martyr, Nicodemus, Gamaliel, and Alibon, the feast of whose Invention we this day keep. Through.

FEAST OF OUR LADY, *ADNIVES.*

¶ *Probably the Mass of Our Lady from Purif. to Advent was said. See Comm. B.V.M.*

S. OSWALD, Mart. King.

¶ *The* Office iii., *the* Epistle *and* Grad. i., Alleluia *and* Offert. v., Gospel iv., *and* Comm. vi. *in the Common.*

The Collect.

Almighty and everlasting God, Who hast hallowed the sacred joy and gladness of this day, in memory of the passion of Thy servant, S. Oswald, increase in our hearts Thy love and charity, that we may have a sense of his guardianship in heaven, the shedding of whose blood we commemorate on earth. Through.

Secret. We beseech Thee, O Lord, graciously accept the gifts which we offer to Thy Majesty in commemoration of Thy King and Martyr, S. Oswald, and of Thy goodness inspire us with that mighty love which burned in him. Through.

P. Comm. We that are prepared by the Bread of Life beseech Thee, Almighty God, that at the prayers of S. Oswald, Thy King and Martyr, whose glorious victory we reverence with yearly devotion, we may find Thy justice satisfied in us. Through.

The Transfiguration of Our Lord.

THE BLESSING OF THE GRAPES.

Bless, O Lord, this fruit of the new grape which Thou hast vouchsafed to ripen by the dew of heaven, the watering of rain, and calm and quiet seasons, and hast given it us to be used with thanksgiving. In the Name of our Lord + Jesus Christ, by Whom Thou dost ever create all good things. Who.

AT MASS.

The Office. Ps. lxxx.

Come and shew the light of Thy countenance, *O Lord,* Thou that sittest upon the cherubims, and we shall be whole.

Ps. Hear, O Thou Shepherd of Israel, Thou that leadest Joseph like a sheep.

The Collect.

O God, Who on this day didst reveal from heaven Thy Only Begotten Son, transfigured in a wonderful manner, to the fathers of both Testaments, grant unto us, we beseech Thee, that by actions acceptable unto Thee we may attain unto the perpetual contemplation of his glory in Whom Thou hast testified that Thou, the Father, wast well pleased. Through.

The Epistle. 2 Peter i. 16-19.

Brethren, we have not followed .... arise in you hearts.

Gradual. Ps. cx. In the day of Thy power shall the people offer Thee free-will offerings with a holy worship. The dew of Thy birth is of the womb of the morning.

℣. The Lord said unto My Lord, Sit Thou on My right hand until I make Thy enemies Thy footstool.

Alleluia! ℣. The hallowed day hath lightened upon us; come ye nations and adore the Lord, for a great light hath this day descended upon the earth.

¶ *The* Sequence, "Let us with lowly voice." (See p. 188, *or the following is said.*)

The Sequence.

Blest be the Holy Trinity for ever,
Deity, Unity, in glory equal,
Father, Son, and Holy Ghost,
Threefold in name, and all of the same substance—

The Father God, the Son God, in both the Holy Spirit in Deity associate;
Yet there are not three Gods, but one true God.
So is the Father Lord, the Son Lord, and the Holy Ghost Lord,
And yet the Son Himself is one true God;
And so from both proceeds the noble Spirit—
Persons distinct, and unity in essence,
Majesty, power, glory, honour equal,
Ruling stars, seas, earth, all created things;
At Whom hell trembles, and the lowest pit
Pays homage; to Whom sun and moon give praise,
And the angelic virtues all adore;
Whom now let every voice and tongue confess.
Let us, too, with uplifted voices sing
Harmonious chants with organ softly blended;
Let us with acclamations cry, All hail,
Praise in the highest to the Lord exalted!
O Trinity adorable
By Thee we are redeemed:
O Love ineffable
Do Thou Thy Universal Church
Protect, save, rescue, liberate and cleanse.
We worship Thee, Almighty, sing to Thee:
To Thee be praise and glory now and ever.

The Gospel. Matt. xvii. 1-9.

At that time Jesus taketh Peter .... from the dead.

The Creed.

Offert. Ps. xciii. *God* hath made the round world so sure that it cannot be moved. Ever since the world began hath Thy seat been prepared, *O God;* Thou art from everlasting.

Secret. O Lord, Heavenly Father, Almighty, everlasting God, receive, we beseech Thee, the gifts which we present on the glorious Transfiguration of Thy Son; and mercifully grant that by them we may be delivered from the disquietude of this world, and may be knit together in happiness eternal. Through.

Comm. Ps. cx. The dew of Thy birth is of the womb of the morning.

P. Comm. O God, Who hast hallowed this day by the Transfiguration of Thy Incarnate Word, and by the voice of Thee, the Father, sent down to Him, grant we beseech Thee, that we who have been fed with the Bread of Heaven, may be found meet to become members of Him Who gave commandment that this should be done in remembrance of Him, Jesus Christ, Thy Son, our Lord. Who.

SS. SIXTUS, FELICISSIMUS, AND AGAPITUS, MM.

¶ *The* Office vii. *in the Common;* Grad. iv., Alleluia *and* Gospel vi., Offert ii., *and* Comm. v. *in the same;* Epistle ii. *Comm. Mart.*

The Collect.

O God, Who permittest us to keep the day of Thy Martyrs, SS. Sixtus, Felicissimus, and Agapitus, grant us to rejoice in their fellowship in everlasting happiness. Through.

Secret. We beseech Thee, O Lord, let the gifts offered to Thy Majesty, at the intercession of Thy Martyrs, SS. Sixtus, Felicissimus, and Agapitus, be made profitable to our eternal salvation. Through.

P. Comm. Grant, we beseech Thee, O Lord, at the intercession of Thy Martyrs, SS. Sixtus, Felicissimus, and Agapitus, that we may receive to our eternal salvation the holy Mysteries which we celebrate in this service on earth. Through.

The Name of Jesus.

The Office. Philipp. ii.

At the Name of Jesus every knee should bow, of things in heaven and things in earth, and things under the earth, and every tongue should confess that Jesus Christ is Lord, to the glory of God the Father.

Ps. cxxxv. O praise the Lord, for the Lord is gracious: O sing praises unto His Name, for it is lovely.

¶ *In Easter-tide,* Alleluia.

The Collect.

O God, Who hast caused the most glorious Name of our Lord Jesus Christ, Thy Only Begotten Son, to be loved with the greatest affection by Thy faithful, and to be terrible and fearful to evil spirits, mercifully grant that all they who devoutly reverence this Name of JESUS on earth may have part in the sweetness of holy consolations in this present life, and in the world to come may attain unto the fulness of joy and eternal praise. Through.

The Lesson. Acts iv. 8-12.

At that time Peter, filled with the Holy Ghost, said, Ye rulers .... whereby we must be saved.

Gradual. Ephes. i. *God the Father* hath set *Jesus Christ* at His own Right Hand in the heavenly places, far above all principality, and power, and might, and dominion, and every name that is named not only in this world, but also in that which is to come, and hath put all things under His feet.

℣. Ps. lxxix. Help us, O God of our salvation; for the glory of Thy Name, *O Lord*, deliver us, and be merciful unto our sins for Thy Name's sake.

Alleluia! ℣. Sweet to the heart the Name of Jesus Christ,
To the ear music, honey to the taste;
Causing the heart foi joy to sing,
The world's despite discomfiting.

¶ *At a Commemoration in Easter-tide the second* Alleluia *is* ℣. Luke xxiv., "Jesus *our Lord arose* and stood in the midst of *His disciples*, and said unto them, Peace be unto you."

¶ *At a Commemoration from LXX. to Easter is said—*

Tract. Jesu Christ, Name sweet to hear,
To the sad an omen dear,
With joy Thou fill'st the mind.
℣. Grief from It flies, we find a prize,
And clouded eyes see light arise,
And truth the erring find.
℣. To speak that Name, or to proclaim,
Or give It fame, is still the same—
It ever sweetly sounds.
℣. Foul deeds of sin and guilt within,
Cleansed by that Name do pardon win,
Which gently heals our wounds.
℣. It scares our foes, It goodness sows,
It soothes our woes, the proud o'erthrows,
It gives protection sure.
℣. This Name defends, and vigour lends,
Our will amends, our aim extends
To joys which aye endure.

The Sequence.

Jesu, the gentle Nazarene,
King of the Jews, of kindly mien,
Gracious in life's fair bloom,
That He might His own people save
Himself to death and torment gave,
Borne pallid to the tomb.

Sweet is the Name, sweet the Surname,
No one such title can proclaim,
Surpassing all beside.
It sinners soothes, and gives them cure,
Comforts the just, and makes them sure,
Whatever may betide.

Under the banner of this King
Thy life doth cease from troubling,
Thy foes before thee flee:
If thou but think upon this Name,
Warlike array is put to shame,
And thou shalt conqueror be.

Unto this Name be honour paid,
Which evil spirits, sore afraid,
Dread, and before it quail:
This is the Name which brings salvation,
The only certain consolation
To aid when sad hearts fail.

This we are bound to venerate,
In our heart's storehouse to instate,
Think on it with affection great,
But with heroic love.
Ignatius this lesson taught:
When his good fight the Martyr fought,
Upon his riven heart was wrought
Jesus, the Lord above.

No higher can our wishes tend
Than to have Jesus for our friend,
Whose love doth every love transcend,
And never doth upbraid.
He loves us, O how fervently!
He loves us, O how constantly!
He loves us, O how faithfully!
Eager to give us aid.

So wondrous hath He made His Name,
That it the hearts of all doth claim,
First in importance, chief in fame,
Sweet to our inmost will.
Our human nature's laws ordain
That him who loves we love again,
And all our powers delight to strain
His pleasure to fulfil.

All good doth in that Name abound;
Its utterance makes the sweetest sound,
In it is royal merit found,
To hear it gives delight.
In it a father's brightness shines,
A mother's beauty it enshrines,
A brother's honour it combines,
Brethren it clothes with might.

By Jesu's Head, Heart, Hands, and Mind,
Bruises and Wounds incarnadined,
Feet, Body, vigour for mankind
Are graciously applied.
They grievous pains and tortures bear;
Our sins by these all cleansèd are,
Our fall'n estate His pious care
Doth to revival guide.

Wherefore whoe'er desires to see
Why Jesu's Name so wondrously
Doth cause the good to long that He
May deign in them to dwell;

(*Division.*)

Jesus in beauty is most fair,
In goodness is without compare;
His gentle sweetness all doth bear,
His mercy none can tell.

Jesus is King of noble line,
Jesus is comeliness divine;
Jesus in word doth mighty shine,
In deeds most marvellous.
Jesus, courageous and high-souled;
Jesus, the gladiator bold;
Jesus, Whose gifts can ne'er be told,
In bounty plenteous.

Jesus, compassionate and kind;
Jesus, bright leader of the blind;
Jesus, all sweets in Him we find—
In Him is our delight.
Jesus, in glory high renowned;
Jesus, by all men fruitful found;
Jesus, with every virtue crowned,
Gives comfort infinite.

Above all might, the mightiest;
Above all honour, lordliest;
Above all love, the loveliest—
All praise to Him pertains.
In knowledge He doth all transcend,
His circuit doth to all extend,
His love all hearts doth apprehend,
And captive made detains.

Hail! Name so precious to the ear!
Sweet Jesus! Name which all revere:
May nought on earth prevail to tear
 This title from our heart.
By this let sin be done away,
To this let each one homage pay,
Through this in heavenly bliss we pray
 May we obtain a part.

¶ *Or the following Hymn may be used as a* Sequence.*

JESU!—The very thought is sweet!
In that dear Name all heart-joys meet;
But sweeter than the honey far
The glimpses of His Presence are.

No word is sung more sweet than this;
No name is heard more full of bliss;
No thought brings sweeter comfort nigh,
Than Jesus, Son of God most High.

Jesu! the hope of souls forlorn!
How good to them for sin that mourn!
To them that seek Thee, oh, how kind!
But what art Thou to them that find?

Jesu, Thou sweetness, pure and blest!
Truth's Fountain, Light of souls distress'd,
Surpassing all that heart requires,
Exceeding all that soul desires!

No tongue of mortal can express,
No letters write its blessedness:
Alone who hath Thee in his heart
Knows, love of Jesus! what Thou art.

I seek for Jesus in repose,
When round my heart its chambers close:
Abroad, and when I shut the door,
I long for Jesus evermore.

With Mary, in the morning gloom,
I seek for Jesus at the tomb;
For Him, with Love's most earnest cry,
I seek with heart, and not with eye.

Jesus, to God the Father gone,
Is seated on the Heavenly Throne:
My heart hath also passed from me,
That where He is, there it may be.

We follow Jesus now, and raise
The voice of prayer, the hymn of praise,
That He at last may make us meet
With Him to gain the Heavenly Seat.

* From the *Gradual.*

The Gospel. Matt. i. 20-23.

At that time the Angel of the Lord .... God with us.

The Creed.

Offert. Mark xvi. In My Name shall they cast out devils; they shall speak with new tongues, they shall take up serpents: and if they drink any deadly thing, it shall not hurt them; they shall lay hands upon the sick and they shall recover. *Alleluia.*

Secret. We present our Sacrifice unto Thee with devout mind, O God, the Father of mercies, in reverence of the most beloved Name of Thy Son our Lord Jesus Christ, humbly praying that by virtue thereof help may be vouchsafed to all that are in need, so that they, delighting in that Name, may obtain a saving performance of their desire. Through.

Preface. Because by the Mystery.

Comm. Rev. ii. To him that overcometh will I give to eat of the hidden Manna; and will give him a white stone, and in the stone a new name written, which no man knoweth saving he that receiveth it.

P. Comm. O Lord, we, calling to mind with inward devotion the holy Mysteries which we have received in honour of the most acceptable Name of Thy Son our Lord Jesus Christ, beseech Thee that they may increase and multiply our spiritual gladness, and may both light up our affections, and engrave on them continually this saving Name of JESUS, and stir us up to rejoice with our whole heart in Jesus our sweetest Saviour. Through.

¶ *Let the same Mass be said through the Octave without* Creed, *also in* Commemorations, *with the second part of the* Sequence.

S. DONATUS, Mart. Bp

¶ *All as* iii. *Comm. Conf. Bp., except* Epistle v., Offert i., *and* Comm vi. *in Comm. Mart.*

The Collect.

O God, Who art the glory of Thy priests, grant, we beseech Thee, that we may perceive the aid of S. Donatus, Thy Martyr and Bishop, whose feast we celebrate. Through.

Secret. Hear our prayers, O Lord, and bestow on us the succour of Thy compassion, that the gifts which we offer before Thy Majesty may be worthy of Thee, at the intercession of S. Donatus, Thy Martyr and Bishop. Through.

P. Comm. We beseech Thee, O Lord, mercifully be present at our worship, that at the intercession of S. Donatus, Thy Martyr and Bishop, the service which we attend with due reverence in honour of Thy Name may heal and save us. Through.

S. CYRIACUS AND HIS COMPANIONS, MM.

¶ *The* Office ii., Grad. iii., Alleluia vii., Offert. iii. *in the Common.*

The Collect.

O God, Who causest us to rejoice in the yearly feast of Thy Martyrs, SS. Cyriacus and his companions, mercifully grant that we may follow their steadfastness in sufferings, whose day we keep. Through.

The Lesson. Ecclus. ii. 7-11.

Ye that fear the Lord .... For the Lord *our God* is full of compassion and mercy.

The Gospel. Mark xvi. 15-18.

At that time Jesus said unto His disciples, Go ye into all the world .... and they shall recover.

Secret. We offer unto Thee the sacrifice of praise, O Lord, for the noble martyrdom of Thy Saints Cyriacus and his companions, and tell of Thy marvellous acts whereby such a victory was won. Through.

Comm. Mark xvi. These signs shall follow them that believe *in Me:* they shall cast out devils, they shall lay hands on the sick and they shall recover.

P. Comm. We, who put our trust in the prayers of Thy Martyrs, SS. Cyriacus and his companions, beseech Thee, O Lord, that we may attain unto everlasting restoration through that Sacrament which we have received. Through.

THE VIGIL OF S. LAURENCE, Mart.

¶ *When the Vigil of S. Laurence occurs on a week-day, let the Mass of the Octave of the Name of Jesus be said after Terce, with a Memorial of S. Romanus; and after Sext let the Mass of the Vigil be said; both at the High Altar. When it occurs on a Sunday, then let the Mass of the Vigil be said in the Chapter-house, with a Memorial of S. Romanus; and at High Mass let a Mass of the Octave of the Name be said, with a Memorial of the Sunday and of the Trinity; and on Wednesday let the Sunday Mass be said in the Chapter-house.*

The Office. Ps. cxii.

He hath dispersed abroad, and given to the poor, and his righteousness remaineth for ever : his horn shall be exalted with honour.

Ps. Blessed is the man that feareth the Lord : he hath great delight in His commandments.

The Collect.

Grant, we beseech Thee, Almighty God, that we may reverence with fervent faith the triumph, shining in the perpetual light of heaven, which S. Laurence, Thy Martyr, accomplished on earth in the flames which he despised. Through.

¶ *Memorial of S. Romanus, Mart.*

(See *Coll.* ii., Comm. Mart.)

The Lesson.

(See ii. Comm. Virg. Mart.)

Gradual. Ps. cxii. He hath dispersed abroad and given to the poor, and his righteousness remaineth for ever.

℣. His seed shall be mighty upon earth, the generation of the faithful shall be blessed.

If Sunday—Alleluia, ℣. *The Deacon Laurence wrought a good work, who by the sign of the Cross caused the blind to see, and gave the treasures of the Church to the poor.*

The Gospel.

(See iii. Comm. Mart.)

Offert. Job. xvi. My prayer is pure, *therefore I seek that utterance be given to my voice* in heaven, *because there is* my *Judge* and my record : *let my prayer ascend up unto the Lord for ever.*

Secret. Let our oblation, O Lord, we beseech Thee, be as pleasing unto Thee as the good deeds of S. Laurence, Thy Martyr, on whose feast it is offered. Through.

Secret of S. Romanus. We beseech Thee, O Lord, receive our gifts and our prayers, and both cleanse us by these heavenly Mysteries, and mercifully hear us at the intercession of S. Romanus, Thy Martyr. Through.

Comm. (See i. Comm. Mart.)

P. Comm. Continue in us, O Lord, the effect of Thy gift, that the Sacrament we have received of Thy bounty on the feast of S. Laurence, Thy Martyr, may work in us peace and salvation. Through.

P. Comm. of S. Romanus. Grant, we beseech Thee, Almighty God, that like as we give Thee thanks in the Office of S. Romanus, Thy Martyr, upon earth, so we may be gladdened by his countenance for ever. Through.

S. LAURENCE, *Mart.*

The Office. Ps. xcvi.

Glory and worship are before Him, power and honour are in His sanctuary.

Ps. O sing unto the Lord a new song, sing unto the Lord all the whole earth.

The Collect.

Grant, we beseech Thee, Almighty God, that we may quench the flames of our sins, as Thou didst give grace to S. Laurence to overcome his torments in the fire. Through.

¶ *Memorial of the Name of Jesus.*

The Epistle. 2 Cor. ix. 6-10.

Brethren, he which soweth sparingly .... the fruits of righteousness.

Gradual. Ps. xvii. Thou hast proved me, *O Lord,* and visited mine heart in the night season.

℣. Thou hast tried me, and shalt find no wickedness in me.

Alleluia! As on the Vigil.

The Sequence.

¶ *All as on S. Vincent's Day, changing* Vincent *to* Laurence, *and the following verse for the corresponding* "Thus Dacianus," etc.

Valerianus mocked appears:
With liberal hand the Deacon cheers
(While him they strive to gain)
The poor and needy gathered round,
His loving ministrations found
Free alms to soothe their pain.

The Gospel.
(See iii. Comm. Mart.)

Offert. Ps. xvi. Glory and worship are before Him; power and honour are in His sanctuary.

Secret. O Lord, that we may be made meet to receive Thy Mysteries, we beseech Thee, let that truth ever animate and enlighten us which kindled a flame in the heart of S. Laurence, Thy Martyr, enabling him to confess Thee: Jesus Christ Thy Son our Lord. Who.

Comm. John xii. If any man serve Me, let him follow Me; and where I am, there shall also My servant be.

P. Comm. We that are satiated with the holy gift, humbly pray Thee, O Lord, that at the intercession of S. Laurence, Thy Martyr, we may find in this, our bounden duty and service, the increase of Thy salvation. Through.

S. TIBURTIUS, Mart.

¶ *All as* i. *in the Common, except* Grad. *and* Gosp. iii., Offert. ii. *in the same;* Epistle ii. *Comm. Mart. Bp.*

The Collect.

O Lord, let the continual guardianship of S. Tiburtius, Thy Martyr, protect us, forasmuch as Thou never failest to look favourably upon those on whom Thou hast bestowed the ministration of such aid. Through.

¶ *Memorial of S. Laurence.**

Secret. Let this Sacrifice, O Lord, which is presented on the passion of S. Tiburtius, Thy Martyr, be pleasing unto Thee, and at his intercession, we beseech Thee, let it be profitable to our salvation. Through.

P. Comm. We beseech Thee, Almighty God, at the intercession of S. Tiburtius, Thy Martyr, both increase and multiply in us Thy gifts, and of Thy mercy preserve that which Thou dost bestow. Through.

S. HIPPOLYTUS AND HIS COMPANIONS, MM.

¶ *The* Office *and* Grad. iv., Epistle *and* Alleluia iii., Gospel vii., Offert. v. *in the Common;* Collects ii. *Comm. Conf. Bp.*

¶ *Memorials of the Name of Jesus and of S. Laurence.*

Comm. Luke xii. And I say unto you my friends, be not afraid of them which *persecute you.*

* (*Sic*) But (?) Memorials of the Name of Jesus and of S. Laurence.

THE VIGIL OF THE ASSUMPTION OF BLESSED MARY.

¶ *All as in the Common, except that the* Office *is only repeated after the* "Glory be."

The Collect.

O God, Who didst deign to choose Blessed Mary as a virgin shrine wherein Thou wouldst dwell, grant, we beseech Thee, that we, being defended by her protection, may be present at her feast with joy. Who.

Memorial of S. Eusebius, Conf.

O God, Who causest us to rejoice in the yearly feast of S. Eusebius, Thy Confessor, mercifully grant that by his example whose day we keep we may draw nearer unto Thee. Through.

¶ *Memorial of S. Laurence.*

Offert. Happy art thou, O holy Virgin Mary, and most worthy of all praise, for from thee sprang the Sun of Righteousness, Christ our God.

℣. *Blessed art thou, Virgin Mary, who didst bear the Lord, didst give birth to the Creator of the world, Who made thee, and ever remainest Virgin.**

Secret. We beseech Thee, O Lord, let the prayers of the Mother of God commend our gifts to Thy mercy whom Thou for this cause hast translated from this present world that she may intercede with Thee in hope and confidence for our sins. Through.

Secret of S. Eusebius. Let our service be pleasing unto Thee, O Lord, at the intercession of S. Eusebius, Thy Confessor, and let the oblation of these present gifts be the protection of the faithful. Through.

Comm. Gentle Mother of God, succour all that pray; we, too, with them, humbly entreat that by the aid of thy prayers we may sing praises unto the Trinity.

P. Comm. We beseech Thee, O merciful God, to strengthen our frailty, that we who keep the requiem of the Holy Virgin Mother of God, may by her intercession rise again from our iniquities. Through.

P. Comm. of S. Eusebius. O Lord, we have joyfully received the heavenly Sacrament: let us find it the more profitable at the intercession of S. Eusebius, Thy Confessor. Through.

* This is said without *Alleluia*, except it be Sunday.

¶ *If the Vigil occur on a week-day, then let the Mass of the Octave of the Name be said after Terce, with Memorials of SS. Eusebius and Laurence, and after Sext the Mass of the Vigil. If it occur on a Sunday, then let the Mass of the Vigil be said in the Chapter-house, with Memorials of SS. Eusebius and Laurence; and for High Mass the Mass of the Octave of the Name; with Memorials of the Sunday and of the Trinity; and let the Sunday Mass be said on the following Tuesday in the Chapter-house.*

The Assumption of Blessed Mary.

The Office.

As on the Visitation, inserting the word *Assumption.*

The Collect.

We beseech Thee, O Lord, let us be continually aided by the sacred feast of this day, whereon the Holy Mother of God underwent death in this world, and yet could not be holden by the chains of death: who did bring forth Thy Son our Lord. Who.

The Lesson. Ecclus. xxiv. 7-15.

With all these I sought rest, and in *the* inheritance *of the Lord* I shall abide .... like the best myrrh.

Another Lesson through the Octave. Cant. iii., iv., v., vi., vii.*

Go forth, O ye daughters of Jerusalem .... clusters of grapes.

¶ *These two Lessons are said alternately through the Octave, but on the Octave Day and Sunday in the Octave is said the first.*

Gradual. As v. Comm. Virg. Mart.

Alleluia! ℣. *This day the Virgin Mary entered heaven: rejoice, for she reigneth with Christ for ever.*

¶ *The following* Alleluia *is said daily, except on the Sunday in the Octave and the Octave Day.*

Alleluia! Mary is taken up into heaven: angels rejoice, praise, and bless the Lord.

The Sequence.

From our first Mother Eva's sickly branch
Mary the blooming rose proceedeth forth;
Bright as amidst the stars the Morning Star,
And fair in beauty as the moon she came;

* Chap. iii. 11; iv. 1, to "Within thy locks;" 7 and 8, to "Lebanon," 11, 12, 13, to "fruits," and 15; v. 1, to "spice;" vi. 8 and 9; vii. 6 and 7.

Sweet beyond balsam, ointments, frankincense;
As violet glowing, dewy as the rose,
White as the lily, she who was preferred
To bear the highest Father's holy Child,
That of a Virgin's flesh immaculate
He might upon Him take flesh hallowed.
Great Gabriel brings the message of new joy,
Th' arising of the eternal King on earth.
And to His Mother thus gives salutation:
Blessed art thou, Queen of the universe! *
Thou shalt bring forth the Everlasting King.
She answered, How can I fruitful be,
Seeing a man I know not, from my birth
Ever a Virgin chaste continuing?
Fear not (the Angel answered), upon Thee,
Chaste as thou art, the Holy Ghost shall come,
Whereby thou shalt bear God and Man in one.
O truly holy, truly to be loved!
Of whom redemption hath for us arisen,
Salvation of the world, and our true life.
Mother of God, accept our prayers this day,
Whereon to heaven's portals thou wast borne.
Dear to the Father, Jesus' Mother pure,
The Holy Spirit's temple thou wast made.
Fair Spouse of God, thou Christ the King hast borne:
Lady thou art in heaven and in earth.
This day hosts met thee from the court of heaven,
And to the starry palace led thee up.
Jesus Himself, to welcome Thee His Mother,
Came with the angels forth, and set thee up
With Him for ever in His Father's seat.
With God now reigning, mercifully pardon
Our evil deeds, and ask for us all good.
O gracious Mediatrix, next to God
Our only hope, commend us to thy Son,
That we in highest heaven may Alleluias sing.

The Gospel. Luke x. 38-42.

At that time Jesus entered .... which shall not be taken away from her.

The Creed.

Offert. (See iv. Comm. Virg. Mart.)

Secret. We beseech Thee, O Lord, that the prayers of the Blessed Mother of God may make our gifts acceptable to Thee, that albeit we know her to have departed this life in respect of this flesh we may perceive her prayers for us continually in the glory of heaven. Through.

* This verse is to be said thrice.

Comm. Blessed is the womb of the Virgin Mary, which bare the Son of the Everlasting Father.

P. Comm. We that have partaken of the heavenly Table implore Thy mercy, O Lord our God, that we who keep the feast of the Mother of God may at her intercession be delivered from all evils which beset us. Through.

¶ *Let the same Mass be said daily through the Octave, with the* Sequences *as in the Octave of the Visitation.*

THE OCTAVE OF S. LAURENCE, Mart.

The Office. Ps. xvi.

Thou hast proved and visited my heart in the night-season, *O Lord:* Thou hast tried me, and shalt find no wickedness in me.

Ps. Hear the right, O Lord : consider my complaint.

The Collect.

We beseech Thee, O Lord, let the adorable death of S. Laurence, Thy Martyr, gladden and make us more ready worthily to rehearse the same. Through.

¶ *The* Epistle *as on S. Laurence Day;* Grad. i., Offert. i., *and* Comm. iii. *in Comm. Mart.*

Alleluia! As on the Vigil.

¶ *If the Vigil occur on the Sunday,* And hath .... poor *is omitted.*

The Gospel. Matt. x. 37-42.

At that time Jesus said to His disciples, He that liveth ...... lose his reward.

Secret. O Lord, we celebrate again the death of S. Laurence, Thy Martyr, with an oblation, which, albeit in its own origin it is much to be remembered, remaineth still glorious for ever. Through.

P. Comm. We beseech Thee, O Lord, let the intercession of S. Laurence, Thy Martyr, succour us, that so the receiving of the heavenly Banquet may bestow on us renewed joy. Through.

¶ *This Mass is said in the Chapter-house: if the Octave of S. Laurence occur on the Sunday, let the Mass of the Octave be said there nevertheless, and the Sunday Mass on the Vigil of S. Bartholomew in the same place, unless there be twenty-six or twenty-seven Sundays after Trinity, when a Sunday Mass is transferred.*

THE FOURTH DAY WITHIN THE OCTAVE.

Memorial of S. Agapitus.

Let Thy Church, O God, trusting in the glorious help and prayers of St. Agapitus, Thy Martyr, ever remain devout, and stand sure and steadfast. Through.

Secret. We beseech Thee, O Lord, let the sacrifice of praise which we present unto Thee on the revered passion of S. Agapitus, Thy Martyr, be pleasing to Thee at his intercession for whose sake it is offered. Through.

P. Comm. Grant, we beseech Thee, O Lord our God, that we who have received the virtue of Thy Sacrament may, at the intercession of S. Agapitus, Thy Martyr, be made worthy of so great a gift. Through.

THE FIFTH DAY WITHIN THE OCTAVE.

Memorial of S. Magnus, M.

Be present, O Lord, at our supplication, and at the intercession of S. Magnus, Thy Martyr, mercifully defend us from the assaults of our enemies. Through.

Secret. Graciously look down, O Lord, we beseech Thee, on the gifts and offerings of the faithful; and that the prayers of none be in vain, the desires of none without effect, bestow upon us, at our petition, the succour of Thy glorious Martyr, Magnus. Through

P. Comm. We that have received Thy holy Mysteries beseech Thee, O Lord, that the continual guardianship of S. Magnus, Thy Martyr, may succour us. Through.

THE OCTAVE OF THE ASSUMPTION OF BLESSED MARY.

¶ *All as on the day.*

Memorial of SS. Timothy and Simphorianus.

We beseech Thee, O Lord, mercifully bestow Thy aid upon us, and at the intercession of Thy Martyrs, SS. Timothy and Simphorianus, stretch out over us the right hand of reconciliation to Thee. Through.

The Sequence.

Hail Mary! of the sea bright Star, arising
By power Divine to give the nations light,
Hail! Gate of Heaven, who bring'st into the world,
Though closed thyself, the very Light of Truth,
The Sun of Righteousness, in flesh arrayed.
Pride of the world, Virgin, thou Queen of Heaven!
Exalted as the sun, fair as the moon,
Behold, how all look up to thee with love.
For thy birth, faithful rod of Jesse's stem,
The ancient Fathers and the Prophets longed;
Thee Gabriel did show forth, the tree of life,
Which overshadowed by the Holy Ghost
Should of a bloom divine the Almond yield.
From rock of Moabitish wilderness
Unto Mount Sion's daughter Thou hast led
The Lamb, the King and Ruler of the land.
Leviathan, that crooked, piercing serpent,
Crushing, thou hast the sinful world delivered.
We for this cause, the remnant that are left,
Revering thee, who in a wondrous way,
Didst bear the Lamb Who reigneth in the heavens,
Eternally repeat upon the Altar
His mystical atoning Sacrifice.
Hereby the Manna true, which Moses erst
Beheld in figure, now, the veil withdrawn,
Before the eyes of the true Israelites,
True Abraham's sons, is to their marvel set.
O Virgin pray for us, that of that Bread
Of Heaven we may indeed be worthy found.
Help us with foot unsandaled, with clean lips,
And with pure heart, O Virgin, Mother made,
To draw nigh to the sacred Fire, the Word,
Which, as the bush did bear the flame, thou bearedst.
By true faith let us taste the water sweet
Which in the wilderness the rock foreshowed.
Baptized in the sea, gird up our loins;
Look to the brazen Serpent on the Cross.
Hear us: Thy Son to thee doth nought deny.
Save, Jesus, those for whom Thy Mother prays.
O grant us to behold the Well of Life,
And fix on Thee our mind's eyes purified;
By good works to adorn our Christian Faith,
That so we may from this world's sojourn pass,
O Author of our life, in peace to Thee.

Secret. O Lord, let that oblation of the peculiar people be acceptable to Thee, in honour of Thy Saints, for whose sake they confess that they have received help in trouble. Through.

P. Comm. We that are satisfied with the holy gift, beseech

Thee, Almighty God, grant that we all may, at the intercession of Thy Martyrs, SS. Timothy and Simphorianus, have a place in the assembly of Thy Saints. Through.

THE VIGIL OF S. BARTHOLOMEW, Ap.

¶ *All as in the Common, with a Memorial of S. Timothy and Appollinaris out of Comm. Many Mart. If it occur on the Sunday there is only a Memorial of the Vigil.*

S. Bartholomew, *Ap.*

¶ *All as* i. *in the Common, except* Grad. *and* Offert. ii., Gosp., v. *in the same; the* Creed *is said.*

The Collect.

Almighty and everlasting God, Who hast made this day joyous by the feast of S. Bartholomew, Thy Apostle, grant, we beseech Thee, unto Thy Church to love that which he believed, and to preach that which he taught. Through.

Memorial of S. Audoenus, Bp.

O God, Who hast bestowed on the soul of Thy most holy Bishop and Confessor, Audoenus, everlasting glory, grant, we beseech Thee, that we may be so aided by his guardianship, that with him we may have life everlasting. Through.

Secret. We who celebrate the feast of S. Bartholomew, Thy Apostle, implore Thy mercy, O Lord, that we may receive Thy benefits, aided by him in reverence for whom we offer unto Thee the sacrifice of praise. Through.

Secret of S. Audoenus. We beseech Thee, O Lord, let the gifts offered by Thy faithful people be made acceptable unto Thee for the sake of S. Audoenus, Thy Confessor and Bishop, that we may mercifully be cleansed from all defilement of sin by those very Mysteries at which we pay our service. Through.

P. Comm. We humbly pray Thee, O Lord, that we who have received the Sacrament of Salvation on the feast of S. Bartholomew, Thy Apostle, may alike believe and follow that which he preached. Through.

P. Comm. of S. Audoenus. We that have partaken of the fulness of the heavenly Table, humbly beseech Thee, Almighty God, that like as we rejoice in the everlasting glory of S.

Audoenus on its yearly commemoration, so at his intercession before Thee we may be defended from all adversity. Through.

S. RUFUS, Mart.

¶ *The* Office ii., Epistle *and* Grad. iii., Alleluia, *and* Comm. vi.; Gospel v. *and* Offert. i. *in the Common.*

The Collect.

Be present, O Lord, at our supplications, that we who trust in the intercessions of S. Rufus, Thy Martyr, may be disturbed neither by the threatenings of our adversaries nor any that may assault us. Through.

Secret. We present our Sacrifice unto Thee, O Lord, in honour of S. Rufus, Thy Martyr, humbly beseeching Thee, that as Thou didst give grace unto him to confess the holy faith, so Thou wouldst abundantly bestow upon us pardon and peace. Through.

P. Comm. We that are satisfied with the heavenly gift, beseech Thee, O Lord our God, help us in every place, for the sake of S. Rufus, Thy Martyr. Through.

S. Augustine, *Conf. Doct.*

¶ *The* Office *and* Alleluia i., Grad. iv., Comm. ii. *Comm. Conf Bp.; the rest as in the Common. The* Creed *is said.*

The Collect.

O God, Who didst provide for Thy Church S. Augustine to be a Catholic Doctor to expound the mysteries of Holy Scripture, grant, we beseech Thee, that we may ever be instructed by his doctrine and supported by his prayers. Through.

Memorial of S. Hermes.

O God, Who didst strengthen S. Hermes, Thy Martyr, with the virtue of constancy in suffering, grant unto us, for love of Thee, to despise the favours of this world, and to fear none of its adversities. Through.

Secret. We beseech Thee, O Lord, let not the favourable prayers of S. Augus ine, Thy Bishop and Confessor, fail us, both to make our gifts acceptable unto Thee, and ever to obtain Thy pardon for us. Through.

Secret of S. Hermes. We beseech Thee, O Lord, graciously accept our gifts; and that we may serve worthily at Thy Altar, guard us by the intercession of S. Hermes, Thy Martyr. Through.

P. Comm. Grant, O Lord, we beseech Thee, that we, receiving the Sacrament of Salvation, may follow the teachings of him whose glorious feast we keep. Through.

P. Comm. of S. Hermes. We, being filled with Thy heavenly benediction, beseech Thy mercy, O Lord, that at the intercession of S. Hermes, Thy Martyr, we may perceive that service to be for our salvation which we humbly perform. Through.

THE BEHEADING OF S. JOHN BAPTIST.

¶ *The Mass of S. Sabina is said after Prime or Terce in the Chapter-house, and the Mass of the Decollation after Sext.*

AT MASS OF S. SABINA.

The Office. Ps. cxix. 75, 120.

I know, O Lord, that Thy judgments are right; and that Thou of very faithfulness hast caused me to be troubled: my flesh trembleth for fear of Thee, and I am afraid of Thy judgments.

Ps. Blessed are those that are undefiled in the way, and walk in the law of the Lord.

The Collect.

Trusting in the prayers of S. Sabina, Thy Virgin and Martyr, we beseech Thy mercy, O Lord, that for her sake and prayers we may attain unto everlasting joys. Through.

¶ *All as* i. *in the Common, except* Grad. *and* Alleluia iii., *and* Comm. ii. *in the same.*

Secret. We magnify Thee, O Lord, with our gifts and offerings: let them procure for us both the guardianship of S. Sabina, Thy Martyr, and joys everlasting. Through.

P. Comm. We who celebrate the Mysteries of our redemption, beseech Thee, O Lord our God, that for the sake of S. Sabina, Thy Martyr, we may both be protected and have fruition of the unspeakable glory of the vision of Thyself. Through.

AT HIGH MASS.

¶ *The* Office iii., Grad. i., Offert. ii., *and* Comm. vi. *in the Common.*

The Collect.

O Lord, we beseech Thee, let the hallowed feast of S. John, Thy Baptist and Martyr, bestow on us aid for the furtherance of our salvation. Through.

The Lesson. Prov. x. 28-32; xi. 3, 8-11.

The hope of the righteous .... the city is exalted.

Alleluia! ℣. *Herod* sent an executioner and commanded *him to cut off the head of John* in the prison.

The Sequence.

As on the Nativity of S. John Baptist, inserting the proper verse.

The Creed.

The Gospel. Mark. vi. 17-29.

At that time Herod *the King* sent .... in a tomb.

Secret. We beseech Thee, O Lord, let the gifts which we offer on the martyrdom of S. John, Thy Baptist and Martyr, be profitable to our salvation, at his presentation, who, now that his course is finished on earth, hath an everlasting seat in heaven. Through.

P. Comm. O Lord, we beseech Thee, let the feast of S. John Baptist bestow on us a double benefit, that we may reverence the mighty Sacrament which we have received as betokened in our prayers, and may rejoice as it is more evidently set forth in us. Through.

SS. FELIX AND ADAUCTUS, MM.

¶ *The* Office *and* Alleluia v., Epistle ii., Grad. iv., Gospel vii., Offert iii., *and* Comm. x. *in the Common.*

The Collect.

O Lord, we humbly beseech Thy Majesty, that as Thou causest us to rejoice on the commemoration of SS. Felix and Adauctus, Thy Martyrs, so Thou wouldst ever defend us at their prayers. Through.

Secret. Mercifully receive, O Lord, we beseech Thee, the Sacrifice which we present on the yearly commemoration of the Martyr Saints; and grant that we may obtain forgiveness of sins at their intercession in whose honour it is offered. Through.

P. Comm. We that are refreshed with the holy gifts beseech Thee, O Lord, that at the intercession of Thy holy Martyrs, SS. Felix and Adauctus, we may give Thee thanks unceasingly. Through.

S. CUTHBURGA, Virg. Mart.

¶ *All as* i. *in the Common, except* Offert. ii. *and* Epistle i. *Comm. Virg. not Mart.*

The Collect.

O God, Who didst in divers ways adorn Thine handmaiden Cuthburga with the grace of exceeding chastity, grant to us, Thy servants, at her prevailing intercession, that we may prosper in either life; that like as we do keep her feast on earth, so by her intercession we may ever be had in remembrance in heaven. Through.

Secret. We lay our mystic gifts upon Thy Altar, O Lord, humbly beseeching Thy Majesty, that for her sake and by her assistance we may escape all pollution. Through.

P. Comm. We that are refreshed with the Sacrament of Heaven, bow down before Thy Altar, and entreat Thy Majesty, O Lord, that what we have received with joy on the feast of S. Cuthburga, may by the aid of her intercession be profitable to our salvation in either life. Through.

S. GILES, *Conf. Abb.*

¶ *All as in the Common, except* Comm. ii. *Conf. Bp.*

The Office

O God, Who on this day didst cause S. Giles, Thy Confessor and Abbat, to enter the courts of the kingdom of heaven, grant, we beseech Thee, that we may be sensibly succoured by his prayers in whose deeds we reverently rejoice. Through.

Memorial of S. Priscus, Mart.

Almighty and everlasting God, the strength of them that contend, and the palm of Martyrs, mercifully look down upon this day's feast, and cause Thy Church to rejoice in its celebration continually; and, at the intercession of S. Priscus, Thy Martyr, fulfil the desires of all that believe in Thee. Through.

Secret. O Lord, we beseech Thee, mercifully pour forth upon our gifts the grace of reconciliation, at the intercession of S. Giles, Thy Confessor and Abbat, both watching over the benefits that Thou hast conferred upon us, and in Thy mercy increasing the same. Through.

Secret of S. Priscus. We thankfully offer, O Lord, our gifts upon Thy Altar in memory of S. Priscus, Thy Martyr, and pray Thee, that at his intercession the same may further our reward in heaven. Through.

P. Comm. Defend, O Lord, Thy people that trust in Thy mercy, and at the intercession of S. Giles, Thy Confessor and Abbat, make them whom Thou hast refreshed with heavenly Mysteries more fervent in following after Thy gifts. Through.

P. Comm. of S. Priscus. We beseech Thee, O Lord, look upon Thy people whom Thou hast refreshed by partaking of this holy Mystery, and give unto them the abundance of Thy grace as they celebrate the feast of Thy Martyr, S. Priscus, that being aided by visible consolation, they may be more earnestly stirred up to seek the good things which are invisible. Through.

THE TRANSLATION OF S. CUTHBERT, *Conf. Bp.*

¶ *All as* i. *in the Common, except* Grad. *and* Comm. ii. *in the same.*

The Collect.

Grant, we beseech Thee, Almighty and merciful God, that we who keep the day of the translation of Thy Confessor and Bishop S. Cuthbert, may ever obtain, at his intercession, the benefits of Thy loving-kindness. Through.

Secret. We beseech Thee, O Lord, sanctify these gifts at the intercession of S. Cuthbert, Thy Confessor and Bishop, and mercifully cleanse us from the stains of all our sins. Through.

P. Comm. We beseech Thee, O Lord, let S. Cuthbert, Thy Confessor and Bishop, the day of whose translation we keep, obtain for us, by the help of his holy intercession, that this Communion may make us worthy in Thy sight. Though.

S. BERTINUS, Conf. Abb.

¶ *All as in the Common, except* Alleluia, *which is* ii. *Conf. Bp.*

The Collect.

Almighty and ever-living God, Who shinest forth wondrously in Thine elect, whom Thou, by Thy indwelling, art pleased to glorify, grant us, we beseech Thee, so worthily to reverence the feast of S. Bertinus, Thy Confessor and Abbat, that for his sake and prayers we may be found worthy to be a temple unto Thyself. Through.

Secret. O Lord, we beseech Thee, let the grace of the Holy Ghost receive these our gifts, and at the intercession of S. Bertinus, Thy Confessor and Abbat, both keep us without rebuke in this life, and bring us unto the kingdom of heaven. Through.

P. Comm. O Lord, we beseech Thee, let Thy holy Mysteries continually help us, and at the intercession of S. Bertinus, Thy Confessor and Abbat, protect us from all adversities. Through.

The Nativity of Blessed Mary.

The Office.

As on the Assumption, changing it to *Nativity.*

The Collect.

As on the Conception of Our Lady.

The Lesson. Ecclus. xxiv. 17-22.

As the vine brought I forth .... do amiss.

Another Lesson through the Octave. Wisdom iv. 1-7.

Better is it to have no children and to have virtue .... shall be in rest.

¶ *Let these two Lessons be read alternately through the Octave. On Sunday and the Octave Day, however, the last is always read.*

Gradual. As iv. Comm. Virg. Mart.

Alleluia! The Nativity of the glorious Virgin Mary of the seed of Abraham, of the tribe of Judah, of the famous root of Jesse.

¶ *The following* Alleluia *is said daily, except on Sunday and the Octave Day.*

Alleluia! ℣. By thee, O Mother of God, is our lost life restored; thou who didst conceive a Child from Heaven, and didst bear a Saviour to the world.

The Sequence.

Pour forth divine, unceasing Alleluias;
With simple acclama ions, harmonized.
Let the shrill trumpet give the echo back,
For all creation on this day rejoices

That she, the Mother of our Lord, was born,
Through whom life, forfeit once, hath been restored.
She, born of David's line, conceived a Son
Who should o'er David's kingdom wield the sceptre;
Yet by faith only doth her womb conceive.
From highest heaven the angel speeding saith,
"Hail, Mary! full of grace, holy and blessed
Among all women, thou shalt bear the King,
Who by His might hath doomed the chains of death,
By His own will His own work setting free,
And gifting it with life and blessedness."
The maiden doth believe his words forthwith,
Yet marvels she should Maid and Mother be.
She doth conceive a Son of beauteous form,
The Governor of all the universe.
This is the dry rod, blooming by God's grace;
This is the only Mistress of mankind,
Casting a veil o'er the first mother's guilt,
As the rose doth the thicket decorate,
E'en so in Mary nought is found to harm.
The Sin which Christ's first Spouse, Eve, brought on us,
The Virgin Mary wholly puts to flight.
O Virgin! who alone chaste Mother art,
Loose thou our bands of sin, and grant us part
In realms where reign the armies of the saints;
For thou, terrestial Queen, all power dost hold,
With Thy Son ruling over all for ever,
Exalted far above the glittering bands
Of Cherubim and Seraphim in glory:
For near Thy Son installed, at His Right Hand
Thou sitt'st, in virtue and in wisdom shining.
For this cause, thy Nativity this day
Brings to us yearly joys; the courts resound
With hymns in praise of thee, O Virgin Mary!
Through every clime the Church cries, Alleluia!
And Heaven's pavilions swell the panegyric,
Unto the highest eminence uprising.

The Gospel. Matt. i. 1-16.

The book of the generation .... is called Christ.

The Creed.

¶ *Throughout the week and on the Octave Day let the second Gospel be said.*

The Gospel. Luke xi. 27, 28.

At that time, as Jesus spoke to the multitude, a certain woman .... and keep it.

¶ Offert., Secret, Comm., *and* P. Comm. *as on the Conception.*

THE SECOND DAY WITHIN THE OCTAVE.

Memorial of S. Gorgonius, Mart.

We beseech Thee, O Lord, let S. Gorgonius, Thy Martyr,

gladden us by his intercession, and cause us to rejoice in his holy feast. Through.

Secret. O Lord, we beseech Thee, let the service and Sacrifice be pleasing unto Thee which the devotion of Thy family presenteth, on whose behalf let Thy Martyr, S. Gorgonius, intercede. Through.

P. Comm. We beseech Thee, O Lord God, let Thy family have part and increase of that sweetness whereby it is continually replenished by the excellent favour of Thine anointed, in Thy Martyr, S. Gorgonius. Through.

THE FOURTH DAY WITHIN THE OCTAVE.

Memorial of SS. Prothus and Hyacinth, MM.

We beseech Thee, O Lord, let the precious confession of Thy Martyrs, SS. Prothus and Hyacinth, comfort us; and let their devout intercession ever protect us. Through.

Secret. Grant, we beseech Thee, O Lord, that the gifts which of our bounden duty we present unto Thee in reverence of Thy Martyrs, SS. Prothus and Hyacinth, may work in us continually restoration and salvation. Through.

P. Comm. We beseech Thee, O Lord, let Thy Martyrs, SS. Prothus and Hyacinth, pray that Thy holy Sacrament which we have received cleanse us. Through.

SUNDAY WITHIN THE OCTAVE.

¶ *All as on the Day, except the* Gospel "At that time, as Jesus spake."

The Exaltation of the Holy Cross.

The Office.

As on the Invention of the Cross.

The Collect.

O God, Who wast pleased to redeem mankind with the precious Blood of Thy Only Begotten Son, our Lord Jesus Christ, mercifully grant that they who draw nigh to adore the life-giving Cross may be set free from the bonds of their sins. Through.

Memorial of SS. Cornelius and Cyprian, MM.

As on SS. Felix, Simplicius, Faustinus, and Beatrice's Day.

¶ *Memorial of the Octave of the Nativity.*

The Epistle.

As on the Invention of the Cross.

Gradual, Philip. ii. *Christ* became obedient unto death *for us*, even the death of the Cross.

℣. Wherefore God also hath highly exalted Him, and given Him a Name which is above every name.

Alleluia! As on the Invention of the Cross.

The Sequence.

Let us extol the Cross's praise,
And in its special glory raise
Exultingly our voice;
Let dulcet sound to heaven resound,
O'er the sweet wood of holy Rood
'Tis fit we should rejoice.

Let life and words concordant be:
When life at one with words we see,
The symphony is sweet.

The Cross let all its servants praise,
By which new life and healthful days
Upon them are bestowed;
Let each and all together cry,
Hail, Cross, the world's recovery,
Salvation-bearing Rood!

O how blessed, how renowned
Is this saving Altar found
On which the Lamb was slain—
Spotless Lamb, by Whom mankind
Full deliverance doth find
From sin's primeval stain.

The ladder this to sinners given,
By means of which Christ, King of Heaven,
Drew to Him all our race;
This doth the form thereof display—
The arms outstretching every way,
The world's four parts embrace.

These are not novel mysteries,
Not newly doth the cross uprise
Its mighty power to show:
This sweetened erst the bitter well;
Moses did from the rock compel
Water by this to flow.

No safety in the house abides
Till by the Cross who there resides
His threshold doth secure:
No danger from the murderous foe,
No sad bereavement doth he know,
Who thus doth help procure.

The widow, lacking fire and food,
Who at Sarepta gathered wood,
The hope of safety gained:
Without two sticks for faith to use,
Barrel of meal and scanty cruse
Had increase ne'er obtained.

In ancient writ the Cross lay hid,
Yet types did show what now we know;
To us 'tis brought to light.
Kings credence give, foes cease to strive;
By this alone, Christ leading, one
Doth thousands put to flight.

The Cross doth make its servants brave,
And ever victory to have;
Heals weakness and diseases grave;
Before it devils cower.
This to the captive freedom gives,
Regenerates our vicious lives,
All ancient dignity revives
Beneath the Cross's power.

O holy Cross, triumphant Tree!
The world's true health, all hail to thee!
Amidst the trees none such can be
In leaf, or flower, or bud.
Medicine of the Christian soul,
Heal thou the sick, preserve the whole;
Things which no mortal may control
Thy power cannot elude.

Thou, Who the Cross didst hallow, hear
Us who that holy Cross revere:
The servants of Thy Cross convey
Unto the realms of changeless day,
When this life's toils are o'er.
Those whom by pain Thou makest pure
Strengthen the anguish to endure;
And when the day of wrath shall come,
Of Thy vast mercy fetch us home
To joys for evermore.

The Gospel. John xii. 31-36.

At that time Jesus said to the multitude of the Jews, Now is the judgment of this world .... the children of light.

The Creed.

Offert. As on the Invention of the Cross.

Secret. Let Thy merciful aid, O Lord, prevent our humble prayers and offerings on this feast, and let faith in the Tree open again the door of salvation to us, which Eve's presumptuous touching of the tree in Paradise had shut against us. Through.

Secret of SS. Cornelius and Cyprian. Grant, we beseech Thee, Almighty God, that our humble oblation may both be acceptable to Thee in honour of Thy Saints, and purify us alike in mind and body. Through.

Comm. As on the Invention of the Cross.

P. Comm. We who have been satisfied with the Body and Blood of our Lord Jesus Christ, by Whom the banner of the Cross is sanctified, beseech Thee, O Lord our God, that as we have been found meet to adore It, so we may have our portion in Its everlasting glory and saving power. Through.

P. Comm. of SS. Cornelius and Cyprian. O Lord, we beseech Thee, ever to feed us with the joys of Thy Saints, seeing that our own salvation is furthered as often as honour is paid to them in whom Thy wondrous works are set forth. Through.

THE OCTAVE OF THE NATIVITY.

¶ *All as on the Day, except the* Lesson *and* Gospel, *which are the second.*

Memorial of S. Nichomedes, Mart.

Be present, O Lord, with Thy people, that they, declaring the noble deeds of Thy Martyr, S. Nichomedes, may by his protection be ever aided in seeking Thy compassion. Through.

Secret. Mercifully accept, O Lord, the gifts offered to Thee, and let the prayers of S. Nichomedes, Thy Martyr, commend them unto Thy Majesty. Through.

P. Comm. We beseech Thee, O Lord, let the Sacrament we have received purify us, and at the intercession of S. Nichomedes, Thy Martyr, absolve us from all our sins. Through.

S. EDITH, *Virg. not Mart.*

¶ *All as* i. *in the Common, except* Grad. *and* Alleluia ii. *in the same.*

The Collect.

O God, Who hast vouchsafed to Thy faithful examples of chastity, forasmuch as Thou didst will Thy Son our Lord to be born of a Virgin, grant us at the prayers of S. Edith, Thy Virgin, purity of mind and body, whereby we may receive the happiness that Thou hast promised us. Through.

Memorial of SS. Euphemia, Lucina, and Geminianus, MM.

Grant, we beseech Thee, O Lord, to our prayers that we may press forward with joy, and imitate the constancy of their faith whose passion we keep this day with yearly piety. Through.

Secret. We beseech Thee, O Lord, let Thy blessing come down upon this our oblation, and let S. Edith obtain of Thee that we may be made a sacrifice well pleasing to Thyself. Through.

Secret of SS. Euphemia, Lucina, and Geminianus. Graciously look down upon the gifts of Thy people, O Lord, and gladden us in the assistance of Thy Martyrs, SS. Euphemia, Lucina, and Geminianus, whose feast Thou permittest us to keep. Through.

P. Comm. Let our partaking at Thy ghostly Table, O Lord, be the salvation of our body and soul: and let the prayers of S. Edith, Thy Virgin, commend us to Thee. Through.

P. Comm. of SS. Euphemia, Lucina, and Geminianus. We that have received the Divine Mysteries, O Lord, beseech Thee to hear our prayers; and let us be comforted by the continual help of Thy Martyrs, SS. Euphemia, Lucina, and Geminianus, whose victory we celebrate in due order. Through.

S. LAMBERT, Mart. Bp.

¶ *The* Office *and* Grad. iii. *Conf. Bp.*; Alleluia iv. *in the same*; Epistle, Gospel, *and* Comm. i. *in the Common*; Offert. i. *Comm. Mart.*

The Collect.

We beseech Thee, O Lord, let the prayers of S. Lambert, Thy Martyr and Bishop, commend us unto Thee; and as his

[illegible]

¶ If [illegible] fall on a Sunday, the Mass of the Vigil is said in the Chapter [illegible] on Feast Day, there is only a Memorial of the Vigil at the [illegible] Day Mass.

S. Matthew, *Ap.*

¶ *All as in the Common, except—*

The Collect.

Assist us, O Lord, at the prayers of S. Matthew, Thy Apostle and Evangelist, that what of ourselves we cannot attain may be bestowed upon us at his intercession. Through.

Memorial of S. Laudus, Bp. and Conf.

Grant, we beseech Thee, Almighty God, that we who keep the feast of S. Laudus, Thy Bishop and Confessor, may at his intercession attain unto everlasting blessedness. Through.

The Gospel. Matt. ix. 9-13.

At that time, as Jesus passed forth .... sinners to repentance.

The Creed.

Secret. We beseech Thee, O Lord, let the oblation of Thy Church be commended to Thee at the prayers of S. Matthew, Thy Apostle and Evangelist, by whose glorious preaching she is instructed. Through.

Secret of S. Laudus. We beseech Thee, O Lord, that like as Thou hast translated S. Laudus, Thy Bishop and Confessor, unto eternal glory, so for his sake Thou wouldst sanctify this present Sacrifice unto our salvation. Through.

P. Comm. We that have received with joy the adorable Sacrament on the yearly feast of S. Matthew, Thy Apostle and Evangelist, beseech Thee that he may obtain for us, by his glorious prayers, ever to believe and to follow that which the blessed Evangelist preached and taught. Through.

P. Comm of S. Laudus. We that have been fed with the Bread of Thy Heavenly Table, beseech Thee, O Lord our God, that at the intercession of S. Laudus, Thy Bishop and Confessor, whose feast we keep, Thou wouldst defend us from all adversities.

S. MAURICE AND HIS COMPANIONS, *MM.*

¶ *All as* i. *in the Common, except* Alleluia viii., Gosp. v., Offert. iii., *and* Comm. iv. *in the same.*

The Collect.

We beseech Thee, Almighty God, let the joyful feast of Thy Martyrs, SS. Maurice, Exuperius, Candidus, Victor, Innocentius, Vitalis, and the companions of the same, make us to be glad, and glory in their day on whose protection we lean. Through.

Secret. We beseech Thee, O Lord, let this present Sacrifice find acceptance with Thee for the sake of the glorious Theban Martyrs, for whose precious blood it is hallowed unto Thee. Through.

P. Comm. We that have received the heavenly Sacrament, beseech Thee, O Lord, that, at the intercession of Thy holy Theban Martyrs, we may obtain pardon of our sins. Through.

S. THECLA, Virg. not Mart.

¶ *All as* i. *in the Common, except* Grad. *and* Alleluia ii. *in the same; the* Office ii., Offert iii., *and* Comm. iv. *Comm. Virg. Mart.*

S. FERMINUS, Conf. Bp.

¶ *The* Office iii., Grad. *and* Offert. ii., Alleluia v., *and* Comm. i. *in the Common; the* Epistle *and* Gospel i. *Comm. Mart. Bp.*

SS. CYPRIAN AND JUSTINA, MM.

¶ *The* Office vii., Collects, Epistle, *and* Gospel iii., Grad. vi., Alleluia v., Offert. iv., *and* Comm. ii. *in the Common.*

SS. COSMAS AND DAMIAN, MM.

¶ *The* Office v., Grad. *and* Offert. ii., Alleluia iv., Gosp. i., Comm. iii. *in the Common; the* Epistle ii. *Comm Mart.*

The Collect.

Let the blessed feast of Thy Martyrs, SS. Cosmas and Damian, magnify Thee, O Lord, wherein Thou hast both bestowed upon them eternal glory, and of Thy unspeakable providence hast also aided us. Through.

Secret. We beseech Thee, O Lord, let that Sacrifice out of which all martyrdoms took their beginning, which we offer on the precious death of Thy just ones, obtain for us the favour of reconciliation with Thee. Through.

P. Comm. Let the tasting of Thy Sacrament, O Lord, be our sure salvation, for which we earnestly pray, for the sake of Thy Martyrs, SS. Cosmas and Damian. Through.

Michaelmas Day.

The Office. Ps. ciii.

O praise the Lord, all ye angels of His, ye that excel in strength: ye that fulfil His commandment, and hearken unto the voice of His Word.

Ps. Praise the Lord, O my soul, and all that is within me praise His holy Name.

The Collect.

O God, Who hast ordained the services of angels and men in a wonderful order, mercifully grant that, as they alway do Thee service in heaven, so our life may be defended by them on earth. Through.

The Lesson. Rev. i. 1-5.

In those days, Jesus signified by His angel unto His servant John things which must shortly came to pass; .... *Who* loved us, and washed us from our sins in His own Blood.

Gradual. As the Office.

Alleluia! ℣. Ps. cxxxviii. Even before the gods* will I sing unto Thee, *O Lord my God.*

The Sequence.

To celebrate Thy praise, O King of Heaven,
Let all our band harmonious unite,
Our whole assembly singing hymns to Thee
On the renewal of high festival
In Michael's honour, he whose ministry
Gives lustre to the mighty universe.
Nine are the orders of the heavenly hosts
By Thee created, and these angel forms
Thou makest flames of fire at Thy pleasure.
These are the work of Thy primeval Hand
We latest in Thine Image fashioned.

* The Latin is *Angelorum.*

Nine orders, each retaining its own office,
So teach divines, of heavenly hosts are reckoned—
The Angel Host, the Archangelic Phalanx,
The Principalities, the Heavenly Powers,
Might gracious-mouthèd, high names of Dominion,
And Thrones divine, and Cherubim ethereal,
And Seraphim with hair that glows as fire.
Do ye, O Michael, first of heavenly princes,
And Gabriel, the Word's true messenger;
And Raphael, once on earth a hired servant,
Bear us to those who rest in Paradise.
All the Commandments of the Father ye
Fulfil, sent forth by Wisdom of the same,
And the coequal Spirit, One in substance,
Which God ye serve, ten thousand times ten thousand.
In twice ten thousand ministering courses
Your hundred thousands in the Palace wait,
To which the King brought back the hundredth sheep,
Born of the Word; and tenth piece of silver,
Over which found ye do rejoice together,
Ye in the heaven, we on the earth below.
A chosen band, let us our vows upraise
With harmony of tuneful harp and lute,
That so, the glorious wars of Michael ended,
The incense of our prayers may be accepted
Upon the golden Altar before God;
To Whom in glory sing we Alleluia.

The Gospel. Matt. xviii. 1-10.

At that time came the disciples .... which is in heaven.

The Creed.

Offert. Rev. viii. *An* angel stood by the Altar *of the temple,* having a golden censer *in his hand;* and there was given unto him much incense, and the smoke of the incense ascended up before God. *Alleluia!*

Secret. We beseech Thee, O Lord, graciously receive the gift of Thy people, and let it be acceptable to Thee, not for our sake, but for the prayers of S. Michael, Thy Archangel, and all the blessed spirits. Through.

P. Comm. O all ye angels of the Lord, bless ye the Lord: praise Him and magnify Him for ever.

P. Comm. We, trusting in the prayers of S. Michael, Thy Archangel, humbly beseech Thee, O Lord, that we may in heart and mind attain unto that after which we seek in rendering him honour. Through.

S. Jerome, *Conf. Doct.*

¶ *All as in the Common, except* Alleluia vi., Offert. ii., Comm. i. *Comm. Conf. Bp. The* Creed *is said.*

The Collect.

O God, Who hast been pleased to make known to us the truth of Holy Scripture and the mysteries of the Sacraments by S. Jerome, Thy Priest and Confessor, grant, we beseech Thee, that we may ever be instructed by his doctrine whose feast we keep, and aided for his sake. Through.

Secret. O Lord, we beseech Thee, of Thy mercy look upon our gifts, and at the prayers of S. Jerome, Thy Priest and Confessor, graciously purify us thereby. Through.

P. Comm. Grant, we beseech Thee, O Lord, that S. Jerome, Thy Priest, may both instruct Thy Church in the doctrines of the faith, and being instructed therein, may she, at his pious intercession, be made worthy of the Mysteries of God. Through.

SS. REMIGIUS, GERMANUS, VEDASTUS, AND BAVO, *Conff. Bps.*

¶ *All as in the Common, with Memorial of S. Melorus, Mart., in Comm. Mart. Bp.*

The Collect.

Hearken, O Lord, we beseech Thee, to the supplications of Thy people, with the protection of Thy Bishops and Confessors, SS. Germanus, Remigius, Vedastus, and Bavo; and grant that in this life we may rejoice in peace and find an eternal refuge. Through.

Secret. We beseech Thee, O Lord, look upon our prayers, and the oblations of Thy faithful, that they may be acceptable to Thee on the feast of Thy Saints, and advance our reconciliation with Thee. Through.

P. Comm. We, who have been fed with the Sacrament which restoreth mankind, on the feast of Thy Confessors, SS. Germanus, Remigius, Vedastus, and Bavo, beseech Thee, O Lord our God, that as Thou art pleased to bestow upon us heavenly gifts, so we may thereby abide in the favour of Heaven. Through.

S. LEDGER, Mart. Bp.

¶ *The* Office *and* Grad. iii., Alleluia iv., Offert i., *and* Comm. ii. *in Comm Conf. Bp.*; Gospel ii. *Comm. Mart.*

The Collect.

O God, Who on this day didst crown Thy Martyr and Bishop, S. Ledger, with glory and honour; mercifully grant that we who deserve not glory may at his intercession obtain pardon. Through.

The Epistle. 2 Tim. ii. 8-10; iii. 10-12.

Dearly beloved, Remember .... shall suffer persecution.

Secret. We beseech Thee, O Lord, maintain Thy gifts in us for the sake of S. Ledger, Thy Martyr and Confessor, in honour of whose confession we offer unto Thee the Sacrifice of praise. Through.

P. Comm We that are refreshed by the receiving of Thy holy gift beseech Thee, O Lord our God, that at the intercession of S. Ledger, Thy Martyr and Bishop, we may perceive the effect of his aid whose service we perform. Through.

S. FAITH, Virg. Mart.

¶ *All as* ii. *in the Common, except* Epistle i., Alleluia v., Comm. iv., *in the same.*

The Collect.

O God, Who dost hallow this day by the martyrdom of S. Faith, Thy Virgin, grant unto Thy Church the assistance of the prayers of her in whom she doth glory. Through.

Secret. Receive, O Lord, the prayers and oblations dedicated unto Thee for the sake of S. Faith, Virgin and Martyr; and grant that they may be profitable to our salvation for the intercession of her in whose reverence they are set apart. Through.

P. Comm. We that have been refreshed at Thy Altar humbly beseech Thee, O Lord, that we may perceive the protection of S. Faith, Thy Virgin and Martyr, on whose day we have communicated. Through.

SS. MARK, MARCELLUS, AND APULEIUS, MM.

¶ *The* Office *and* Alleluia vii., Epistle i., Grad., Offert., *and* Comm. iv., Gospel vi. *in the Common.*

The Collect.

We beseech Thee, O Lord, let the blessed deeds of Thy Martyrs, SS. Mark, Marcellus, and Apuleius, be with us, and ever fill us with fervent love towards Thee. Through.

Secret. We beseech Thee, O Lord, let the oblation to be offered reconcile us unto Thy Majesty, for the worthiness of the prayers of Thy Saints in commemoration of whom it is presented. Through.

P. Comm. We beseech Thee, O Lord, let us be defended by the Sacrament which we have received, and for the sake of Thy Martyrs, SS. Mark, Marcellus, and Apuleius, let us be shielded by the armour of Heaven from the wickedness which assaileth us. Through.

S. DENYS AND HIS COMPANIONS, *MM.*

¶ *The* Office *and* Grad. i., Alleluia *and* Gospel v., Offert iii., *and* Comm. ii. *in the Common.*

The Collect.

O God, Who on this day didst strengthen S. Denys with the virtue of constancy in suffering, and wast pleased to join in fellowship with him Rusticus and Eleutherius to preach Thy glory to the Gentiles; grant unto us, we beseech Thee, that we, following their example, may for the love we bear Thee despise the good things of the world, and fear none of its adversities. Through.

The Lesson. Acts xvii. 16-34.

Now, while Paul waited for *Silas and Timotheus* at Athens .... and believed *on the Lord Jesus Christ*, among the which was Dionysius the Areopagite.

[illegible]

[illegible] S. [illegible] and [illegible].

[illegible] the prayers and [illegible] of Thy [illegible] [illegible] Saints, [illegible], [illegible] [illegible] praying unto Thee, and obtain for [illegible]

[illegible] feast of S. Agapitus, Mart.

The Translation of S. Edward, *Conf. King.*

¶ *The* Office *as on Trans. of S. Thomas, altering the Name;* Epistle *and* Gospel *in Comm. Abbat;* Grad. iv., Alleluia, *and* Sequence i. *Comm. Conf. Bp.;* Offert. ii. *and* Comm. vi. *Comm. Mart. The* Creed *is said.*

The Collect.

O God, Who hast crowned Thy King and Confessor, S. Edward, with eternal glory, make us, we beseech Thee, so to reverence him on earth that we may reign with him in heaven. Through.

Secret. Pour forth, we beseech Thee, O Lord, the light of the Holy Ghost upon us who serve at Thy Altar, that our devout offering unto Thee in honour of King S. Edward, may at his intercession both restore and save us. Through.

P. Comm. We that have been filled with the Banquet of Living Bread beseech Thee, O God our Lord, that for the sake and prayers o' Thy King and Confessor, S. Edward, we may be made partakers of the heavenly Feast. Through.

ANOTHER MASS.

¶ *All as above, except:—*

The Collect.

Almighty and everlasting God, Who hast numbered S. Edward, Thy Confessor, in the company of Thy Saints, grant of Thy mercy that we who commemorate his glorious Translation may perceive his protection of us with Thee. Through.

Secret. Let Thy grace, O Lord, increase the joy of us who are gladdened by the holy Translation of King Edward, and make us feel the sweetness of Thy presence in this Sacrifice. Who.

P. Comm. O Lord, let the most blessed King Edward, Thy Confessor, on whose holy Translation Thou permittest us yearly to offer prayer with joy, be our intercessor, that the Sacrament which we have received may be profitable to our salvation. Through

---

S. CALIXTUS, Mart. Pope.

¶ *All as* iii. *Comm. Conf. Bp., except* Alleluia iv., Offert. i., *and* Comm. ii. *in the same;* Epistle ii. *in the Common.*

The Collect.

O God, Who seest that in our frailty we fall short of love

towards Thee, mercifully renew us after the example of S. Calixtus, Thy Bishop and Martyr. Through.

Secret. Let the offering of these Mysteries be profitable unto us, O Lord, and for the sake of S. Calixtus set us free from guilt, and confirm us in everlasting salvation. Through.

P. Comm. Grant, we beseech Thee, O Lord, that we may perfectly follow the faith of him whose suffering we keep in memory as we partake of the Sacrament. Through.

S. WULFRAN, *Conf. Bp.*

¶ *All as* i. *in the Common, except* Collects *and* Comm. ii., *and* Grad. iv. *in the same.*

S. MICHAEL IN THE MOUNTAIN TOMB.

¶ *All as on Michaelmas Day, except as follows. The* Creed *is said.*

The Lesson. Rev. xii. 7-12.

There was war in heaven .... ye that dwell in them.

Alleluia! ℣. *The sea was shaken and the earth trembled when the Archangel Michael descended from heaven.*

S. ETHELDREDA, *Virg. not Mart.*

¶ *All as* i. *in the Common, except* Grad. ii. *in the same.*

S. Luke, *Evang.*

¶ *All as in the Common, with this Memorial.*

Memorial of S. Justus.

O God, Who gavest to S. Justus such courage, that in the weak body of a child he endured a glorious martyrdom for love of Thee, mercifully grant for his sake and intercession that we may be absolved from all our sins. Through.

Secret. We beseech Thee, O Lord, that like as the gifts offered on the martyrdom of S. Justus bear witness to Thy Divine power and glory, so they may bestow on us our effectual salvation. Through.

P. Comm. We that are refreshed by the heavenly benediction beseech Thee, O Lord, that at the intercession of Thy Martyr, S. Justus, the healing power of Thy Sacrament may be profitable to both our bodies and souls. Through.

S. FRIDESWIDE, *Virg. not Mart.*

¶ *All as* i. *in the Common, except* Epistle, Grad., *and* Alleluia ii. *in the same.*

THE ELEVEN THOUSAND VIRGINS, *MM.*

¶ *All as* i. *in the Common, except* Epistle ii. *in the same.*

The Collect.

O God, Who hast hallowed this day's feast by the glorious sufferings of Thy Virgin Saints and Martyrs, be present at the prayers of Thy family, and help us for their sake and intercession whose feast we this day keep. Through.

Secret. As in Comm. Mart.

P. Comm. As the *P. Comm.* for SS. Christopher and Cucufatus on S. James's Day.

S. ROMANUS, Conf. Bp,

¶ *All as* i. *in the Common, except* Epistle, Gospel, *and* Comm. iii., *and* Alleluia v. *in the same.*

The Collect.

O God, unto Whom the Bishop S. Romanus, being endued with the grace of holiness, was so pleasing that he was counted worthy to have fellowship with the Saints in heaven, grant to Thy Church, we beseech Thee, to attain everlasting happiness at his intercession the day of whose burial she thankfully celebrates. Through.

Secret. We beseech Thee, Almighty God, mercifully to behold this our Sacrifice of devotion, and at the intercession of S. Romanus, Thy Bishop and Confessor, of Thy goodness grant us thereby health of mind and body. Through.

P. Comm. Grant, we beseech Thee, O Lord our God, that the holy Mysteries we have received may, at the intercession of S. Romanus, Thy Confessor and Bishop, both obtain for us the grace of devotion and in the end a blessed eternity. Through.

SS. CRISPIN AND CRISPINIAN, *MM.*

¶ *The* Office *and* Grad. vii., Epistle *and* Alleluia v., Gospel xiii., Offert. ii., *and* Comm. vi., *in the Common.*

The Collect.

O God, Who hast bestowed upon Thy Martyrs, SS. Crispin and Crispinian, the crown of martyrdom, grant, we beseech Thee, that at their intercession we may obtain remission of our sins, and the everlasting joys of the blessed. Through.

Memorial of the Translation of S. John de Beverley, Conf. Bp.

O God, Who hast hallowed this day by the Translation of the most holy John, Thy Bishop and Confessor, we beseech Thee, for his sake and prayers, to let us be translated into the fellowship of his saints. Through.

Secret. Grant, we beseech Thee, Almighty God, that by the presenting of these gifts which we offer in honour of Thy Martyrs, SS. Crispin and Crispinian, we may be reconciled unto Thee, and by receiving them may be quickened unto life. Through.

Secret of S. John de Beverley. Mercifully look down, we beseech Thee, O Lord, on this our simple and humble service, and at the intercession of S. John, Thy Bishop and Confessor, whose Translation we keep, graciously receive the oblations which we offer in his honour on Thy Holy Altar. Through.

P. Comm. We beseech Thee, O Lord, to help us, for the prayers of Thy Martyrs, SS. Crispin and Crispinian, and cause us who keep their feast with these holy Mysteries to be ever devoted to Thy Name. Through.

P. Comm. of S. John de Beverley. Succour us, we beseech Thee, O Lord, for the sake and prayers of S. John, Thy Bishop and Confessor, that by his protection that which in this present service we celebrate may obtain the joys of everlasting salvation. Through.

THE VIGIL OF SS. SIMON AND JUDE, App.

¶ *The* Office i., Epistle, *and* Alleluia ii. *(if Sunday)*, Grad. vi. Gospel, "I am the true vine;" Offert. *and* Com. iv. *in Comm. Many Mart.*

The Collect.

Grant, we beseech Thee, Almighty God, that like as we anticipate the glorious feast of Thy Apostles, Simon and Jude, so they themselves may prevent Thy Majesty in our behalf, that we may be found worthy of Thy bounties. Through.

Secret. As in the Common.

P. Comm. We that have been filled with Thy saving Mysteries, beseech Thee, O Lord, that we may be aided by the prayers of those whose feast we anticipate by fasting. Through.

The Feast of SS. Simon and Jude, *App.*

¶ *All as* i. *in the Common, except* Alleluia iv. *in the same.*

The Collect.

O God, Who, by Thine Apostles, SS. Simon and Jude, hast suffered us to come to the knowledge of Thy Name, grant us both to celebrate their everlasting glory by our growth in grace, and by our Celebration to make progress in the same. Through.

The Epistle. Romans viii. 28-36.
Brethren, we know .... Christ Jesus our Lord.

Secret. We, O Lord, having in reverence the eternal glory of Thy Apostles, SS. Simon and Jude, beseech Thee, that being cleansed by the holy Mysteries, we may the more worthily celebrate the same. Through.

P. Comm. The Divine Mystery having been consecrated, we beseech Thee, Almighty God, that their prayers for us fail not whose protection Thou hast bestowed on us for our governance. Through.

THE VIGIL OF ALL SAINTS.

¶ *The* Office ii., Grad. v., Alleluia vii. *(if Sunday)*, Offert. iii., *and* Comm. iv. *in Comm. Many Mart.*

The Collect.

O Lord our God, increase and multiply upon us Thy grace,

and grant that in a holy profession we may follow after the joys of Thy Saints whose glorious feast we anticipate. Through.

The Lesson. Rev. v. 6-12.

In those days, lo, S. John beheld .... and blessing *for ever and ever. Amen.*

The Gospel. John xvii. 11-26.

In those days, Jesus, looking upon His disciples said, Holy Father .... and I in them.

Secret. O Lord, we place upon Thine Altar our gifts and offerings; grant, we beseech Thee, that at the prayer of all Thy Saints, whose coming festival we anticipate, they may be profitable unto our salvation. Through.

P. Comm. We, O Lord, having accomplished with joy the Sacrament of the feast we look for, beseech Thee to grant us the aid of their prayers in commemoration of whom it is appointed. Through.

¶ *If the Vigil fall on Sunday, the Mass of the Vigil is said in the Chapter-house, and the High Mass is of the Sunday, with a Memorial of S. Quintinus.*

S. QUINTINUS, Mart.

The Collect.

O God, Who dost glorify Thy Church with the yearly feast of S. Quintinus, Thy Martyr, mercifully grant that we who reverence his memory with due service may be accounted worthy to have him ever as an intercessor with Thee. Through.

Secret. O Almighty God, we offer unto Thee the Sacrifice of praise in reverence of S. Quintinus, Thy Martyr, and pray that he who died a glorious death for Thy Name may ever live to intercede for us. Through.

P. Comm. We beseech Thee, O Lord, let Thy people receive, at the intercession of S. Quintinus, Thy Martyr, the mercy which they implore, that they may ever be found worthy of Thy Sacrament. Through.

The Feast of All Saints.

The Office.

As on the Visitation B. V. M., changing it to *All Saints.*

The Collect.

Almighty and everlasting God, Who hast granted to us under one feast, to reverence the good deeds of All Saints, we beseech Thee give largely unto these manifold intercessors the abuundant reconciliation of us unto Thyself, after which we long. Through.

The Lesson. Rev. vii. 2-12.

Lo, S. John saw another angel .... for ever and ever. Amen.

Gradual. As iii. Comm. Many Mart.

Alleluia ! ℣. Wisdom iii. *The Saints* shall judge the nations and have dominion over the people, and their Lord shall reign for ever.

The Sequence.

To Christ, the Glorious, let our white-robed bands
Sing hymns upon this holy festival,
Extolling all the company of Saints.
First, let our voice be heard in Mary's praise,
Through whom the Prize of Life to us accrues.
O Queen, who art both Mother and pure Virgin,
Gain pardon through Thy Son for our transgressions.
May the blest angels' holy congregation,
And glorious archangelic company,
Blot out our sins and set us high in heaven.
Thou prophet, herald, light, and more than Prophet,
Lighten our path, and purify our bodies;
Prince of Apostles, with thy holy band,
Confirm, we pray, the hearts of all in truth.
O glorious Stephen, with thy glittering crown,
And all the noble army of the Martyrs,
Grant us bold hearts, strengthen our mortal bodies,
That Holy Cross the enemy may vanquish.
Great Martin, and the company of Bishops,
Our meek petitions graciously accept.
Queen of the Virgin band, highly exalted,
Mother intact, Virgin once great with child,
Holy, and chaste, devoted to the Lord,
Preserve our souls and purify our bodies.
May monks, uplifting venerable voices,
And all the confraternities of Saints,
Govern our times by their unceasing prayers,
And lead us to true joys in heaven above:
Let the redeemed devoutly say, Amen.

¶ *The* Gospel ii., Offert., *and* Comm. i. *in Comm. Many Mart. The* Creed *is said.*

Secret. We offer Thee, O Lord, our gifts and prayers: let them both be pleasing to Thee in honour of All Saints, and of Thy mercy be made profitable to our salvation. Through.

P. Comm. Grant, we beseech Thee, O Lord, that through the partaking of this Sacrament, Thy faithful people may ever rejoice in reverencing all Thy Saints, and be defended by their perpetual supplications. Through.

The Commemoration of All Souls.

¶ *All as* i. *in the Masses for the Dead, except the* Gradual *and* Tract ii. *in the same. Let the* Epistle *be read in the pulpit, and let the* Gradual *be said by the Clergy of the second grade. Let the* Tract *be said by Clergy of the upper grade at the steps of the Quire. The* Gospel *is said as on Sunday.*

The Collect.

O God, the Creator and Redeemer of all that believe, grant unto the souls of all the faithful departed remission of all their sins, that by devout supplications they may obtain the forgiveness for which they have ever longed. Who.

¶ *Let no Memorial be made.*

Offert. O Holy God, Who hast called back the first man unto eternal glory; O Good Shepherd, Who hast brought back the lost sheep to the fold on Thy gracious shoulders; O just Judge, when Thou shalt come to judge us, deliver from death their souls whom Thou hast redeemed; give not the souls that confess Thee a portion with the beasts; abandon them not for ever.

Secret. O Lord, mercifully look upon the oblations which we offer unto Thee for the souls of all the faithful departed, and to those on whom Thou hast bestowed the excellence of the Christian faith give also its reward. Through.

P. Comm. We beseech Thee, O Lord, let our prayers and supplications be profitable to the souls of all the faithful departed; deliver them from all their sins, and make them partakers of Thy redemption. Through.

¶ *If this Commemoration fall on Sunday, let it be put off till next day, and let a Memorial be made of S. Eustachius at the Sunday Mass.*

Memorial of S. Eustachius and his Companions, MM.

Grant to us, O Lord, we beseech Thee, at the intercession of

Thy Martyrs, S. Eustachius and his companions, joy and peace, and let us be protected by the prayers of those in whose victories we rejoice. Through.

Secret. Receive, we beseech Thee, Almighty God, these our oblations in honour of Thy Martyrs, S. Eustachius and his companions, for the sake of whose holy prayers be pleased to grant us pardon for our past offences, and security for the future. Through.

P. Comm. We that in reverence of Thy Martyrs, S. Eustachius and his companions, have received the Divine Mysteries, beseech Thee, O Lord, to grant that we may both be ever guarded by their faithful aid, and profit by their noble example. Through.

S. WENEFRID, *Virg. Mart.*

¶ *All as* i. *in the Common, except the* Alleluia *and* Offert. i. *in the same. If All Souls' Day fall on a Sunday, then let this feast be on Tuesday.*

S. LEONARD, *Conf. Abb.*

¶ *All as in the Common, except* Offert. i. *Comm. Conf. Bp.*

The Collect.

We beseech Thee, O Lord, further our prayers by the heavenly gift, that we who glory in the guardianship of S. Leonard, Thy Confessor and Abbat, may ever be succoured for his sake and prayers. Through.

Secret. Receive, O Lord, the gifts to be humbly offered to Thy loving-kindness, and let them be profitable to our salvation at the intercession of S. Leonard, Thy Confessor and Abbat, on whose day we trust they have been accepted. Through.

P. Comm. We beseech Thee, O Lord, let the receiving of Thy Sacrament purify us, and let our service on the holy feast of Thy Confessor and Abbat, S. Leonard, for his sake and by his protection, avail for our eternal forgiveness. Through.

THE FOUR CROWNED MARTYRS.

¶ *The* Office i., Epistle ii., Grad. *and* Gospel vi., Alleluia vii., Offert. iv., *and* Comm. iii. *in the Common.*

The Collect.

As on the Day of the Seven Brothers, MM.

Secret. Let Thy abundant blessing, O Lord, we beseech Thee, descend, and make our gifts acceptable to Thee, at the intercession of Thy holy Martyrs, SS. Claudius, Nichostratus, Simphorianus, Castorius, and Simplicius, and work out for us the Sacrament of Redemption. Through.

P. Comm. We that are refreshed with the joy of the Heavenly Sacrament, humbly beseech Thee, O Lord, that we may be aided and protected by those in whose victory we rejoice. Through.

S. THEODORE, Mart.

¶ *The* Office iv., Epistle i., Grad. *and* Alleluia ii., Gospel iii., Offert. v., *and* Comm. vi. *in the Common.*

The Collect.

O God, Who dost compass about and protect us with the glorious confession of S. Theodore, Thy Martyr, grant that we may profit by his example, and be supported by his prayers. Through.

Secret. We that have offered our gifts in reverence for the feast of S. Theodore, Thy Martyr, beseech Thee, O Lord, that albeit, we are let and hindered by our own conscience, for his sake we may be made acceptable. Through.

P. Comm. Let the Holy Sacrament we have received purify us, O Lord, and at the intercession of S. Theodore, Thy Martyr, bring us to the fellowship of perpetual bliss. Through.

S. MARTIN, *Conf. Bp.*

¶ *All as* i. *in the Common, except* Grad. iv. *and* Comm ii. *in the same.*

The Collect.

O God, Who seest that in our own strength we cannot stand upright, mercifully grant that, at the intercession of S. Martin, Thy Confessor and Bishop, we may be defended against all adversity Through.

Memorial of S. Menna, Mart.
As *Coll.* ii. in Comm. Mart.

Alleluia! This Martin, poor and of low estate, entereth heaven rich, and is honoured with Divine hymns.

The Sequence.

As on the Translation of S. Martin.

Secret. O God, Whose will is that all good things be comprehended in the Mystery of Thy Sacred Body, mercifully grant that, at the intercession of Thy Bishop and Confessor, S. Martin, we may perceive the benefits of the gifts which, in reverence of him, we offer unto Thee. Through.

Secret of S. Menna. O Lord, do Thou sanctify the Sacrifice which is offered to Thee, the true High Priest for ever, and at the intercession of S. Menna, Thy Martyr, make us, we beseech Thee, so to handle this Mystery, that we ourselves may be a temple and Sacrifice well pleasing to Thee. Who.

P. Comm. Succour Thy people, we beseech Thee, O Lord, that they going forward in the strength of Thy Sacrament may, at the intercession of S. Martin, Thy Bishop and Confessor, both be ever governed by Thy gift, and under Thy guidance attain their portion in eternal redemption. Through.

P. Comm. of S. Menna. We beseech Thee, O Lord, let Thy grace ever work in us renewal of heart, and cause us to rejoice on the feast of S. Menna, Thy Martyr. Through.

¶ *The same Mass is said daily throughout the Octave, unless a feast or Commemoration of Our Lady, or Salus, occur.*

S BRITIUS, Conf. Bp.

¶ *The* Office, Epistle, *and* Comm. iii., Grad, i., Alleluia, *and* Offert. ii. in *the Common; the* Gospel ii. *Comm. Mart. Bp.*

The Collect.

We beseech Thee, O Lord, at the intercession of S. Britius, Thy Confessor and Bishop, to keep Thy people that trust in Thy love, that for his prayers we may be meet to have fellowship in the joys of heaven. Through.

¶ *Memorial of S. Martin.*

Secret. We beseech Thee, O Lord, let the yearly feast of Thy Confessor and Bishop, S. Britius, commend us unto Thy loving-

[illegible] that by his holy Office and [illegible] we may be [illegible] of this present world, and attain the [illegible] of Thy grace. Through.

P. Comm. We being refreshed with the Divine Mysteries, beseech Thee, O Lord our God, that Thou wouldst ever protect us by the intercession of Thy Confessor and Bishop, on whose [illegible] we reverently offer this Sacrament unto Thee. Through.

THE TRANSLATION OF S. ERKENWALD, *Conf. Bp.*

¶ *In the Diocese of London all as in the Common.*

S. MACHUTUS, *Conf. Bp.*

¶ *All as in the Common, except Grad. ii. and Comm. ii. in the same; the* Gospel i. Comm. *Mart. Bp.*

The Collect.

Almighty and everlasting God, Who didst endue S. Machutus, Thy Confessor and Bishop, with the grace of fortitude, and didst receive him this day into the glory of heaven, hear the prayers of Thy people. Through.

¶ *Memorial of S. Martin.*

Secret. We pray Thee, O Lord, mercifully look on the oblations which we present to Thee to be consecrated in honour of S. Machutus, Thy Confessor and Bishop, beseeching Thee that, for his sake and intercession, we may of Thy goodness have pardon of all our sins and negligences. Through.

P. Comm. O Lord, mercifully exalt by the protection of S. Machutus, Thy Confessor and Bishop, those whom Thou hast filled with heavenly gifts, that we being delivered from all things which may hurt us, may run in the way of Thy salvation with our whole heart. Through.

S. EDMUND, *Conf. Abp.*

¶ *The* Office *as on the Translation,* Epistle, Gospel, *and* Offert. i., Grad. iv., Sequence, *and* Comm. ii. *in the Common.*

The Collect.

O God, Who in the bountiful goodness of Thy counsels has adorned Thy Church with the noble life of S. Edmund, Thy Bishop and Confessor, and gladdened it by his glorious miracles, mercifully grant unto us Thy servants that we may both be amended by his example, and protected from all adversities by his guardianship. Through.

¶ *Memorial of S. Martin.*

Alleluia! This Edmund, poor and of low estate, entereth heaven rich, and is honoured by Divine hymns.

Secret. We beseech Thee, O Lord, let the gifts to be offered be pleasing unto Thee, for the prayers of S. Edmund, Thy Bishop and Confessor, and being presented, let them be profitabe to our salvation. Through.

P. Comm. We beseech Thee, O Lord, strengthen our minds with the Sacrament we have received, and as Thou hast been pleased to comfort them by the miracles of S. Edmund, Thy Bishop and Confessor, so vouchsafe to help them also by his prayers, and enlighten them by his example. Through.

S. HUGH, *Conf. Bp.*

¶ *The* Office Alleluia *and* Offert i., Epistle *and* Gradual iv., Gospel *and* Comm. ii. *in the Common.*

The Collect.

O God, Who didst excellently adorn S. Hugh, Thy Confessor and Bishop, with exceeding good deeds and renowned miracles, mercifully grant that his example may stir us up, and his virtues shed lustre upon us. Through.

¶ *Memorial of S. Anianus, Conf. Bp.*

As on S. Nicasius' Day.

¶ *Memorial of S. Martin.*

Secret. We beseech Thee, O Lord, let S. Hugh, Thy Bishop and Confessor, commend the gifts which we have offered, that we, being aided for his sake, may thereby attain unto grace and glory. Through.

Secret of S. Anianus. O Lord, we beseech Thee, mercifully accept our prayers, and let the supplications of S. Anianus, Thy Bishop and Confessor, commend the Sacrifice dedicated unto Thee. Through.

P. Comm. We beseech Thee, O Lord God, let S. Hugh, Thy Bishop and Confessor, make our duty and service acceptable to Thee; and let not our guilt make the Heavenly Sacrament of none effect to us. Through.

P. Comm of S. Anianus. Almighty and merciful God, Who dost ordain us to be partakers and ministers of Thy sacraments, grant, we beseech Thee, that at the intercession of S. Anianus, Thy Bishop and Confessor, we may both increase in faith, and have part and lot in his blessedness. Through.

THE OCTAVE OF S. MARTIN, Conf. Bp.

¶ *All as on S. Martin's Day, except—*

The Collect.

Grant, we beseech Thee, Almighty God, that the feast of S. Martin, Thy Bishop and Confessor, which we have attended, may further the eternal salvation of Thy people; that we may ever have his protection in heaven to whom we oftentimes pay reverence on earth. Through.

Secret. We beseech Thee, O Lord, let this oblation which we offer again to Thy Majesty on the feast of S. Martin, Thy Bishop and Confessor, avail us for pardon; that thereby we may be delivered from our sins, and be made meet to stand at Thy sacred Altar. Through.

P. Comm. O Lord, we beseech Thee, let the Sacrament which we have received be our defence from all adversity, at the intercession of S. Martin, Thy Confessor and Bishop, and enable us to serve Thee alone in continual well-doing. Through.

¶ *If the Octave Day fall on Saturday or Sunday, let a Memorial only be had of it, and no Mass be said in the Chapter-house.*

S. EDMUND, King, Mart.

¶ *The Office and Alleluia* iii., *Epistle and* Grad. i., Gospel iv., Offert. v., *and* Comm. vi. *as in the Common.*

The Collect.

O God of unspeakable mercy, Who didst give grace unto the most blessed King Edmund to overcome his enemy by dying for Thy Name; mercifully grant unto Thy family that at his intercession they may mortify and destroy the enticements of the old enemy in themselves. Through.

Secret. We beseech Thee, Almighty God, mercifully behold this Sacrifice of our redemption, and at the intercession of S. Edmund, Thy King and Martyr, for the sake of this Thy family favourably receive the same. Through.

P. Comm. Let our dutiful service be acceptable to Thee, Almighty God, and let the holy Mysteries we have received, at the intercession of S. Edmund, Thy King and Martyr, further our attaining the reward of eternal life. Through.

S. CECILIA, *Virg. Mart.*

¶ *The* Office, Alleluia, *and* Offert ii., Epistle *and* Gospel i., Grad. iv. *in the Common.*

The Collect.

O God, Who dost gladden us by the yearly feast of S. Cecilia, Thy Virgin-Martyr, grant us to follow the example of her pious conversation whom in this Office we reverence. Through.

Secret. Grant, we beseech Thee, Almighty and merciful God, that like as we offer the Divine Sacrament on the feast of S. Cecilia, Thy Virgin-Martyr, so at her holy prayers we may obtain a free pardon of Thee. Through.

Comm. Ps. cxix. 78. Let the proud be confounded, for they go wickedly about to destroy me, but I will be occupied in Thy commandments *and statutes, that I be not confounded.*

P. Comm. We that have been made partakers of Thy Sacrament entreat Thy mercy, O Lord, that at the intercession of S. Cecilia, Thy Virgin-Martyr, we may have pardon of all our sins. Through.

S. CLEMENT, *Mart. Pope.*

The Office. Isa. lix.

The Lord saith, My words, which I have put in thy mouth, shall not depart out of thy mouth, *for thy name is there, and thy gifts shall be accepted upon My Altar.*

Ps. cii. Hear my prayer, O Lord, and let my crying come unto Thee.

The Collect.

O God, Who makest us glad on the yearly feast of S. Clement, Thy Martyr and Bishop, mercifully grant that we may also imitate his fortitude in suffering whose day we keep. Through.

Memorial of S. Felicitas, Mart.

Grant, we beseech Thee, Almighty God, that we may be protected for the sake and prayers of S. Felicitas, Thy Martyr, whose feast we keep. Through.

The Epistle. Philip. iv. 1-3.

I beseech you, my brethren .... book of life.

Gradual. As ii. Comm. Conf. Bp.

Alleluia! ℣. That Saint is worthily had in remembrance of mankind, who hath been translated unto the joy of angels.

The Sequence.

As in the Common.

The Gospel.

ii. in the Common.

¶ Offert. *and* Comm. ii. *in Comm. Conf. Bp.*

Secret. We thanfully offer unto Thee, O Lord, this gift on the martyrdom of S. Clement, Thy Bishop; and trust that as we know he liveth in glory in Thy presence, so he may intercede for us. Through.

Secret of S. Felicitas. We offer Thee these gifts, O Lord, on the glorious feast of S. Felicitas, and pray that she who by her confession and blood has made this day holy for her commemoration may implore for us the continual aid of Thy mercy. Through.

P. Comm. We beseech Thee, O Lord, let the partaking of the Divine Sacrament and the glorious prayers of S. Clement, Thy Bishop and Martyr, cleanse us. Through.

P. Comm. of S. Felicitas. We that receive this Sacrament beseech Thee, O Lord, that at the intercession of Thy Martyr S. Felicitas, it may minister to us the food of eternal life. Through.

S. CHRYSOGONUS, Mart.

¶ *The* Office *and* Comm. iii., Grad. i., Alleluia vi., *and* Offert. v. *in the Common. The* Lesson ii. *in Vig. Ap.*

The Collect.

Be present at our prayers, O Lord, that we who know that of our own wickedness we are guilty may at the intercession of S. Chrysogonus, Thy Martyr, be delivered. Through.

Secret. We beseech Thee, O Lord, receive our gifts with a favourable countenance, that at the intercession of S. Chrysogonus, Thy Martyr, all the defilement of our sins may be washed away. Through.

P. Comm. Grant, we beseech Thee, O Lord, that we who have been refreshed with Thy Mysteries may ever be strengthened by the help of Thy Martyr, S. Chrysogonus. Through.

S. KATHERINE, *Virg. Mart.*

¶ *The* Office iii., Epistle *and* Grad. ii., Alleluia vi., Gospel *and* Offert. i., *and* Comm. iv. *in the Common.*

The Collect.

Almighty and ever-living God, Who didst command the body of Thy glorious Virgin, Katherine, to be carried by angels unto Mount Sinai, grant, we beseech Thee, that by her aid we may be carried unto the city of the principalities, and there be counted worthy to behold the shining vision of Thyself. Through.

The Sequence.

On this day to Christ their King
Every age doth praises sing,
  With heart, and voice, and lute:
Katherine's worthy name we raise
With o'erflowing notes of praise;
  No human tongue is mute.

Costus' daughter, this is she,
Whose illustrious family
  Greece her own doth claim.
The pound committed to her care,
Tenfold increase to Christ she bare,
  By her rhetoric fame.

While studying scholastic art
To higher things she lifts her heart,
  Enlightened by the Word;
Discerns in either Testament
Of life the one true aliment,—
  In manger laid the Lord.

Nourished by this pleasant food,
Her earnest longing is renewed
The more its sweets she tastes;
Strengthened by this heavenly fare
The suffering of Christ's Cross to bear,
To martyrdom she hastes.

The King now threatens, now cajoles:
She fears not threats, nor is her soul's
Firm constancy abused:
Threats fall as dust before the wind,
Handmaidens, state, and offers kind
As valueless refused.

Wise men by her are put to shame;
In furnace cast for Jesu's Name,
Their garments are unharmed.
Into the dungeon angels press
The Virgin's stripes with balm to dress;
Forthwith her pangs are charmed.

She, while the Queen compassionates,
The controverted faith debates;
And when the third day terminates,
Triumphant wins the crown.
A gentle dove the Virgin feeds,
The cruel wheel on which she bleeds
Is rent in pieces; when she pleads,
Awe-struck the crowd falls down.

'Midst tortures winning victory,
She sends Porphyrius to the sky:
With him two hundred go.
Her prayer is granted by the Lord,
Her neck she offers to the sword:
Milk follows at the blow.

Her body angels bear away,
And reverently in Syna lay;
Oil from her tomb doth flow,
The wonder illustrates the place,
While in the heavens a new-born grace
A golden star doth show

Virgin, fair star of modesty,
Chief honoured in Thy dignity,
Sinners against Christ's Majesty
To Christ restore again.
Vessel of holy conversation,
Flower sweet above all distillation,
Protect us, grant to us translation
Thither where Christ doth reign.

Secret. O Lord, we beseech Thee, graciously accept the oblations which we Thy faithful people joyfully present this day in honour of S. Katherine, Thy Virgin-Martyr, and at her intercession let this Sacrifice enter with such favour into Thy presence, that Thou of Thy mercy mayest deliver us out of the perils of this life, and mercifully pardon all our sins. Through.

P. Comm. Grant, we beseech Thee, O Lord, unto Thy people health of mind and body by this holy Sacrament which we have received; and at the intercession of S. Katherine, Thy Virgin-Martyr, in whose honour we rejoice, fill the hearts of Thy faithful with everlasting consolations, that they being upheld by Divine protection may both please Thee with holy devotion, and ever obtain a part in the benefits which Thou bestowest. Through.

S. LINUS, Mart. Pope.

¶ *The* Office, Offert., *and* Comm. ii. *in Comm. Conf. Bp.;* Grad. iii., Alleluia iv. *in the same;* Collects *and* Epistle i., Gospel ii. *as in the Common.*

THE END OF THE PROPER OF SAINTS

The Common of Saints.

THE VIGIL OF AN APOSTLE OR EVANGELIST.

The Office. Ps. lii.

As for me, I am like a green olive-tree in the house of God; my trust is in the tender mercy of God for ever and ever. I will always give thanks unto Thee for that Thou hast done; and I will hope in Thy Name, for Thy saints like it well.

Ps. Why boastest thou thyself, thou tyrant: that thou canst do mischief.

The Collect.

Grant, we beseech Thee, O Almighty God, that our service preceding the day of Saint *N.*, Thy Apostle, may more and more obtain for us the aid of his intercession. Through.

The Lessons.

I.

Ecclus. xliv. 22-23, xlv. 1-7.

The blessing *of the Lord is* upon the head of *the righteous. Therefore* He gave him an heritage, and divided his portion among the twelve tribes. And he found favour in the sight of all flesh; and He magnified him so that *the* enemies stood in awe of him. By his words He caused the wonders to cease; He made him glorious in the sight of kings, and shewed him His glory. He sanctified him in His faithfulness and meekness, and chose him out of all men. He gave him commandments before His face, even the law of life and knowledge, *and* exalted *him*. An everlasting covenant He made with him; He beautified him with comely ornaments, and clothed him with the robe of glory.

II.

Proverbs iii. 13-20.

Happy is the man .... the clouds drop down the dew.

Gradual. Ps. xcii. The righteous shall flourish like a palm-tree; and shall spread abroad like a cedar in Libanus, *in the House of the Lord.*

℣. To tell of Thy loving-kindness early in the morning: and of Thy truth in the night-season.

¶ *The* Alleluia, *if Sunday, is taken from the Common of an Apostle.*

The Gospels.

I.

John xv. 1-7.

At that time Jesus said to his disciples, I am the true vine ...... it shall be done unto you.

II.

John xv. 5-7.

I am the vine .... unto you.

Offert. Ps. viii. Thou hast crowned him with glory and worship, and madest him to have dominion over the works of Thy hands, *O Lord.*

Secret. Let the offering of our worship be acceptable to Thee, O Lord, that we may thereby come to the feast of Thy Apostles with purer minds. Through.

Comm. Ps. xxi. His honour is great in Thy salvation : glory and great worship shalt Thou lay upon him, *O Lord.*

P. Comm. Grant to us, eternal Benefactor, that we may everywhere be protected by his pious intercession, whose day we have anticipated with devotion in these holy Mysteries which we have received. Through.

THE COMMON OF AN APOSTLE.

The Office. Ps. cxxxix.

How dear are Thy counsels unto me, O God : O how great is the sum of them.

Ps. O Lord, Thou has searched me out and known me, Thou knowest my downsitting and mine uprising.

The Collect.

Hear Thy people, O Lord, who entreat Thee under the guardianship of Thy Apostle, Saint *N.*, that they being ever defended by Thy help, may serve Thee in all godly quietness. Through.

I. *The Epistle.* Ephes. ii. 19-22*

Brethren, ye are no more strangers and foreigners .... an habitation of God through the Spirit.

II. *The Lesson.* Acts v. 12-16.

In those days, by the hands of the Apostles .... and the were healed every one.

I. *Gradual.* Ps. cxxxix. How dear are Thy counsels unto me, O God : how great is the sum of them.

℣. If I tell them, they are more in number than the sand.

* In some Missals are added verses 40-42.

II. *Gradual.* Ps. xix. Their sound is gone out into all lands; and their words into the ends of the world.

℣. The heavens declare the glory of God, and the firmament sheweth his handiwork.

III. *Gradual.* Ps. xlv. Thou *shalt* make *them* princes in all lands. I will remember Thy Name, *O Lord.*

℣. Instead of Thy fathers thou shalt have children: therefore shall the people give thanks unto Thee.

I. *Alleluia!* ℣. Ps. cxxxix. How dear are Thy counsels unto me: O God, how great is the sum of them.

II. *Alleluia!* ℣. Ps. xix. Their sound is gone out into all lands, and their words into the ends of the world.

III. *Alleluia!* ℣. Acts v. By the hands of the Apostles were many signs and wonders wrought among the people.

IV. *Alleluia!* ℣. John xv. Ye have not chosen Me, but I have chosen you, and ordained you that ye should go and bring forth fruit, and that your fruit should remain.

¶ *In LXX. is said—*

Tract. Ps. cxii. Blessed is the man that feareth the Lord; he hath great delight in His commandments.

℣. His seed shall be mighty upon earth: the generation of the faithful shall be blessed.

℣. Riches and plenteousness shall be in his house; and his righteousness endureth for ever.

The Sequences.

I.

Illustrious council of Apostles holy,
Ruling the divers kingdoms of the world,
The Churches guide in life and conversation,
Which, by thy doctrines, in the faith stand fast.
Lo! Antioch and Rome yield unto thee,
O Peter, both their kingdom and their throne:
Greece, Alexander's realm, thou Paul hast seized.
The savage Ethiopians, Matthew, thou
Hast with the white fleece of the Lamb invested,
Which with no spot or blemish is defiled.
Thomas, Bartholomnw, John, Philip, Simon,
James both the Great and Less, Andrew, Thaddæus,
Ye warriors of God of high renown,
The East and West, yea, and the whole round world,
Account it joy that they may call you Fathers
For whom they look to sit in judgment on them;
For which cause unto you, ye holy men,

The universe, as is its bounden duty,
Doth tribute pay of reverence and honour.

II.

Let the Church Catholic sing Alleluia!
Extolling high the Apostolic band;
Of whom, by virtue of the Holy Cross,
Peter, their Prince, ascended up to heaven.
The Doctor of the world his triumph wins
In Nero's time, in Romulus' great city.
The Cross on Andrew glory doth confer,
And both the Jameses wear the martyr wreath;
The one Ægeas' hand, the other twain
The nation of the Jews to heaven consigned.
In token of their Master's approbation
Matthew and John have each a special favour:
The one by Hyrtacus is slain, the other
Jesus Himself to His own Banquet bids.
Philip, that learned teacher of the truth,
In Scythia, preaching, finished his course.
Thomas in India by a lance was slain;
Simon and Jude, whilst they the holy message
Entrusted to their lips to Persia bear,
Each in the blood-red martyr robe are clad;
Bartholomew speaks words of life to Ind;
By lot Matthias was Apostle named.
Then let the earth, the courts of heaven, applaud,
The Church here present add her acclamations,
The Apostles' high and holy acts extolling.
These are the candlesticks before God's Face;
These in the Palace of the Mighty King
Exalted sit, in place pre-eminent.
Salt of the earth, light of the world, are these,
Like heavenly luminaries brightly shining
These bear the palm, these wear the crown already;
Already for them is the table set.
O then how great, how glorious, how joyous
Their festal day, which now we celebrate!
Let this, our annual commemoration,
Our mention of their acts, our praises due,
Be pleasing to them in the courts above.

The Gospels.

I.

John xv. 17-25.

At that time Jesus said unto His disciples, These things I command you .... they hated Me without a cause.

II.

Matt. x. 16-22.

At that time Jesus said to His disciples, Behold, I send you forth as sheep in the midst of wolves .... but he that endureth to the end shall be saved.

III.

Matt. xix. 27-29.

At that time Simon Peter said to Jesus, Behold, we have left all ...... inherit everlasting life.

IV.

Matt. xvi. 13-19.

At that time, Jesus came into the coast .... shall be loosed in heaven.

V.

Luke xxii. 24-30.

At that time there was also a strife ...... twelve tribes of Israel.

The Creed.

I. *Offert.* Ps. xix. Their sonnd is gone out into all lands, and their words into the end of the world.

II. *Offert.* Ps. xlv. Thou *shalt* make them princes in all lands; *they shall* remember Thy Name from one generation to another.

III. *Offert.* Ps. cxxxix. How dear are Thy counsels unto me, O God: how great is the sum of them.

Secret. We beseech Thee, O Lord, that we who keep the feast of Thy Apostle, S. *N.*, may receive Thy favours through his aid for whom we offer Thee the sacrifice of praise. Through.

Comm. Matt. xix. Ye that have followed Me shall sit upon twelve thrones judging the tribes of Israel, *saith the Lord.*

P. Comm. Defend us, O merciful God, by these holy Mysteries we have received, and ever rule us under the guardianship of Thy Apostle, S. *N.*, whose day we celebrate.

THE COMMON OF AN EVANGELIST.

The Office. Ps. xxxvii.

The mouth of the righteous is exercised in wisdom: and his tongue will be talking of judgment, the law of his God is in his heart.

Ps. Fret not thyself because of the ungodly: neither be thou envious against the evil doers.

The Collect.

We beseech Thee, O Lord, let Thy Evangelist Saint *N.*, intercede for us, who continually bore about in his body the mortification of the Cross for the honour of Thy Name. Through.

The Lesson. Ezekiel i. 10-14.

As for the likeness of *the* faces *of the four living creatures* .... a flash of lightning.

Gradual. Ps. xxxvii. The mouth of the righteous is exercised in wisdom: and his tongue will be talking of judgment.

℣. The law of his God is in his heart: and his going shall not slide.

Alleluia! ℣. Isa. xli. The first *shall say* to Zion, Behold, behold them: and I will give to Jerusalem one that bringeth good tidings.

The Sequence.

To Christ your voices raise
In glorifying praise,
  Ye reverential choir;
Who the Evangelists,
Truth's steadfast dogmatists,
  Did with His grace inspire;

Who, as Him doth beseem
Who by the lightnings gleam
  Unto the world gives light;
By these whom He chose out,
All heresies doth rout,
  And schism put to flight.

These are the fountains four
From whence the rivers pour
  O'er hill and vale to reach;
From Paradise they spring,
The world illumining
  With undivided speech.

Four living creatures show
These four to us below—
  So holy vision says—
Each differing in form,
In action uniform
  Before the Prophet's gaze.

With wings of fashion fair,
Poised o'er the earth in air
  Forth with their wheels they go;
Calm and composed of mien
And full of eyes, and keen
  The Word of God to show:

In these we may behold
The twice two rings of gold
  Which Israel's Ark did bear;
Their doctrines wholesome sound,
The Church, wherever found,
  Its Keeper, doth declare.

[illegible]

Comm. [illegible] Almighty God, [illegible] at the Holy Altar, may, by the prayers of [illegible] further the salvation of our souls, that we may be preserved for ever. Through.

THE COMMON OF A MARTYR.

The Offices.

I. Ps. xcii. The righteous shall flourish like a palm-tree, and shall spread abroad like a cedar in Libanus. Such as are planted in the house of the Lord: shall flourish in the courts of the house of our God.

Ps. It is a good thing to give thanks unto the Lord: and to sing praises unto Thy Name, O Most Highest.

II. *Ps.* xxxvii. *The righteous* shall not be cast away: for the Lord upholdeth him with His hand. He is ever merciful, and lendeth: and his seed is blessed, they are preserved for ever.

Ps. Fret not thyself because of the ungodly; neither be thou envious against the evil doers.

III. *Ps.* viii. Thou hast crowned him with glory and worship, and Thou makest him to have dominion of the works of Thy hands.

Ps. O Lord our Governor, how excellent is Thy Name in all the world!

IV. *Ps.* xxi. *The righteous* shall rejoice in Thy strength, O Lord: exceeding glad shall he be of Thy salvation. Thou hast given him his heart's desire.

Ps. For Thou shalt prevent him with the blessings of goodness: and shalt set a crown of pure gold upon his head.

V. *Ps.* lxiv. The righteous shall rejoice in the Lord, and put his trust in Him: and all they that are true of heart shall be glad.

Ps. Hear my voice, O God, in my prayers: preserve my life from fear of the enemy.

VI. *Ps.* lxiv. Hide me, *O God*, from the gathering together of the froward. *Alleluia.* And from the insurrection of wicked doers. *Alleluia, Alleluia.*

Ps. Hear my voice, etc.

The Collects.

I.

Be present with us in our prayers, O Lord, and at the intercession of Saint *N.*, Thy Martyr, graciously bestow upon us Thy everlasting mercy. Through.

II.

Grant, we beseech Thee, Almighty God, that we who keep the feast of Saint *N.*, Thy Martyr, may, at his intercession, be strengthened in the love of Thy Name. Through.

I. *The Lesson.* Ecclus. xiv. 20-21; xv. 3-6.

Blessed is the man .... *The Lord our God shall* inherit an everlasting name.

II. *The Epistle.* Eph. i. 3-8.

Brethren, blessed be the God and Father .... hath abounded towards us, *through Jesus Christ our Lord.*

III. *The Lesson.* Ecclus. xxxi. 8-11.

Blessed is the rich .... the congregation *of saints* shall declare his alms.

IV. *The Epistle.* 2 Tim. iv. 1-8.

Dearly beloved, I charge *thee* before God and the Lord Jesus Christ .... unto all them also that love His appearing.

V. *The Epistle.* 2 Tim. ii. 4-10.

Dearly beloved, no man that warreth entangleth himself with the affairs of this life .... salvation which is in Christ Jesus with eternal glory.

VI. *The Epistle.* Gal. v. 10-12; vi. 12-14.

Brethren, I have confidence .... I unto the world.

I. *Gradual.* Ps. xxi. Thou hast set, *O Lord,* a crown of pure gold upon his head.

℣. Thou hast given him his heart's desire; and hast not denied him the request of his lips.

II. *Gradual.* Ps. cxii. Blessed is the man that feareth the Lord: he hath great delight in His commandments.

℣. His seed shall be mighty upon earth: the generation of the faithful shall be blessed.

III. *Gradual.* Ps. xxxvii. The righteous shall not be cast away: for the Lord upholdeth him with His hand.

℣. He is ever merciful, and lendeth: and His seed is blessed.

IV. *Gradual.* Ps. xcii. The righteous shall flourish like a palm-tree: and shall spread abroad like a cedar in Libanus *in the house of the Lord.*

℣. To tell of Thy living kindness early in the morning: and of Thy truth in the night season.

I. *Alleluia!* ℣. Ps. xxi. Thou hast set, *O Lord,* a crown of pure gold upon his head.

II. *Alleluia!* ℣. Ps. xxi. The righteous shall flourish like a palm-tree, and shall spread abroad like a cedar in Libanus.*

III. *Alleluia!* ℣. Ps. liv. The righteous shall rejoice in the Lord, and put his trust in Him: and all they that are true of heart shall be glad.

* Gradual.

IV. *Alleluia!* ℣. *That saint is worthily had in memory of men, who hath passed unto the joy of angels.**

V. *Alleluia!* ℣. Jam. i. 12. Blessed is the man that endureth temptation, for when he is tried he shall receive the crown of life.

VI. *Alleluia!* ℣. Ps. cxii. Blessed is the man that feareth the Lord: he hath great delight in His commandments.

VII. *Alleluia!* ℣. Ps. viii. Thou crownest him with glory and worship: Thou makest him to have dominion of the works of Thy hands.

VIII. *Alleluia!* ℣. Ps. xxxvii. The righteous shall not be cast away, for the Lord upholdeth him with His hand.

Tract. Ps. xxi. Thou hast given him his heart's desire, and hast not denied him the request of his lips.

℣. For Thou shalt prevent him with the blessing of goodness.

℣. Thou shalt set a crown of pure gold upon his head.

The Sequence.

Now let us sing, with instruments well tuned
The feast of *N.*, in divers kinds of voice,
Praying our due thanksgivings to the Lord,
Much to be had in reverence of His saints,
Whom, with high gifts and virtues manifold,
He doth adorn and richly beautify.
In them, as though in instruments of music,
Faith doth with her own finger touch the strings,
Discoursing high of virtues excellent—
As on each single string she lays her hand
She blends it in the fourfold melody
Which she, that mother of all grace, evokes;
Composing thus harmonious symphony!
Without whom all is dissonant,
Yea, trifling, poor, and vain;
With whom all is unisonant,
Yea, fraught with endless gain;
Aided by whom the just, in holy lives
Seeking to climb the heights of starry heaven,
Sing forth new songs, and tune their harps in gladness.
May we who keep their feast be counted meet
To hold with them in heaven communion sweet.

¶ *In LXX. is said—*

The Gospels.

I.

John xii. 24-26.

At that time, Jesus said to His disciples, Verily, verily, I say unto you .... him will My Father honour *Who is in heaven.*

* Gradual.

II.

Luke x. 16-20.

At that time, Jesus said to His disciples, He that heareth you heareth Me .... because your names are written in heaven.

III.

Matt. xvi. 24-28.

Then said Jesus unto His disciples, If any man will come after Me .... Son of Man coming in His Kingdom.

IV.

Luke xiv. 26-33.

At that time, Jesus said to His disciples, If any man come to Me .... he cannot be My disciple.

V.

Matt. x. 26-32.

At that time, Jesus said to His disciples, There is nothing covered .... My Father which is in Heaven.

¶ *In Easter-tide,* "I am the true Vine."

I. *Offert.* Ps. xxi. The righteous shall rejoice in Thy strength, O Lord: exceeding glad shall he be of Thy salvation. Thou hast given him his heart's desire.

II. *Offert.* Ps. xxi. Thou hast set a crown of pure gold upon his head. He asked life of Thee, and Thou gavest *it* him. *Alleluia.*

III. *Offert.* Ps. xcii. The righteous shall flourish like a palm-tree, and shall spread abroad like a cedar in Libanus.

IV. *Offert.* Ps. lxxxix. The very heavens shall praise Thy wondrous works, *O Lord,* and Thy truth in the congregation of the saints. *Alleluia, Alleluia.*

V. *Offert.* Ps. viii. Thou hast crowned him with glory and worship, and made him to have dominion over the works of Thy hands, *O Lord.*

Secret. We beseech Thee, O Lord, look with loving-kindness upon these gifts which we present unto Thee, that the blessing of the Holy Ghost may be poured forth upon them, to the intent they may the more strongly infuse into our hearts that love through which Thy Martyr, Saint *N.*, overcame all bodily tortures. Through.

I. *Comm.* Matt. xvi. *He that* will come after Me, let him deny himself, and take up his cross and follow Me.

II. *Comm.* John xii. If any man serve Me, let him follow Me; and where I am, there also shall My servant be.

III. *Comm.* Ps. xxi. Thou hast set, *O Lord*, a crown of pure gold upon his head.

IV. *Comm.* Ps. lxiv. The righteous shall rejoice in the Lord, and shall put his trust in Him, and all they that are true of heart shall be glad.

V. *Comm.* John xv. I am the Vine, ye are the branches. He that abideth in Me, and I in him, the same bringeth forth much fruit. *Alleluia, Alleluia.*

VI. *Comm.* Ps. xxi. His honour is great in Thy salvation: glory and great worship shalt Thou lay upon Him, *O Lord.*

P. Comm. We beseech Thee, O Lord, mercifully to absolve from all their sins those whom Thou hast refreshed with the heavenly Mystery, that, by the intercession of Thy Martyr, Saint *N.*, we may, with purified hearts, have the full fruition of Thy gifts. Through.

THE COMMON OF A MARTYR AND BISHOP.

The Office. Ps. viii.

Thou hast crowned him with glory and worship: Thou makest him to have dominion of the works of Thy hands.

Ps. O Lord, our Governor, how excellent is Thy Name in all the world.

The Collect.

O God, Who hast sanctified the joy of this day for the commemoration of Thy Martyr and Bishop, Saint *N.*, be present at the prayers of Thy family, and grant that we may be succoured for his sake and intercession whose feast we this day celebrate. Through.

The Epistles.

I.

Hebrews v. 1-6.

Brethren, every high priest taken from among men .... a priest for ever after the order of Melchisedec.

II.

Hebrews xiii. 9-16.

Brethren, be not carried about with divers and strange doctrines .... with such sacrifices God is well pleased.

The Gospels.

I.

Matt. ix. 35-38; x. 7, 8, 16.

At that time Jesus went about .... and harmless as doves.

¶ Gradual *and* Alleluia, Sequence, *and* Tract *as* i. *Com. Mart. The following* Gospel *is said on all feasts of exiled Bishops, whether Martyrs or Confessors.*

II.

Luke xix. 12-28.

At that time Jesus spake to His disciples this parable: A certain nobleman went into a far country .... ascending up to Jerusalem.

¶ *In Easter-tide*, Gospel, "I am the true Vine;" Offert. *as* ii. *Comm. Mart.*

Secret. Graciously regard, we beseech Thee, O Lord, these gifts offered unto Thee; and at the prayers of Saint *N.*, Thy Martyr and Bishop, on whose commemoration we present them, sanctify both us and them. Through.

Comm. As iii. Com. Mart.

P. Comm. O Lord, we who have received the holy Sacrament upon the feast of Thy blessed Martyr and Bishop *N.*, beseech Thee to grant us that, by his aid, this our temporal service may be consummated in joys everlasting. Through.

THE COMMON OF MANY MARTYRS.

The Offices.

I. *Ps.* lxxix. O let the sorrowful sighing of the prisoners come before Thee: reward Thou them, O Lord, seven-fold into their bosom. *Avenge* the blood of Thy *saints* which is shed.

Ps. O God, the heathen are come into Thine inheritance: Thy holy Temple have they defiled, and made Jerusalem an heap of stones.

II. *Ps.* xxxiv. O fear the Lord, ye that are His saints: for they thar fear Him lack nothing. The lions do lack, and suffer hunger: but they who seek the Lord shall want no manner of thing that is good.

Ps. I will always give thanks unto the Lord: His praise shall ever be in my mouth.

III. *Ps.* xxxiv. The poor crieth, and the Lord heareth him, yea, and saveth him out of all his troubles.*

Ps. I will always.

IV. *Ps.* lxviii. Let the righteous be glad and rejoice before God: let them also be merry and joyful.

Ps. Let God arise, and let His enemies be scattered: let them also that hate Him flee before Him.

V. *Ecclus.* xliv. 15. The people will tell of the wisdom *of the saints*, and the congregation will shew forth their praise: their name liveth for evermore.

Ps. xxxiii. Rejoice in the Lord, O ye righteous: for it becometh well the just to be thankful.

VI. *Wisd.* iii. 8. *The saints* shall judge the nations, and have dominion over the people, and their Lord shall reign for ever.†

Ps. Rejoice in the Lord.

VII. *Ps.* xxxvii. But the salvation of the righteous cometh of the Lord: Who is also their strength in the time of trouble.

Ps. Fret not thyself because of the ungodly; neither be thou envious against the evil doers.

VIII. Ps. cxlv. Thy saints give thanks unto Thee, *O Lord.* They shew the glory of Thy kingdom. *Alleluia!*

Ps. I will magnify Thee, O God, my King: and I will praise Thy Name for ever and ever.

Of Many Martyrs not Bishops.

Almighty and everlasting God, grant us so to reverence the excellence of Thy Martyrs, SS. *N.* and *N.*, that we may both be set free from present dangers, and made meet for everlasting joys. Through.

Of Many Martyrs Bishops.

Almighty and everlasting God, Who didst kindle in the hearts of Thy Martyr Bishops, SS. *N.* and *N.*, the flame of Thy love, give unto our souls the same power of faith and charity, that so we may profit by their examples in whose triumphs we rejoice. Through.

I. *The Epistle.* Hebrews xi. 33-39.

The Saints through faith subdued kingdoms ...... and these all *were found to have* obtained a good report through faith *in Jesus Christ our Lord.*

* Gradual. † Gradual.

II. *The Lesson.* Wisdom iii. 1-8.

The souls of the righteous are in the hand of God .... and their Lord shall reign for ever.

III. *The Lesson.* Wisdom v. 15-20.

But the righteous shall live for evermore .... His severe wrath shall He sharpen for a sword. *Then shall the promises have an end, and the Lord our God shall lead them to the appointed place.*

IV. *The Epistle.* Hebrews x. 32-38.

Brethren, call to remembrance the former days .... Now the just shall live by faith

V. *The Epistle.* 1 Cor. iv. 9-14.

Brethren, we are made a spectacle unto the world, and to angels, and to men .... but as my beloved sons I warn you *in Christ Jesus our Lord.*

VI. *The Lesson.* Proverbs xv. 2-4, 6-9.

The tongue of the wise useth knowledge aright .... but he loveth him that followeth after righteousness.

VII. *The Lesson.* Wisdom x. 17-20.

God shall render to the righteous .... magnified with one accord Thy Name *O Lord our God.*

VIII. *The Lesson.* Ecclus. xliv. 10-15.

These were merciful men .... show forth their praise.

I. *Gradual.* Exod. xv. The Lord is glorious in *His saints, marvellous in His Majesty,* doing wonders.

℣. Thy right hand, O Lord, is become glorious in power: Thy right hand, O Lord, hath dashed in pieces the enemy.

II. *Gradual.* Ps. xxxiv. The poor crieth, and the Lord heareth him: yea, and saveth him out of all his troubles.

℣. The Lord is nigh unto them that are of a contrite heart: and will save such as be of an humble spirit.

III. *Gradual.* Ps. xxxiv. O fear the Lord, ye that are His saints: for they that fear Him lack nothing.

℣. But they who seek the Lord shall want no manner of thing that is good.

IV. *Gradual.* Wisdom iii. The souls of the righteous are in the hand of God, and there shall no torment touch them

℣. In the sight of the unwise they seemed to die; but they are in peace.

V. *Gradual.* Ps. cxlix. Let the saints be joyful with glory: let them rejoice in their beds.

℣. O sing unto the Lord a new song: let the congregation of saints praise Him.

VI. *Gradual.* Ps. lxxix. *Avenge, O Lord,* the blood *of Thy saints* which is shed.

℣. The dead bodies of Thy servants have they given to be meat unto the fowls of the air: and the flesh of Thy saints unto the beasts of the land.

VII. *Gradual.* Ps. cxxxiii. Behold, how good and joyful a thing it is: brethren to dwell together in unity!

℣. It is like the precious ointment upon the head, that ran down unto the beard: even unto Aaron's beard.

℣. For there the Lord promised His blessing; and life for evermore.

VIII. *Gradual.* Ps. cxxiv. Our soul is escaped even as a bird out of the snare of the fowler.

℣. The snare is broken and we are delivered.

℣. Our help standeth in the Name of the Lord: Who hath made heaven and earth.

I. *Alleluia!* ℣. Ps. cxlv. Thy saints give thanks unto Thee, *O Lord;* they shew the glory of Thy kingdom.

II. *Alleluia!* ℣. *Thy saints, O Lord, shall flourish as a lily, and as the odour of balsam shall they be before Thee.*

III. *Alleluia!* ℣. Ps. xxxiii. Rejoice in the Lord, O ye righteous *and saints; God hath chosen you to be His inheritance.*

IV. *Alleluia!* ℣. Ps. cxviii. The voice of joy and health is in the dwellings of the righteous.

V. *Alleluia!* ℣. Ps. lxviii. But let the righteous be glad and rejoice before God; let them also be merry and joyful.

VI. *Alleluia!* ℣. Wisd. x. *God* rendered to the righteous a reward of their labours, *and* guided them in a marvellous way.

VII. *Alleluia!* ℣. Ps. lxviii. *Our* Lord is wonderful in *His saints.*

VIII. *Alleluia!* The noble army of martyrs praise Thee, O *Lord.*

¶ *In LXX. is said—*

Tract. Ps. cxxvi. They that sow in tears : shall reap in joy.

℣. He that now goeth on his way weeping, and bearing forth good seed.

℣. Shall doubtless come again with joy, and bring his sheaves with him.

The Sequences.

I.

Lo sweetly sounds the deep-toned Alleluia,
Closing the Martyr's glorious requiem.
The blessed angels' radiant host stands round
In triumph, crying, Holy! Holy! Holy!
In the Apostles' brilliant habitation,
Judging all peoples, nations. languages,
Enthroned high, a shining company,
Who counted all the pomp of life as loss,
Like stars they glitter in the firmament.
Clothed in white robes the Martyrs make them ready,
Warriors who fought the battle of the world.
Lo, with white coronals the saints are crowned
Who witnessed righteously a good confession,
And lying words disdained,
Contending for the faith;
Now in the heavenly kingdom they have place,
Most excellently uttering words of triumph,
Or chanting forth their hymns of exultation—
With skill to praise attuned,
And voice of accent sweet—
To Christ their King bowing their heads submissive:
Much do the spirits praise Thy Holy Name,
By virgin choirs much art Thou glorified;
To Thee, the undefiled,
In sweetest harmony,
The hosts of Heaven sing ever, Alleluia,
Praise ever be to Thee, O Christ, by all—
Thou Who to those that praise Thee givest aid.
We, too, with tuneful voice,
With them in harmony,
Would unto Christ pour forth loud Alleluias.
Grant us that Kingdom, ever fair and shining,
Where we may all chant forth our Alleluias.

II.

God is to be admired in His Saints,
Who by His grace wrought great and wondrous acts:
Who by the excellency of their faith
Subdued the world and its most grievous perils;
The threatening of the judges, cruel stripes,
And blandishments, with steadfast soul despising,
They for their King poured out their souls to death.

With victor's laurel crownèd, now they triumph—
Christ's holy footsteps duly following,
That spotless Lamb, to Whom unceasingly
They pour forth sweetest hymns, fulfilled with His grace.
May Christ, Who is our glory, grant that we
Who celebrate their festival to-day
May be found meet to be with them united.

The Gospels.

I.

Luke vi. 20-23.

At that time Jesus lifted up His eyes on His disciples, and said .... your reward is great in heaven.

II.

Matt. v. 1-12.

At that time Jesus, seeing the multitudes, He went up into a mountain .... for great is your reward in heaven.

III.

Matt. x. 23-26.

At that time Jesus said to His disciples, But when they persecute you in this city, flee ye into another .... fear them not therefore.

IV.

Luke xxi. 14-19.

At that time Jesus said to His disciples, Settle it therefore in your hearts .... in your patience possess ye your souls.

V.

Luke vi. 17-23.

At that time Jesus came down with them .... your reward is great in heaven.

VI.

Luke xxi. 9-19.

At that time Jesus said to His disciples, When ye shall hear of wars .... in your patience possess ye your souls.

VII.

Luke xii. 1-8.

At that time Jesus said unto His disciples, Beware ye of the leaven of the Pharisees .... confess before the angels of God.

VIII.

Matt. xxiv. 3-13.

At that time, as Jesus sat upon the Mount of Olives .... the same shall be saved.

IX.

Luke xi. 47-54.

At that time Jesus said to the multitude of the Jews and the chief of the Pharisees, Woe unto you .... that they might accuse Him.

X.

Mark xiii. 1-13.

At that time, as Jesus went out of the Temple, one .... the same shall be saved.

XI.

Mark xiii. 5-13.

At that time Jesus said to His disciples, take heed that no man .... the same shall be saved.

XII.

Matt. x. 34-42.

At that time Jesus said to His disciples, Think not that I am come .... he shall in no wise lose his reward.

XIII.

Matt. x. 16-22.

As ii. Comm. Ap.

XIV.

Matt. xxiv. 1-13.

At that time, Jesus went out .... the same shall be saved.

¶ *In Eastertide,* Gospel, "I am the Vine," *as* ii. *Vig. Ap.*

I. *Offert.* Ps. lxviii. O God, wonderful art Thou in Thy holy places: even the God of Israel, He will give strength and power unto His people; blessed be God. *Alleluia.*

II. *Offert.* Ps. v. They that love Thy Name shall be joyful in Thee; for Thou, Lord, wilt give Thy blessing unto the righteous; and with Thy favourable kindness wilt Thou defend him as with a shield.

III. *Offert.* Ps. xxxii. Be glad, O ye righteous, and rejoice in the Lord: and be joyful, all ye that are true of heart.

IV *Offert.* Ps. cxlix. Let the saints be joyful with glory; let them rejoice in their beds. Let the praises of God be in their mouth.

V. *Offert.* Ps. cxxiv. Our soul is escaped even as a bird out of the snare of the fowler: the snare is broken, and we are delivered.

VI. *Offert.* Ps. lxxxix. O Lord, the very heavens shall praise Thy wondrous works: and Thy truth in the congregation of the saints. *Alleluia, Allelluia.*

VII. *Offert.* Ps. xc. O satisfy us with Thy mercy, and that soon: so shall we rejoice and be glad. *Alleluia.*

Secret of Martyrs not Bishops. Receive, we beseech Thee, O Lord, the gifts of Thy people in honour of the feast of Thy Martyr Saints, and enable us with pure heart to take part in their commemoration. Through.

Secret of Martyr-Bishops. We offer, O Lord, unto Thy Majesty these gifts, in veneration of the glorious deeds of Thy holy Martyr-Bishops *N.* and *N.*, entreating that by showing reverence to them we may obtain pardon for ourselves. Through.

I. *Comm.* Ps. xxxiii. Rejoice in the Lord, O ye righteous, *Alleluia* for it becometh well the just to be thankful. *Allleluia.*

II. *Comm.* Luke vi. A great multitude *of sick*, and they that were vexed with unclean spirits came unto Him; for there went virtue out of Him and healed them all.

III. *Comm.* Ps. lxxix. The dead bodies of Thy servants have they given to be meat unto the fowls of the air, and the flesh of Thy saints unto the beasts of the land: according to the greatness of Thy power, preserve Thou those that are appointed to die.

IV. *Comm.* Wisd. iii. The souls of the righteous are in the hand of God, and there shall no torment touch them. In the sight of the unwise they seemed to die: but they are in peace.

V. *Comm.* John xv. I have chosen you and ordained you, that ye should go and bring forth fruit, and that your fruit should remain.

VI. *Comm.* Wisd. iii. For though they be punished in the sight of men, God proved them. As gold in the furnace hath He tried them, and received them as a burnt offering.

VII. *Comm.* Ps. cxxiv. Our soul is escaped as a bird out of the snare of the fowlers.

VIII. *Comm.* John xv. I am the *true* vine, ye are the branches: he that abideth in Me and I in him, the same bringeth forth much fruit. *Alleluia, Alleluia.*

IX. *Comm.* Luke xii. I say unto you, my friends, Be not afraid of them *which persecute you.*

X. *Comm.* Matt. x. What I tell you in darkness, that speak ye in light, *saith the Lord;* and what ye hear in the ear, that preach ye upon the house-tops.

XI. *Comm.* Matt. xxv. Verily I say unto you, inasmuch as ye have done it unto one of the least of these My brethren, ye have done it unto Me. Come, ye blessed of My Father, inherit the kingdom prepared for you from the foundation of the world.

P. Comm. of Martyrs not Bishops. We, rejoicing in the reception of Thy Sacrament, O Lord, humbly pray that Thou wouldst enable us to imitate their constancy whose deeds Thou vouchsafest to us to celebrate. Through.

P. Comm. of Martyr-Bishops. O God, Who purifiest us by the participation of Thy adorable Sacrament, grant us, we beseech Thee, the continued guardianship of Thy Saints; whereby we may have a portion in the Mystery of Salvation. Through.

Another of Martyrs not Bishops, in Sarum Missal of 1527.

Collect. O God, Who permittest us to celebrate the day of Thy Martyrs, SS. *N.* and *N.*, grant us the enjoyment of their fellowship in eternal bliss. Through.

Secret. We offer unto Thee, O Lord, our gifts and worship: grant that in honour of Thy Saints they may be pleasing to Thee, and by Thy mercy further our salvation. Through.

P. Comm. Grant, we beseech Thee, O Lord, at the intercessions of Thy Martyrs, *N.* and *N.*, that what we have partaken of with our mouth we may receive with a pure heart. Through.

THE COMMON OF A CONFESSOR AND BISHOP.

The Offices.

I. *Ecclus.* xlv. Therefore was there a covenant of peace made with him *by the Lord* that he should be the chief of the sanctuary and of his people, and that he and his posterity should have the dignity of the priesthood for ever.

Ps. lxxxix. My song shall be alway of the loving-kindness of the Lord.

II. *Ps.* cxxxii. Let Thy priests be clothed with righteousness, *O Lord*: and let Thy saints sing with joyfulness. For Thy servant David's sake turn not away the presence of thine Anointed.

Ps. Lord, remember David: and all his troubles.

III. *Dan.* iii. O ye priests of the Lord, bless ye the Lord: O ye holy and humble men of heart, praise the Lord.

Ps. O all ye works of the Lord, bless ye the Lord: praise Him, and magnify Him for ever.

The Collects.

I. O Almighty and ever-living God, Who causest us to rejoice this day in the feast of Thy Bishop and Confessor, *N.*, we humbly pray Thy mercy, that by the holy prayers of him whose feast we reverently keep we may obtain the recompense of eternal life. Through.

II. Grant, we beseech Thee, Almighty God, that the revered feast of Thy Confessor and Bishop, Saint *N.*, may increase our devotion and further our salvation. Through.

The Lessons.

I.

Ecclus. xliv. 16, 17, 19-23; xlv. 3, 7, 16.

Behold a High Priest who in his day pleased the Lord, and was found righteous; in the time of wrath he was taken in exchange. In glory there was none like unto him; who kept the law of the Most High; therefore He assured him by an oath that He would *make him increase among his people. Therefore did* He establish likewise the blessing of all men, and the covenant, and made it rest upon his head. He acknowledged him in His blessing, and He brought out of him a merciful man, which found favour in the sight of *the Lord*, and He made him glorious in the sight of kings, and gave him a *crown of glory*. An everlasting covenant He made with him, and gave him the priesthood among the people; and clothed him with a robe of glory, to execute the office of the priesthood, and to bless the people in His Name; to offer to *Him* incense, and a sweet savour.

II.

Ecclus. l. (1, 4, 5, 6-12, 15, 23.*)

Behold a high priest who in his life *cared for his people, and delivered them from destruction.* He repaired the house again, and in his days fortified the temple : *he enlarged the state and gained glory.* How was he honoured in the midst of the people .... He stretched out his hands to the cup, and poured out a sweet-smelling savour unto the Most High King of all. And *he* bowed *himself* down to worship the second time, that *he* might receive a blessing from the Most High, *Who* dealeth with us according to His mercy. He grant us joyfulness of heart, and that peace may be in our days in Israel for ever.

III.

Wisdom x. 10-14.

The Lord guided the just in right paths, shewed him the kingdom of God .... and *the Lord our God* gave him perpetual glory.

IV.

Ecclus. xlv. 1-5.

He was beloved of God and men *and his* memorial is blessed .... even the law of life and knowledge.

I. *Gradual.* Ecclus. xliv. *Behold a high priest who in his days* pleased *God.*

℣. There is none like him who kept the law of the Most High.

II. *Gradual.* Ps. cx. The Lord sware and will not repent : Thou art a priest for ever after the order of Melchisedech.

℣. The Lord said unto my Lord : Sit Thou on My right hand.

III. *Gradual.* Ps. lxxxix. I have found David My servant : with My holy oil have I anointed him. My hand shall hold him fast : and My arm shall strengthen him.

℣. The enemy shall not be able to do him violence : the son of wickedness shall not hurt him.

IV. *Gradual.* Ps. xxi. *O Lord,* Thou shalt prevent him with the blessings of goodness ; and shalt set a crown of pure gold upon his head.

* This Lesson is said on both feasts of S. Edmund, Archbp.

℣. He asked life of Thee, and Thou gavest him a long life: even for ever and ever.

I. *Alleluia!* ℣. *The righteous shall grow up as a rose, and blossom for ever before the Lord.**

II. *Alleluia!* ℣. Ecclus xliv. *The Lord loved and adorned him,* and clothed him with a robe of glory.

III. *Alleluia!* ℣. Ps. lxxxix. I have made a covenant with My chosen: I have sworn unto David My servant.

IV. *Alleluia!* ℣. *The Lord hath chosen thee to be a high priest among His people.*

V. *Alleluia!* ℣. Ps. lxxxix. I have found David My servant, and with My holy oil have I anointed him.

VI. *Alleluia!* ℣. Ps. lxxxix. I have laid help upon one that is mighty; I have exalted one chosen out of the people.

¶ *The* Tract *in LXX., as in Comm. Ap.*

The Sequences.

I.

The festive day is come ¶
Which brings to us great joy,
When Holy Church gives thanks acceptable to God.
This day the Heavenly Host sings, Glory in the highest
With voice and symphony melodious.
This day the holy armies of the heavens
Unite with us in praise of God our King,
Christ, of the holy Virgin Mary born.
Hail, noble Prelate (*or* great Confessor) *N.*, thou flower of saints!
With steadfast faith, Christ's footsteps following,
Thou hast attained the everlasting Kingdom;
Already to their courts the blessed welcome thee.
To thee unitedly our suit we make,
Our frail life by Thy blest protection aid.
Praise, glory to thee, blessed, holy *N.*
Entreat for us, O blessed, holy *N.*,
That in the heavenly Temple we may stand,
Fulness of joy beholding in thy presence.
Praise, honour, and thanksgiving pure
Be unto God, Who doth for evermore endure.
Let all things say, Amen.

II.

Now, holy band, tell out your highest praise abroad,
To give resplendent honours unto *N.*,
Who shines above the moon, and sun, and stars,
And glitters with high deeds in place pre-eminent;

* ? Isai. xxxv.

For this is he whom wisdom's mystic lore
Did marvellously grace, and gave him lustre,
Which richly lighted the whole universe.
Upon the field of souls he scattered wide
The seed prolific of the Word divine,
Dispersing all the darkness of the night.
Earnest in speech, as bearing in himself
A heavenly inspiration, by his preaching
The whole Church Catholic he builded up.
Now set on high, in glory he exults,
Midst the bright tents of angels triumphing.
There, lifted up to loftiest place, he stands,
In full fruition of exhaustless life,
In Christ's rich pastures of salvation.
O worthy praise most eminent,
Prelate, that hath such joys attained
For excellency of his deeds,
Whereby he shone resplendent as a torch.
We, with loud voice, rejoicingly
Pour forth our willing supplications to him,
That he would bring us aid, and by his prayer
Obtain for us eternal recompense.
Thou gem of prelates, such the boon we crave
With meet devotion, and with minds sincere,
Instantly for thy favour making prayer
That we may pass beyond the sacred threshold,
And, standing there within the lofty palace,
Find joyful welcome in that kingly realm
In this thy court we, holy Prelate, wait,
And with great joy and festal jubilee
Sing now our sweet and lofty Alleluias.

The Gospels.

I.

Matt. xxv. 1-23.

At that time Jesus spake to His disciples this parable, A *certain* man travelling into a far country .... enter thou into the joy of thy lord.

II.

Mark xiii. 33-37.

At that time Jesus said to His disciples, Take ye heed, watch and pray .... What I say unto you I say unto all, Watch.

III.

Matt. xxiv. 42-47.

At that time Jesus said to His disciples, Watch, therefore .... ruler over all his goods.

IV.

Luke xix. 12-28.

As ii. Comm. Mart. Bp.

¶ *In Eastertide*, Gospel, "I am the true vine."

I. *Offert.* Ps. lxxxix. My truth also and My mercy shall be with him : and in My Name shall his horn be exalted.

II. *Offert.* Ps. lxxxix. I have found David My servant : with My holy oil have I anointed him. My hand shall hold him fast : and My arm shall strengthen him.

I. *Secret.* O Lord, we beseech Thee, graciously receive these our supplications, and grant that we who attend this heavenly Sacrament may, at the intercession of Thy Confessor and Bishop, Saint *N.*, be delivered from all sin, and through Thy purifying grace be cleansed by these same Mysteries at which we serve. Through.

II. *Secret.* Regard, we beseech Thee, O Lord, the gifts of Thy people presented to Thee in honour of Saint *N.*, Thy Confessor and Bishop, and let the witness of Thy truth be profitable to our salvation. Through.

I. *Comm.* Matt. xxv. Lord, thou deliveredst unto me five talents : behold, I have gained beside them five talents more. Well done, thou good and faithful servant : thou hast been faithful over a few things, I will make thee ruler over many things : enter thou into the joy of thy lord.

II. *Comm.* Matt. xxiv. Blessed is that servant whom his lord, when he cometh, shall find watching.

III. *Comm.* Matt. xxiv. A faithful and wise servant, whom his lord hath made ruler over his household, to give them meat in due season. Verily I say unto you, that he shall make him ruler over all his goods.

I. *P. Comm.* Grant, we beseech Thee, O Lord our God, that we being cleansed by the Divine Mystery may, at the intercession of Saint *N.*, Thy Confessor and Bishop, reach forth unto the fulness of that heavenly Sacrament, of which we have partaken. Through.

II. *P. Comm.* O Lord, graciously raise up us whom Thou refreshest with Thy Sacrament, at the prayers of Saint *N.*, Thy Confessor and Bishop, that we may attain, in these Mysteries and our intention, unto the end of our redemption. Through.

THE COMMON OF A CONFESSOR AND DOCTOR.

The Office.

As *Offert.* iii. in Comm. Conf. Bp.

The Collect.

Hear, O Lord, we beseech Thee, the prayers we offer on the feast of Saint *N.*, Thy Confessor and Doctor; and by his intercession, who worthily served Thee, deliver us from all our sins. Through.

The Lessons.

I.

Ecclus. xlvii. 7, 8, 9-11; xxiv. 1-4.

In all his works he praised the Holy One .... *In the midst of the people shall she be exalted, and she shall be admired in the fulness of holiness: in the multitude of the elect she shall have honour, and amongst the blessed she shall be blessed.*

II.

Wisd. vii. 7-13.

Wherefore I prayed, and understanding was given me .... I do not hide her riches.

¶ Sequence *and* Tract *in LXX.*, Gradual *and* Alleluia ii. *in Comm. Conf. Bp.*

The Gospel. Matt. v. 13-19.

At that time Jesus said to His disciples, Ye are the salt of the earth .... great in the kingdom of heaven.

Offert. As i. in Comm. Conf. Bp.

Secret. Sanctify, we beseech Thee, O Lord, the gifts dedicated unto Thee, and by the same, at the intercession of Saint *N.*, Thy Confessor and Doctor, turn Thy Face in reconciliation unto us. Through.

Comm. As iii. in Comm. Conf. Bp.

P. Comm. Grant, we beseech Thee, Almighty God, that we rendering thanks unto Thee for the gifts we have received, may, at the intercession of Saint *N.*, Thy Confessor and Doctor, obtain further benefits. Through.

THE COMMON OF A CONFESSOR AND ABBAT.

The Office. Ps. xxxvii.

The mouth of the righteous is exercised in wisdom : and his tongue will be talking of judgment. The law of his God is in his heart.

Ps. Fret not thyself because of the ungodly : neither be thou envious against the evil doers.

The Collect.

O God, Who didst endue Saint *N.*, Thy Confessor and Abbat, with the grace of holiness, make us, for his sake, to abound in good works, that so we may be counted worthy to obtain from Thee the Highest Good, all that is needful for us. Through.

The Lesson. Ecclus. xxxix. 5-9.

The righteous will give his heart to resort early to the Lord .... shall live from generation to generation.

Gradual. Ps. xxxvii. The mouth of the righteous is exercised in wisdom : and his tongue will be talking of judgment.

℣. The law of his God is in his heart, and his goings shall not slide.

Alleluia! Ps. lxxxix. I have laid help upon one that is mighty : I have exalted one chosen out of *My* people.

¶ *The* Sequence *as in Comm. Conf. and Bp.* Tract, *in LXX., as in Comm. Mart.*

The Gospel. Luke xi. 33-36.

At that time Jesus said to His disciples, No man, when he hath lighted a candle .... shining of a candle doth give thee light.

Offert. Ps. xxi. Thou hast given him his heart's desire, *O Lord,* and hast not denied him the request of his lips : Thou hast set a crown of pure gold upon his head.

Secret. We beseech Thee, O Lord, that the Sacrifice which we offer on the feast of Saint *N.*, Thy Confessor and Abbat, may be acceptable unto Thee; and that, for his pleading sake, the favour Thou bearest unto us may be increased. Through.

Comm. As iii. in Comm. Conf. and Bp.

P. Comm. We, who partake of the holy Mysteries, beseech Thee, O Lord, to extend Thy mercy to us; that those things which we seek in prayer, we may, at the intercession of Saint *N.*, Thy Confessor and Abbat, obtain in a conversation well pleasing unto Thee. Through.

THE COMMON OF ANY CONFESSOR.

¶ *All as in Comm. Conf. Abbat, except the* Epistle iii. *and* Gospel ii. *in Comm. Conf. Bp.*

The Collect.

Give ear, O Lord, to the prayers we present to Thee on the feast of Saint *N.*, Thy Confessor; that we, who put not our trust in our own righteousness, may be helped for his sake and prayers, who was pleasing unto Thee. Through.

Secret. Receive, O Lord, the Sacrifice of reconciliation and praise, and at the intercession of Saint *N.*, Thy Confessor, grant that it may both lead us unto pardon, and establish us in perpetual thanksgiving. Through.

P. Comm. Grant, we beseech Thee, Almighty God, that by his intercession on whose feast this Sacrament is offered, the same may be made profitable unto our salvation. Through.

THE COMMON OF MANY CONFESSORS.

The Office. Ps. cxxxii.

Let Thy priests be clothed with righteousness: and let Thy saints sing with joyfulness.

Ps. Lord, remember David: and all his trouble.

The Collect.

I. Defend us, we beseech Thee, O Lord, by the protection of SS. *N.* and *N.*, Confessors; that, at the intercession of those whose feast we celebrate yearly with worship, we may be delivered from all adversities. Through.

II. O God, Who dost compass and protect us by the glorious witness of Thy Confessors, SS. *N.* and *N.*, grant that we may both profit by their example and rejoice in their intercession. Through.

The Epistle. Heb. vii. 23-27.

Brethren, they truly were many priests .... for this *our Lord Jesus Christ* did once when He offered up Himself.

Gradual. Ps. cxxxii. Let *His* priests be clothed with righteousness : let *His* saints sing with joyfulness.

℣. There shall I make the horn of David to flourish : I have ordained a lantern for Mine Anointed.

Alleluia! ℣. Wisd. iii. *The righteous* shall shine, and run to and fro like sparks among the stubble, *for ever.*

¶ *No* Sequence *is said, even though it be a feast of Nine Lessons.*

The Gospels.

I.

Luke xii. 35-40.

At that time Jesus said to His disciples, Let your loins be girded about .... the Son of Man cometh at an hour when ye think not.

II.

Matt. x. 5-8.

At that time Jesus sent forth *His* twelve *disciples* .... freely ye have received, freely give.

Offert. Ps. cxlix. Let the saints be joyful with glory : let them rejoice in their beds. Let the praises of God be in their mouth.

Secret. Be present, O Lord, with the prayers and gifts of Thy people; and let the oblations of the holy Mysteries, at the intercession of Thy Saints, be pleasing in Thy sight. Through.

Comm. John xv. I have chosen you out of the world, that ye should go and bring forth fruit, and that your fruit should remain.

P. Comm. Let Thy faithful people, O Lord, be refreshed by the healing of the heavenly gift; and, at the prayers of Thy Confessors and Saints, we pray that they may be cleansed from all sin. Through.

THE COMMON OF A VIRGIN AND MARTYR.

The Offices.

I. Ps. xlv. Thou hast loved righteousness, and hated iniquity; wherefore God, even thy God, hath anointed thee with the oil of gladness above thy fellows.

Ps. My heart is inditing of a good matter: I speak of the things which I have made unto the King.

II. Ps. cxix. 4, 6, 7. I will speak of Thy testimonies also, even before kings, and will not be ashamed: and my delight shall be in Thy commandments, which I have loved.

Ps. Blessed are those that are undefiled in the way: and walk in the law of the Lord.

III. Ps. cxix. 95-6. The ungodly laid wait for me to destroy me: but I will consider Thy testimonies, *O Lord*. I see all things come to an end: but Thy commandment is exceeding broad.

Ps. I will speak.

The Collect.

Give ear to us, O God of our salvation, that as we celebrate with joy the feast of Saint *N.*, Thy Virgin Martyr, so we may be perfected in love and devotion. Through.

The Lessons.

I.

Ecclus. li. 9-12.

Then lifted I up my supplication .... and bless Thy Name, O Lord my *God*.

II.

Ecclus. li. 1-8.

I will thank Thee, O Lord and King .... and savest them out of the hands of the enemies, *O Lord my God*.

III.

Ecclus. xxiv. 1-3; 15, 16.

Wisdom shall praise herself .... branches of honour and grace.

I. *Gradual.* Ps. xlv. Thou hast loved righteousness, and hated iniquity.

℣. Wherefore God, even thy God, hath anointed thee with the oil of gladness.

II. *Gradual.* Ps. xlv. According to thy worship and renown, good luck have those with thine honour .... ride on.

℣. Because of the word of truth, of meekness, and righteousness; and thy right hand shall teach thee terrible things.

III. *Gradual.* Ps. xlv. Full of grace are thy lips, because God hath blessed thee for ever.

℣. Because of the word of truth ...... things.

IV. *Gradual.* Ps. xlv. Hearken, O daughter, and consider; incline thine ear. So shall the King have pleasure in thy beauty.

℣. According to thy worship and renown ...... ride on.

V. *Gradual.* Ps. xlv. Because of the word ...... terrible things.

℣. Hearken, O daughter ...... thy beauty.

I. *Alleluia!* ℣. 2 Cor. xi. For I am jealous over you with a godly jealousy, for I have espoused you to one husband that I may present you as a chaste virgin to Christ.

II. *Alleluia!* ℣. Ps. xlv. *Come, my chosen one, and I will set thee on my throne:* so shall the King have pleasure in thy beauty.

III. *Alleluia!* ℣. Ps. xlv. According to thy worship and renown ...... ride on.

IV. *Alleluia!* ℣. Ps. xlv. Full of grace ...... for ever.

V. *Alleluia!* ℣. *This is the wise virgin* whom the Lord *found* watching.

VI. *Alleluia!* Ps. cxix. 46. I will speak of Thy testimonies before kings, and will not be ashamed, *O Lord.*

¶ *In LXX. is said—*

Tract. Full of grace ...... for ever.

℣. According ...... ride on.

℣. Because of ...... things.

℣. Hearken, O daughter, and consider ...... beauty.

The Sequence.

Let us exult upon this festive day,
The mighty acts commending of the Lord,
Who in His Saints His greatest works doth show—
Whose power in virgin deeds most brightly shineth;
For by His grace they the world's pomp despised,
And virgin courage kings' commands withstood.
Wrath madly rages; vanquished spite, embittered
'Gainst tender flesh, more torments doth devise.
But now more steadfast do the virgins stand,
While tortures new are multiplied upon them,
Rejoicing that their bodies are afflicted
For everlasting glory, which they look for,
Seeing the joys of this world pass away,
And suddenly glide by and fade as flowers.

[illegible]
[illegible]
[illegible]
[illegible]
[illegible]
[illegible] with God,
[illegible]
[illegible] the Lord
[illegible] peace.

The Gospel. Matt. xiii. 44-52.

At that time Jesus spake unto His disciples this parable, The kingdom of heaven is like unto treasure ...... things new and old.

I. *Offert.* Ps. xlv. Kings' daughters were among thy honourable women: upon thy right hand did stand the Queen clothed in a vesture of gold, wrought about with divers colours.

II. *Offert. Lesser.* Ps. xlv. The virgins that be her fellows shall bear her company, and shall be brought unto thee.

III. *Offert. Greater.* Ps. xlv. The virgins that be her fellows shall bear her company, and shall be brought unto thee. With joy and gladness shall they be brought: and shall enter into the King's palace.

IV. *Offert.* Ps. xlv. Full of grace ...... for ever.

Secret. O Lord, favourably regard the offerings we present; and, at the intercession of Saint *N.*, Thy Virgin Martyr, loose the chains of our sins. Through.

I. *Comm.* Full of grace ...... for ever.

II. *Comm.* Ps. cxix. 161, 2, 7. Princes have persecuted me without a cause, but my heart standeth in fear of Thy Word. I am glad of Thy Word as one that findeth great spoils: my soul hath kept Thy testimonies, *O Lord*, and loved them exceedingly.

III. *Comm.* Ps. cxix. 122, 128. I deal with the thing that is lawful and right, *O Lord:* O give me not over unto mine oppressors. Therefore hold I straight all Thy commandments: and all false ways I utterly abhor.

IV. *Comm.* Matt. xiii. The kingdom of heaven is like unto a man seeking goodly pearls, who, when he had found one pearl of great price, sold all that he had and bought it.

V. *Comm.* Matt. xxv. The *five wise virgins* took oil in their vessels with their lamps. And at midnight there was a cry, Behold the Bridegroom cometh: go ye out to meet *Christ the Lord.*

P. Comm. We beseech Thee, merciful God, let our obedience and service be pleasing unto Thee, that the most holy Mysteries which we have received may, at the intercession of Saint *N.*, Thy Virgin Martyr, both procure for us Thy grace, and minister unto us the joy of eternal happiness. Through.

THE COMMON OF A VIRGIN NOT MARTYR.

The Office.

As i. Comm. Virg. Mart.

The Collect.

Almighty and everlasting God, the source of virtue and lover of virginity, grant, we beseech Thee, that we may be commended to Thee for the sake of Saint *N.*, Thy Virgin, whose life of chastity was well pleasing unto Thee. Through.

I. *The Epistle.* 2 Cor. x. 17, 18; xi. 1, 2.

Brethren, he that glorieth .... virgin to Christ.

II. *The Lesson.* Wisd. vii. 36; viii. 1-4.

Vice shall not prevail against wisdom .... and a lover of His works.

III. *The Lesson.* Isaiah lxi. 10-11; lxii. 5.

I will greatly rejoice in the Lord .... so shall thy God rejoice over thee, *saith the Lord Almighty.*

I. *Gradual.* As iii. Comm. Virg. Mart.

II. *Gradual.* As i. in the same.

I. *Alleluia!* As iv. Comm. Virg. Mart.

II. *Alleluia!* As i. in the same.

The Sequence.

A holy Virgin, worthy to be reckoned
Amongst the wise, O friends, we celebrate;
A daughter she of the King's Mother, Mary,
Adopted Sister of the Son of God.
She, with the curb of fasting, tamed her flesh,
And cut off luxury by suffering's sword.
With all the enemy's assaults she wrestled;
Trusting in Christ, she smote and vanquished him.

With joyous spirit following the Bridegroom,
Who from the courts of Heaven did visit her,
Into His chamber hasted she to enter.
O thou, in fulness of delights abiding,
Plead before Christ our present low estate,
And ask for us a plenteous consolation.

The Gospel. Matt. xxv. 1-13.

At that time Jesus spake unto His disciples this parable, The kingdom of heaven shall be likened unto ten virgins .... ye know neither the day nor the hour.

Offert As ii. Comm. Virg. Mart.

Secret. We offer unto Thee, O Lord, our prayers and gifts with joyfulness of heart in honour of Saint *N.*, Thy Virgin; grant, we beseech Thee, that we may both fitly perform our service, and may attain unto the everlasting healing. Through.

Comm. As i. Comm. Virg. Mart.

P. Comm. We beseech Thee, O Lord, let the Mysteries we have received be profitable to us; and at the intercession of Saint *N.*, Thy Virgin, both deliver us out of our sins, and exalt us by the protection of Thy favour. Through.

THE COMMON OF MANY VIRGINS.

The Office. Ps. xlv.

The rich also among the people shall make their supplication before thee. The virgins that be her fellows shall be brought unto *the King*. With joy and gladness shall they be brought *unto thee.*

Ps. My heart is inditing of a good matter: I speak of the things which I have made unto the King.

Of Virgins Martyrs.

O God, Who, that Thou mightest provoke mankind to the confession of Thy Name, hast bestowed even on the weak sex the victory of martyrdom; grant, we beseech Thee, that Thy Church, being established by this example, may never fear to suffer for Thy sake, and may long after the glory of the heavenly reward. Through.

Of Virgins not Martyrs.

Almighty and ever-living God, tried in Whose balance we are not fit to worship Thy Majesty as is due; let Thy Virgins,

SS. *N.* and *N.*, intercede for our sins, and for their sakes grant us pardon. Through.

I. *The Epistle.* 1 Cor. vii. 25-34.

Brethren, concerning virgins .... in body and in spirit, *in Christ Jesus our Lord.*

II. *The Lesson.* Wisd. iv. 1-7.

Better it is .... yet shall he be in rest.

I. *Gradual.* Ps. cxlix. Let the saints be joyful with glory: let them rejoice on their beds.

℣. O sing unto the Lord a new song: let the congregation of saints praise Him.

II. *Gradual.* Exod. xv. *God* is glorious in holiness, *marvellous in majesty*, doing wonders.

℣. Thy right hand, O Lord, is become glorious in power: Thy right hand, O Lord, hath dashed in pieces the enemy.

I. *Alleluia!* ℣. Ps. xlv. The virgins that be her fellows shall be brought *unto the King*. With joy and gladness shall they be brought *unto thee.*

II. *Alleluia!* ℣. Matt. xxv. *The five wise virgins* took oil in their vessels with their lamps: and at midnight there was a cry made, Behold the Bridegroom cometh; go ye out to meet Him, *Christ the Lord.**

The Gospel.

As in Comm. Virg. not Mart.

Offert. As ii. Comm. Virg. Mart.

Secret of Virgin Martyrs. Grant, we beseech Thee, O Lord, that we may be aided by the continual protection of Thy Virgin Martyrs, SS. *N.* and *N.*, in whose revered commemoration we offer these gifts to be dedicated to Thy Majesty. Through.

Secret of Virgins not Martyrs. We beseech Thee, O Lord, at the intercession of Thy Virgins *N.* and *N*, sanctify the gifts of Thy people, that they being freed from all things hurtful, may obtain those things which are profitable for them both here and for ever. Through.

Comm. As v. Comm. Virg. Mart.

P. Comm. of Virgin Martyrs. Grant, we beseech Thee, Almighty God, that we who have received the Divine Mysteries on the feast of Thy Holy Virgin Martyrs, *N.* and *N.*, may at their

* Gradual.

intercession be found worthy to attain unto eternal restoration, Through.

P. Comm. of Virgins not Martyrs. We beseech Thee, O Lord our God, that the gift of these holy Mysteries vouchsafed to us, may, at the intercession of Thy Holy Virgins, *N.* and *N.*, abundantly bestow upon us succour in this present life, and consummation of life eternal. Through.

THE COMMON OF A HOLY WOMAN.*

The Office.

Let us all rejoice in the Lord, and celebrate this feast in honour of Saint N., *on whose festival Angels rejoice and praise the Son of God.*

Ps. xlv. My heart is inditing .... unto the King.

The Collect.

Hear us, we beseech Thee, O God of our salvation, that like as we do rejoice in the feast of Saint *N.*, so we may be instructed by her love and prayers. Through.

The Lesson. Proverbs xxxi. 10-31.

Who can find a virtuous woman? .... Her own works praise her in the gates.

Gradual. As v. Comm. Virg. Mart.

Alleluia! As iv. Comm. Virg. Mart.

The Sequence.

A woman justly praised,
  A parent firm and chaste,
With no reproach to vex her
  Which barrenness doth cast.

Fruit thirty-fold she yielded
  While yet a wedded wife;
But sixty-fold she rendered
  When in a widowed life.

Her loins with strength she girded,
  And practised self-command;
Her candle went not out by night,
  So busy was her hand.

Her marriage honourable was,
  Pure was her widow's grief;
Amongst the aged reverence
  Was paid to her in chief.

* Missal of 1527.

As Holy Scripture teacheth us,
  A virtuous woman's price
Is far above the richest gems
  Of earthly treasuries.

In silence it was her delight
  To learn in Wisdom's school,
Nor sought in any wise to gain
  Over her husband rule.

Not she a widow who is said
In wanton pleasure to be dead,
  But doing good alway;
Finding a holy occupation
In acts of prayer and supplication
  Throughout the night and day.

Strangers with hospitality
She lodged, and washed with charity
  The saints' wayfaring feet;
And those on whom affliction weighed,
With kind relief and holy aid
  She graciously did greet.

O holy *N.*, whom we revere,
Whose feast with the revolving year
  Hath now returned again;
Chaste, prudent, faithful matron, pray
For us, that, this life o'er, we may
  In joys eternal reign. Amen.

¶ *In LXX. is said—*

Tract. ℣. Ps. xlv. Full of grace are thy lips, because God hath blessed thee for ever.

℣. Gird Thee with Thy sword upon Thy thigh, O Thou most mighty.

℣ According to thy worship and renown .... ride on.

The Gospel.

As in Comm. Virg. Mart.

I. *Offert.* As iv. Comm. Virg. Mart.

II. *Offert.* As i. Comm. Virg. Mart.

Secret. Let the offering of Thy holy people be acceptable unto Thee, O Lord, in honour of Thy Saints, for whose sake they acknowledge they have received succour in tribulation. Through.

Comm. As iv. Comm. Virg. Mart.

P. Comm. Thou hast satisfied Thy family, O Lord, with the sacred gifts: we beseech Thee, comfort us by her intercession whose feast we celebrate. Through.

[illegible]

THE [illegible] OF THE HOLY TRINITY.

[illegible] Alleluia.

The [illegible] Romans [illegible]

[illegible] to Whom be glory for [illegible]

[illegible]

[illegible] be with you all in *Christ* [illegible]

[illegible] Praise the Lord, ye servants : O [illegible] Blessed be the Name of the Lord : [illegible] for evermore.

THE [illegible] OF THE ANGELS.

[illegible] Powers, Effects, and Canons [illegible]

The [illegible]

[illegible] O Lord, unto us whom Thou [illegible] ministrations of Angels. Through.

The [illegible]

[illegible] worship [illegible]

The [illegible] John v. 1-4.

[illegible] of the Jews [illegible] whatsoever disease he had.

[illegible] We offer unto Thee, O Lord, this Sacrifice of praise, [illegible] that, at the intercession of angels on our [illegible] Thou wouldest mercifully receive the same, and grant that [illegible] to our salvation. Through.

[illegible] We, being fortified with the heavenly benediction, [illegible] beseech Thee, O Lord, that the service which we celebrate in weakness, may, by the aid of the holy angels and archangels, and all the heavenly spirits, be profitable unto us. Through.

THE MASS FOR ANY NECESSITY, COMMONLY KNOWN AS "SALUS POPULI."

The Office.

I am the salvation of the people, saith the Lord: in whatsoever distress they shall call on Me, I will hear them, and will be their Lord for ever.

Ps. lxxviii. Hear my law, O my people; incline your ears unto the words of my mouth.

¶ *The* Gloria in Excelsis *is not said.*

The Collect.

O God, Who by the grace of the Holy Ghost dost pour the gift of charity into the hearts of Thy faithful people, grant unto Thy servants, our brethren and sisters, for whom we entreat Thy mercy, health of mind and body, that they may love Thee with their whole strength, and may accomplish that which is pleasing unto Thee with a perfect love. Through.

The Lesson. Isaiah xviii., xix.

Thus saith the Lord God, In that day shall the present be brought unto the Lord of Hosts, and a fierce king shall rule over them. In that day shall there be an altar to the Lord in the midst of the land; and the Lord shall be known, and they shall do sacrifice and oblation; yea, they shall vow a vow unto the Lord and perform it; and they shall return even to the Lord, and He shall be entreated of them, and shall heal them. In that day shall Israel be a blessing in the midst of the land, whom the Lord of hosts shall bless, saying, Blessed be My people and the work of My hands, Israel My inheritance, *saith the Lord Almighty.*

Gradual. Ps. lxxix. Be merciful to our sins, *O Lord:* wherefore do the heathen say, Where is now their God?

℣. Help us, O God of our salvation; for the glory of Thy Name deliver us, *O Lord.*

Alleluia! ℣. Ps. lxxxv. Shew us Thy mercy, O Lord: and grant us Thy salvation.

¶ *In Easter-tide, when there is a Station in a Procession, the second* Alleluia *is not said, and this is also changed in the* Mass for Peace *and other similar ones.*

The Gospel. Mark xii. 41-44.

At that time Jesus sat over against the treasury .... even all her living.

Offert. Ps. lv. Hear my prayer, O God : and hide not Thyself from my petition. Take heed unto me, and hear me.

¶ *In Advent and from LXX. to L. the following verses are said alternately :—*

℣. Ps. lv. I am vexed ; the enemy crieth so ; I would make haste to escape.

℣. Ps. lv. As for me, I will call upon God, *deliver* my soul : *Thou shalt* put forth *Thy* hands against *them.*

Secret. Have mercy, O Lord, we beseech Thee, upon Thy servants and handmaids, for whom we offer this Sacrifice of praise unto Thy Majesty ; and grant that by this Holy Sacrament they may receive the grace of heavenly benediction, and attain unto the glory of everlasting happiness. Through.

Comm. Mark ii. Verily, I say unto you, what things soever ye desire when ye pray, believe that ye receive them, and he shall have them.

P. Comm. We that have received with our lips the Divine Mysteries, beseech Thee, O Lord, that this saving Sacrament may be profitable to the peace and prosperity of those in love for whom we have offered the same unto Thy Majesty. Through.

THE MASS OF THE HOLY GHOST.

The Office.

As on Whitsun-Day.

¶ *From LXX. to Easter, the* Office, Ezek. xxxvi., *is said :—*

When I shall be sanctified in you I will gather you out of all countries and sprinkle clean water upon you, and ye shall be clean from all your filthiness : a new heart also will I give you.

Ps. xxxiv. I will alway give thanks unto the Lord : His praise shall ever be in my mouth.

The Collect.

As on Whitsun-Day, omitting *as on this day.*

The Lesson. Acts viii. 14-17.

In those days, when the Apostles which were in Samaria ...... received the Holy Ghost.

Gradual. Ps. xxxiii. Blessed are the people whose God is the Lord Jehovah : and blessed are the folk that He hath chosen to Him to be His inheritance.

℣. By the Word of the Lord were the heavens made : and all the hosts of them by the breath of His mouth.

Alleluia ! ℣. *Come, Holy Ghost, fill the hearts of Thy faithful people, and kindle in them the fire of Thy love.*

In *Eastertide*—I. *Alleluia !* ℣. Ps. civ. When Thou lettest Thy breath go forth they shall be made, and Thou shalt renew the face of the earth.

II. *Alleluia !* ℣. *Come, Holy Ghost.*

The Sequence.

Come, O Holy Ghost, inspire
Hallowed thought, and pure desire,
With Thy bright celestial fire.

Come, Thou Parent of the poor,
Come, Thy blessed gifts assure ;
Come, Thou heart-enlightener pure !

Comforter, with us condole ;
Kind Host of the pilgrim soul,
Sweetest Refuge of our fears :

Thou, Who art in toil a Rest,
Shade, when with the heat oppressed,
Solace in this vale of tears.

O Thou very blessed Light,
Make our hearts' recesses bright ;
Knowledge of Thyself bestow ;

For without Thy rays divine
Nought can e'er unsullied shine,
Nought escape from guilt and woe.

Wash all that is vile away,
With soft dews our drought allay,
Heal the wounds of Satan's fray :

Bend the stubborn to obey,
Warm these icy frames of clay,
Guide the erring lest they stray.

Grant Thou to the pure and just,
Who in Thy protection trust,
Of thy sevenfold gifts the store:

O'er them grace and virtue pour,
Open wide Salvation's door,
Give us joys for evermore.

¶ Gospel, Offertory, Secret, *and* Preface *as on Whitsun-Day, omitting as* on this day; Comm. *and* P. Comm. *as on the same.*

THE MASS OF THE BLESSED SACRAMENT.

¶ *All as on Corpus Christi.*

THE MASS OF THE HOLY CROSS.

¶ *All as on Holy Cross Day. No* Gloria in Excelsis *is said.*

The Office.

As on Maundy Thursday.

The Collect.

O God, Who by the Precious Blood of Thy Only-Begotten Son, our Lord Jesus Christ, hast willed to sanctify the banner of the life-giving Cross; grant, we beseech Thee, that they who rejoice in honour of the same Holy Cross, may also everywhere have joy in Thy protection. Through.

The Epistle. Phil. ii. 8-11.

Brethren, Christ became obedient unto death .... glory of God the Father.

In Eastertide—II. *Alleluia!* ℣. Gal. vi. *But us it becometh* to glory in the Cross of our Lord Jesus Christ.

The Gospel. Matt. xx. 17-19.

At that time Jesus going up to Jerusalem .... the third day He shall rise again.

Secret. We beseech Thee, O Lord, let this Sacrifice purify us from all sin, which having been offered upon the Altar of the Cross did bear the offences even of the whole world. Through.

Preface. Who hast established.

P. Comm. Be present with us, O Lord our God, and grant

that those whom Thou causest to rejoice in honour of the Holy Cross may ever be defended by its continual aid. Through.

THE MASS OF THE FIVE WOUNDS OF THE LORD JESUS CHRIST.*

The Office. Philippians ii.

Our Lord Jesus Christ humbled Himself and became obedient unto death, even the death of the Cross. Wherefore God also hath highly exalted Him, and given Him a Name which is above every name.

Ps. lxxxix. My song shall be alway of the loving kindness of the Lord.

¶ *The* Gloria in Excelsis *is said, except in Advent, and from LXX. to Easter.*

The Collect.

O Lord Jesu Christ, Son of the living God, Who didst come down from Heaven to earth from the bosom of the Father, and didst bear five wounds on the Cross; and didst pour forth Thy precious Blood for the remission of our sins; we humbly beseech Thee that at the day of judgment we may be set at Thy Right Hand, and hear from Thee that most comfortable word, Come, ye blessed, into My Father's Kingdom. Who.

The Lesson. Zech. xii. 10, 11; xiii. 6, 7.

Thus saith the Lord God, I will pour upon the house of .... the Man that is My fellow, saith the Lord of hosts.

Gradual. Ps. lxix. Thy rebuke hath broken My heart; I am full of heaviness: I looked for some to have pity on Me, but there was no man, neither found I any to comfort Me.

℣. They gave Me gall to eat: and when I was thirsty they gave Me vinegar to drink.

Alleluia! ℣. *Hail, our King, Jesus Christ, Thou alone has pitied our sins and wickednesses; in obedience to the Father, Thou wast led to the Cross as a gentle lamb to the slaughter. Glory to Thee, Hosanna to Thee, O Most High, in the choir of praise and honour.*

Tract. Ps. xliii. Give sentence with me, O God, and defend my cause against the ungodly: O deliver me from the deceitful and wicked man.

* See Appendix D.

[illegible] For Thou art the God of my strength: why hast Thou cast Me from Thee? and why go I so heavily, while the enemy oppresseth Me?

[illegible] * For there are false witnesses risen up against Me, and such as speak wrong.

† The plowers plowed upon My back, and made long furrows.

‡ They stand staring and looking upon Me. They part My garments among them, and cast lots upon My vesture.

‡ They pierced My hands and My feet. I may tell all My bones [illegible].

The Sequence

Thou, Christ, with Thy disciples the Feast didst celebrate,
Thy death [illegible] didst clearly relate;
And [illegible] didst foreshow,
And afterwards thence departing didst to the Garden go.
[illegible] the Lord didst prostrate lie,
And prayed that the night [illegible], if possible, pass by.
[illegible] commended all,
And [illegible] the ground did fall.
[illegible] did presume;
[illegible] wherefore art thou come?
[illegible] dost thou betray?
Forthwith the soldiers seized Him and led the Lord away.
Therefore through those night hours sleepless the Lord remained,
Nor [illegible] detained.
By magistrates unjustly reviled and mocked He stands;
And innocent, is buffeted and smitten by men's hands.
Whilst Jesus [illegible] Pilate himself marvelled,
The madness of the people more fiercely is aroused;
And crowds a mighty uproar stirred up on every side,
In which their voices thundered, and Crucify Him! cried.
Captive and bound, the Saviour away the soldiers bore,
With cruel blows His body they mangled then full sore;
Upon the King of Glory they set a thorny crown;
Then all to [illegible] Him deride, with bended knees bowed down.
The mighty Redeemer, Who in tender flesh was found,
With thongs is to the pillar [illegible] bound.
The torturer's vile scourging He then doth undergo,
His precious Blood in rivers on every side doth flow.
Next Jesus through the city in slow procession came,
Bearing upon His shoulder the Cross of bitter shame.
Unto the gates of outlet streamed forth the populace,
To all men was revealed His manifold disgrace.
Indignity most crowning, of clothing all bereft,
To winds and cold, O Jesu, exposed Thou wert left;
The curse of sin, all sinless, Thou on the Cross didst bear,
And 'midst the malefactors chief obloquy dost share.

* Ps. xxvii. † Ps. cxxix. ‡ Ps. xxii.

With outstretched arms, His hands, lo! are nailèd to the tree;
Flesh, nerves, and veins. with iron are tortured piteously;
His feet and soles transfixèd in like wise torn we see.
Then, after these things speaking, I thirst, the Saviour said;
Forthwith one ran, and vinegar with gall commingled,
And on a sponge he put it unto His mouth with haste,
And yet He would not drink it, but scarce thereof would taste.
O Jesus, Wonder-worker, how dost Thou this explain?
Thou of the Cross art silent, yet dost of thirst complain—
Didst Thou feel thirst more keenly than all that bitter pain?
Or, rather, our salvation didst Thou so thirst to gain?
Then, on the Father calling, of words Thou mad'st an end,
And to His holy keeping Thy Spirit didst commend.
At length, with loud voice crying, Thou gavest up the ghost,
And so Thy work didst finish—the saving of the lost.
Now I, alas! deal proudly, Thou dost full lowly lie;
Mine are the foul transgressions, Thine is the penalty.
I eat the fruit forbidden, Thou drink'st the cup of gall;
I seek mine ease and pleasure, dread sorrows on Thee fall.
What mind or tongue, moreover, of living man can tell
The bitter pain and grief which the Virgin's heart befell
When she beholds them pierce His already lifeless side,
And her Son's holy Body by a lance riven wide?
That lifeless Body, truly, no more the pang could feel,
But her sad heart was piercèd by the soldier's spear of steel,
When standing by she saw it in her Son's side infixed,
And forthwith thereout flowing came Blood and Water mixed.
Rivers of Blood most precious the Saviour's fountains give;
With speedy steps run hither, O sinner's soul, and live.
Let all with thirsty longing that sacred draught drink in,
That each may oft gain healing of all the wounds of sin.
Unto that Saviour's fountain betake thee then with speed,
That on the sweets thence flowing thy inmost soul may feed;
Purchased by that Blood's shedding, the Fount of Life we see:
May healing for thy sickness thence flow eternally.

The Gospel. John xix. 28-35.

At that time Jesus, knowing that all things were now accomplished .... and his record is true.

Offert. Ps. xxxv. *False witnesses did rise up against Me: without mercy they have sought to slay Me: and they spared not to spit upon My face: with their lances they have wounded Me, and all My bones have been out of joint.*

Secret. O Lord Jesu Christ, Who wast lifted up upon the wood of the Cross that all the world, which was in darkness, might be enlightened; pour forth, we beseech Thee, that light upon our souls and bodies, through which we may attain unto light everlasting. Through.

Preface. Who hast established.

Comm. Ps. xxii. They pierced My hands and My feet: I may tell all My bones.

P. Comm. O Lord Jesu Christ, Who at the sixth hour of the day didst ascend the Cross for the redemption of the world, and didst shed Thy precious Blood for the remission of our sins; grant, we humbly beseech Thee, that by the merits of Thy Passion and wounds we may, after our death, enter with joy the gates of Paradise. Who.

THE FEAST OF THE CROWN OF OUR LORD.

The Office.

Let us all rejoice in the Lord who celebrate the feast in honour of the Crown of the Lord, on which festival angels rejoice and praise the Son of God.

Ps. Angels rejoice, and archangels are glad; and all the saints are joyful and full of mirth.

The Collect.

Grant, we beseech Thee, Almighty God, that we, who in memory of the Passion of our Lord Jesus Christ adore upon earth His Crown of Thorns, may be accounted worthy to be crowned by Him with honour and glory in Heaven. Who.

The Epistle. Cant. iii. 7-11; iv. 1, 8.

Threescore valiant men are about *the bed of Solomon*, of the valiant of Israel .... Come with Me from Lebanon, My Spouse, with Me from Lebanon, *come and Thou shalt be crowned.*

I. *Alleluia!* ℣. *We reverence Thy Crown, O Lord; we celebrate Thy glorious triumph.*

II. *Alleluia!* ℣. *A Crown of Thorns this day we venerate,*
By which is won a wreath of glorious state.

The Sequence.

Wouldst thou boast thyself aright,
And by God with glory bright
In eminence be crowned?
Learn this Crown to venerate,
And His course to imitate
Whose Brow it did surround.

The King of Heaven wore this Crown.
And gave it honour and renown
By His own sanctity;
In this casque he fought the fight,
And put the ancient foe to flight,
And triumphed on the Tree.

A knightly helm in this we see,
In this a palm of victory—
The High Priest's mitre, too;
Though with thorns 'twas first arrayed,
Hallowed by that sacred Head,
It bare a golden hue.

For the sharpness of the thorns,
By His Passion Christ adorns
With rays of golden light;
Souls beset with thorns of sin,
Hopeless ever life to win,
Find blessings infinite.

For the sinner thorns arise;
Of his own iniquities
A thorny crown is twined;
But the thorns are changed to gold,
When he turns and seeks the fold,
That he may mercy find.

These are right mysterious joys;
But the matter which employs
Our gratulations now
Is the tale which doth convey
Signal fame to France to-day
To decorate her brow.

To her care the Holy Crown
Is entrusted as her own,
Whereof we keep the day:
All the honour that is due,
With devotion yearly new,
Unto this feast we pay.

Holding such a priceless treasure,
To be longed for above measure,
Thou art enriched indeed;
Happy land beyond compare,
To the Lord exceeding dear,
Unequalled is thy meed.

Other realms to thee concede
Three distinctions that exceed
The honours they can claim:
Faith unfeigned, Valour great,
Oil thy kings to consecrate—
So flourisheth thy fame.

MASSES OF THE BLESSED VIRGIN MARY.*

FROM ADVENT TO CHRISTMAS, EXCEPT ON THE CONCEPTION B.V.M.

¶ *This is said for the* Daily Mass *in her Chapel and in the Quire when there is High Service.*

The Office. Isaiah xlv.

Drop down, ye heavens, from above, and let the skies pour down righteousness : let the earth open, and let them bring forth salvation.

Ps. And let righteousness spring up together : I the Lord have created it.

The Collect.

As on p. 284.

¶ *Let Memorials be made,* I. *of the Trinity as on Trinity Sunday,* II. *of Bps. as in occasional Collects.* III. *of Benefactors as in* Mass of Dead, IV. *the 4th of general Collects. The second Collect at the* Daily Mass *in Our Lady's Chapel is always of the Saint to whom the Altar or Church is dedicated.*

. *The Lesson.* Isaiah vii. 10-15.

In those days the Lord spake unto Ahaz, saying .... refuse the evil and choose the good.

Gradual. Ps. xxiv. Lift up your heads, O ye gates ; and be ye lift up, ye everlasting doors : and the King of Glory shall come in.

℣. Who shall ascend into the hill of the Lord : or who shall rise up in His holy place ?

¶ *The* Gradual *is never repeated at the* Daily Mass of our Lady, *nor at* Votive Masses *except at High Service.*

Alleluia ! ℣. Luke i. Hail, *Mary*, that art highly favoured ; the Lord is with thee : blessed art thou among women.

The Sequences.

¶ *One of these* Sequences *is always said at the* Daily Mass.

I.

From Heaven Gabriel was sent,
The Word's envoy intelligent,
To speak in accents reverent
  With Mary, blessed Maid :
An excellent and kindly word
Is in that lowly chamber heard :
Eva the Angel doth discard,
  And Ave saith instead.

* See Appendix E.

The fulness of the time is come,
Behold the Word is Flesh become,
Yet to that Holy Virgin's womb
Is no dishonour done;
She bears who doth no husband know;
No pains of travail or of woe
Doth the unsullied Virgin show,
When she brings forth a Son.

New is the thing and strange to see—
Believe, it is enough for thee;
For such as thou it may not be
To loose the sandal's tie:
A sign beyond thy power to know,
The unconsumèd Bush doth show;
Lest any with unloosened shoe
Dare rashly to draw nigh.

The sapless Rod, devoid of dew,
By a new rite, a manner new,
Decked both with flower and fruit we view,
So did the Virgin bear.
Right blessèd is such fruit, I trow—
Fruit of rejoicing, not of woe:
Adam had triumphed o'er his foe
If such had been his fare.

Jesus our Saviour, Lord alone,
A Holy Mother's Holy Son,
Who hath in highest Heaven His Throne,
Is in a stable laid.
May He Who came in such a guise
Blot out all our iniquities,
Seeing our earthly sojourn is
With dangers overspread.

II.

No one lower in grade
To the Virgin is sent,
But an Archangel dread,
Mighty Gabriel, went,
On that message of love.
Such a herald renowned
Might such message explain,
And the new grace expound;
And a forecast most plain
Of her child-bearing prove.

For the glorious King,
Nature's order and laws
In subjection did bring,
The old leaven and dross
Casting out in His might.

The high looks of the proud
  To confusion He turned,
And the arrogant crowd
  Underneath Him He spurned,
    As one valiant in fight.

The world's Prince in His pride
  Let Him cast forth in shame,
And give part to His Bride
  Of the kingdom and fame
Of His Father on high.
On thy embassage go
  These great gifts to narrate,
Back the curtain to throw
  From the mystery great
    Which in Scripture doth lie.

With thy message draw nigh,
  Say, "Hail," reverently,
"Full of grace from on high,
  Lo! the Lord is with thee:
    Fear not, thou blessed one.
Do thou, Virgin, comply
  With what God doth reveal;
So thy vowed chastity
  Shall keep sacred its seal,
    Yet His will shall be done."

The chaste maiden believes
  When the word she doth hear,
And forthwith she conceives,
  And a Son she doth bear—
    Him of wonderful Name:
Him the Counsellor grave,
  All the world for to guide;
God, the mighty to save;
  Father, aye to abide
    In peace ever the same.

III.

Now let that good and gracious word,
Ave, with our sweet strains accord,
Which makes Thy chamber ready, Lord,
  The Virgin, Mother, Child.
She, to that Ave giving heed,
Virgin of David's stock decreed,
Without delay conceived seed,
  Lily midst briars wild.

Hail, Mother of true Solomon,
Hail, wondrous Fleece of Gideon,
The Magi to thine Infant Son
  Their triple offerings bring.

Hail, thou of whom the Son is born,
Hail, thou who to the world forlorn,
And lost by sin, a Child hast borne
  Who is both God and King.

Hail, Mother of the Word Divine;
Safe Harbour, of the Bush the sign;
Pillar of smoke of incense fine,
  Mistress of angel bands;
We supplicate thee, us amend,
And when amended, us commend;
Let us have joys that never end
  At Thy Son's bounteous hands.

The Gospel. Luke i. 26-38.

At that time the Angel Gabriel was sent from God .... be it unto me according to Thy word.

¶ *The* Creed, *when it is said in the Mass for the day.*

Offert. Luke i. Hail, *Mary*, that art highly favoured, the Lord is with thee: blessed art thou among women, and blessed is the fruit of thy womb.

Secret. As on p. 284.

Preface. And thee.

Comm. Isaiah vii. Behold, a Virgin shall conceive and bear a Son, and shall call His Name Emmanuel.

P. Comm. As on p. 285.

¶ *It is to be noted that the same* Mass *is to be said in all feasts of S. Mary through the year in her Chapel that is said in the Quire, except through* Octaves, *in which, however, the* Epistle *is the same.*

ON CHRISTMAS DAY AND UNTIL THE PURIFICATION.

The Office.
As in Comm. Many Virg.

The Collect.
See p. 205.

The Epistle. Titus iii. 4-7.

Beloved, the kindness .... the hope of eternal life *in Christ Jesus our Lord.*

Gradual. Ps. xlv. Thou art fairer than the children of men: full of grace are thy lips.

℣. My heart is inditing of a good matter: I speak of the things which I have made unto the King. My tongue is the pen of a ready writer.

Alleluia! ℣. *After child-bearing thou remainedst a Virgin undefiled: O Mother of God, intercede for us.*

¶ *The following* Sequence, *or else one of the six in the Mass of the Assumption, is said throughout the year.* *See pp.* 390-2

The Sequence.

Hail, holy Parent, Rose
On which thorn never grows;
Hail, thou fair ocean star,
Deliver us from war.
Mother, do thou increase
The gift of real peace;
Our miseries relieve,
Reverse the name of Eve.
Our ills and troubles stay,
Draw us in thy sweet way:
Gain pardon for our sin,
All blessings for us win.
By thee, our Mother kind,
We Son and Father find;
E'en as He, born of thee,
Deigned also thine to be.
Cast down high-mindedness,
O Saviour limitless!
Make Thou the haughty mild,
Exalt the undefiled.
So let thy grace prevail,
O Virgin Mother, hail,
Let us on high with thee
Sing praises endlessly.
O Father, I this day
To Thee due homage pay,
And to Thy gracious Son,
In mystic union.

Let us praise God, the Father's Son,
Whom Mary in her womb hath borne;
Whom let the earth, the sea, and sky,
Praise and adore incessantly.
Let all arise with one consent
To turn away His anger bent;
Each one acknowledging His sway,
Whom moon, and stars, and all obey.

Blest Mother, in thy low estate,
Us by thy prayers exalted high,
Above the heavens elevate,
Blest in the gift bestowed on thee.

O Virgin, most compassionate,
Full of the Holy Spirit's grace:
Protect us, to thy Son present,
Blest in the message to thee sent.

[illegible]

Hail, Holy [illegible] King [illegible] for ever and ever.*

R. Blessed art thou among women, and blessed is the fruit of thy womb.†

* Sedulius Carm. Pasch. ii 63.

† Luke i.

The Collect.

As on p. 285.

The Lesson. Ecclus. xxiv. 9-12.

He created me from the beginning .... in the portion of the Lord's inheritance, *and my abode is in the full congregation of the saints.*

Gradual. Blessed and worthy of honour art thou, O Virgin Mary; who without touch of shame wast found the Mother of the Saviour.

℣. *O Virgin, Mother of God, He Whom the whole world cannot contain was made Man and abode in thy womb.*

¶ *From Purification to LXX., and from second Sunday after Trinity to Advent is said—*

Alleluia! ℣. Hail, Virgin, Mother of God, temple of the Holy Ghost, who alone wast worthy to be called Queen and Mistress of Heaven.*

¶ *In Eastertide is said—*

I. *Alleluia!* ℣. Through Thee, Mother of God, the life we had lost is given to us: who didst conceive seed from Heaven, and bare a Saviour to the world.

II. *Alleluia!* ℣. Of the Resurrection as on a Feast with Rulers of Choir (*see* p. 191).

¶ *In the Chapel of B. V. M. one of the following is said from the Purification to Advent, except from LXX. to Easter.*

On Sunday.

Alleluia! ℣. Obtain for thy suppliants, O gentle Mother of God, pardon of sin, through thy holy prayers.

On Monday.

Alleluia! ℣. Through thee, etc.

On Tuesday.

Alleluia! ℣. Pray for us, gentle Virgin Mary, of whom Christ was born; pray for us sinners.

On Wednesday.

Alleluia! ℣. The powers of Heaven reverence thee, O Virgin Mary, as they behold thy only Son at the right hand of God the Father in power and great majesty.

* This, together with what follows in this Mass, and the next, is in the ordinary type, though not in the Bible.

On Thursday.

Alleluia! ℣. Ps. xiv. *Come, my chosen one, and I will set thee on my throne*, so shall the King have pleasure in thy beauty.

On Friday.

Alleluia! ℣. Hail, Virgin. *As above.*

On Saturday.

Alleluia! ℣. The rod of Jesse hath budded: a Virgin hath borne God and Man: God hath given peace again, reconciling in Himself the lowest with the highest.

¶ *In Eastertide is said in the chapel—*

I. *Alleluia!* ℣. Through thee, etc.

II. *Alleluia!* (*One of the above in order, but on Monday the second will be*)—℣. After childbirth thou remainest a Virgin undefiled: O Mother of God, intercede for us.

¶ *No* Tract *is ever said, but a* Sequence: *in Advent one of the three on pp. 521-4, at other times one of the six on p. 525.*

The Gospels.

I.

Luke xi. 27, 28.

At that time it came to pass, as He spake these things .... Word of God, and keep it.

II.

John xix. 25-27.

At that time there stood by the Cross of Jesus .... took her unto his own home.

Offert. Happy art thou, O holy Virgin Mary, and most worthy of all praise, because of thee hath risen the Sun of Righteousness, Christ our God. Alleluia.

¶ Alleluia *is always said here except from LXX. to Easter, and on the Vigil of the Assumption.*

Secret. As on p. 285.

Comm. Blessed is the womb of the Virgin Mary, which bare the Son of the Eternal Father.

¶ *In Eastertide.*

Comm. The true faith of the Son cleansed away the sins of the world, and thy virginity remaineth to thee inviolate. Alleluia, Alleluia.

P. Comm. As on p. 285.

A MASS IN REMEMBRANCE OF THE FEASTS OF THE BLESSED VIRGIN MARY.

The Office. Ps. xiv.

Let us all rejoice in the Lord, and celebrate this feast in honour of the Virgin Mary, in whose festivals angels rejoice and praise the Son of God.

Ps. My heart is inditing of a good matter: I speak of the things which I have made unto the King.

The Collect.

O God, Who causest us to rejoice in celebrating the joys of the blessed and glorious Virgin Mary's Conception, Nativity, Annunciation, Visitation, Purification, and Assumption; grant us so worthily to devote ourselves to her praise and service, that we may perceive her presence and assistance in all necessities and straits, especially in the hour of death; and after death may by her and with her be found worthy to joy with Thee in Heaven. Through.

The Lesson. Cant. ii. 13, 14; iv. 1-20.*

Arise, my love .... like the smell of Lebanon.

Gradual. Thou shalt shine in glorious light, and all the ends of the world shall worship thee.

℣. The nations from afar shall come to thee and bring gifts; shall in thee adore the Lord, and shall account thy land holiness.

Alleluia! ℣. Blessed are all they that love thee, O Virgin, and rejoice in thy peace. Blessed be the Lord that hath exalted thee, and set His dominion upon thee for ever and ever.

The Sequence.

No messenger mean
To the barren is sent,
But an angel of might
Most refulgent in light,
From the Lover of men.

* *i.e.*, 1, 2, *to* washing; 7, 8, *to* Lebanon; 9, 10, honey *to the end.*

She wonders, believes,
And in joy she conceives,
The blest Mother of God,
Whom exulting she bore,
  Most beloved of all.

The most excellent Maid
In seclusion abides,
Serving God in her heart,
Sweetly singing apart,
  Born a blessing to man.

Her mind's pious intent
With a vow she confirmed
Angels associate
Best befit her estate
  Who came us to restore.

From the city above
The Archangel He sends;
To the message of love
The Maid meekly attends,
  Believes and conceives.

Then the Virgin with child
Rises up in her haste;
He Whom none can declare
Doth the barren who bare
  His Forerunner salute.

Undefiled she brought forth
The Redeemer of earth;
Vast advantage to men,
Angel-heralded birth—
  To the vanquished a palm.

In her meekness the Babe
Unto God she presents,
And the gift offers there
Which the Law bade prepare
  While Symeon stood by.

Mistress she of the world
In assumption is seen
Beyond angels to shine—
Of the heavens the Queen,
  Favoured Mother of God.

There the Son sets her down
With Himself on His Throne,
And the Virginal Crown
To the glory of God
  Deigns to put on her head.

These most marvellous acts
We Thy people recite;
To thee sing in our hearts
In thy praises unite,
Whom the fatherless love.

O then for us obtain
Pardon, Mother benign!
Let our guilt melt away,
Let that City divine
Be our dwelling for aye.
Amen.

The Gospel. Luke i. 39-47.

At that time Mary arose .... in God my Saviour.

Offert. Luke i. All generations shall call *thee* blessed. For He that is mighty hath done to *thee* great things: and holy is His Name.

Secret. O Lord Jesu Christ, from Whom good thoughts do proceed; Who hast taught Thy servant to honour Thy glorious Mother; mercifully grant that we may with solemn Sacrifice devoutly celebrate Thine own due praise on earth, and at her intercession be found worthy to reign in joy in Heaven. Who.

Preface. And Thee.

Comm. Bless God, ye heavens with fear, and rejoice before Him with trembling; for He hath shewn us mercy, forasmuch as He hath been pleased to make His Mother our advocate in Heaven.

P. Comm. Grant, we beseech Thee, Almighty God, that we may keep with a pure heart the Sacraments which we have received in honour of the Blessed Virgin-Mother Mary, that we who now celebrate her feast, may, when we depart out of this life, pass to a fellowship with her. Through.

A MASS FOR PEACE.

The Office.

As on the Eighteenth Sunday after Trinity.

The Collect.

See p. 286

The Lesson.

As on Ember Saturday in Lent.

Gradual. Ps. cxxii. I was glad when they said unto me, We will go into the house of the Lord.

℣. Peace be within thy walls, and plenteousness within thy palaces.

Alleluia! ℣. Ps. cxlvii. He maketh peace in thy borders: and filleth thee with the flour of wheat.

The Gospel. John xvi. 32, 33.

At that time Jesus said to His disciples, Behold, the hour cometh .... I have overcome the world.

Offert. Ps. lxxxv. Wilt thou not turn again and quicken us; that Thy people may rejoice in Thee? Shew us Thy mercy, O Lord, and grant us Thy salvation.

Secret. See p. 286.

Comm. Mark xi. Verily, I say unto you, what things soever ye desire when ye pray, believe that ye receive them and ye shall have them.

P. Comm. See p. 287.

A MASS FOR THE KING.

The Office. Ps. lxxxiv.

Behold, O God, our defender; and look upon the Face of Thine Anointed. For one day in Thy courts is better than a thousand.

Ps. O how amiable are Thy dwellings: Thou Lord of Hosts. My soul hath a desire and longing to enter into the courts of the Lord.

The Collect.

We beseech Thee, Almighty God, that Thy servant our Sovereign *N.*, who by Thy mercy hath taken upon himself the government of the kingdom, may also be endued plenteously with all virtues; that being therewith meetly arrayed, he may be graciously enabled to flee from vice, to overcome his enemies, and finally to attain unto Thee, Who art the way, the truth, and the life. Through.

The Lesson.

As in the Mass for Peace.

Gradual. Ps. lxxxvi. My God, save Thy servant that putteth his trust in Thee.

℣. Give ear, O Lord, unto my prayer.

Alleluia! ℣. Ps. lix. Deliver me from mine enemies, O my God: defend me from them that rise up against me.

The Gospel. Mark xi. 23-26.

At that time Jesus said to His disciples, Verily I say unto you .... forgive your trespasses.

Offert. Ps. lv. Hear my prayer, O Lord, and hide not Thyself from my petition; take heed unto me and hear me.

Secret. Sanctify, O Lord, we beseech Thee, the gifts offered to Thee, that they may become unto us the Body and Blood of Thy Only-Begotten; and may of Thy bounty ever be profitable unto Thy servant, our King *N.*, to obtain health of soul and body, and to perform the duty enjoined upon him. Through.

Comm. As in the Mass for Peace.

P. Comm. O Lord, we beseech Thee, let the receiving of the saving Sacrament preserve Thy servant our King *N.* from all adversities, to the end that he may obtain peace and tranquillity for the Church, and after the course of this life is passed away may attain unto an eternal inheritance. Through.

A MASS FOR THE GRACE OF THE HOLY GHOST.

¶ *All as in the* Mass of the Holy Ghost, *except—*

The Epistle. 1 Cor. xii. 7-11.

Brethren, the manifestation of the Spirit .... severally as He will.

The Gospel. John iv. 21-24.

At that time Jesus saith *unto the woman of Samaria,* Woman, believe Me .... in spirit and in truth.

Offert. Ps. civ. When Thou lettest Thy breath go forth they shall be made: and Thou shalt renew the face of the earth. The glorious Majesty of the Lord shall endure for ever.

Secret. We beseech Thee, O Lord God, let this oblation wipe away the sins of our heart, that it may become a worthy habitation of the Holy Ghost. Through.

Comm. John xiv. The Holy Ghost will teach you all things, *Alleluia,* whatsoever I have said unto you. *Alleluia, Alleluia.*

P. Comm. We that offer Thee the Sacrifice of our salvation, beseech Thee, O Lord, to grant that, our minds being purified by the grace of the Holy Spirit, we may celebrate more frequently this Mystery of Thy loving-kindness. Through.

A MASS FOR ONESELF.

The Office. Ps. liv.

Save me, O God, for Thy Name's sake; avenge me in Thy strength. Hear my prayer, O God.

Ps. For strangers are risen up against me: and tyrants seek after my soul.

The Collect.

Almighty and everlasting God, Who hast seen fit that I, a sinner, should stand at Thy Holy Altar and praise the might of Thy Holy Name; grant unto me, I beseech Thee, by the Mystery of this Sacrament, pardon for my sins, that I may worthily minister before Thy Majesty. Through.

The Epistle. Romans vii. 22-25.

Brethren, I delight in the law of God .... through Jesus Christ our Lord.

Gradual. Ps. lxxi. Be Thou my strong rock and house of defence: that Thou mayest save me.

℣. In Thee, O Lord, have I put my trust: let me never be put to confusion.

Alleluia! Ps. lix. Deliver me from the hands of mine enemies, *O Lord my God,* and from them that persecute me.

The Gospel. John xv. 7-11.

At that time Jesus said to His disciples, If ye abide in Me ...... that your joy might be full.

Offert. Ps. v. O hearken Thou unto the voice of my calling, my King and my God: for unto Thee will I make my prayer, *O Lord.*

℣. Ponder my words, O Lord; consider my meditation.

Secret. O God, who commandest that Thou shouldest be entreated of sinners, and that the sacrifice of a contrite heart should be offered Thee, vouchsafe to accept this Sacrifice which with my unworthy hands I offer, and that I myself may be a worthy offering and sacrifice to Thee, mercifully grant that by setting forth this Mystery I may receive forgiveness of all my sins. Through.

Comm. Ps. xix. O cleanse Thou me from my secret faults, *O Lord.* Keep Thy servant also from presumptuous sins.

P. Comm. Incline Thy pitiful ears, most merciful God, to my prayers; and through the Mystery of this Divine Sacrament of the Body and Blood of Thy Son, our Lord Jesus Christ, which I, unworthy, have received; enlighten my heart by the grace of the Holy Ghost, that I may worthily minister at Thy Holy Mysteries, and love Thee with an everlasting love, and finally be a partaker of eternal happiness. Through.

A MASS FOR THE GIFT OF THE HOLY GHOST.

The Office. Romans v.*

The love of God is shed abroad in our hearts, *Alleluia*, by the Holy Ghost which is given unto us. *Alleluia, Alleluia.*

Ps. lxxxviii. O Lord God of my salvation, I have cried day and night before Thee.

The Collect.

Almighty and everlasting God, Who with Thy finger writest in the hearts of believers the righteousness of Thy law, give unto us the increase of faith, hope, and charity; and that we may attain that which Thou dost promise, make us to love that which Thou dost command. Through.

The Epistle. 1 Cor. xiii. 4-13.

Brethren, charity suffereth long .... but the greatest of these is charity.

Gradual. Ps. viii. O Lord our Governour, how excellent is Thy Name in all the world.

℣. Thou that hast set Thy glory above the heavens.

Alleluia! ℣. Ps. lxxxviii. O Lord God of my salvation, I have cried day and night before Thee.

The Gospel. John xiii. 33-36.

At that time Jesus said to His disciples, Little children, yet a little while .... shall follow Me afterwards.

* *From LXX. to Easter this is as on p.* 533

Offert. Ps. cxlvi. Praise the Lord, O my soul; while I live will I praise the Lord: yea, as long as I have any being I will sing praises unto my God.

Secret. Send forth, we beseech Thee, O Lord, the Spirit of Love; and let Him both make these our present gifts Thy Sacrament unto us, and cleanse our hearts to receive the same. Through.

Comm. Matt. vi. Seek ye first the Kingdom of God, and His righteousness; and all these things shall be added unto you, *saith the Lord.*

P. Comm. Pour forth the Spirit of Thy Love upon us, O Lord; and those whom Thou hast satisfied with the Bread and Wine of Heaven, in Thy loving-kindness, make to be of one mind. Through.

A MASS FOR SINNERS.

The Office. Ps. cxxx.

If Thou, Lord, wilt be extreme to mark what is done amiss: O Lord, who may abide it? For there is mercy with Thee; *O God of Israel.*

Ps. Out of the deep have I called unto Thee, O Lord: Lord, hear my voice.

The Collect.

Hear, we beseech Thee, O Lord, the prayers of Thy suppliants, and spare those that confess their sins unto Thee; and of Thy mercy grant us alike pardon and peace. Through.

The Epistle. Romans v. 8-11.

Brethren, while we were yet sinners .... Our Lord Jesus Christ.

Gradual. Ps. lxxix. Be merciful unto our sins, *O Lord,* for Thy Name's sake. Wherefore do the heathen say: Where is now their God?

℣. Help us, O God of our salvation, for the glory of Thy Name; *O Lord,* deliver us.

Alleluia! ℣. Ps. lxxxv. Shew us Thy mercy, O Lord, and grant us Thy salvation.

The Gospel. Luke v. 27-32.

At that time Jesus saw a publican .... but sinners to repentance.

Offert. Ps. lxxxv. Wilt Thou not turn again, and quicken us, O God: that Thy people may rejoice in Thee? Shew us Thy mercy, O Lord: and grant us Thy salvation.

Secret. We present unto Thee, O Lord, the oblation of reconciliation, entreating Thee of Thy mercy to forgive our sins, and direct our wavering hearts. Through.

Comm. Ps. xxxi. Bow down Thine ear; make haste to deliver us.

P. Comm. Grant us, O eternal Saviour, that we by this gift receiving pardon, hereafter may flee from sin. Through.

A MASS FOR PENITENTS.

The Office. Ps. cxix. 137, 124.

Righteous art Thou, O Lord and true is Thy judgment. O deal with Thy servant according unto Thy loving mercy.

Ps. Blessed are those that are undefiled in the way: and walk in the law of the Lord.

The Collect.

Almighty and everlasting God, of Thy loving-kindness pardon the sins of Thy servant *N.*, who confesseth unto Thee, that his conscience which accuseth him may not prevail more for his punishment than Thy merciful forgiveness for his pardon. Through.

The Epistle. Gal. vi. 1, 2.

Brethren, if a man be overtaken .... fulfil the law of Christ.

Gradual. Ps. lxxxvi. My God, save Thy servant that putteth his trust in Thee.

℣. Give ear, O Lord, unto my prayer.

Alleluia! ℣. Ps. cxiv. Ye that fear the Lord, put your trust in the Lord: He is their helper and defender.

The Gospel. Matt. ix. 10-13.

At that time, as Jesus sat .... but sinners to repentance.

Offert. Ps. ix. And they that know Thy Name will put their trust in Thee: for Thou Lord, hast never failed them that seek Thee. O praise the Lord which dwelleth in Sion, for He forgetteth not the complaint of the poor.

Secret. Grant, we beseech Thee, Almighty and merciful God, that this saving offering may both unceasingly deliver Thy servant *N.* from his own guilt, and defend him from all adversity. Through.

Comm. Mark xi. Verily, I say unto you, what things soever ye desire when ye pray, believe that ye receive them, and ye shall have them.

P. Comm. Almighty and merciful God, Who wouldst rather amend than destroy every penitent soul that confesseth; mercifully look upon this Thy servant *N.*, and by the Sacrament which we have received turn from him Thy wrath and indignation, and forgive him all his sins. Through.

A MASS FOR THE INSPIRATION OF HEAVENLY WISDOM.

The Office. Ps. xix.

The law of the Lord is an undefiled law, converting the soul; the testimony of the Lord is sure, and giveth wisdom unto the simple.

Ps. The heavens declare the glory of God: and the firmament sheweth His handy-work.

The Collect.

O God, Who by Wisdom co-eternal with Thyself didst create man who was not, and when lost didst mercifully renew him; grant, we beseech Thee, that our souls being inspired by the same, we may love Thee with our entire will, and run after Thee with our whole heart. Through.

The Epistle. James i. 5-7.

Beloved, if any of you lack wisdom, let him ask of God ...... receive anything of the Lord.

Gradual. Ps. xxxiv. Come, ye children, and hearken unto me: I will teach you the fear of the Lord.

℣. They had an eye unto Him, and were lightened: and their faces were not ashamed.

Alleluia! ℣. Ps. lxxxv. Shew us Thy mercy, O Lord, and grant us Thy salvation.

The Gospel. John xvii. 1-3.

At that time Jesus lifted up his eyes to Heaven, and said, Father .... Whom Thou hast sent.

Offert. Ps. cxix. 12, 13. Blessed art Thou, O Lord: O teach me Thy statutes. *Blessed art Thou, O Lord; O teach me Thy statutes.* With my lips have I been telling of all the judgments of Thy mouth.

Secret. We beseech Thee, O Lord, let the gift of this our oblation be sanctified by the operation of Thy wisdom, that it may please and glorify Thee, and be profitable to our salvation. Through.

Comm. Ps. cxix 4, 5. Thou hast charged that we shall diligently keep Thy commandments. O that my ways were made so direct that I might keep Thy statutes.

P. Comm. We beseech Thee, O Lord our God, pour into our hearts the light of Thy wisdom by this holy Sacrament which we have received, that we may truly know and faithfully love Thee. Through.

A MASS FOR THOSE IN TROUBLE OF HEART.

The Office.

As in the Mass for Penitents.

The Collect.

O God, that despisest not the sighing of a contrite heart, nor the desire of such as be sorrowful; assist our prayers that we make before Thee in our trouble, imploring Thee, that Thou wouldst graciously hear us, and of Thy accustomed loving-kindness wouldst grant that those evils which the craft and subtilty of the devil or man worketh against us be brought to nought, and by the providence of Thy goodness they may be dispersed; that we, being hurt by no persecution, but delivered from all straits and tribulation, may give thanks unto Thee, for our consolation, in Thy Church. Through.

The Epistle. 2 Cor. i. 3-5.

Brethren, blessed be God, even the Father .... our consolation also aboundeth by Christ.

Gradual. Ps. cxx. When I was in trouble, I called upon the Lord : and He heard me.

℣. Deliver my soul, O Lord, from lying lips : and from a deceitful tongue.

Alleluia! ℣. Ps. cxv. Ye that fear the Lord, put your trust in the Lord : He is their helper and defender.

The Gospel. John xvi. 20-22.

At that time Jesus said to His disciples Verily, verily, I say unto you .... your joy no man taketh from you.

Offert. Ps. xxxiv. The angel of the Lord tarrieth round about them that fear Him : and delivereth them. O taste, and see how gracious the Lord is.

Secret. O God, who healest those that are broken in heart, and turnest the sadness of the sorrowful to joy : favourably look upon this offering by which Thou willest to remit the sins of the whole world, and mercifully accept it in our trouble ; pardon all our sins, take away our tribulation, banish our cares, and remove our straits and affliction, that we, being delivered from all the evils which we suffer, may evermore delight in giving thanks for Thy blessings. Through.

Comm. Ps. cxxx. Redeem *me, O God of* Israel, from all *my* sins.

P. Comm. Put away our sins, we beseech Thee, O Lord God, and grant us Thy mercy ; hearken unto the words of our mouth, and give heed to us in our low estate ; loose our bonds, blot out our misdeeds, look upon our affliction, put away adversity, and, vouchsafing an abundant answer to our petition, continually of Thy mercy hear us. Through.

A MASS FOR A SICK PERSON.

The Office.

As in the last Mass.

The Collect.

Almighty and everlating God, the eternal salvation of them that believe, hear us in behalf of Thy servant *N.*, for whom we humbly implore the help of Thy mercy, that he may be restored to health, and give thanks unto Thee in Thy Church. Through.

The Epistle. James v. 13-16.

Beloved, is any among you afflicted ? .... that ye may be healed.

Gradual. Ps. vi. Have mercy upon me, O Lord, for I am weak : O Lord, heal me.

℣. For my bones are vexed. My soul also is sore troubled.

Alleluia ! ℣. Ps. cxlvii. He healeth those that are broken in heart : and giveth medicine to heal their sickness.

The Gospel. Luke iv. 38-40.

At that time Jesus arose out of the synagogue .... and healed them.

Offert. Ps. vi. Turn Thee, O Lord, and deliver my soul: O save me for Thy mercy's sake.

Secret. O God, at Whose pleasure the moments of our life are numbered, receive the prayers and offerings of Thy servant *N.*, for whom in his sickness we implore Thy merciful aid; that we may rejoice in the health of him for whose danger we are in fear. Through.

Comm. Ps. xxv. Deliver *me, O God of Israel,* out of all *my* troubles.

P. Comm. O God, the special protector of the frailty of man, show the power of Thy help upon our sick one; that he, being assisted by Thy mercy, may be found worthy to be presented again in health unto Thy holy Church. Through.

A MASS FOR THE WELFARE OF A FRIEND.

The Office.

As in the last Mass.

The Collect.

Almighty and everlasting God, have mercy on Thy servant *N.*, and dispose him according to Thy mercy in the way of everlasting salvation; that of Thy gift he may desire what is pleasing unto Thee, and perform it with his whole heart. Through.

The Lesson.

As in the Mass for Peace.

Gradual. Ps. lxxxvi. My God, save Thy servant that putteth his trust in Thee.

℣. Give ear unto my prayer.

Alleluia! ℣. Ps. cxv. Ye that fear the Lord, put your trust in *Him:* He is their helper and defender.

The Gospel.

As in the Mass for the King.

Offert. Ps. ix. *All* they that know Thy Name will put their trust in Thee; for Thou, Lord, hast never failed them that seek Thee. O praise the Lord which dwelleth in Sion, for He forgetteth not the complaint of the poor.

Secret. We beseech Thee, O Lord, let this oblation which we humbly offer unto Thy Majesty be for the welfare of Thy servant *N.*, that by Thy providence his life may in all places be directed both in prosperity and adversity. Through.

Comm. As in the Mass for Penitents.

P. Comm. We, receiving the Sacrament of our everlasting salvation, entreat Thy mercy, O Lord, that by it Thou wouldst preserve Thy servant *N.* from all adversity. Through.

A MASS FOR FAIR WEATHER.

The Office.

As in the Mass *Salus Populi.*

The Collect.

Hear us, O Lord, who cry unto Thee, and grant us, Thy humble servants, fair weather; that we who are justly afflicted for our sins, may by Thy preventing pity find mercy. Through.

The Lesson. Lament. ii. 19, 20; iii. 47-50, 54-58.

In those days Jeremiah the prophet spake, saying, Arise, cry out in the night .... Thou has redeemed my life, *O Lord my God.*

Gradual. As in the Mass *Salus Populi.*

Alleluia! ℣. Ps. xc. Lord, Thou hast been our refuge: from one generation to another.

The Gospel. Luke viii. 22-25.

At that time, it came pass on a certain day that *Jesus* went .... and they obey Him.

Offert. Ps. cxxxviii. Though I walk in the midst of trouble, yet shalt Thou refresh me, *O Lord;* Thou shalt stretch forth Thy hand upon the furiousness of mine enemies, and Thy right hand shall save me.

Secret. O Lord, hear our prayers and accept the vows of Thy people: bid the immoderate outpourings of rain to cease, and turn this plague of waters to the setting forth of Thy Mystery; that they who rejoice to have been born again in the water of regeneration may also rejoice in their correction by this chastisement. Through.

Comm. As in the Mass *Salus Populi.*

P. Comm. O Lord, we beseech Thee, graciously hear the prayers of Thy people; and, by virtue of this Sacrament, let a calm change of weather bring to us the message of Thy peace: and do Thou, Who scourgest us for our offences, spare those who confess their sins. Through.

A MASS FOR RAIN.

The Office. Ps. cv.

Let the heart of them rejoice that seek the Lord. Seek the Lord and His strength : seek His Face evermore.

Ps. O give thanks unto the Lord, and call upon His Name : tell the people what things He hath done.

The Collect.

O God, in Whom we live, and move, and have our being, grant us seasonable rain; that we, enjoying a sufficiency of support in this life, may with more confidence reach after the things which are eternal. Through.

The Lesson. Jer. xiv. 19-22.

In those days Jeremiah the prophet prayed, saying, Hast Thou utterly rejected Judah? .... Thou hast made all those things, *O Lord our God.*

Gradual. Ps. cxlv. The eyes of all wait upon Thee, O Lord : and Thou givest them their meat in due season.

℣. Thou openest Thine hand : and fillest all things living with plenteousness.

Alleluia! ℣. Ps. cxxx. Out of the deep have I called unto Thee, O Lord : Lord, hear my voice.

The Gospel. Matt. vi. 31-33.

At that time Jesus said unto His disciples, Take no thought, saying .... all these things shall be added unto you.

Offert. Ps. lxxviii. *The Lord* opened the doors of heaven; He rained down manna also upon them for to eat : and gave them food from Heaven. So man did eat angels' food.

Secret. O Lord, be favourable to us through the gifts we offer, and grant us the seasonable aid of sufficient rain. Through.

Comm. Ps. civ. *O Lord,* the earth is filled with the fruit of Thy works, that *Thou mayest* bring food out of the earth, and wine That maketh glad the heart of man : and oil to make him a cheerful countenance, and bread to strengthen man's heart.

P. Comm. O God, Who sendest rain upon the just and upon the unjust, we beseech Thee that we, being delivered from our offences by this Sacrament, may receive abundantly of Thy bounty the rain we have looked for, whereby both health and nourishment may be bestowed on us. Through.

A MASS IN THE TIME OF WAR.

The Office. Ps. xxv.

Call to remembrance, O Lord, Thy tender mercies : and Thy loving kindnesses, which have been ever of old. Let not our enemies have dominion over us. Deliver *us, O God of* Israel, out of all *our* troubles.

Ps. Unto Thee, O Lord, will I lift up my soul : my God, I have put my trust in Thee, let me not be confounded.

The Collect.

O God, the Sovereign of all kings and kingdoms, Who by smiting healest and by forgiving sparest us ; extend unto us Thy mercy, that we may use for our restoration and correction the peace and quietness established by Thy power. Through.

The Lesson. Esther xiii. 9-17.

In those days Esther prayed to the Lord, saying, O Lord, Lord, the King Almighty .... destroy not the mouths of them that praise Thee, O Lord *our God.*

¶ *The* Gradual *and* Alleluia *as in the Mass* Salus Populi.

The Gospel.

As in Mass for the King.

Offert. Ps. lxxxv. *O God,* wilt Thou not turn again, and quicken us : that Thy people may rejoice in Thee ? Shew us Thy mercy, O Lord, and grant us Thy salvation.

Secret. O Lord, we beseech Thee, mercifully be present with Thy people ; and as Thou dost instruct them by the Mysteries of thy heavenly Sacraments, so by these gifts which they devoutly present unto Thee, defend them of Thy pity from the fury of all their enemies. Through.

Comm. Ps. xxxi. Bow down Thine ear : make haste to deliver *us.*

P. Comm. We that have been strengthened with the holy Food of the Body and Blood of our Lord Jesus Christ, humbly beseech Thee, Almighty God, to cleanse us by this special remedy from all pollution of sin, and guard us from the assault of all dangers. Through.

A MASS FOR ONE IN PRISON.

¶ *All as on the feast of S. Peter's Chains.*

The Collect.

O God of pardon, God of all comfort, we humbly entreat Thee of Thy goodness, loose Thy servant *N.* from the chains of all his sins, and from the bonds in which he is held captive by his enemies, and at the intercession of Mary, the blessed Mother of God, and Thy holy Apostles, Peter, Paul, and John, take under Thy care him whom Thou hast corrected by Thy fatherly goodness, and bring him to everlasting joy. Through.

Secret. O Lord, let this Sacrifice of praise and reconciliation cleanse Thy servant *N.*, who putteth his trust in Thee, from all the defilements of sin; and, at the intercession of S. Mary, and of Thy blessed Apostles, Peter, Paul, and John, cause him to be set at liberty without hurt or let, from all the snares and bondage wherewith his enemies oppress him. Through.

P. Comm. Grant, we beseech Thee, O Lord, that this gift of our redemption, which we, unworthy as we are, have received, may, at the intercession of Mary, the blessed Mother of God, and of Thy Apostles, Peter, Paul, and John, preserve Thy servant *N.* from all danger, and give him safe deliverance from the straitness and bondage which he endureth. Through.

A MASS IN THE TIME OF PESTILENCE.

The Office.

As in the Mass *Salus Populi.*

The Collect.

O God, Who of Thy sole mercy didst put away the destruction which hung over the Ninevites, to whom, that Thou mightest show Thy pity, Thou gavest repentance and conversion; have respect, we beseech Thee, unto Thy people who fall down before Thy merciful presence; and, for Thy loving-kindness sake, suffer not those whom Thou hast redeemed with the Blood of Thine Only-Begotten to perish by the plague of pestilence. Who.

The Lesson. Jerem. xiv. 7, 8, 9.*

In those days Jeremiah prayed, saying, O Lord, though our

* *i.e.*, 7, 8, *to* trouble; 9, yet Thou *to the end.*

iniquities testify against us, *deliver us:* do it, *we beseech Thee,* for Thy Name's sake .... leave us not, *O Lord our God.*

Gradual. As in the Mass *Salus Populi.*

Alleluia! As in the Mass for Fair Weather.

The Gospel. Luke xi. 9-13.

At that time Jesus said to His disciples, Ask, and it shall be given you .... to them that ask Him.

Offert. As in the Mass for Penitents.

Secret. Almighty God, we beseech Thee, favourably to look upon the gift of Thy Church, and prevent us with Thy mercy rather than Thine anger; for if Thou shouldst be extreme to mark our iniquities, no creature could abide; but for the sake of the marvellous loving-kindness wherewith Thou hast made us, suffer not the works of Thine hands to perish. Through.

Comm. As in the Mass *Salus Populi.*

P. Comm. Almighty and merciful God, look upon the people now lying under the hand of Thy Majesty, and let the receiving of Thy holy Sacrament prevent the deadly sickness from overtaking us. Through.

A MASS IN THE TIME OF MURRAIN.

¶ *All as in the last* Mass, *except—*

The Collect.

O God, Who hast supplied relief to man's labours, even by dumb animals, we humbly beseech Thee suffer not them, without which mankind cannot subsist, to fail us in our need and perish. Through.

Secret. O Lord, we beseech Thee, let the oblation of this Sacrifice succour us, mightily setting us free from all sin, and delivering us from all calamities which assail us; that so the beasts which do us service in our need may by Thy power be preserved. Through.

P. Comm. O Lord, we beseech Thee, by this holy Sacrament which we have received, of Thy pity turn away temptation from Thy faithful people, and drive far from us the pestilence which has seized upon the beasts of the field; and as Thou dost according to their deserts scourge those who err, so, when Thou hast corrected them, comfort them in Thy compassion. Through.

A MASS IN ANY TROUBLE.

¶ *All as in the Mass for those in Trouble of Heart.*

The Collect.

Graciously shew us, O Lord, Thy unspeakable mercy; and both cleanse us from all sin, and of Thy goodness rescue us from the punishment which we deserve for the same. Through.

Secret. We beseech Thee, O Lord, let the Sacrifice to be offered unto Thee purify our hearts, and cause our gifts to find acceptance of Thy loving-kindness, and after Thou hast plagued restore us to prosperity. Through.

P. Comm. O Lord, defend by Thy Divine power those whom Thou dost refresh with the heavenly gift; that they who have the fruition of Thy Mysteries, may not be cast down by any adversity. Through.

A SERVICE FOR THOSE GOING ON A JOURNEY.*

¶ *First let* Ps. xxv., Unto Thee, O Lord; li., Have mercy; and xci., Whoso dwelleth, *be said over them as they kneel before the Altar after having confessed.*

Lord, have mercy.
Christ, have mercy.
Lord, have mercy.
Our Father.

℣. And lead us not into temptation.
℟. But deliver us from evil.

℣. I said, Lord, be merciful unto me.
℟. Heal my soul, for I have sinned against Thee.
℣. The Lord shew thee His ways,
℟. And teach thee His paths.
℣. The Lord direct thy steps according to His word,
℟. That no unrighteousness get the dominion over thee.
℣. O that thy ways were made so direct,
℟. That thou mightest keep the statutes of the Lord.
℣. The Lord uphold thy goings in His paths,
℟. That thy footsteps slip not.

* This and the next two Services, although they are in all Missals, strictly belong to the Manual, the text of which is therefore followed in preference to that of the Missal.

℣. Praised be the Lord God daily.

℟. The God of our salvation prosper thy way before thee.

℣. The good Angel of the Lord accompany thee.

℟. And dispose thy way and thine actions aright, that thou mayest return to thy own place with joy.

℣. Blessed are those that are undefiled in the way,

℟. And walk in the law of the Lord.

℣. Let the enemy have no advantage over thee,

℟. Nor the wicked approach to hurt thee.

℣. Arise, O Lord, and help us;

℟. And deliver us for Thy Name's sake.

℣. Turn us again, O Lord God of Hosts.

℟. Shew the light of Thy countenance, and we shall be whole.

℣. Lord, hear my prayer;

℟. And let my crying come unto Thee.

℣. The Lord be with you,

℟. And with thy spirit.

Let us pray.

Assist us, O Lord, in these our supplications, and dispose the way of Thy servant *N.* towards the attainment of Thy salvation; that among all the changes and chances of this life, he may ever be defended by Thy help. Through.

Let us pray.

O God, Who art the guide unto life, and keepest those that trust in Thee under Thy fatherly protection, we beseech Thee, grant unto Thy servants here present, who are setting forth from amongst us, the company of guardian angels, that they, being protected by Thy aid, may be seized by no fear of evil, nor be smitten by any grievous sickness, nor be troubled by any enemy lying in wait to assail them; but let them prosperously accomplish the course of their appointed journey, and returning unto their own homes be received in safety, and pay due thanks unto Thy Name. Through.

Let us pray.

O God, Who ever bestowest Thy mercy on those that love Thee, and art not far from those that serve Thee in any place; direct the way of this Thy servant *N.* according to Thy will, that

Thou being his protector and guide, he may walk without stumbling in the paths of righteousness.* Through.

¶ *This ended, let them rise, and let Mass follow, after the manner of a feast of Nine Lessons.*

The Office. Ps. xxxi.

Be Thou my strong rock and house of defence : that Thou mayest save me. For Thou art my strong rock and my castle : be Thou also my guide, and lead me for Thy Name's sake.

Ps. In Thee, O Lord, have I put my trust, let me never be put to confusion; deliver me in Thy righteousness.

The Collect.

Assist us, *as above.*

The Lesson. Genesis xxiv. 7.

In those days Abraham spake and said, The Lord God of heaven, which took me from my father's house, and from the land of my kindred, and which spake unto me, and that sware unto me, saying, Unto thy seed will I give this land ; He shall send His angel before thee.

Gradual. Ps. xxxi. Be Thou .... save me.

℣. In Thee, O Lord .... confusion.

Alleluia! ℣. Ps. cxv. Ye that fear the Lord put your trust in the Lord ; He is their helper and defender.

¶ *In Eastertide the second Alleluia will be one of those on pp.* 191-2.

The Gospel. Matt. x. 7-15.

At that time Jesus said to His disciples, As ye go preach ...... than for that city.

Offert. Ps. ix. And all they that know Thy Name will put their trust in Thee : for Thou, Lord, hast never failed them that seek Thee. O praise the Lord which dwelleth in Sion. For He forgetteth not the complaint of the poor.

Secret. Be favourable, O Lord, we beseech Thee, to our supplications, and graciously accept these offerings which we present unto Thee in behalf of Thy servants ; that Thou wouldst vouchsafe to direct their way by Thy grace preventing and following

* In the case of Pilgrims, here follows the blessing of the Scrip and Staff; and if they are going to Jerusalem, of the Cross. See the last two amongst the Benedictions, pp. 595-6.

them, and that we may rejoice in their safe performance thereof by thy merciful protection. Through.

Comm. Ps. cxix. 4, 5. Thou hast charged that we shall diligently keep Thy commandments; O that my ways were made so direct that I might keep Thy statutes.

P. Comm. We beseech Thee, O Lord, let the receiving of the Sacrament of the heavenly Mystery further the good success of Thy servants' journey, and bring them to all things profitable to their salvation. Through.

¶ *After the Mass, let the Priest say the following prayers over them, kneeling. These prayers may be said whether they be pilgrims going to Jerusalem, to the shrine of St. James of Compostello, or on any other journey:—*

℣. The Lord be with you.

℟. And with thy spirit.

Let us pray.

O God of infinite mercy and boundless majesty, Whom neither space nor time divide from those whom Thou defendest, be present with Thy servant (*or* servants) who in all places putteth his trust (*or* who trust) in Thee, and vouchsafe to be his (*or* their) guide and companion in every way by which he is (*or* they are) going; let no adversity harm him (*or* them), no difficulty hinder him (*or* them); let all things be healthful and prosperous for him (*or* them) that, whatsoever he (*or* they) shall ask rightly he (*or* they) may by the aid of Thy Right Hand speedily and effectually obtain. Through.

Let us pray.

The Almighty and everlasting God, Who is the Way, the Truth, and the Life, dispose your journey according to His good pleasure; send His Angel Raphael to keep you in this your pilgrimage, and both conduct you in peace on your way to the place where you would be, and bring you back again on your return to us in safety. May Mary, the blessed Mother of God, with all angels, archangels, patriarchs, and prophets, intercede for you; may the holy Apostles Peter and Paul, with the rest of the apostles, martyrs, confessors, and virgins, intercede for you; and may the saints whose prayers you ask, with all the saints, obtain for you your just desires, prosperity, and forgiveness of all sins, and life everlasting. Through.

¶ *Then let them be communicated, and so depart in the Name of the Lord.*

The Order of the Solemnization of Matrimony.*

¶ *Let the man and woman be placed before the door of the church, or in the face of the Church, before the presence of God, the Priest, and the people: let the man stand on the right of the woman, and the woman on the left of the man, because she was formed from the rib of the left side of Adam. Then let the Priest ask the banns, and, in the bearing of all, let him say in the mother tongue—*

Brethren, we are gathered together in the sight of God and His angels, and all the saints, in the face of the Church, to join together two persons—to wit, this man and this woman (*here let him look upon them*), that whatsoever they may have done aforetime henceforth they may be one body, yet two souls, in the faith and law of God, to the end they may together attain eternal life.

¶ *Then let a charge be made to the people in the mother tongue, thus:—*

I charge you all, by the Father, and the Son, and the Holy Ghost, that if any of you know any cause why these two persons cannot lawfully make contract of matrimony, he do presently confess it.

¶ *Let the same charge be made to the man and woman; that, if they have done aught secretly, or made any vow, or know any impediment concerning themselves why they may not lawfully contract matrimony, they do then confess it. If any person shall allege any impediment and shall give security for the proof of it, let the marriage be deferred until such time as the truth of the thing be known. If no impediment is alleged, let the Priest enquire of the woman's dower. The Priest shall not betroth or consent to a betrothal between the man and woman before the third publication of the banns, which ought to be asked on three distinct and separate Holy-days, so that one week-day at the least intervene. Then let the Priest say to the man, in the mother tongue, in the audience of all—*

N., wilt thou have this woman to thy wedded wife; wilt thou love, honour, hold, and cherish her, in health and in sickness, as a husband should a wife, and, forsaking all other, keep thee only unto her, so long as ye both shall live?

¶ *Let him answer—*

I will.

* Here follows a long note, which it is unnecessary to print, concerning the seasons in which the Church forbids persons to marry—viz., from Advent Sunday to the morrow of the Octave of Epiphany; from LXX. to the morrow of the Octave of Easter; and from Rogation Monday to the morrow of Trinity Sunday.

¶ *Then let the Priest say unto the woman—*

N., wilt thou have this man to thy wedded husband, wilt thou obey and serve him; love, honour, and cherish him in health and sickness, as a wife should a husband, and forsaking all other, keep thee only unto him, so long as ye both shall live?

¶ *Let her answer—*

I will.

¶ *Then let the woman be given by her father or a friend; if a maid, with her hand uncovered; if a widow, covered; and let the man receive her, to be kept in God's faith and his own according to his vows before the Priest; and let him hold her by the right hand in his right hand, and let the man give his troth to the woman, saying thus, after the Priest presently, by word of mouth—**

Ich *N.* take the *N.* to my wedded wyf, to haven and to holden fro this day forward, for betre for wors, for rychere for porere in syknesse and in helthe, til deth us departe, and thereto y plight the my trewthe (*withdrawing his hand*).

¶ *Then let the woman say, after the Priest—*

Ich *N.* take the *N.* to my wedded hosebund, to haven and to holden fro this day forward, for betre for wors, for rychere for porere, in siknesse and in helthe, to be boneyre and buxum in bedde and at borde, till dethe us departe, and thereto y plith the my trewthe (*withdrawing her hand*).

¶ *Then let the man lay gold, silver, and a ring on a dish or book; and let the Priest ask if the ring hath been blessed already; if it be answered not, then let the Priest bless the ring, thus:—*

℣. The Lord be with you,

℟. And with thy spirit.

Let us pray.

O Creator and preserver of mankind, giver of spiritual grace, bestower of eternal salvation, do Thou, O Lord, send Thy bles+sing on this ring (*looking at it*), that she who shall wear it may be armed with the strength of heavenly defence, and that it may be profitable unto her eternal salvation. Through.

Let us pray.

Bl+ess, O Lord, this ring (*looking at it*) which we hallow in

* The *English* here is taken from Maskell's *Mon. Rit.*; the *Text* followed, however, is that of the Manual of 1537.

Thy Holy Name, that whosoever she be that shall wear it may be steadfast in Thy peace and abide in Thy will, and live, increase, and grow old in Thy love, and let the length of her days be multiplied. Through.

¶ *Then let Holy Water be sprinkled over the ring.*

¶ *But if the ring shall have been already blessed, then, as soon as the man have laid it on the book, let the Priest take the ring and deliver it to the man; and let the man receive it in his right hand, with the first three fingers, holding the right hand of the Bride with his left hand, and say, after the Priest—*

With this ryng ich the wedde, and with my body ich the honoure, and with al my gold ich the dowere.*

¶ *And then let the Bridegroom put the ring on the thumb of the Bride, saying—*

In the Name of the Father; (*on the first finger*) and of the Son; (*on the second finger*) and of the Holy Ghost; (*on the third finger*) Amen.

¶ *And there let him leave it, because in that finger there is a certain vein which reaches to the heart;* † *and by the purity of the silver is signified the inward affection which ought ever to be fresh between them. Then, whilst they bow their heads, let the Priest say a blessing over them—*

Bles + sed be ye of the Lord, Who made the world out of nothing. Amen.

¶ *Then let* Ps. lxviii. *be said:—*

Thy God hath sent forth strength for thee: stablish the thing, O God, that Thou hast wrought in us;

For Thy temple's sake at Jerusalem: so shall kings bring presents unto Thee.

When the company of the spear-men, and multitude of the mighty are scattered abroad among the beasts of the people, so that they humbly bring pieces of silver.

Glory.

Lord, have mercy.

Christ, have mercy.

Lord, have mercy.

Our Father.

℣. And lead us not into temptation.

℟. But deliver us from evil.

* From the Lincoln (Sarum) MS. Pontifical at Cambridge.

† According to Decretal xxx.

℣. Let us bless the Father, and the Son, and the Holy Ghost.

℟. Let us praise and exalt Him for ever.

℣. Let us praise the Lord, Whom angels praise.

℟. To whom cherubim and seraphim cry, Holy, Holy, Holy.

℣. Lord, hear my prayer.

℟. And let my cry come unto Thee.

℣. The Lord be with you,

℟. And with thy spirit.

Let us pray.

The God of Abraham, the God of Isaac, the God of Jacob, be with you; may He Himself unite you and pour the fulness of His blessing upon you. Who.

Let us pray.

God the Father bl + ess you; Jesus Christ keep you; the Holy Ghost enlighten you; the Lord make His face to shine upon you and be merciful unto you; turn His countenance unto you and give you peace; and so fill you with all spiritual benediction for the remission of your sins, that ye may have eternal life and live for ever.

℟. Amen.

¶ *Here let them go into church, to the step of the Altar, and let the Priest and his ministers, as they go, say* Psalm cxxviii. *without note.*

Lord, have mercy.
Christ, have mercy.
Lord, have mercy.

¶ *Then, the Bride and Bridegroom kneeling at the Altar-step, the Priest shall desire those present to pray for them, saying—*

Our Father.

℣. And lead us not into temptation.

℟. But deliver us from evil.

℣. Save Thy servant and Thy handmaid,

℟. My God, who put their trust in Thee.

℣. O Lord, send them help from Thy holy place,

℟. And defend them out of Sion.

℣. Be unto them, O Lord, a tower of strength,
℟. From the face of their enemy.
℣. Lord, heard my prayer,
℟. And let my cry come unto Thee.
℣. The Lord be with you,
℟. And with thy spirit.

Let us pray.

The Lord bless you out of Sion, that ye may behold Jerusalem in prosperity all the days of your life, and see your children's children and peace upon Israel. Through.

Let us pray.

O God of Abraham, God of Isaac, God of Jacob, ble+ss these young persons, and sow the seed of eternal life in their hearts; that whatsoever they shall profitably learn, they may indeed fulfil the same. Through Jesus Christ Thy Son, restorer of man. Who.

Let us pray.

Look down from Heaven, O Lord, and bless+this congregation; and as Thou sentest Thy holy Angel Raphael to Tobias, and to Sarah, the daughter of Raguel, so vouchsafe, O Lord, to send Thy bles+sing upon these young persons, that they, obeying Thy will and alway being in safety under Thy protection, may live, increase, and grow old in Thy love; and may be worthy, and peacemakers, and that the length of their days may be multiplied. Through.

Let us pray.

Favourably regard, O Lord, this Thy servant and this Thy handmaid, that in Thy Name they may receive a heavenly bene+diction, see the children of their sons and daughters to the third and fourth generations in safety, ever remain steadfast in Thy will, and at length attain unto the Kingdom of Heaven. Through.

Let us pray.

The Almighty and merciful God, Who by His own power did create our first parents Adam and Eve, and by His own consecration did knit them together; Himself sanctify and ble+ss your souls and bodies, and join you together in the union and love of true affection. Through.

¶ *Then let him bless them, saying—*

God Almighty bl+ess you with all heavenly benediction, and make you worthy in His sight, pour upon you the riches of His grace, and instruct you in the Word of Truth, that ye may be enabled to please Him alike in body and soul. Through.

¶ *These prayers being ended, and the Bride and Bridegroom being brought to the Presbytery* (i.e., *between the Quire and the Altar*) *on the south side of the Church, and the woman being set at the man's right hand between him and the Altar, let Mass begin.*

The Office.

As in the Mass for Trinity Sunday.

¶ *The* Kyrie *is sung with its verses, and the* Gloria in Excelsis. *Let the Mass be celebrated as on a double feast.*

The Collect.

As on Trinity Sunday.

Memorial of the Bride and Bridegroom.

Hear us, O Almighty and merciful God; that what we according to our office, minister, may be abundantly fulfilled with Thy blessing. Through.

The Epistle. 1 Cor. vi. 15-20.

Brethren, know ye not .... which are God's.

¶ Gradual *and* Alleluia *as in the* Mass for the Trinity.

The Sequence.

As on Whitsun Thursday.

The Gospel. Matt. xix. 3-6.

At that time the Pharisees came unto *Jesus* .... let no man put asunder.

The Creed.

Offert. As on Trinity Sunday.

¶ *The Bride and Bridegroom are never censed in the Church with incense which has been blessed. Therefore, when such incense is offered at the Altar, if the censer be passed down to the clergy or laity, other incense must be put in for that purpose.*

I. *Secret.* As on Trinity Sunday.

II. *Secret.* Of Thy goodness and mercy be present, O Lord, with our supplications, and accept this oblation which we offer unto Thee in behalf of Thy servants whom Thou hast seen fit to bring to man's estate and the day of espousal. Through.

¶ *After the* Sanctus, *let the Bride and the Bridegroom kneel in prayer at the step of the Altar, a pall or veil being held over them, which four of the clergy in surplices hold at the four corners, unless one or both shall have been espoused and blessed already; in which case no pall is held over them and no sacramental benediction given. Then before* The Peace of the Lord, *after making the Eucharistic fraction in the usual manner, and having left the Host on the paten in three pieces, let the Priest turn to them and say these prayers reading, as they kneel under the pall—*

℣. The Lord be with you,

℟. And with thy spirit.

Let us pray.

Be favourable, O Lord, unto our supplications, and of Thy goodness assist the ordinances whereby Thou has appointed that mankind should be increased; that they who are joined together by Thy allowance may be preserved by Thy succour. Through.

Let us pray.

O God, Who by Thy mighty power madest all things out of nothing; Who also, after other things set in order, didst create for man, made after the image of God, the inseparable help of the woman, that out of man's flesh woman should take her beginning, teaching that what Thou hast been pleased to make one it should never be lawful to put asunder. O God, Who hast consecrated the state of matrimony to such an excellent mystery, that in it is signified the sacramental union and marriage of Christ and the Church;* O God, by Whom woman is joined to man, and the union, instituted in the beginning, is gifted with that bles+sing which alone has not been taken away either through penalty of original sin or the judgment of the deluge; look graciously (*regarding them*), we beseech Thee, on this Thine handmaid now to be joined in wedlock, who earnestly desireth to be guarded by Thy protection. Let the yoke of love and peace be upon her; let her be faithful and chaste; let her wed in Christ and ever remain a follower of holy matrons. Let her be loving to her husband as Rachel, wise as Rebecca, long-lived and

* This last clause, beginning, *O God, Who hast*, is termed the *Sacramental Blessing*, and is not said at a second marriage.

faithful as Sara. Let not the father of lies get advantage over her through her doings; let her abide in the bond of faith and precept; being wedded to one man, let her flee all unlawful conversation, and fortify her weakness with the strength of discipline. Let her be grave and bashful, severe and modest, well-instructed in heavenly doctrine. Let her be fruitful in child-bearing, well reported of, and innocent, and attain to a desired old age, seeing her children's children unto the third and fourth generation, and finally attaining unto the rest of the blessed and the Kingdom of Heaven. Through.

¶ *After this let the Priest turn to the Altar and say* The Peace *and* Agnus Dei *as usual; then, the pall being removed, let the Bridegroom and Bride rise, and let the Bridegroom receive* The Peace *from the Priest and give it to the Bride, kissing her, and no one else; but let the clergy receive* The Peace *from the Priest, and pass it on to the rest after the accustomed manner.**

Comm. and *P. Comm.* as on Trinity Sunday.

II. *P. Comm.* We beseech Thee, O Almighty God, further the ordinance of Thy Providence with compassion and love, and keep in peace unto old age those whom Thou joinest together in lawful union. Through.

¶ *After Mass let bread and wine, or any liquid, be blessed, and let them drink it in the Name of the Lord, the Priest first saying—*

℣. The Lord be with you,

℟. And with thy spirit.

Let us pray.

Ble+ss, O Lord, this bread, and this wine, and this vessel, as Thou didst the five loaves in the wilderness, and the six waterpots in Cana of Galilee; that all they who taste thereof may be discreet, sober, and undefiled, O Thou Saviour of the World. Who.

* Here follows a long dissertation regarding blessing a second marriage (by which is meant only the Sacramental Blessing), a practice forbidden apparently by the Canon Law. It appears, however, that many priests *were* in the habit of blessing second marriages, and in 1321 the case was brought by an English priest, John Waystede, before Pope John XXII., who forbade the practice; but in the case of either or both the parties of a second marriage not having been before blessed, he henceforth permitted them to receive the Benediction. He also mitigated somewhat the penalties against priests who *had* erred in this respect.

¶ *At night let the Priest bless the marriage chamber.*

℣. The Lord be with you,

℟. And with thy spirit.

Let us pray.

Ble + ss, O Lord, this chamber and all that dwell therein, that they may be established in Thy peace and stand fast in Thy will, and live and grow in Thy love, and let the length of their days be multiplied. Through.

¶ *And then the couch.*

℣. The Lord be with you,

℟. And with thy spirit.

Let us pray.

Ble + ss, O Lord, this couch, Thou who neither slumberest nor sleepest; Thou Who keepest Israel, keep Thy servants who rest in this bed from all phantoms and illusions of devils; keep them waking, that they may meditate on thy precepts; keep them sleeping, that in their slumber they may have a sense of Thee; and let them here and everywhere be defended by the aid of Thy protection. Through.

¶ *Then let him bless them.*

Let us pray.

God bless + your bodies and your souls, and send a blessing upon you as He blessed Abraham, Isaac, and Jacob. Amen.

Let us pray.

The hand of the Lord be upon you, and let Him send His holy angel to keep and comfort you all the days of your life. Amen.

Let us pray.

The Father, the Son, and the Holy Ghost ble + ss you, Trine in number, One in Name. Amen.

¶ *Then let the Priest sprinkle them with Holy Water and depart.*

THE PURIFICATION OF A WOMAN AFTER CHILD-BIRTH BEFORE THE CHURCH PORCH

¶ *First let the Priest say* Ps. cxxiii., "I will lift up mine eyes;" *and* Ps. cxxviii., "Blessed are all they."

Lord, have mercy upon us
Christ, have mercy upon us.
Lord, have mercy upon us.

Our Father.

℣. And lead us not into temptation.

℟. But deliver us from evil.

℣. O Lord, my God, save this woman Thy servant,

℟. Who putteth her trust in Thee.

℣. Send her help from the holy place,

℟. And defend her out of Zion.

℣. Be Thou to her, O Lord, a strong tower,

℟. From the face of her enemy.

℣. Lord, hear my prayer,

℟. And let my cry come unto Thee.

℣. The Lord be with you,

℟. And with thy spirit.

The Collect.

O God, Who has delivered this Thy servant from the peril of childbirth, and made her faithful to Thy service; grant that after she hath faithfully finished the course of this life she may obtain life and rest eternal under the wings of Thy mercy. Through.

¶ *Then let the woman be sprinkled with Holy Water, the Priest saying,* Purge me with hyssop; *then let him lead her by the right hand into Church, saying—*

Enter into the temple of God, that thou mayest have eternal life and live for ever and ever. Amen.

Common Memorials.

FOR A FRIEND.

The Collect.

O God, Who justifiest the ungodly, and wouldst not the death of a sinner; we humbly entreat Thy Majesty graciously to preserve Thy servant *N.*, who trusteth in Thy mercy, by Thy heavenly aid, and keep him under Thy continual protection; that he may both constantly serve Thee, and be separated from Thee by no temptations. Through.

Secret. We beseech Thee, O Lord, by virtue of this Mystery both to cleanse us from our own offences, and to absolve Thy servant *N.* from all his sins. Through.

P. Comm. We beseech Thee, O Lord, let the Sacrament which we have received purify us, and grant that Thy servant *N.* may be freed from all sin; that he whose conscience by sin is accused, may glory in the fulness of heavenly healing. Through.

FOR A SICK PERSON NEAR DEATH.

The Collect.

Almighty and everlasting God, preserver of souls, Who dost correct those whom Thou dost love, and for their amendment dost tenderly chastise those whom Thou dost receive, we call upon Thee, O Lord, to bestow Thy healing, that the soul of Thy servant, at the hour of his departure from the body, may by the hands of Thy holy angels be presented without spot unto Thee. Through.

Secret. Assist us mercifully, O Lord, in our supplications, and receive the oblation which we offer to Thee in behalf of Thy servant, who seeketh the health, not of his body, but of his soul: grant him, we beseech Thee, pardon of all his sins, that through this Sacrifice which we present to Thee, his soul may be received by the holy angels, and be counted worthy to attain unto the kingdom of Thy glory. Through.

P. Comm. We, being refreshed by Thy saving Sacrament, whereby Thou art wont to satisfy the souls of them that trust in Thee, yield Thee thanks, O Lord; and leaning on Thy tender mercy, we devoutly pray Thee deign to have mercy on Thy servant, that the enemy may not get advantage over him in the hour of his departure from the body, but that he may be found meet to pass unto life. Through.

FOR THOSE ON A JOURNEY.

As in the Mass for the same

FOR THE POPE.

O God, the Shepherd and Ruler of all the faithful, look down in Thy mercy on Thy servant *N.*, whom Thou hast appointed to be Chief Pastor over Thy Church; grant, we beseech Thee, that he may edify, by word and example, those over whom he is set; and, together with the flock committed to him, attain unto life everlasting. Through.

Secret. Look with favour, O Lord, on the gifts offered unto Thee: and govern Thy servant *N.*, whom Thou hast chosen to be the shepherd of Thy people, with Thy continual protection. Through.

P. Comm. We beseech Thee, O Lord, let this receiving of the Divine Sacrament be our protection: and let It ever save and defend Thy servant *N.*, whom Thou hast appointed shepherd over Thy Church, together with the flock committed unto him. Through.

FOR THE BISHOP.

We beseech Thee, O Lord, govern Thy servant *N.*, our Bishop, and at the intercession of Mary, the Blessed Mother of God, and all Thy saints, multiply upon him the gifts of Thy grace; that he being delivered from all evil, may not be left destitute of temporal aid, and may rejoice in ordinances which endure for ever. Through.

Secret. Receive, we beseech Thee, O Lord, the gifts offered to Thee; and at the intercession of Mary, the Blessed Mother of God, and all Thy saints, in Thy mercy everywhere preserve Thy servant *N.*, our Bishop; save him from all adversities which he deserveth, that he being delivered from the snares of all his enemies, visible and invisible, may serve Thee in godly quietness. Through.

P. Comm. We beseech Thee, O Lord, at the intercession of Mary, the Blessed Mother of God, and all Thy saints, let the favour of Heaven be multiplied upon Thy servant *N.*, our Bishop, who is subject unto Thee; that he may be delivered out of the perils of this present life, and be strengthened with everlasting gifts. Through.

ANOTHER FOR THE BISHOP.

The Collect.

Grant, we beseech Thee, O Lord, to Thy servant our Bishop, that by preaching and doing such things as be rightful, he may by the example of good works edify the minds of those under his authority, and receive of Thee, most tender Shepherd, an everlasting recompense and reward. Through.

Secret. We beseech Thee, O Lord, favourably to accept our gifts, and in Thy goodness in every time and place protect Thy servant *N.*, our Bishop, and the flock committed to him. Through.

P. Comm. We beseech Thee, O Lord, let this Communion cleanse us from sin, and of Thy loving-kindness preserve Thy servant *N.*, our Bishop, and the flock committed unto him. Through.

FOR BISHOPS AND THEIR FLOCKS.

The Collect.

Almighty and everlasting God, Who alone workest great marvels, send down upon Thy servants the Bishops, and all congregations committed to their charge, the healthful spirit of Thy grace; and that they may truly please Thee, pour upon them the continual dew of Thy blessing. Through.

Secret. O Lord, we beseech Thee, graciously accept the oblations of Thy servants; and let them perceive in themselves the saving effect of that which we devoutly celebrate on their behalf, to the honour of Thy Name. Through.

P. Comm. O Lord, further with Thy continual protection those whom Thou dost refresh with the heavenly gift; and grant that they, whom Thou dost never fail to comfort, may be made worthy of eternal redemption. Through

---

FOR ONESELF (NOT SARUM).

The Collect.

O God, Father Almighty, Who art the Maker of all things, I humbly implore Thee, that whilst I confess before Thine Almighty Majesty that I, Thy servant, have grievously offended, Thou wouldst stretch out unto me the right hand of Thy compassion; to the end that while I present to Thy loving-kindness this offering for my sins, Thou, O most merciful, wilt be pleased to absolve me from the wickednesses which I have committed. Through.

Secret. O God of mercy, compassion, and pardon, forgive, I beseech Thee, and pity me Thy servant; graciously be pleased to accept the offering which I present for my sins; of Thy favourable pity and tender mercy, pardon whatsoever defilement I have contracted by carnal will and frailty; and grant unto me space for repentance and plenteous tears, that I may be counted worthy to receive of Thee the forgiveness of my offences. Through.

P. Comm. O God, Who art the Saviour of all that live, Who desireth not the death of sinners, neither hast pleasure in the perdition of those that die; I humbly implore Thee to grant me pardon of my offences, that I may weep over my trespasses, and hereafter sin no more; that whensoever the last day and end of my life shall come, the holy angel may receive me cleansed from all sin. Through.

AGAINST TEMPTATIONS OF THE FLESH.

The Collect.

Kindle, O Lord, in our reins and our heart the fire of the Holy Ghost; that we may serve Thee with a chaste body, and please Thee with a pure mind. Through.

Secret. Unloose, O Lord, the chains of our sins by the fire of the Holy Ghost; and that we may offer Thee this Sacrifice of praise with perfect freedom, restore that which Thou didst formerly bestow upon us; and by Thy pardon save us whom Thou hast vouchsafed to save by grace. Through.

P. Comm. O Lord God, our helper and defender, help us who receive Thy Holy Sacrament by the power of the Holy Ghost; let the strength of chastity and newness of holiness be revived in our flesh, that being snatched out of the hand of Hell, it may be presented by Thy command in the joy of the resurrection. Through.

AGAINST EVIL THOUGHTS.

The Collect.

Almighty and merciful God, regard in Thy goodness our prayers, and deliver our hearts from the temptation of evil thoughts; that we may be found worthy to be made an habitation of the Holy Ghost. Through.

Secret. O Lord God, we offer these oblations unto Thee for our salvation; and pray that Thou wouldst vouchsafe to enlighten our souls with the grace of the Holy Ghost, that so by Thy mercy we may be delivered from evil thoughts. Through.

P. Comm. Cleanse our hearts, we beseech Thee, O Lord, from all temptations, through this Sacrifice which we have offered unto Thy Majesty, that we may be made worthy of the grace of the Holy Ghost. Through.

FOR TEARS OF CONTRITION.

The Collect.

Almighty and merciful God, Who, to quench the thirst of Thy people, broughtest a spring of living water out of the stony rock; draw from our hard hearts tears of contrition, that we may bewail our sins, and through Thy mercy obtain pardon for them. Through.

Secret. Mercifully look down, O Lord, on this offering which we present unto Thy Majesty for our sins, and draw from our eyes plenteous floods of tears, whereby we may be able to quench the fiery flames which we deserve. Through.

P. Comm. We, being satisfied with Thy Body and Blood, beseech Thee, O Lord, ever freely to bestow upon us repentance and sorrow of heart for our sins, and abundant tears; to the end that we may hereafter find heavenly comfort. Who.

IN THE TIME OF STORMS.

The Collect.

We beseech Thee, O Lord, let spiritual wickedness be driven away from Thy habitation, and the fierceness of tempests depart Through.

Secret. We offer unto Thee, O Lord, the gifts of praise; rendering thanks to Thee for benefits already bestowed upon us, and humbly praying for those which Thou shalt confer. Through.

P. Comm. Almighty and ever-living God, Who by chastening dost heal, and by pardon dost preserve us; grant unto us, Thy humble servants, that we may be gladdened by the quiet and comfort we desire, and may evermore use the gift of Thy loving-kindness. Through.

AGAINST THOSE WHO ASSAIL THE CHURCH.

The Collect.

Almighty and most merciful God, with Whom is no unrighteousness, grant unto us, that they who assail and lay waste the possessions of this Thy sanctuary may speedily be corrected by Thy chastisement. Through.

Secret. We offer unto Thee, O Lord, the Sacrifice of reconciliation and praise, beseeching Thee in Thy pity to correct those whom the adversary, by his persuasion, hath stirred up to make assault on the possessions of Thy sanctuary. Through.

P. Comm. O Lord, we beseech Thee favourably to hear our prayers, and of Thine accustomed mercy defer not speedily to accomplish that which we ask concerning the enemies and plunderers of Thy Holy Church. Through.

FOR THOSE AT SEA.

The Collect.

O God, Who didst bring our fathers through the Red Sea, and bear them through the great waters, we praise Thy Name, and humbly beseech Thee to vouchsafe to turn away all adversities from Thy servants at sea, and to bring them with a calm voyage unto the haven where they would be. Through.

Secret. Accept, we beseech Thee, O Lord, the prayers and oblations of Thy people; and graciously defend from all adversities Thy servants who in Thy Name are travelling by water. Through.

P. Comm. We, being sanctified by the Divine Mystery, humbly entreat Thy Majesty, O Lord, by the wood of the Holy Cross, graciously to protect from all perils Thy servants at sea who trust in Thee. Through.

FOR OUR BENEFACTORS, AND THE HEALTH OF THOSE OF THEM WHO ARE LIVING.

The Collect.

O Lord, stretch forth the right hand of Thy heavenly help unto Thy servants and handmaidens; that they may seek Thee with their whole heart, and what they ask rightly, let them obtain. Through.

Secret. Be favourable, O Lord, unto these our supplications, and graciously accept these oblations of Thy servants and handmaidens which we present to Thee for their health and safety; and that the prayer of none be in vain, the request of none unavailing, grant, we beseech Thee, that what we ask faithfully we may obtain effectually. Through.

P. Comm. We beseech Thee, O Lord, give unto Thy servants and handmaidens constancy and sincerity in Thy faith; that they being grounded in Divine charity, may not be removed from the integrity of the same by any temptation. Through.

AGAINST THOSE WHO RISE UP AGAINST US.

The Collect.

We beseech Thee, O Lord, cast down the pride of our enemies, and lay them low by the might of Thy right hand; that iniquity prevail not against righteousness, but that falsehood ever give place to truth. Through.

Secret. We beseech Thee, O Lord, by virtue of this Holy Mystery, let us be cleansed from our secret faults, and delivered from the snares of our enemies. Through.

P. Comm. We beseech Thee, O Lord, let the partaking of Thy holy Mystery purify us, and bestow upon us alike pardon and protection. Through.

FOR A WOMAN WITH CHILD.*

The Collect.

O God, Who didst sanctify the blessed Virgin-Mother, Mary, both in her conception and delivery; and by Thy mighty power didst deliver Jonah from the whale's belly, protect Thy servant who is great with child, and visit her with Thy salvation that the child she beareth may be safely delivered, and may attain unto the grace of the laver of salvation. Through.

Secret. Receive, O Lord, we beseech Thee, our humble prayers and oblations, and preserve Thy servant under the shield of Thy protection; and as Thou hast ordained of Thy grace that she be with child, so, when the time of her travail draweth near, graciously deliver her, and mercifully keep her, and her child, from all disquietude. Through.

* This was composed by Pope Celestine for his sister. He granted a hundred days' indulgence to any priest who said it.

P. Comm. Almighty God, be present with our supplications, and grant unto Thine handmaid the gift of Thy bountiful protection; that when the time of her labour is at hand, she may receive the protection of Thy grace; and that the child she may have borne be brought to the laver of salvation, and increase and grow in grace. Through.

MEMORIALS OF SS. KATHERINE, MARGARET, AND MARY MAGDALENE.

The Collect.

O God, Who hast granted unto Thy most holy Virgins SS. Katherine and Margaret the palm of martyrdom, and to S. Mary Magdalene pardon of her sins, mercifully vouchsafe unto us, for their sake and prayers, both to be adorned with the grace of chastity, and to be loosed from the bands of our sins. Through.

Secret. O Lord, let this gift which we have offered be pleasing unto Thee, ; and that we may be enabled worthily to minister unto Thee, let the holy Virgins Katherine and Margaret obtain for us purity of mind, and the blessed Mary Magdalene a saving penitence. Through.

P. Comm. We that have been partakers of heavenly food beseech Thee, Almighty God, that, for the sake and prayers of Thy holy Virgins SS. Katherine, Margaret, and Mary Magdalene, we may serve Thee with a chaste body, and alway cleave unto Thy love. Through.

FOR THOSE SICK OF A FEVER.*

The Collect.

Almighty and everlasting God, Who by Thy holy Apostles and Martyrs wast pleased to bestow divers gifts of healing, vouchsafe, we beseech Thee, to raise up to health by Thy medicine Thy servant *N.*, who is grievously vexed by fever (at the intercession of Thy servant Sigismund, King and Martyr), and mercifully restore him whole as before. Through.

Secret. We offer Thee the holy gifts, O Lord, in the name of Sigismund, Thy chosen King and Martyr, that Thou wouldst abate the burning fever of this sick person, and ever defend him by Thy aid. Through.

* A Memorial of S. Sigismund, King and Martyr, when he lay in the city of Sens.

P. Comm. Almighty and everlasting God, Who hast granted to those who minister before Thee the fulfilment of all those things which they ask aright; mercifully receive our prayers which we offer in behalf of Thy servant *N.*, in honour of S. Sigismund, Thy King and Martyr, and grant that what we ask for him with a devout mind we may speedily obtain by Thy favour. Through.

AGAINST INFIDELS.

The Collect.

O everlasting Trinity, one God, to Whose power it belongeth to put down the mighty and exalt the meek, we humbly entreat Thy mercy in this holy ordinance, grant Thy aid unto Thy whole Church; and as Thou didst deliver the children of Israel from the hands of the Egyptians, so deliver Thy Christian people from the oppression of infidels, and give victory unto Thy servants, that the estate of Thy Church may be exalted on high, and the infidels entirely cast down by faith, that Christians may rejoice in Thy inheritance, and the Catholic Church ever give thanks for Thy Right Hand, which doth in all things protect her. Through.

Secret. Almighty and ever-living God, accept our unworthy prayers, and give heed to our petitions in these holy offerings; and as Thou was present with Moses and Aaron in Egypt, so vouchsafe to be with us and with all the Christian host, and deliver us from the yoke of the oppressor. Through.

P. Comm. Grant, we beseech Thee, O Lord, that we whom Thou hast satisfied with the heavenly gift may be cleansed from our secret faults, and delivered from the snares of the enemy, that through Thy aid we may evermore rejoice in Thy comfort. Through.

OF THE LORD'S INCARNATION.

The Collect.

We beseech Thee, O Lord, let the holy brightness of Thy Son's Incarnation, Nativity, Passion, Resurrection, Ascension, and the coming of the Holy Ghost, illuminate our hearts as we think on them; that thereby we may be freed from the darkness of this world, and by His guidance attain unto the land of everlasting light. Through.

Secret. We beseech Thee, O Lord, confirm in our hearts the Mysteries of the true faith, that we who confess Him Who was conceived of a Virgin to be very God and Man, may by the power of His life-giving Incarnation, Nativity, Passion, Resurrection, Ascension, and the coming of the Holy Ghost, attain unto the country which abideth for ever. Through.

P. Comm. Grant, we beseech Thee, Almighty God, that we who celebrate with due praise and veneration the memory of Thy Son our Lord Jesus Christ's Incarnation, Nativity, Passion, Resurrection, Ascension, and the coming of the Holy Ghost, may by the grace of the same Holy Spirit ourselves rise from the death of the soul, and live for ever in sanctification by Thee. Through.

FOR THE KING AND QUEEN.

The Collect.

O God, in Whose hand are the hearts of Kings, Who art the Comforter of the meek, the Strength of the faithful, and the Protector of all that trust in Thee, give unto our King *N.* and Queen *N.*, and all Christian people, to discern and acknowledge Thy over-ruling authority, that by Thee they may ever have renewed strength and pardon. Through.

Secret. Receive, O Lord, we beseech Thee, the prayers and oblations of Thy Church, which we offer unto Thy Majesty for the welfare of Thy servants our King and Queen, and for the protection of their faithful people; entreating Thee to work the ancient wonders of Thine arm, that Christendom, being delivered out of the hands of her enemies, may serve Thee in freedom and quietness. Through.

P. Comm. Grant, we beseech Thee, Almighty God, that by these Holy Mysteries which we have received, our King and Queen, and all Christian people may ever think such things as be rightful, and both in word and deed follow after that which is well-pleasing unto Thee. Through.

Masses for the Dead.

BEFORE THE DAY OF BURIAL WHEN THE CORPSE IS PRESENT.*

¶ *It is to be noted that a Mass is said daily in the Chapter-house through Advent (when the Choir is not ruled) till Christmas Eve, and from the Octave of the Epiphany to Wednesday in Holy Week, and from Trinity Monday to Advent, for the faithful departed, with Deacon and Subdeacon, in albs and amices only, unless a double Feast or Octave with Rulers occur the day before, or the corpse be present, or it be the Anniversary of a Bishop, for then the* Mass *is said at the special Altar, or at an Altar near which the body is buried. Also no* Mass for the Dead *is said in the Chapter-house in Eastertide unless the body be present, or it be an Anniversary or Trental.*

The Office.

Grant them, O Lord, eternal rest, and let light perpetual shine upon them.

Ps. lxv. Thou, O Lord, art praised in Sion; and unto Thee shall the vow be performed in Jerusalem. Thou that hearest prayer, unto Thee shall all flesh come.

¶ *At the* Office *let the Deacon cense the corpse on either side, beginning at the head, but let him not go round it.*

The Collect.

O God, Whose property is always to have mercy and to forgive, we humbly pray Thee in behalf of the soul of Thy servant which Thou hast this day commanded to depart out of this world: deliver it not into the hands of the enemy, nor forget it at the last, but command it to be received by the holy angels, and to be carried into the land of the living; and forasmuch as he hoped and believed in Thee, let him be accounted worthy to rejoice in the communion of Thy saints. Through.

¶ *Memorials are said of Bishops, Brethren, Parents, and all the Faithful Departed, if any person other than the King, Queen, or great Noble.*

The Epistle. 1 Thess. iv. 13-18.

I would not have you be ignorant .... comfort one another with these words.

¶ *The following* Gradual *is said for a Bishop only,*† *and that whether the body is present or not, by three Clerks of the second bench, standing at the head of the corpse. But if the body be not present, they stand at the step of the Quire.*

* If the body be not present, all as in the Daily Mass. (See p. 575.)

† This rubric is corrected according to the Defensorium Directorii, which states the one as it stands in the Missal to be wrong.

Gradual. Ps. xxiii. Yea, though I walk through the valley of the shadow of death, I will fear no evil: for Thou art with me, O *Lord.*

℣. Thy rod and Thy staff comfort me.

¶ *In all other Masses the following* Gradual *is sung by three Clerks of the second bench at the head of the corpse, if present; if it be not, it is said at the step of the Quire, the Choir sitting and chanting it.*

Gradual. Grant them, O Lord, eternal rest, and let light perpetual shine upon them.

℣. Ps. xxv. *Their* souls shall dwell at ease, and *their* seed shall inherit the land.

¶ *This is said by four Clerks of the highest bench, standing at the head of the corpse, if present; if not, at the step of the Quire, two singing each* ℣., *but all four beginning and ending it together. In the meantime, after censing the Altar, let the Deacon cense the corpse.*

Tract. Ps. xlii. Like as the hart desireth the water-brooks, so longeth my soul after Thee, O God.

℣. My soul is athirst for God, yea, even for the living God: when shall I come to appear before the presence of *my* God?

℣. My tears have been my meat day and night, while they daily say unto me, Where is now thy God?

The Gospel. John xi. 21-27.

At that time Martha said to Jesus .... which should come into the world.

Offert. O Lord Jesus Christ, King of Glory, deliver the souls of all the faithful departed from the hand of hell, and from the deep pit; deliver them from the lion's mouth, that hell swallow them not up, that they fall not into the blackness of darkness; but let S. Michael the Standard-bearer bring them into the holy light which thou promisedst of old to Abraham and his seed.

¶ *Here again the Priest shall cense the corpse, and after washing his hands shall say,* We offer to Thee (*see p.* 299).

Secret. Accept, we beseech Thee, O Lord, merciful Father, the oblation which we offer unto Thee in behalf of the soul of Thy servant *N.*, which Thou hast delivered this day from the corruption of the flesh; and grant that he may be restored and absolved from all the errors of this mortal state, and in eternal rest may await the day of resurrection. Through.

Comm. Grant unto those, O Lord, in memory of whom the Body of Christ is received, eternal rest.

℣. And let light perpetual shine upon them. Grant unto those, O Lord, in memory of whom the Blood of Christ is received, eternal rest.

P. Comm. Grant, we beseech Thee, Almighty God, that the soul of Thy servant *N.* may be received by the angels of light, and carried to the habitations prepared for the blessed. Through

---

MASS ON THE DAY OF BURIAL.

¶ *All as in the last Mass.*

The Collect.

Almighty and everlasting God, we humbly entreat Thy mercy that Thou wouldst command that the soul of Thy servant *N.*, for whose body we perform the due Office of Burial, be laid in the bosom of Thy Patriarch, Abraham; that when the day of Thy recognition shall arrive, he may be raised up at Thy bidding among the saints and Thine elect. Through.

Secret. Receive, O Lord, in behalf of the soul of Thy servant the Sacrifice which Thou hast graciously offered unto God the Father for us; and because for the sake of men Thou didst come down from Heaven, when Thou shalt come again let It be counted worthy to be united to the assembly of Thy saints. Through Thee, O Saviour of the world, Who.

P. Comm. Grant, we beseech Thee, O Lord, that the soul of Thy servant, for whose body we have this day performed the duty of man to man, may be cleansed by this Sacrifice, and give thanks unto Thee for the perpetual gift of Thy salvation. Through.

MASS IN TRENTALS AND ON THE THIRTIETH DAY.

The Office.

As in the first Mass for the Dead.

The Collect.

O God, Whose property is ever to have mercy and to forgive, be favourable unto the soul of Thy servant, and forgive all *his* sins, that *he* being loosed from the chains of death may be found meet to pass unto life. Through.

¶ *The catafalque is not censed. If Mass is said for a body that is pres*[illegible] *or an Anniversary come in a Trental, then* I. *Collect of* Anniversar[illegible] Burial, II. Trental, III. Bishop, IV. Brethren, V. All Fa[illegible] Departed.

The Lesson. 2 Macc. xii. 43-45.

In those days a mighty man of valour, Judas, made a gather[illegible] .... that they might be delivered from sin.

¶ *In Trentals of Bishops the* Epistle *is as in the first Mass for the Dea*[illegible]

Gradual. Grant them. (See p. 572).

¶ *But it is sung by the whole Choir sitting, and only begun by the C*[illegible] *standing at the step of the Quire. If it is for a Bishop it is as* [illegible] *first Mass, only the Clerks sing it at the step of the Quire.*

Tract. If for a Bishop, as above; if not, as in the Daily M[illegible] (see p. 575).

¶ *The rest as in the first Mass for the Dead; but the* Gospel *is one of* [illegible] *in the Daily Mass (see p. 576), if the Mass is not for a Bishop.*

Secret. Look down, we beseech Thee, Almighty God, [illegible] vouchsafe favourably to receive this Sacrifice which we [illegible] unto Thee in behalf of the soul of Thy servant; and grant [illegible] perpetual peace and everlasting rest. Through.

P. Comm. We beseech Thee, O Lord, let the celebration [illegible] the Divine Sacrament be profitable unto the soul of Thy servant[illegible] that of Thy mercy he may have eternal fellowship with Him [illegible] Whom he trusted and believed. Through.

MASS ON ANNIVERSARIES.

The Office.

As above in the first Mass for the Dead.

¶ *The catafalque is censed if it be the Anniversary of a Bishop or Dea*[illegible]

The Collect.

O Lord God of pardon, grant unto the soul of Thy servant[illegible] the anniversary of whose burial we keep, a place of refreshing[illegible] a blessed rest, and the light of glory. Through.

¶ *The remaining* Memorials *as above.*

The Epistle.

As in the Daily Mass, except it be for a Bishop; then as in the first Mass for the Dead.

Gradual and Tract. As in the Daily Mass, unless it be for a Bishop, then as in the first Mass for the Dead.

The Gospel.

One of those in the Daily Mass, unless it be for a Bishop, then as in the first Mass for the Dead.

¶ *The rest as in the first Mass for the Dead.*

Secret. O Lord, we beseech Thee, mercifully to hear our humble prayers in behalf of the soul of Thy Servant whom as on this day we yearly commemorate; in behalf of whom we offer unto Thee the Sacrifice of praise; that Thou wouldst vouchsafe to admit him unto the fellowship of Thy saints. Through.

P. Comm. Grant, we beseech Thee, O Lord, that the soul of Thy servant, the anniversary of whose burial we keep, may be cleansed by this Sacrifice, and alike obtain pardon and eternal rest. Through.

THE DAILY MASS FOR THE DEAD.*

The Office.

As above.

The Collects.

¶ *The first is for* Bishops; *the second for* Brethren; *the third for* All the Faithful Departed.

¶ *At the Mass in the Chapter-house no incense is offered.*

The Lesson. Rev. xiv. 13.

In those days I heard .... their works do follow them.

The Epistle. 1 Cor. xv. 20-23.

Brethren, Christ is risen .... every man in his own order.

¶ *This last* Lesson *and* Epistle *are said alternately through the year.*

Gradual. As above, but it is sung by the whole Choir sitting, the Precentor beginning it.

Tract. Ps. cxxx. Out of the deep have I called unto Thee, O Lord: Lord, hear my voice.

℣. O let Thine ears consider well: the voice of my complaint.

* To be used at all times except on the above occasions.

℣. If Thou, Lord, wilt be extreme to mark what is done amiss: O Lord, who may abide it?

℣. For there is mercy with Thee, therefore shalt Thou be feared, *O Lord.*

SUNDAY AND MONDAY.

The Gospel.

As in the first Mass for the Dead.

TUESDAY.

The Gospel. John vi. 37-40.

At that time Jesus said to His disciples and to the multitude of the Jews, All that the Father giveth Me .... at the last day.

WEDNESDAY.

The Gospel. John v. 24-29.

At that time Jesus said to His disciples and to the multitude of the Jews, Verily, verily .... resurrection of damnation.

THURSDAY.

The Gospel. John v. 21-24.

At that time Jesus said to His disciples and to the multitude of the Jews, As the Father raiseth up the dead .... from death unto life.

FRIDAY.

The Gospel. John vi. 51-54.

At that time Jesus said to His disciples and to the multitude of the Jews, I am the Living Bread .... at the last day.

SATURDAY.

The Gospel. John vi. 53-54.

At that time Jesus said to His disciples and to the multitude of the Jews, Verily, verily .... at the last day.

¶ We offer Thee *is not said;* Offert. *as above.*

Comm. Let light eternal shine upon them, O Lord, together with Thy saints, for ever, for Thou art holy.

℣. *Grant them, O Lord, eternal rest; and let light perpetual shine upon them, together with Thy saints, for ever, for Thou art holy.*

¶ *In the last Service before Easter, the* Comm. *is as in the first Mass for the Dead.*

Memorials for the Dead.

FOR BISHOPS.

The Collect.

O God, Who hast caused Thy servants to be reckoned among those of Episcopal dignity in the Apostolic ministry, grant, we beseech Thee, that they may rejoice in the everlasting fellowship in heaven of those whose office they bore awhile on earth. Through.

Secret. We offer unto Thee, O Lord, our service and oblations in behalf of the souls of Thy servants, our Bishops, beseeching Thee that they may have a portion of everlasting blessedness, together with the Apostolic Prelates whose office they executed. Through.

P. Comm. We beseech Thee, O Lord, let the celebration of the Divine Mystery be profitable to the souls of Thy servants, our Bishops, that those whom whilst on earth Thou madest dispensers of this gift may by Thy command be numbered with Thine elect priesthood. Through.

FOR BRETHREN AND SISTERS.

The Collect.

O God, the bestower of pardon and the author of the salvation of mankind, we beseech Thee, of Thy mercy, that the brethren and sisters of our congregations who are departed this life may at the intercession of Blessed Mary, ever Virgin, S. Michael the Archangel, and all saints, attain unto fellowship in eternal happiness. Through.

Secret. O God, Whose mercy is infinite, graciously receive our humble prayers, and grant unto the souls of the brethren and sisters of our congregations to whom Thou didst give grace to confess Thy Name, the pardon of all their sins by this Sacrament of our salvation. Through.

P. Comm. Grant, we beseech Thee, O Almighty and merciful God, that the souls of the brethren and sisters of our congregations in whose behalf we have offered this Sacrifice of praise unto Thy Majesty, being by virtue of this Sacrament purified from all sin, may through Thy mercy receive the blessedness of perpetual light. Through.

FOR BENEFACTORS.

The Collect.

Almighty and merciful God, the only salvation of mankind, we humbly entreat Thee in behalf of the souls of Thy servants and handmaidens our parents and benefactors, that at the intercession of Mary, the Blessed Mother of God, with all Thy saints, Thou wouldst deign to bestow abundantly upon them pardon of their sins, and in the last day the joy of a blessed resurrection. Through.

Secret. Sanctify, we beseech Thee, O Lord, this life-giving Sacrament of all the faithful, and grant that, at the intercession of Mary, the Blessed Mother of God, with all Thy saints, It may profit the souls of Thy servants and handmaidens, our parents and benefactors, that they may be cleansed from all their sins, and refreshed with the Food of everlasting life. Through.

P. Comm. We beseech Thee, O Lord, let the saving Sacrament upon which we have fed quicken us; and at the intercession of Mary, the Blessed Mother of God, with all Thy saints, grant that it may be profitable to the souls of Thy servants and handmaidens, our parents and benefactors, procuring for them Thy grace and pardon, and the attainment of the everlasting glory of a future resurrection. Through.

FOR AN ABBAT.

The Collect.

Grant, we beseech Thee, O Lord, that the soul of Thy servant and Abbat, whom whilst he abode in this world Thou didst adorn with Thy holy gifts, may ever rejoice in a glorious seat in heaven. Through.

Secret. Receive, we beseech Thee, O Lord, the oblation which we humbly present unto Thee in behalf of the soul of Thy servant and Abbat, entreating of Thy mercy that he upon whom Thou didst lay the office, may also have the reward of a Priest. Through.

P. Comm. Grant, we beseech Thee, Almighty God, that by these holy Mysteries the soul of Thy servant and Abbat, who faithfully ministered unto Thee, may stand pure in Thy sight. Through.

FOR A PRIEST.

The Collect.

O God, Whose mercies are without number, accept our prayers for the soul of Thy servant and Priest, and vouchsafe him the fellowship of Thy saints in the land of light and joy. Through.

Secret. We beseech Thee, O Lord our God, graciously receive the offering which we present unto Thee in behalf of the soul of Thy servant and Priest, and grant that he whom Thou didst suffer to serve at Thy Altar may attain at Thy bidding unto the fellowship of Thy Priests in bliss. Through.

P. Comm. We beseech Thee, Almighty God, by these holy Mysteries to bestow upon the soul of Thy servant and Priest, whom Thou didst permit to minister at the holy Altar, a part and lot in eternal happiness. Through.

FOR A FATHER AND MOTHER.

The Collect.

O God, Who hast commanded us to honour father and mother, of Thy mercy have compassion on the souls of my father and mother; forgive them all their sins, and let me behold them in the joy of eternal light. Through.

Secret. Accept, O Lord, this Sacrifice which is offered to Thee in behalf of the souls of my father and mother, and grant them endless joy in the land of the living, and make me to be numbered with them in the blessedness of the saints. Through.

P. Comm. O Lord, let the partaking of the heavenly Sacrament obtain everlasting repose and light for the souls of my father and mother, and let me with them have through Thy grace a share in the heavenly crown. Through.

FOR ANYONE DECEASED.

The Collect.

O God, Who alone canst heal after death, grant, we beseech Thee, that the soul of Thy servant, being cleansed from all sin, may be gathered into the company of Thine elect. Through.

Secret. Accept, O Lord, we beseech Thee, this oblation which we present unto Thee in behalf of the soul of Thy servant, and grant him eternal rest amongst saints elect, that so he may have the full fruition of their fellowship in life eternal. Through.

P. Comm. O Lord, let our prayers ascend unto Thee, and through this holy Sacrament which we have received let the soul of Thy servant have eternal joys, that he whom Thou madest Thine by adoption may also by Thy command have a share in Thy heritage. Through.

FOR A DEAD FRIEND.

The Collect.

Help us, O God of our salvation, and at the prayers of Mary, the most Blessed Mother of God, ever Virgin, let the soul of Thy servant have a place in the light of everlasting blessedness. Through.

Secret. Accept, we beseech Thee, O Lord, the Sacrifice of reconciliation and praise which we present unto Thee to be consecrated to Thy Name in honour of the Blessed Mary, Mother of God, and the repose of Thy servant, for which we humbly entreat Thee. Through.

P. Comm. Let our prayers, O Lord, come up before Thee, and let the soul of Thy servant *N.* have eternal joys; and at the intercession of Mary, the Blessed Mother of God, let him whom Thou hast made Thy own by adoption have part in Thine inheritance. Through.

FOR ONE OVERTAKEN BY SUDDEN DEATH.

The Collect.

Almighty and merciful God, in Whose power is the estate of man; absolve the soul of Thy servant, we beseech Thee, from all sins, that although overtaken by death he may not lose the benefit of the repentance which he desired. Through.

Secret. O Lord, we beseech Thee, let the offering of this Sacrifice be acceptable unto Thee in behalf of the soul of Thy servant, and let him find that pardon for his sins which he sought; and forasmuch as he could not fulfil it with his lips, let him attain by Thy bounty unto the benefit of the penitence after which he longed. Through.

P. Comm. O God, by Whom every good thing is given to the hearts of men, vouchsafe by this holy Sacrament which we have received, as Thou didst give unto the soul of Thy servant the will to repent, so in Thy pity Thou wouldst bestow upon him the pardon he desired. Through.

FOR MALE RELATIONS.

The Collect.

Almighty and everlasting God, unto Whom no prayer is made without hope of compassion, be favourable unto the souls of Thy servants, and cause those who have departed out of this life in the confession of Thy Name to be gathered into the number of Thy saints. Through.

Secret. Have mercy, we beseech Thee, O Lord, on the souls of Thy servants in whose behalf we have offered Thee the Sacrifice of reconciliation; and forasmuch as in the light of this world they abode in the Catholic Faith, let a most merciful recompense be bestowed upon them in the life to come. Through.

P. Comm. Let this Communion, O Lord, cleanse us from sin, and bestow upon the souls of Thy servants a portion in the joy of Heaven, that before the judgment-seat of Christ's glory Thy people may be set apart with those at the Right Hand, and have no part with those on the left. Through.

FOR FEMALE RELATIONS.

The Collect.

Have mercy, we beseech Thee, O Lord, of Thy goodness, on the souls of Thine handmaidens; and grant that they, being purified from the corruptions of this mortal life, may have a share in eternal salvation. Through.

Secret. O Lord, let the souls of Thine handmaidens be cleansed from all sin by this Sacrifice, without which none is free from guilt; and grant that by this office of holy reconciliation they may obtain perpetual mercy. Through.

P. Comm. We beseech Thee, O Lord, let the souls of Thine handmaidens have a part in the eternal Light, the Sacrament whereof they have, of Thy perpetual mercy, attained unto. Through.

FOR A DEPARTED WOMAN.

The Collect.

We humbly beseech Thy Majesty, O Lord, that the soul of Thine handmaiden, being cleansed from the sins which in this life she hath committed, may be numbered in the lot of Thy just ones. Through.

Secret. We present unto Thee, O Lord, this oblation with humble supplication, entreating Thy Majesty that the soul of Thine handmaiden may through this office of holy reconciliation be accounted meet to attain unto eternal rest. Through.

P. Comm. Grant, we beseech Thee, O Lord, unto the soul of Thine handmaid eternal compassion; that being set free from the bondage of the flesh, eternal Light may have it in possession. Through.

DURING TRENTALS.

The Collect.

Incline Thine ear, O Lord, unto our prayers, whereby we humbly entreat Thy mercy that Thou wouldst give unto the souls of Thy servants and handmaidens, who at Thy command have departed this life, a place in the land of peace and light, and ordain them a communion with Thy saints. Through.

Secret. We beseech Thee, O Lord, let this oblation release the souls of Thy servants and handmaidens from all evils of this mortal life; forasmuch as when offered It also bare the sin of the whole world. Through.

P. Comm. Vouchsafe unto us, O Lord, by this Sacrifice which we have received, that the souls of Thy servants and handmaidens may be counted worthy to obtain that remission of sins which they have ever desired. Through.

FOR BENEFACTORS.

The Collect.

Have mercy, O Lord, we beseech Thee, upon the souls of all our departed benefactors, and in return for the benefits which they bestowed upon us on earth let them obtain an eternal reward in Heaven. Through.

Secret. Let the oblation of this Sacrifice be pleasing unto Thee, O Lord, for our own salvation, and that of all our benefactors whose memory we call to mind with especial affection, and graciously have mercy upon all Christians quick and dead. Through.

P. Comm. Let the Sacrament we have received, O Lord, set us free from the chains of sin, and obtain for the souls of all our departed benefactors fellowship with blessed spirits. Through.

FOR THOSE WHO REPOSE IN A CEMETERY.

The Collect.

O God, in Whose tender mercy the souls of the faithful are at rest; of Thy favour give unto the souls of all Thy servants and handmaidens who here and everywhere sleep in Christ pardon of sin, that they being absolved from all guilt may evermore rejoice with Thee. Through.

Secret. Mercifully accept, O Lord, this Sacrifice which is presented unto Thee in behalf of the souls of all Thy servants and handmaidens who here and everywhere sleep in Christ, that being delivered by this one only offering from the dread bonds of death they may be found meet to attain unto eternal life. Through.

P. Comm. O God, the Light of faithful souls, graciously be present when we call upon Thee, and grant unto Thy servants and handmaidens whose bodies here and everywhere repose in Christ a place of refreshment, the blessing of rest, and brightness of light. Through.

FOR THOSE WE ARE BOUND TO PRAY FOR.

The Collect.

Grant, we beseech Thee, O Lord our God, that the souls of Thy servants and handmaidens, the commemoration of whom we keep with special reverence, and for whom we are bidden and are bound to pray, and the souls of all our benefactors, relations, and connections, and all the faithful, may rest in the bosom of Thy saints, and being presently raised from the dead may please Thee in the land of the living. Through.

Secret. We beseech Thee, O Lord, let these gifts which we offer in presence of Thy Majesty be profitable to the souls of all Thy servants and handmaidens, commemoration of whom we keep with special reverence, and for whom we are bidden and are bound to pray, as also for the souls of all our benefactors, relations, and friends, and all the faithful, that they being delivered by Thy loving-kindness from the dread bonds of death, may be found meet to be partakers of eternal happiness. Through.

P. Comm. O God, Who of Thine unspeakable mercy dost cause the souls of men to pass from trouble to rest: favourably hear our supplications in behalf of the souls of Thy servants and handmaidens commemoration of whom we keep with special reverence, and for whom we are bidden and are bound to pray;

as also for the souls of all our benefactors, relations, and friends, and of all the faithful; restore them to Paradise, and number them in the lot of Thy just ones. Through.

FOR ALL THE FAITHFUL DEPARTED.

The Collect.

O God, the Creator and Redeemer of all, grant unto the souls of all the faithful departed pardon of all their sins; that through the help of holy supplications they may obtain the forgiveness they have ever desired. Who.

Secret. Look down mercifully, we beseech Thee, O Lord, on the oblation we offer in behalf of the souls of all the faithful departed; and as Thou wast pleased to bestow on them the gift of Christian faith, grant them also the reward of the same. Through.

P. Comm. We beseech Thee, O Lord, let our humble prayers be profitable uuto the souls of all the faithful departed; deliver them from all their sins, and make them partakers of Thy redemption. Through.

THE TRENTAL OF S. GREGORY.*

The Collect.

O God, the supreme hope of our redemption, Who didst choose before all lands to be born in the Land of Promise, and there didst suffer death; graciously deliver the soul of Thy servant *N.* out of the hands of evil spirits, and that same land out of the power of the infidels; and that the people that believe not in Thee may receive correction by Thy power do Thou of Thy great loving-kindness succour all those who trust in Thee. Who.

Secret. Almighty and everlasting God, Redeemer of souls that shall be saved, and price of the redemption of mankind; in Thy

* Whoever may desire to keep the Trental of S. Gregory must celebrate three Masses of the Lord's Nativity, three of the Lord's Epiphany, three of the Purification of S. Mary, three of the Annunciation of the same, three of the Lord's Resurrection, three of the Lord's Ascension, three of Whitsun-Day, three of the Trinity, three of the Assumption of S. Mary the Virgin, three of her Nativity· and let these Masses be celebrated within the Octaves of the above feasts, all as on their day, but with these Collects after the Collect for the day. Let him also say daily *Placebo* and *Dirige*, with nine Psalms, Lessons, and Anthems, except in Eastertide, when the Service must be said with three; and let the Commendation of Souls be said so many times. Let the first Collect be the following; let him also say it every day at Mass throughout the year.

pity have mercy on the soul of Thy servant *N.*, and whatsoever defilements it hath contracted by the fraud of the Devil, or through its own iniquity, do Thou of Thy pity mercifully pardon and cleanse away; deliver also the land which Thou hast hallowed by Thine own Blood from the hands of the enemies of the Cross, and mercifully dispose the desires of the children of Israel who are instant in prayer for its freedom after the way of everlasting salvation. Who.

P. Comm. O God, Whose mercies are without number, to Whom only it belongeth to heal after death; Who art the Life of the living, the Hope of the dying, and the Salvation of all that trust in Thee; Who didst deign to consecrate by Thy precious Blood the land of Thine inheritance polluted by the sins of the sons of Esau; do Thou cleanse the soul of Thy servant *N.* from all sins by virtue of this Sacrament, and deliver it from all pains which for them it deserveth; make the unbelieving and rebellious Thine own peculiar people by Thy grace; and pitifully stretch out the hand of Thine aid unto all those who put their trust in Thy mercy. Who.

A PROSE FOR THE DEPARTED.

WHICH MAY BE SAID IF ANY DESIRE IT.

Day of wrath, O Day of mourning,
Lo, the world in ashes burning—
Seer and Sybil gave the warning.

O, what fear man's bosom rendeth,
When from Heaven the Judge descendeth,
On Whose sentence all dependeth.

Wondrous sound the trumpet flingeth,
Through earth's sepulchres it ringeth,
All before the Throne it bringeth.

Death is struck, and Nature quaking,
All creation is awaking—
To its Judge an answer making.

Lo, the Book, exactly worded,
Wherein all hath been recorded—
Thence shall judgment be awarded.

When the Judge His seat attaineth,
And each hidden deed arraigneth,
Nothing unavenged remaineth.

What shall I, frail man, be pleading?
Who for me be interceding
When the just are mercy needing?

King, of Majesty tremendous,
Who dost free salvation send us,
Fount of pity, then befriend us.

Think, kind Jesu, my salvation
Caus'd Thy wondrous Incarnation—
Leave me not to reprobation.

Faint and weary Thou hast sought me—
On the Cross of suff'ring bought me;
Shall such grace be vainly brought me?

Righteous Judge of Retribution,
Grant Thy gift of absolution
Ere that Reck'ning Day's conclusion.

Guilty, now I pour my moaning,
All my shame with anguish owning:
Spare, O God, Thy suppliant groaning.

Thou the sinful Mary savest,
Thou the dying thief forgavest—
And to me a hope vouchsafest.

Worthless are my prayers and sighing,
Yet, good Lord, in grace complying,
Rescue me from fires undying.

With Thy favour'd sheep, O place me;
Nor among the goats abase me—
But to Thy Right Hand upraise me.

While the wicked are confounded,
Doom'd to flames of woe unbounded,
Call me, with Thy saints surrounded.

Low I kneel, with heart-submission:
See, like ashes, my contrition—
Help me in my last condition.

Ah, that day of tears and mourning,
From the dust of earth returning,
Man for Judgment must prepare him.

Spare, O God, in mercy spare him;
Lord, Who didst our souls redeem,
Grant a blessed Requiem. Amen.

A MASS TO TURN AWAY PESTILENCE.*

The Office. 2 Sam. xxiv.

Remember Thy covenant, O Lord, and say to Thy destroying angel, Stay thou thy hand, that the earth be not laid waste; slay not every living soul.

Ps. lxxx. Hear, O Thou Shepherd of Israel, Thou that leadest Joseph like a sheep.

* Composed by Pope Clement at Avignon.

The Collect.

O God, Who desireth not the death, but the repentance of sinners, we beseech Thee graciously turn Thy people unto Thyself; and, forasmuch as their devotion unto Thee is steadfast, in Thy mercy put away from them the rod of Thy wrath. Through.

The Lesson. 2 Sam. xxiv. 15-19.

In those days the Lord sent a pestilence .... as the Lord commanded.

Gradual. Ps. cvii. *The Lord* sent His word and healed them, and they were saved from their destruction.

℣. O that men would therefore praise the Lord for His goodness, and declare the wonders that He doeth for the children of men.

Alleluia! ℣. *I will save My people in the midst of Jerusalem; and I will be to them a God in truth and justice.*

The Sequence.

With pious minds let us rejoice,
Our hearts responding to our voice,
The Trinity to praise;
The Father and the Son entreat,
And Holy Ghost, with reverence meet,
While lauding hymns we raise.

To Him together let us cry,
Beseeching of the Lord on high
That He will pitying hear:
Our hearts are faint, our souls oppressed,
The nation now is sore distressed,
The plague strikes all with fear.

Fierce pestilence doth taint the air,
Disease prevails, and none doth dare
To hope for safety more;
The waves with poison mingled flow,
And storms and tempests wildly blow;
The people mourn full sore.

If Thou dost for our sins chastise,
Now it is time Thou shouldst arise—
Have mercy, Jesu kind:
The lion seeks the flock to tear,
Good Shepherd, if Thou art not there
No succour can we find.

The earth, the sea, the firmament,
And each obedient element,
Thy Hand Divine declare:
As Thou didst walk the sea confessed
Thy footsteps on her waters pressed;
The floods their Maker bare.

At Thy command all tumults cease,
And in a moment there is peace,
Nought moves, and all is still;
All rests on Thee, all reverence pays,
The whole creation Thee doth praise,
O Power of kindly will.

Send us propitious gales, we pray,
And bear us to the goal of life;
The pestilence drive far away,
And rid us of the tempest's strife.

We that were long time bound by sin,
Turn back to Thee, regaining strength;
Chastised, and sad of heart within,
In Thee alone we trust at length.

Converted sinners the old law
Ne'er to receive refused;
And mercifully did chastise
Those who its grace abused.

As Joab after Abner went,
Pursuing him with fierce intent,
Good words for peace prevailed;
In safety o'er the mountain height
Joab, returning, marched by night,
Else life for all had failed.

According to the appointed word,
Pardon the prophet doth accord
To David's great offence;
His grievous crime is cleansed away,
When "I have sinned," he doth say,
In tones of penitence.

King Hezekiah sore doth weep;
Forthwith at his repentance deep,
His sin is put aside;
He weeps, and profits by his tears,
For God doth add unto his years
A longer term beside.

The gentle Esther seeks relief
Of Assuerus in her grief,
Her nation's life to win:
Hence Mordecai deliverance found:
On his own gallows, Haman, bound,
Doth expiate his sin.

Whilst heavenly valour from on high
Judith illuminates,
Headless she leaves her enemy,
And captives liberates.

Then, Mother of the highest King,
The true Anointed One we see
You both, the Law prefiguring,
Thou Esther, Assuerus He.

O blessed Virgin, intercede,
  Us from the pestilence to save;
Those whom Thy Son redeemed and freed,
  Let Him deliver from the grave.

O Virgin Mother, the Word's Cell,
Star of the Sea, thou Garden Well,
The pestilential storm dispel;
  Let us poor sinners live;
O Mother, wipe our tears away,
The raging tempest still this day;
Now in our trouble for us pray,
  Our drooping hearts revive.

Thy Son doth spare if thou dost pray,
O Mother then no more delay,
  Thy Holy Child implore;
Let the fell plague, the deadly blast,
Together cease, and now at last
  Health to our land restore.

Our guilt and punishment, we pray,
Let Thy Son wholly take away,
  And us with comfort greet;
And grant us of His realm a share
Whose citizens eternal are:
  Let all Amen repeat.

The Gospel. Luke iv. 38-44.

At that time Jesus arose out of the synagogue ...... synagogues of Galilee.

Offert. Numb. xvi. *The high priest* stood between the living and the dead, *and, offering the oblation of incense, appeased the* wrath *of* the Lord, and the plague was stayed *from the house and people of Israel.*

Secret. O Lord, we beseech Thee, let this Thy Sacrifice succour Thy people; mightily deliver us from all things which affright us, and keep and defend us from all calamities which assail us. Through.

Comm. Luke vi. A multitude *of diseased*, and they that were vexed with unclean spirits, *came to Jesus*, for there went virtue out of Him and healed them all.

P. Comm. Hear us, O God, of our salvation, and at the intercession of Mary, the Blessed Mother of God. set Thy people free from the terrors of Thy wrath, and of Thy mercy cause them to rest securely in Thy bountiful goodness. Through.

THE PASSION OF OUR LORD JESUS CHRIST ACCORDING TO JOHN.*

† *At that time* Pilate took Jesus and scourged Him. And the soldiers platted a crown of thorns, and put it on His head, and they put on Him a purple robe, and said, Hail, King of the Jews: and they smote Him with their hands. ‡ And they spit upon Him, and took the reed, and smote Him on the head. § And *the soldiers* took Jesus, and He, bearing His Cross, went forth into a place called the place of a skull: where they crucified Him, and two other with Him, on either side one, and Jesus in the midst. After this, Jesus knowing all things *which should come to pass*, said, I thirst; and they filled a sponge with vinegar, and put it upon hyssop, and put it to His mouth. ‖ And when He had tasted thereof, He would not drink, *but* said, ¶ It is finished; and He bowed His head, and gave up the ghost. ** And *immediately* the earth did quake, and the sun was darkened. And the veil of the Temple was rent, and the rocks rent, and the graves were opened, and *those who* slept arose; *which things*, when the centurion saw, *he* said, Truly, this was the Son of God. †† *At length* one of the soldiers with a spear pierced His side, and forthwith came thereout blood and water. And he that saw it bare record, and *we know that his* record is true.

℣. The Lord be with you.

℟. And with thy spirit.

Let us pray.

O Lord Jesu Christ, Who for us sinners didst place Thy hands and Thy feet, and Thy whole Body upon the wood of the Cross; and didst bear the crown of thorns, set upon Thy head by the Jews in dishonour of Thy most Holy Body; and hanging upon the Cross didst suffer five wounds for the sake of us sinners, and hast redeemed us by Thy sacred Blood; grant us, we beseech Thee, O Lord, this day, and every day, the practice of penitence, abstinence, patience, humility, and chastity; and light, sense, understanding, and knowledge of the truth, even unto the end. Through Thee, Jesu Christ, Saviour of the world, King of Glory. Who.

* This Passion was compiled by Pope John XXII., at Avignon, three days before his death; for which he granted to all who said or heard it, being truly contrite penitents, three hundred days' indulgence.

† John xix. 1-3. ‡ Matt. xxvii. 30. § John xix. 16-18; 28, 29. ‖ Matt. xxvii. 34. ¶ John xix. 30. ** Matt. xxvii. 51-54. †† John xix. 34, 35.

Divers Benedictions.*

THE BLESSING OF SALT AND WATER.

¶ *On all Sundays after Prime and the Chapter, let the Blessing** *be made of salt-water at the step of the Quire, on this wise*—

I exorcise thee, O creature of salt, by the living God, + by the true God, + by the holy God, + by the God Who commanded thee to be cast into the water by Elias the prophet, that the barrenness of the same might be healed, that thou become salt for the preservation of them that believe, and be to all who take thee salvation of soul and body; and from the place wherein thou shalt be sprinkled let every delusion and wickedness of the Devil, and all unclean spirits, when adjured, fly and depart, by Him; Who shall come to judge the quick and the dead, and the world by fire. Amen.

Let us pray.

We humbly implore Thy boundless loving-kindness, Almighty and everlasting God, that of Thy bounty Thou wouldst deign to ble + ss and sanc + tify this creature of salt, which Thou hast given for the use of mankind; let it be unto all who take it health of mind and body; that whatsoever shall be touched or sprinkled with it be freed from all manner of uncleanness, and from all assaults of spiritual wickedness. Through.

¶ *Then let the* Exorcism of the Water *be said.*

I exorcise thee, O creature of water, in the Name of God + the Father Almighty; and in the Name of Jesus Christ, + His Son, our Lord; and in the power of the Holy + Ghost; that thou mayest become water exorcised for the chasing away of all the power of the enemy; that thou mayest have strength to cast out the enemy himself and his apostate angels, by the power of the same, our Lord Jesus Christ, Who shall come to judge the quick and dead, and the world by fire. Amen.

Let us pray.

O God, Who for the salvation of mankind hast hidden one of Thy greatest sacraments in the element of water, graciously give ear when we call upon Thee, and pour upon this element, prepared for divers purifications, the power of Thy blessing; let Thy creature serve in Thy Mysteries, by Divine grace be effectual for casting out devils and for driving away diseases,

* The place of these varies in the editions: they are all put together here.

that on whatsoever in the houses or places of the faithful this water shall be sprinkled, it may be freed from all uncleanness, and delivered from hurt. Let not the blast of pestilence nor disease remain there; let every enemy that lieth in wait depart; if there be ought which hath ill-will to the safety and quietness of the inhabitants, let it flee away at the sprinkling of this water, that they being saved by the invocation of Thy Holy Name, may be defended from all that rise up against them. Through.

¶ *Here let the Priest cast salt into the water in the form of a Cross, saying—*

Let this become a mixture of salt and water, in the Name of the Father, + and of the Son, + and of the Holy Ghost. + Amen.

℣. The Lord be with you,

℞. And with thy spirit.

Let us pray.

O God, Author of invincible might, King of a dominion which cannot be moved and ever a Conqueror, Who puttest down the strength of all that rise up against Thee, overcomest the rage of the adversary, and by Thy power dost cast down his wickedness; we, O Lord, with fear, humbly entreat and implore Thee mercifully to look upon this creature of salt and water; after Thy loving-kindness graciously illumine and sanctify + it, that wheresoever it shall be sprinkled, by the invocation of Thy holy Name all unclean spirits which lie in wait may be cast out, and the dread of the serpent be chased far away; and let the presence of the Holy Ghost vouchsafe to be with us who ask Thy mercy in every place. Through.

¶ *Whilst the water is sprinkled, is said—*

Ant. Thou shalt purge me with hyssop, and I shall be clean; Thou shalt wash me, and I shall be whiter than snow.

Ps. li. Have mercy upon me, O God, after Thy great goodness.

Ant. Thou shalt purge me with hyssop, and I shall be clean; Thou shalt wash me, and I shall be whiter than snow.

℣. According to the multitude of Thy mercies do away mine offences.

Ant. Thou shalt purge me with hyssop, and I shall be clean; Thou shalt wash me, and I shall be whiter than snow.

℣. Glory be. As it was.

Ant. Thou shalt wash me, and I shalt be whiter than snow.

¶ *After the sprinkling of the Holy Water, let the Priest say at the step of the Quire—*

℣. Shew us Thy mercy, O Lord.

℟. And grant us Thy salvation.

Let us pray.

Graciously hear us, O Lord, Holy Father, Almighty, everlasting God; and vouchsafe to send Thy holy angel from Heaven to keep, cherish, protect, visit, and defend all who dwell in this place. Through.

THE BLESSING OF BREAD.

Ps. O all ye works of the Lord.

℣. The Lord be with you.

℟. And with thy spirit.

Let us pray.

Ble + ss, O Lord, this creature of bread, as Thou didst bless the five loaves in the wilderness, that all who taste of it may receive alike health of body and soul. Through.

¶ *Then let the bread be sprinkled with Holy Water.*

ANOTHER.

℣. Our help is in the Name of the Lord.

℟. Who hath made heaven and earth.

℣. The Lord be with you.

℟. And with thy spirit.

Let us pray.

O Lord, Holy Father, Almighty and everlasting God, deign to ble + ss this bread with Thy spiritual benediction, that it may be health of mind and body to all who receive it, and a defence against all diseases and snares of the enemy; through Jesus Christ, Thy Son, our Lord, Who didst come down from Heaven and give us Bread which is the life and salvation of mankind. Who.

THE BLESSING OF BREAD ON SUNDAYS.

¶ *First let the Priest read the* Gospel, "In the beginning."*

℣. Blessed be the Name of the Lord,

℟. From this time forth for evermore.

℣. Let us give thanks unto the Lord.

℟. Thanks be to God.

℣. The Lord be with you.

℟. And with thy spirit.

Let us pray.

The Collect.

Bless, O Lord, *as above.*

¶ *Then let the Priest sprinkle the bread with Holy Water.*

THE BLESSING OF THE PASCHAL LAMB, OF EGGS AND HERBS, AT EASTER.†

℣. The Lord be with you.

℟. And with thy spirit.

Let us pray.

O God, ruler of heaven and earth, Who givest food to all flesh, and fillest every living thing with Thy blessing, ble + ss and sancti + fy this Paschal lamb, and grant us who receive Thy gifts health both of mind and body. Through.

O God, Who art the Maker of all flesh, Who didst give laws unto Noah and his sons concerning clean and unclean animals: and as Thou didst give eggs and herbs to mankind, didst allow them to eat of clean beasts; and also didst command Moses and Thy people in Egypt on the evening of the Passover to eat the Paschal lamb as a type of our Lord Jesus Christ, by Whose Blood Thou didst redeem to Thyself out of the world all the first-born, and in that night didst command all in Egypt to be smitten, preserving Thy people, marked out beforehand with the blood of the lamb; vouchsafe, O Lord God Almighty, to bl + ss and sancti + fy this Paschal lamb, that whosoever of Thy faithful people shall eat

* *i.e.*, this being the last Gospel at Mass, the bread was probably blessed in the sacristy afterwards.

† '4 P.V. Missal.

of it may, of Thy goodness, be filled with Thy grace and heavenly benediction, O Lord, Saviour of the world, by Whom all things were made and created from the beginning. Who.

¶ *Then let all the things be sprinkled with Holy Water, and censed by the Priest.*

THE BLESSING OF A SCRIP AND STAFF.*

℣. The Lord be with you,

℟. And with thy spirit.

Let us pray.

O Lord Jesu Christ, Who of Thy unspeakable mercy, at the bidding of the Father, and by the co-operation of the Holy Ghost, wast willing to come down from Heaven, and to seek the sheep that was lost by the deceit of the Devil, and to carry him back on Thine own shoulders to the flock of the Heavenly Country; and didst command the sons of Mother Church by prayer to ask, by holy living to seek, and by knocking to persevere; that so they may the more speedily find the reward of saving life; we humbly call upon Thee, that Thou wouldst be pleased to ble+ss these scrips (*or* this scrip), and these staves (*or* this staff), that whosoever for the love of Thy Name shall desire to wear the same at his side, or to hang it at his neck, or to bear it in his hands, and so on his pilgrimage to seek the aid of the saints, with the accompaniment of humble prayer, being protected by the guardianship of Thy Right Hand, may be found meet to attain unto the joys of the everlasting vision, through Thee, O Saviour of the world. Who.

¶ *Here let the scrip be sprinkled with Holy Water, and let the Priest put it round each Pilgrim's neck, saying—*

In the Name of our Lord Jesus Christ, receive this scrip, the habit of thy pilgrimage, that after due chastisement thou mayest be found worthy to reach in safety the shrine of the saints to which thou desirest to go; and after the accomplishment of thy journey mayest return to us in health. Through.

¶ *Here let him give the staff to the Pilgrim, saying—*

Receive this staff for thy support in the travail and toil of thy

* This and the next are generally found after the Service for those going a journey.

pilgrimage, that thou mayest be able to overcome all the hosts of the enemy, and reach in safety the shrine of the saints whither thou desirest to go; and having obediently fulfilled thy course, may return again to us with joy. Through.

THE BLESSING OF A CROSS FOR ONE ON A PILGRIMAGE TO JERUSALEM.

℣. The Lord be with you.

℟. And with thy spirit.

Let us pray.

O God, Whose power is invincible and pity cannot be measured, the aid and sole comfort of pilgrims; Who givest unto Thy servants armour which cannot be overcome; we beseech Thee be pleased to ble+ss this Cross which is humbly devoted to Thee, that the banner of the venerated Cross, the figure whereof is upon it, may be a most mighty strength to Thy servants against the wicked temptations of the old enemy; a defence by the way, a protection in Thy house, and a security to us on every side. Through.

¶ *Here let the garment marked with the Cross be sprinkled with Holy Water, and given to the Pilgrim, the Priest saying—*

Receive this dress whereupon the sign of the Cross of the Lord our Saviour is traced, that through it safety, benediction, and strength to journey in prosperity, may accompany thee to the Sepulchre of Him Who, with God the Father and the Holy Ghost, liveth and reigneth one God, world without end. Amen.

THE END.

VARIATION between the text of the Sarum Pontifical at Cambridge and the Exeter one, are found at the end of the Blessing of the Oil for the Sick, the first and second of the Blessings of the Oil for Catechumens, and in the latter part of the third Blessing of the Chrism. Reference has already been made, in the Introduction, to the state of the English MS. Missals, etc., previous to the discovery of printing. Perhaps nothing illustrates the remarks there made better than the case of the English Pontificals. None were ever printed; hence it cannot be determined for certain what the Sarum or any other Use was. In the library at Cambridge are four MS. Pontificals, all assuming to be *Secundum Usum Sarum.* Of these, one is in text Roman (!); but it follows the English Use in consecrating the Oil of Catechumens before and not after the Chrism. The other three are, a MS. of the xiith. century, which belonged to Winchester Cathedral; one of the xiiith. century, which belonged to Ely; and a third of the xvth. century, which probably belonged to Lincoln, (this is *the* Sarum Pontifical so often mentioned in Appendix A. as well as by Maskell and others; it is preferable, however, to call MSS. by the name of the Church or district to which they belong, if ascertainable). Now, the Exeter Pontifical—the text of which is followed in Appendix A.—contains, in addition to the Exeter Consecration of Holy Oils, a section at the end, *Qualiter consecretur Crisma in Ecclesiâ Sarum*; and it was this circumstance, coupled with the fact that the above deviations (being mostly at the end of the prayers) did not at once catch the eye, which induced the belief that the text was the same in both MSS. Dismissing from the mind, as one must, in the case of all English MS. Missals, etc., any such supposition as that because they profess to be *Secundum Usum Sarum*, they therefore are,* there appear to be three different texts, and two kinds of ceremonial in the service in question, in English Pontificals, Winchester, Ely, and Lincoln agree in the above-mentioned deviations in *text*, in opposition to Exeter, and the fourth MS. Pontifical at Cambridge, which is totally distinct. In *ceremonial*, Exeter, Winchester, Ely, and the fourth MS. at Cambridge, agree in respect to the procession taking place at *Te igitur*, and not at *Per quem* as at Sarum; whilst the Lincoln MS. stands alone, coinciding with the description of Sarum ceremonial in the Exeter Pontifical, and in the *Tractatus*. These last two descriptions are, of course, the only real guide to Sarum Use; and as the majority of MSS. agree in the deviations in text in opposition to that of Exeter, it may be assumed that the Lincoln M.S. best represents in text and ceremonial the Sarum Use.

* The fact is, this term was used, just as the term *Secundum Usum Romanum* was abroad, simply to signify that that was the standard Missal of the country; the conclusion that if it was, it must therefore be exactly followed, seems never to have occurred to the compilers of these MSS.

APPENDIX A.*

THE CONSECRATION OF HOLY OILS.

¶ *Let the Bishop go at the Office of Mass with a procession as on other Doubles; let two assist him, in copes, on the right and left, at the Confession, and afterwards retire. Then let the Service proceed until* Thee, therefore; *at which let three Ministers get ready in albs and amices, and with banners; and three Deacons with veils over their shoulders, each bearing one of the three oils, and one to carry the silk canopy; also let the three Archdeacons in silk copes fill the Holy-oil stocks.*

¶ *Before* By Whom, O Lord, *let the Bishop withdraw a little from the Altar, and let the Archdeacon of Berkshire say thrice aloud,* The Oil of the Sick, *and the Deacon who carries the same, and is preceded by a banner, following him; and let the Deacon† present the oil-stock to the Bishop, and the Bishop make the sign of the Cross over it thrice, and breathe thrice upon it, saying in the hearing of those about him—*

I exorcise thee, most unclean spirit; and put thee to flight with all thy assaults, Satan, and every illusion of wicked enemies, by the majesty of God the Father, Almighty, Who by His marvellous power created the heavens, the earth, the sea, and all that in them is; that, together with all thy poisonous lies, thou mayest depart far from this creature of oil at the coming benediction. In the Name of the Father +, and of the Son +, and of the Holy Ghost +, let this oil be to all who shall be anointed therewith a spiritual unction and perfect medicine, to confirm in the Lord the temple of man's estate, by the co-operation therein of the grace and virtue of the Holy Ghost, through Jesus Christ, our Redeemer; to Whom, with the Father, be all praise and honour for ever and ever. Amen.

THE BLESSING OF THE OIL OF THE SICK.

Let us pray.

Almighty God, Who for the need of the sick didst visit the world to show forth Thy healing power, and by Thy presence didst cause every pain and sickness to flee away; regard these Thy servants, that what this day in the commemoration of the Holy Supper is to be done by our ministry, may be perfected by Thy power; and let not a sinner's blessing displease Thee, forasmuch as Thou art the purifier and pardoner of all Thy priests. Do Thou also, O Lord, Who, according to the word of Elisha, didst so heal Naaman the Syrian, after he had washed in Jordan seven times, that his flesh came again as the flesh of a little child, and he was cleansed of leprosy; heal and cleanse all that are anointed with this oil from all leprosy both spiritual and bodily; grant, also, O Lord, that they who are touched by this oil, may remain holy and undefiled vessels, and may ever abound with the sevenfold grace of the Holy Ghost. Who.

We beseech Thee, O Lord, Holy Father, Almighty, everlasting God, send forth Thy Holy Spirit from on high upon this fatness of the olive, which Thou hast been pleased to bring out of the green tree, and through the present influence of the Holy Ghost let it be enriched with heavenly benediction, to the refreshment of bodies, and salvation of souls; we pray Thee, O Lord, Who art the true Saviour and Physician, Who also hast said they that are whole need not a physician, but they that are sick; pour forth upon this oil the healing power of Thy bene+diction for us that are

* The text followed is that of the Exeter Pontifical. The rubrics have been compared with the Sarum one at Cambridge and the Registrum S. Osmundi.

† Sarum Pontifical, *Archdeacon*.

in sickness and in need of Thy Divine remedies, that it may be to all who touch it, and are anointed therewith, the salvation of their souls, the protection of their bodies, the stilling of their passions, and the restoration of saving health. Let this oil, O Father Almighty, be sancti+fied, as Thou saidst by the Apostle, Is any sick among you? let him be anointed with holy oil in the Name of the Lord, and He shall raise him up; and if he have committed sins, they shall be forgiven him; to the end that we, O Lord, trusting in this Thy sanction, may all receive the same for an holy unction and spiritual cure, to the banishing of our infirmities, and the obtaining forgiveness of all our sins. In the Name of Jesus Christ, Thy Son, our Lord.

¶ *Then let the Archdeacon and his ministers retire in the same order in which they came.*

¶ *A little before the Blessing over the people, let the Archdeacon of Wiltshire, saying thrice aloud* Holy Oil, *approach in the same manner, the second Deacon* preceding him with the Oil of the Catechumens and a banner; and let the Bishop make the sign of the Cross over it thrice, and breathe thrice upon it, saying—*

I exorcise thee, creature of oil, in the Name of God the Father + Almighty, by this invocation + of Jesus Christ, and by the power of the Holy Ghost; that by this adjuration of the Trinity most high and one Godhead, all the wicked power and malice of the Devil, and all fierce assaults and hurtful illusions of enemies, may be turned back and put to flight, and utterly depart from thy substance, which was created for man's use; that in the Name of the Lord thou mayest become a holy oil, a saving unction, purified also by holy mysteries, for the sanctification of flesh and of spirit, and for the remission of sins to all who shall be anointed of thee, to the end that they may obtain in Baptism the grace of the Holy Spirit; that like as the breasts and shoulders of all receive the outward sign of Confirmation, so through thee their minds and souls may be inwardly sanctified with a heavenly benediction, in the Name of the Father +, and of the Son +, and of the Holy Ghost +,

℣. For ever and ever.
℟. Amen.
℣. The Lord be with you.
℟. And with thy spirit.

THE BLESSING OF THE OIL OF CATECHUMENS.

Let us pray.

O Lord God, Father Almighty, Whose Only-Begotten, that He might show Himself to be the Lord, worked numberless miracles on the Jews, healed the paralytic, cleansed the lepers, cast out devils, raised the dead, and at the last was crucified that He might crucify evil spirits and quicken the dead; sanctify this oil, and let all who shall be anointed therewith be enriched with the grace of eternal sanctification, and be made fruitful with all the fatness of the earth and the dew of Heaven. Grant also, Lord God, that our benediction may abide sure and mighty in His Name, Whom all creation serveth; Whom Cherubim and Seraphim, and all the orders of Heaven, unite in praising, saying, Holy, Holy, Holy, Lord God of Hosts, Who livest and reignest in the Holy Trinity, One God, world without end.

Let us pray.

O God, Who by the power of Thy Holy Spirit dost strengthen the very beginnings of tender minds, we pray Thee to ble+ss and sanctify this oil,

* Sarum Pontifical, *Archdeacon.*

grant unto those who by the anointing of this creature shall come unto the laver of blessed regeneration, cleansing of mind and body, that, if any spirits of the enemy remain and cleave unto them, at the touch of this hallowed oil they may depart. Let no place be left for spiritual wickedness; no advantage be given to apostate powers; no occasion to lie in wait be permitted for evil visitants; but to Thy servants who come near, and by the operation of Thy Holy Spirit, let this be an unction for their cleansing, favourable and profitable unto the salvation of those who shall also obtain the birth of heavenly regeneration in the Sacrament of Baptism. Through.

¶ *After this let the Bishop go back to his chair, and the Deacon carry back the Holy-oil stock to its place; then let the Archdeacon of Dorset say thrice aloud* The Oil of Chrism, *and let the Ministers prepare to bring the same. Let them proceed in the following order: First, three banners; then two Acolytes in albs; thirdly, two Thurifers; fourthly, two Sub-Deacons (from the Bishop) with Texts; fifthly, the Deacon with the Chrism, over which is carried a silk canopy; and let three boys in surplices precede him, singing the following hymn, an Acolyte with a Cross being on either side of him, and behind him the Archdeacons, with the Archdeacon of Dorset in the midst*—

℣. O Redeemer, hear, we pray Thee;
We who hold us fast by Thee.

Choir. O Redeemer.

℣. Hear, thou Judge of the departed,
Only hope of all mankind;
Hear their cry who plead before Thee,
The gift of peace the faithful find.

Ch. O Redeemer.

℣. May the Father here be present,
Who, albeit invisibly,
Above Thy fellows with the unction
Of gladness hath anointed Thee.

Ch. O Redeemer.

℣. May the Holy Ghost be present,
Who, when ceased the deluge rain,
To the Ark, the Church's figure,
Brought the olive branch again.

Ch. O Redeemer.

℣. This, the Tree of Light the parent
Did present for consecration:
This, our lowly band adoring,
Brings to Him, the world's salvation.

Ch. O Redeemer.

℣. Duly vested at the Altar,
Suppliant the Bishop stands;
Rightly ordering the Chrism
With his consecrating hands.*

Ch. O Redeemer.

* The Exeter Pontifical makes the Bishop stand at the right side of the Altar at this verse, and then sit again; and in the Service of that Church for the Consecration of Holy Oils which it contains asserts that this is the Sarum use.

℣. Thou this Oil vouchsafe to hallow,
King of the eternal land;
Sign of living power to vanquish
Satan and his demon band.

Ch. O Redeemer.

℣. Sin, from souls by Holy Water
Hallowed, doth flee apace;
Brows, by Holy Oil anointed,
Gifts adorn of special grace.

Ch. O Redeemer.

℣. In the Virgin's womb indwelling,
Son unto her heart most dear;
Light bestow, prevent the darkness
Of all who anointed are.

Ch. O Redeemer.

℣. Let this be a feast-day to us,
Through the ages evermore;
With meet praises consecrated,
Nor wax old till time be o'er.

Ch. O Redeemer.

¶ *Let the Bishop return to the Altar, and let the vessel with the Oil of Chrism be brought him; with which let him mix the balsam, previously prepared and blessed, saying—*

Let this mixture of balsam and oil be to all anointed therewith a propitiation and saving defence for ever and ever. In the Name of the Father, and of the Son, and of the Holy Ghost. Amen.

¶ *Then let the Bishop turn to the East; let him make the sign of the Cross over the oil-stock thrice, and breathe thrice upon it, and begin the Hymn,* Come, Holy Ghost,* *genuflecting, the Choir and Clergy singing alternate verses; which being ended, let him say—*

I exorcise thee, creature of oil, by the power of God Almighty, Who made heaven, earth, the sea, and all that in them is. Let all power of the enemy, all the host of the Devil, and all assailiants, together with every illusion of Satan, be rooted out and put to flight from before thee; that thou mayest become, to all who shall be anointed with thee, the adopter of children by the power of the Holy Ghost. In the Name of the Father, Almighty ✠, and in the love of His Son Jesus Christ our Lord ✠. Who.

℣. The Lord be with you.
℟. And with thy spirit.

Let us pray

dearly beloved brethren, unto the Lord, the Father Almighty, Maker of heaven and earth, Who, in the marvellous power of His Only-Begotten Son, did succour the world which was miserably perishing, to the intent that upon us, unworthy and without merit, who should call upon His Holy Name, He might vouchsafe to bestow the aid of His heavenly compassion, and to purify our hearts by the sevenfold gifts of the Holy Spirit; that we, being cleansed from the stain of our sins, may be made meet to prepare the saving Christ; that the grace of Almighty God may aid us in this office; that what is to be obediently performed by us may be perfected by His own most holy bene✠diction, and the Divine co-operation of the Holy Ghost; and that this oil, sanc✠tified and renewed by God, may by the life-

* See p. 290.

giving droppings of fragrant balsam be made a holy + Chrism for confirming the Orders of the Church, for promoting to offices of dignity, for sanctifying the laver of Baptism, and for signing with the sign of the Cross the children newly regenerate; that it be also a Chrism and assurance of eternal safety to all who shall be anointed therewith for the everlasting salvation of souls; our Lord Jesus Christ, the Only-Begotten of The Same, and the Holy Ghost from Both proceeding, thereto agreeing and assisting, Who in the Holy Trinity liveth and reigneth, One True God, world without end. Amen.

O Lord God of Hosts, lively hope of mankind, salvation and life of all that live godly, Who of Thy righteousness and for the praise of Thy glory hast ordained that the estate of Catholic Orders and royal dignities should be consecrated with the oil of gladness and the Chrism of salvation; we bow before Thee, entreating Thee, most merciful, to enlighten our senses and consciences with Thy pleasant brightness, and further us in these holy ceremonies with the fulness of heavenly blessings, for the preparation of the healing medicines of our souls. For the consecration of this health-giving unction, Thou, O Lord, hast provided for the use of man all things which spring out of the earth, but more especially hast Thou appointed the fruit of the olive for the salvation of men under both dispensations; seeing that Thou hast promised by Thy Prophet, that upon unction with holy oil we shall be cleansed from all sin, and as the Most High Priest for ever hast consecrated the rank and dignity of the Church's Orders with the oil of Chrism, we beseech Thee, O Lord, let Thy invisible Presence be with us, and send forth Thy Holy Spirit from on high upon us, who confess Thee in One Nature and substance of Three Persons, to make by our office and ministry a fragrant balsam of living odours, and pour it in bless+ing upon the oil of Consecration, and by the soothing commingling of both make perfect a saving Chrism for the salvation of them that believe. Sanctify+, we beseech Thee, O Lord God, this oil and balsam with the benediction of Thy Godhead, whereby, being made a Chrism of salvation, let it cause Thy children renewed unto Thee in the hope of adoption to rise unto the newness of heavenly regeneration. Let this Chrism, O Lord, be sanc+tified in the presence of Thy Godhead, be redolent of the sweet scent of angelic odours, and be a spiritual medicine and restoration of soul and body, and by the abundant outpouring of the Holy Ghost become the salvation of all; and let all who shall be worthily anointed with this holy oil be made partakers of eternal gladness, through the same Holy Ghost. Who.

Almighty and unsearchable God and Father, Who, when Thou didst purpose to send on earth Thine Only-Begotten Son, Who, was co-eternally with Thee before the world, didst also bestow upon the world the fulness of grace; Whom Thou didst also graciously anoint with holy oil, royal oil, the oil of Chrism, above His fellows, that He might have none co-equal with Him among all the prophets, kings, and priests, and might alone appear more perfect in the flesh; and that it might be plainly shown that none shall ascend into the Kingdom of Heaven except he be sanctified by the putting on of holy Chrism: do Thou, by that same Jesus Christ of Nazareth, Whom John baptized in Jordan for our salvation, pour upon this Chrism Thy consecrating grace, and shed forth upon all the dew of the most Holy Spirit Himself; defend them from the malice and power of the perpetual enemy, and from the prison of hell: and give them part in the joys of the Kingdom of Heaven, of His bounteous gift Who sitteth at Thy Right Hand, God and Lord, and with Thee and the Holy Ghost co-equally liveth and reigneth.

¶ *Here let him change his tone, and chant the Preface following*—

℣. For ever and ever.
℟. Amen.
℣. The Lord be with you.
℟. And with thy spirit.
℣. Lift up your hearts.
℟. We lift them up unto the Lord.
℣. Let us give thanks unto our Lord God.
℟. It is meet and right so to do.

It is very meet, right, just, and our bounden duty that we should, at all times and in all places, give thanks unto Thee, O Lord, Holy Father, Almighty, Everlasting God; Who, in the beginning, amongst other gifts of Thy goodness and loving-kindness, didst command the earth to bring forth trees yielding fruit, among which sprang up olives bearing this rich liquid the fruit whereof should minister unto the holy Chrism. For David also, foreknowing in the spirit of prophecy the Sacrament of Thy grace, made mention also of oil to make us of a cheerful countenance; and when of old the sins of the world were washed out by the outpouring of a deluge, the dove, manifesting the similitude of the gift to come, by an olive branch brought tidings of the restoration of peace to the earth. Which thing hath in the last times been declared by manifest tokens, forasmuch as, when the waters of Baptism have washed away the guilt of all sin, this Anointing of Oil maketh our countenances cheerful and calm. Then, too, Thou gavest commandment to Moses Thy servant, that, after he had washed Aaron his brother with water, he should, by pouring on him this oil, ordain him priest. To this a higner honour was given when Thy Son Jesus Christ our Lord required of John to baptize Him in the waters of Jordan, in that Thou didst send down from above the Holy Ghost, in the likeness of a dove, upon Thy Only-Begotten, in Whom, by witness of the voice which followed, Thou didst declare Thyself well pleased. This it was Thou didst most clearly show, which the Prophet David sang of, that He should be anointed with the oil of gladness above His fellows. Thee, therefore, we entreat, O Lord, Holy Father, Almighty, Everlasting God, by the same Thy Son Jesus Christ, vouchsafe to bl+ess the fatness of this creature with Thy bene+diction, and mingle with it the power of the Holy + Ghost, by the co-operation of the might of Thine Anointed, from Whose Holy Name Chrism has received its title; wherewith Thou hast anointed priests, kings, prophets, and martyrs, that they, being lifted up by these degrees, according to the Sacrament of Ordination, and anointed with the consecration of unction, might put on the robe of incorruption. Therefore, O Lord, we entreat Thy almighty power that the creature of this holy Chrism may be an anointing of salvation to those who have been born again of water and of the Holy Ghost, and that Thou wouldst make them partakers of eternal life, and to have part and lot in heavenly glory. *(In a low voice)*—Through the same our Lord Jesus Christ Thy Son. Who.

¶ *After this, let the Deacon with the Chrism hold it covered in the veil on the right of the Altar till after the* Agnus Dei. *Then let the Bishop proceed with the Fraction, and after the Blessing over the people let him say,* And His peace be ever with you. ℟. And with thy spirit. *Then let the Precentor begin the* Agnus Dei, *and let the Chrism be brought to the Bishop to kiss, he saying,* Hail, Holy Chrism; *and let it then be sent round and kissed as the* Pax. *Then let the procession with the Oils return in the same order to the Sacristy, and Mass proceed as in the Missal (see p. 139).*

APPENDIX B.

A COMPARATIVE TABLE OF THE EPISTLES, SEQUENCES AND GOSPELS IN THE PROPER OF SEASONS, AS THEY STAND IN THE SARUM, YORK, AND HEREFORD MISSALS RESPECTIVELY.*

	SARUM.	YORK.	HEREFORD.
Advent Sunday	*Ep.* Rom. xiii. 11-14	As Sarum	As Sarum
	Gos. Matt. xxi. 1-9	As Sarum	Mark i. 1-8
Monday and Tuesday aft.	*Ep.* As on Sunday	As Sarum	As Sarum
	Gos. As on Sunday	Mark i. 2-8	As York
Wednesday	*Ep.* Jas. v. 8-10	As Sarum	Is. li. 1-6
	Gos. Mark i. 1-8	Matt. iii. 7-11	As York
Friday	*Ep.* Is. li. 1-8	Is. xxviii. 16, 17, 29; xxx. 18	Is. xlii. 1-13
	Gos. Matt. iii. 1-6	Luke iii. 7-17	Luke iii. 7-18
2 Sun. in Advent.			
Wednesday	*Ep.* Zach. viii. 3-8	Is. li. 1-6	Is. xliii. 5-3
	Gos. Matt. xi. 11-15	As Sarum	As Sarum
Friday	*Ep.* Is. lxii. 6-12	Is. xli. 27; xlii. 1-13	Is. li. 1-6
	Gos. John i. 15-18	As Sarum	Mark i. 1-8
3 Sun. and Ember Days.			
4 Sun. in Advent.			
Wednesday	*Ep.* Joel. ii. 23-27, iii. 17-21	Is. xvi. 1-5	2 Pet. iii. 8-14
	Gos. Luke vii. 17-28	Matt. iii. 1-6	Matt. iii. 1-6
Friday	*Ep.* Zach. ii. 10-13	Is. xxviii, 16, 17, 29, xxx. 18	Is. xvi. 1-5
	Gos. Mark viii. 15-26	Luke iii. 7-17	As on 4th Sunday
1 Mass Christmas Day		No "Laudes Deo dicam."	
2 Mass	"Sonant Regi"	"Lætabundus exultet"	"Cœleste organum"
3 Mass	"Cœleste Organum"	"Christi Hodierna Celebramus Natalitia"	As York
S. Thos. Cant.	"Solenne Canticum"	"Spe Mercedis"	"Mundo Christus oritur"
VIth. Day	"Christi Hodierna"	"Cœleste Organum."	"Lux Fulgebit." As 2nd Mass Christmas, but if Sun. then as Sarum
Circumcision	"Eja Recolemus"	"Lætabundus"	"Eja Recolemus"
Vigil Epiphany		"Lætabundus"	*Gosp.* As 2nd Mass Christmas
In Octave		*Sequence* divided into three parts, at "Balaam" and "Magi"	As Sarum, with iv. *Sequences* to be used alternately — *i.e.*, "Verbum Bonum," "Lætabundus," "Gaude Virgo Ecclesia," "Gaudele vos Fideles"

* Where there are Latin words they are the first words of Sequences; it so happens that when the Epistles and Gospels are the same the Sequences often differ.

	SARUM.	YORK.	HEREFORD.
Sunday in Octave	As on Day, but Gosp. John i.	Rom. iii. 19-26. All the Sequence is said Matt. iii. 13-17	As Sarum, with the Sequence.
Octave Day	Is. xxv. etc.* Matt. iii. 13-17	As on Epiphany As on Epiph., with all the Sequences	As Sarum As Sarum
1 Sun. aft. Oct. Epiph.		"Cœleste Organum"	"Lætabundus" or "Cœleste"
Wednesday	Rom. x. 1-4 Matt. iv. 12-17	1 Tim. ii. 1-7 Matt. xxi. 28-32	Rom. iii. 19-26 Mark i. 4-11
Friday	Rom. xiii. 1-6 Luke iv. 14-22	2 Pet. ii. 16-21 Matt. iv. 12-17	As York As York
2 Sun. aft. Oct. Epiph.		"Lætabundus" or "Cœleste"	As York
Wednesday	1 Tim. i. 15-17 Mark vi. 1-6	Coloss. i. 25-28 Matt. iv. 23-25	As York Luke iv. 14-22
Friday	Rom. xiv. 14-26 Luke iv. 31-37	1 Tim. i. 15-17 As Sarum	As York Mark i. 40-44
3 Sun. aft. Oct. Epiph.		"Cœleste" or "Voce Jubilantes," if after Pur. B.V.M.	"Lætabundus" or "Cœleste"
Wednesday	Rom. xv. 30-33 Mark iii. 1-5	Heb. iii. 1-6 Mark iii. 6-15	As York As York
Friday	1 Cor. iii. 16-23 Matt. iv. 23-25	1 John ii. 9-13 Luke v. 12-15	As York Mark iii. 6-15
4 Sun. aft. Oct. Epiph.			
Wednesday	1 Cor. vii. 1-5 Luke ix. 57-62	Rom. v. 18-21 Mark vi. 1-6	As York As Sarum
Friday	1 Cor. vii. 20-24 Mark x. 12-16	2 Tim. i. 8-13 Luke ix. 57-62	Rom. xi. 25-35 As Sarum
5 Sun. aft. Oct.	Matt. xiii. 24-30	Luke iv. 14-22	As Sarum
Wednesday	1 Tim. ii. 1-7 Matt. xxi. 28-32	Rom. v. 18-21 Mark vi. 1-6	None None
Friday	None	As on previous Friday	None
LXX.			
Wednesday	2 Cor. iv. 3-12 Mark ix. 30-37	Heb. vi. 4-9 As Sarum	Heb. iv. 11-16 As Sarum
Friday	2 Cor. iv. 13-18 Matt. xii. 30-37	Heb. iv. 11-16 Luke ix. 51-56	1 John v. 10-20 As York
LX.			
Wednesday	2 Cor. i. 23, 24, ii. 1-11 Mark iv. 1-9	Heb. xii. 3-9 Matt. xii. 30-37	As York As York
Friday	2 Cor. v. 11-15 Luke xvii. 20-37	Heb. xii. 11-17 As Sarum	As York As Sarum
L.			
Ash-Wednesday	The differences between the three Missals are unimportant, though numerous.		
Maundy Thursday	According to Hereford, all; according to York, the principal persons are to be communicated.		

* See p. 39.

	SARUM.	YORK.	HEREFORD.
Good Friday.	In Hereford the Priest communicated himself, saying nothing except *In the Name of the Lord*, only saying the Confession previously; in York, the *Confiteor* and prayers for communicating, but no *Let the obedient performance* is said.		
Holy Saturday	V. Lesson—Isaiah lv. 1-11	No *Rex Sanctorum*, but a long Litany is said.	
Easter Day.			
Monday	"Zyma Vetus"	"LaudesSalvatori"	"Prome Casta Concio."
Tuesday	"Prome CastaConcio"	"VictimæPaschali"	"ConcinatOrbis."
Wednesday	"Concinnat Orbis"	As Sarum	"VictimæPaschali"
Thursday	"Dic Nobis Quibus"	"Prome Casta"	As Sarum
Friday	"Victimæ Paschali"	"Zyma Vetus"	"PsalleLyricaCarmina."
Saturday	"Mane Prima Sabbati"	As Sarum	As York
Low Sunday	All as on Easter Day. "Laudes Salvatori"	Quasimodo Mass "Mane Prima"	Quasimodo Mass. "LaudesSalvatori"
Wednesday	1 Cor. xv. 12-23 Mark xvi. 9-13	As Sarum As Sarum	Heb. xiii. 17-21 As York
Friday	Heb. xiii. 17-21 Matt. xxviii. 8-15	As Sarum As Sarum	1 John v. 4-10 As York
2 Sunday	No *Sequence**	"VictimæPaschali"	As York
Wednesday	1 Peter i. 18-25 Luke xxiv. 1-12	As Sarum As Sarum	1 Cor. xv. 12-21 As York
Friday	Rom. v. 18-21 Matt. ix. 14-17	As Sarum As Sarum	1 Cor. xv. 22-28 As York
3 Sunday	No *Sequence*	"Victimæ"	As York
Friday	1 Thess. v. 5-11 John xii. 46-50	As Sarum As Sarum	Rom. xiv. 7-12 As York
4 Sunday	No *Sequence*	"Victimæ"	As York
Wednesday	Jas. ii. 1-13 John xvii. 11-15	1 Thess. v. 5-11 As Sarum	As York As York
Friday	Jas. ii. 24-26 John xiii. 33-36	Coloss. i. 12-18 As Sarum	Coloss. i. 12-20 As York
5 Sunday	No *Sequence*	"Victimæ"	As York
Rog. Tues.	James v. 16-20 Luke xi. 5-13	1 Tim. ii. 1-7 Mark xi. 23-26	As York Matt. vii. 7-14
Vigil		"Omnes Gentes Plaudite" is used for weekly Office at Mass	As Sarum
Ascension Day			
Friday	As on Day	"Sonet Vox Fidelium with "Lætetur Orbis"	*Ep.* Ephes. ii. 4-7
Saturday	As on Day	Ditto	Mon. Sat. *Ep.* Heb. ii. 9-18 Tu. Wed. iii. 1
Octave Day	All as on Day	Ephes. iv. 7-13	Mass as Sarum, but *Gosp.* Luke xxiv. 49-53
Whitsun Day			
Monday	"Resonet Sancta"	"Alma Chorus Domini"	As York

* *i.e.*, at the Mass of the Sunday, for at the Mass of the Resurrection *Victimæ* is said.

	SARUM.	YORK.	HEREFORD.
Tuesday	"Eja Musa"	"Laudes Deo" or "VeniSancteSpiritus"	As York
Wednesday	"Lux Jocunda"	"ResonetSancta" or "Alma Chorus"	"Veni Spiritus"
Thursday	"Alma Chorus"	"Lux Jocunda"	"Veni Sancte Spiritus"
Friday	"Laudes Deo"	"Laudes Deo" or "ConsolatorAlmæ"	"Alma Chorus"
Saturday	"Alma Chorus"	"VeniSancteSpiritus"	"Laudes Deo"
In York	*Less.* I., Is. xliv. 1-3, with an interpolation. *Coll.* "Illo vos igne." *Less.* II., Joel ii. 23-26. *Coll.* "Deus qui discipulis." *Less.* III. (i. Sarum.)* *Less.* IV. (ii. Sarum.)† *Less* V. (v. Sarum.) *Ep.* Rom. v. 1-5. *Seq.* "Veni Sancte Spiritus."		
Trinity Sunday.			
Corpus Christi		*Seq.* in iii. parts in Oct. "Quod in Cœna," "Sumunt boni"	As Sarum
1 Sun. aft. Trinity (Sun. in Oct.)		1 Sund. after Octave of Whitsun-Day (SundayinOctave.)‡	Sun. in Oct., "Voci vita sit unita" Service for Sun. as Sarum
Wednesday	2 Pet. i. 16-19 Matt. v. 17-19	Coloss. iii. 5-11 As Sarum	As York As Sarum
Friday	None	Heb. xii. 11-14 Luke xvii. 1-10	None
2 Sun. aft. Trin.			
Wednesday	Ephes. iv. 17-24 Matt. xxi. 23-27	1 Cor. xv. 14-23 Luke xx. 27-40	Rom. vi. 12-14 As Sarum
Friday	None	Rev. xviii. 1-24 Luke xii. 11-21	1 John i. 5-10 Luke viii. 49-56
3 Sun. aft. Trin.			
Wednesday	2 Tim. iv. 17, 18 Matt. v. 25-30	Coloss. iii. 17-24 As Sarum	As York As York
Friday	None	1 John iii. 1-3 Mark xi. 15-23	As York As York
4 Sun. aft. Trin.			
Wednesday	1 John ii. 3-6 Matt. xvii. 10-18	1 Pet. iv. 12-19 Luke xiii. 31-35	Rom. v. 12-21 As York
Friday	None	1 John iii. 21-24 Mark x. 2-9	James v. 8-11 As York
5 Sun. aft. Trin.			
Wednesday	1 Tim. ii. 1-7 Luke viii. 23-25	Rev. x. 8-11; xi. 1-4 Mark vii. 24-30	Rom. iii. 28-31, iv. 1-3 Matt. xxi. 28-32
Friday	None	1 Thess. iv. 9-11 Luke xii. 54-59, xiii. 1-3	Malachi iii. 5-18, and iv. Matt. xvii. 10-17
6 Sun. aft. Trin.			
Wednesday	1 John ii. 21-25 Mark x. 17-21	Heb. xii. 18, 19, xiii. 1-8 As Sarum	As York As York

* *Coll.* Da nobis quæsumus. † *Coll.* Præsta quæsumus ut a nostris.

‡ During Trinity-tide (except the xith Sunday after Trinity) one of the following Sequences is said:—*Voce jubilantes. Trinitatem Simplicem. Quicunque vult salvus esse. Adoremus Unitatem. Profitemus Unitatem.*

	SARUM.	YORK.	HEREFORD.
Friday	None	Rom. vi. 12-14	1 John ii. 1-7
		Mark v. 2-20	As York
7 Sun. aft. Trin.			
Wednesday	Rom. viii. 1-6	As Sarum	As Sarum
	Matt. xii. 1-7	Mark xvi. 1-6	As York
Friday	None	Rom. viii. 7-12	As York
		Matt. xii. 1-7	As York
8 Sun. aft. Trin.			
Wednesday	Rom. v. 8-11	As Sarum	Rom. v. 3-11
	Mark ix. 38-48	As Sarum	As Sarum
Friday	None	1 Cor. i. 26-31	As York
		Matt. xxiii. 3-23	As York
9 Sun. aft. Trin.			
Wednesday	Rom. vi. 16-18	As Sarum	As Sarum
	Luke xvi. 10-15	As Sarum	As Sarum
Friday	None	1 Cor. i. 17-25	1 Cor. xv. 22-28
		Luke v. 38-46	As York
10 Sun. aft. Trin.			
Wednesday	1 Cor. xv. 39-46	As Sarum	As Sarum
	Luke xxi. 34-36	Luke xxi. 20-26	As York
Friday	None	Rom. viii. 24-27	As York
		Luke xxi. 34-36	As York
11 Sun. aft. Trin.		*Seq.* Stans a longe	
Wednesday	1 Cor. vi. 15-20	James iv. 7-11	As Sarum
	Luke xviii. 1-8	As Sarum	Matt. xii. 30-37
Friday	None	1 Cor. vi. 15-20	1 Cor. v. 11-13 vi. 1-8
		Luke xii. 48-53	John vi. 15-21
12 Sun. aft. Trin.			
Wednesday	2 Cor. iv. 5-11	As Sarum	As Sarum
	Matt. xi. 20-24	Matt. ix. 27-35	As York
Friday	None	2 Cor. iv. 11-18	As York
		Matt. xi. 20-24	As York
13 Sun. aft. Trin.			
Wednesday	1 Thess. ii. 9-13	2 Cor. v. 1-11	As York
	Matt. xii. 14-21	As Sarum	As York
Friday	None	Rom. vii. 14-24	As York
		Luke xiii. 23-30	Luke xii. 13-24
14 Sun. aft. Trin.			
Wednesday	2 Cor. vi. 14-18; vii. 1.	As Sarum	As Sarum
	Luke xii. 13-24	Luke v. 12-15	Mark xi. 11-18
Friday	None	1 Cor. vi. 9-14	As York
		Luke viii. 1-3	As York
15 Sun. aft. Trin.			
Wednesday	1 Tim. i. 8-14	Ember Days	Coloss. i. 12-18
	Luke xx. 1-8		As Sarum
Friday	None	Ember Days	1 Tim. vi. 7-16
			Matt. xvii. 23-26
16 Sun. aft. Trin.			
Wednesday	Coloss. ii. 8-13	Coloss. i. 12-18	As Sarum
	Mark viii. 22-26	Matt. v. 33-42	Luke vii. 28-53

	SARUM.	YORK.	HEREFORD.
Friday	None	1 Tim. vi. 7-16	Coloss. iii. 23-25 iv. 1-6
		Luke xx. 2-8	Luke viii. 22-25
17 Sun. aft. Trin.			
Wednesday	Rom. v. 17-21	Coloss ii. 8-13	Ember Days
	Matt. xvii. 24-27	Matt. v. 33-48	
Friday	None	Coloss. iii. 22-25, iv. 1-6	Ember Days
		Mark viii. 22-26	
18 Sun. aft. Trin.			
Wednesday	Rom. xv. 30-33	Eph. i. 16-21	1 Cor. iii. 16-21
	Matt. xiii. 31-35	Matt. xiii. 24-26	Luke xi. 47-54
Friday	None	1 Cor. iv. 20, 21, v. 1-5	As York
		Matt. xiii. 31-35	Mark viii. 22-26
19 Sun. aft. Trin.			
Wednesday	2 Thess. ii. 15-17 iii. 1-5	As Sarum	As Sarum
	Matt. xiii. 37-43	As Sarum	As Sarum
Friday	None	Rom. xiii. 1-4	As York
		Matt. vii. 12-14	As York
20 Sun. aft. Trin.			
Wednesday	2 Tim. ii. 1-7	2 Thess. iii. 6-13	As York
	Luke xiv. 12-15	As Sarum	As Sarum
Friday	None	1 Tim. vi. 17-19	As York
		Luke vi. 22, 23	Matt. xiii. 33-35
21 Sun. aft. Trin.			
Wednesday	1 Thess. i. 4-10	1 Tim. i. 5-12	As York
	Luke vi. 6-11	As Sarum	Mark xi. 23-26
Friday	None	1 Tim. ii. 7-15	1 Cor. ii. 12-14
		Matt. viii. 14-17	Mark iv. 24-29
22 Sun. aft. Trin.			
Wednesday	Rom. iii. 19-26	1 Tim. ii. 1-7	1 Tim. iii. 16. iv. 1-8
	Matt. xi. 23-26	As Sarum	Matt. xiii. 31-35
Friday	None	1 Tim. i. 15-20, ii. 1-3	As York
		Matt. viii. 14-17	As York
23 Sun. aft. Trin.			
Wednesday	Rom. v. 17-21	2 Tim. i. 8-11	1 Tim. i. 15-18
	Matt. xvii. 24-27	As Sarum	Luke xiv. 12-15
Friday	None	1 Tit. i. 15, 16. ii. 1-10	As York
		Mark vii. 3-8	Mark i. 21-31
24 Sun. aft. Trin.			
Wednesday	2 Cor. x. 20-31	Rom. xi. 25-36	Heb. iii. 12-19 iv. 1-8
	Matt. xxi. 28-32	Mark xii. 28-34	Luke vi. 6-11
Friday	None	Heb. x. 19-27	As York
		Matt. xxi. 28-32	Luke vi. 6-11
25 Sun. aft. Trin.			
Wednesday	Ember Days	2 Thess. i. 3-10	1 James v. 8-10
		Luke x. 3-9	Matt. viii. 14-22
Friday	Ember Days	Zech. ii. 10-13	2 Pet. iii. 8-15
		Mark xiii. 33-37	Luke xii. 13-24
Ded. of Ch.	"Jerusalem et Zion filiæ"	Psallat Ecclesia	Rex Salomon

APPENDIX C.

THE KALENDARS OF YORK AND HEREFORD.

According to York, the Saints' Days were—

January.—v., The Depos. of S. Edward, King Conf.; Trans. of S William on the Sunday in Octave of Epiphany. viii., S. Lucian. x., S. Paulinus, First Hermit, Mem. only. xiii., SS. Sixtus, Hilary, Remigius, Mem. only. xvii., S. Anthony, Monk. Conf. xix., S. Germanicus, Mart. xxiii., S. Emerentiana, Virg. Mart. xxiv., S. Babille, with Three Children, MM. xxvi., S. Polycarp, Mart. Bp., together with the Sarum Feasts; except those on v., xvii., and xix.

February.—iv., S. Gilbert, Conf.; together with the Sarum Feasts, except no S. Frideswide.

March.—i., S. Albinus, Bp. Conf.; together with SS. Gregory, Cuthbert, Benedict, and the Annunciation. No others.

April.—No Feast of SS. Richard, Alphege, or Erkenwald. xxiv., Trans. of S. Wilfrid; together with the Sarum Feasts.

May.—xxv., Only S. Urban. xxvi., Mem. of Ven. Bede (but it is not in the Proper of Saints); the rest as Sarum. No Feast of SS. Nicholas, or Aldhelm.

June.—iv., S. Petrocus, Conf. viii., S. William, with an Octave. ix., No Trans. of S. Edmund. xv., Octave of S. William. xvi., No Trans. of S. Richard. xvii., S. Botulph, Abb. xx., No Trans. S. Edward. xxi., S. Leofrid, Abb. Two Masses for Nativ. of St. John Bapt, to be said alternately through Octave, and three through Octave of SS. Peter and Paul; together with the Sarum Feasts.

July.—No Visit. B.V.M.; then as Sarum till viii., S. Grimbald, Conf. ix., S. Everilda. No Saints' Days till S. Margaret, then as Sarum, but xxvii. S. Martha.

August.—Feast of S. Peter's Chains has an Octave; no Transfiguration or Name of JESUS. xxv., S. Hilda, Virg. Mart. xxxi., S. Aidan, Conf. Bp. No S. Cuthburga; together with the Sarum Feasts.

September.—iv., Mem. of S. Birinus. vii., S. Evurtius, Conf. Bp. x., S. Maurilius. No S. Edith; together with the Sarum Feasts.

October.—iv., S. Francis, Conf. viii., S. Pelagia. x., S. Paulinus. xii., Depos. of S. Wilfrid; no Trans. of S. Etheldreda. xix., Feast of Relics. xx., S. Austreberta, Virg. xxi., S. Hilarion. xxv., Trans. of S. John de Beverley. xxx., S. Germanus; the rest as Sarum, except no S. Frideswide.

November.—vii., S. Willebrode. x., S. Martin, Pope; the rest as Sarum, except SS. Winifrid, Erkenwald, and Hugh.

December.—i., SS. Crisantius and Daria; the rest as Sarum.

According to HEREFORD, the Saints' Days were—

January.—v., No. S. Edward, Conf. viii., No S. Lucian. xxvii., SS. John and Paul; Mem. of S. Paula. No S. Batildis; together with the Sarum Feasts.

February.—xxiii., S. Milburga Virg. xxviii., S. Oswald; with the Sarum Feasts.

March.—v., S. Pieranus, Conf. Bp.; and the other Sarum Feasts, except SS. Patrick and Edward.

April.—As Sarum, except no SS. Alphege or Erkenwald. xi., S. Guthlac.

May.—ix., No Trans. S. Nicholas; the rest as Sarum, except xi., The Ded. of Hereford Cath. xx., S. Ethelbert, King Mart.; with an Octave. xxviii., No S. Germanus.

June.—v., No S. Boniface. xv., Mem. S. Eadburga. xvi., No. S. Richard. xvii., S. Botulph, Abb. xx., No S. Edward. xxi., S. Leofrid., Abb.; the rest as Sarum.

July.—viii., S. Grimbald. xii., S. Cletus, Pope. xxviii., S. Panthaleon, Mem. Sampson. No Trans. S. Martin; SS. Swithin, Osmund or Arnulph, and the Visit. B.V.M. has no Octave; the rest as Sarum.

August.—All as Sarum, but no Feast of our Lady *ad Nives*. Transfiguration, Name of JESUS, and Octave, or Romanus. xxv., Depos. S. Thomas of Hereford.

September.—No Trans. SS. Cuthbert or Cyprian and Justin. xvi., No S. Edith; the rest as Sarum.

October.—ii., S. Thomas of Hereford, with an Octave. iv., S. Francis, S. Raphael.* vii., S. Ositha. x., S. Paulinus. xii., S. Wilfrid; no S. Gereon, Trans. of Etheldreda or Wulfran. xxv., Trans. S. Thomas of Hereford, with Octave; the rest as Sarum.

November.—All as Sarum, but no SS. Eustachius, Erkenwald, or Hugh

December.—i., SS. Crisantius and Daria; no S. Osmund. xi., Damasus, Mem. only; the rest as Sarum.

At the end of the Hereford Missal is appended a Mass for S. John de Bridelstowe (? Bridlington), whose day is May ii.

The following particulars respecting the Saints' Days observed in England may be interesting:—

747 A.D. By the Council of Cloveshoe, the feasts of S. Gregory and of S. Augustine are ordered to be kept.

1240. In a Constitution of William de Cantilupe, Bp. Worcester, the following feasts are said to be observed as doubles—"ad Usum Sarum:" —All principal and greater doubles except Ded. of a Ch., Feast of the Place, Corpus Christi, Visit. B.V.M., Name of JESUS, and S. Andrew's Day.

Work is prohibited on Jan. i., vi., xix., xxv.; Feb. ii. xxii., xxiv., xxviii.; March xxv.; Easter Day and two days after, Ascension Day, Whitsun Day, and two following days; April xxv.; May i., iii.; June xxiv., xxix.; July vii., xxii., xxv.; August i., x., xv., xxiv., September viii., xiv., xxi., xxix.; October xviii., xxviii.; November i., xi., xxx.; December v., xxi., xxv., Sundays, Ded. of Ch., Feast of Place.

On the following days no work is allowed except ploughing, *i.e.*:

SS. Vincent, John ante Port., Barnabas, Leonard, Clement, Trans. S. Oswald, Katherine.

* See Proper of Saints, Hereford.

The following days are to be observed by women, *i.e.*,

SS. Agnes, Margaret, Lucy, Agatha. *Conf.* also Giles, De Bridport's Constit. Bp. of Sarum, 1256 A.D.

1287. The Synod of Exeter adds to the above, March xii., April xxiii., May xxvi., August xxix., December viii.* This is confirmed by the Constits. of Ranulph de Salop, 1342, Bishop of Bath and Wells, but these omit SS. Gregory and George.

1305. Constits. Woodlake, Bp. of Winton, order Feasts of SS. Swithin, Britius, Edmund Archbp., and Richard, to be kept solemnly.

1332. The Council of Mayfield adds Corpus Christi to the above days, and omits Feb. xxiii., March xii., May vi., June xi., August x., xxix., November xi., xxv.

1351. Constits John de S. Paul, confirm December viii. and November xxv., and add July xxvi.

1354. S. Augustine's Day is raised by a Bull into a Double.

1386. Mandate, Bp. of London, to keep the two Feasts of S. Erkenwald better. The service is stated here to be taken from the Comm. Conf. Bp., but it is not Sarum.

1398. Archbp. Arundel. SS. David and Chad to be feasts of ix. lessons. Commemoration of S. Thomas in Province of Canterbury on Tuesdays if possible.

1400. Constits. Archbp. Arundel, order the same feasts to be observed as the Constits. of Cantilupe do (see above), but add SS. Chad, Gregory, All Souls', SS. Wenefride, and Katherine.

1415. Archbp. Chichely makes SS. David and Chad Doubles. (?)

1453. Edmund Lacy, Bp. of Exeter, institutes Office and Feast of S. Raphael, November xxii.

1480. The Convocation of Canterbury enacts that the Sarum Feast of Visit. B.V.M. be kept, also October xvii. and xix.

1518. Council of York. If Vig. S. John Bapt. occur on Corpus Christi, the Vigil is to be kept on previous Wednesday.

—— Dedication of Churches in London Diocese to be October iii.

1528. At Ely Cath., Trans. of S. Mary Magd. to be kept March xix.

1536. Dedication of Churches to be kept on the first Sund. in October.

APPENDIX D.†

The legend which precedes this Mass in the original is briefly this:—S. Boniface lay on his death-bed; to him appeared the Archangel Raphael with the said Mass. "Rise and write out this Office," saith he, "and say it five times, and thou shalt be healed; and whosoever shall say it for himself or any sick person five times, shall be healed, and if for a soul in Purgatory it shall be delivered." S. Boniface then enquired who he was, and on learning, conceded to all, *Rite confessis et Bene contritis*, who should say this Mass five times the seventh part of the forgiveness of all their sins; and to all who got it said, 40 days' indulgence of mortal, and a year's of venial sins.

* *Conf.* for this Feast Constit. Simon Islip. Archbp. Cantuar, 1328.

† See p. 515.

APPENDIX E.*

The reasons assigned at the beginning of this Mass for the origin of the Saturday in commemoration of our Lady are 1st.—That at Constantinople the veil before her image was drawn aside every Friday evening at Vespers, and replaced at the same hour the following night; 2nd. That when all the disciples forsook our Lord and fled, she only who had borne him without pain, and knew that He was God, remained; 3rdly. Because the Sabbath is a day of rest, and she is the door of Heaven; 4thly. Because the Feast of the Mother should follow that of the Son; † 5thly. For that on the day our Lord rested from labour the Service should be more joyous.

APPENDIX F.‡

"Le Célebrant avec ses ministres sortoit de la Sacristie au *Gloria Patri* de *l'Introït* comme à Lyon. Après le *Confiteor* le Célebrant baisoit le Diacreet le Soûdiacre .... Puis le Célebrant montoit à l'Autel et le Diacre aussi .... présentoit le Livre des Saints Evangiles à baiser au Célebrant qui baisoit aussi le milieu de l'Autel ...... Ils s'asseïoient dès qu'on commençoit le *Kyrie*, marqué que le Célebrant ne lisoit pas à l'Autel l'Introït ni le *Kyrie* .. .. après l'Oraison les Ceroferaires plaçoient les cierges du côté de l'Orient vers l'Occident .... Au *Gloria in Excelsis* le Célebrant encensoit l'Autel. C'est presentement (1717) pendant le *Kyrie*, et l'Acolythe va encenser le Clergé durant le *Gloria in Excelsis* et durant le *Credo*. Dès que le Soûdiacre commençoit l'Epître, le Célebrant s'asseïoit, et faisoit signe au Diacre de s'asseoir aussi .... On voit par là que le Prêtre ne la lisoit pas à l'Autel......L'Epître et l'Evangile aux jours de fêtes étoient chantez au Jubé, aussi-bien que le Graduel et l'*Alleluia*, qui étoient chantez comme à Lyon *per Rotulos*, dans des tables d'y voire. C'est ce me semble ce que l'ancient Ordinaire appelle, *Tabulas osseas quas tenent in manibus* § ...... Puis le Diacre ...... alloit au Jubé ‖ ...... L'Antienne de l'Offertoire avoit toujours des versets comme à Lyon ......Le Calice étoit couvert non d'une Palle mais du Corporal comme on fait encore *aujourd'hui* à Lyon et chez les Chartreux...... Le Diacre prenoit sur l'Autel la Patene la présentoit au Soûdiacre et le Soûdiacre la donnoit à garder dans une voile à un Acolythe, s'il y en avoit, comme à Paris et à Tours; sinon il la tenoit lui-même, comme cela se fait *aujourd'hui* à Rouen. J'ai dit que c'etoit le Diacre qui la prenoit de dessus l'Autel, *non licet enim* (dit l'ancien Ordinaire) *quidquam sacri ab altari auferre alicui nisi Diacono vel Sacerdoti.*¶ Cela s'observe encore aujourd'hui exactement dans l'Eglise Cathedrale ...... Dans l'ancien Ordinaire de Rouen ni dans l'Ordre Romain ni dans aucun des anciens Interpretes des Offices Divins, il n'est fait aucune mention de

* See p. 521. † *i.e.*, Friday. ‡ See Introd. p. xi.
§ Conf. *Reg. S. Osm.* Sec. xxi.
‖ But for this, see quotation in the Introduction.
¶ Canon xxi., Council of Laodicea.

'alice séparément ; mais seulement de celle avant
dans le Missel de Rouen, de l'an 1516, que le
e rogamus étoit incliné profondément devant
jointes (comme *aujourd'hui*) mais croisées, la
squ'à *ex hac altaris participatione.* La même
Missels d'Angleterre, et d'Ecosse, dans ceux
de 1519, de Lyon de 1530, et on peut dire
us les Missels de France jusqu'au tems de
hæc omnia, le Diacre ......ôtoit le corporal de
'est point dit dans l'ancien Ordinaire que le
inte Hostie, mais seulement que les Diacres et
ez depuis le *Te igitur* jusqu'à *Sed libera nos*
trois Missels d'Angleterre et d'Ecosse que le
Hostie l'adorera par une inclination de tête, de
autrefois à S. Jean de Lyon ...... Aussi la
quée dans leur Missel de 1530, non plus que
es d'Ecosse : car on y lit ; *Omnes clerici post*
ltare quousque completur totum Officium Missæ.
the présentoit la Patene au Soûdiacre puis le
acre au Célebrant ...... Le Prêtre après la
e ablution mais un Acolythe apportoit un
s du Prêtre et cela se faisoit encore à Rouen
. Le Soûdiacre aidoit au Diacre à purifier
le *Diacre aujourd'hui** pendant que le Soû-
côté de l'Autel). Et un Acolythe recevoit
ppez dans un grand voile."—De Moleon,
92.

ies with English Missals will be found which
following are a few :—The reading of the
mas, and the Epiphany ; the processions ; the
rangement in regard to reading the Lessons ;
ek ; and the still more minute peculiarity
rpent-rod to hold the taper which was to
translator will only add that there is scarcely
the English Missals with which a parallel
ouen, elsewhere in France ; and that a care-
urgies on any obscure English Rubric, or
... any one desirous of attaining to a thorough
knowledge of the rites and ceremonies of the Church of our Fathers.

* *Conf.* Sarum Missal, p. 320.

Lightning Source UK Ltd.
Milton Keynes UK
UKOW021934280513
211386UK00005B/104/P

9 781144 134141